High-Value Natural Resources and Post-Conflict Peacebuilding

Edited by Päivi Lujala and Siri Aas Rustad

First published 2012
by Earthscan
2 Park Square, Milton Park, Abingdon, Oxon OX14 4RN

Simultaneously published in the USA and Canada
by Earthscan
711 Third Avenue, New York, NY 10017

Earthscan is an imprint of the Taylor & Francis Group, an informa business

© 2012 Environmental Law Institute and United Nations Environment Programme

The right of the editors to be identified as the authors of the editorial material, and of the authors for their individual chapters, has been asserted in accordance with sections 77 and 78 of the Copyright, Designs and Patents Act 1988.

All rights reserved. No part of this book may be reprinted or reproduced or utilised in any form or by any electronic, mechanical, or other means, now known or hereafter invented, including photocopying and recording, or in any information storage or retrieval system, without permission in writing from the copyright holders.

Trademark notice: Product or corporate names may be trademarks or registered trademarks, and are used only for identification and explanation without intent to infringe.

British Library Cataloguing in Publication Data
A catalogue record for this book is available from the British Library

Library of Congress Cataloging in Publication Data
High-value natural resources and post-conflict peacebuilding/edited by Päivi Lujala and Siri Aas Rustad.
    v.; cm. – (Peacebuilding and natural resoues series)
   Includes bibliographical references and index.
   Contents: Extraction and extractive industries – Commodity and revenue tracking – Revenue distribution – Allocation and institution building – Livelihoods – Lessons learned.
   ISBN 978-1-84971-230-9 (pdk : alk. paper) – ISBN 978-0-203-87848-4 (ebk.) 1. Natural resources–Co-management–Case studies.
2. Natural resources–Management–Case studies. 3. Natural resources–Political aspects–Case studies. 4. Peace-building–Case studies. I. Lujala, Päivi. II. Rustad, Siri Aas.
HC85.H54 2012
333.7–dc23

2011036001

Printed and bound in Great Britain by
CPI Antony Rowe, Chippenham, Wiltshire

Table of contents

List of figures and tables vii
Preface ix
Foreword xiii
Acknowledgments xv

High-value natural resources: A blessing or a curse for peace? 3
Päivi Lujala and Siri Aas Rustad

Part 1: Extraction and extractive industries **19**

Introduction 21

Bankrupting peace spoilers: Can peacekeepers curtail belligerents' access to resource revenues? 25
Philippe Le Billon

Mitigating risks and realizing opportunities: Environmental and social standards for foreign direct investment in high-value natural resources 49
Jill Shankleman

Contract renegotiation and asset recovery in post-conflict settings 69
Philippe Le Billon

Reopening and developing mines in post-conflict settings: The challenge of company-community relations 87
Volker Boege and Daniel M. Franks

Diamonds in war, diamonds for peace: Diamond sector management and kimberlite mining in Sierra Leone 121
Kazumi Kawamoto

Assigned corporate social responsibility in a rentier state: The case of Angola 147
Arne Wiig and Ivar Kolstad

Part 2: Commodity and revenue tracking **155**

Introduction 157

The Kimberley Process at ten: Reflections on a decade of efforts to end the trade in conflict diamonds 159
J. Andrew Grant

iv High-value natural resources and post-conflict peacebuilding

The Kimberley Process Certification Scheme: A model negotiation? 181
Clive Wright

The Kimberley Process Certification Scheme: The primary safeguard
for the diamond industry 189
Andrew Bone

A more formal engagement: A constructive critique of certification as
a means of preventing conflict and building peace 195
Harrison Mitchell

Addressing the roots of Liberia's conflict through the Extractive
Industries Transparency Initiative 201
Eddie Rich and T. Negbalee Warner

Excluding illegal timber and improving forest governance: The European
Union's Forest Law Enforcement, Governance and Trade initiative 211
Duncan Brack

Part 3: Revenue distribution 221

Introduction 223

Sharing natural resource wealth during war-to-peace transitions 225
Achim Wennmann

Horizontal inequality, decentralizing the distribution of natural resource
revenues, and peace 251
Michael L. Ross, Päivi Lujala, and Siri Aas Rustad

The Diamond Area Community Development Fund: Micropolitics and
community-led development in post-war Sierra Leone 261
Roy Maconachie

Direct distribution of natural resource revenues as a policy for
peacebuilding 275
Martin E. Sandbu

Part 4: Allocation and institution building 291

Introduction 293

High-value natural resources, development, and conflict: Channels
of causation 297
Paul Collier and Anke Hoeffler

Petroleum blues: The political economy of resources and conflict
in Chad 313
John A. Gould and Matthew S. Winters

Leveraging high-value natural resources to restore the rule of law:
The role of the Liberia Forest Initiative in Liberia's transition to
stability 337
Stephanie L. Altman, Sandra S. Nichols, and John T. Woods

Forest resources and peacebuilding: Preliminary lessons from Liberia
and Sierra Leone 367
Michael D. Beevers

An inescapable curse? Resource management, violent conflict,
and peacebuilding in the Niger Delta 391
Annegret Mähler

The legal framework for managing oil in post-conflict Iraq: A pattern
of abuse and violence over natural resources 413
Mishkat Al Moumin

The capitalist civil peace: Some theory and empirical evidence 437
Indra de Soysa

Part 5: Livelihoods 461

Introduction 463

Counternarcotics efforts and Afghan poppy farmers: Finding the right
approach 467
David M. Catarious Jr. and Alison Russell

The Janus nature of opium poppy: A view from the field 491
Adam Pain

Peace through sustainable forest management in Asia: The USAID
Forest Conflict Initiative 503
Jennifer Wallace and Ken Conca

Women in the artisanal and small-scale mining sector of the Democratic
Republic of the Congo 529
Karen Hayes and Rachel Perks

Forest user groups and peacebuilding in Nepal 545
Binod Chapagain and Tina Sanio

Lurking beneath the surface: Oil, environmental degradation, and
armed conflict in Sudan 563
Luke A. Patey

Part 6: Lessons learned

Building or spoiling peace? Lessons from the management of
high-value natural resources 571
Siri Aas Rustad, Päivi Lujala, and Philippe Le Billon

Appendices 623

List of abbreviations 623
Author biographies 629
Table of contents for *Post-conflict peace building and
natural resource management* 641

Index 657

List of figures and tables

FIGURES

The economic role of the extractive sector in selected post-conflict and conflict-affected countries	4
Armed civil conflicts involving high-value natural resources, 1970–2008	7
Diamond deposits in Sierra Leone (Map)	123
Diamond deposits in Sierra Leona (Map)	160
Diamond deposits in Angola (Map)	161
Oil in Sudan and South Sudan (Map)	237
Oil and tribal concentrations in Chad (Map)	319
Forest cover in Liberia (Map)	339
Forest cover in Sierra Leone and Liberia (Map)	370
Ethnic groups in Iraq (Map)	416
Oil in Iraq (Map)	417
Economic freedom and the risk of internal armed conflict (>25 battle deaths), 1970–2008	444
Effects of economic freedom on political repression in oil-exporting states and non-oil-exporting states	450
Effects of democracy on political repression in oil-exporting states	451
Effects of democracy and economic freedom on political repression	452
Poppy cultivation in Afghanistan, 1994–2009	471
Poppy cultivation in Uruzgan Province, 1994–2009	482
Supply chain for wood-based products	510
Oil in Sudan and South Sudan (Map)	565

TABLES

Control of conflict resources by UN peacekeeping missions, 1988–2009	32
Voluntary social and environmental standards	57
Renegotiation of Mittal iron-ore mining contract in Liberia: Summary of changes	76
Effects of a top-down mineral certificate-of-origin scheme	198
Income-sharing schemes	233
Oil, gas, and mineral resources and secessionist movements	253
The effect of economic freedom on the onset of civil war, 1946–2005	447
The effect of economic freedom on political repression, 1981–2006	449
Variables that influence forest conflict	512
Forest conflict and armed conflict in the countries profiled during the Conflict Timber Project	513
Actors and strategies involved in conflict management	551
Case studies: summary data tables (Forest User Groups and Peacebuilding in Nepal)	553
Approaches to managing high-value natural resources in post-conflict situations	610

Preface

Decades of civil wars, international wars, and wars of secession demonstrate the strong relationship between natural resources and armed conflict. Disputes over natural resources and their associated revenues can be among the reasons that people go to war. Diamonds, timber, oil, and even bananas and charcoal can provide sources of financing to sustain conflict. Forests, agricultural crops, and wells are often targeted during conflict. Efforts to negotiate an end to conflict increasingly include natural resources. And conflicts associated with natural resources are both more likely to relapse than non-resource-related conflicts, and to relapse twice as fast.

Immediately after the end of a conflict, a window of opportunity opens for a conflict-affected country and the international community to establish security, rebuild, and consolidate peace—or risk conflict relapse. This window also presents the opportunity to reform the management of natural resources and their revenues in ways that would otherwise be politically difficult to achieve. Capitalizing on this opportunity is particularly critical if natural resources contributed to the onset or financing of conflict—and, if this opportunity is lost, it may never reappear. Moreover, poorly informed policy decisions may become entrenched, locking in a trajectory that serves the interests of a limited few.

Since the end of the Cold War, and particularly since 2000, substantial progress has been made in establishing institutional and policy frameworks to consolidate peacebuilding efforts. In 2005, the United Nations established the Peacebuilding Commission to identify best practices for peacebuilding. The commission is the first body to bring together the UN's humanitarian, security, and development sectors so that they can learn from peacebuilding experiences.

The Peacebuilding Commission has started to recognize the importance of natural resources in post-conflict peacebuilding. In 2009, along with the UN Environment Programme, the commission published a pioneering report—*From Conflict to Peacebuilding: The Role of Natural Resources and the Environment*—that framed the basic ways in which natural resources contribute to conflict and can be managed to support peacebuilding. Building on this report, the commission is starting to consider how natural resources can be included within post-conflict planning and programming in Sierra Leone, the Central African Republic, Guinea-Conakry, and other countries.

Since the establishment of the Peacebuilding Commission, the policies governing post-conflict peacebuilding have evolved rapidly. In his 2009 *Report of the Secretary-General on Peacebuilding in the Immediate Aftermath of Conflict*, UN Secretary-General Ban Ki-moon articulated five priorities for post-conflict peacebuilding, all of which have natural resource dimensions. The following year, in an update to that report, Ban Ki-moon noted the pressing need to improve post-conflict natural resource management to reduce the risk of conflict relapse, and urged "Member States and the United Nations system to make questions of natural resource allocation, ownership and access an integral part of peacebuilding strategies." And a 2011 UN report, *Civilian Capacity in the Aftermath of Conflict*, highlighted approaches for mobilizing civil society to support peacebuilding in many realms, including natural resources.

The World Bank has also begun focusing on natural resources: the Bank's 2011 *World Development Report*, for example, placed the prevention of fragility, conflict, and violence at the core of the Bank's development mandate. Drawing on the Bank's experiences around the world, the report focuses on jobs, justice, and security, and highlights the contribution of natural resources to these goals.

Despite growing recognition of the importance of post-conflict natural resource management, there has been no comprehensive examination of how natural resources can support post-conflict peacebuilding. Nor has there been careful consideration of the risks to long-term peace caused by the failure to effectively address natural resources. Practitioners, researchers, and UN bodies have researched specific resources, conflict dynamics, and countries, but have yet to share their findings with each other at a meaningful scale, and limited connections have been drawn between the various strands of inquiry. As a result, the peacebuilding community does not know what works in what circumstances, what does not, or why.

Given the complexity of peacebuilding, practitioners and researchers alike are struggling to articulate good practice. It is increasingly clear that natural resources must be included as a foundational issue; many questions remain, however, regarding opportunities, options, and trade-offs.

Against this backdrop, the Environmental Law Institute, the UN Environment Programme, the University of Tokyo, and McGill University launched a research program designed to examine experiences in post-conflict peacebuilding and natural resource management; to identify lessons from these experiences; and to raise awareness of those lessons among practitioners and scholars. The program has benefitted from broad support, with the government of Finland—one of the few donor governments to explicitly recognize the role of natural resources in both conflict and peacebuilding efforts—playing a catalytic role by providing core financing.

The research program has been guided by the collective experiences of the four members of the Steering Committee: as the coordinators of the program and the series editors, we have drawn on our work in more than thirty post-conflict countries. Our experiences—which include leading environmental assessments in Afghanistan, developing forest law in Liberia, supporting land reform in Mozambique, and fostering cooperation around water in Iraq—have led to a shared understanding that natural resource issues rarely receive the political attention they merit. Through this research program and partnership, we hope to catalyze a comprehensive global effort to demonstrate that peacebuilding substantially depends on the transformation of natural assets into peacebuilding benefits—a change that must occur without mortgaging the future or creating new conflict.

Since its inception in 2007, the program has grown dramatically in response to strong interest from practitioners, researchers, and policy makers. Participants in an initial scoping meeting suggested a single edited book consisting of twenty case studies and cross-cutting analyses. It soon became clear, however, that the undertaking should reflect a much broader range of experiences, perspectives, and dimensions.

The research program yielded more than 150 peer-reviewed case studies and analyses written by more than 230 scholars, practitioners, and decision makers from almost fifty countries. The case studies and analyses have been assembled into a set of six edited books, each focusing on a specific set of natural resources or an aspect of peacebuilding: high-value natural resources; land; water; resources for livelihoods; assessment and restoration of natural resources; and governance. Examining a broad range of resources, including oil, minerals, land, water, wildlife, livestock, fisheries, forests, and agricultural products, the books document and analyze post-conflict natural resource management successes, failures, and ongoing efforts in more than fifty-five conflict-affected countries. In their diversity and number, the books represent the most significant collection to date of experiences, analyses, and lessons in managing natural resources to support post-conflict peacebuilding.

In addition to the six edited books, the partnership has created an overarching book, *Post-Conflict Peacebuilding and Natural Resources: The Promise and the Peril*, which will be published by Cambridge University Press. This book draws on the six edited books to explore the role of natural resources in various peacebuilding activities across the humanitarian, security, and development sectors.

These seven books will be of interest to practitioners, researchers, and policy makers in the security, development, peacebuilding, political, and natural resource communities. They are designed to provide a conceptual framework, assess approaches, distill lessons, and identify specific options and trade-offs for more effectively managing natural resources to support post-conflict peacebuilding.

Natural resources present both opportunities and risks, and postponing their consideration in the peacebuilding process can imperil long-term peace and undermine sustainable development. Experiences from the past sixty years provide many lessons and broad guidance, as well as insight into which approaches are promising and which are problematic.

A number of questions, however, still lack definitive answers. We do not always understand precisely why certain approaches fail or succeed in specific instances, or which of a dozen contextual factors are the most important in determining the success of a peacebuilding effort. Nevertheless, numerous discrete measures related to natural resources can be adopted now to improve the likelihood of long-term peace. By learning from peacebuilding experiences to date, we can avoid repeating the mistakes of the past and break the cycle of conflict that has come to characterize so many countries. We also hope that this undertaking represents a new way to understand and approach peacebuilding.

Carl Bruch
Environmental Law Institute

David Jensen
United Nations Environment Programme

Mikiyasu Nakayama
University of Tokyo

Jon Unruh
McGill University

Foreword

Ellen Johnson Sirleaf
President of Liberia

In Liberia, we face a paradox similar to that of many post-conflict developing countries described in this book: our country is endowed with rich natural resources, yet our people live in poverty. The story of Liberia's recent history is well known. Despite our abundant natural heritage, for fourteen years Liberia was ravaged by a horrific civil war that disintegrated the nation and brought us near the bottom of the United Nations' Human Development Index. By 2003, our economy had collapsed, our infrastructure was destroyed, and our young people knew only war and want. And once again we faced a paradox: our timber, minerals, and other natural resources promised a way out of poverty and conflict, but they also threatened to pull our country back to the destructive path of patronage, corruption, and violence.

When I became President, in 2006, we faced herculean challenges of where to start the transition from war to peace, from devastation to recovery. Although the transitional government had made important steps, unemployment was at an all-time high, and inflation was driving up food and fuel prices. The war had devastated our economic structures and undermined the government's capacity to implement the sound economic policies necessary to recover. The diamond and timber sectors, key sources of revenue for the country, were frozen under UN sanctions. A whole generation of children was traumatized and had missed the opportunity to go to school. We needed to reintegrate former soldiers and find a way for almost one million Liberians to return home. We had inherited an entrenched, criminalized value system—a system in which impunity and mismanagement of our natural resources had been the norm.

Peace brings promise, and with it high expectations—especially in a country with abundant natural resources. We needed to provide for the basic needs of our people, give them jobs, rebuild our economy, restore governance and government, and reweave the fabric of society. The revenues from our diamonds and timber had been used to fuel conflict, yet we knew that to move our country forward, we had to turn this natural resource "curse" into a blessing. But where to start?

Throughout Liberia, our abundant natural resources offered the promise for consolidating peace and building a better future for our country and our people. Diamonds, iron ore, gold, and other minerals are among Liberia's many buried treasures. Above the soil, millions of hectares of valuable forests cover our landscape. And beneath the sea, our offshore continental shelf may well harbor oil and gas. We needed to figure out how to manage these resources for the transition to peace. We needed to harness these resources to provide our people with tangible peace dividends in the form of jobs, schools, and improved living standards. At the same time, we had to devise a way to reverse the entrenched corruption and mismanagement in order to prevent a relapse into war. While we had considerable international support, we had no model to follow for how to put back the pieces of our broken country.

In order to fulfill the promise of our natural heritage, we realized that better management of natural resources had to become a centerpiece of Liberia's postwar development strategy. A large part of the problem lay in the lack of information about money that companies extracting timber and other natural resources had paid to the government. This money belonged to all the citizens of Liberia, not just to the rulers, business elites, and soldiers.

I vowed to ensure national growth, development, and reconciliation through accountable management of our extractive industry and the revenue it generates. To put this principle into practice, we immediately took steps to rein in uncontrolled extraction of our natural resources and to combat the cancerous vice of corruption. We continued the efforts of the Governance and Economic Management Assistance Program begun by the transitional government; joined the Kimberley Process; established the Land Reform Commission; reformed the timber sector from top to bottom; and joined the Extractive Industries Transparency Initiative (EITI).

My first executive order, in February 2006, cancelled all timber concessions until new standards could be put in place. Six months later, we passed a pioneering new forestry law that provides for sustainable and beneficial use of Liberia's forests. The new law helps ensure that local communities play an active role in approving timber contracts, monitoring timber operations, and benefiting from timber revenues. To overcome the legacy of mistrust, we have made a special effort through the Liberia EITI to be inclusive by widely publicizing revenues from the mining, petroleum, rubber, and forestry sectors.

Trust is the greatest asset that any country can have. After war, however, trust was perhaps our scarcest resource. By restoring transparency, empowerment, and accountability in our core natural resource sectors, we have started to rebuild that trust. These efforts are central to Liberia's conflict reduction strategy.

In reforming management of our high-value natural resources, we are finding our way along the path from conflict to peace and sustainable development. We are not alone on this path. This book examines many of the initiatives that Liberia has undertaken, as well as experiences from other countries. When Liberia was first emerging from conflict, we had no model and little guidance for how to transform our natural resource sectors to rebuild our country. This book provides valuable insights for making peacebuilding more effective through natural resource management. As we learned directly, timber and other high-value natural resources were important for a surprising number of the tasks we faced in rebuilding our country. The experiences and analyses in this book are an essential resource for everyone working in post-conflict peacebuilding. I only wish that this book had been available when I became President.

Acknowledgments

This volume, the culmination of a three-year research project, would not have been possible without the efforts and contributions of many people and organizations.

The volume editors are grateful to Peter Whitten, managing editor, and Sandra F. Chizinsky, manuscript editor, for their peerless editorial assistance. We are also thankful for the support of assistant managing editors Sarah Wegmueller and Annie Brock, who skillfully shepherded the volume through the publication process. Nick Bellorini, of Earthscan, provided guidance throughout; Matt Pritchard, Elan Spitzberg, and Arthur Green created the maps; and Joelle Stallone proofread the manuscript. We are also grateful to our colleagues at the Department of Economics, Norwegian University of Science and Technology, and the Centre for the Study of Civil War, Peace Research Institute Oslo, for their comments and support.

Research assistance and publishing support was provided by numerous research associates, interns, legal interns, and visiting attorneys at the Environmental Law Institute: Elliott August, Andrew Beckington, Susan Bokermann, Daniel Brindis, Heather Croshaw, Akiva Fishman, Caitlin Fogarty, Mona Funicello, Sara Gersen, Adam Harris, Farah Hegazi, Katelyn Henmueller, Emily Jorgensen, Sean Joyner, Rachel Kenigsberg, Masumi Kikkawa, Seda Kojoyan, Vrinda Manglik, Shanna McClain, Mark McCormick-Goodhart, KJ Meyer, Joseph Muller, Rachel Parks, Katarina Petursson, Jessica Renny, Doug Sharp, Sarah Stellberg, John Stokes, Ben Tannen, Carley Wigod, and Louise Yeung.

Peer reviewers were essential to ensuring the analytical rigor of contributions to this volume. The authors would like to acknowledge the assistance of the scholars and practitioners who contributed anonymous peer reviews.

Some chapters in this volume were adapted from earlier publications: "High-Value Natural Resources, Development, and Conflict: Channels of Causation," by Paul Collier and Anke Hoeffler, is an updated and adapted version of Paul Collier, "Natural Resources, Development, and Conflict: Channels of Causation and Policy Interventions," in *Economic Integration and Social Responsibility*, ed. Francois Bourguignon, Pierre Jacquet, and Boris Pleskovic (Washington, D.C.: World Bank, 2007), and is printed with permission from the International

Bank for Reconstruction and Development, The World Bank. "Horizontal Inequality, Decentralizing the Distribution of Natural Resource Revenues, and Peace," by Michael Ross, Päivi Lujala, and Siri Aas Rustad, is based on Michael L. Ross, "How Can Mineral Rich States Reduce Inequality?" in *Reversing the Resource Curse*, ed. Macartan Humphreys, Jeffrey Sachs, and Joseph Stiglitz (New York: Columbia University Press, 2007), and is printed with permission from Columbia University Press. "Counternarcotics Efforts and Afghan Poppy Farmers: Finding the Right Approach," by David Catarious Jr. and Alison Russell, and "Peace through Sustainable Forest Management in Asia: The USAID Forest Conflict Initiative," by Jennifer Wallace and Ken Conca, are printed with the permission of the Environmental Law Institute.

Financial support for the project was provided by the United Nations Environment Programme; the government of Finland; the U.S. Agency for International Development; the Research Council of Norway; the European Union; the University of Tokyo (including the Graduate School of Frontier Sciences and the Alliance for Global Sustainability); the John D. and Catherine T. MacArthur Foundation; the Canadian Social Science and Humanities Research Council; the Philanthropic Collaborative; the Center for Global Partnership of the Japan Foundation; the Ploughshares Fund; the Compton Foundation; the Global Infrastructure Fund Research Foundation Japan; Zonta Club Tokyo; the International Union for Conservation of Nature Commission on Environmental Law; the Nelson Talbott Foundation; and an anonymous donor.

The cover was designed by Nikki Meith. Cover photography is by Christophe Smets/Luna/Visum/Sill Pictures.

High-Value Natural Resources and Post-Conflict Peacebuilding

High-value natural resources: A blessing or a curse for peace?

Päivi Lujala and Siri Aas Rustad

High-value natural resources have the potential to promote and consolidate peace. Too often, however, they make the path to sustainable peace long and hazardous. Valuable resources can help to jump-start development, secure sustained growth, raise living standards, and increase economic equality. They are also an important source of foreign currency for cash-strapped governments, can reduce dependence on international aid, and can support compensation and post-conflict relief for war-affected populations. But the promise of a brighter and more peaceful future is often spoiled by deep-rooted corruption and patronage, which confer benefits on small groups rather than on the population as a whole, and by shortsighted management of the resources and the revenues they generate.[1] In addition, the mere presence of high-value resources can jeopardize peace, if the resources become the focus of violent disputes or provide financing for groups that seek to ignite (or resume) armed conflict.

In many post-conflict countries, revenues from high-value natural resources—such as oil, natural gas, minerals, gemstones, and timber—are an integral (and even dominant) part of the national economy and state budget. In post-conflict Algeria, Angola, and Sudan, for example, oil and gas account for more than 60 percent of government revenues and over 90 percent of all export revenues (see figure 1). In Sierra Leone, in the wake of a brutal civil war that ended in 2002, diamonds accounted for 96 percent of all exports (IMF 2009b). And in Chad, Iraq, Libya, and Nigeria—all of which were affected by armed conflict during the early years of the twenty-first century—oil and gas account for as much as 70 percent of gross domestic product and more than 80 percent of government revenues. In

---

Päivi Lujala is an associate professor of geography at the Norwegian University of Science and Technology (NTNU) and a senior researcher at the Department of Economics, NTNU, and the Centre for the Study of Civil War (CSCW) at the Peace Research Institute Oslo (PRIO). Siri Aas Rustad is a researcher at CSCW, PRIO, and a Ph.D. candidate in political science at NTNU.

[1] Although many patronage systems are corrupt, the phenomenon of patronage is distinct from that of corruption.

4 High-value natural resources and post-conflict peacebuilding

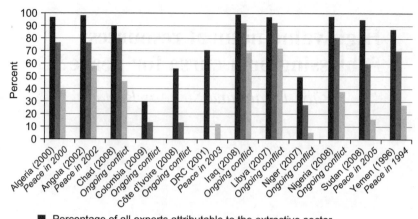

- Percentage of all exports attributable to the extractive sector
- Percentage of government revenues derived from the extractive sector
- Percentage of gross domestic product attributable to the extractive sector

Figure 1. The economic role of the extractive sector in selected post-conflict and conflict-affected countries
Sources: End dates for conflict: Gleditsch et al. (2002); Harbom and Wallensteen (2010). All other data: IMF (2001, 2005, 2007, 2008, 2009a, 2010b, 2010c, 2010d, 2010e, 2011a, 2011b, 2011c).
Notes:
1. Numbers in parentheses indicate the year for which the data were obtained.
2. Where there are two columns instead of three, the data for the third column were unavailable.
3. For post-conflict countries, data were obtained for the year following the end of hostilities or for the first year for which they were available. (In some cases, conflict reignited after the period included in the figure.) For conflict-affected countries, the data are for the latest year for which they were available.
4. Country data reflect various resource sectors, as follows: Algeria, oil and gas; Angola, oil, gas, and diamonds; Chad, Colombia, Libya, Nigeria, Sudan, and Yemen, oil and gas; Côte d'Ivoire, oil, gas, and coffee; the Democratic Republic of the Congo (DRC), mining; Iraq, oil and gas. For Niger, export share data are based on uranium and gold, government revenues data are based on uranium, and gross domestic product data are based on mining.

Niger, uranium and gold are important revenue sources (IMF 2009a), as are oil, cocoa, and coffee in Côte d'Ivoire (IMF 2010d), and diamonds and timber in the Central African Republic (IMF 2010a). In Burma in 2008–2009, gas exports made up one-quarter of all exports; forest products and gemstones were other important exports (Turnell 2010; Talbott, Akimoto, and Cuskelly 2012).

When peace comes, the revenues from high-value natural resources—when managed well—can help finance reconstruction and other vital peace-related needs. When mismanaged, however, resource revenues can undermine both economic performance and the quality of governance, and thereby increase the risk of renewed violence.

Recent high-profile reports by the UN Secretary-General, the World Bank, the UN Environment Programme, and the United Nations have highlighted the need to more effectively harness high-value natural resources for development and peacebuilding (see sidebar) (UNSG 2009, 2010; World Bank 2011; UNEP 2009; UN 2011). If managed effectively, high-value natural resources constitute substantial assets that national and international actors can use to support core peacebuilding objectives, including macroeconomic recovery, livelihood generation and support, the reform of governance and political processes, and improved security.[2]

The fact that so many resource-rich countries are unable to achieve long-term peace, however, raises some difficult questions about how high-value resources should be managed in post-conflict settings. How can post-conflict governments cut through corruption and patronage and reform their extractive sectors? How can leaders who are more interested in personal benefit than in improving the lives of their citizens be reined in? How can post-conflict governments make the best use of the potential created by foreign direct investment? What responsibilities do extractive industries have in post-conflict countries? How can the environmental effects of resource extraction be minimized? How can a balance be struck between large-scale production, which can provide considerable revenues for the state, and small-scale and artisanal production, which may be the backbone of local livelihoods? How can illegal extraction be curtailed without damaging livelihoods? How can one ensure that revenues are used to advance long-term development objectives? How should potential peace spoilers be dealt with?

The goal of this volume is to provide insight into these and similar questions—for the benefit of national and local governments,

---

Post-conflict peacebuilding and natural resources: Key terms and concepts

Following conflict, peacebuilding actors leverage a country's available assets (including natural resources) to transform the country, with the aim of achieving security, service, economic, and governance objectives. Peacebuilding actors work at the international, national, and subnational levels, and include national and subnational government bodies; United Nations agencies and other international organizations; international and domestic nongovernmental organizations; the private sector; and the media. Each group of peacebuilding actors deploys its own tools, and there are a growing number of tools to integrate the peacebuilding efforts of different types of actors.

A post-conflict period typically begins after a peace agreement or military victory. Because a post-conflict period is often characterized by intermittent violence and instability, it can be difficult to pinpoint when the post-conflict period ends. For the purposes of this book, the post-conflict period may be said to end when political, security, and economic discourse and actions no longer revolve around armed conflict or the impacts of conflict, but focus instead on standard development objectives. Within the post-conflict period, the first two years are referred to as the *immediate aftermath of conflict* (UNSG 2009), which is followed by a period known as *peace consolidation*.

According to the United Nations, "Peacebuilding involves a range of measures targeted to reduce the risk of lapsing or relapsing into conflict by strengthening national capacities at all levels for conflict management, and to lay the foundations for sustainable peace and development" (UNSG's Policy Committee 2007). In many instances, this means addressing the root causes of the conflict.

There are many challenges to peacebuilding: insecurity, ethnic and political polarization (as well as marginalization), corruption, lack of governmental legitimacy, extensive displacement, and loss of property. To address these and other challenges, peacebuilding actors undertake diverse activities that advance four broad peacebuilding objectives:

- *Establishing security*, which encompasses basic safety and civilian protection; security sector reform; disarmament, demobilization, and reintegration; and demining

Cont'd on page 6

---

[2] The conceptual framework adopted in this book draws substantially from the *Report of the Secretary-General on Peacebuilding in the Immediate Aftermath of Conflict* (UNSG 2009), but the activities have been regrouped and supplemented by activities articulated in USIP and U.S. Army PKSOI (2009), Sphere Project (2004), and UN (2011).

6 High-value natural resources and post-conflict peacebuilding

> **Post-conflict peacebuilding and natural resources: Key terms and concepts (cont'd)**
>
> - *Delivering basic services*, including water, sanitation, waste management, and energy, as well as health care and primary education
> - *Restoring the economy and livelihoods*, which includes repairing and constructing infrastructure and public works
> - *Rebuilding governance and inclusive political processes*, which encompasses dialogue and reconciliation processes, rule of law, core government functions, transitional justice, and electoral processes.

Although they are sometimes regarded as distinct from peacebuilding, both peacemaking (the negotiation and conclusion of peace agreements) and humanitarian assistance are relevant to peacebuilding, as they can profoundly influence the options for post-conflict programming. Peacemaking and humanitarian assistance are also relevant to this book, in that they often have substantial natural resource dimensions.

Successful peacebuilding is a transformative process in which the country and the international community seek to address past wrongs and proactively lay the foundation for a lasting peace. As part of this process, peacebuilding actors seek to manage the country's assets—as well as whatever international assistance may be available—to ensure security, provide basic services, rebuild the economy and livelihoods, and restore governance. The assets of a post-conflict country include natural resources; infrastructure; and human, social, and financial capital. Natural resources comprise land, water, and other renewable resources, as well as extractive resources such as oil, gas, and minerals. The rest of the book explores the many ways in which natural resources affect peacebuilding.

national and transnational civil society organizations, extractive industries, and the international community. To this end, policy makers, field researchers and practitioners, and scholars—all of whom have close knowledge of the issues at hand—have been asked to share their views on the challenges associated with the management of high-value resources in post-conflict and conflict-affected countries.

FROM POTENTIAL PROSPERITY TO CONFLICT: WHAT GOES WRONG?

High-value natural resources have been associated with dozens of armed conflicts, millions of deaths, and the collapse of several peace processes—and case study and statistical evidence confirms that such resources play a role in sparking and fuelling armed civil conflict.[3] According to data gathered by Siri Aas Rustad and Helga Malmin Binningsbø, between 1970 and 2008 the portion of armed civil conflicts

---

[3] For the purposes of this chapter, the term *armed civil conflict* refers to both internal and internationalized internal conflicts included in the Uppsala Conflict Data Program/ Peace Research Institute Oslo (UCDP/PRIO) Armed Conflict Dataset. According to the UCDP/PRIO data set (Gleditsch et al. 2002; Harbom and Wallensteen 2009), from 1989 to 2008 there were only eight armed conflicts between independent countries, including Pakistan and India (1989–2003); the Iraqi invasion of Kuwait (1990–1991); Ecuador and Peru (1995); and the invasion of Iraq by a coalition led by the Unites States and the United Kingdom (2003). During the same period, more than 120 internal conflicts occurred, although some of these were internationalized in the sense that other countries provided military support for the government or for the rebels (Gleditsch et al. 2002; Harbom and Wallensteen 2010). Examples of internationalized internal conflict include the conflicts in the Balkans (1991–2001), Afghanistan (2001–present), Iraq (2004–present), and the Democratic Republic of the Congo (1996–2001). The preponderance of internal conflicts is reflected in this volume, which focuses on resource management in the wake of such conflicts. Among the issues not addressed in this volume, for example, is the joint management of resources that straddle national borders.

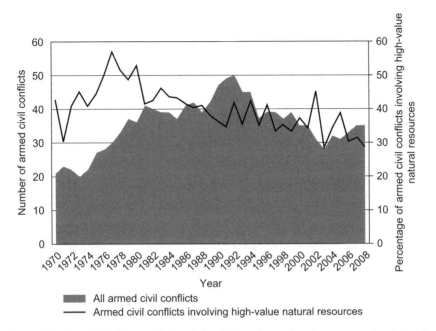

Figure 2. Armed civil conflicts involving high-value natural resources, 1970–2008
Sources: Conflict data: Gleditsch et al. (2002); Harbom and Wallensteen (2007, 2009). Resource data: Rustad and Binningsbø (2010).
Notes: The Uppsala Conflict Data Program/Peace Research Institute Oslo Armed Conflict Dataset defines *conflict* as an armed contestation between the government in a country and a rebel organization in which more than twenty-five battle-related deaths occur (Gleditsch et al. 2002). The figure includes all armed civil conflicts active from 1970 to 2008.

that were related, in some way, to high-value natural resources ranged from 29 to 57 percent (see figure 2) (Rustad and Binningsbø 2010).

Why is peace so difficult to achieve and sustain in the presence of these resources?[4] High-value natural resources increase the risk of conflict in a number of ways. The risk of conflict can be directly increased when access to revenues motivates or finances belligerent movements, or when grievances are created (1) by unmet expectations or inequalities in the distribution of revenues, jobs, and other benefits, or (2) by the negative side effects of resource exploitation. The risk of conflict can be indirectly increased when resource sectors undermine economic performance and the quality of institutions. Thus, the three main avenues that lead from natural resources to armed conflict are resource capture, resource-related grievances, and adverse effects on the economy and institutions.

---

[4] In a later chapter in this volume, "High-Value Natural Resources, Development, and Conflict: Channels of Causation," Paul Collier and Anke Hoeffler consider the links between conflict and high-value natural resources in more detail.

8 High-value natural resources and post-conflict peacebuilding

Paul Collier and Anke Hoeffler (2004, 2006) and Päivi Lujala (2010) suggest that the capture of resources for personal or regional enrichment is a possible motivation for rebel uprisings and violent secessionist movements.[5] Although resource capture can be one of the goals of armed rebellion, it is rarely, if ever, the sole motivation for conflict. Even in Sierra Leone, where the Revolutionary United Front has been represented as the classic example of a predatory, greed-driven movement, the reality is far more complex.[6] More often, resource capture is a means of financing warfare and attracting supporters. For example, the Revolutionary Armed Forces of Colombia (Fuerzas Armadas Revolucionarias de Colombia, or *FARC*) has relied on kidnapping and drugs to finance its insurgency for decades. As efforts to curtail FARC's access to income from these activities have met with some success, FARC has turned to gold mining to support its violent campaign against the government (*Economist* 2011; *New York Times* 2011).

Grievances can motivate armed conflict, particularly when the parties to a resource-related dispute are divided along ethnic, religious, or other lines. Among the events that may spark violent uprisings are land appropriation, environmental degradation, population displacement, large inflows of migrants, and frustration over unfulfilled economic expectations. Examples of grievance-based conflicts include Aceh, in Indonesia; Bougainville, in Papua New Guinea; Kurdistan, in Iraq; northern Niger; and southern Sudan. Grievances do not necessarily arise in the context of potential regional autonomy, as was the case in Aceh and southern Sudan; they may also occur in response to the abuse of power by local elites, as was the case in Sierra Leone.

With respect to economic growth and developmental outcomes, many resource-rich countries perform poorly in comparison to their less resource-rich counterparts. This phenomenon, often referred to as the *resource curse* or the *paradox of plenty*, is exemplified in countries such as Algeria, the Democratic Republic of the Congo, Iraq, and Nigeria.[7] The resource curse has a number of potential causes, including the following:

- A government that is able to finance its budget through natural resource revenues rather than public taxation can easily become detached from, and therefore less accountable to, the populace.

---

[5] The numerous examples of secessionist movements in resource-rich areas include Aceh, in Indonesia; Biafra, in Nigeria; Bougainville, in Papua New Guinea; Cabinda, in Angola; Kurdistan, in Iraq; and southern Sudan.

[6] For further discussion of the conflict in Sierra Leone, see, for example, Roy Maconachie, "The Diamond Area Community Development Fund: Micropolitics and Community-led Development in Post-war Sierra Leone," in this volume.

[7] The term *resource curse* was coined by Richard M. Auty (1993); *paradox of plenty* was coined by Terry Lynn Karl (1997). At its broadest, the phrase *resource curse* refers not only to poor economic development, but also to other negative political and social outcomes that have been associated with abundant natural resources, including detachment from the electorate and increased risk of armed conflict.

- Resource revenues often fuel patronage, corruption, and rent seeking, all of which may promote the interests of a small and predatory elite.[8] In Nigeria, for example, it is estimated that 1 percent of the population enjoys 80 percent of the oil revenues (Kalu 2008).
- When the group in power focuses on short-term gains (sometimes in an effort to meet popular demands), the results may include overspending, poor investment decisions, and ill-conceived economic policies.
- In countries whose economies depend on a few valuable resources, the weakness of political and economic institutions may be compounded by exposure to price shocks, which occur when rapid shifts in raw material prices lead to abrupt fluctuations in resource revenues.

Political and economic underperformance is endemic in many resource-rich countries—which, according to empirical studies, renders them vulnerable to conflict. Several studies have documented that armed civil conflict is more likely to occur in poor countries than in rich ones.[9] Research also shows that dysfunctional institutions and low state capacity are positively correlated with an increased likelihood of conflict.[10]

Supporting the case study evidence (Ross 2004a, 2004b), several statistical studies document strong and significant relationships between particular natural resources and conflict, but few have been able to disentangle the possible mechanisms behind the relationships. James Fearon and David Laitin (2003), for example, have found that oil increases the likelihood of conflict—a finding that has been confirmed by the work of Indra de Soysa and Eric Neumayer (2007), Macartan Humphreys (2005), and Päivi Lujala (2010). Lujala has found that when oil and gas are located in the conflict area, conflicts tend to be longer and more severe (Lujala 2009, 2010). Taken together, Lujala shows that (1) oil-producing countries are 1.5 to 2 times more likely to experience armed civil conflict than nonproducers, and that (2) when internal conflict occurs in a region that has oil reserves, it lasts twice as long as conflicts that occur in areas without oil reserves, and combatant deaths are twice as high. Collier and Hoeffler's 2006 study of conflict types links oil to higher risk of secessionist conflict, and Lujala (2009) shows that secessionist conflicts in regions with oil reserves tend to be more severe than any other conflicts.

---

[8] *Rent seeking* refers to attempts to capture economic benefits without contributing to overall economic production. In the case of high-value natural resources, where revenues are extraordinarily high in relation to the costs of extraction, rent seekers may attempt to capture rents through such means as corrupt practices and patronage. Apart from the fact that rent seeking does not contribute to overall economic activity, it can directly undermine economic outcomes—by, for example, weakening economic institutions or diverting revenues from education and other activities that are crucial for economic growth.

[9] See, for example, Collier and Hoeffler (2004), Fearon and Laitin (2003), and Hegre and Sambanis (2006).

[10] See, for example, Collier et al. (2003).

Diamonds and other gemstones have also been subject to statistical studies. Fearon (2004) and Lujala (2009, 2010) have shown that gemstones have effects similar to those of oil—namely, conflict is more likely and tends to last longer. The role of timber, opium, and other high-value crops is less clear. There is some evidence that opium cultivation makes conflicts last longer (Fearon 2004; Lujala 2010), but little systematic evidence links timber production to civil war (Rustad et al. 2008).

RESOURCES FOR CONFLICT

Because natural resources have varying characteristics, they are not equally relevant to conflict—and those that are relevant may be so for different reasons. High-value resources, for example, may be either renewable or nonrenewable, although most—such as oil, gas, rutile, coltan, cobalt, diamonds, and gold—are nonrenewable, and tend to be located in geographically limited areas. What all high-value resources have in common, however, is the potential to yield substantial revenue.

Some high-value resources are limited to confined areas and depend on sophisticated and expensive extraction methods or require special types of transportation (e.g., pipelines). Because such resources are difficult to loot and are generally securely controlled by the government during both peace and war, they provide fewer opportunities for conflict financing.[11] Thus, the revenues from resources such as oil, natural gas, kimberlite diamonds, copper, and rutile are likely to accrue to the central government and those who control it. Such resources may nevertheless play a role in conflict: rebel movements may seek to oust the government to gain control of them, and if the resources are located in more remote areas, they may play a role in secessionist uprisings (Le Billon 2001). Rebels may also loot existing stockpiles of commodities or may attempt to bring extraction or transportation to a halt, in order to cut off the central government from its revenue source. Finally, the large revenues derived from high-value resources may increase the risk of conflict through adverse effects on political and economic institutions.

Some high-value resources are linked to conflict because of their financing potential.[12] However deep grievances may be, rebellion is unlikely to begin or to be sustained without financing opportunities. Since the end of the Cold War,

---

[11] An extreme case is offshore oil and gas drilling, in which the product can be exported by pipelines or ships without ever being present on land in the producing country.

[12] Resources that are used to finance conflict are sometimes referred to as *conflict resources*. Although definitions of the term vary, one widely used definition is that of Global Witness (n.d.): "Conflict resources are natural resources whose systematic exploitation and trade in a context of conflict contribute to, benefit from or result in the commission of serious violations of human rights, violations of international humanitarian law or violations amounting to crimes under international law." Because this definition applies only to conflicts in which there are specific violations of international law, it has a somewhat narrower scope than others.

High-value resources: A blessing or a curse? 11

financing from the superpowers has declined, and revenues from valuable natural resources have gained importance as a source of conflict financing.[13]

The resources most suitable for wartime looting have extremely high value-to-weight ratio and can be easily extracted, concealed, smuggled, and sold. Easy extraction is a particular advantage: a resource that can be extracted by individuals or small groups using simple tools (that is, through artisanal mining techniques) can be readily exploited by rebels who either undertake the mining themselves or use forced labor. Among the commodities with high price-to-weight ratios that can be artisanally mined are alluvial gold, alluvial diamonds, and gemstones such as rubies and sapphires.[14] Rebels do not need to rely on extraction directly; they also engage in illegal taxation of trade and export routes. And in some cases, including Colombia and Nigeria, rebels have succeeded in obtaining ransoms from extractive firms by threatening to blow up oil pipelines or by kidnapping personnel working on installations.

When it comes to conflict financing, many natural resources have another advantage: they are generic, which means that their origins cannot be traced as easily as those of manufactured products. Because generic illegal commodities can be readily integrated into legal trade channels, they are a particularly lucrative form of contraband, with trade prices that differ only marginally from those of their legal counterparts.

Another advantage of some high-value resources is their scarcity. Some occur in only a small number of countries and have few substitutes, and are therefore of strategic importance. Demand for such resources may sometimes override other considerations, such as the legality of the exploitation, the behavior of the government that has granted exploitation rights, and the role of the commodities in financing warfare.

Of course, resources other than high-value minerals may play a role in conflict or have adverse effects on economic and political institutions. Most notable are coca and opium, which have been linked to conflicts in Latin America and Asia, respectively, and timber, which has been connected to a number of conflicts in Africa and Southeast Asia. Fisheries have also been used to finance conflict; in Somalia, for example, some warring groups have sold false fishing licenses for offshore tuna reserves (Webersik and Crawford 2012).

FROM CONFLICT TO PROSPERITY: WHAT CAN BE DONE?

When conflict ends, many of the original causes often remain unresolved—whether they relate to resources or not—and may even have been aggravated by the

---

[13] There are, of course, other financing sources, including payments from nationals living abroad and voluntary and nonvoluntary support from civilians.

[14] Alluvial deposits are found in sand, clay, and gravel discharged by rivers. Existing or ancient riverbeds can be mined using simple tools such as shovels, buckets, and pans.

12 High-value natural resources and post-conflict peacebuilding

grievances and economic and political havoc associated with the conflict itself.[15] Post-conflict countries thus face daunting challenges when it comes to building peace, reducing poverty, and managing natural resources—particularly when poor resource management may be undermining both peacebuilding and poverty reduction. As is clear from both the chapters in this volume and the literature in general, many resource-rich post-conflict countries are unable to sustain peace. This observation has been confirmed by empirical studies: for example, Rustad and Binningsbø's analysis of 285 episodes of armed civil conflict shows that when natural resources play a role, the period of post-conflict peace is 40 percent shorter than when they do not (Rustad and Binningsbø 2010).[16]

The difficulty of sustaining peace when high-value natural resources are involved has two key implications: (1) the conflicts involving such resources are generally harder to resolve; and (2) thus far, the measures that have been used to manage natural resources and their associated revenues are generally unsatisfactory. Improved management of high-value natural resources and the associated revenues is thus fundamental to peacebuilding.

This volume addresses the full range of challenges associated with high-value resources in post-conflict settings. Its thirty chapters reflect the perspectives of forty-one contributors and consider the experiences of eighteen countries (see map on page 13); the book also includes analyses of additional countries. The chapters vary in their approach: some focus on particular cases, such as Afghanistan, Sierra Leone, or Sudan; and others on particular resources, such as oil, diamonds, or timber. Still others consider specific policy options, such as conflict-sensitive resource extraction or decentralized revenue distribution; such options are often discussed in light of one or more case examples.

Broadly speaking, the organization of the volume reflects the successive stages in the chain that extends from resource extraction to final allocation and expenditure of revenues. The chapters are grouped into five sections that examine specific challenges and opportunities within each stage of the resource chain.

Part 1 focuses on the ways in which host governments, extractive industries, and the international community can strengthen the management of extraction to promote peace. Once a peace agreement is signed, one of the crucial tasks is to prevent potential peace spoilers from obtaining access to the resources that

---

[15] It is important to note that in some cases, high-value resources have nothing to do with triggering or financing the conflict—but as the conflict winds down, they become important issues to be addressed in the peacebuilding process.

[16] The term *conflict episode* refers to how a conflict is reported in the UCDP/PRIO Armed Conflict Dataset: a peace period is defined as the absence of conflict for more than two calendar years, and begins the first day that hostilities end (e.g., after military victory by one side) (Gleditsch et al. 2002; Harbom and Wallensteen 2007, 2009). The Rustad and Binningsbø 2010 study considers oil, gas, diamonds, minerals, forest resources, land, and agricultural products (including crops used to produce drugs), and all internal conflicts from the UCDP/PRIO Armed Conflict Dataset from 1946 through 2006.

High-value resources: A blessing or a curse? 13

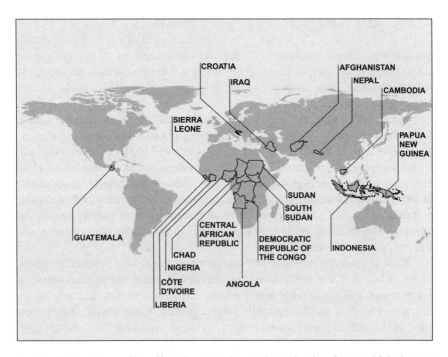

Post-conflict and conflict-affected countries and territories from which lessons have been drawn in this book, either through case studies or broader thematic analyses

had been used to finance the conflict or that could be used to finance a renewed conflict. Post-conflict countries may also need to deal with contracts signed by previous governments, transitional governments, or rebel groups, in which the shortsighted interests of the few may have trumped the long-term development needs of the population as a whole. Extractive companies, which may be reluctant to conduct their business in ways that take post-conflict fragility into account, which intentionally enter post-conflict countries in order to take advantage of weak governance structures, or which may simply be unsure how to develop conflict-sensitive projects, pose yet another challenge.[17]

Part 2 focuses on the instruments used to track commodities and revenues. In both cases, transparency is critical. If conflict resources are to be prevented from entering markets, their origins must be known; similarly, to curtail corruption and patronage, revenue flows between extractive industries and governments

---

[17] Conflict-sensitive projects take into consideration the causes and impacts of past conflicts, and try to minimize further negative impacts by developing extraction strategies that, at the very least, do not contribute to renewed conflict—and, ideally, contribute to the peace process.

14　High-value natural resources and post-conflict peacebuilding

must be made public. Specifically, part 2 considers the Kimberley Process Certification Scheme, which tracks the origin and trade of rough diamonds; the Extractive Industries Transparency Initiative, which supports transparency in the management of oil, gas, and mining revenues; and the Forest Law Enforcement, Governance and Trade initiative of the European Union, which seeks to curb illegal timber harvesting and trade.

Many high-value resources generate substantial revenues that the central government distributes, by means of budgetary allocations or direct transfers, to lower-level administrative units. The chapters in part 3 explore the pros and cons of various options for revenue distribution and address one of the most contentious issues associated with high-value resources: whether producing regions should receive preferential treatment in revenue distribution. Because many post-conflict countries are riddled with corruption, which diverts revenues from economic and social development needs, most of the chapters in part 3 also consider measures that can help stem corruption.

Even if resource revenues are distributed in a way that producing regions regard as fair, this does not ensure long-term development and peace. Long-term development and sustainable peace require that the revenues accruing to the central government and lower administrative units be spent wisely. But because many post-conflict countries are burdened by weak institutions and corrupt practices, it is difficult to ensure that revenue spending will have the desired effect on long-term development. Institution building is therefore crucial to natural resource management. Part 4 examines the role of revenue allocation and institution building, and includes several in-depth case studies on various approaches.

Resource management decisions promoted by donors and made by the central government may have strong and unintended effects on local livelihoods. Resources that have fueled conflict may also be central to the survival of local communities; hence, interfering with the extraction of such resources may create new grievances and conflicts. Part 5 highlights the importance of taking local livelihoods and economies into account in the design and implementation of approaches to managing high-value natural resources. The chapters address sustainable forest management, the precarious position of women in artisanal mining, the effects of environmental degradation on the peace process, and the vulnerability of farmers who cultivate opium poppy.

A concluding chapter distills lessons from the preceding chapters and identifies sequencing options for various approaches to high-value natural resource management.

Taken together, the chapters in this volume offer a consistent message: proper management of high-value natural resources is crucial in the aftermath of armed conflict. Effective management of these key assets can support a range of peacebuilding objectives—from livelihood and macroeconomic recovery, to good governance and inclusive political processes, to improved security. But the chapters also demonstrate that there is no single, universally applicable approach to natural resource management in post-conflict settings.

On the one hand, the many strategies presented in this volume are not mutually exclusive but complementary. At the same time, not all strategies are appropriate for all post-conflict countries or for all natural resources. Resource management initiatives must take into account a number of factors, including the type of resources involved; past, current, and potential linkages with conflict; both regional and international dynamics and trade patterns; institutional quality and capacity with respect to resource management; and conditions that may have shaped resource management in the past. For example, where pre-conflict patronage systems and customary rules still exert strong influence, they should be attended to. Similarly, institutional capacity may limit the types of approaches that can be adopted; there may be little point, for instance, in putting time, money, and effort into comprehensive contract reviews when the political will to act on the results is lacking. Thus, decisions about how to improve the management of high-value natural resources in post-conflict settings require, first and foremost, thorough knowledge of the context, including the limitations on institutional capacity and political will. Only then is it possible to choose the appropriate strategies, determine how they will be implemented, and assign them priority within the overall post-conflict peacebuilding process.

One must always keep in mind the opportunities that lie, sometimes well hidden, in high-value resources. With improved governance, resource-rich countries can turn the resource curse into a blessing. Although many of the cases in this book depict missed opportunities and failed efforts to bring countries and people to peace, the hope is that this volume, by recounting past successes as well as failures, will help readers grasp the many opportunities that high-value natural resources offer to war-torn countries.

REFERENCES

Auty, R. M. 1993. *Sustaining development in mineral economies: The resource curse thesis.* London: Routledge.

Collier, P., L. Elliot, H. Hegre, A. Hoeffler, M. Reynal-Querol, and N. Sambanis. 2003. *Breaking the conflict trap: Civil war and development policy.* World Bank Policy Research Report. Oxford, UK: Oxford University Press.

Collier, P., and A. Hoeffler. 2004. Greed and grievance in civil war. *Oxford Economic Papers* 56 (4): 563–596.

———. 2006. The political economy of secession. In *Negotiating self-determination*, ed. H. Hannum and E. F. Babbitt. Lanham, MD: Lexington Books.

de Soysa, I., and E. Neumayer. 2007. Resource wealth and the risk of civil war onset: Results from a new dataset on natural resource rents, 1970–99. *Conflict Management and Peace Science* 24 (3): 201–218.

Economist. 2011. Guerrilla miners: The FARC turn to gold. January 27. www.economist.com/node/18013780?story_id=18013780.

Fearon, J. D. 2004. Why do some civil wars last so much longer than others? *Journal of Peace Research* 41 (3): 275–301.

Fearon, J. D., and D. D. Laitin. 2003. Ethnicity, insurgency, and civil war. *American Political Science Review* 97 (1): 75–90.

Gleditsch, N. P., P. Wallensteen, M. Eriksson, M. Sollenberg, and H. Strand. 2002. Armed conflict 1946–2001: A new dataset. *Journal of Peace Research* 39 (5): 615–637.

Global Witness. n.d. Definition of a conflict resource. www.globalwitness.org/campaigns/conflict.

Harbom, L., and P. Wallensteen. 2007. Armed conflicts, 1946–2006. *Journal of Peace Research* 44 (5): 623–634.

———. 2009. Armed conflicts, 1946–2008. *Journal of Peace Research* 46 (4): 577–587.

———. 2010. Armed conflicts, 1946–2009. *Journal of Peace Research* 47 (4): 501–509.

Hegre, H., and N. Sambanis. 2006. Sensitivity analysis of the empirical literature on civil war onset. *Journal of Conflict Resolution* 50 (4): 508–535.

Humphreys, M. 2005. Natural resources, conflict and conflict resolution: Uncovering the mechanisms. *Journal of Conflict Resolution* 49 (5): 508–537.

IMF (International Monetary Fund). 2001. Republic of Yemen: Selected issues. IMF Country Report No. 01/61. April. www.imf.org/external/pubs/ft/scr/2001/cr0161.pdf.

———. 2005. Algeria: Statistical appendix. IMF Country Report No. 05/51. February. www.imf.org/external/pubs/ft/scr/2005/cr0551.pdf.

———. 2007. Angola: Selected issues and statistical appendix. IMF Country Report No. 07/355. October. www.imf.org/external/pubs/ft/scr/2007/cr07355.pdf.

———. 2008. Socialist people's Libyan Arab Jamahiriya: Statistical appendix. IMF Country Report No. 08/301. September. www.imf.org/external/pubs/ft/scr/2008/cr08301.pdf.

———. 2009a. Niger: Selected issues and statistical appendix. IMF Country Report No. 09/70. February. www.imf.org/external/pubs/ft/scr/2009/cr0970.pdf.

———. 2009b. Sierra Leone: Selected issues and statistical appendix. IMF Country Report No. 09/12. January. www.imf.org/external/pubs/ft/scr/2009/cr0912.pdf.

———. 2010a. Central African Republic: Sixth review under the arrangement under the extended credit facility and financing assurances review—staff report; debt sustainability analysis; staff supplement; press release on the executive board discussion; and statement by the executive director for Central African Republic. IMF Country Report No. 10/332. www.imf.org/external/pubs/ft/scr/2010/cr10332.pdf.

———. 2010b. Chad: 2010 article IV consultation—staff report; staff supplements; public information notice on the executive board discussion; and statement by the executive director for Chad. IMF Country Report No. 10/196. June. www.imf.org/external/pubs/ft/scr/2010/cr10196.pdf.

———. 2010c. Colombia: Arrangement under the flexible credit line and cancellation of the current arrangement—staff report; staff supplement; press release on the executive board discussion; and statement by the authorities of Colombia. IMF Country Report No. 10/156. May. www.imf.org/external/pubs/ft/scr/2010/cr10156.pdf.

———. 2010d. Côte d'Ivoire: Second review under the three-year arrangement under the extended credit facility, request for waivers of nonobservance of performance criteria, and financing assurances review—staff report; staff statement; press release on the executive board discussion; and statement by the executive director for Côte d'Ivoire. IMF Country Report No. 10/228. July. www.imf.org/external/pubs/ft/scr/2010/cr10228.pdf.

———. 2010e. Democratic Republic of the Congo: Statistical appendix. IMF Country Report No. 10/11. January. www.imf.org/external/pubs/ft/scr/2010/cr1011.pdf.

———. 2011a. Iraq: Second review under the stand-by arrangement, requests for waiver of applicability, extension of the arrangement, and rephasing of access—staff report; press release on the executive board discussion; and statement by the executive director for Iraq. IMF Country Report No. 11/75. March. www.imf.org/external/pubs/ft/scr/2011/cr1175.pdf.

———. 2011b. Nigeria: 2010 – article IV consultation—staff report; debt sustainability analysis; informational annex; public information notice on the executive board discussion; and statement by the executive director for Nigeria. IMF Country Report No. 11/57. February. www.imf.org/external/pubs/ft/scr/2011/cr1157.pdf.

———. 2011c. Sudan: Second review under the 2009–10 staff-monitored program—staff report; staff supplement; and statement by the executive director for Sudan. IMF Country Report No. 11/86. April. www.imf.org/external/pubs/ft/scr/2011/cr1186.pdf.

Kalu, K. N. 2008. *State power, autarchy, and political conquest in Nigerian federalism.* Lanham, MD: Lexington Books.

Karl, T. L. 1997. *The paradox of plenty: Oil booms and petro-states.* Berkeley: University of California Press.

Le Billon, P. 2001. The political ecology of war: Natural resources and armed conflicts. *Political Geography* 20 (5): 561–584.

Lujala, P. 2009. Deadly combat over natural resources: Gems, petroleum, drugs, and the severity of armed civil conflict. *Journal of Conflict Resolution* 53 (1): 50–71.

———. 2010. The spoils of nature: Armed civil conflict and rebel access to natural resources. *Journal of Peace Research* 47 (1): 15–28.

New York Times. 2011. In Colombia, new gold rush fuels old conflict. March 3. www.nytimes.com/2011/03/04/world/americas/04colombia.html?_r=2&hp.

Ross, M. 2004a. How do natural resources influence civil war? Evidence from thirteen cases. *International Organization* 58 (Winter): 35–67.

———. 2004b. What do we know about natural resources and civil war? *Journal of Peace Research* 41 (3): 337–356.

Rustad, S. A., and H. M. Binningsbø. 2010. Rapid recurrence: Natural resources, armed conflict and peace. Working Paper, Center for the Study of Civil War. Oslo: Peace Research Institute Oslo.

Rustad, S. A., J. K. Rød, W. Larsen, and N. P. Gleditsch. 2008. Foliage and fighting: Forest resources and the onset, duration and location of civil war. *Political Geography* 27 (7): 761–782.

Sphere Project. 2004. Humanitarian charter and minimum standards in disaster response. www.sphereproject.org/content/view/720/200/lang,english/.

Talbott, K., Y. Akimoto, and K. Cuskelly. 2012. Burma's cease-fire regime: Two decades of unaccountable natural resource exploitation. In *Governance, natural resources, and post-conflict peacebuilding*, ed. C. Bruch, C. Muffett, and S. S. Nichols. London: Earthscan.

Turnell, S. 2010. Finding dollars and sense: Burma's economy in 2010. In *Finding dollars, sense, and legitimacy in Burma*, ed. S. L. Levenstein. Washington, D. C.: Woodrow Wilson International Center for Scholars.

UN (United Nations). 2011. *Civilian capacity in the aftermath of conflict: Independent report of the Senior Advisory Group.* www.civcapreview.org/LinkClick.aspx?fileticket =K5tZZE99vzs%3d&tabid=3188&language=en-US.

UNEP (United Nations Environment Programme). 2009. *From conflict to peacebuilding: The role of natural resources and the environment.* Nairobi. http://postconflict.unep.ch/publications/pcdmb_policy_01.pdf.

UNSG (United Nations Secretary-General). 2009. Report of the Secretary-General on peacebuilding in the immediate aftermath of conflict. A/63/881-S/2009/304. June 11. New York: United Nations.
———. 2010. Report of the Secretary-General on peacebuilding in the immediate aftermath of conflict. A/64/866–S/2010/386. July 16. New York: United Nations.
UNSG's (United Nations Secretary-General's) Policy Committee. 2007. Conceptual basis for peacebuilding for the UN system. May. New York: United Nations.
USIP (United States Institute of Peace) and U.S. Army PKSOI (Peacekeeping and Stability Operations Institute). 2009. *Guiding principles for stabilization and reconstruction.* Washington, D.C.: Endowment of the United States Institute of Peace. www.usip.org/publications/guiding-principles-stabilization-and-reconstruction.
Webersik, C., and A. Crawford. 2012. Commence in the chaos: Charcoal, bananas, fisheries, and conflict in Somalia. In *Livelihoods and natural resources in post-conflict peacebuilding*, ed. H. Young and L. Goldman. London: Earthscan.
World Bank. 2011. *World development report 2011*. Washington, D.C. http://wdr2011.worldbank.org/sites/default/files/pdfs/WDR2011_Full_Text.pdf.

PART 1
Extraction and extractive industries

Introduction

In post-conflict countries, proper management of high-value natural resources can yield the necessary revenues to put the economy back on track and allow recovery from conflict. But such resources can also be a source of tension and even violence: for example, former belligerents who are unsatisfied with the terms of the peace agreement may seek opportunities to finance a new uprising; extractive companies may attempt to take advantage of disarray to secure lucrative resource concessions; and corrupt government officials may seek opportunities to enrich themselves and their constituencies. Local populations, meanwhile, are desperate to rebuild their homes and their lives; often depend on natural resources for their livelihoods; and may be suffering not only from the effects of conflict, but also from the negative side effects of resource extraction.

It is imperative, in post-conflict settings, to curtail potential peace spoilers' access to resources that have previously financed conflict or that could be used to finance renewed conflict. At the same time, to avoid exacerbating old grievances or creating new ones, it is important to minimize the harmful social and environmental consequences of extraction, to ensure that local residents participate in decision making about extraction projects, and to maximize benefits to local communities. Finally, it is essential to ensure that contracts for large-scale resource extraction are fair, and that the state receives a fair share of revenues. Each of the six chapters in part 1 approaches these issues from different angles.

In most post-conflict countries, peace is fragile at first, and some groups may actively seek to destabilize it. Whatever the motivations for such actions, they can be financed by readily extractable resources; curtailing these groups' access to resources may thus be crucial to promoting peace. In "Bankrupting Peace Spoilers: Can Peacekeepers Curtail Belligerents' Access to Resource Revenues?" Philippe Le Billon evaluates United Nations initiatives designed to prevent peace spoilers from gaining access to resource revenues. Drawing on examples from eight countries, Le Billon concludes that the UN should mandate peacekeeping missions to engage more directly with resources that could finance conflict, both at extraction points and along transit routes, and that such efforts should be backed up by targeted commodity sanctions and careful monitoring.

Foreign direct investment in the natural resource sector is common in resource-rich countries, and post-conflict countries are no exception. From a peacebuilding perspective, foreign direct investment is important because it brings private sector resources to bear on the reconstruction of post-conflict economies and societies. While it is often in a company's best interest to act responsibly—whether to enhance its reputation, secure financing, or avoid costly conflicts with local populations and host governments—firms sometimes need to be compelled to adhere to corporate social responsibility standards. In other cases, companies may have the will but may lack understanding of the particular challenges posed by resource extraction in post-conflict situations. The voluntary standards outlined in Jill Shankleman's chapter, "Mitigating Risks and Realizing Opportunities: Environmental and Social Standards for Foreign Direct Investment in High-Value Natural Resources," are designed to help extractive companies engage in responsible natural resource exploitation. Although the standards were not developed specifically for post-conflict settings, they are relevant to peacebuilding because, among other requirements, they call for investors to evaluate, monitor, and respond to risks to the environment, land rights, migration, employment, and security. The chapter describes the standards, illustrates their application in post-conflict countries, and evaluates their strengths and weaknesses with respect to peacebuilding.

The phrase *odious contracts* is used to refer to contracts that grant extractive companies unduly high profit margins, generous tax exemptions, or other benefits; that are signed under conditions that lack transparency and accountability; that are not approved by local communities; or that fail to stipulate appropriate environmental and social standards. Such contracts can not only lead to significant losses of public revenues, but can also generate grievances and conflict. In "Contract Renegotiation and Asset Recovery in Post-Conflict Settings," Philippe Le Billon uses two case examples—Liberia and the Democratic Republic of the Congo—to consider the challenges involved in reviewing such contracts. The chapter also examines the theft of revenues during conflict, either by rebels or corrupt government officials. Le Billon argues that although asset recovery (which involves tracking, freezing, and repatriating stolen revenues) has a mixed record, it is an important means of signaling an end to impunity for war profiteering.

The topics of transparency, accountability, participation, and environmental and social responsibility are further developed in "Reopening and Developing Mines in Post-Conflict Situations: The Challenge of Company-Community Relations," by Volker Boege and Daniel M. Franks. Many post-conflict governments are weak—and, in some regions, virtually absent. Where state institutions lack capacity and effectiveness, local populations may adhere to local traditions and customary laws, under which resource concessions granted by the central government lack legitimacy. In such cases, company-community relations become crucial in obtaining local consent for extraction projects. Focusing on case examples from Papua New Guinea and Guatemala, Boege and Franks illustrate the importance of dialogue, consultation, and public participation in efforts to gain legitimacy in the eyes of the population. The chapter also examines the role of company-community relations in finding solutions that are not only beneficial for extractive firms, local communities, and host governments, but that also contribute to peace.

Company-community relations are explored further in Kazumi Kawamoto's "Diamonds in War, Diamonds for Peace: Diamond Sector Management and Kimberlite Mining in Sierra Leone." The first portion of this chapter traces the history of the relationship between diamonds and conflict in Sierra Leone. The second focuses on an industrial diamond-mining site where forced relocations, contention over promised amenities, and failure to take local communities' concerns into account led to a violent riot. Although this one incident does not seem to have jeopardized long-term peace, Kawamoto's chapter provides a cautionary tale about the importance of taking grievances seriously and including local residents in decisions about extraction. When such incidents are allowed to proliferate, they may not only create serious tensions, but may also divert attention and revenues from other pressing issues, and thereby prolong or even destabilize peacebuilding.

In the final chapter of part 1, "Assigned Corporate Social Responsibility in a Rentier State: The Case of Angola," Arne Wiig and Ivar Kolstad discuss the responsibility of international oil companies in a nation where the government has failed to meet the socioeconomic needs of the population. Wiig and Kolstad argue, on the basis of the assigned-responsibility model, that because the government has failed to meet its responsibility, and the international community and civil society have failed (or were unable) to take secondary responsibility, the large multinational oil companies doing business in Angola are morally obligated to step into the breach and advocate improved governance. This obligation is especially strong because the companies have been financing the country's patronage system, have benefited from the dysfunctional institutions that are in place, and have sufficient power to push for improved governance.

Taken together, the chapters in part 1 focus on the ways in which governments, extractive industries, the international community, and civil society can strengthen the management of high-value resource extraction to promote peace. The principal areas of focus are preventing potential peace spoilers from obtaining access to resources, reviewing and addressing contracts signed by previous governments, developing conflict-sensitive extraction projects, and ensuring community participation in decision making about extraction projects.

Bankrupting peace spoilers: Can peacekeepers curtail belligerents' access to resource revenues?

Philippe Le Billon

High-value natural resources—such as timber, minerals, and opium—are often sources of tension and violence during post-conflict transition periods. Resource production areas and trade routes are commonly hot spots for armed groups, including security forces that have been demobilized but not disarmed and reintegrated; they also tend to be theaters for clashes between competing groups that run protection rackets for illegal activities. Armed groups rely on resource sectors for survival; they may also engage in resource-related human rights abuses—as, for example, when security forces forcibly displace local residents or migrant workers, or compel them to engage in forced labor in order to open up land for resource projects.

Curtailing belligerents' access to weapons has been a major focus of international security actors. Although weapons embargoes and disarmament initiatives are important, they are difficult to implement and generally insufficient to secure long-term peace. Curtailing belligerents' access to resource revenues provides a complementary and possibly more effective approach, particularly when it is combined with reforms that address both the "enabling effect" of resources on armed violence and the broader economic, political, and environmental causes of conflict associated with resource sectors.

One approach to curtailing belligerents' access to revenues and reducing the human rights abuses associated with resource sectors is to mandate peacekeeping missions whose express responsibility is to prevent peace spoiling and protect civilians. Such a mandate could be backed by commodity sanctions that are contingent on (1) the achievement of peace-process benchmarks and (2) adherence to legal (or at least specified) practices in a given resource sector. A logging sector, for example, can be closed for exports until sound regulatory institutions are in place and until the state has the capacity, legitimacy, and stability to ensure

---

Philippe Le Billon is an associate professor at the University of British Columbia, where he is affiliated with both the Department of Geography and the Liu Institute for Global Issues.

their effectiveness. Although there are major obstacles to deploying peacekeeping forces to curtail access to resources, which will be discussed in the course of the chapter, the approach nonetheless offers a number of benefits.[1]

The chapter is divided into five major parts: (1) a brief review of the principal instruments that the United Nations Security Council (UNSC) has used to address "conflict resources";[2] (2) a discussion of strategies for controlling access to conflict resources; (3) a summary of the work of eight UN peacekeeping missions in contexts that involved conflict resources, with particular attention to the Democratic Republic of the Congo (DRC); (4) a summary discussion of the issues associated with the deployment of peacekeepers in efforts to curtail access to conflict resources; and (5) a brief conclusion.

UN INITIATIVES

UN initiatives to address the links between high-value natural resources and armed conflicts have included economic sanctions, expert panels, and specific measures undertaken as part of the peacemaking, peacekeeping, or peacebuilding tasks carried out by UN missions.[3] Through resolutions passed in the UNSC and General Assembly, the UN has also supported a number of other initiatives, such as the Kimberley Process Certification Scheme, which is designed to stem the trade in conflict diamonds. And through the UN Global Compact, the UN has supported corporate social responsibility—most notably by raising awareness and standards of practice among extractive companies operating in conflict zones.

Commodity sanctions have targeted rebel groups by curtailing their access to resource revenues; examples include the Khmer Rouge, in Cambodia (logs); the National Union for the Total Independence of Angola (União Nacional para a Independência Total de Angola, or UNITA), in Angola (diamonds); the Revolutionary United Front (RUF), in Sierra Leone (diamonds); the Taliban, in Afghanistan (opium production); and the New Forces (Forces Nouvelles), in Côte d'Ivoire (diamonds). Resource-focused sanctions have also targeted the governments of Iraq, Liberia, and Libya (the third for its involvement in the Lockerbie

---

[1] The analysis in this chapter draws on primary and secondary sources, personal communications with staff at the UN Department of Peacekeeping Operations, and on direct observation of, or participation in, peacekeeping operations in Angola, Cambodia, the Democratic Republic of the Congo, Sierra Leone, and the former Yugoslavia. The chapter does not present a comprehensive record of peacekeeping.

[2] *Conflict resources* are defined as "natural resources whose systematic exploitation and trade in a context of conflict contribute to, benefit from or result in the commission of serious violations of human rights, violations of international humanitarian law or violations amounting to crimes under international law" (Global Witness n.d.).

[3] *Peacemaking* seeks to facilitate the resolution of a conflict; *peacekeeping* seeks to prevent further violence; and *peacebuilding* is a long-term process that seeks to promote reconciliation and prevent future conflicts.

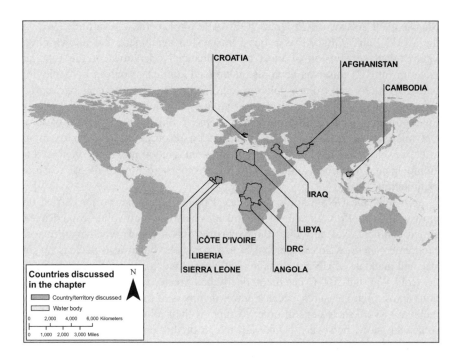

bombing, rather than for its training and funding of insurgent groups in civil wars) (Cortright and Lopez 2002).

With the exception of Cambodia, Iraq, and Libya, all these sanction regimes were associated with investigations by UN expert panels—consultants hired by the UN Secretariat to investigate war economies and sanction busting.[4] Because the panels' reports are made public, they have been instrumental in successful "naming and shaming" campaigns. Even though fewer than a handful of sanction busters had been successfully prosecuted by 2006, the public reports had the desired chilling effect.

UN transitional authorities and specialized UN agencies have also engaged in other activities that are related to conflict resources, including partnering with national authorities and international aid agencies to reform resource sectors and build local institutional capacity in post-conflict settings.[5] For example, the UN Transitional Authority in Timor-Leste renegotiated the maritime boundary between Timor-Leste and Australia, which had implications for petroleum exploitation; and the UN Mission in Liberia (UNMIL) supported the Governance and Economic

---

[4] The first such panel was launched in 1999 by Robert Fowler, chair of the Angola Sanction Committee. The UN Commission of Inquiry on Rwanda, established in 1994 (Boucher and Holt 2009), predated the investigation of the Angola Sanction Committee.

[5] The UN Food and Agriculture Organization, the UN Environment Programme, and the UN Development Programme are among the UN agencies involved in such efforts.

Management Assistance Program (GEMAP) for Liberia. An initiative led by the World Bank, GEMAP is a quasi-trusteeship agreement that allows direct international supervision of most of the financial operations of the Liberian government. UN missions have also addressed conflict resources by deploying border monitors and troops; policing (e.g., deploying UN troops as backup for resource management officials); and providing supervision and technical assistance for economic reforms and resource management. Finally, the activities of some UN missions have had an indirect impact on resource sectors: for example, effective disarmament, demobilization, and reintegration programs often lead to employment for former soldiers, who might otherwise turn to illegal resource exploitation.[6]

Overall, the UNSC holds the greatest potential and has so far carried the most weight in efforts to address the linkages between high-value resources and armed conflicts. Not only does the Security Council decide whether to impose economic sanctions and dispatch UN expert panels, but it also decides on the size and mandate of UN missions in conflict-affected countries. Since the end of the Cold War, the UNSC has theoretically had greater freedom to impose sanctions and similar measures, because fewer members of the Security Council were inclined to veto such steps in order to support their allies. The UNSC has been somewhat slow, however, to take advantage of this potential. Meanwhile, the importance of resources to armed groups has grown rapidly since the late 1980s, as belligerents turned to natural resources to replace external political sponsorship. For most of the 1990s, the UNSC made increasing use of arms sanctions, negotiated settlements, and regional or UN peacekeeping missions, but rarely of commodity sanctions. Although arms sanctions may be more effective than commodity sanctions and may therefore continue to be the principal sanction strategy, that is not to say that the two approaches cannot be combined.[7]

Between 1989 and 2006, the UNSC used commodity sanctions in only about one-third of the conflicts involving resources (Le Billon 2007). Most of these sanctions have been imposed since the late 1990s, nearly a decade after resources came to play a major role in belligerents' finances. When the use of commodity sanctions finally increased, it was given a further boost by a more proactive use of sanctions committees and expert panels. Because of broader engagement on the part of nongovernmental organizations (NGOs), conflict analysts, and resource industries, sanctions are now better targeted, monitored, and enforced, while their humanitarian impact is more carefully considered. The UNSC is now considering bolstering the authority and capacity of UN peacekeeping missions to more directly intervene in the control of resource sectors—a step that was recently taken in the DRC.

---

[6] UN involvement in disarmament, demobilization, and reintegration dates back to the UN's first major, multidimensional peacekeeping mission, which was established in Cambodia in the early 1990s. (This mission is discussed later in the chapter.)

[7] On the cases of Liberia and Côte d'Ivoire, see Strandow (2006).

STRATEGIES FOR CONTROLLING ACCESS TO CONFLICT RESOURCES

Experience with the imposition of sanctions, and understanding gained through investigations conducted by expert panels, conflict analysts, and NGOs, suggests that efforts to address the links between high-value natural resources and armed conflicts will be more effective if the approach is explicitly shaped by what is known about the situation, including the following factors:

- The characteristics of the resources (legality, accessibility, and geographical distribution).
- The structure of the industry and of the commodity chain (that is, the chain of supply between production and consumption): transportation routes, transformation sites, relative monopoly within the sector, level of concentration, and consumer awareness.
- The motivation and capacity of intermediaries and authorities along the commodity chain (e.g., domestic and regional governments, trade associations).
- The type of conflict and the types of armed groups being targeted.

Taking direct control of production sites allows peacekeepers to more readily prevent connections between resource production and armed groups. Control of production sites is extremely difficult, however, when resource operations are transient and when both workers and armed groups move rapidly. For example, mining operations that target easily reached minerals may be as short as a few days. Logging ventures may also be transient, especially when they can take advantage of an existing transportation network.

The sheer number, remoteness, insecurity, and transient character of production sites may render mapping difficult (Spittaels and Hilgert 2009); this not only increases labor demand but also increases the risk of casualties for both UN troops and the civilians who are brought in to regulate resource activities. Moreover, when peacekeepers attempt to control transient production sites in rebel-controlled areas, it may be difficult to distinguish between civilians and combatants. Finally, there is a risk of "mission creep," in which the UN assumes responsibility for an increasing number of tasks, thereby creating further dependence on UN troops. Nevertheless, the presence of armed groups often increases poverty and the likelihood of abuse of local populations (Weinstein 2006); hence, for lack of an alternative, the direct deployment of UN peacekeeping troops in resource production areas may make sense.

A second, related approach is to control key points in trade and transportation routes, such as trading houses; storage locations; and major roads, bridges, rivers, and airports. This approach has two main difficulties, however: determining where resources have come from and whether they are legitimate, and avoiding delays for legitimate entrepreneurs (Crossin, Hayman, and Taylor 2003). Working with expert panels and local authorities, peacekeeping missions can help identify and, if given the necessary authority, arrest traders who are dealing in conflict resources. Trade controls at national borders, in particular, can simultaneously stem the flow of revenues to armed groups and assist the government to improve revenue collection. Peacekeepers posted at control points may also support sanction schemes or verify that certification measures are in effect. It is important to note, however, that most UN missions have limited mandates and operational scope. Border controls, for example, have focused mostly on controlling imports (such as incoming weapons), rather than exports (such as smuggled natural resources), although there have been some exceptions, most notably in the case of missions that assume governing functions, including the provision of border security (Walsh et al. 2007).

The first two approaches—taking control of production sites and of key points in trade routes—involve *direct* control over natural resources; a third approach should be considered when belligerents obtain funding through *indirect* control over natural resources. For example, armed groups may impose "taxes" on supplies destined for mining camps; extort funds from municipalities that are in proximity to natural resources (or that receive revenue from natural resources); or engage in other forms of extortion and racketeering. In such cases, peacekeeping forces are needed to improve security, severing the indirect control of resources and decreasing belligerents' opportunities to threaten, intimidate, or harm civilians, companies, or government institutions. Peacekeepers may also step in for local police forces when it is necessary to make politically charged arrests.[8] Field investigations have revealed dangerous complicities with belligerents—notably among local officials—that must be taken into account in the peacebuilding process (e.g., when officials are engaging in sanction busting or providing fuel to armed groups).

While the first three approaches deal with supply-side issues, a fourth approach is needed to tackle the demand side—that is, helping importing countries implement resource control measures such as sanctions or certifications. Typically, demand-side enforcement mechanisms include sanctions on specific commodities from particular countries (e.g., timber from Liberia); information sharing between peacekeeping forces, customs offices, importing governments, UN missions, and UN expert panels; and the monitoring of both upstream and downstream channels, through due diligence processes, to determine the legality of the extraction process and identify any human rights abuses.

Although the lack of territorial and institutional access to neighboring countries has so far prevented peacekeeping missions from implementing these approaches, specific mandates for peacekeeping missions, combined with formal

---

[8] When organizations or individuals are attempting to survive (or even prosper) in the midst of conflict, boundaries between belligerent groups, government officials, and civilians may become blurred; this is particularly the case when the belligerent groups' "frontlines" are shifting or nonexistent.

requests to neighboring governments from the UNSC, may secure such access. As noted earlier, sanctions are one of the Security Council's main tools; thus, the UNSC has, on occasion, imposed so-called secondary sanctions on neighboring states. These secondary sanctions target countries that have failed to block the import of conflict resources and continue to export them as a legal commodity, or that have refused access to peacekeeping missions attempting to implement sanctions on a commodity. Although secondary sanctions are effective when targeted to very specific commodities (as was the case in Liberia, where diamond exports were sanctioned as a result of the government's support of the rebellion in Sierra Leone), broader secondary sanctions raise ethical issues.

On the basis of past UN experience, a possible strategy for controlling access to conflict resources would involve the following sequence of initiatives:

1. An investigation by an expert panel.
2. The imposition of targeted commodity sanctions.
3. The establishment of peacekeeping missions authorized to engage in resource control.
4. If necessary, the imposition of secondary sanctions on sanction busters.

One way to strengthen this sequence is to encourage greater collaboration between expert panels and peacekeeping missions (Holt and Boucher 2009). Efforts to curb access to conflict resources are often combined with a post-conflict review of all resource sectors, and support for local authorities' efforts to recover looted assets and renegotiate resource contracts signed during hostilities.[9]

UN PEACEKEEPING MISSIONS AND CONFLICT RESOURCES

UN peacekeeping operations have been established in at least eight countries where conflict resources contributed to prolonging hostilities. This section briefly reviews the mandates, specific measures, and effectiveness in each case; examples are presented in chronological order (see table 1).

Angola

UNAVEM, the UN Angola Verification Missions (1988–1997), and MONUA, the UN Observer Mission in Angola (1997–1999), had limited mandates (mostly observation and facilitation of demobilization) and little military capacity. Neither mission took major steps to prevent diamonds from financing UNITA, either before or after 1997, when the UN imposed an export ban on diamonds that were not certified by the government (uncertified diamonds were presumed to come

---

[9] For further discussion of contract renegotiation and asset recovery, see Philippe Le Billon, "Contract Renegotiation and Asset Recovery in Post-Conflict Settings," in this volume.

Table 1. Control of conflict resources by UN peacekeeping missions, 1988–2009

Mission	Type of mandate	Measures	Outcomes
Angola: UNAVEM[a] (1988–1997), MONUA[b] (1997–1999)	Observation	Ban on noncertified diamond exports	The missions had very limited effectiveness, but the ban was effective—partly because of military pressure on UNITA from the Angolan government, and partly because the governments in Kinshasa (DRC) and Brazzaville (Republic of the Congo), which had provided conduits for UNITA's diamond smuggling, were toppled; peacekeepers provided some assistance to UN expert panels.
Cambodia: UNTAC[c] (1992–1993)	Transitional authority	Ban on logging exports (sawn timber exempt)	Limited effectiveness because the ban was not implemented for long enough, and there was no UN enforcement of the ban in Khmer Rouge areas along the Thai border; the UN mission provided some assistance as a transitional authority in the area of environmental and resource management.
Croatia UNTAES[d] (1996–1998)	Transitional authority	Border monitoring	Limited support for local police forces.
Sierra Leone: UNAMSIL[e] (1999–2005)	Assistance	Ban on noncertified diamond exports	Peacekeepers provided some assistance with monitoring and conflict resolution in the diamond sector.
DRC: MONUC[f] (1999–2010), MONUSCO[g] (2010–present)	Assistance	Curtailing financing of illegal groups	Monitoring, border control at airports, some military assistance to Congolese army to curtail armed groups' access to natural resources.
Afghanistan: UNAMA[h] (2002–present)	Assistance	Counternarcotics operations	Policy coordination and technical cooperation; no military component.
Liberia: UNMIL[i] (2003–present)	Assistance	Ban on timber and all diamond exports	Limited assistance in key areas; UNMIL also maintains an Environment and Natural Resources Unit, which assists UN expert panels.
Côte d'Ivoire: MINUCI[j] (2003–2004), UNOCI[k] (2004–présent)	Assistance	Ban on all diamond exports	Embargo-monitoring unit; no mandate to address key resource sectors (e.g., cocoa) from which rebels obtain financing.

Notes:
a. UN Angola Verification Missions.
b. UN Observer Mission in Angola.
c. UN Transitional Authority in Cambodia.
d. UN Transitional Administration in Eastern Slavonia, Baranja, and Western Sirmium.
e. UN Assistance Mission in Sierra Leone.
f. UN Mission in the Democratic Republic of the Congo.
g. UN Stabilization Mission in the Democratic Republic of the Congo.
h. UN Assistance Mission in Afghanistan.
i. UN Mission in Liberia.
j. UN Mission in Côte d'Ivoire.
k. UN Operation in Côte d'Ivoire.

from UNITA-controlled areas). MONUA did, however, provide logistical assistance to a UN panel of experts in 1999.

Cambodia

In Cambodia, the Khmer Rouge (also known as the Party of Democratic Kampuchea, or PDK) was financed by logging and, to a lesser extent, gem mining. Using military observers and aerial surveys, UNTAC, the UN Transitional Authority in Cambodia (1992–1993), documented the extent of the exploitation, thereby increasing the (mostly ineffective) pressure that environmental and human rights groups had been putting on the transitional government, the Supreme National Council, to declare a moratorium on the export of logs from Cambodia—which it did, on September 22, 1992. On November 30, 1992, the UNSC supported the moratorium through resolution 792, which requested "States, especially neighbouring States, to respect . . . [the] moratorium by not importing such logs" and further requested "UNTAC to take appropriate measures to secure the implementation of such moratorium" (UNSC 1992). The resolution also extended the moratorium to the export of minerals and gems.

Although the resolution was carefully phrased as an effort to protect Cambodia's natural resources, the fact that it was not vetoed by China, the PDK's main backer, sent an important political signal to the PDK. Nevertheless, the resolution was largely useless: UNTAC was unable to gain access to smuggling areas, either from PDK-controlled territory or from the Thai side; the transitional government's implementation of the moratorium was erratic; and sawn-timber exports were exempt from the moratorium. Moreover, immediately after the UN-sponsored elections in May 1993, the transitional government expanded exemptions even further. In addition to its limited involvement in the moratorium, UNTAC provided some guidance to local authorities in environmental and resource management, as part of its mandate as a transitional authority.

Croatia

Like UNTAC, the UN Transitional Administration in Eastern Slavonia, Baranja, and Western Sirmium, or UNTAES (1996–1998), also had to deal with illegal logging, but on a much smaller scale; as Serbian-held territories reverted to Croatia, local "mafia" groups engaged in a pattern of "looting before leaving." Timber smuggling appeared to be mostly criminally motivated, with limited consequences for the evolution of the conflict. While border monitors were checking for incoming weapons, valuable hardwoods, including oak, were being smuggled to Serbia for eventual export to Europe. Trafficking routes were known, but neither UN border officers nor UNTAES military personnel were authorized to take action, other than to provide limited support for local police forces; Serbian militias also refrained from intervening. Joint Serbian-Croatian police forces, however, did conduct some operations, including border patrols, which apparently had some success in countering illegal logging and smuggling (UNSC 1997).

Sierra Leone

The UN Assistance Mission in Sierra Leone, or UNAMSIL (1999–2005), actively engaged in diamond sector regulation only in the last stages of its operation. Before that point, peacekeeping forces had intervened in an ad hoc fashion to prevent the escalation of resource-related conflicts,[10] but the UN mission remained wary of overstepping its mandate,[11] antagonizing local interest groups, exposing UN troops to criminal violence, or reinforcing rumors that peacekeeping forces were involved in diamond deals (UNAMSIL 2001). Although some of these concerns were legitimate, reports from military observers about diamond-related conflicts (including ongoing armed skirmishes) and requests for assistance from the government and from the donors who were funding diamond reforms eventually led UNAMSIL to take on a more proactive role. In 2003, two years after hostilities had ceased, UNAMSIL began conducting aerial surveys, deploying foot patrols, and engaging in targeted conflict-settlement interventions in the diamond sector—most notably, working with local youths who were in conflict with mining groups made up of former RUF soldiers. These efforts were often undertaken jointly with the Ministry of Mines, but UNAMSIL occasionally served in a supervisory capacity for that ministry (DFID 2006).

Democratic Republic of the Congo

Since its establishment in 1999, the UN mission in the Democratic Republic of the Congo (Mission de l'Organisation des Nations Unies en République Démocratique du Congo, or MONUC) repeatedly confronted conflict-related resources issues. During the first war (1996–1997), the second war (1998–2003), and the aftermath of the second war, mineral resources financed both local and foreign armed groups, especially in the eastern part of the country. Although the UN has used expert panel investigations and public reporting to address this connection, it has not imposed sanctions on conflict resources.[12]

By 2008, MONUC was already planning joint operations with the Congolese army, the Forces Armées de la République Démocratique du Congo (FARDC), to disrupt the presence of the Democratic Forces for the Liberation of Rwanda

---

[10] Peacekeepers intervened, for example, in the clashes between local youths and demobilized rebel soldiers during the 2001 diamond rush in Koidu, Sierra Leone's diamond capital.

[11] This reluctance was despite the fact that the mandate included coordinating with, and assisting, Sierra Leonean law enforcement in the discharge of its responsibilities (UNAMSIL 2005).

[12] The DRC is part of the Kimberley Process Certification Scheme; thus, its official exports ought to exclude diamonds that come from rebel-controlled areas.

(Forces Démocratiques de Libération du Rwanda, or FDLR) "in mining areas ... [to drive] them away from their most important trading routes" (Doss n.d.).[13] In December 2008, with Resolution 1856 the Security Council gave MONUC a mandate to

> coordinate operations with the FARDC integrated brigades deployed in the eastern part of the Democratic Republic of the Congo and support operations led by and jointly planned with these brigades in accordance with international humanitarian, human rights and refugee law with a view to ... preventing the provision of support to illegal armed groups, including support derived from illicit economic activities (UNSC 2008f, para. 3(g)).

MONUC was also given authority to "use its monitoring and inspection capacities to curtail the provision of support to illegal armed groups derived from illicit trade in natural resources" (UNSC 2008f).

In Resolution 1857, the UNSC extended the list of individuals and companies subject to travel sanctions, financial sanctions, or both, to "individuals or entities supporting the illegal armed groups in the eastern part of the Democratic Republic of the Congo through illicit trade of natural resources," thus sending a strong signal to companies involved in trading conflict resources (UNSC 2008g para. 4(g)).[14] The UNSC also requested that MONUC, governments in the region, and the group of experts "cooperate intensively, including by exchanging information regarding ... the illegal trafficking in natural resources" (UNSC 2008g, para. 11).[15] Military cooperation between MONUC and the Congolese government has not been straightforward, however; in a joint Congolese-Rwandan operation undertaken in January and February 2009 against the FDLR, for example, MONUC was largely excluded from planning and implementation.

Implementation of Security Council Resolution 1856 involves some major difficulties:

- The resolution calls for MONUC to work "in close collaboration" with the Congolese government and to intervene "in support of" FARDC-led operations (Peleman 2009). While this requirement recognizes the sovereignty of the Congolese state, it has led to delays that might not have occurred if MONUC troops been able to intervene autonomously.
- Many of the new FARDC officers are former members of armed groups that continue to have a stake in illegal exploitation, and some FARDC units are directly involved in such exploitation. As noted by Global Witness, "in parts of Mwenga and Kalehe, Congolese army units ... have started taking over

---

[13] The FDLR is a militia made up of chiefly Rwandan Hutus, many of whom have lived in the DRC since the 1994 Rwandan genocide.
[14] An earlier resolution, 1807, had established the initial list (UNSC 2008d). The only companies on the list were from the DRC, Rwanda, or Uganda (UNSC 2009a).
[15] "Group of experts" is the new name for UN expert panels.

mining sites after dislodging the FDLR" (2009b, 3). In response to criticism of such actions, Joseph Kabila, the president of the DRC, ordered all military personnel to vacate mining sites (Global Witness 2009a).[16]

- The situation in the DRC is complicated by the fact that natural resources are not the only source of finance for armed groups. Some militias also derive income from illegally taxing the local population. Curtailing access to resource revenues may therefore, at least in the short term, increase predatory behavior toward local populations—which might, in turn, increase the workload of the UN mission, whose main task is to protect the civilian population. MONUC has limited capacity, and needs to prioritize its activities. As of this writing, MONUC is placing priority on protecting civilians and curbing the activities of armed groups (chiefly the FDLR), even if curtailing armed groups' access to resources would improve medium-term prospects.
- Not all mining sites and links in the trading network can be brought under control. Systematic mapping of mining- and mineral-trade routes in North Kivu and South Kivu (in the eastern DRC) identified 215 mining sites, 45 trading houses, 10 airports, and 6 major border crossings (IPIS 2008). In July 2009, Lt. Col. Jean-Paul Dietrich, a MONUC military spokesperson, noted that while Kimia II, a joint FARDC-MONUC military operation undertaken in 2009, "aimed at recovering the main mining sites ... there are other sources of income [still available] for the FDLR and the armed groups" (IRIN 2009). A report from Global Witness also stressed that while Kimia II

    appears to have temporarily disrupted the FDLR's mining activities in certain other areas, ... the longer-term effect is not yet clear. The FDLR have abandoned some mines in parts of Mwenga (South Kivu), in anticipation of the deployment of [Kimia II], only to continue mining in nearby areas. The FDLR have turned increasingly violent against the civilian population since the start of [Kimia II] (2009b, 3).

- Despite nearly a decade of media, UN expert panel, and NGO reports stressing the importance of conflict resources, and despite the UNSC resolutions of late 2008 (UNSC 2008a, 2008b, 2008d)—which encouraged MONUC, more strongly than ever before, to cooperate with the FARDC to curtail the illegal resource trade—the UN has not taken the step of imposing sanctions, which would have made it easier to distinguish between legal and illegal

---

[16] Because MONUC is required to collaborate with the Congolese army, President Kabila's order effectively prevented MONUC troops from intervening at mine sites, giving a potential advantage to illegal armed groups that have sufficiently reduced their military presence to prevent the president from reversing his policy (and sending Congolese troops back to the mines), but that are nevertheless continuing their economic activities.

resources, exploitation, and trade.[17] In the absence of official sanctions, many resource companies, faced with accusations of complicity in war crimes, claim to have stopped importing minerals from conflict zones in the DRC—in particular, tantalite, from the eastern DRC. Thus, a poorly implemented de facto sanction regime is currently in place that obstructs even the legal traders, who then shift toward, or are replaced by, informal (and in some cases criminal) trading networks. The economic ascendance of informal or criminal networks, in turn, drags down miners' incomes (because these networks are associated with both lower prices and lower demand), and undermines the formal economy, governing institutions, and government revenues.

- Finally, implementation of UNSC Resolution 1856 is complicated by the involvement of Congolese military, political, and business leaders in "illegal" trade—an issue that is rendered even more complex by the difficulty of defining legality in the DRC, where political legitimacy (that is, the standing of the authorities that passed the laws) is uncertain, and where international, national, provincial, and customary laws may simultaneously apply (Cuvelier 2004). A 2009 UN report noted that "conducting random checks at port, airport or border posts can ... have serious consequences for the Mission's relations with the Government and the FARDC" (JMAC 2009, 4). In 2008, a UN expert panel argued that "targeting companies complicit in systematically trading minerals with FDLR and promoting due diligence within the international minerals supply chain represent effective ways of cutting off the financial support of FDLR" (UNSC 2008h, 19). Such efforts are complicated, however, by the fact that many of the businesspeople involved in conflict resources are also major subcontractors or landlords for MONUC and aid agencies. Thus, MONUC is in a somewhat difficult position: to accomplish its mandate, it must maintain a good relationship with the government of the DRC; but it may not always be in the interests of the government to have MONUC on board.

To address these problems, MONUC staff have recommended the following strategies (JMAC 2009):

- Training MONUC staff, especially military observers and civil police, in the monitoring of conflict resource trade (e.g., how to identify trade vectors—such as vehicles, planes, and companies—and how to recognize legal documentation).

---

[17] There were three reasons for the UN's resistance to the imposition of an embargo: concerns about its feasibility in the absence of support from neighboring countries; concerns about the embargo's effects on livelihoods and the overall economy; and the fact that regional political and economic elites—upon which both the political process and the logistics of the UN mission depend—may have been implicated in questionable activities.

- Deploying military observers at key locations (including airports), and providing support for unannounced inspections (e.g., of aircraft) by Congolese security forces.
- Removing armed groups and army checkpoints that are illegally taxing the resource trade.
- Assisting with capacity building for Congolese police, military personnel, and customs officers, through the provision of training and equipment.
- Profiling peace spoilers and key economic actors who are likely to be involved in the production and trading of conflict commodities.
- Undertaking satellite observation of mining sites and transportation corridors.
- Undertaking centralized data gathering and analysis.
- Building awareness, among local businesses, of illegal exploitation.[18]
- Engaging in broader collaboration with development agencies and local authorities to regulate and bring trade into the formal economy.

The Congolese government has also given attention to resource issues as part of its Programme of Stabilization and Rebuilding of Former Conflict Zones (STAREC). The program calls for Congolese security forces to monitor mining sites operated by armed groups; for government services (specifically, the mining registry; the Center of Evaluation, Expertise, and Certification, the DRC's regulatory mining body; and the Ministry of Mines' antifraud office) to be strengthened in the provinces; and for controls to be established on airfields and roads leading to mine sites (Custers 2009). As part of the STAREC initiative, the Congolese prime minister has asked MONUC to assist in the transportation and deployment of mining inspectors, but MONUC staff does not feel that such an effort can be undertaken until road projects are completed and police forces and credible public administrators are in place in areas where mines are located.

Afghanistan

UNAMA, the ongoing UN Assistance Mission in Afghanistan, was established in 2002 and faces the most difficult conflict resource issue of any current peacekeeping operation: in 2008 alone, opium is estimated to have provided between US$250 and US$470 million to the Taliban (UNODC 2008).[19] UNAMA's mandate is to cooperate with the Afghan government in "identifying individuals and

---

[18] This would involve, for example, helping businesses to understand that conflict resources are used to finance armed groups, to grasp the importance of legitimate government taxation, and to be aware of the risk of being sanctioned for dealing in conflict resources.

[19] Timber and other resources are also at issue, but to a much smaller degree (UNODC 2008).

entities participating in the financing or support of acts or activities of al Qaeda and the Taliban using proceeds derived from illicit cultivation, production and trafficking of narcotic drugs and their precursors" (UNSC 2009b, para. 31).[20]

Narcotics—in Afghanistan, most notably opium production and trafficking—have long been monitored by the UN Office on Drugs and Crime (UNODC), which closely cooperates with UNAMA and with a growing number of international development organizations. UNAMA's director for narcotics is also the UNODC director, and both organizations engage in policy coordination and technical cooperation but have no peacekeeping military component; most of the international troops in Afghanistan are part of the UNSC-mandated International Security Assistance Force (ISAF), which is under the command of the North Atlantic Treaty Organization (NATO).[21]

Until 2008, the ISAF limited its role to the support of Afghan-government drug-eradication policies, most visibly through the military protection of crop eradication units. Since then, NATO has taken a more direct approach, targeting drug laboratories and traffickers; however, each country that sends troops to the ISAF can choose its own level of involvement in counternarcotics activities, and interventions "can be taken only upon request of the Afghan Government and with the consent of the national authorities of the forces involved" (NATO n.d.).[22]

Several studies have pointed out that unless eradication programs improve the broader agricultural, economic, and, most importantly, institutional context of narcotics production, they are counterproductive (Byrd 2008; Goodhand 2008).[23] Although opium poppy cultivation declined in 2008, opium production had exceeded external demand for several years, primarily because of a lack of effective counternarcotics policies;[24] the resulting massive stockpiles have led to a drop in prices, which has contributed to an increase in the use of opium within Afghanistan (UNODC 2009).

---

[20] See also UNSC Resolutions 1267, 1735, 1806, and 1822 (UNSC 1999, 2006, 2008c, 2008e).

[21] For further discussion of counternarcotics policies and the organizations that are implementing them, see David M. Catarious Jr. and Alison Russell, "Counternarcotics Efforts and Afghan Poppy Farmers: Finding the Right Approach," in this volume.

[22] ISAF describes its direct military intervention in this area as "providing in-extremis support to the Afghan National Security Forces' counter-narcotics operations," although it will also provide "enhanced support" that includes "the destruction of processing facilities and action against narcotic producers if there is a clearly established link with the insurgency" (NATO n.d.).

[23] For more information on the role of opium in Afghanistan, see Adam Pain, "The Janus Nature of Opium Poppy: A View from the Field," in this volume.

[24] During the initial years of NATO's presence in Afghanistan, the primary focus was on political stability and antiterrorism—which led NATO countries to turn a blind eye to the involvement of supposed allies in the opium trade. NATO also wished to avoid upsetting the opium-based rural economy in many parts of the country.

Liberia

UNMIL, the ongoing UN Mission in Liberia, was established in 2003; its mandate is "to assist the transitional government in restoring proper administration of natural resources," as part of the implementation of the peace process (UNSC 2003, para. 3(r)). Conflict resources—mostly timber, but also rubber and diamonds—had played a major role in the Liberian conflicts between 1989 and 2003.

Because of the rapid cessation of hostilities and improving security after 2003, UNMIL did not confront extensive problems with conflict commodities—which was a positive factor, considering that UNMIL's full deployment took nine months, largely because UN member countries failed to provide the pledged troops.[25] Nevertheless, UNMIL was subject to criticism for failing to do more to address the problem of conflict resources. Among its critics was Global Witness, the leading NGO in the realm of resources and armed conflicts. In 2005, Global Witness wrote a letter to the UNSC, stating that UNMIL had failed to implement its mandate because

> they have not been given the legal authority to act as independently and pro-actively as they need to effectively seek out and stop illegal timber or diamond operations. . . . UNMIL's ability to fulfill its mandate is further undermined by its lack of deployment in diamond- and timber-rich areas, particularly along Liberia's porous border regions with Côte d'Ivoire, Guinea and Sierra Leone (Global Witness 2005).

If UNMIL did not undertake sufficient efforts to secure conflict commodities, it did create an environment and natural resources unit, although the unit's work on conflict resources is largely limited to assisting with the investigations of UN expert panels.[26] Arguably, other UN agencies—such as the UN Environment Programme, the UN Food and Agriculture Organization, and the UN Development Programme—have a more general mandate to engage in environmental protection and resource management, but the creation of the environment and natural resources unit was in line with UNMIL's quasi-trusteeship functions during the transition period from 2003 to 2005.

UNMIL did carry out some aerial reconnaissance to monitor mining, along with occasional (but rare) ground patrols. On some occasions, it also deployed troops in resource-rich areas—for example, to remove artisanal diamond miners operating illegally within an oil palm plantation; to close a large artisanal diamond mining site that had been identified by an expert panel but had not been shut down by the transitional government (allegedly, diamonds were being stockpiled

---

[25] The deployment of UNAMSIL, in contrast, was delayed in part because the RUF maintained control of diamond-rich territories, notably in Kono District.

[26] The unit has also helped the mission to minimize the environmental impact of peacekeeping operations and has conducted an environmental baseline survey; see Ravier (2008) and UNMIL (n.d.).

at the site while the owners waited for sanctions to be lifted) (UNSC 2004; Powell and Yahya 2006);[27] and to protect the interests of a U.S. diamond company and restore calm and order after demonstrations at a Firestone rubber concession in 2007. Some troop deployments have sparked controversy; in particular, Liberian mining interests and company employees have accused UNMIL of protecting the interests of foreign companies over those of local populations (Mines and Communities 2007; *News* 2007). Such accusations demonstrate that UN peacekeeping deployment in resource sectors can generate new conflicts, and should therefore be considered from a political perspective instead of being narrowly conceived as a law-and-order measure.

Côte d'Ivoire

The UN Mission in Côte d'Ivoire, MINUCI (2003–2004) and the UN Operation in Côte d'Ivoire, UNOCI (2004–present), faced limited direct hostilities between the government and the Forces Nouvelles, the rebel group that controlled the northern part of the country. A UNSC resolution banned all diamond exports in 2005, and a UNOCI embargo-monitoring unit was established in 2006 to collaborate with UN expert panels; however, most of the funding for belligerents—especially the Forces Nouvelles—comes from illegal taxes on primary commodities (primarily cocoa, but also coffee, timber, and cotton) and transportation fuel (Global Witness 2007; Powell and Yahya 2006; UNSC 2005).

The cocoa sector has been singled out for its contribution to a parallel economy that feeds corruption and hostilities, but because of massive employment in that sector, cocoa sanctions would have devastating consequences. Although UN expert panels and NGOs have recommended the investigation of rebel financing, corruption, land conflicts, and human rights abuses in the cocoa sector, UN officials have expressed reluctance to work on such politically sensitive subjects (Global Witness 2007). MINUCI did take some limited actions with regard to the cocoa sector—to help reduce poverty among farmers, for example, MINUCI provided training in income management—but these measures did not directly address other, potentially controversial issues associated with resources (APO 2009; ONUCI 2009).

ISSUES AND PERSPECTIVES

As an international military force deployed to keep the peace, UN peacekeeping operations—and, more broadly, non-UN peacekeeping forces (such as regional peacekeeping forces)—have a unique ability to help sever links between resources and peace spoilers. Although peacekeepers could theoretically be deployed to

---

[27] UN sanctions were imposed on diamond exports from 2001 to 2007, and on timber exports from 2003 to 2006.

control diamond mining, logging, or drug trafficking operations that finance armed groups, the governments that are mandating peacekeeping operations—through the UNSC, for example—are often reluctant to assign peacekeepers such roles.

At the mission level, operational staff, both at headquarters and on the ground, recognize the importance of curtailing peace spoilers' access to high-value resources, but they are also aware of the difficulties associated with intervention. Mission staff, including military observers monitoring military activities and, to a lesser extent, UN civil police monitoring and assisting local police forces, often report on the role of resources in local skirmishes—not only between armed groups but also between rival government security agencies, private militias, and criminal gangs. This low-level violence rarely receives political attention, but political affairs officers at UN missions have nevertheless warned of the potential for escalation; they have also noted the broader implications of resource revenues for relations within and between armed groups. Such issues have also received greater consideration because UN intelligence efforts have been boosted by Joint Mission Analysis Cells, which are charged with assessing the overall political and security situations of UN missions and reporting to the Special Representatives of the UN Secretary-General that head the missions.

The deployment of UN troops for combat operations intended to curtail rebel access to resources raises a number of questions. Is direct intervention legal? How might it affect relations between the UN mission, the host government, and local populations? Might such intervention further military dependence on UN troops? Do the peacekeeping missions have the necessary capacity to intervene successfully? Finally, is it worth the risk—both for the troops and for civilians in the targeted area?[28]

Answers to these questions depend, in large part, on the specific circumstances. Legally, local authorities have the right to prohibit unilateral deployment, unless the country is under a UN trusteeship mandate, under which sovereign authority is vested in a UN administrative body. Moreover, because most missions prior to 2000 were carried out under chapter VI of the UN Charter, which addresses pacific settlement of disputes, rather than chapter VII, which addresses forceful settlement of disputes, peacekeeping missions are prevented from engaging in any "offensive" combat role—including taking control of resource production areas. Despite the recent use of chapter VII authorizations, out of the half-dozen peacekeeping missions established since 1988 in countries where hostilities had been financed, in large part, by conflict commodities, only one—MONUC—has been specifically mandated to address the financing of illegal groups by illicit economic activities, which included the provision of military support to DRC government troops. Although the UN Head of Mission and the UN

---

[28] Some regional and UN peacekeeping units have allegedly been involved in resource trafficking (diamonds in Sierra Leone, and arms for gold in the DRC) (Montague 2002; Basanisi 2008). Thus, there is the additional risk that, through closer involvement with conflict resources, UN personnel will become embroiled in corruption.

Mission Chief of Staff, as well as individual UN-mandated military contingents, or even officers, have used their room for maneuver to investigate, report on, or stop illegal practices,[29] decision makers within UN missions have generally been wary of overstepping their mandate, overextending or diverting resources, alienating economic or political stakeholders, or putting both peacekeepers and civilians at risk by interfering with the economic interests of criminals and armed groups.

Sovereignty issues (including sovereignty over resources) have also discouraged sending and receiving governments from assigning UN peacekeepers an active role in preventing conflict resources from funding peace spoilers.[30] Furthermore, because the economic interests of governments and companies may conflict (either because a company and a host government are competing producers, or because a sending government also happens to be the home government of investors), there is a risk that, if peacekeepers are directly involved in conflict resources issue, there may be allegations that the peacekeepers are serving the interests of their home countries—specifically by protecting those countries' access to resources. Although the U.S. invasion of Iraq was not a "peacekeeping" mission, the non-UN mandated and U.S.-led "coalition of the willing" was the subject of such allegations. On the other hand, shared economic interests could create an incentive for granting peacekeeping missions broader mandates and thereby increasing their effectiveness.[31]

Most governments provide troops to UN missions on the assumption that the risk of casualties is very low. In addition, the military capacity of most UN contingents is usually limited, especially for offensive combat operations. Many

---

[29] Given the wide variations in the behavior of individual missions or elements within those missions, the review provided in this chapter is only preliminary; a systematic assessment of the involvement of UN missions in resource sectors could contribute to more effective future peacekeeping operations.

[30] For example, Russia was initially very reluctant to support and participate in the Kimberley Process Certification Scheme because it viewed transparency about production volume and diamond prices as an infringement on its sovereignty and commercial interests.

[31] Most accusations of resource appropriation have been made under the following circumstances: when mining was being undertaken by mercenary companies (as was the case with the South African mercenary group Executive Outcomes, in the mid-1990s); when neighboring countries have conducted military interventions (as both Uganda and Rwanda did during the late 1990s, in the former Zaire/DRC); and when non-UN-mandated foreign military interventions have been conducted, as was the case with the United States in Colombia and Iraq (Le Billon 2005). Concerns about resource appropriation may be valid for UN-mandated peacekeeping contributors with large mining investments. In the case of the DRC, relative stability in the most significant mining areas (especially in Katanga) may have contributed to the neglect of "local" violence, most of which was concentrated in the eastern part of the country and affected artisanal mining. As long as key mining projects were not under threat, the country was considered "at peace." For the argument that peacekeeping in the DRC failed largely because the broader implications of local conflicts and local violence were ignored, see Autesserre (2006).

governments that send troops to UN peacekeeping missions view resource control not only as a high-risk option, but as a distraction from, or even as counterproductive to, peacekeepers' principal political and humanitarian mandates. "Robust" peacekeeping—entailing combat operations in mining or logging areas, for example—is thus unlikely, in part because of the risk of casualties among both civilians and UN troops.[32] Nevertheless, in some cases, the deployment of UN troops in resource areas has been viewed as a necessity.[33] Where such efforts have been undertaken, however, they have occasionally met with determined resistance from armed groups, and the resource-rich areas have often been the last ones to come under UN control.[34]

One of the most pressing issues is whether intervention will make a substantial contribution to a speedier end to the conflict, without creating harmful consequences in the future—loss of livelihoods, for example, or abuse by rebel groups. When armed groups' access to conflict resources is curtailed, they sometimes turn on the local populations, either to obtain funding or simply for revenge—events for which the UN would bear some responsibility. There is another perspective on this problem, however: Weinstein (2006) has found that rebel groups that emerge in resource-rich environments tend to commit worse abuses against civilians. This behavior appears to be associated with a membership pool of "consumers" rather than "investors"—that is, combatants who are drawn to the rebellion by short-term, opportunistic economic objectives rather than by long-term political objectives.[35] In the short term, UN military interventions in resource sectors may risk exacerbating abuses by rebels against civilian populations; but in the long term, such interventions may not only reduce the capacity of rebel groups but may also help focus rebel movements on political objectives—and therefore on negotiations, rather than on survival and profiteering.[36] Thus, intervention needs to be carefully considered from a number of perspectives, including ethical, military, political, and economic.

---

[32] Potential alternatives include targeted interventions at key sites and backing for judicial procedures against traders involved in conflict-resource trafficking.

[33] For example, Jean-Marie Guéhenno, Special Representative of the Secretary-General for Peacekeeping Operations, has stressed that peacekeeping deployment should take mining areas into account, a consideration that he considered particularly important in the case of the DRC (UNSC 2007).

[34] This was the case, for example, in Sierra Leone, where the RUF maintained control of the Kono diamond mines. Resources are not the only consideration, however. In Angola, UNITA units moved from diamond-rich areas to the homeland of its leader—a choice that was criticized from within the movement (UNITA 2001).

[35] In resource-rich areas, a higher incidence of abuses against civilians may also be linked to low dependence on local populations for sustenance; this is in contrast to rebellions that operate in resource-poor areas or that lack access to external sponsors.

[36] This effect works by weeding out "consumers," including those in leadership positions. Such "repoliticization" of rebel movements, however, may foreclose the option of "buying out" movement leaders through economic and security incentives—an approach that has sometimes led to key defections.

CONCLUSION

Requiring peacekeepers to prevent resources from financing peace spoilers is part of a growing effort, since the early 1990s, to strengthen peacebuilding by improving the developmental outcomes of resource exploitation. Overall, much can be achieved if peacekeeping missions directly address conflict resources. Attention must be paid, however, to the characteristics of the resource sectors, the specific incentives that shape the post-conflict situation, and the capacity and determination of local and international institutions. Although much experience has been gained, the establishment of study groups, within UN missions, that have specific expertise on resource sectors in the post-conflict setting would help to identify further constraints and opportunities.

The preliminary review provided in this chapter gives rise to several general observations and recommendations. Most broadly and most importantly, peacekeeping forces can play a role in curtailing peace spoilers' access to resource revenues. Meeting this objective requires identifying actors in the extractive industries, demilitarizing resource production areas, and closing down activities that benefit spoilers. The capacity of peacekeepers should be reinforced so that they can more effectively engage in observation, mediation, and policing. Further attention should be given to the resource areas in which peacekeepers can be more efficiently deployed. The experience of MONUC, in the DRC, will be of major interest in this regard, especially given its specific mandate from the UNSC. The investigative role of expert panels should be further strengthened through greater collaboration with peacekeeping missions; expert panels should also engage in the collection of evidence for the purpose of prosecution.

As part of their peacebuilding mandate, UN mission staff should seek to address broader linkages between resource revenues and conflicts by assisting (1) local authorities who are in charge of resource sectors and (2) international transitional authorities and aid agencies that are engaged in these sectors. Monitoring, logistical support, and the "good offices" of the UN Head of Mission can all contribute to such efforts. In the DRC, for example, MONUC shares information collected on illegal logging with several UN agencies, NGOs, and government authorities.

The UNSC has an extensive, if controversial, track record in seeking to curtail belligerents' access to resource revenues. The experience of peacekeeping forces, in contrast, remains very limited. Peacekeepers have only recently been specifically mandated by Security Council resolutions to address resource financing; previously, such efforts were generally ad hoc measures undertaken at the mission level or at the direction of local UN commanders.

The evidence reviewed in this chapter suggests that traditional peacekeeping missions are generally poorly prepared to forcefully and effectively curtail peace spoilers' access to resource revenues. Such interventions must be (1) carefully considered from humanitarian, political, and economic standpoints before being carried out; (2) preceded by careful operational planning; and (3) conducted by adequately trained, equipped, and disciplined international forces—so that the risks of human rights abuses, military failure, and corruption are minimized. Collaboration with local forces should also be monitored, and should be subject to stringent guidelines. Short of engaging in interdiction, peacekeepers do have the potential to help collect information on resource sectors, remove peace spoilers from important resource extraction areas, and back up police efforts to arrest illicit traders.

REFERENCES

Autesserre, S. 2006. Local violence, national peace? Postwar "settlement" in the eastern D.R. Congo (2003–2006). *African Studies Review* 49 (3): 1–29.

Basanisi, M. 2008. Who will watch the peacekeepers? *New York Times*, May 23.

Boucher, A. J., and V. K. Holt. 2009. *Targeting spoilers: The role of United Nations panels of experts.* Washington, D.C.: Stimson Center.

Byrd, W. A. 2008. *Responding to Afghanistan's opium economy challenge: Lessons and policy implications from a development perspective.* Washington, D.C.: World Bank.

Cortright, D., and G. A. Lopez. 2002. *Sanctions and the search for security: Challenges to UN action.* Boulder, CO: Lynne Rienner.

Crossin, C., G. Hayman, and S. Taylor. 2003. Where did it come from? Commodity tracking systems. In *Natural resources and violent conflict: Options and actions*, ed. I. Bannon and P. Collier. Washington, D.C.: World Bank.

Custers, R. 2009. *Le plan STAREC du gouvernement congolais: Une analyse préliminaire.* Antwerp: IPIS.

Cuvelier, J. 2004. Linking the local to the global: Legal pluralism in the DRC conflict. In *Conflict and social transformation in eastern DR Congo*, ed. K. Vlassenroot and T. Raeymakers. Ghent: Academia Press.

DFID (Department for International Development). 2006. Interview, DFID-sponsored diamond advisor to the president of Sierra Leone. July.

Doss, A. n.d. Letter from the Special Representative of the UN Secretary-General. Cited in Global Witness, *Faced with a gun, what can you do? War and the militarisation of mining in Eastern Congo* (London, 2009).

Global Witness. 2005. Open statement to the Security Council details the critical need for the maintenance of sanctions on Liberian diamonds and renewal and extension of the mandate of MONUC. March 18. www.globalwitness.org/media_library_detail.php/372/en/open_statement_to_the_security_council_details_the.

———. 2007. *Hot chocolate: How cocoa fuelled the conflict in Côte d'Ivoire.* London.

———. 2009a. *Faced with a gun, what can you do? War and the militarisation of mining in Eastern Congo.* London.

———. 2009b. *Bisie killings show minerals at heart of Congo conflict.* London.

———. n.d. Definition of conflict resources. www.globalwitness.org/pages/en/definition_of_conflict_resources.html.

Goodhand, J. 2008. Corrupting or consolidating the peace? The drugs economy and post-conflict peacebuilding in Afghanistan. *International Peacekeeping* 15 (3): 405–423.

Holt, V., and A. Boucher. 2009. Framing the issue: UN responses to corruption and criminal networks in post-conflict settings. *International Peacekeeping* 16 (1): 20–32.

IRIN (Integrated Regional Information Networks). 2008. Mapping conflict motives in war areas. www.ipisresearch.be/mapping.php.
———. 2009. DRC: Charcoal profits fuel war in east. *IRIN Humanitarian News and Analysis*, 28 July. www.irinnews.org/report.aspx?reportId=85462.
JMAC (Joint Mission Analysis Cell). 2009. *Talking points; SRSG Doss on illegal exploitation: MONUC*. Kinshasa: MONUC.
Le Billon, P. 2005. *Fuelling war: Natural resources and armed conflict*. Adelphi Paper No. 373. London: Routledge.
———. 2007. Natural resources, armed conflicts, and the UN Security Council. Liu Institute for Global Issues. May 30. http://liu.xplorex.com/sites/liu/files/Publications/30May2007_Natural_Resources_Armed_Conflicts_UNSC07-001.pdf.
Mines and Communities. 2007. Africa update. April 18. www.minesandcommunities.org/article.php?a=115.
Montague, D. 2002. The business of war and the prospects for peace in Sierra Leone. *Brown Journal of World Affairs* 9 (1): 229–237.
NATO (North Atlantic Treaty Organization). n.d. NATO's role in Afghanistan. www.nato.int/cps/en/natolive/topics_8189.htm.
News (Monrovia). 2007. Liberia: UNMIL deploys extra security in Firestone. December 11. http://allafrica.com/stories/200712110877.html.
ONUCI (Opération des Nations Unies en Côte d'Ivoire). 2009. L'ONUCI finance la formation de 500 producteurs de cacao de Bloléquin. August 10. www.onuci.org/spip.php?article2433&var_recherche=cacao.
Peleman, J. 2009. Personal communication with the chief of Joint Mission Analysis Cell, Office of the Special Representative of the UN Secretary-General. August.
Powell, R., and M. Yahya. 2006. *The current state of diamond mining in the Mano River region and the use of diamonds as a tool for peace building and development*. London: International Alert.
Ravier, S. 2008. Environment in UN peacekeeping operations. University of Geneva/UN Environment Programme. www.unige.ch/formcont/environmentaldiplomacy/TheseSophieRAVIER.pdf.
Spittaels, S., and F. Hilgert. 2009. *Accompanying note on the interactive map of militarised mining areas in the Kivus*. Antwerp: International Peace Information Service.
Strandow, D. 2006. Sanctions and civil war: Targeted measures for conflict resolution. Department of Peace and Conflict Research, Uppsala University. www.smartsanctions.se/literature/strandow_content060926.pdf.
UNAMSIL (United Nations Assistance Mission in Sierra Leone). 2001. Interviews, UNAMSIL officers. April.
———. 2005. Sierra Leone—UNAMSIL—Mandate. United Nations. www.un.org/en/peacekeeping/missions/unamsil/mandate.html.
UNITA (União Nacional para a Independência Total de Angola). 2001. Interviews, UNITA officials, Luanda.
UNMIL (United Nations Mission in Liberia). n.d. Environmental and natural resources unit. http://unmil.org/1content.asp?ccat=environmental&zdoc=1.
UNODC (United Nations Office on Drugs and Crime). 2008. Afghanistan opium survey 2008. www.unodc.org/documents/crop-monitoring/Afghanistan_Opium_Survey_2008.pdf.
———. 2009. Global decrease in opium due to a decrease in Afghanistan. UNODC Afghanistan. www.unodc.org/afghanistan/en/frontpage/2009/may/global-decrease-in-opium-cultivation-due-to-a-decrease-in-afghanistan.html.

UNSC (United Nations Security Council). 1992. Resolution 792. S/RES/792 (1992). November 30.
———. 1997. *Security Council official records, fifty-second year, supplemental for April, May and June 1997.*
———. 1999. Resolution 1267. S/RES/1267 (1999). October 15.
———. 2003. Resolution 1509. S/RES/1509 (2003). September 19.
———. 2004. Expert panel report on Liberia, pursuant to resolution 1521. S/2004/955. December 6.
———. 2005. Resolution 1643. S/RES/1643 (2005). December 15.
———. 2006. Resolution 1735. S/RES/1735 (2006). December 22.
———. 2007. Natural resources and armed conflicts. Seminar. May.
———. 2008a. Resolution 1797. S/RES/1797 (2008). June 30.
———. 2008b. Resolution 1804. S/RES/1804 (2008). March 13.
———. 2008c. Resolution 1806. S/RES/1806 (2008). March 20.
———. 2008d. Resolution 1807. S/RES/1807 (2008). March 31.
———. 2008e. Resolution 1822. S/RES/1822 (2008). June 30.
———. 2008f. Resolution 1856. S/RES/1856 (2008). December 22.
———. 2008g. Resolution 1857. S/RES/1857 (2008). December 22.
———. 2008h. UN group of experts report on the DRC, pursuant to resolution 1533. S/2008/773. December 12. New York: United Nations.
———. 2009a. Report of panel of experts on Liberia. S/2009/290. June 5. New York: United Nations.
———. 2009b. Resolution 1868. S/RES/1868 (2009). March 23.
Walsh, K., K. N. Andrews, B. L. Hunt, and W. J. Durch. 2007. *Post-conflict borders and UN peace operations.* Stimson Center Report No. 62. Washington, D.C.: Stimson Center.
Weinstein, J. 2006. *Inside rebellion: The politics of insurgent violence.* Cambridge, UK: Cambridge University Press.

Mitigating risks and realizing opportunities: Environmental and social standards for foreign direct investment in high-value natural resources

Jill Shankleman

This chapter addresses a significant aspect of resource extraction in post-conflict settings: the way in which extractive companies operate resource concessions. In the wake of conflict, there is a risk that resource extraction will have destabilizing impacts—by, for example, damaging the environment, preventing local people from accessing the resources that they depend on, or fostering tension about the distribution of jobs and other project benefits. Responsible resource extraction requires companies to minimize such risks, and thereby render their activities more likely to contribute to post-conflict stability and economic development.

The main focus of the chapter is on three sets of voluntary standards that have been developed, since the early 2000s, to improve the environmental and social performance of major investment projects:

- The International Finance Corporation's Performance Standards on Social and Environmental Sustainability (IFC-PS), which extended and provided a private sector focus to the World Bank safeguard policies that had been introduced in the late 1990s (IFC 2006).[1]
- The Equator Principles (EPs), which were developed by commercial banks in concert with the IFC and largely followed previously established IFC standards (Equator Principles 2006).[2]
- The Voluntary Principles on Security and Human Rights (VPSHR, or VPs), which were developed by the United States and United Kingdom (UK), in collaboration with some large oil and mining companies and international nongovernmental organizations (NGOs) (VPSHR n.d.).

Jill Shankleman is director of J. Shankleman Limited, a business consulting firm that assists oil and gas companies to assess the social impact of their investments.

[1] The IFC is the private sector lending and investment arm of the World Bank Group. As of March 2010, the IFC-PS was under revision, following consultations conducted in 2009. For a description of the World Bank safeguard policies, see World Bank (n.d.b).

[2] Any bank involved in project financing can become an EP signatory. See Equator Principles (2006).

50   High-value natural resources and post-conflict peacebuilding

These three sets of standards are interlinked and cross-referenced: the IFC-PS refers to the VPs, and the EPs incorporate the IFC-PS. In that they are applied to investment projects in addition to host-country legal requirements, the standards are voluntary. But some companies make formal commitments to apply the standards, and adherence is often a condition of project financing from banks.

The chapter explores what these standards mean for extractive industry projects in general, and for projects in post-conflict settings in particular.[3] Although the standards were not developed specifically for projects in post-conflict countries, they can help ensure that companies investing in extractive industry projects in such settings take seriously the risk of social and environmental damage, and position themselves to support post-conflict peacebuilding by providing economic (and sometimes social) development opportunities.[4]

On the one hand, the standards are a useful tool for helping to make foreign direct investment in the natural resource sector a stronger contributor to post-conflict peacebuilding: they provide a framework that enables firms to be more aware of the complexities of post-conflict environments and to behave more responsibly than might otherwise be the case. On the other hand, because of their voluntary nature and the absence of requirements for systematic follow up on implementation, the standards have not been as effective as they might otherwise have been. In order to have greater impact, the standards should be revised to require companies to publish regular and detailed progress reports. Further, environmental regulations in most developing countries, especially those emerging from conflict, need to be revised and updated to incorporate the social, labor, health, and security requirements included in the voluntary standards.

The chapter is divided into five major sections: (1) background information on foreign direct investment in post-conflict settings; (2) a description of project financing methods and the role of environmental and social standards

---

[3] Because this chapter is focused on the environmental and social management of natural resource operations, it does not consider other important initiatives, such as the Extractive Industries Transparency Initiative and the Kimberley Process Certification Scheme, which address revenue management and product trading, respectively. Both are important aspects of natural resource exploitation and are addressed in a number of chapters in this volume: Eddie Rich and T. Negbalee Warner, "Addressing the Roots of Liberia's Conflict through the Extractive Industries Transparency Initiative"; Harrison Mitchell, "A More Formal Engagement: A Constructive Critique of Certification as a Means of Preventing Conflict and Building Peace"; J. Andrew Grant, "The Kimberley Process at Ten: Reflections on a Decade of Efforts to End the Trade in Conflict Diamonds"; Clive Wright, "The Kimberley Process Certification Scheme: A Model Negotiation?" and Duncan Brack, "Excluding Illegal Timber and Improving Forest Governance: The European Union's Forest Law Enforcement, Governance and Trade Initiative."

[4] The Natural Resource Charter initiative, which is designed to help governments and societies effectively harness the opportunities created by natural resources, recognizes the importance of environmental and social standards in natural resource management; such standards are reflected in one of the twelve precepts developed by the Natural Resource Charter to inform and improve natural resource management (Natural Resource Charter n.d.).

in project financing; (3) a description of the origins and requirements of the key voluntary standards; (4) a discussion of the application of the standards in post-conflict settings; and (5) a concluding discussion of the standards as peacebuilding tools.

BACKGROUND: NATURAL RESOURCE PROJECTS IN POST-CONFLICT ENVIRONMENTS

In post-conflict countries with high-value natural resources, the first foreign direct investments are often in the resource extraction sector. There are four principal reasons for this pattern:

- Oil, gas, minerals, and metals firms have to locate where the resources are, whereas investors who are more free to choose their location are likely to delay investment until conditions are stable.
- Natural resource investments are usually governed by direct agreement between investors and the government, which are enforceable through the laws of third-country legal systems, often those of the United States, the United Kingdom, or the Netherlands.[5] Such arrangements enable investors to circumvent the weaknesses of legal institutions in post-conflict states.
- Large-scale natural resource projects can be operated as enclaves, insulated from the deficiencies of post-conflict infrastructure; they often have their own power generation, water treatment, housing compounds, and even airstrips.
- A skilled workforce can be brought in from outside, especially when oil fields and pipelines are being constructed; the local workforce can then be trained, over time, to undertake most of the operational work.

However, most developing countries lack the knowledge, the laws, and the institutions to ensure that resource extraction projects are carried out responsibly,

---

[5] For example, the production-sharing agreement between the State Oil Company of Azerbaijan (SOCAR) and a consortium of oil companies, which provides the legal basis for oil production from the Azeri Chirag Guneshli field, includes the following provision regarding disputes: "in the event a dispute arising between SOCAR and any or all of the Contractor Parties . . . , the disputing Parties shall meet in an attempt to resolve the dispute to their mutual satisfaction by reference to the terms of this Contract applying the principles of contractual interpretation under Azerbaijan law; if mutual satisfaction is not so achieved the disputing Parties will apply the principles of contractual interpretation under English law. If satisfactory mutual agreement is not achieved within thirty (30) days after receipt by a Party of notice of such dispute, such dispute shall be settled in accordance with the arbitration provisions of Appendix VI and the applicable law provisions of Article 23.1" (State Oil Company of Azerbaijan et al. 1994, 61). Arbitration is through application of the Arbitration Rules of the United Nations Commission on International Trade Law (State Oil Company of Azerbaijan et al. 1994).

in ways that protect people and the environment. Since the mid-1990s, resource companies, the banks that finance resource projects, donor nations and agencies, and NGOs have become increasingly aware that in the absence of effective social and environmental protection measures, the viability of resource extraction operations is at risk. The leading example of such risks is in the Niger Delta, where about one-quarter of potential oil production is lost to theft, violence, or sabotage.[6] There are many less dramatic cases in which companies have faced opposition or found it slower, more costly, or more controversial to operate than expected.[7]

Investments in resource sectors have the potential to help stabilize post-conflict countries by generating government revenues, creating employment, and demonstrating to other businesses that countries are safe to invest in. Host governments receive payments when they sell the rights to explore for oil or minerals, and generally receive a regular income flow when production is under way.[8] Especially in oil-rich areas, such as Angola or Southern Sudan, government revenues from oil far outstrip all other income sources, including donor assistance and non-oil taxation.

However, as is discussed elsewhere in this volume, unless carefully and transparently managed, resource revenues can also fuel corruption and conflict. Similarly, unless the potential impacts are carefully assessed in advance, resource extraction can damage the environment and undermine social stability, especially in fragile post-conflict contexts. Responsible investing minimizes harmful effects, ensures that communities are compensated fairly and transparently for any land taken or damage caused, and recognizes and addresses the possibility of unintended consequences.[9]

The laws of most developing countries require environmental impact assessments of new projects (Craik 2008), but conventional assessments—that

---

[6] According to the U.S. Energy Information Administration (EIA), "the instability in the Niger Delta has caused significant amounts of shut-in production and several companies declaring *force majeure* on oil shipments. EIA estimates Nigeria's nameplate oil production capacity to be around 2.7 million barrels per day (bbl/d), but as a result of attacks on oil infrastructure 2008 monthly oil production ranged between 1.8 million bbl/d and 2.1 million bbl/d" (EIA n.d.).

[7] For examples from mining, see Volker Boege and Daniel M. Franks, "Reopening and Developing Mines in Post-Conflict Settings: The Challenge of Company-Community Relations," in this volume.

[8] Once investment costs have been covered through oil sales, oil projects typically generate some revenue flow to governments through profit-sharing arrangements between the company and the government. Mining projects generally involve some sort of royalty payment to the government. For further discussion of revenue sharing between companies and governments, see Achim Wennmann, "Sharing Natural Resource Wealth during War-to-Peace Transitions," in this volume.

[9] An example of an unintended consequence is the sudden and overwhelming influx of people seeking jobs and opportunities amid the "gold rush" mood that may develop around new or reopened production areas.

is, those that do not apply the new standards—typically afford little consideration of the social context, such as a legacy of disputed land rights, displaced persons, or intergroup tensions. In the words of a mining ministry official in a resource-rich post-conflict country,

> these impact assessments look like cut-and-paste jobs by consultants. They tell us nothing—and anyway, we do not have the technical skills to interpret them, or the people and vehicles enabling us to go and inspect and see what is happening on the ground.[10]

When resource companies claim to respect local law, this often means that they undertake environmental impact assessments primarily as administrative tasks designed to secure the necessary permits, not as tools for understanding the physical and social environment into which they are entering. Ideally—and as required under the standards discussed in this chapter—impact assessment is an iterative process used to gain a detailed understanding of the full range of project impacts, both positive and negative. The assessment should influence siting and design so as to avoid negative impacts where possible, and it should provide the basis for an investor's commitment to systematic management and monitoring of impacts.

Companies that wish to establish extractive projects in post-conflict environments must anticipate, understand, and address a number of particularly destabilizing social and environmental issues that are often associated with such settings; chief among these are land rights and ownership, migration, employment, and security. Conflict is likely to have displaced people from the land, and it is often unclear who owns the land, who has rights to it, and who should be negotiated with (and compensated) when land is lost to an oil field, a mine, or a pipeline. Land issues are particularly important in many parts of rural Africa, where formal legal title is rare and people hold land under customary tenure. Under local laws, in many cases, those who hold customary rights would not be compensated or receive replacement land if the land that they were farming and living on were appropriated for a natural resource project.

Large projects usually encourage migration. Although migration can have destabilizing effects by putting pressure on resources and facilities, in some cases it can contribute to stability. In Sierra Leone, for example, many people would like to see new investment in mining (or in other sectors, such as biofuel), drawing young men back to their villages of origin, where they can take up employment in resource extraction projects; the fear is that if the young men remain in the cities, rootless and unemployed, they will be ideal recruits for future charismatic but destructive leaders. Circumstances like these are ideal opportunities for resource extraction firms to reserve unskilled jobs for local residents, and to define "local" to include family members who are temporarily residents elsewhere. In

---

[10] Personal communication with the author.

post-conflict environments, it is particularly important for jobs—one of the key local benefits of investment—to be distributed fairly, transparently, and without exacerbating the tensions that contributed to the original conflict (by, for example, unintentionally favoring one ethnic group or community over another).

Oil and mining projects invariably require extensive security. During construction, the projects bring in large amounts of valuable equipment and materials; once the facilities are up and running, oil wells, mines, and pipelines are valuable assets that are potentially vulnerable to theft or sabotage. Projects can draw criminals (or even rebels) to the area, putting local residents at risk—and, particularly in conflict-ridden areas in Ethiopia, the Niger Delta, and parts of Latin America, workers may also be subject to kidnapping and other attacks.

Typically, the company that is in charge of the project has its own guard force, which is backed up on a permanent or incident-response basis by government forces, police, or the military. While such arrangements may improve security for the local population—for example, by bringing in a police presence for the first time—they can also have the opposite effect: ill trained, unpaid, or hostile security forces may prey on local residents, for example. In an extreme case that occurred in 2004, in Katanga, in the Democratic Republic of the Congo (DRC), a number of security issues came together: a rebel group took over a small town; the army requisitioned transport from the mining company in the area, then put down the rebellion with extreme force, killing a number of civilians. Twelve soldiers and three expatriate employees of the mining company were charged with war crimes and complicity in war crimes in connection with the massacre; all were acquitted (*CNW* 2007).

PROJECT FINANCING

Private sector investment in natural resources is capital intensive. Whereas a company may use its own resources to undertake exploration to determine whether a site offers resources worth extracting, the cost of developing oil fields, pipelines, and mines runs from the hundreds of millions of dollars to billions, depending on the scale and location of the resources, and requires outside investment. The first phase in the development of the huge Tenke Fungurume copper mine in the DRC, for example, is estimated to cost over US$2 billion (Tenke Fungurume Mining n.d.).[11] On a smaller scale, the Kinsevere Stage II mining project, also in the DRC, is expected to require a capital investment of US$400 million (Anvil Mining n.d.).

With the exception of the very largest oil and mining firms, companies that have successfully explored for oil or minerals generally need to obtain financing—that is, to secure equity investment, loans, or both—in order to have sufficient capital to progress from exploration to resource development. The project financing structure typically involves both equity investors, known as sponsors, and bank

---

[11] More information about this project can be found at www.tenke.com.

loans.[12] The loans are often obtained through multilateral or bilateral development banks,[13] but commercial banks are also significant suppliers of project financing. Frequently, natural resource projects secure financing from a mix of development and commercial banks.[14] Export credit agencies provide credit and insurance for foreign investors, including insurance against political risks, which can be necessary in post-conflict countries.[15]

Since profits are the means by which loans are repaid and investors rewarded, the identification and evaluation of any risks that might jeopardize those profits are key parts of securing project financing. Before banks agree to finance a project, they undertake extensive due diligence to assess its technical and commercial viability. Because banks have come to recognize that environmental damage or social conflict can put a project at risk—and expose the lender to criticism—the due diligence process is increasingly likely to include an assessment of environmental and social risks. Bankers are aware, for example, that oil fields in Nigeria are "shut in" (that is, not producing) because of violence and sabotage, and that disputes over land acquisition or other issues can prevent projects from being developed on time and within budget. Thus, even though the companies that are developing resource extraction projects may not consider it necessary to thoroughly investigate the environmental and social impacts of their activities, they may find that their bankers require it. Banks are now key actors in the promotion of higher environmental and social standards for natural resource investments in post-conflict countries.

---

[12] According to the Basel Committee on Banking Supervision, "Project finance may take the form of financing of the construction of a new capital installation, or refinancing of an existing installation, with or without improvements. . . . In such transactions, the lender is usually paid solely or almost exclusively out of the money generated by the contracts for the facility's output, such as the electricity sold by a power plant. The borrower is usually an SPE [special purpose entity] that is not permitted to perform any function other than developing, owning, and operating the installation. The consequence is that repayment depends primarily on the project's cash flow and on the collateral value of the project's assets" (2006, pt. 3, secs. 221–222).

[13] The Inter-American Development Bank and the IFC are examples of multilateral development banks. Bilateral banks based in the Netherlands and in Germany, respectively, are the Nederlandse Financierings-Maatschappij Voor Ontwikkelings Landen n.v., known as FMO; and the Deutsche Investitions- und Entwicklungsgesellschaft mbH, known as DEG.

[14] Although development banks make public some information on the projects they invest in, clear and comprehensive information on overall project financing is rarely available; hence, it is difficult to obtain an accurate breakdown of the relative importance of commercial and development banks in project financing.

[15] Export credit agencies are multilateral, bilateral, or private bodies that provide credit and insurance for groups investing in foreign countries. Examples of export credit agencies include the Overseas Private Investment Corporation (OPIC) in the United States and the Corporación Andina de Fomento (CAS) of the Andean countries. For a listing of export credit agencies and a discussion of their functions and operations, see Harvard Business School (2010).

THE KEY VOLUNTARY STANDARDS

Taken together, the IFC-PS, the EPs, and the VPs provide a set of tools with the potential to help make foreign direct investment in natural resources a stronger contributor to post-conflict peacebuilding. Table 1 summarizes the origins, applicability, objectives, and key elements of each set of standards.

Origins of the standards

The voluntary standards being applied today developed from three roots. The overall approach was established by the environmental safeguard policies that the World Bank developed during the 1990s, in response to criticism that some of the bank's investments—in large dams, for example—had caused environmental and social damage that could have been avoided (Siebenhüner 2008). The second root was the World Bank's Extractive Industries Review, which was conducted from 2000 through 2004 and resulted, among other things, in commitments to more demanding environmental and social standards for oil and mining projects supported by the bank.[16] The third root was the dialogue between the U.S. and UK governments, the major Western oil and mining companies, and international NGOs, which resulted in the creation of the VPs. This dialogue originated in concerns that the security provided by governments and security contractors for extractive industry operations could have unintended consequences—specifically, that people living near the projects could experience a reduction in security and the violation of their human rights. Such consequences could occur, for example, if security forces behaved in a predatory way, or if equipment that had been provided to protect a site was commandeered by criminals or militias. Thus, the principles that emerged from this dialogue specifically address the provision of security for oil, gas, and mining projects.

Between 2000 and 2006, extensive collaboration between the IFC and other banks, as well as companies and NGOs, led the IFC to develop a set of social and environmental policies for private sector projects that (1) expanded and clarified the World Bank policies that it had previously applied and (2) incorporated the key elements of the VPs. These standards, which became known as the Equator Principles, or EPs, have since been adopted by sixty-seven commercial banks. Over the past few years, a growing number of organizations—including most of the Western bilateral development banks and export credit agencies—have subscribed to these standards, either by becoming signatories to the EPs or by incorporating the IFC-PS into their organizational policies. In 2008, the Industrial Bank Co. Ltd. became the first Chinese bank to adopt the EPs; that same year, China EXIM (China's export credit bank) announced that where host countries'

---

[16] For information on the Extractive Industries Review (EIR) and links to EIR reports, see World Bank Extractive Industries Review Advisory Group (n.d.).

Table 1. Voluntary social and environmental standards

Origin	Applicability	Objective	Key elements
International Finance Corporation's Performance Standards on Social and Environmental Sustainability			
July 2006	All IFC projects	To create a comprehensive system for identifying and managing social and environmental risks	Eight specific standards, plus requirements for consultation and public disclosure of information
Created by the IFC in consultation with companies, donor nations and agencies, NGOs, and other entities			
Equator Principles			
June 2003	Financing for major projects carried out in non-OECD countries[a]	To apply IFC environmental and social standards to projects financed by signatory banks	A common framework and standards for assessing and managing environmental and social risk in project financing
Initiated by a group of ten commercial banks			
Voluntary Principles on Security and Human Rights			
December 2000	Oil, gas, and mining	To provide guidance to companies on maintaining the safety and security of their operations while respecting human rights and fundamental freedoms	General requirements addressing risk assessment; use of security contractors; working with government security forces
Created by the U.S. and UK governments; seven oil and mining companies; eight NGOs			

a. The thirty-member OECD (Organisation for Economic Co-operation and Development) represents democratic, market-economy countries, most of which are developed countries.

environmental regulations are inadequate, "We should refer to our country's standards or international practices" (China EXIM Bank 2007, art. 12).[17]

Collectively, the three sets of standards compel investors to examine carefully the economic, environmental, social, and political context of their investments, and to evaluate and respond to the risks of damage to community health, safety, and security, among other matters. But because of their heavy emphasis on risk management, the standards are a stronger tool for evaluating and avoiding negative impacts than for securing positive ones. For example, the standards provide no explicit guidance on whether, or how, investors should support social development projects.

Requirements of the standards

The requirements of the IFC-PS, the EPs, and the VPs are more onerous than typical national legislation and push companies into extensive engagement with governments and communities on a range of issues—such as human rights standards associated with security provision—that are not routine aspects of project development. For example, the IFC-PS requires compensation for anyone who loses access to land because of a resource project, regardless of whether legal title is held (IFC 2006).[18] Companies are also responsible for ensuring that community members' homes and livelihoods are at least as good as whatever they may have lost because of the project. Finally, unlike most national legislation, the standards address labor issues: they have strong systems in place to protect worker health and safety, and they require evidence that projects will abide by the core labor standards of the International Labour Organization.

Typically, applying the IFC-PS, the EPs, or the VPs to a large (multimillion-dollar) natural resource project in a post-conflict country will require at least one year of work, which is spent preparing impact assessments and developing management plans. Applying the standards also means that in addition to the engineers and accountants who typically form the core of a management team, the investors will have to include environmental specialists and community relations staff. Because applying the standards requires judgment—and social rather than physical-science skills—external consultation on impact assessments and management plans can be important in ensuring that plans are realistic, appropriate, and acceptable.

Some banks and businesses that apply the IFC-PS, the EPs, or the VPs use their websites to publish impact assessments and explain the steps that are being taken to mitigate risks. Before committing to a particular project, the IFC and

---

[17] Reportedly, the winning bid by China's MCC Corporation to develop the Ayrak copper mine in Afghanistan included the commitment to apply the EPs, though no documentation showing this has been published. See Wines (2009).
[18] IFC-PS 5 addresses land acquisition and resettlement.

Environmental and social standards for foreign direct investment 59

the Multilateral Investment Guarantee Agency,[19] for example—both of which are members of the World Bank Group—disclose information about the project.[20] The disclosures include social and environmental impact assessments, social and environmental management plans, and the strategies that the company and the World Bank plan to use to manage social and environmental risks.[21] When the IFC is considering financing a project, it releases a short description of the investment and identifies any performance standards that apply to it. In most cases, the IFC provides a link to the impact assessment, which shows the findings from the analysis conducted by the project's consultants. The IFC has released detailed information, for example, on the Chad-Cameroon and the Baku-Tbilisi-Ceyhan pipelines.[22] Because they identify the kinds of issues that may arise and suggest how they might be managed, such online repositories provide a useful resource for other businesses working in comparable environments.

The International Finance Corporation Social and Environmental Performance Standards

The IFC-PS is based on a four-step business management model: assess, define actions, monitor, and reassess.[23] First, the standards define the scope of the assessments that should be undertaken before a project starts, in order to identify the following:

- The potential impacts of the project.
- The risks the project presents to the environment and local communities.
- The risks that the physical and social environment present to the success of the project.

---

[19] For more information about the projects of the Multilateral Investment Guarantee Agency, see MIGA (n.d.).
[20] For project disclosure documents, see IFC (n.d.a).
[21] Examples of planned projects to which the IFC-PS, the EPs, or the VPs are being applied—and for which impact assessments are in the public domain—include the Addax Bioenergy project, which is producing ethanol for export and electricity for the domestic market in Sierra Leone; the Kingamyambo Musonoi Tailings project, which is using waste from abandoned mines in the DRC to produce copper; and the Tenke Fungurume copper mine, also in the DRC. For environmental, social, and health impact assessments and management plans for the Addax Bioenergy project, see CES (n.d.). As of December 2009, environmental documentation for the Kingamyambo Musonoi Tailings project was available at www.ifc.org/disclosure; this information will not remain available beyond the official disclosure period unless the IFC decides to invest in the project. For more information on the Tenke Fungurume copper mine, see Tenke Fungurume Mining (n.d.).
[22] Online information is available for IFC natural resource (and other) projects since the 1990s, though in the case of older projects the information is sometimes limited to statements noting where the hard copies of the documents can be found.
[23] Through their incorporation of the IFC-PS, the EPs follow the same model.

Second, the standards define what the company that is investing in the project must do in order to limit negative impacts and mitigate risks. For example, investors are required to communicate with stakeholders, and to consult on proposed management strategies to ensure that they are relevant to local circumstances and needs. Third, the standards require the company to set up a program to monitor and measure the effectiveness of the management system, and to provide periodic progress reports to the communities affected by the project. The standards also identify several issues that, if mismanaged, can trigger conflict, such as land acquisition, community access to natural resources, pollution, and risks to community safety. But they do not require any proactive measures to improve the local benefits of projects—through employment or philanthropic social initiatives, for example.

The accompanying sidebar lists the IFC performance standards. PS 1 is the foundation and applies to every project. The initial (scoping) stage of the impact assessment required under PS 1 determines which of the remaining standards are relevant to the project. Every private sector natural resource project will employ labor (PS 2) and involve potentially polluting activities (PS 3); most will trigger PS 4 by having some potential impacts on communities. But some types of projects—such as offshore oil production—might not involve land acquisition (PS 5), and many others are in locations where no indigenous peoples (as defined in the standard) are living (PS 7), and where cultural heritage (PS 8) is not an issue. In the context of peacebuilding, it is important to note that PS 4, which addresses community health, safety, and security, specifically requires investors to consider the potential interactions between their investment and local conflict.

International Finance Corporation's social and environmental performance standards

PS 1 Social and environmental impact assessment and management systems*
PS 2 Labor and working conditions
PS 3 Pollution prevention and abatement
PS 4 Community health, safety, and security
PS 5 Land acquisition and involuntary resettlement
PS 6 Biodiversity conservation and sustainable natural resource management
PS 7 Indigenous peoples
PS 8 Cultural heritage

* PS 1 includes requirements for consultation with affected communities and disclosure of information to stakeholders that also apply to all the other standards.

Source: IFC (2006).

The Voluntary Principles on Security and Human Rights

The VPs—which, like the IFC-PS, are based on a four-phase model—include more detailed requirements concerning security for extractive industries. Under the VPs, companies operating in conflict areas (which are not specifically defined in the principles, but are generally understood to mean areas of recent or current conflict) must consider (1) what impacts predicted, current, or recent conflict might have on the project and (2) what impact the project might have on conflict or post-conflict stabilization. Thus, the VPs state that

> identification of and understanding the root causes and nature of local conflicts, as well as the level of adherence to human rights and international humanitarian law standards by key actors, can be instructive for the development of strategies

for managing relations between the Company, local communities, Company employees and their unions, and host governments. Risk assessments should also consider the potential for future conflicts (VPSHR n.d.).

The principles go even further, however, by setting out provisions for companies to apply when transferring equipment to private or public security forces. Companies developing oil or gas resources or operating pipelines usually need to hire security guards and provide them with equipment. At its most benign, such protection may involve horseback patrols, but it may also include armed guards. The requirements on the transfer of equipment were developed in the wake of allegations, in the 1990s, that equipment (specifically, night-vision goggles) provided by oil companies in Colombia to their security guards was being transferred to paramilitary organizations, which enabled them to launch attacks against local populations.[24] With respect to equipment transfers, the VPs state that

Voluntary Principles for Security and Human Rights
Signatories to the Voluntary Principles for Security and Human Rights must do the following:
1 Undertake risk assessments for specific locations they are investing in; these assessments must evaluate • Security risks • The potential for violence • The human rights records of government and private security forces • Extent to which the rule of law prevails • The history and causes of any local conflict • Potential risks associated with transferring equipment to security forces or contractors.
2 In relations between companies and public security forces, efforts should be made to reach agreements addressing the following: • Security arrangements • Deployment and conduct consistent with United Nations norms • Consultation and advice.
3 Contracts with private security providers should include requirements addressing the following issues: • Ethical conduct and human rights • Appropriate conduct and the use of force (i.e., rules of engagement) • Technical and professional proficiency • Compliance with the UN Basic Principles on the Use of Force and Firearms by Law Enforcement Officials and the UN Code of Conduct for Law Enforcement Officials • Monitoring of adherence to principles and of environmental and social impacts • Limitation of private security to preventive and defensive services • Ineligibility for employment of any individuals who have been credibly implicated in human rights abuses • Recording and investigation of any cases in which physical force has been used.
Source: Author's summary of VPSHR (n.d.).

where Companies provide equipment (including lethal and non-lethal equipment) to public or private security, they should consider the risk of such transfers, any

---

[24] The wider issues related to the interaction between security for oil facilities and ongoing civil conflict were set out by Human Rights Watch in a report that influenced the development of the VPSHR. Specifically, Human Rights Watch noted that "oil companies that deploy security forces to protect their installations and personnel bear responsibility for the actions those forces undertake. In Arauca and Casanare, the army has dedicated entire brigades . . . to protecting oil production. The companies cannot ignore the human rights violations committed by those units; indeed the companies' dependence on the army and police for their survival gives them a tremendous moral responsibility. In both departments, the army units—albeit to different degrees—have been allegedly involved in extrajudicial executions which have not been resolved" (Human Rights Watch, Colombia 1998).

relevant export licensing requirements, and the feasibility of measures to mitigate foreseeable negative consequences, including adequate controls to prevent misappropriation or diversion of equipment which may lead to human rights abuses. In making risk assessments, companies should consider any relevant past incidents involving previous equipment transfers (VPSHR n.d.).

The VPs are particularly innovative in requiring companies to consider (1) whether their presence could potentially undermine the security of local communities (for example, by triggering the arrival of military detachments whose role is to protect investments, but who may behave in a predatory way toward the population) and (2) how such effects could be avoided. Under the VPs, companies are required to apply strict contractual rules to private sector security contractors and to ensure that if the government provides security, the forces have the requisite procedures, training, and equipment to respond to threats such as thefts, community demonstrations, roadblocks, and labor disputes in a competent, proportional, and appropriate way.

APPLYING ENVIRONMENTAL AND SOCIAL STANDARDS IN POST-CONFLICT SETTINGS

Application of environmental and social standards is important in post-conflict settings because there is some evidence that countries are particularly vulnerable to renewed conflict during the decade after peace.[25] Two oil projects in conflict areas, both supported by the IFC, were important developmental arenas for the approaches that became embodied in the IFC-PS. Both the Chad-Cameroon and the BTC projects involved the construction of very large pipelines that would be taking oil from landlocked production sites to export terminals in another country.[26] Developed at the end of the 1990s, these projects were by far the largest foreign direct investment projects in Chad, Cameroon, Azerbaijan, and Georgia up to that point. In cooperation with the financial institutions that were providing financing for the investors, a huge amount of information was collected, and many meetings were held in the project areas, in other parts of the host countries, and internationally.[27] The investors associated with both projects made

---

[25] See Collier (2001).
[26] The Chad-Cameroon project had two innovative components: (1) conditions requiring the government of Chad to enact a revenue management law that committed the majority of oil revenues to development-related spending and (2) detailed requirements designed to achieve environmentally and socially sustainable project development. The revenue management component was not successful: once revenues started to flow, the government modified the law and eventually paid back its loan from the World Bank, removing any obligations under that loan. The project-level environmental and social performance was judged to have been more successful. For more information on the Chad-Cameroon project, see John A. Gould and Matthew S. Winters, "Petroleum Blues: The Political Economy of Resources and Conflict in Chad," in this volume.
[27] Chad-Cameroon lenders included the World Bank and the IFC.

detailed public commitments describing how they would limit social and environmental damage and provide social and environmental benefits. As part of their management plans, the investors also established elaborate systems for monitoring and dispute resolution.[28]

The assessment of potential impacts and the development of social and environmental management plans focused on issues that had not been previously recognized as requiring systematic assessment and management. Such issues included the following:

- Avoiding risks to the health and safety of local people (whether from large, temporary construction workforces—well-paid men with money to spend on bars and prostitutes—or from large numbers of heavy vehicles transporting materials into the sites).
- Ensuring worker safety throughout the chain of contractors and subcontractors.
- Ensuring that workers had proper contracts that were compliant with the core standards of the International Labour Organization.[29]

How successful have efforts been to apply new environmental and social standards? In the case of the Chad-Cameroon and BTC projects, one indisputable impact was that innovations in the scope of the impact assessments were incorporated into the new IFC-PS. And, since 2006, impact assessments and management plans for extractive industry projects to which the IFC-PS has been applied have improved in both scope and depth. One indicator of this shift is that when banks that apply the IFC-PS begin due diligence on projects that have been prepared according to the requirements of host-government legislation, one of the banks' first requirements is for supplementary impact assessments to ensure that social impacts—such as potential labor issues and effects on community health and safety—are evaluated.

The scope of the voluntary standards is sufficient to ensure that predictable risks associated with resource extraction in post-conflict environments (such as pollution, displacement, and predation by security forces) will be identified—and, if appropriate actions are taken, mitigated. Where follow-up includes external monitoring and the results are published—as is the case for the Chad-Cameroon and BTC pipelines, though not for many other projects—there is evidence that investors have made substantial efforts to implement their social and environmental commitments and to address any critical findings reported by auditors or monitors.[30]

---

[28] For investor materials relating to the Chad-Cameroon pipeline, see World Bank (n.d.a); for materials relating to BTC, see IFC (n.d.b).

[29] The eight core standards of the International Labour Organization address child labor, equality and discrimination, forced labor, freedom of association, and the right to collective bargaining (ILO n.d.).

[30] Monitoring reports for the Chad-Cameroon and BTC, respectively, can be found at ExxonMobil (n.d.) and BP (n.d.). Both firms provide far more extensive and detailed monitoring information, and over a longer time period, than is generally available for natural resource projects in developing countries.

In one of the only evaluations of project-level effects, the World Bank's Independent Evaluation Group assessed the Chad-Cameroon project and found that "[World Bank Group] involvement resulted in stronger environmental and social protections . . . than would have been the case otherwise," and that in Cameroon in particular,

> the arrangements put in place for compliance with environmental specifications at the project level (especially the Environmental Management Plan) and addressing the social implications, and their monitoring through an independent entity, may be regarded as among the best in extractive industries projects in Africa (IEG 2009, iv).

The evaluation found less success in Chad, where the high environmental and social standards that had been applied to the original project were not fully replicated as the project expanded into other oil fields (IEG 2009); the evaluation was also critical of the World Bank's efforts to influence revenue management.

Conflict-related questions for inclusion in impact assessments

1 What happened in the project area during the recent conflict? For example,
   - Were community members displaced?
   - Was there combat?
   - Are there land mines in the area?
   - Were traditional or elected leaders replaced?
2 Were ethnic, religious, or generational divisions a factor in the conflict?
3 What steps have been taken or planned for recovery (e.g., resettlement of displaced persons, demobilization of combatants, formal reconciliation processes, war crimes trials)?
4 What infrastructure and services existed in the area before the conflict? Which of these are still operational?

Adherence to the standards would be facilitated by the development of simple guidelines describing the information that investors and their consultants should gather for projects in post-conflict settings. The accompanying sidebar lists some questions that should be asked during the planning phase for resource projects in such settings. Gaining clarity on the issues addressed by these questions would help investors and other stakeholders avoid misunderstandings related to land tenure, ensure that project-related employment is distributed fairly and does not exacerbate existing tensions, and recognize the long-term effects of conflict and the time that is required to repair the associated social and physical damage.

CONCLUSION: ENVIRONMENTAL AND SOCIAL STANDARDS AS PEACEBUILDING TOOLS

The key strengths of the IFC-PS, the EPs, and the VPs as tools for peacebuilding is that they raise the quality of the projects to which they are applied, and can therefore set benchmarks for other businesses in the host country. The time that is required in order to plan projects to meet these standards, the amount of information that is disclosed, and the extent of the consultations that are held also contribute to greater understanding among host-country officials, communities, NGOs, and consultants about the potential impacts of projects and about international standards for impact mitigation. This knowledge may then feed into the revision and updating of environmental laws—as is currently underway in

Angola, for example, under a joint project between the African Development Bank and the government of Angola (African Development Bank Group n.d.). Thus, by building capacity in host countries, the standards help lay the foundations for effective long-term regulatory regimes.

Written standards also provide a basis for correcting problems. In the case of the DRC mining project in which vehicles requisitioned from a company were used to transport troops, the company and its lenders subsequently undertook extensive analysis of the problem and developed a new security management system designed to prevent any similar events. The company has since shared its handbook and training techniques with other mining companies in Katanga and internationally (Multilateral Investment Guarantee Agency, Japan Environmental and Social Challenges Fund, and Anvil Mining 2008). As of yet, however, there has been little rigorous assessment of effectiveness in avoiding risks at the project level.

With respect to peacebuilding, the IFC-PS, the EPs, and the VPs have several weaknesses, however:

- Because they are voluntary, the standards are inherently limited. Businesses can choose whether to apply the standards, and are bound to do so only if they seek financing from lenders that are committed to their implementation.
- The standards are not easy to apply, and require effective consultation, expertise, and resources. The author's experience as a consultant (both implementing the standards and assessing the quality of the implementation on behalf of banks and insurers) suggests that although expertise is being developed, implementation is still of variable quality.
- The standards require only limited evaluation of previous conflict and its implications. Thus, it is unclear to what extent they are capable of directly addressing key post-conflict issues, such as the reintegration of former soldiers, through the large-scale development of high-value resources. Foreign direct investors and consultants are usually reluctant to consider conflict issues in other than a superficial way—owing in part to the optimism that is common among investors, and in part to a reluctance to delve into political complexities that are regarded as almost indecent for foreigners to probe.

Ultimately, the standards can be only a part of the necessary conditions for natural resource development that supports, rather than undermines, effective peacebuilding. Without effective revenue management and institutions that are capable of deploying resource wealth to support peacebuilding, the environmental and social standards applied at the project level cannot overcome the risks of the "resource curse."[31]

---

[31] The *resource curse* refers to the poor development outcomes experienced by many resource-rich countries. For more information on this topic, see Collier and Goderis (2007).

REFERENCES

African Development Bank Group. n.d. Support to environment sector. www.afdb.org/en/projects-operations/project-portfolio/project/p-ao-cz0-001/.
Anvil Mining. n.d. Kinsevere Stage II. www.anvilmining.com/ go/operations/kinsevere.
Basel Committee on Banking Supervision. 2006. International convergence of capital measurement and capital standards: A revised framework. June. www.bis.org/publ/bcbs128.pdf.
BP (British Petroleum). n.d. Baku-Tbilisi-Ceyhan pipeline. www.bp.com/subsection.do?categoryId=9006630&contentId=7013422.
CES (Coastal and Environmental Services). n.d. Reports available for public review & information. www.cesnet.co.za/publicdocs.htm.
China EXIM Bank (China Export and Import Bank). 2007. Guidelines for environmental and social impact assessments of the China Export and Import Bank's (China EXIM Bank) loan projects. August 28. Unofficial translation by International Rivers Network. Quoted in Jill Shankleman, *Going global: Chinese oil and mining companies and the governance of resource wealth*. Washington, D.C.: Woodrow Wilson International Center for Scholars, 57. www.wilsoncenter.org/topics/pubs/DUSS_09323Shnkl_rpt0626.pdf.
CNW. 2007. Anvil and its employees acquitted in Kilwa incident. www.newswire.ca/en/releases/archive/June2007/28/c2026.html.
Collier, P. 2001. Policy for post-conflict societies: Reducing risks of renewed conflict. The economics of civil wars, crime, and violence project. World Bank. www.worldbank.org/research/conflict/papers.htm.
Collier, P., and B. Goderis. 2007. Commodity prices, growth, and the natural resource curse: Reconciling a conundrum. CSAE WPS/2007-15. Centre for the Study of African Economies. www.csae.ox.ac.uk/workingpapers/pdfs/2007-15text.pdf.
Craik, N. 2008. *The international law of environmental impact assessment*. Cambridge, UK: Cambridge University Press.
EIA (U.S. Energy Information Administration). n.d. Oil. www.eia.doe.gov/cabs/Nigeria/Oil.html.
Equator Principles. 2006. The "Equator Principles": A financial industry benchmark for determining, assessing and managing social & environmental risk in project financing. July. www.equator-principles.com/documents/Equator_Principles.pdf.
ExxonMobil. n.d. Chad/Cameroon—Doba Basin. www.exxonmobil.com/Corporate/energy_project_chad.aspx.
Harvard Business School. 2010. Export credit agencies (ECAs). www.people.hbs.edu/besty/projfinportal/ecas.htm.
Human Rights Watch, Colombia. 1998. Human rights concerns raised by the security arrangements of transnational oil companies. Mimeo. New York: Human Rights Watch.
IEG (Independent Evaluation Group). 2009. The World Bank Group program of support for the Chad-Cameroon petroleum development and pipeline construction. Report No. 53015. http://siteresources.worldbank.org/INTOED/Resources/ChadCamReport.pdf.
IFC (International Finance Corporation). 2006. Performance standards on social and environmental sustainability. www.ifc.org/ifcext/sustainability.nsf/Content/ PerformanceStandards.
———. n.d.a. IFC disclosure. www.ifc.og/disclosure.
———. n.d.b. Baku-Tbilisi-Ceyhan oil pipeline project. Project documents. www.ifc.org/ifcext/btc.nsf/Content/Project_Documents.
ILO (International Labour Organization). n.d. International labour standards by subject. www.ilo.org/ilolex/english/subjectE.htm.

MIGA (Multilateral Investment Guarantee Agency). n.d. Projects overview. www.miga.org/projects/index_sv.cfm.

Multilateral Investment Guarantee Agency and Japan Environmental and Social Challenges Fund, in partnership with Anvil Mining. 2008. The Voluntary Principles on Security and Human Rights: An implementation toolkit for major project sites. Working Paper. Multilateral Investment Guarantee Agency. www.miga.org/documents/VPSHR_Toolkit_v3.pdf.

Natural Resource Charter. n.d. Precept 6. www.naturalresourcecharter.org/index.php/en/the-precepts/precept-6.

Siebenhüner, B. 2008. Learning in international organizations in global environmental governance. *Global Environmental Politics* 8 (4): 92–116.

State Oil Company of Azerbaijan; Amoco Caspian Sea Petroleum Limited; BP Exploration (Caspian Sea) Limited; Delta Nimir Khazar Limited; Den Norske Stats Ojeselskap a.s; Lukoil Joint Stock Company; McDermott Azerbaijan, Inc.; Pennzoil Caspian Corporation; Ramco Hazar Energy Limited; Turkiye Petrolleri A.O.; Unocal Khazar, Ltd. 1994. Agreement on the joint development and production sharing for the Azeri and Chirag fields and the deep water portion of the Gunashli field in the Azerbaijan sector of the Caspian Sea. www.bp.com/liveassets/bp_internet/bp_caspian/bp_caspian_en/STAGING/local_assets/downloads_pdfs/pq/ACG_PSA.pdf.

Tenke Fungurume Mining. n.d. Tenke Fungurume Mining: An investment in the future of the Democratic Republic of the Congo. www.fcx.com/operations/downloads/TFM_CONTRACT_FACTS.pdf.

VPSHR (Voluntary Principles on Security and Human Rights). n.d. Risk assessment. http://voluntaryprinciples.org/principles/risk_assessment.

Wines, M. 2009. China willing to spend big on Afghan commerce. *New York Times*, December 29. www.nytimes.com/2009/12/30/world/asia/30mine.html?ref=uneasy_engagement.

World Bank. n.d.a. The Chad-Cameroon petroleum development and pipeline project. http://go.worldbank.org/WPW0WXBR00.

———. n.d.b. World Bank safeguard policies. http://go.worldbank.org/QL7ZYN48M0.

World Bank Extractive Industries Review Advisory Group. n.d. Extractive industries review. http://go.worldbank.org/PMSHHP27M0.

Contract renegotiation and asset recovery in post-conflict settings

Philippe Le Billon

Properly managed, high-value natural resources can help consolidate peace by providing jobs, revenues, and infrastructure. Sharing resource wealth can also provide an incentive for cease-fire agreements between belligerents. But when high-value resources are subject to unfair contracts or diverted to war profiteers, they can undermine the transition to a durable peace. This chapter describes two principal means of addressing such problems: (1) reappraising and renegotiating resource exploitation contracts and (2) freezing, recovering, or claiming compensation for stolen assets.

Contract reappraisal and renegotiation can increase public revenues, provide greater transparency and accountability, and support the regulation of the social and environmental impacts of resource sectors. Over the long term, through the cancellation of poorly run concessions, reappraisal can also attract higher-quality investments that are more fiscally advantageous for the government. Finally, a well-run reappraisal scheme that yields demonstrably successful development outcomes can strengthen trust in, and improve the legitimacy of, the government.

To deal with war profiteering, the United Nations Security Council (UNSC) has made increasing use of (1) asset freezing, in which assets are rendered inaccessible to their (illegitimate) owners, most notably to curtail funding for further hostilities, and (2) asset recovery, in which assets are returned to their rightful owners or allocated to victims who require compensation. Such measures are often undertaken on the basis of investigations conducted by sanctions committees and panels of experts. The objective of asset recovery is not only to shore up public revenues for post-conflict recovery,[1] but also to signal an end to impunity for war profiteering and to discourage extractive companies and banking institutions from

---

Philippe Le Billon is an associate professor at the University of British Columbia, where he is affiliated with both the Department of Geography and the Liu Institute for Global Issues.

[1] Although some funds may be recovered through the repatriation of assets, others may be irretrievable because of contractual provisions inherited from previous governments. International aid can temporarily mask these losses, but they will become more apparent when foreign aid declines and countries are most in need of sustained revenues.

participating in resource looting. In some cases, host governments have sued individuals and firms that have profited from the exploitation of conflict resources (Harwell and Le Billon 2009).

This chapter is divided into three parts: (1) a discussion of the reasons for, and approaches to, contract reappraisal and renegotiation; (2) a consideration of efforts to freeze, recover, or claim compensation for stolen assets; and (3) a brief conclusion.

CONTRACT REAPPRAISAL AND RENEGOTIATION

During or shortly after a conflict, resource concessions are often awarded by authorities that have questionable legitimacy. Politicians, cronies, rebel groups, mercenary outfits, or members of the armed forces may receive resource rights, either on their own or as part of power-sharing agreements. Even in peaceful times, the negotiation of contracts for high-value resource projects is often marred by secrecy, corruption, and lack of expertise, resulting in terms that are unfavorable both for the state and the populace. Moreover, such negotiations rarely involve consultation with, or the approval of, local communities; as a result, the most vulnerable local residents may be taken advantage of by local leaders and by wealthier households eager to tap into the new revenue streams.

The drive for post-conflict contract reappraisal stems, in part, from concerns, largely among development nongovernmental organizations (NGOs), about the effects of the liberalization of extractive sectors.[2] Such liberalization has been promoted since the 1980s, most notably by the World Bank, as a means of increasing foreign direct investment and economic output; it has also been promoted by the home governments of international mining companies, which provide substantial support to facilitate overseas ventures.[3] One problem with contracts made under conditions of liberalization, however, is that the terms may reflect the limited bargaining power of post-conflict states; specifically, the host countries are often at a disadvantage because of the obvious risk of investing in a post-conflict setting (Emel and Huber 2008).

More generally, high risk and low returns tend to operate in a vicious cycle. The risks associated with damaged physical infrastructure, the potential for renewed conflict, and regulatory uncertainty not only put the host government at a disadvantage in its negotiations with investors,[4] but also tend to attract

---

[2] Liberalization generally involves the opening of resource sectors to foreign investment, easier profit repatriation, and weaker environmental and social regulations (Bridge 2004; Christian Aid 2009).
[3] On the case of Canada, see Campbell (1998).
[4] For some companies, hostilities and high risk may be considered an advantage. For example, the stock market dropped in response to the cessation of hostilities in Angola, probably because peace would bring about more intense competition and stronger government bargaining power (Guidolin and La Ferrara 2007). (The authors sampled seven companies listed on the exchanges of Toronto, Canada; Johannesburg, South Africa; and Australia.)

high-risk companies that may be more inclined to use bribery, deploy private armed protection, and come up short in the realm of corporate social responsibility.

Both local government and development agencies—eager to fast-track foreign direct investment—may turn a blind eye to the backgrounds and records of these companies, a decision that has implications both for new contracts and for older ones in need of renegotiation. For example, contracts may be awarded to companies that have poor records in terms of corporate social responsibility; ventures may be permitted that are mostly "mining the market"—that is, speculating on the future value of concessions, rather than bringing in investment, creating jobs, and generating tax revenues; or companies may be allowed to cherry-pick—to take the most profitable ore or timber out of the concession in the shortest time, while diminishing the long-term commercial value of the entire reserve. In some cases, the emphasis on foreign investment is political in origin: domestic rulers may favor foreign companies and businesspeople out of a desire to avoid creating a business class that could fund (or become) a source of political opposition.

Yet another problem is that decisions with long-term impacts are often based on short-term considerations. Warlords focus on winning the next battle—and when warlords become politicians, they focus on winning the next election (meanwhile securing their futures through corruption, in case of defeat). Thus, both warlords and politicians may ignore long-term economic interests in favor of resource contracts that bring quick returns; such returns can then be used, for example, to pay soldiers and civil servants whose salaries are in arrears—an important move for staying in power. As an election approaches, announcements of massive incoming foreign investment may help win votes and secure the backing of foreign donors. It is essential to build safeguards again such short-term incentives.

Host-country leaders may also be more eager to pursue investment on the part of a foreign company, which can jump-start operations, than to promote the development of domestic champions within the extractive sector. Foreign companies have many advantages; for example, they are generally in a better position to fast-track investment, ramp up exploitation, and build infrastructure. In addition, foreign companies may be more likely to incorporate socially responsible initiatives into their business practices, although the extent of such initiatives will depend on the demands of local communities, on the firms' relationship to the government, and on the extent to which overseas constituencies hold companies accountable for meeting their official standards for corporate social responsibility. In fact, foreign companies are often the only option, especially in capital- and technology-intensive resource extraction: there are simply no domestic companies able to take on the work. When the capacity of local companies has been worn away by the conflict and its aftermath, partnership between foreign and domestic companies—including the employment and training of local workers—may help revive such capacity.

Nevertheless, the pursuit of foreign investment may have several disadvantages for a post-conflict government, and for the effective transition to a peaceful and prosperous society:

- It may lock the resource sector into an arrangement with a poorly regulated foreign company (although it may admittedly be better regulated than a domestic one, especially if the foreign company is publicly listed and subject to minimum disclosure requirements).
- Foreign companies, preferring to concentrate on their core activities, may have little interest in spawning upstream or downstream businesses within the resource sector because of the significant risks involved.
- Foreign companies may choose to diversify into entirely different sectors (as many domestic oil companies have done, with various degrees of success).[5] In addition, foreign companies may not be interested in investing in local communities or may be prevented from doing so by the government.

Thus, while foreign companies may help jump-start the local economy, their long-term impacts, particularly with respect to economic diversification, are more problematic. Finally, there is the matter of taxes. Host governments often provide major tax incentives to attract large-scale investment and demonstrate that the country is "open for business" (Le Billon and Levin 2009). Although the overall impact on host governments' tax revenues has varied, observers have pointed to the long-term risk of lower fiscal returns on nonrenewable resources (Bridge 2004; Otto 2006).

Arguably, whether the resource companies are public or private, national or foreign may matter less than the capacity of the host-country institutions that are regulating them; this concern is relevant to both new contracts and to renegotiation. To avoid rushing projects into inadequate institutional settings, donor agencies, local authorities, companies, and civil society groups must cooperate to strengthen institutional capacity and to implement resource projects that are capable of delivering broad development outcomes.

Strategies

The reappraisal and renegotiation of resource exploitation contracts signed during or immediately after a conflict offer a valuable opportunity to improve the development outcomes of resource exploitation. But there are important questions about the timing of such undertakings. On the one hand, the earlier reappraisal and renegotiation are implemented, the better: first, allowing the contracts to remain as they are implies tacit acceptance by post-conflict authorities; second, the interest and influence of external actors, who may be able to assist in bringing about

---

[5] On the cases of national oil companies based in the Middle East, see Marcel (2006); on Angola's oil company, Sonangol, see Soares de Oliveira (2008).

better contracts, is the greatest during the early post-conflict phase. On the other hand, given the background and incentives of transitional authorities (especially domestic authorities, such as "governments of national unity," which bring all armed factions into a power-sharing agreement), rushing into reappraisal and renegotiation may leave the door open for a new round of poorly negotiated contracts. One option is a two-phase process in which audits, reappraisal, and discussions of reforms would occur under the transitional authorities, and renegotiations would occur under, and be put in place by, a post-transition government—that is, a government that is brought to power through a general election of both the chief executive and the legislature.[6]

Reappraisals may result in the cancellation, renegotiation, or confirmation of existing contracts. Donor agencies and other international organizations should help sustain reappraisal and renegotiation processes by providing technical assistance and supporting the host-country civil society groups that demand and monitor such efforts. To gain the support of domestic authorities, donors may consider providing funding to make up for revenue losses during review periods.

Contract reappraisal and renegotiation generally involve a systematic review of extractive sector activities and contracts, including those that involve state companies, by interministerial, parliamentary, or tripartite commissions (government, NGO, and donor-agency representatives). Contracts that are determined to fit the definition of "odious contracts" may be canceled.[7] The reappraisal and renegotiation process may also include reappraisal, for tax purposes, of business activities conducted during the war, and the imposition of penalties on companies that knowingly traded in "conflict resources."[8] Reappraisal and renegotiation are challenging, primarily because of the stakes involved and the risk of costly and lengthy legal battles.

One of the first steps is to ensure the legality of the contracts that are already in place. In Liberia, for example, none of the logging contracts that were due for reappraisal could be proven to be legal; thus, it was relatively easy to cancel them (Blundell 2008). Most importantly, ensuring legality requires the full disclosure of contracts (including any confidential clauses), corporate structure, and ownership.[9] Contracts must also be closely reviewed for evidence of tax

---

[6] It would be naive, however, to think that elections alone can bring transition to a close.

[7] An odious contract, like "odious debt," is undertaken against the interests of the people, without their consent, and with the full awareness of the creditor. For a discussion of these two concepts, see Khalfan (2006) and Alvarez-Plata and Brück (2008).

[8] According to Global Witness, an international NGO whose work focuses on breaking the link between natural resources and conflict, *conflict resources* are those "whose systematic exploitation and trade in a context of conflict contribute to, benefit from or result in the commission of serious violations of human rights, violations of international humanitarian law or violations amounting to crimes under international law" (Global Witness n.d.).

[9] Confidential clauses may be suspended if they are superseded by the reappraisal legislation.

evasion and of abusive practices such as tax holidays, transfer pricing, biased commodity-pricing mechanisms, and the sheltering of liabilities; provisions allowing such practices should be revoked.[10] In the course of reappraisal, conflicts can emerge on a number of levels; for example, companies and governments may disagree about confidentiality clauses or about the validity of new legislation in the resource sector (especially if the contract currently in place includes stabilization clauses that effectively freeze the legal setting and preclude the application of new legislation).

Among the concerns associated with contract reappraisal is the risk that renegotiations will give way to, or even be motivated by, corruption (Chêne 2007). Another is that if reappraisal criteria are not clear, companies may be deterred from future investments out of concern that they might be subject, at a later date, to unpredictable criteria. This concern can be addressed by the adoption of international standards, such as those included in the Natural Resource Charter.[11] Other measures that can help in this area include an assessment of institutional vulnerability, to identify the risk of corruption; the creation of an autonomous regulatory agency that is separate from the ministries that are in charge of the daily management of resource sectors; and the selection of reappraisal teams that have strong expertise and as few conflicts of interest as possible.[12] Another risk is that disgruntled companies, especially those that have lost contracts, will seek compensation through international arbitration. Although compensation has been standard practice where industries have been nationalized, companies that have signed contracts during hostilities are often on very weak legal grounds; in Liberia, for example, contracts with all logging companies were canceled after they failed to demonstrate that they had been operating legally during Charles Taylor's administration.

Yet another risk is that reappraisal may delay projects—and thereby delay investment, jobs, and tax revenues. Concerns about delay may be intensified by

---

[10] Under transfer pricing, prices declared at export are set artificially low, to reduce tax liability; the importing entity (which is often located in a tax haven) then resells the commodity at a higher price. The same approach can be used in reverse for the importation of staff and materials. Under biased commodity-pricing mechanisms, prices are determined and indexed to the advantage of the company, thereby reducing taxes. Companies shelter liabilities by creating "independent" subsidiaries and subcontractors; so, for example, a subsidiary that owed compensation for environmental damages would simply declare bankruptcy. For purposes of tax evasion, subsidiaries can be headquartered in territories with lax regulations.

[11] See www.naturalresourcecharter.org.

[12] Reappraisal teams are diverse but generally include legislative representatives from the major political parties; officials from relevant ministries; prominent members of civil society organizations; and experts on taxes, the resource sector in question, and contractual law (such experts are often paid for by donor agencies). Nominations to reappraisal teams are often made by political parties and civil-society umbrella organizations, in consultation with donor agencies and international financial institutions, but may also be made by the head of state.

the cyclical character of resource prices, creating an incentive to rush projects when prices are high or rising.[13] Finally, there is the risk that reappraisal will further undermine the legitimacy of the political class without providing a suitable alternative—which could, in turn, further radicalize elements in the population. As will be seen in the following section, Liberia provides an example of relatively successful reappraisal and renegotiation, but this was not the case in the Democratic Republic of the Congo (DRC), where the reappraisal and renegotiation process further tarnished the reputation of the political class and caused the country to largely miss the commodity boom that occurred between 2003 and 2008.

Examples

The next two sections describe contract reappraisal and renegotiation efforts in Liberia and the DRC.

Liberia

Liberia has had a number of successes with contract reappraisal and renegotiation.[14] President Ellen Johnson Sirleaf not only canceled logging concessions, but also renegotiated an iron-ore mining contract that had allowed the company to determine the price of iron ore—and thereby control its own taxation level.[15] A number of factors contributed to the substantially improved terms of the new contract, including Johnson Sirleaf's background in banking, her personal involvement in the renegotiation, and her international profile as Africa's first elected female president; finally, there was the effort undertaken by Global Witness to publicly expose the inequities in the previous contract (Global Witness 2006, 2007) (see table 1).

The renegotiation of a second major contract, a Firestone rubber concession, also yielded significant improvements, including a quadrupling of the lease price; a reduction in the risk of transfer pricing, accomplished through the use of international market prices;[16] a fifty-year reduction in the duration of the contract; and improved housing for workers (Kaul and Heuty 2009; Stier 2009). Critics had a number of concerns about the Firestone contract: inadequate time for public consultation (only two days); a reduction in the U.S.-based parent company's

---

[13] From the perspective of investors, the incentive to expedite projects may be offset, however, by the fact that development prices are higher during boom periods. The link between boom-and-bust cycles and investments is not straightforward.

[14] For a detailed analysis of the renegotiation process, including challenges and outcomes, see Kaul and Heuty (2009). On international oversight of renegotiations, see Ford and Tienhaara (2010).

[15] The contract was originally made between Mittal Steel and the previous transition government.

[16] Transfer pricing is a means of accounting for the value of goods and services transferred within a company; when applied across tax jurisdictions, however, it is often used to evade taxation.

Table 1. Renegotiation of Mittal iron-ore mining contract in Liberia: Summary of changes

Initial contract	Renegotiated contract
Mittal sets iron-ore price.	Iron-ore price determined by international market price.
Five-year tax holiday, with unlimited extension.	No tax holiday.
Obligations are guaranteed only by the concessionaire (a subsidiary of Mittal).	Obligations are guaranteed by the parent company.
The ownership of the main national railway line and deep-sea port were transferred to Mittal.	No transfer of railway or port; no exclusive rights to use of railway or port.
Extended and backdated the equitable-treatment clause, which required that Mittal be treated similarly to all past and future companies in sectors other than iron ore.	Equitable-treatment clause limited to the iron-ore sector; no backdating.
Concessionaire has rights to all minerals in the concession area.	Concessionaire has rights to iron ore only.
Contract governed by United Kingdom law.	Contract governed by Liberia law.
Minimal social obligations.	Recruitment of senior managers from within Liberia; health care obligations toward workers.

Sources: Global Witness (2006, 2007).

direct social and environmental liability; government regulation of pricing; and the inclusion of a clause that limits future government regulation of the industry (Global Witness 2008a). More generally, formal consultations with NGOs, easier public access to contracts, and stronger backing from international donors and agencies would likely have improved the process. Nevertheless, contract renegotiations in Liberia stand as models of success, thanks largely to an engaged leadership, a collaborative and unified government negotiation team, and "world-class" technical assistance (Kaul and Heuty 2009, 14).

Democratic Republic of the Congo

Three main processes influenced the renegotiation of mining contracts in the DRC: a World Bank–sponsored liberalization of the mining sector and two sequential contractual review processes undertaken by parliamentary and interministerial commissions. In 2002, the World Bank established a new mining code to increase foreign direct investment and to facilitate the partial privatization of a largely publicly owned sector (Mazalto 2005). This donor-driven effort also sought to reassure foreign investors by providing greater contractual stability and regulatory predictability, particularly in light of the DRC's past history of nationalizing industries; contract renegotiations and cancellations (apart from those of targeted public companies) were not a priority. In contrast, the goal of the two contractual review processes was to reassess the legality and fairness of past contracts,

Contract negotiation and asset recovery 77

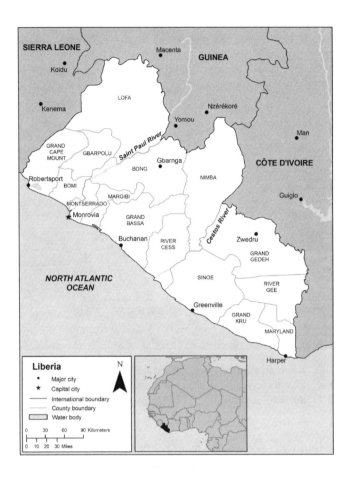

including those of foreign investors, and to develop clear recommendations for renegotiation or cancellation. Final renegotiations, however, remained firmly under the prerogative of the Congolese president—and proved to be limited in scope.

Although the Transitional Parliament Commission was established on April 2, 2003, to reassess contracts passed in the DRC during the civil wars of 1996–1997 and 1998–2003, it did not begin its work until May 2004.[17] The commission, which was chaired by opposition leader Christophe Lutundula, had a limited budget from the DRC government (only US$8,000), but it had significant financial support from the World Bank (US$443,000). Nevertheless, the commission faced several problems. First, there were delays in nominating members because some political parties were initially excluded, and there were intraparty negotiations

---

[17] The commission was established by resolutions 16 and 19 (DIC/CEF/01 and DIC/CEF/04) of the Inter-Congolese Political Negotiations: Final Act, which was signed in Sun City, South Africa, on April 2, 2003.

78 High-value natural resources and post-conflict peacebuilding

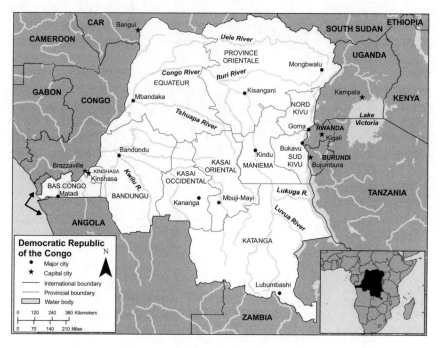

Note: The DRC constitution, which was ratified in 2005 and came into effect in 2006, mandated that within three years the eleven provinces be redivided into twenty-six. As of August 2011, the redivision had not yet taken place.

over the nominations. Second, the main political parties, including those in the government—the People's Party for Reconstruction and Democracy, the Movement for the Liberation of the Congo, and Rally for Congolese Democracy–National— refused to collaborate with the commission; only the smallest party in the transition parliament, the Rally for Congolese Democracy–Movement for Liberation, co-operated (NIZA 2006).

The commission submitted its report to the Bureau of the National Assembly in June 2005, but debate within the assembly was repeatedly postponed, allegedly by senior politicians who were implicated in the contracts (Human Rights Watch 2005).[18] The report was finally provided to parliament (and leaked on the Internet) in mid-February 2006. The commission recommended the renegotiation or cancellation of sixteen contracts, judicial investigation of twenty-eight Congolese or international companies, and the prosecution of seventeen people for fraud. Neither parliament nor the executive branch of the government took heed of the report.

---

[18] The Bureau of the National Assembly is the secretariat for the legislative body.

Further undermining the commission's work, the report was politicized by Lutundula's affiliation with the Alliance for the Renewal of the Congo, a political party that presented itself as seeking to break from the practices of the principal parties. In the view of some politicians, Lutundula's political affiliation gave him a vested interest in tarnishing the principal parties.

The Interministerial Commission for the Revisitation of Mining Contracts (Revisitation Commission), launched by the Minister of Mines in April 2007, reviewed sixty-one contracts that had been signed with Congolese state companies during the two wars (1996–1997 and 1998–2003) and under the transition government (2003–2006).[19] The Revisitation Commission received limited assistance from foreign donors; only Belgium provided significant support (about US$100,000, through the Carter Center, for legal advice). Several domestic and international civil society organizations also provided advice.

The Revisitation Commission's report, completed in November 2007 but not publicly released until March 2008, stated that of the sixty-one contracts that had been reviewed, thirty-eight had been renegotiated and twenty-three had been canceled for irregularities.[20] An independent review by the Carter Center (2009), which had access to some of the renegotiated contracts, assessed the renegotiations as a "missed opportunity," arguing that

- The "vast array of divergent obligations" would make the contracts difficult to oversee and enforce, especially given the DRC's weak regulatory apparatus.
- Although the renegotiations increased one-time upfront payments, the payments were contingent on economic conditions (such as resource prices and the profitability of mining ventures) and therefore unlikely to be made.
- The renegotiations offered no clear long-term benefits in terms of stronger tax regulation.

In addition to the three major initiatives discussed so far, the Congolese judicial system also reviewed—and canceled—a number of mining and logging concessions. This initially gave credence to the notion that existing institutions (in this case, the judiciary) had the independence and capacity to review the legality of previously awarded contracts, unlike the two commissions that had so far attempted to do so. The involvement of the courts, however, raised concerns about the absence of a concerted approach to contract review that would bring

---

[19] See Minister of Mines (2007). The thirty members of the Revisitation Commission were drawn from the office of the president and the office of the prime minister; the ministries of mines, finance, budget, justice, and industry; and specialized agencies such as the Mining Cadastre. Members of national civil-society organizations were invited as observers.

[20] The initial mandate had allowed for a category of contracts that could remain unaltered, but none qualified (IPIS 2008).

together all three branches of government. Finally, because of the particular company that had been targeted by the judicial procedure, there were concerns about political interference.[21]

Overall, given the lack of transparency and independent review that characterized the situation before (and, to some extent, during) the efforts of the commissions, the contractual reappraisal initiatives appear to have yielded minimal long-term benefits for the DRC, while further undermining the credibility of the political class and all branches of government. Moreover, the DRC's inability to bring the reappraisal and renegotiation process to a positive conclusion increases the risk that international arbitration will vindicate the ousted companies that have challenged the decisions of the Congolese government (*Le Potentiel* 2009).

FREEZING, RECOVERING, AND CLAIMING COMPENSATION FOR STOLEN ASSETS

While contract negotiations seek to direct current and future natural resource revenues to the state, the goal of asset recovery is to track down and repatriate the proceeds generated by illegal resource exploitation, as defined by domestic legislation or international sanction regimes. The principal steps in the recovery process are to find the assets, freeze them, identify their rightful owners, and determine the conditions for their repatriation.

Many governments and courts—or, in some cases, the UNSC—impose conditions on repatriation. Despite the difficulties involved, post-conflict political transitions offer a major opportunity for asset recovery because of the confluence of a number of factors, including a change in regime, the presence of international security forces and international courts, and financial and diplomatic support from international donors—not to mention media coverage.

Tracking down assets requires expertise, judicial support, and collaboration from financial institutions (Winer and Roule 2003).[22] Recovery is often slow and costly, and efforts are often ineffective—notably because of lack of material evidence, the high speed of fund transfers, lack of collaboration between jurisdictions, the immunity of perpetrators who are still in power (or are protected by current governments), and legal loopholes and inconsistencies (Smith, Pieth, and Jorge 2007). Even when the assets are still within the country and there has been a change in government, seizure may be difficult. The government of Liberia, for

---

[21] Boss Mining's contract was canceled and awarded to Katanga Mining because Boss Mining was about to take over Katanga Mining (Kabemba 2008).
[22] In 2006, in one of the rare cases of legal prosecution, a Dutch timber merchant, Guus van Kouwenhoven, was initially sentenced to eight years of imprisonment for breaking the UN arms embargo on Liberia. A Dutch court of appeals overturned the sentence in 2008 (Global Witness 2008b). In April 2010 the Dutch Supreme Court overruled the court of appeal's acquittal and ordered a new trial.

example, was for a long time reluctant to freeze the domestic assets of Liberian politicians, for fear of political backlash from supporters of the profiteers (UNSC 2009).

A landmark 2005 civil case in the International Court of Justice (ICJ) focused attention on the justiciability of the pillage of natural resources as a war crime (Harwell and Le Billon 2009). In *Democratic Republic of the Congo v. Uganda*, the ICJ found that although there was no evidence of a state strategy to use the military to pillage the resources of the DRC, the Ugandan state nevertheless failed, in its obligation as an occupying power, to prevent its armed forces and their nonstate collaborators from pillaging natural resources in the occupied Congolese province of Ituri, which is rich in gold and other minerals.

Because the two countries had previously agreed that they would decide on any damages through bilateral negotiation, the court did not award damages to the DRC; the negotiations that will determine how the DRC will be compensated for its loss of property were still under way at the time of writing. It would, in any case, have been nearly impossible for the ICJ to enforce a compensation ruling: first, such rulings are contentious because of the subjective nature of valuing the impacts of war; second, the ICJ's reach and enforcement capacity are limited by the principle of sovereignty.

Liberia's Truth and Reconciliation Commission (TRC) can recommend reparations for victims of human rights abuses. In its final report, the TRC recommended that the government of Liberia

> also hold responsible individuals and entities that were responsible for committing tax evasion. In particular, the TRC recommends that corporate officers in the timber, mining and telecommunications sector be prosecuted for their willingness to avoid the payment of tax revenues to Liberia during the civil conflict in Liberia. Government agents that knowingly facilitated and colluded in tax evasion must also be held accountable (TRC 2009, 41).

The TRC also called for the government of Liberia to set up a reparation trust fund financed through

> judgments against economic criminals through three ways: (1) recovering tax arrears from timber, mining, petroleum and telecommunications companies that evaded tax liability under the Taylor regime; (2) obtaining funds from economic criminals that are sentenced by Liberian courts to pay restitution or other fees; and (3) utilizing criminal and civil confiscation schemes in foreign jurisdictions to repatriate Liberian assets (TRC 2009, 43).

One of the most ambitious ongoing compensation schemes is the attempt, by the Republic of Iraq, to sue multinational corporations for having "conspired with the former regime of Saddam Hussein to corrupt the United Nations Oil-for-Food Program" (Bernstein Liebhard LLP n.d.). According to the plaintiffs, companies not only provided Saddam Hussein's regime with kickbacks, but also benefited from advantageous terms, thus doubly depriving the Iraqi people of billions of dollars in aid while simultaneously busting sanctions.

The return of stolen assets is a central principle of the UN Convention against Corruption (UNCAC), which came into force in 2005.[23] Since 2007, this principle has received further backing from the Stolen Asset Recovery (StAR) Initiative, a joint effort of the World Bank and the UNODC.[24] Although StAR's main focus so far has been on policy analysis for the regulatory reform of the international financial system (World Bank and UNODC 2009), it has also developed training materials, undertaken capacity building, and developed programs in about half a dozen countries. StAR collaborates with the main international corruption and money-laundering initiatives, such as the Financial Action Task Force, as well as with specialized organizations, such as the International Centre for Asset Recovery.[25]

Generally speaking, asset recovery focuses on major investors, traders, and exporters who have profited from conflict resources; other targets include politicians, government officials, and leaders of armed groups that have been linked to human rights abuses. Given the risk that some actors, such as the leaders of armed groups, may spoil the peace in order to avoid facing justice, preventive measures are required; for example, asset recovery should be postponed until any military units or armed supporters associated with the accused have been disbanded. The freezing of assets—and, to a lesser extent, the recovery of assets, which demands a higher level of evidence regarding ownership—also involves specific legal risks: breaching the right to judicial review (because decisions to freeze assets are taken outside of court, and are not easily challenged by courts) and breaching the principle of presumption of innocence (Godinho 2009).

As of this writing, most post-conflict asset recovery has focused on allegedly corrupt heads of state, rather than on businesses or rebel groups funded by conflict resources (Dulin 2007), and most of the assets frozen by the UN have been those of suspected financiers of terrorism. Among political leaders who ruled during armed conflicts, successful asset recovery procedures have been undertaken against Mobutu Sese Seko (DRC), Alberto Fujimori and Vladimiro Montesinos (Peru), and Saddam Hussein (Iraq). Procedures are under way against José Eduardo dos Santos (Angola) and Charles Taylor (Liberia). Although a number of rebel groups are believed to have accumulated large amounts of funds, little information is available on the whereabouts of these funds.

---

[23] For an analysis of the challenges facing UNCAC, see Smith, Pieth, and Jorge (2007).
[24] For more information on the joint effort, see www.worldbank.org/StAR.
[25] The Group of Seven (G-7) established the Financial Action Task Force in 1989 to address money laundering; more recently, it has begun to address terrorism financing (see www.fatf-gafi.org). The International Centre for Asset Recovery is based at the Basel Institute of Governance (see www.baselgovernance.org/big/) and provides various resources, including assistance and training for asset recovery (see www.assetrecovery.org).

CONCLUSION

This chapter has considered two complementary options for improving the impact of high-value resources on peacebuilding and post-conflict transitions: reappraising and renegotiating resource contracts, and freezing, recovering, and claiming compensation for looted assets. Both options have been experimented with: Liberia has renegotiated the contract on a major iron-mining project, and asset recovery is the focus of ongoing judicial procedures in Angola, Iraq, and Liberia.

As a general rule, revenues from resource sectors should be placed under international supervision during the post-conflict transition period, and transitional authorities, whether national or international, should be prohibited from awarding long-term contracts in extractive sectors.[26] Beyond the transition period, long-term monitoring by a tripartite commission (local authorities, civil society, and international donors) should be put in place, and the UNSC should maintain its authority to intervene in revenue management. It is also important to ensure that the intervening parties lack vested interests in the outcome; questions might otherwise arise about motives. The Australian intervention in Timor-Leste and the American intervention in Iraq offer cautionary examples with regard to the oil sector.

Contract renegotiation and asset recovery have rarely yielded substantial benefits. Both approaches are costly, legally complex, and potentially tainted by political interference—and outcomes are often uncertain. These obstacles should not deter such initiatives, however. Investigations by UN panels of experts and NGOs have demonstrated that it is possible to track down embezzled revenues. More systematic investigations, strengthened by collaboration among governments and UN bodies, can further improve efforts to find and prosecute war profiteers.

Contract renegotiations have also yielded some positive outcomes, as in the case of Liberia. In the DRC, in contrast, the president has yet to follow through on the recommendations made by two major commissions. Poor management of resource sectors, inadequate funding for domestic resource-management authorities, and the failure of the commissions' efforts have been particularly frustrating for the Congolese, who could otherwise have benefited from a major mineral boom that occurred between 2003 and 2008.

The experience of the DRC suggests that the first and most important step is for transitional or post-conflict authorities to open the books and to make existing contracts public at the earliest possible stage in the transition. UN

---

[26] This principle could be legally based on the consideration that a transitional authority is akin to an occupying state unless specific powers are legally granted to it. For a description of the rights of the occupying state as "administrator and usufructuary," see Hague Convention (1907, art. 55). The Hague principle, which was upheld by a 1976 memorandum from the U.S. Department of Justice concerning oil exploitation by Israel in the Sinai (Bowen 1997), can be applied to domestic transitional governments through local legislation, through a peace agreement, or through a UNSC resolution.

missions, the UNSC, and donor nations should use their influence to achieve this aim. The second step is to gather sufficient expertise to assess the legality and fairness of the contracts. Contracts signed during conflicts are likely to include flaws that render them illegal—obviating the need for accusations of unfairness or complicity in war crimes. Independent experts, parliamentary commissions, and public hearings can prove valuable during this phase. The third step is to strengthen the legal framework and the institutions that oversee resource exploitation and revenue management, so that revised contracts can be more effectively implemented.

Most resource exploitation contracts are of long duration, stretching thirty years or more. Moreover, many include stabilization clauses that "freeze" legal conditions at the time of signature, thereby locking war-torn countries into arrangements that may have consequences for several generations. Finally, because most high-value natural resources are nonrenewable, most, if not all, of the resources can be tied up in contracts that are unfavorable to domestic authorities and local populations.

Host governments and international transitional authorities are becoming increasingly aware of the problems that can be associated with resource extraction contracts; at the same time, companies are recognizing the risk that glaringly unfair contracts and the growing resentment of host populations may lead to outright contract cancellation and expropriation. Contract renegotiation offers a means for both governments and extraction companies to reevaluate controversial deals and seek new arrangements that will be mutually beneficial over the long term. As discussed in this chapter, such renegotiations are not without risk, and the pressure, participation, and support of civil society groups and international agencies are often crucial in ensuring a positive outcome.

REFERENCES

Alvarez-Plata, P., and T. Brück. 2008. External debt in post-conflict countries. *World Development* 36 (3): 485–504.

Bernstein Liebhard LLP. n.d. Bernstein Liebhard LLP files first amended complaint on behalf of the Republic of Iraq against multinational corporations for Saddam Hussein era oil-for-food program fraud scheme. www.bernlieb.com/news/iraq-oil-food-lawsuit/index.html.

Blundell, A. 2008. Personal communication from the former chair of the United Nations panel of experts on Liberia.

Bowen, S. 1997. *Human rights, self-determination and political change in the Occupied Palestinian Territories.* The Hague: Kluwer.

Bridge, G. 2004. Mapping the bonanza: Geographies of mining investment in an era of neoliberal reform. *Professional Geographer* 56 (3): 406–421.

Campbell, B. 1998. Liberalisation, deregulation, state promoted investment: Canadian mining interests in Africa. *Raw Materials Report* 13 (4): 14–34.

Carter Center. 2009. *The mining review in the Democratic Republic of the Congo: Missed opportunities, failed expectations, hopes for the future.* Atlanta.

Chêne, M. 2007. Corruption and the renegotiation of mining contracts. U4 Anti-Corruption Resource Centre. www.u4.no/helpdesk/helpdesk/query.cfm?id=156.
Christian Aid. 2009. *Breaking the curse: How transparent taxation and fair taxes can turn Africa's mineral wealth into development.* London: Christian Aid.
Dulin, A. 2007. *Biens mal acquis . . . profitent trop souvent: La fortune des dictateurs et les complaisances occidentales.* Paris: Comité Catholique contre la Faim et pour le Développment.
Emel, J., and M. T. Huber. 2008. A risky business: Mining, rent and the neoliberalization of "risk." *Geoforum* 39 (3): 1393–1407.
Ford, J., and K. Tienhaara. 2010. Too little, too late? International oversight of contract negotiations in post-conflict Liberia. *International Peacekeeping* 17 (3): 361–376.
Global Witness. 2006. Heavy Mittal? A state within a state. The inequitable mineral development agreement between the Government of Liberia and Mittal Steel Holdings NV. London.
———. 2007. Update on the renegotiation of the mineral development agreement between Mittal steel and the Government of Liberia. London.
———. 2008a. *Recommendations for future concession contract negotiations drawn from the amended Firestone contract.* London.
———. 2008b. Dutch Court of Appeal finds insufficient evidence to convict conflict timber trader. www.globalwitness.org/media_library_detail.php/631/en/dutch_court_of _appeal_finds_insufficient_evidence_.
———. n.d. Definition of conflict resources. www.globalwitness.org/pages/en/definition_ of_conflict_resources.html.
Godinho, J. 2009. When worlds collide: Enforcing United Nations Security Council asset freezes in the EU legal order. *European Law Journal* 16 (1): 67–93.
Guidolin, M., and E. La Ferrara. 2007. Diamonds are forever, wars are not: Is conflict bad for private firms? *American Economic Review* 97 (5): 1978–1993.
Hague Convention (Convention [IV] respecting the Laws and Customs of War on Land and its annex: Regulations concerning the Laws and Customs of War on Land). 1907. October 18. www.icrc.org/ihl.nsf/385ec082b509e76c41256739003e636d/ 1d1726425f6955aec125641e0038bfd6.
Harwell, E., and P. Le Billon. 2009. Natural connections: Linking transitional justice and development through a focus on natural resources. In *Transitional justice and development*, ed. P. de Greiff and R. Dutie. New York: Social Science Research Council.
Human Rights Watch. 2005. *The curse of gold.* New York.
IPIS (International Peace Information Service). 2008. *Democratic Republic of the Congo, mining contracts: State of affairs.* Antwerp.
Kabemba, C. 2008. Is a genuine and transparent process of mining contracts renegotiation possible in the DRC? Paper presented at the Revenue Watch Institute conference "How Can Africa Get a Better Deal for Its Natural Resources?" February 7, Dakar, Senegal.
Kaul, R., and A. Heuty. 2009. *Getting a better deal from the extractive sector: Concession negotiation in Liberia, 2006–2008.* New York: Revenue Watch Institute.
Khalfan, A. 2006. Odious debt: Definition, application and context. Paper presented at the EURODAD Annual Conference 2006, "From Illegitimacy to Responsibility: Transforming Development Finance." October 30. www.odiousdebts.org/odiousdebts/publications/ ODashfaqEURODAD.pdf.
Le Billon, P., and E. Levin. 2009. Building peace with conflict diamonds? Merging security and development in Sierra Leone's diamond sector. *Development and Change* 40 (4): 693–715.

Le Potentiel. 2009. Congo-Kinshasa: Contrats miniers; L'heure de vérité a sonné. October 27. http://fr.allafrica.com/stories/200910270491.html.

Marcel, V. 2006. *Oil titans: National oil companies in the Middle East.* Washington, D.C.: Brookings Institution Press.

Mazalto, M. 2005. La réforme des législations minières en Afrique et le rôle des institutions financières internationales: La République Démocratique du Congo. *Annuaire de l'Afrique des Grands Lacs* (2004–5):7–31.

Minister of Mines, Democratic Republic of the Congo. 2007. Ministerial archive. CAB. MIN/Mines/01/296/2007. April 20.

NIZA (Netherlands Institute for Southern Africa). 2006. *The state vs. the people: Governance, mining and the transitional regime in the Democratic Republic of Congo.* Amsterdam.

Otto, J. 2006. *Mining royalties: A global study of their impact on investors, government, and civil society.* Washington, D.C.: World Bank.

Smith, J., M. Pieth, and G. Jorge. 2007. *The recovery of stolen assets: A fundamental principle of the UN Convention against Corruption.* U4 Brief No. 2. February. Bergen: U4 Anti-Corruption Resource Centre.

Soares de Oliveira, R. 2008. Business success, Angola-style: Postcolonial politics and the rise and rise of Sonangol. *Journal of Modern African Studies* 45 (4): 595–619.

Stier, K. 2009. Stretching a contract. *Time.* August 3.

TRC (Republic of Liberia Truth and Reconciliation Commission). 2009. Final report volume three: Appendices, title III: Economic crimes and the conflict, exploitation and abuse. www.trcofliberia.org/reports/final/volume-three-3_layout-1.pdf.

UNSC (United Nations Security Council). 2009. Report of panel of experts on Liberia. S/2009/290. June 5. New York: United Nations.

Winer, J. M., and T. J. Roule. 2003. Follow the money: The finance of illicit resource extraction. In *Natural Resources and Armed Conflicts: Actions and Options,* ed. I. Bannon and P. Collier. Washington, D.C.: World Bank.

World Bank and UNODC (United Nations Office of Drugs and Crime). 2009. StAR Progress Report. July. Washington D.C.: World Bank. http://siteresources.worldbank.org/EXTSARI/Resources/ProgressReport2009.pdf?resourceurlname=ProgressReport2f009.pdf.

Reopening and developing mines in post-conflict settings: The challenge of company-community relations

Volker Boege and Daniel M. Franks

Every mine that is reopened or developed in a fragile post-conflict setting becomes a part of that setting; as such, it can either intensify that fragility, and perhaps even trigger a recurrence of conflict, or help stabilize the situation and thereby contribute to peacebuilding.[1] Drawing from case studies in Papua New Guinea and Guatemala, this chapter explores the conditions that are essential for avoiding renewed conflict and for supporting peacebuilding and development, with particular emphasis on the role of community relations practice. In addition to presenting the case studies, the chapter describes problems typically associated with mining in a post-conflict environment; discusses fragility and hybridity, two aspects of the sociopolitical context that have significant influence on mining ventures; explores the interaction between companies, communities, and the state in post-conflict environments; considers the goals and limitations of community relations practice; and discusses lessons learned.

Any attempt to reopen or develop mines in a post-conflict environment not only confronts financial, logistical, and technical difficulties, but—even more important—tremendous social and political challenges. A range of specific, highly sensitive issues that originate from the violent conflict, from its aftereffects, and from post-conflict peacebuilding must be addressed. Specifically, the development or reopening of a mine in a post-conflict situation must be *conflict sensitive* (that is, must minimize the potential of the project to provoke or intensify conflict) and *conflict relevant* (that is, must directly contribute to peacebuilding and to

---

Volker Boege is a research fellow at the Australian Centre for Peace and Conflict Studies, University of Queensland, Australia. Daniel M. Franks is a senior research fellow at the Centre for Social Responsibility in Mining, Sustainable Minerals Institute, University of Queensland, Australia.

[1] Although there is considerable scholarly debate about the definition of *fragile states*, there is general agreement that they lack the capacity or the will (or both) to do the following: uphold law and order and control violence throughout the state's territory; ensure adequate provision of basic goods and services; and adequately generate, control, and allocate resources.

the prevention of new conflict) (Bagwitz et al. 2008).[2] In practical terms, this means

- Reconstructing infrastructure destroyed by prior violent conflict.
- Establishing mutually beneficial relations between all stakeholders.
- Securing positive and sustainable outcomes that reflect the interests of companies, communities, and host governments.

Thus, beyond solving the practical problems associated with reopening old or developing new mines, companies must obtain or reestablish a *social license* to operate. Community relations practice, which focuses on shaping companies' actions so that they are responsive to the people and places that may be affected by a project, is central to obtaining a social license.

MINING IN A POST-CONFLICT ENVIRONMENT

Many states in the Global South are facing the challenges of post-conflict peacebuilding in the wake of protracted internal violent conflicts.[3] Such conflicts have devastating consequences, and it is civilians who suffer most. Civilian casualties are much higher than combatant casualties, and civilians may be subject to human-rights violations as well as to loss of housing, property, basic services, and social and physical infrastructure. Forced from their homes, many civilians may have been internally displaced or forced to flee into neighboring countries. After the cessation of hostilities, survivors are typically impoverished, traumatized, and in bad health.

Companies that wish to develop or reopen mining projects in a post-conflict setting face a host of difficulties. First, conditions often remain insecure, putting staff and assets at risk. Second, infrastructure (roads, transport, communication,

---

[2] Conflict sensitivity and peacebuilding are not the same thing: conflict sensitivity works *in the context of conflict* "to minimize negative and maximize positive impacts of programming," whereas peacebuilding works *on conflict,* "seeking to reduce key drivers of violent conflict and to contribute to Peace Writ Large (the broader societal-level peace)" (Chigas and Woodrow 2009, 10). This chapter focuses primarily on conflict-sensitive activities that can contribute to peacebuilding without being targeted directly toward peacebuilding. The chapter also addresses conflict prevention, which is similarly distinct from peacebuilding. In the context of this chapter, the goal of conflict prevention is to avoid relapse into violent conflict stemming from the reopening or development of new mining projects.

[3] *Global South* and *Global North* are geopolitical terms that refer to the economic and development disparities between the industrialized states of Europe, North America, and parts of Asia (the Global North), and the postcolonial states of Africa, South and Central America, and Asia (the Global South). The terms are an alternative to the distinctions made by Alfred Sauvy between the First (capitalist), Second (aligned with the Soviet Union) and Third (nonaligned) worlds, and to the description of states as either "developed" or "developing."

etc.) is usually in disrepair, and the technical and engineering problems involved in reconstruction are often immense. Third, government institutions are likely to be lacking in capacity, competence, and reliability. Finally, and most important, relations with communities in the project area have to be established. Community residents are still in the process of rebuilding their lives, not only in material but in social and psychological terms, and the prospect of having to deal with the opening or reopening of a resource project can be a significant additional strain. Because communities are at once particularly vulnerable and particularly suspicious of outsiders, companies must find ways to build or rebuild trust.

Where the previous conflict was not related to mining, it will still be difficult to develop new projects simply because of security issues, damaged infrastructure, limited state capacity, and traumatic community history. Nevertheless, not having contributed to violent conflict may create something of an advantage. The chapter therefore differentiates between two scenarios:

- Post-conflict development of new mines or reopening of old mines where mining was a factor in prior violent conflict.[4]
- Post-conflict development of new mines where mining was not a cause of the violent conflict, or where there was no pre-conflict mining.

FRAGILITY AND HYBRIDITY

To understand the problems of company-community relations in a post-conflict environment, it is first necessary to understand the larger context. This section outlines the general sociopolitical conditions likely to be encountered by companies that are developing or reopening mining projects in post-conflict regions of the Global South.

Fragility and hybridity are significant features of the post-conflict environment.[5] In fragile states, the governmental institutions are usually relatively weak, with inadequate capacity to uphold law and order; provide basic goods and services; and generate, allocate, and control resources. In addition, avenues for political representation and citizen participation are generally insufficient. As a consequence of these deficiencies, state institutions typically suffer from a lack of legitimacy in the eyes of the people.[6] Fragility weighs heavily on company-community relations in the post-conflict environment—and in some cases, the state's lack of capacity,

---

[4] This type can be further divided into newcomers and companies that were already in operation before the conflict.
[5] In addition to Papua New Guinea and Guatemala, the subjects of the case studies, other states characterized by post-conflict fragility and hybridity include Cambodia, Timor-Leste, Indonesia, Liberia, Sierra Leone, and the Solomon Islands.
[6] There is a vast literature on fragile post-conflict states. For more recent overviews, see Andersen, Moeller, and Stepputat (2007); Anten (2009); Brinkerhoff (2007); Call (2008); Ghani and Lockhart (2008); OECD/DAC (2008); and Woodward (2006).

effectiveness, and legitimacy may push company-community relations to center stage.

A hybrid political order combines traditional societal structures;[7] elements of the Western model of the state; and contemporary institutions, movements, and groups that have their origins in the effects of, and reactions to, globalization (and, in the case of post-conflict societies, the preceding conflict) (Boege et al. 2008a, 2008b; Boege, Brown, and Clements 2009). In fragile post-conflict situations, the state is only one actor among others, and state order is only one of a number of political orders claiming to provide security, social services, and frameworks for the nonviolent conduct of conflict. Although state institutions may claim authority within the boundaries of a given territory, in large parts of that territory, only outposts of the state can be found; the sociopolitical environment is, to a large extent, stateless. Statelessness, however, does not imply the sort of disorder envisioned by Hobbes, with *bellum omnium contra omnes* (war of all against all). Instead, customary and communal institutions are often central to everyday life.[8]

Particularly in rural or remote areas, which often happen to be the sites of mining projects, customary actors and institutions have maintained their significance, showing remarkable resilience despite colonialism and postcolonial state building. They coexist alongside of, and intertwine with, state institutions; and they often shape local resource use (Schlichte and Wilke 2000; Schlichte 2005; Boege et al. 2006; Buur and Kyed 2007). Governance in post-conflict contexts is further complicated by the aforementioned institutions, movements and formations that have their origins in the effects of and reactions to the conflict, and in globalization more generally. Warlords and their militias in outlying regions, gangs in townships and squatter settlements, vigilante organizations, ethnically based protection rackets, millenarian religious movements, transnational networks of extended family relations, organized crime, and new forms of tribalism may all thrive in the fragile post-conflict context. Occasionally, these new formations succeed in seizing power in certain regions of a given state's territory, be it a remote mountain location or a squatter settlement in the capital city (Schetter 2007; von Trotha 2000, 2005).

In sum, post-conflict environments are generally places in which diverse and competing sets of rules, claims to power, types of behavior, and understandings of order coexist, overlap, and intertwine. Mining companies, however, are generally unaware of the hybridity that shapes post-conflict environments—or, to the extent that they are aware of hybridity, they regard it as an impediment to development and to the good governance of resources.

---

[7] In this context, "traditional" structures have precolonial roots but may have been shaped, through historical change, to achieve their current, postcolonial form.

[8] The phrase *customary and communal institutions* refers, for example, to traditional social structures (e.g., extended families, clans, and villages) and to traditional authorities (e.g., elders, healers, and religious leaders) that exist within the postcolonial context.

COMPANIES, COMMUNITIES, AND THE STATE IN HYBRID POLITICAL ORDERS

Following independence, newly created postcolonial states followed the example of the former colonial establishment and institutionalized modern, Western European legal systems—including, for example, mining laws. The new political elite regarded customary law as anachronistic; in fact, many states in the Global South fail to acknowledge customary law, despite the legal pluralism that, in practice, regulates access to land, water, and other natural resources (Kyed and Buur 2006; Buur and Kyed 2007).

Whereas statutory law governs the deals between companies and governments, customary law still plays a crucial role at the community level. Local populations often perceive the state as an alien external force that is not only physically distant (in the capital city) but removed from their everyday reality. In the eyes of community members, state authorities do not necessarily have the legitimacy to negotiate with external parties on behalf of local residents. In explaining this perspective, people refer to the customary laws of their communities (Buur and Kyed 2007). Hence, a license to operate—granted to a company by state authorities and based on modern statutory law—is not necessarily meaningful in the eyes of local residents who adhere to customary law.

None of this is to suggest, however, that state institutions are irrelevant. In principle, the host state sets the conditions for the resource extraction—and, for better or for worse, local, provincial, and central government agencies have significant influence on resource extraction projects. The extent to which the state maintains a presence in the area, the rules it sets, and its ability to enforce those rules shape company-community relations and affect the ways in which companies pursue their projects.[9]

Thus, company-community relations occur in the context of state structures and institutions, however fragile these may be. At the same time, the companies themselves figure prominently in the post-conflict setting. Often, they are better equipped, better organized, and more capable than state authorities. In post-conflict areas, state agencies may barely function—and may therefore deliver few, if any, services in areas such as education, health, and security—whereas the company may be all too present. Under such conditions, residents may not only expect the company to step in for the state, but may transfer their grievances against the state to the company (Switzer 2001; Zandvliet 2004; Boege et al. 2006).

Finally, company-community relations in the post-conflict environment are subject to the influence of civil society. Although many civil society organizations (such as nongovernmental organizations [NGOs], trade unions, chambers of commerce, women's associations, and youth associations) are relatively weak under conditions of hybridity, they must nevertheless be reckoned with. Organizations

---

[9] It also matters whether communities perceive state institutions as siding with outside companies or as defending local interests.

that are rooted in the local context—religious institutions, for example—often have a more visible presence than state institutions, as do community-based organizations that are allied to international NGOs. In the era of the Internet, there are no "faraway places": big international NGOs can influence events and public opinion, both in host countries and in the companies' home countries, and local organizations and activists in remote areas can link up with international NGOs and with the outside world in general. Both local and international civil society groups can therefore be expected to play a role in company-community relations, particularly during the first stages of peacebuilding, when two things are likely to occur: (1) a great deal of international attention may be focused on humanitarian assistance, reconstruction, and reconciliation, and (2) a broad spectrum of external actors—including donor agencies, United Nations agencies, and international NGOs—may make their presence felt.

COMMUNITY RELATIONS PRACTICE: GOALS AND LIMITATIONS

Because of controversy about the relationship between extractive industries and sustainable development, the mining industry has assigned increasing prominence—and resources—to the practice of community relations. Companies have begun to employ community relations specialists (including sociologists, communications experts, and anthropologists) and have developed procedures and initiatives to respond to environmental and community concerns. Voluntary standards and policies—and to a lesser extent, the procedures, practices, and internal management systems of mining companies—have come to reflect a community relations perspective.

The goal of community relations is to shape companies' actions to be socially, culturally, and environmentally responsive to the people and places that may be affected by development.[10] Community relations practitioners attempt to resolve real and perceived community concerns, impacts, and risks; their work emphasizes increased communication, improved understanding, and stronger relationships with stakeholders. By resolving disputes between local populations and mining companies, the practice of community relations reduces the risk of actions such as blockades, protests, campaigns, legal suits, and sabotage, which might otherwise be the only forms of influence stakeholders can exert, and can destabilize the peace process.

In this chapter, community relations is conceived as having three dimensions (Kemp 2009):

- Assisting mining companies to understand the community's perspective.
- Fostering dialogue and cooperation between the community and the company.
- Driving organizational change in order to improve practice within mining companies.

---

[10] This is in contrast to public relations, where the primary motive is for the company to communicate its perspective to the public—and, ultimately, persuade the public to adopt the company's perspective.

In practical terms, company-community relations can be improved through the following means (Kemp 2009; Franks et al. 2009):

- Formal and informal opportunities for consultation, engagement, and participation (e.g., community panels and boards, and community monitoring programs).
- Initiatives that foster an understanding of the community (e.g., stakeholder analysis and impact assessment).
- The establishment of procedures for responding to complaints and resolving disputes.[11]
- Community- and enterprise-development initiatives designed to improve the balance between the costs and benefits of mining (e.g., community development funds).
- Procedures for seeking consent from affected communities and customary landowners who hold sovereignty over land.

There are, of course, limits to community relations practice. On the company side, community relations are constrained by the imperatives of commerce and production, and by the governance structures under which companies operate. Mining companies' economic orientation is global; their interest in a given locality is based merely on the existence of an ore deposit that can be extracted and marketed for profit. Thus, within the constraints of the political and geographical context, the management strategies of each mining operation are shaped primarily by the demands of the market and the internal economics of the company as a whole. Because the goal of a mining operation is to extract a single, high-value resource (ore), the company does not depend on the broader environmental and social conditions of a locality, beyond what is needed for the immediate support of the operation (e.g., labor, water, energy). Thus, when companies undertake corporate social responsibility initiatives—by, for example, adhering to voluntary standards—their actions have value only to the extent that they support the primary objective: to provide shareholders with a return on their investment through the mining, extraction, and processing of resources (Franks 2007).

On the community side, company-community relations depend on the community's acceptance of the mining activity, either in its current or in some less intrusive form. But where developers are extracting resources without consent—regardless of whether the land is held by indigenous peoples who hold sovereign rights, or even by communities that do not hold recognized sovereign rights—the very presence of the operation may be in dispute. In other words, what the community may want is the *absence* of any company-community relationship.

---

[11] The Special Representative of the UN Secretary-General on the issue of human rights and transnational corporations and other business enterprises has stressed the importance of mechanisms to address complaints and grievances early, before they escalate (Ruggie 2008). The mining industry is beginning to implement such mechanisms more widely (Kemp and Gotzmann 2008).

Under such conditions, it is not always possible to negotiate a mutually beneficial arrangement. Even when mining reflects best practice, resource extraction may simply be incompatible with community life. The attitudes of local communities toward development and the environment often differ substantially from those of mining companies that enter the local context for the sole purpose of resource extraction. This is particularly the case where communities depend on subsistence agriculture, and local, market-related economic activities play only a minor role. Because resource extraction has the potential to undermine functioning ecosystems, it may be perceived as incompatible with the sustainability of both livelihoods and culture.

The wide-ranging effects of mining, which commonly extend well beyond the mining lease, can pose exceptional challenges for community relations efforts. Mining can trigger inflation; induce migration (because of the availability of employment opportunities); place pressure on (but also support) social services; affect the cost and availability of housing; and lead to ecological and cultural change. Tailings discharged into a river, for example, may transform ecosystems hundreds of kilometers downstream; the demands of mining employment may cause shifts in traditional family roles; the introduction of a cash economy may break down customary patterns of exchange; and, where cultural and religious practices are tied to specific features of the landscape, the transformation of that landscape may have cultural repercussions.

Company-community relations are also shaped by the history of an operation —in particular, by the exploration and feasibility phases of projects. Whereas multinational mining companies may have competent community relations teams (including anthropologists and other culturally sensitive experts), the junior companies that conduct much of the exploration work rarely do. Junior companies are intently focused on generating a return on investment by rapidly finding and demonstrating the feasibility of ore bodies. As a consequence, they often give short shrift to community relations and local decision making, and are thus more likely to spark conflicts. When larger companies punchase prospective mines from the juniors, they also inherit any tensions and conflicts that were created during exploration (Bebbington et al. 2008).

In post-conflict situations, fragility and hybridity intensify the constraints on community relations practice. Communities in post-conflict settings are typically fragmented, complex, and host people that have been internally displaced. They may harbor distrust of institutions and particular social groups and lack the time or capacity to engage with the mining project. They may also include groups, such as militias, that were associated with the conflict. Under these conditions, the issue of consent poses particular problems: Who makes up the "relevant" community? Who is entitled to speak for it? What constitutes community consent (Laplante and Spears 2008)? In hybrid political orders, companies are well-advised to seek the participation of nonstate (customary) actors, but the practicalities of obtaining consent in such situations are far from straightforward.

In sum, the techniques that are designed to foster mutual understanding, encourage participation, and avoid conflict may be severely hampered in fragile post-conflict settings or where there is a history of conflict between the community and the mining company. Efforts to prevent conflict—through improved communication, understanding, and engagement—can be undermined by distrust, unresolved grievances, and the residual effects of past trauma. Acknowledging the limits of community relations practice and the unique challenges of post-conflict settings will help companies make more relevant, responsive, and focused decisions.

CASE STUDY: BOUGAINVILLE, PAPUA NEW GUINEA

The Panguna gold and copper mine, on the island of Bougainville, in Papua New Guinea (PNG), was a decisive contributing factor in a protracted violent conflict that began in 1988 and ended in 1998. This case study considers the history of the previous project, the post-conflict situation, the current efforts to recommence mining, and the associated difficulties.

Mining and violent conflict on Bougainville

In the 1970s and 1980s, the Panguna mine was one of the largest open-pit mines in the world. It was operated by Bougainville Copper Limited (BCL), a subsidiary of Conzinc Rio Tinto of Australia, one of the world's leading mining companies.[12] The Panguna project brought enormous profits to the British-Australian company, as well as considerable revenues to the central government of PNG, in the faraway capital city of Port Moresby, on mainland New Guinea. In fact, the mine was the largest single source of income for the government and the backbone of PNG's economy. As such, it enjoyed unwavering support from the Australian government, which viewed Panguna as essential for the economic stability of the young nation-state. (PNG gained its independence from Australia in 1975.)

Area residents, however, took a different view. Land had been taken from local communities on a scale that destroyed the basis of their subsistence economy, and mining wastes were discharged directly into the local river, harming downstream ecosystems. To communities near the mine site, land was important not only economically but also as the core of their social, cultural, and spiritual life.[13] Both central government authorities and the mining company management, however, largely ignored the social and cultural significance of the land.[14]

---

[12] Conzinc Rio Tinto has since become Rio Tinto.
[13] For an overview of the various aspects of social, economic, cultural, and political conditions in Bougainville before the conflict, see Regan and Griffin (2005).
[14] For a comprehensive account of the construction, operation, legal context, and impact of the Panguna mine, see Wesley-Smith (1988) and Denoon (2000). For BCL's perspective, see Quodling (1991). For a brief overview of the mine's operation and associated problems, see Vernon (2005). For the environmental degradation caused by the mine, see the early assessment by Brown (1974); also see Wesley-Smith (1988) and Connell (1991).

96 High-value natural resources and post-conflict peacebuilding

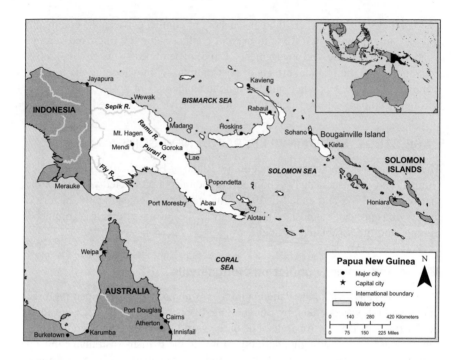

A substantial influx of workers from outside Bougainville, along with large amounts of cash, added even more pressure to local social structures. Local people blamed outsiders—workers, expatriate Australian company managers, and the agents of the central government—for failing to respect indigenous culture and the rights of community members as the original owners of the land.[15] Moreover, many residents felt that the costs and benefits of mining were distributed unevenly: the bulk of the mining revenues flowed to outsiders, while the residents were left with the negative environmental and social effects. Islanders demanded meaningful environmental protection measures, compensation for past environmental damage, and a larger share of the revenues.[16] The mining company and the PNG government, backed by the Australian government, rejected the demands, triggering the longest and bloodiest conflict in the South Pacific since the end of World War II. Out of a total population of 200,000 in Bougainville, nearly 20,000 were killed.

In late 1988, clan members from the mine area sabotaged the mine, bringing operations to a standstill, and established a guerrilla force, the Bougainville Revolutionary Army (BRA). Fighting between the BRA and the government's

---

[15] On the damaging social effects of the Panguna mine in particular and of mining in a Melanesian context in general, see Filer (1990, 1992); Wesley-Smith and Ogan (1992); and Denoon (2000).

[16] For the politico-economic context of the mining project, see Regan (2003).

Reopening and developing mines in post-conflict settings 97

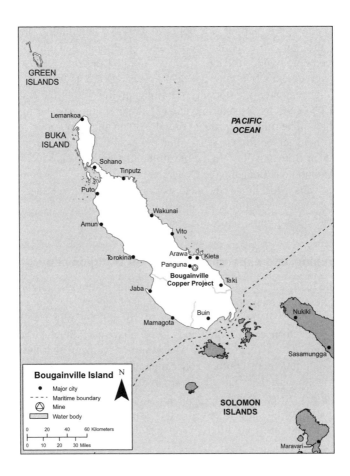

security forces began in the mine area but soon spread across the whole island. The BRA called for independence for Bougainville, taking up a secessionist stance that had last surfaced in the 1960s and 1970s, during early protests against the development of the Panguna mine.[17]

The BRA managed to overrun the Panguna mine at an early stage of the war, during 1989 and 1990, and the mine has remained closed ever since.[18] Currently, the mine site remains in the hands of the Meekamui Movement, a hard-core secessionist faction that has yet to join in the peace process that began in 1998.

---

[17] On the triggers, early stages, and escalation of the conflict, see Connell (1991) and Howard (1991); for a history of the conflict, see Parliament of Australia (1999).
[18] Production was suspended in May 1989, and the last remaining staff were evacuated from Bougainville in March 1990.

By the late 1990s, neither side believed there was anything to be gained by continuing the war. Post-conflict peacebuilding ensued, and the Bougainville Peace Agreement, signed in August 2001,[19] marked the final settlement of the war.[20] The agreement's two core political provisions are as follows: (1) for the time until the referendum, autonomy for Bougainville within the framework of the state of PNG and its constitution; and (2) a referendum to determine whether Bougainville will be fully independent or will remain an autonomous entity within PNG, to be held ten to fifteen years after the establishment of an autonomous government for Bougainville.[21] In the meantime, Bougainville has its own government, the Autonomous Bougainville Government (ABG) which has comprehensive governing powers. Most important, a number of highly sensitive issues—including land, natural resources, mining, the environment, oil and gas, trade, commerce, and industry—are to come under the sole control of the ABG.

Reestablishing and expanding mining on Bougainville

Bougainville today clearly exhibits the characteristic features of a hybrid political order: specifically, elements of the Western model of statehood (e.g., a constitution, a president and a parliament, free and fair elections), combined with elements of customary governance (e.g., chiefs and elders, village assemblies, customary law) and modern nonstate actors (e.g., the Meekamui Movement) that have complex relations—including both conflict and cooperation—with state and customary institutions. Although there have been some efforts at deliberate integration, to a certain degree these domains—with all their complementarities, synergies, and incompatibilities—simply coexist. Thus, governance involves a complicated interplay of institutions from different spheres: the state, traditional communities, and nonstate actors.

The ABG is aware that, given the fragility and hybridity of the post-conflict environment, mining has the potential to ignite conflict. Joseph Kabui, the late president of the ABG, nevertheless strongly advocated the reestablishment and expansion of mining.[22] At the time of writing, preliminary talks were under way

---

[19] For an overview of the peace process, see Parliament of Australia (1999), Carl and Garasu (2002), BCC (2004), and Wolfers (2006).

[20] The text of the peace agreement can be found in Carl and Garasu (2002). For an analysis of the peace agreements, see Regan (2002a, 2002b).

[21] The Autonomous Bougainville Government was established in 2005.

[22] In particular, a group within the ABG, including the late president Joseph Kabui, established quite a close relationship with a junior Canadian mining company, Invincible Resources Corporation. Invincible established a presence in Bougainville that included a communication center in the town of Arawa and the financing of a private security company staffed by ex-BRA combatants. It also acquired, for around US$7 million, 70 percent ownership of the Bougainville Resource Development Corporation—which the ABG, under Kabui, had established to foster investment in Bougainville. At the time of writing, Invincible had reduced its presence in Bougainville considerably.

between various stakeholders (government, mining companies, and landowning communities) about the possibility of reopening the Panguna mine and developing new mining projects on the island.[23] The ABG has declared its interest in mining—and mining is viewed, by some members of the ABG, as the most promising option for increasing government revenues and spurring economic growth and development.

So that it will have more room to maneuver in negotiations, the ABG has urged the PNG government to put into effect the transfer of control over mining, gas, and oil provided for in the peace agreement. Furthermore, the ABG wants to lift the current moratorium on new mining explorations conducted outside BCL's lease area (the PNG government had imposed the moratorium at the beginning of the violent conflict). With the World Bank's assistance, the ABG has also established a mining division.[24]

Although BCL is still the official owner of the Panguna mine,[25] BCL officials have not had access to the mine site since it was occupied by the BRA in the late 1980s. BCL has declared its interest in reopening the mine and commissioned a prefeasibility study on the costs and technical requirements of redeveloping Panguna. The study, which was completed in November 2008, found that there is potential for a viable mining operation at Panguna, although the capital costs of redevelopment are likely to be high.[26]

In the meantime, BCL and Rio Tinto keep a low profile in Bougainville. Company representatives are well aware of the profound distrust (and even hatred) still harbored in certain quarters of the populace. They acknowledge that reopening Panguna will mean reestablishing trust and good relations with the communities on Bougainville—an immense effort that will take considerable time.[27] Some Bougainville political leaders want BCL to come back, to "clean up the mess" it left behind and to take over responsibility for mining again ("better to work

---

[23] Much of the information that follows draws on interviews conducted by Volker Boege in 2007 with former combatants, communal and traditional authorities, and representatives from government, civil society, and business. The interviews were part of a case study for a project entitled Towards Effective and Legitimate Governance: States Emerging from Hybrid Political Orders (2007–2008). The project was funded by AusAID, the Australian government's overseas aid program.
[24] The Bank has allocated US$2 million for training and capacity building.
[25] Rio Tinto owns 53.58 percent of BCL; the government of PNG owns 19.06 percent; and public shareholders hold the remaining 27.36 percent.
[26] Redeveloping Panguna will cost about US$3.8 billion. Copper reserves are estimated at almost 3 million tons, and gold production in the range of 400,000 ounces per year. Panguna is potentially one of the world's largest copper and gold mines, with a processing rate of 50 million tons of ore per year and a mine life of at least seventeen years. BCL holds seven exploration licenses in areas adjacent to the Panguna area, and it is widely believed that they also contain large deposits of copper and gold.
[27] The BCL chairman's annual general meeting address noted that it would be "at least four years, and possibly six, before mining could be re-started on Bougainville" (BCL 2009). This seems to be an overly optimistic prognosis.

with the devil we know than getting in somebody new"). Other political figures are more open to alternatives to BCL.

There is general agreement among representatives of the central government, the ABG, the company, and landowning communities that company-community relations are central, and that in areas that will be both directly and indirectly affected by the mines, comprehensive discussions with local landowning communities will be necessary before planning to resume mining can begin. There are divergent views among stakeholders, however, on whether residents are willing to allow mining to resume. While some members of the ABG and political leaders from the mine area say that local communities are interested in reopening the Panguna mine, others have the impression that the communities are still very much opposed to mining; still others say that it is hard to know.

Some NGOs and community-based organizations are concerned that the ABG and the PNG governments will engage in a hasty and superficial consultation process, and that this will trigger renewed conflict. In keeping with the fragility and hybridity of the post-conflict setting, state institutions are relatively weak both at the central level and on Bougainville, while nonstate actors (e.g., those from the local customary sphere and from new social formations, such as the Meekamui Movement) are relatively strong. Under these conditions, inadequate consultation could be particularly risky.

As noted earlier, the mine site and adjacent areas are still controlled by the Meekamui Movement (specifically, by its military arm, the Meekamui Defence Force). In August 2007, meetings between the ABG and the Meekamui Movement yielded the Panguna Communiqué, which has provided the basis for a rapprochement between the two entities. Without either Meekamui consent or the dissolution of the Meekamui Movement, it will be impossible to reopen Panguna. Within the ranks of the Meekamui Movement, views on reopening Panguna and developing new mining projects seem to differ: some movement members are more open to the idea and others are strongly against it. This division mirrors the views of the communities near Panguna and other potential mine sites.

The strongest resistance, however, comes not from the area immediately surrounding Panguna but from more distant communities that suffered the greatest environmental damage from the mine—particularly those that are downstream, along the Jaba River. In these communities, it is the chiefs and elders who maintain peace and order: customary law comes first, and the law of the state second (if it is accepted at all). This legal pluralism has implications for company-community relations, which must be framed not only in terms of state law, but also customary law.

Processes of reconciliation within and between communities in the Panguna mine area and adjacent areas began in earnest only in 2009. Some community leaders and politicians from these areas have put a lot of effort into initiating these processes; other community leaders, however, remain skeptical and have not yet joined. Although reconciliation will take time, it is an essential foundation for meaningful company-community dialogue about reopening the mine.

In December 2008, James Tanis—a former high-ranking BRA commander who had played a crucial role in the peace negotiations—was elected to succeed Joseph Kabui as president of Bougainville. Tanis, who comes from a village downstream of the Panguna mine, has claimed that he will ensure that all the affected communities will have the opportunity to participate in decision making about mining, both with regard to Panguna and any new mining projects. During the first months of his presidency, he held exploratory talks with a variety of stakeholders—including Panguna landowners, representatives of the Meekamui Movement, the PNG government, and BCL. And in October 2009, at Tanis's invitation, BCL company secretary Paul D. Coleman came to Buka, Bougainville's capital, and held talks with the ABG, with former combatants, and with landowners from the Panguna area (although he was unable to go to the mine site itself).[28] President James Tanis committed the ABG to comprehensive and unhurried dialogue on reopening Panguna, and on mining in general. Future discussions will have to include the PNG government and BCL, on the one hand, and local landowning communities (including members of the Meekamui Movement) on the other.

Bougainville: Conclusions and prospects

Given the historical burden of mining in Bougainville, company-community relations will have to take a fresh approach, both to avoid the mistakes of the past and to obtain a new social license to operate. Company-community relations will be more difficult to manage today than they were in the past. A host of different stakeholders must find common ground, despite different interests, needs, values, worldviews, and aspirations.

It remains to be seen how much the various stakeholders have learned so far, and how deep and sustainable the lessons were. The ABG still seems to be focused on the potential economic benefits of mining, but it also acknowledges the importance of a social license to operate; whether the central PNG government has an equally balanced view is unclear. Given the fragility of the sociopolitical context and the hybridity of the political order, it would be dangerous to give undue priority to economic considerations and to set aside social considerations as less important.

So far, Bougainville has been one of the rare success stories of contemporary post-conflict peacebuilding in a fragile state (Boege 2008). Whether the story will culminate in a peaceful future very much depends on how mining is dealt with, particularly with regard to company-community relations. Bougainville also has the potential to become another kind of success story: one in which conflict-sensitive and conflict-relevant redevelopment of mining actually strengthens

---

[28] Tanis extended the invitation in January 2009, but the visit did not occur until October.

102 High-value natural resources and post-conflict peacebuilding

peacebuilding. Any future resource developments in Bougainville, however, must engage all stakeholders in a comprehensive dialogue that addresses the following issues:

- The past: What went wrong with mining on Bougainville, and why? A common understanding of history is required as the basis for reconciliation, compensation, and rehabilitation, and for the reestablishment of trust.
- The present: What are the current grievances and concerns? Once an environment of mutual trust has been established, companies, communities, and other stakeholders can explore their expectations.
- The future: How should the process move forward? Collaborative planning, decision making, and implementation are key to building consent (both within and among communities, and between communities and companies), and to establishing procedures for addressing grievances and solving disputes in the future.

Such a process can decisively strengthen and stabilize peacebuilding. However, it will have to be sequential: without reconciliation, it is impossible to plan for the future. State institutions will provide the framework for engagement, and state actors will present their views and interests, but company-community relations will be at the core. Whether reopening the Panguna mine, developing new mines, or both will contribute to peacebuilding or will destabilize what has been achieved so far hinges on the quality of these company-community relations.

CASE STUDY: SAN MARCOS, GUATEMALA

San Marcos, Guatemala, is an example of the post-conflict development of a new mine in an area where mining was not a cause of violent conflict.[29] The case study describes the history of the conflict and the post-conflict situation, analyzes company-community relations at the mine site, and describes the community relations initiatives currently in place.[30]

History of the conflict in Guatemala

The Marlin gold and silver mine is located in the highlands of western Guatemala, in the municipalities of San Miguel Ixtahuacán and Sipacapa, Department of San Marcos. The mine is owned and operated by *Montana Exploradora de Guatemala*,

---

[29] As with other Cold War–era conflicts, access to natural resources was contested at the macro scale in Guatemala, but extractive resource industries did not directly contribute to the civil conflict.
[30] This case study was based on publicly available material. Where possible, information was confirmed through multiple sources.

Reopening and developing mines in post-conflict settings 103

S.A., a subsidiary of Goldcorp, a Canadian mining company.[31] The deposit was discovered in 1998, construction started in early 2004, and operations began in 2005. The US$254 million mining development was viewed by the international development community as an opportunity for post-conflict economic development and was supported by a US$45 million loan from the International Finance Corporation (IFC), a member of the World Bank Group.

The mine is the first major mining investment in Guatemala since the cessation of a protracted civil conflict (1960–1996) in which more than 200,000 people were killed (Commission for Historical Clarification 1999). The roots of the conflict stemmed from the 1954 overthrow (organized by the U.S. Central Intelligence Agency) of the populist and democratic government of Jacobo Árbenz Guzmán by Colonel Carlos Castillo Armas. After the murder of Castillo Armas,

---

[31] Goldcorp acquired the mine from its acquisition of Glamis Gold in November 2006.

in 1957, a series of short-lived regimes followed, one of which was the autocratic government of General Miguel Ydígoras. In November 1960, discontented army officers attempted to oust Ydígoras in an unsuccessful coup, precipitating a revolutionary movement and a counterinsurgency state.

In the 1960s, state violence involved selective targeting of militants; in the 1970s, the attacks expanded to include prominent members of the political opposition and, ultimately, indigenous Mayan villagers, who were perceived to be supporting the rebels; widespread massacres, which included high percentages of women and small children, peaked in the early 1980s (Ball, Kobrak, and Spirer 1999). Noncombatants, including Mayan villagers, made up 83 percent of the victims of the civil war, and 93 percent of the atrocities were committed by the armed forces (Commission for Historical Clarification 1999). In addition to civilian deaths, Guatemala faced the trauma of disappearances, the destruction of more than 400 villages, and the internal displacement of over a million people; 100,000 more fled to neighboring countries (Colletta and Cullen 2000). Extrajudicial killings by the military continued until 1996, when the UN brokered a peace accord between the government and the guerrillas. By the time the conflict ended, the state and its institutions had been discredited. Writing in 2000, Nat J. Colletta and Michelle L. Cullen noted that "severe social, economic, and political exclusion was a catalyst for the protracted, brutal conflict, and these exclusionary issues remain only partially resolved after the peace accord" (Colletta and Cullen 2000, 100).

The region in the vicinity of the mine is populated by Mam-Mayan and Sipakapense-Mayan indigenous peoples. Between 1960 and 1996, tens of thousands of people were murdered in Guatemala's western highlands, the location of the mine. And the Commission for Historical Clarification (1999) recorded fifteen distinct massacres in the Department of San Marcos—a high concentration relative to other regions.

The contemporary company-community relationship

The post-conflict environment in San Marcos is shaped by the lingering trauma of the conflict and by the Guatemalan government's lack of institutional capacity. It is also influenced by complex allegiances and interactions between Maya communities, Ladino (mixed-race) communities, municipal governments, the Catholic Church, and various arms of the Guatemalan state. Glamis Gold, the former owner of the mine, has described the operating environment as a "culture of distrust" and a "very complex cultural, historical, and political backdrop" (Schenck 2006, 2). Community members who are opposed to the mine argue, similarly, that the mine must be understood within the social and political context of Guatemala—which, thirteen years after the end of the civil war, "is in danger of becoming a failed state, plagued by drug-fueled violence, government corruption, and the absence of the rule of law" (Frente de Defensa San Miguelense and Center for International Environmental Law 2009, 2). Some NGOs have argued that the company's presence has ultimately done more harm than good; Rights

Action, for example, has observed that "rather than strengthening the collective social fabric of impoverished indigenous communities, weakened by the enduring legacy of the internal armed conflict, the company's engagement with local actors further weakened the social fabric" (Rights Action 2008).

The operators of the Marlin mine have encountered a number of difficulties, some of which stem from the post-conflict environment. Conflicts have arisen over issues such as consent for resource development, respect for indigenous worldviews and decision-making structures, compensation for land purchases, water security, the regulation of mining, damage to housing allegedly caused by blasting, company and government responses to community protests, and the potential for, and the alleged occurrence of, environmental pollution.

Consent and consultation are common issues for mining operations outside the post-conflict context;[32] but in Guatemala, where indigenous people and their lands were the target of the pre-mining conflict, these issues are particularly acute. Opponents of the mine claim that in 2003, the Guatemalan Ministry of Energy and Mines violated the International Labour Organization (ILO) Convention 169 on Indigenous and Tribal Peoples (ratified in June 1996 as part of the peace accords, but not enacted through legislation) by failing to gain the consent of indigenous communities before granting a mining license. Although the spirit of the convention emphasizes the need to protect and recognize indigenous peoples agreement or the precise wording requires only consultation "with the objective of achieving consent."[33]

The failure to gain the acceptance of nearby communities triggered conflict as early as the exploration stage. In December 2004, in the town of Los Encuentros,

---

[32] Free, prior, and informed consent (FPIC) of indigenous communities affected by development projects is emerging as an international legal norm, as reflected in the recent UN Declaration on the Rights of Indigenous Peoples (UN 2008). The mining industry, however, has yet to systematically embrace the concept, beyond what is enforced by host states.

[33] Article 6 of the ILO Indigenous and Tribal Peoples Convention states:

1. In applying the provisions of this Convention, governments shall: (a) consult the peoples concerned, through appropriate procedures and in particular through their representative institutions, whenever consideration is being given to legislative or administrative measures which may affect them directly. . . . 2. The consultations carried out in application of this Convention shall be undertaken, in good faith and in a form appropriate to the circumstances, with the objective of achieving agreement or consent to the proposed measures.

Article 15 (2) states:

In cases in which the State retains the ownership of mineral or sub-surface resources or rights to other resources pertaining to lands, governments shall establish or maintain procedures through which they shall consult these peoples, with a view to ascertaining whether and to what degree their interests would be prejudiced, before undertaking or permitting any programmes for the exploration or exploitation of such resources pertaining to their lands. The peoples concerned shall wherever possible participate in the benefits of such activities, and shall receive fair compensation for any damages which they may sustain as a result of such activities (ILO 1989).

mining equipment en route to the Marlin site was blockaded for forty days (Fulmer, Godoy, and Neff 2008). The standoff ended in a clash with Guatemalan military and police forces, the death of one man, and the injury of twenty others (Eccarius-Kelly 2007).[34] In March 2005, residents of Sipacapa lodged a formal complaint with the Office of the Compliance Advisor/Ombudsman (CAO) of the IFC about the consultation process and the operation's potential environmental impact.[35] The CAO found that the residents were not at significant risk of environmental contamination from the project; however, the CAO also found the following:

- A number of technical breaches of procedure had occurred.
- "A more thorough consideration of the governance and country context and the balance of risks and benefits accruing as a result of this investment would have been helpful" (iii).
- Consultation had not met the community's expectations, which were that the mine should seek their consent.
- The environmental impact statement had failed to provide adequate information to the community (CAO 2005).[36]

In December 2009, the Frente de Defensa San Miguelense, a coalition of Mayan and Catholic community groups in San Miguel Ixtahuacán, filed a further complaint on the basis of the Guidelines for Multinational Enterprises of the Organisation for Economic Co-operation and Development (OECD). The complaint alleged human-rights violations—in particular, the failure to obtain free, prior, and informed consent from indigenous communities; structural damage to housing from mine blasting; water contamination and associated health issues; and the criminalization of community protest. At the time of writing, the outcome was still pending (Frente de Defensa San Miguelense and Center for International Environmental Law 2009).

---

[34] In a separate clash, a mining security guard was implicated in a shooting death.

[35] IFC investment in the Marlin mine closely followed the completion of the World Bank Extractive Industries Review (EIR), an effort to respond to civil society concerns about the links between natural resource development, human rights, and sustainability. The EIR recommended changes in the assessment process for World Bank involvement in projects. Under the recommendations, environmental and social criteria, in addition to economic factors, would be taken into account (World Bank 2004). This has led many to regard Marlin as a test case of the World Bank's new approach. The IFC involvement in the Marlin project, however, had already begun before World Bank management adopted responses to the EIR recommendations.

[36] Changes implemented at the Marlin operations since the complaint to the CAO include operational changes to water management systems, the establishment of a community monitoring committee (Asociación de Monitoreo Ambiental Comunitario), the adoption of the Voluntary Principles on Security and Human Rights (IFC 2005), and certification under the International Cyanide Management Code for the Transport, Manufacture and Use of Cyanide for the Production of Gold.

The legal basis for obtaining indigenous consent for resource development in Guatemala is also grounded in articles 58, 66, and 67 of the Guatemalan constitution, which recognize indigenous cultural identity, customs, and lands, and in the municipal codes that outline processes for consultation with local communities and indigenous peoples. In June 2005, exercising its powers under the municipal codes, Sipacapa organized a referendum on the Marlin operations, in which residents overwhelmingly rejected the presence of the mine (Eccarius-Kelly 2007). A series of referenda were subsequently held in San Miguel Ixtahuacán, with similar results. The legality of such procedures was challenged in the Guatemalan courts by Montana Exploradora, a subsidiary of Goldcorp; in May 2007, the Constitutional Court ruled that although the referenda were legal, their results were nonbinding because they encroached on provisions of the Guatemalan constitution, including articles on the exploitation of nonrenewable natural resources.

While Goldcorp and the Guatemalan government may or may not be in compliance with the Convention ILO 169, the IFC guidelines, the OECD Guidelines for Multinational Enterprises, and the Guatemalan constitution, the legalistic approach—especially one that fails to recognize the legal pluralism that shapes everyday life in San Marcos—has failed to address the core issues in the dispute. Regardless of law, a strong argument can be made that prior consultation with, and consent of, affected communities and indigenous peoples is a precondition for gaining a social license to operate, particularly in post-conflict settings. Without a social license, the risk of disruption to the operation is significantly increased. The case demonstrates the limits of relying on statutory structures under conditions of political hybridity.

Community-relations initiatives

Goldcorp has undertaken a number of initiatives designed to build a constructive company-community relationship (Montana Exploradora de Guatemala 2009):

- A seventeen-member community-relations unit that includes Mam- and Sipakapense-speaking staff (residents of San Miguel Ixtahuacán and Sipacapa).
- Seven public information offices.
- A formal process for addressing community grievances.
- A community development foundation (Fundación Sierra Madre).
- Support for community development projects (activities are identified and assigned priority by local development councils and local government representatives from each community).

At the urging of a group of "socially responsible" investors (the Public Service Alliance of Canada Staff Pension Fund [PSAC], the Ethical Funds Company, the First Swedish National Pension Fund, and the Fourth Swedish National Pension Fund), Goldcorp also agreed to a human rights impact assessment

(HRIA) as a means of further improving company-community relations; the HRIA was in progress at the time of writing.

HRIAs are designed to help resource developers consider the human rights implications of their actions in greater depth; they also help ensure compliance with international and national obligations (International Alert 2005; International Business Leaders Forum and International Finance Corporation 2007; Lenzen and d'Engelbronner 2009). These assessments generally proceed along the same lines as other impact assessments;[37] where HRIAs differ is that they explicitly evaluate the human rights impacts of laws, conflicts, and social and economic practices in relation to the Universal Declaration on Human Rights, the International Covenant on Civil and Political Rights, and the International Covenant on Economic, Social and Cultural Rights.

But standards of human rights, however universal they appear, cannot be substituted for an understanding of local norms; moreover, HRIAs may simply be incompatible with the hybridity of post-conflict settings. While it is too early to judge the success of the approach in the Marlin case, the HRIA has already encountered some obstacles. In December 2008, On Common Ground, a Canadian consulting firm, was brought under contract to undertake the HRIA.[38] While the consultants initially proposed involving community-based organizations in the development of the methodology, they subsequently concluded that "the conditions necessary to engage local communities and organizations in open dialogue do not exist in the current circumstances" (HRIA Steering Committee 2009). Although the consultants attributed the refusal to participate to polarization in the community—originating in disagreements over national debates on the revision of the mining law—it is at least as likely that the contemporary mine-community conflict and the and fragile hybrid post-conflict setting were contributing factors to community polarization, opposition to mining, and the decision not to participate.

Further, the HRIA process itself has been subject to criticism from NGOs, community organizations, and the Catholic Church for failing to consult community stakeholders about the decision to undertake an HRIA; and one of the original instigators of the assessment, the PSAC, withdrew from the process, citing concerns over prior community consent (Law 2009). The consultants are proceeding with the assessment but leaving open the prospect of community participation should circumstances change (HRIA Steering Committee 2009). Meanwhile, a parallel HRIA—funded by the Archbishop of Guatemala City and led by the University

---

[37] Standard impact assessments typically have the following elements: a description of the activity and the context, including the legal, regulatory, and administrative standards of host and home governments, financiers, and the corporation itself; predictions, which are developed through scenarios and forecasting methods; an analysis of risks and impacts, including the assignment of priorities; and the development, implementation, monitoring, and reporting of management strategies.

[38] Independent peer review of the HRIA and its methodology is to be undertaken by International Alert.

of Notre Dame's Center for Civil and Human Rights—was also under way at the time of writing (CCHR 2009). Local participation is essential to understanding the views of community members and fostering mutual understanding. Without it, the HRIA fulfills only one of the dimensions of community relations practice: to foster change in corporate practice.

Guatemala: Conclusions

The Marlin case demonstrates the challenges of community relations practice in post-conflict settings; it also demonstrates the intersection between historical and contemporary grievances, even when mining development is not implicated in the original conflict. Although Goldcorp did not have to repair a historically fractured relationship, post-conflict conditions not only generated company-community conflict, but also made it difficult for those conflicts to be resolved. Failure to consult with indigenous peoples, to engage them in decision making, and to obtain their informed consent to actions that would affect their lives were fundamental issues in the Guatemalan civil conflict. Indigenous peoples had been politically marginalized and dispossessed of land and resources; they were also the principal victims during the war. Grievances against the mining companies arose because of a variety of issues, including different values and interests, unequal distribution of costs and benefits, disproportionate influence on decision making, and varied access to information. The fragility and hybridity of the post-conflict setting, however, intensified the difficulties posed by these issues. Moreover, both communities and the state are relatively unfamiliar with mining processes and inexperienced in regulating and negotiating with mining companies.

For company-community relations to thrive, both parties must want a relationship. When this is not the case—and when the community does not even consent to the presence of a resource developer—community relations techniques have reduced efficacy. Goldcorp inherited a situation in which neither the former owners nor the Guatemalan government seems to have paid enough attention to the perspectives of local residents or to the post-conflict context. Goldcorp is attempting to address some of these issues, but is likely to face continued challenges.

LESSONS LEARNED

Reopening or developing mines in post-conflict settings can benefit from three strategies: taking fragility and hybridity into account, assigning priority to reconciliation, and building familiarity.

Taking fragility and hybridity into account

Any mining company that hopes to achieve mutually beneficial company-community relations and strengthen peacebuilding must take into account the fragility and hybridity of the post-conflict setting. In practical terms, this means actively including those informal institutions and actors that represent the political order outside state structures, and acknowledging that the state structure, including the legal system, is not the sole (or even the principal) framework for resource governance in post-conflict environments. Where customary law still holds sway, companies and state institutions that intend to establish extractive resource projects are well advised to take it into account, and to strive for a social license to operate within the framework of customary law. As both the Bougainville and San Marcos cases demonstrate, under conditions of political hybridity, customary rules regarding land and other natural resources must be reconciled with state-based laws. Moreover, in the absence of state enforcement of environmental and social standards, it is essential to uphold high corporate standards.

It is only natural that people who have experienced violent conflict—and who may have had past negative experiences with mining companies, particularly where the mines played a role in the conflict—would be suspicious, and perhaps resentful, of external actors who want to reopen or develop mines. On Bougainville, for example, BCL will initially have to deal with resistance and blame (and perhaps even outright hatred) while attempting to meet the community's expectations and demands.[39]

Both cases demonstrate that it is particularly difficult, under conditions of political hybridity, to provide a secure environment for operations, given the multiplicity of actors and institutions that lay claim to legitimate authority. To address this issue, companies would be well-advised not to think of security in a narrow sense—that is, as something that is achieved by means of police or other security forces. Instead, security should be based on good company-community relations; any remaining needs for the protection of employees and assets should be addressed by locally managed and staffed security services. Locally based security not only meets the security needs of the project but contributes, in a broader way, to peacebuilding.

Giving priority to reconciliation

Regardless of whether mining was implicated in prior conflict, communities must reconcile within themselves and with other communities, even before negotiating with mine operators and government representatives. There can be substantial intracommunity conflict (e.g., between men and women, or between the older and the younger generation), intercommunity conflict (e.g., between those in the immediate project area and those in areas subject to potential impacts), and conflict between religious or ethnic groups. Supporting intra- and intercommunity reconciliation is an essential part of establishing sustainable company-community

---

[39] On the other hand, some Bougainville residents view the reopening or development of mines as an opportunity to improve their economic and social circumstances. (In fact, community members are rarely unanimous about mining, and even a single person may hold simultaneous and conflicting views about it.)

relations, but it requires "long-term commitment and patience" (Nelson 2006, 21) on the part of companies, and an awareness that communities want ongoing relationships, not merely "solutions" and "settlements" (Banks 2008, 32).

Where mining was implicated in the prior conflict, the company must deal with deep wounds, and any attempt to reopen operations will have to address this history and the associated grievances first. To rebuild trust and achieve reconciliation, the company must engage in a genuine and focused dialogue, in which each side presents its perception of the history and its ongoing effects. In Bougainville, for example, BCL will essentially have to behave as if it were another "clan": it must acknowledge its status as a party to the previous violent conflict, participate in traditional Bougainvillean conflict resolution, and accept all the obligations that come with such participation.[40] In practical terms, this means making reparations for environmental damage and finding ways to remediate the damage to the extent possible. A willingness to respect Bougainvillean culture and to be a part of local ways of doing things is essential for building trust, restoring the relationship with the community, and getting back into business. Moreover, it is an alternative to protracted legal proceedings, which can be very costly and do not really enjoy legitimacy in the eyes of the community; solutions achieved through judicial proceedings are much less reliable and sustainable than solutions achieved in the local customary context.

BCL and other companies that might develop mines on the island must be careful not to rush things; to gain the free, prior, and informed consent of all relevant stakeholders, they must be willing to engage in a comprehensive, long-term process that may well take years. BCL has stated that it is committed to reopening Panguna only "if this is the wish of the majority of landowners and Bougainvilleans" (BCL 2009); this commitment will have to be translated into practice. Nor will such a commitment be without problems. If influential minorities continue to oppose the reopening of the mine, the wish of the majority will not be enough: BCL will have to persuade an *overwhelming* majority of the local population of the benefits of mining.[41] Obtaining the free, prior, and informed

---

[40] At the core of customary peacebuilding in Bougainville is the restoration of social harmony among the conflicting parties, which does not necessarily mean a return to the status quo, but may instead involve some sort of transition to new arrangements. Only through extensive talks and negotiation can parties overcome hatred and mistrust and achieve reconciliation. Reconciliation is cemented by the exchange of gifts (compensation) for damage done and wrongs committed. The exchange takes place in the context of peace ceremonies, in which former adversaries may feast, drink, and dance together; chew betel nut together; and symbolically break spears and arrows. Of course, participation in such a process poses extraordinary problems for a modern multinational mining corporation—but it will have to be done in some form. On customary peacemaking and peacebuilding in Bougainville, see Regan (2000), Howley (2002), and Boege (2006, 2008).

[41] As well as providing a strong moral foundation for the project, an overwhelming majority would deliver a practical benefit by ensuring that any groups that were still in opposition would be too small to spoil the project.

consent of an overwhelming majority is just one of the challenges, however; defining the landowners is another. Too narrow a conception of landowners, as fence-line neighbors, was one cause of the previous violent conflict. This time, BCL will need to apply a much broader definition—one that includes, for example, communities that are located downstream of the mining area, well beyond the mine site.

For their part, communities must avoid settling too hastily on monetary compensation packages that may seem attractive at first but that may generate new problems, such as intracommunity disputes about the division of funds. To avoid potentially destructive intracommunity and intercommunity conflict, communities must learn to speak with one voice in their negotiations with companies, state institutions, and other external actors; in practical terms, this means working to resolve their own disagreements before they attempt to deal with outsiders. Last but not least, communities will have to adjust their customary ways of doing things to meet the challenges that accompany large-scale mining projects: as Glenn Banks has noted, "conflicts are created precisely because tradition cannot deal with the new questions or issues that come about with resource developments" (Banks 2008, 30–31).

Building familiarity

Although a mining company whose presence predates a violent conflict may be burdened by the weight of that history, it also has the advantage of a deeper understanding of the place and the people; in many cases, mining companies have managed to retain some sort of relationship with the local community, and some residents may even have retained a positive view of the old operation. Newcomers, on the other hand, must establish a company-community relationship from scratch and gain familiarity with the social, political, historical and environmental context. Conflict-sensitive context analysis is indispensable to any attempt to reopen or develop mines in post-conflict situations. Two dimensions of the context must be analyzed: the overall post-conflict setting—that is, the political, economic, social, and cultural context, including issues related to security, reconciliation, law and justice, and legislation—and the specific post-conflict setting of the mine. During the early development of the Marlin mine, no such analysis appears to have been undertaken, and the mining operation continues to grapple with issues historically rooted in the prior conflict, including marginalization, exclusion, and the failure to have obtained the free, prior, and informed consent of indigenous stakeholders.

At the same time that companies must familiarize themselves with the post-conflict setting, they must also provide support for the communities whose lives may be affected by mining projects. The communities may be unfamiliar with what mining entails, and the government may lack the experience and capacity to effectively regulate operations. Lack of familiarity with mining can create fear and influence residents' views on whether and how mining should proceed. To help the community understand the planned project and its potential impact, and to bolster the community's capacity to undertake community development and participatory roles, the company must make a deliberate effort to increase the community's familiarity with mining. In addition to maintaining ongoing and transparent communication, consultation, and engagement, the company might arrange community training sessions and site visits to similar operations. The company should also help build capacity in government departments that have a role in regulating mining, while being careful to respect the independence of the agencies performing their oversight functions.

CONCLUSION

As the Bougainville case demonstrates, a company that attempts to reopen a mine that played a role in a previous conflict is likely to be greeted with suspicion, if not resentment, by community residents. Working with and through community leaders, and in the context of customary forms of dispute resolution, the company will have to take responsibility for past wrongs, show willingness to make reparations, and strive for reconciliation. It must respect the outcome of reconciliations and must at the same time be aware that reconciliation is an ongoing process: conflicts may never be really "over" (Banks 2008). A company that attempts to establish a new extractive resource project in a post-conflict setting, as in the case of San Marcos, is burdened by different issues: although there is no unpleasant history associated with mining, newcomers are less familiar with the communities with whom they are planning to develop a relationship. The communities, for their part, are unfamiliar with what mining entails, and the various levels of government lack experience with mining and may lack the capacity to effectively regulate operations.

In addition to engaging in conflict-sensitive community relations practices, companies in post-conflict settings also have an obligation to actively assist peacebuilding through conflict-relevant policies. In practical terms, this means creating policies and engaging in activities that are specifically designed to support peacebuilding. For example,

- Providing former combatants with mining jobs, or hiring them to help repair or rebuild infrastructure in communities on both sides of the prior conflict.
- Building the capacity of state institutions to effectively regulate mining projects.
- Providing community services in an impartial and inclusive manner.
- Partnering with civil society groups and communal institutions to address issues that are of particular relevance for peacebuilding, such as corruption; human rights abuses; job creation; and access to education, health care, and economic opportunity.

In addition, companies should participate proactively in the broader post-conflict policy dialogue, in order to strengthen peacebuilding and prevent new conflict. Given the hybridity of the political context, such dialogue should involve central government, local governments, and civil society organizations, particularly at the local level; the participation of traditional authorities and customary leaders is of particular importance. In other words, NGOs, community-based organizations, and chiefs and village elders should not be perceived as nuisances or threats, but as partners. There is no question that this level of engagement can be costly and time-consuming. But to take one's time is perhaps the most important recommendation for post-conflict situations.

REFERENCES

Andersen, L., B. Moeller, and F. Stepputat, eds. 2007. *Fragile states and insecure people? Violence, security, and statehood in the twenty-first century.* New York: Palgrave Macmillan.

Anten, L. 2009. *Strengthening governance in post-conflict fragile states.* Clingendael Issues Paper. The Hague: Netherlands Institute of International Relations.

Bagwitz, D., R. Elges, H. Grossman, and G. Kruk. 2008. *Private sector development in (post-)conflict situations: Guidebook.* Eschborn, Germany: GTZ. www.gtz.de/de/dokumente/en-PSD-conflict-guidebook-2008.pdf.

Ball, P., P. Kobrak, and H. F. Spirer. 1999. State violence in Guatemala,1960–1996: A quantitative reflection. Washington, D.C.: American Association for the Advancement of Science.

Banks, G. 2008. Understanding "resource" conflicts in Papua New Guinea. *Asia Pacific Viewpoint* 49 (1): 23–34.

BCL (Bougainville Copper Limited). 2009. Chairman's annual general meeting address. February 20, Port Moresby.

BCC (Bougainville Constitutional Commission). 2004. Report of the Bougainville Constitutional Commission. Report on the third and final draft of the Bougainville Constitution, prepared by the Bougainville Constitutional Commission (BCC). Arawa and Buka.

Bebbington, A., L. Hinojosa, D. Humphreys-Bebbington, M. L. Burneo, and X. Warnaars. 2008. Contention and ambiguity: Mining and the possibilities of development. *Development and Change* 39 (6): 887–914.

Boege, V. 2006. *Bougainville and the discovery of slowness: An unhurried approach to state-building in the Pacific.* ACPACS Occasional Papers Series No. 3. Brisbane: Australian Centre for Peace and Conflict Studies.

———. 2008. *A promising liaison: Kastom and state in Bougainville.* ACPACS Occasional Papers Series No. 12. Brisbane: Australian Centre for Peace and Conflict Studies.

Boege, V., A. Brown, and K. Clements. 2009. Hybrid political orders, not fragile states. *Peace Review* 21 (1): 13–21.

Boege, V., A. Brown, K. Clements, and A. Nolan. 2008a. *On hybrid political orders and emerging states: State formation in the context of "fragility."* Berghof Handbook Dialogue No. 8. Berlin: Berghof Research Center for Constructive Conflict Management.

———. 2008b. *States emerging from hybrid political orders: Pacific experiences.* ACPACS Occasional Paper No. 11. Brisbane: Australian Centre for Peace and Conflict Studies.

Boege, V., C. Fitzpatrick, W. Jaspers, and W.-C. Paes. 2006. *Who's minding the store? The business of private, public and civil actors in zones of conflict.* BICC Brief 32. Bonn: Bonn International Center for Conversion.

Brinkerhoff, D. W., ed. 2007. *Governance in post-conflict societies: Rebuilding fragile states.* London: Taylor and Francis.

Brown, M. J. F. 1974. A development consequence: Disposal of mining waste on Bougainville, Papua New Guinea. *Geoforum* 5 (2): 19–27.

Buur, L., and H. M. Kyed, eds. 2007. *State recognition and democratization in sub-Saharan Africa: A new dawn for traditional authorities?* New York: Palgrave Macmillan.

Call, C. T., ed. 2008. *Building states to build peace.* Boulder, CO: Lynne Rienner.

CAO (Office of the Compliance Advisor/Ombudsman). 2005. Assessment of a complaint submitted to CAO in relation to the Marlin mining project in Guatemala. International Finance Corporation/Multilateral Investment Guarantee Agency. September 7. www.cao-ombudsman.org/cases/document-links/documents/CAO-Marlin-assessment-English-7Sep05.pdf.

Carl, A., and L. Garasu, eds. 2002. Weaving consensus: The Papua New Guinea-Bougainville peace process. *Accord* 12 (2002).

CCHR (Centre for Civil and Human Rights). 2009. A human rights impact assessment of the Marlin Mine, San Miguel Ixtahuacán, Guatemala. http://law.nd.edu/center-for-civil-and-human-rights/independent-international-panel.

Chigas, D., and P. Woodrow. 2009. *A distinction with a difference: Conflict sensitivity and peacebuilding.* CDA Collaborative Learning Projects. www.cdainc.com/cdawww/pdf/article/RPP_Differentiating%20Conflict%20Sensitivity%20and%20Peacebuilding_20091026.pdf.

Colletta, N., and M. Cullen. 2000. *Violent Conflict and the Transformation of Social Capital: Lessons from Cambodia, Rwanda, Guatemala and Somalia.* Washington, D.C.: World Bank.

Commission for Historical Clarification. 1999. Guatemala memory of silence: Report of the Commission for Historical Clarification; Conclusions and recommendations. http://shr.aaas.org/guatemala/ceh/report/english/toc.html.

Connell, J. 1991. Compensation and conflict: The Bougainville copper mine, Papua New Guinea. In *Mining and indigenous peoples in Australasia*, ed. J. Connell and R. Howitt. Sydney: Sydney University Press.

Denoon, D. 2000. *Getting under the skin: The Bougainville copper agreement and the creation of the Panguna mine.* Carlton South, Victoria: Melbourne University Press.

Eccarius-Kelly, V. 2007. Deep and ragged scars in Guatemala. *Peace Review* 19 (1): 51–58.

Filer, C. S. 1990. The Bougainville rebellion, the mining industry and the process of social disintegration in Papua New Guinea. *Canberra Anthropologist* 13 (1): 1–40.

———. 1992. The escalation of disintegration and the reinvention of authority. In *The Bougainville crisis: 1991 update*, ed. M. Spriggs and D. Denoon. Bathurst, NSW, Australia: Crawford House Press.

Franks, D. 2007. Consuming landscapes: Towards a political ecology of resource appropriation. Ph.D. diss., Griffith University, Brisbane.

Franks, D., C. Fidler, D. Brereton, F. Vanclay, and P. Clark. 2009. Leading practice strategies for addressing the social impacts of resource developments. Briefing paper prepared for the Department of Employment, Economic Development and Innovation, Queensland Government. Centre for Social Responsibility in Mining. Sustainable Minerals Institute.

University of Queensland. www.csrm.uq.edu.au/docs/Franks_etal_LeadingPracticeSocial Impacts_2009.pdf.
Frente de Defensa San Miguelense and Center for International Environmental Law. 2009. Specific instance complaint submitted to the Canadian National Contact Point pursuant to the OECD Guidelines for Multinational Enterprises concerning the operations of Goldcorp Inc. at the Marlin Mine in the indigenous community of San Miguel Ixtahuacán, Guatemala. December 9. Ottawa.
Fulmer, A., A. Godoy, and P. Neff. 2008. Indigenous rights, resistance, and the law: Lessons from a Guatemalan mine. *Latin American Politics and Society* 50 (4): 91–121.
Ghani, A., and C. Lockhart. 2008. *Fixing failed states: A framework for rebuilding a fractured world.* Oxford, UK: Oxford University Press.
Howard, M. C. 1991. *Mining, politics and development in the South Pacific.* Boulder, CO: Westview Press.
Howley, P. 2002. *Breaking spears and mending hearts: Peacemakers and restorative justice in Bougainville.* London: Zed Books.
HRIA Steering Committee (Human Rights Impact Assessment Steering Committee). 2009. Steering Committee update: Marlin mine. May. www.hria-guatemala.com/en/docs/Impact %20Assessment/Steering_Committee_Update_May_2009_05_27_09.pdf.
IFC (International Finance Corporation). 2005. IFC response to CAO assessment report: Complaint regarding Marlin mining project in Guatemala. October 14. www.cao-ombudsman.org/ cases/document-links/documents/Marlin-Responsetofinalreport.pdf.
ILO (International Labour Organisation). 1989. Indigenous and tribal peoples convention, 1989. C169. www.ilo.org/ilolex/cgi-lex/convde.pl?C169.
International Alert. 2005. *Conflict-sensitive business practice: Guidance for extractive industries.* London: International Alert.
International Business Leaders Forum and International Finance Corporation. 2007. *Guide to human rights impact assessment and management: Road-testing draft.* London: International Business Leaders Forum; Washington, D.C.: International Finance Corporation.
Kemp, D. 2009. Community relations in the global mining industry: Exploring the internal dimensions of externally orientated work. *Corporate Social Responsibility and Environmental Management* 17:1–14.
Kemp, D., and N. Gotzmann. 2008. *Community grievance mechanisms and Australian mining companies offshore: An industry discussion paper.* Brisbane: CSRM / ConCord UQ.
Kyed, H. M., and L. Buur 2006. Recognition and democratisation: "New roles" for traditional leaders in sub-Saharan Africa. DIIS Working Paper No. 2006/11. Copenhagen: Danish Institute for International Studies.
Laplante, L. J., and S. A. Spears. 2008. Out of the conflict zone: The case for community consent processes in the extractive sector. *Yale Human Rights and Development Law Journal* 11:69–116.
Law, B. 2009. Canada goldmine worries grow. *BBC News*, March 30. http://news.bbc.co.uk/ 2/hi/7968888.stm.
Lenzen, O., and M. d'Engelbronner. 2009. *Human rights in business: Guide to corporate human rights impact assessment tools.* Aim for Human Rights. January. www.aimforhumanrights.org/fileadmin/user_upload/pdf/HRB_Guide_to_corporate_HRIA_2009-def. pdf.
Montana Exploradora de Guatemala, S.A. 2009. *Environmental and social performance annual monitoring report (AMR).* May. www.goldcorp.com/_resources/project_pdfs/marlin/ Marlin_Mine_2008_AMR.pdf.

Nelson, J. 2006. *Operating in insecure environments.* Corporate Social Responsibility Initiative Working Paper No. 25. Cambridge, MA: Harvard University.

OECD/DAC (Organisation for Economic Co-operation/Development Assistance Committee). 2008. Concepts and dilemmas of state building in fragile situations: From fragility to resilience. OECD/DAC Discussion Paper. Paris: OECD.

Parliament of Australia. Joint Standing Committee on Foreign Affairs, Defence and Trade. 1999. Completed inquiry: Bougainville: The peace process and beyond. September 27. www.aph.gov.au/house/committee/jfadt/bougainville/BVrepindx.htm.

Quodling, P. W. 1991. *Bougainville: The mine and the people.* St. Leonards-Auckland, NSW, Australia: Centre for Independent Studies Ltd.

Regan, A. J. 2000. "Traditional" leaders and conflict resolution in Bougainville: Reforming the present by re-writing the past? In *Reflections on violence in Melanesia*, ed. S. Dinnen and A. Ley. Annandale, VA: Hawkins Press; Canberra: Asia Pacific Press.

———. 2002a. Bougainville: Beyond survival. *Cultural Survival Quarterly* 26 (3): 20–24.

———. 2002b: The Bougainville political settlement and the prospects for sustainable peace. *Pacific Economic Bulletin* 17 (1): 114–129.

———. 2003. The Bougainville conflict: Political and economic agendas. In *The political economy of armed conflict: Beyond greed and grievance*, ed. K. Ballentine and J. Sherman. Boulder, CO: Lynne Rienner.

Regan, A. J., and H. M. Griffin, eds. 2005. *Bougainville before the conflict.* Canberra: Pandanus Books.

Rights Action. 2008. Canada's role in supporting the harmful activities of Goldcorp Inc. (previously, Glamis Gold Inc.) in San Marcos, Guatemala. Sign on letter-report to Canadian government about Goldcorp's mining in Guatemala addressed to the Canadian Ambassador to Guatemala. November 21. www.rightsaction.org/urgent_com/Canada_Goldcorp_Guate_111208.html.

Ruggie, J. 2008. *Protect, respect and remedy: A framework for business and human rights.* Report of the Special Representative of the Secretary-General on the issue of human rights and transnational corporations and other business enterprises. A/HRC/8/5. United Nations Human Rights Council. April 7.

Schenck, J. 2006. Letter to Amar Inamdar, Senior Ombudsman, Office of the Compliance Advisor/Ombudsman. May 22. www.goldcorp.com/_resources/project_pdfs/marlin/glamisresponsecao52606.pdf.

Schetter, C. 2007. Talibanistan: der Anti-Staat. *Internationales Asienforum* 38 (3–4): 233–257.

Schlichte, K. 2005. *Der Staat in der Weltgesellschaft: Politische Herrschaft in Asien, Afrika und Lateinamerika.* Frankfurt: Campus.

Schlichte, K., and B. Wilke. 2000. Der Staat und einige seiner Zeitgenossen: Zur Zukunft des Regierens in der "Dritten Welt." *Zeitschrift fuer Internationale Beziehungen* 7 (2): 359–384.

Switzer, J. 2001. Discussion paper for the July 11 2001 experts workshop on armed conflict and natural resources: The case of the mineral sector. www.iisd.org/pdf/2002/envsec_mining_conflict.pdf.

UN (United Nations). 2008. United Nations declaration on the rights of indigenous peoples. March. www.un.org/esa/socdev/unpfii/documents/DRIPS_en.pdf.

Vernon, D. 2005. The Panguna mine. In *Bougainville before the conflict*, ed. A. J. Regan and H. M. Griffin. Canberra: Pandanus Books.

von Trotha, T. 2000. Die Zukunft liegt in Afrika: Vom Zerfall des Staates, von der Vorherrschaft der konzentrischen Ordnung und vom Aufstieg der Parastaatlichkeit. *Leviathan* 28:253–279.

———. 2005. Der Aufstieg des Lokalen. *Aus Politik und Zeitgeschichte* 28–29 (2005): 32–38.

Wesley-Smith, T. A. 1988: Melanesians and modes of production: Underdevelopment in Papua New Guinea with particular reference to the role of mining capital. Ph.D. diss., University of Hawaii.

Wesley-Smith, T. A., and E. Ogan. 1992. Copper, class, and crisis: Changing relations of production in Bougainville. *Contemporary Pacific* 4 (2): 245–267.

Wolfers, E. P. 2006. Bougainville autonomy: Implications for governance and decentralisation. Public Policy in Papua New Guinea Discussion Paper Series No. 5. Canberra: Australian National University-State, Society and Governance in Melanesia.

Woodward, S. L. 2006. *Institutionally fragile states: Fragile states, prevention and post conflict—Recommendations*. Madrid: Fundación para las Relaciones Internacionales y el Diálogo Exterior.

World Bank. 2004. *Striking a better balance: Final report of the Extractive Industries Review*. Vol. 1. Washington, D.C.: World Bank.

Zandvliet, L. 2004. Redefining corporate social risk mitigation strategies. Social Development Notes: Conflict Prevention and Reconstruction No. 16. February. http://siteresources .worldbank.org/INTCPR/214578-1111751313696/20480291/CPRNote16CEP.pdf.

ADDITIONAL RESOURCES

Although the following materials were not cited, they have been listed because they contributed to the conceptual development of the chapter.

Anderson, M. B. 2003. Developing best practice for corporate engagement in conflict zones: Lessons learned from experience. In *Public bads: Economic dimensions of conflict*. Development Policy Forum Summary Report. Berlin: INWENT.

Anderson, M. B., and L. Zandvliet. 2001. *Corporate options for breaking cycles of conflict*. Cambridge, MA: Collaborative for Development Action.

Bais, K., and M. Huijser. 2005. *The profit of peace: Corporate responsibility in conflict regions*. Sheffield, UK: Greenleaf Publishing.

Ballard, C., and G. Banks. 2003. Resource wars: The anthropology of mining. *Annual Review of Anthropology* 32:287–313.

Banfield, J., V. Haufler, and D. Lilly. 2003. *Transnational corporations in conflict-prone zones: Public policy responses and a framework for action*. London: International Alert.

Boege, V. 1998. *Bergbau – Umweltzerstoerung – Gewalt. Der Krieg auf Bougainville im Kontext der Geschichte oekologisch induzierter Modernisierungskonflikte*. Hamburg: LIT Verlag.

———. 2004. Muschelgeld und Blutdiamanten: Traditionale Konfliktbearbeitung in zeitgenoessischen Gewaltkonflikten. *Schriften des Deutschen Uebersee-Instituts* 63.

Castan Centre for Human Rights Law, Monash University. 2008. *Human rights translated: A business reference guide*. http://human-rights.unglobalcompact.org/doc/human_rights_translated.pdf.

Conca, K., and G. D. Dabelko, eds. 2002. *Environmental peacemaking*. Washington, D.C.: Woodrow Wilson Center Press; Baltimore: Johns Hopkins University Press.

Confederation of Norwegian Business and Industry and Peace Research Institute Oslo. 2003. *Corporate actors in zones of conflict: Responsible engagement.* Oslo: PRIO.

Corporate Engagement Project. 2002a. *Working in a changing world: A new approach to risk mitigation in zones of conflict.* Cambridge, MA: Collaborative for Development Action.

———. 2002b. *Corporate options for constructive engagement in conflict zones: Executive summary.* Cambridge, MA: Collaborative for Development Action.

Dauderstaedt, M., and A. Schildberg, eds. 2006. *Dead ends of transition: Rentier economies and protectorates.* Frankfurt: Campus Verlag.

ERM (Environmental Resources Management). 2008. *Community development and local conflict: A resource document for practitioners in the extractive sector.* http://commdev.org/content/document/detail/1801/.

EIR (Extractive Industries Review). 2003. *Striking a better balance: The extractive industries review.* Final report. Washington, D.C.: World Bank.

Feil, M., and J. Switzer. 2004. *Valuable minerals and conflict: Toolkit for practitioners.* Berlin: Adelphi Research.

Franks, D. 2009. Avoiding mine-community conflict: From dialogue to shared futures. In *Proceedings of the First International Seminar on Environmental Issues in the Mining Industry,* ed. J. Wiertz and C. J. Moran. Santiago: Gecamin / Sustainable Minerals Institute.

Giordano, M. F., and M. A. Giordano. 2005. International resource conflict and mitigation. *Journal of Peace Research* 42 (1): 47–65.

Humphreys, M., J. D. Sachs, and J. E. Stiglitz, eds. 2007. *Escaping the resource curse.* New York: Columbia University Press.

Le Billon, P. 2008. Resources for peace? Managing revenues from extractive industries in post-conflict environments. Public Finance in Post-Conflict Environments Policy Paper Series. New York: Center on International Cooperation and Political Economy Research Institute.

Nelson, J. 2000. *The business of peace: The private sector as a partner in conflict prevention and resolution.* London: International Alert, Council on Economic Priorities, and Prince of Wales Business Leaders Forum.

OECD (Organisation for Economic Co-operation and Development). 2006. *OECD risk awareness tool for multinational enterprises in weak governance zones.* Paris.

OECD/DAC (Organisation for Economic Co-operation and Development/Development Assistance Committee). 2005. *Land and violent conflict.* Paris: OECD.

Render, J. M. 2009. *Mining and indigenous peoples issues review.* London: International Council on Mining and Metals.

Schlichte, K. 2005. *The dynamics of states: The formation and crises of state domination.* Burlington, VT: Ashgate Publishing Group.

———. 2007. Administering Babylon: On the crooked ways of state building and state formation. *Politorbis: Zeitschrift fuer Aussenpolitik* 42:34–39.

Schure, J. 2007. Governing the gift of nature: Resource conflict monitor—The links between governance, conflict and natural resources. BICC Concept Paper. Bonn: Bonn International Center for Conversion.

Seck, S. L. 2008. Home state responsibility and local communities: The case of global mining. *Yale Human Rights and Development Law Journal* 11:177–206.

Sherman, J. 2002. *Options for promoting corporate responsibility in conflict zones: Perspectives from the private sector.* New York: International Peace Academy.

Sillitoe, P. 2000. *Social change in Melanesia: Development and history.* Cambridge, UK: Cambridge University Press.
Smith, G. A. 2008. An introduction to corporate social responsibility in the extractive industries. *Yale Human Rights and Development Law Journal* 11:1–7.
Smith, L. T. 1999. *Decolonizing methodologies: Research and indigenous peoples.* London: Zed Books.
Switzer, J., and H. Ward. 2004. Enabling corporate investment in peace: An assessment of voluntary initiatives addressing business and violent conflict, and a framework for policy decision-making. IISD/IIED Discussion Paper. London: Chatelaine.
UNEP (United Nations Environment Programme). 2004. *Understanding environment, conflict, and cooperation.* Nairobi.
Wenger, A., and D. Moeckli. 2003. *Conflict prevention: The untapped potential of the business sector.* Boulder, CO: Lynne Rienner.
Zandvliet, L. 2005. *Opportunities for synergy: Conflict transformation and the corporate agenda.* Berlin: Berghof Forschungszentrum fuer konstruktive Konfliktbearbeitung.

Diamonds in war, diamonds for peace: Diamond sector management and kimberlite mining in Sierra Leone

Kazumi Kawamoto

During Sierra Leone's civil war (1991–2002), the country's diamonds became famous—not for their high quality, but because they were "blood diamonds," gems that were traded and smuggled in support of a brutal and protracted civil war. Widely viewed as having both funded and prolonged the war (Maconachie and Binns 2007b; Smillie, Gberie, and Hazelton 2000; Reno 1997; Hirsch 2001), diamonds are today a key resource in the country's post-conflict reconstruction.

Diamond fields cover 20,000 square kilometers in Sierra Leone (see figure 1).[1] During the height of diamond production, from the late 1930s through the 1970s, diamonds made up about 70 percent of the country's export earnings and almost 25 percent of its gross domestic product (Maconachie and Binns 2007a). Between 1930 and 1968, over 30 million carats of diamonds had been officially mined; by 1998, the cumulative official total was 55 million carats (Smillie, Gberie, and Hazelton 2000).

After the war, the management of the diamond industry became a principal focus of peacebuilding. Since 2000, three major approaches to management have emerged: (1) the Diamond Area Community Development Fund (DACDF), which was created to alleviate grievances by directing a portion of state taxes on diamond revenues to local communities; (2) the Kimberley Process Certification Scheme (KPCS), which was designed to break the link between rough diamonds and

---

Kazumi Kawamoto is a Ph.D. candidate at the Graduate School of Arts and Sciences at the University of Tokyo. The author wishes to thank Heather Croshaw, Brigadier (Ret.) M. K. Dumbuya, Mitsugi Endo, Maya Kai Kai, Ibrahim Kamara, Usman Boie Kamara, Abdul Koroma, Jillian Lewis, Kate Rodgers, and Grant Wilson for their helpful advice and suggestions on conducting the fieldwork and drafting this chapter. The research for this chapter was partially funded by the University of Tokyo. Ibrahim Tamba Fanday, Reu Santigie, Edward Sandy, Jonathan Shekah, and Mohamed B. Mansaray provided indispensable logistical support, without which the research would never have been completed. Finally, the author wishes to thank Fatmata, who was a constant source of encouragement during her stay in Sierra Leone.

[1] Most of Sierra Leone's significant diamond deposits are in the Kono, Kenema, and Bo districts, in the eastern part of the country.

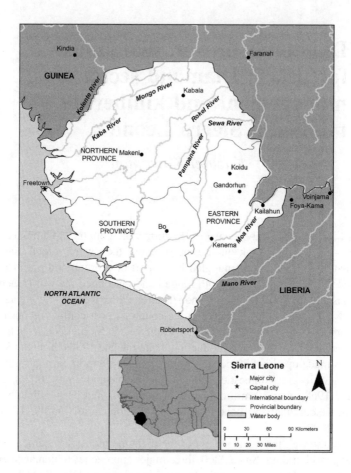

violent conflict; and (3) deep-shaft kimberlite mining, which was undertaken to boost national economic development.

Most of the diamond extraction in Sierra Leone is alluvial diamond mining, also known as secondary diamond mining. Alluvial diamonds are a diffuse and readily obtained (or looted) resource, and therefore difficult to control (Le Billon 2001; Ross 2004). Kimberlite mining, in contrast, is industrial-scale mining that requires extensive infrastructure and investment. In a 2005 interview, Ahmed Tejan Kabbah, then president of Sierra Leone, noted that one of the country's primary goals is to attract bigger mining companies—and with them, greater foreign investment. During the same interview, Kabbah noted that Sierra Leone had had "tremendous success" with the Koidu Holdings, which exploit kimberlite mines. "[Koidu Holdings is] easier to monitor, they keep a paper trail, and they are bringing in a lot of revenue in the form of taxes and employment. The alluvial mines are a problem. They always have been, and will probably continue to be" (PAC and Network Movement for Justice and Development 2005, 1).

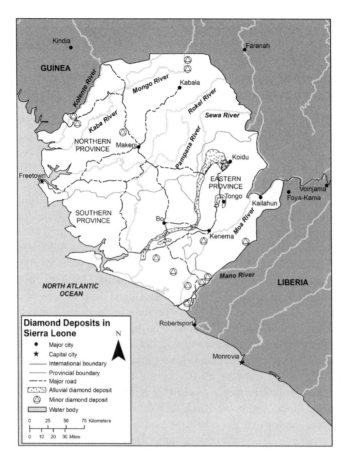

Figure 1. Diamond deposits in Sierra Leone
Source: Based on original map from Aureus Mining.

This chapter considers kimberlite mining in the broader context of Sierra Leone's history—in particular, the history of the link between diamonds and conflict. Unlike alluvial diamond mining, kimberlite mining—which first emerged in Sierra Leone in 2004—has not been associated with the funding of armed rebellion. Nevertheless, as this chapter will demonstrate, it is not free of conflict: in 2007, long-simmering community grievances in Koidu erupted into a riot that left two dead. Because serious disagreements between stakeholders, such as occurred at Koidu, have the potential to destabilize long-term peace in Sierra Leone, it is essential to understand how and why the clash occurred. The kimberlite riot underlines the importance of low-level, local conflicts that make peacebuilding more difficult and can sometimes escalate to larger conflicts.

The chapter is divided into six major sections: (1) a review of the role of diamonds in Sierra Leone's prewar economy; (2) a review of the role of diamonds during Sierra Leone's civil war; (3) a brief discussion of the three major strategies for managing the diamond sector: the DACDF, the KPCS, and kimberlite mining; (4) an analysis of the kimberlite riot; (5) a summary of lessons learned; and (6) a brief conclusion.

DIAMONDS IN THE PREWAR ECONOMY

Since 1930, when diamonds were first discovered in Sierra Leone, the diamond industry has formed the backbone of the economy. In 1935, when Sierra Leone was still a colony of the British Empire, the colonial authorities who controlled the diamond sector awarded the first mining contract to the De Beers' Sierra Leone Selection Trust (SLST), granting it a monopoly for ninety-nine years. Production of rough diamonds began that same year and had reached one million carats by 1937 (Smillie, Gberie, and Hazelton 2000). Thus, in a short time, Sierra Leone went from being a resource-poor nation to being a resource-rich nation.

Most of the diamond production occurred in the Kono and Kenema districts, which had historically been less developed than other parts of Sierra Leone, but which had significant deposits of alluvial diamonds. Initially, revenues from diamond exports were invested in roads, schools, and the provision of clean water in these areas (Maconachie 2009). The regions became economic centers and attracted thousands of workers: anyone who had shovels, sieves, buckets, and picks could engage in alluvial mining (Global Witness and PAC 2004).

By the early 1950s, the diamond-rich regions of Sierra Leone had experienced an influx of diamond miners—mostly young men from Guinea, Liberia, and Sierra Leone, who had formerly worked in agriculture. By 1956, what became known as the Great Diamond Rush had drawn 75,000 illicit miners to the diamondiferous regions of the country—leading to smuggling on a vast scale, effectively ending the SLST monopoly[2] and fostering a general breakdown of law and order in the diamond-mining regions (Smillie, Gberie, and Hazelton 2000). There was also a shift in the trade route: whereas the principal smuggling route had formerly led from Kono to Freetown (the capital of Sierra Leone), increased security along that route led the smugglers to establish a new route, to Monrovia, Liberia (Smillie, Gberie, and Hazelton 2000)—a connection that would prove crucial for rebels and diamond smugglers during the civil war (UNSC 2000a). A number of other factors also contributed to the shift in the trade route: Liberia had no export taxes; money could easily be laundered there; U.S. dollars were the Liberian currency;[3] and there were buyers in Liberia who were willing to pay high prices for diamonds (Smillie, Gberie, and Hazelton 2000; UNSC 2000a).

Aware that they were losing revenue to illicit mining and diamond smuggling, the colonial authorities decided to change their policy. In 1955, the authorities

---

[2] Because De Beers had exclusive mining and prospecting rights for the entire country, all mining that was not being conducted by De Beers was, by definition, illegal.

[3] The use of U.S. dollars facilitates the export of diamonds by lowering transaction costs (the costs of exchanging one currency for another).

dissolved the SLST's monopoly;[4] the following year, they enacted the Alluvial Mining Scheme, which granted mining and trading rights to indigenous and artisanal miners—although the majority of the licenses went to Lebanese traders (Smillie, Gberie, and Hazelton 2000). For several years, the Alluvial Mining Scheme stabilized mining areas and significantly reduced illegal mining; although smuggling continued, it was on a much smaller scale.[5]

In 1961, Sierra Leone gained independence from Britain; the following year, the Sierra Leone People's Party (SLPP), which had co-ruled with the British colonial government since 1952, won the parliamentary elections. In 1967, the All People's Congress (APC) defeated the SLPP in the national elections, but a military coup later that year prevented Siaka Stevens, the new prime minister, from taking office until the spring of 1968—when, in the wake of a military countercoup, the government was handed over to the elected leadership (Gibrill 2007).

In 1971, after becoming president, Stevens formed the National Diamond Mining Company and effectively nationalized the SLST by obtaining a 51 percent stake in it (Maconachie 2008). Stevens tacitly encouraged illegal mining by turning diamonds and the presence of the SLST into a political issue (Smillie, Gberie, and Hazelton 2000). Illicit mining exploded as a consequence, hampering the SLST's efforts to protect its concessions. By 1978, Stevens had solidified political control by making Sierra Leone a one-party state.

Despite early populist promises, Stevens' regime—which was marked by corruption, patronage, poor management, and economic stagnation—brought on the decline of Sierra Leone's diamond industry. Annual legal diamond exports peaked at over 2 million carats in 1970; annual exports declined to 595,000 carats by 1980, and to 48,000 carats by 1988 (Smillie, Gberie, and Hazelton 2000). During the 1980s, as legitimate exports dropped, illicit mining expanded rapidly. Violence erupted in the mining areas, where diamonds were often stolen and smuggled—in many cases by groups with ties to Stevens. Meanwhile, a "shadow state"—a patron-client system operating outside of formal state institutions—emerged, supported by smuggling and illicit mining (Reno 1997, 2000, 2003).[6]

In 1985, Stevens retired from office. Major-General Joseph Saidu Momoh, the APC-appointed successor, became the new head of state. Claiming that he would dissolve the diamond-funded shadow state, Momoh established the Government Gold and Diamond Office, but the formal diamond sector soon became irrelevant (Smillie, Gberie, and Hazelton 2000). As Stevens had before him, Momoh established informal trade and patronage networks, providing access to buyers from Europe, the Middle East, and the United States. The Momoh regime was

---

[4] The SLST was allowed to retain its mining concessions in Yengema and Tongo, its most profitable fields.
[5] One reason that smuggling continued was to avoid the license fees and other costs.
[6] In 1954, De Beers established an office in Monrovia to buy diamonds from smugglers (Smillie, Gberie, and Hazelton 2000).

characterized not only by corruption but also by unruly armed forces, political turmoil, a disgruntled citizenry, and economic decline (ICG 2001b).

In the years leading up to the war, diamond-mining communities remained among the poorest areas in the country. Meanwhile, rural chiefs maintained absolute control over local residents, including access to citizenship and livelihoods;[7] those who lacked patronage—especially the young—remained uneducated and unemployed, and often faced a lifetime of hard labor (Fanthorpe 2001).[8] A set of grievances—including lack of involvement in mining-related decisions and the absence of development and investment in the mining regions—exacerbated general discontent with the government and facilitated the onset of war.

DIAMONDS AND THE CIVIL WAR

A number of scholars have argued that control of the diamond trade was not a direct cause of Sierra Leone's civil war but catalyzed and prolonged the conflict.[9] Although much of the fighting, and many of the atrocities, occurred in and around the diamondiferous areas of Kenema, Kono, and Koidu, the war had complex origins, including decades of rampant corruption, especially in the natural resource sector; impoverished and marginalized rural populations and general economic decline; and a lack of trust in the authoritarian government (ICG 2001b).

In March 1991, a small band of rebels from Liberia's Revolutionary United Front (RUF) crossed into Sierra Leone and attacked the southeastern provinces. The group was led by Foday Sankoh and consisted of only a few hundred men. Initially, the government of Sierra Leone regarded the RUF as no more than a nuisance; but by the following year, that view would change.

The attack was supported by Charles Taylor, a Liberian warlord who was interested in Sierra Leone's natural resources and who was believed to be tied to various criminal activities, including murder, rape, abduction, forced labor, and the use of child soldiers (ICG 2001b; Smillie, Gberie, and Hazelton 2000; Special Court for Sierra Leone n.d.).[10] At first, the RUF rebels attempted to

---

[7] As Richard Fanthorpe notes, "citizenship remains a privilege for those domiciled in old villages registered for tax collection. . . . The young and those of low inherited status inevitably find themselves in attenuating orders of precedence in access to [such] privileges" (2001, 385).

[8] During the war, disaffected young men would offer fertile ground for recruiters from the Revolutionary United Front (Abdullah 1998; Fanthorpe 2001).

[9] See, for example, Maconachie and Binns (2007b); Smillie, Gberie, and Hazelton (2000); Ross (2004); and J. Andrew Grant, "The Kimberley Process at Ten: Reflections on a Decade of Efforts to End the Trade in Conflict Diamonds," in this volume.

[10] Initially, the RUF claimed to have a political agenda: to overthrow the APC government and participate in a radical, pan-African revolution (ICG 2001b; Smillie, Gberie, and Hazelton 2000). But Taylor also had a personal grudge against Sierra Leone because of its involvement in Liberia's civil war, during which the government of Sierra Leone had allowed peacekeeping troops from the Economic Community of West African States Cease-Fire Monitoring Group to be stationed in Freetown.

appeal to anti-Momoh sentiment in Sierra Leone, but it became clear that their real goal was to sever Momoh's control over the diamond fields and to destabilize the regime (Smillie, Gberie, and Hazelton 2000).

On April 29, 1992, the National Provisional Ruling Council (NPRC), a military junta, ousted Momoh, and Captain Valentine Strasser came into power. Strasser vowed to end corruption in government and to defeat the RUF, which was terrorizing the countryside. Like his predecessors, however, Strasser was soon engaged in private dealings, especially in illegal diamond trading (Smillie, Gberie, and Hazelton 2000). As the RUF stepped up its attacks, the NPRC increased the size of the military from 3,000 to over 13,000 (ICG 2001b). To support the expansion, NPRC troops mined diamonds in Kono and traded them for weapons (Smillie, Gberie, and Hazelton 2000). By the end of 1992, despite the army's efforts to control the diamond fields, the RUF had captured the Kono district (Gberie 2002).

Many of the skirmishes that occurred between the army and the RUF in 1992 and 1993 were over control of the diamond fields in the eastern provinces. Some of the first confirmed atrocities also occurred during this time. To instill fear in local populations, exert political and military control, and send a message to any opposition, the RUF targeted civilians (Human Rights Watch 1998); the crimes included rapes, mutilations, and amputations (Smillie, Gberie, and Hazelton 2000; Human Rights Watch 1998). The RUF also kidnapped children to use as soldiers and slaves.

By 1995, the RUF controlled a vast territory and was advancing toward Freetown, and the NPRC hired a private security company, Executive Outcomes, to repel the RUF from the capital and remove the rebel forces from diamond-rich areas (ICG 2001b). The short-lived victory over the RUF allowed the NPRC to conduct presidential and parliamentary elections in February 1996. Despite an invitation from the junta to participate in the democratic election, the RUF refused, and instead continued to engage in brutal attacks on civilians to discourage them from voting (Gberie 2002).

The SLPP earned the majority of seats in parliament, and Ahmed Tejan Kabbah won the presidency. The new government encouraged local communities to protect themselves by establishing their own militias, which were based on traditional hunting societies and were collectively known as the Civilian Defense Force, or CDF (Smillie, Gberie, and Hazelton 2000). The largest of these groups, the Kamajors, often fought on the frontlines against the RUF and, like the rebels, committed human rights violations, including kidnapping children and forcing them to serve as soldiers (IRBC 1999).

In November 1996, in Abidjan, Côte d'Ivoire, the RUF and the Kabbah government signed a peace agreement (Gberie 2002). In May 1997, rogue elements of the Sierra Leone Army (SLA) overthrew the Kabbah government (Gberie 2002), which went into exile in Conakry, Guinea. The new junta, known as the Armed Forces Revolutionary Council (AFRC), was not recognized by the international community. Not long after taking power, the AFRC invited the RUF to control Freetown and the diamond fields (Francis 2005; ICG 2001b). As part of the peace agreement, Executive Outcomes had withdrawn from Sierra Leone. Soon after, the country fell into anarchy, and the AFRC/RUF regime was accused of engaging in atrocities, using forced labor, and child kidnapping (Human Rights Watch 1998).

In the late 1990s, discrepancies between the flow of diamonds out of Liberia and into Antwerp indicated that Charles Taylor was hosting a massive diamond-smuggling ring that led from Sierra Leone to Liberia to Belgium (Smillie, Gberie, and Hazelton 2000).[11] RUF rebels or their Liberian counterparts would carry the diamonds from Foya-Kama to Voinjama, and then to Monrovia, where they would be sold to foreign traders (UNSC 2000a). During the late 1990s, smuggling earned the RUF an estimated US$25 million to US$125 million annually (UNSC 2000a), enabling it to purchase illegal arms from Taylor (Ndumbe and Cole 2005). SLA soldiers—known as *sobels*—were also involved in smuggling, sometimes in cooperation with the rebels (Keen 2000).[12] In addition to overseeing a vast smuggling operation, Taylor appeared to have broader economic and political ambitions (Gberie 2002): his ultimate goal was to institute a form of pan-Africanism and to completely root out any colonial influence in West Africa (ICG 2002). Because of Taylor's involvement, the civil wars of Sierra Leone and Liberia remained closely tied, and diamonds continued to fuel both conflicts.[13]

In July 1997, Taylor was elected president of Liberia, winning approximately 75 percent of the vote. His win may have been attributed, in large part, to the fear that if he lost, he would have resumed the conflict: one of his campaign slogans was "He killed my Ma, he killed my Pa, I will vote for him" (Polgreen 2006). In February 1998, Nigerian forces from the Economic Community of West African States Cease-Fire Monitoring Group (ECOMOG) drove the AFRC/RUF alliance out of Freetown. Kabbah's exiled government was reinstated in May, but the AFRC/RUF militias continued their attacks in the countryside and had regained control of the diamond-rich Kono region by late 1998 (Gberie 2002). Throughout that year, there were increasing reports that both the AFRC/RUF and the CDF/Kamajors were engaging in atrocities and using forced labor, particularly in the AFRC/RUF-controlled Koidu diamond area (Human Rights Watch 1998). Meanwhile, documentation of atrocities by the media and by nongovernmental organizations (NGOs) galvanized the international community, which turned its

---

[11] For example, between 1994 and 1998, Liberian diamond-mining output was estimated at 100,000 to 150,000 carats per year, at most, but during those same years, the Diamond High Council in Antwerp (HRD) recorded Liberian imports to Belgium of over 31 million carats—an average of over 6 million carats per year.

[12] *Sobel* means "soldier by day and rebel by night."

[13] After fighting the Liberian civil war from 1989 to 1996, Taylor became president of Liberia in 1997. Even after August 2003, when Taylor went into exile in Nigeria, he remained a destabilizing force, particularly in Côte d'Ivoire, Ghana, Guinea, Nigeria, and Sierra Leone (Global Witness 2005).

attention not only to blood diamonds but also to the illegal weapons trade that was undermining state security.

In early 1999, the AFRC/RUF attacked Freetown, killing approximately 6,000 and mutilating thousands more (Gberie 2002). Eventually, ECOMOG pushed the rebels out of the city, preserving the Kabbah government. But in the absence of international intervention and amid waning Nigerian support for ECOMOG troops, the weakened government could not continue fighting with the AFRC/RUF; on July 7, 1999, the government of Sierra Leone and the rebels signed the Lomé Peace Agreement (ICG 2001b). The agreement included the following elements:

- The RUF was legitimized and granted a role in the government.[14]
- ECOMOG forces were to depart, to be replaced by the United Nations Assistance Mission in Sierra Leone (UNAMSIL), a peacekeeping mission.[15]
- The RUF were given four cabinet positions, several ambassadorships, and several director-level positions in the public sector (GOSL and RUF 1999; ICG 2001b).
- Foday Sankoh would be given the status of vice president and would serve as chairman of the board of the Commission for the Management of Strategic Resources, National Reconstruction and Development (GOSL and RUF 1999).

In 2000, Partnership Africa Canada (PAC) released a report, *The Heart of the Matter: Sierra Leone, Diamonds & Human Security*, that demonstrated the nexus between illicit diamonds and the weapons trade on the one hand, and the undermining of state security and the commission of atrocities on the other (PAC 2000b). Although the impact was not immediate, the report eventually had profound effects on the diamond industry, fueling international efforts—particularly on the part of the UN Security Council (UNSC)—to curtail the trade in blood diamonds.[16] In the wake of the Lomé Peace Agreement, the UNSC appointed a panel of experts to investigate the connections between the civil war and the illicit diamond trade. The panel's findings, released in December 2000, were similar to those of the PAC report.

In July 2000, through Resolution 1306, the UNSC imposed sanctions on diamond exports from Sierra Leone unless they were accompanied by a certificate of origin (UNSC 2000b). Meanwhile, recognizing the connections between

---

[14] The Lomé Peace Agreement marginalized the AFRC.
[15] Under the Lomé Peace Agreement, the United Nations Observer Mission in Sierra Leone (UNOMSIL) initially shared monitoring responsibilities with ECOMOG. In October 1999, UNOMSIL was succeeded by UNAMSIL, which would eventually deploy 17,000 troops (Gberie 2002).
[16] In 1998, Global Witness, an NGO based in the United Kingdom, released a similar report on the links between the diamond trade and the Angolan civil war: *A Rough Trade: The Role of Companies and Governments in the Angolan Conflict* (Global Witness 1998).

diamonds and civil war in both Angola and Sierra Leone, the international community initiated discussions in Kimberley, South Africa, on how to control the trade in conflict diamonds.[17]

In May 2000, within days of the departure of ECOMOG troops, the RUF captured five hundred peacekeeping troops that had ventured into an RUF-controlled area and held them hostage. That same month, Sankoh was arrested, and documents were recovered that allegedly proved his involvement in the illicit diamond trade. By July, the international community had finally pressured Taylor (who was known to have direct influence over the RUF) and the RUF to release the hostages (ICG 2001b). In November 2000, the RUF and the government negotiated a cease-fire agreement in Abuja, Nigeria, known as the Abuja I Agreement. Nevertheless, RUF forces (including the interim leader Issa Sesay) continued to smuggle rough diamonds; there were also unverified reports that some individual peacekeepers were involved in the illegal diamond trade (Gberie 2002).[18]

In a change of tone, however, the RUF agreed to meet with the UN and the government of Sierra Leone; the result of that meeting was the Abuja II Agreement of May 2, 2001. The RUF consented to disarm, in accordance with the Lomé Peace Agreement, and dropped its requirement that the SLA disarm as well (ICG 2001a). The Abuja II Agreement also set the stage for the resumption, on a wide scale, of disarmament, demobilization, and reintegration; as disarmament progressed, the government gradually regained control of former rebel territory (U.S. Department of State 2010).

In March 2001, through Resolution 1343, the UNSC had banned diamond exports from Liberia; the sanctions became effective five days after the signing of the Abuja II Agreement. In July of the same year, the RUF, the government, and the UN agreed to ban diamond mining in the Kono district, which had been viewed as a cause of the country's civil war; the ban was not implemented, however (Amnesty International USA 2002). With Taylor under international scrutiny, the UN imposed arms embargoes and created barriers to diamond smuggling,[19] thereby making Taylor's war—both in Sierra Leone and in Liberia—much more expensive,[20] and cutting off the RUF's lifeline to Liberia.

---

[17] For more information on what became known as the Kimberley Process, see, in this volume, Clive Wright, "The Kimberley Process Certification Scheme: A model Negotiation?"

[18] Gberie cites reports that individual UNAMSIL peacekeepers were involved in RUF diamond trading (Gberie 2002). Interviews of Kono residents undertaken by the author in 2008 suggest that individual ECOMOG peacekeepers were also involved in diamond trading.

[19] UNSC Resolution 788, of November 1992, imposed an arms embargo on Liberia that ended in March 2001; the embargo was imposed again in May 2001 (by Resolution 1343) and extended in May 2002 and May 2003 (by resolutions 1408 and 1478, respectively) (UNSC 1992, 2001, 2002, 2003). Smuggling was addressed by Resolution 1343, which banned diamond exports from Liberia (SIPRI 2010).

[20] With his war funds diminished significantly, Taylor then faced an insurgency struggling for control of Liberia.

In the wake of the attacks on the United States on September 11, 2001, money laundering—some of which occurred through the illegal diamond trade—surfaced as a source of funding for terrorism (Farah 2001; Global Witness 2003). The United States increased pressure on UNAMSIL to accelerate disarmament, demobilization, and reintegration and enforce the diamond-mining ban (Gberie 2002). By early 2002, approximately 72,000 former combatants had been disarmed and demobilized and were in the process of reintegration (U.S. Department of State 2010; UNDDR Resource Center n.d.).[21]

On January 18, 2002, President Kabbah declared the civil war officially over (U.S. Department of State 2010), and in May 2002, the SLPP and President Kabbah were reelected in a landslide. The Revolutionary United Front Party, the RUF's political arm, received less than 2 percent of the vote and failed to win any seats in parliament (Gberie 2002). After the election, Kabbah turned his attention to economic recovery and sustainable development. The government regarded the diamond sector, on both macro and micro scales, as key to economic growth. By the end of 2005, UNAMSIL had completed its mission in Sierra Leone and was replaced by the UN Integrated Office for Sierra Leone (UNIOSIL), a peacebuilding mission (UNSC 2005). In 2008, UNIOSIL was succeeded by UNIPSIL, the UN Integrated Peacebuilding Office in Sierra Leone (UNSC 2008).

DIAMONDS AND PEACE

Though the conflict ended in 2002, several years would pass before Sierra Leone would realize government revenue through the legal diamond trade. As noted earlier, Sierra Leone has used three approaches to the management of the diamond industry: the Diamond Area Community Development Fund (DACDF), which marshals diamond wealth for post-war peacebuilding; the Kimberley Process Certification Scheme (KPCS), which addresses the connections between diamonds and violent conflict;[22] and kimberlite mining, which has the potential to boost economic growth at a national scale.

The Diamond Area Community Development Fund

Returning revenues to communities and ensuring that they have a say in their own development are essential means of preserving peace. Under the provisions

---

[21] However, several hundred ex-RUF and ex-CDF soldiers either joined Taylor in Liberia or joined Liberians United for Reconciliation and Democracy, his opponents in Liberia's civil war (Gberie 2002).

[22] For additional perspectives on the DACDF and the KPCS, see Roy Maconachie, "The Diamond Area Community Development Fund: Micropolitics and Community-led Development in Post-war Sierra Leone"; J. Andrew Grant, "The Kimberley Process at Ten: Reflections on a Decade of Efforts to End the Trade in Conflict Diamonds"; and Harrison Mitchell, "A More Formal Engagement: A Constructive Critique of Certification as a Means of Preventing Conflict and Building Peace," all in this volume.

of the DACDF, 0.75 percent of the total value of diamond exports is allocated to mining communities. Through the fund, between 2001 and 2006, the government distributed approximately US$3.5 million to chiefdoms where mining occurs (MMR n.d.).[23] Allocations are based on the number of diamond-mining licenses issued and on the value of the diamonds extracted from the territory (MMR 2008a).

One of the goals of the fund is to support local participation in decision making about natural resources and development, and to thereby address the grievances of mining communities—particularly those of marginalized youth.[24] Alisha Eisenstein and Paul Temple (2008) have found that there is indeed a remarkable difference in socioeconomic development between DACDF chiefdoms and non-DACDF ones, and that the fund did create opportunities for youth. For example, reconstructed schools have supported education; guesthouses built with DACDF funds have created employment; and community centers are helping to generate income and "promote peaceful coexistence" (Eisenstein and Temple 2008, 28).

On the other hand, the fund has not been free of criticism. Charges of misappropriation and lack of accountability led to the suspension of disbursements in 2006 (PAC and Network Movement for Justice and Development 2006).[25] New operational procedures and guidelines for the DACDF, introduced in 2008, require more participatory and democratic planning, as well as monitoring and evaluation.

The Kimberley Process Certification Scheme

The KPCS, which requires its members to "certify shipments of rough diamonds as 'conflict-free'" (Kimberley Process n.d.), came into force on January 1, 2003; as a signatory, Sierra Leone implemented the KPCS in its diamond sector.[26] As

---

[23] Sierra Leone is divided into three provinces, each of which consists of several districts. Each district is composed of chiefdoms, which were the basic administrative units during the British protectorate. Each chiefdom is ruled by a paramount chief, with the support of a chiefdom council (chiefdom councils were known as "tribal authorities" before independence) (Fanthorpe 2001, 379).

[24] The fund also indirectly supports the KPCS. As Roy Maconachie has noted, "in addition to providing valuable resources for social and economic development, the fund is supposed to encourage chiefdoms to monitor mining more effectively and eradicate illegal activities, thereby enhancing the [KPCS]" (Maconachie 2009, 75).

[25] For more information on this issue, see Roy Maconachie, "The Diamond Area Community Development Fund: Micropolitics and Community-led Development in Post-war Sierra Leone," in this volume.

[26] With the assistance of Belgium's Diamond High Council, Sierra Leone had earlier implemented its own diamond certification scheme, which began operating in October 2000 (Diamond High Council and Antwerp World Diamond Center 2000).

of December 2009, the KPCS had forty-nine members representing seventy-five countries (Kimberley Process n.d.).

Although international NGOs have raised questions about monitoring and auditing (PAC and Network Movement for Justice and Development 2006; PAC and Global Witness 2005), since the certification scheme was put in place the value of diamonds legally exported from Sierra Leone has skyrocketed from US$10 million in 2000 to US$142 million in 2007 (MMR 2010).[27] It is thus clear that Sierra Leone's participation in the KPCS has reduced diamond smuggling, increased government revenues, and constrained the shadow state.

Kimberlite mining

Kimberlite mining is expected to play an important role in peacebuilding by increasing government revenues, attracting foreign investment, and creating employment. The government of Sierra Leone believes that kimberlite mining has the potential to produce up to 450,000 carats per year (M'cleod 2008)—a significant contribution, given that total exports in 2008 amounted to 40,399 carats (Government Gold and Diamond Office 2008). Nevertheless, kimberlite mining has not been without problems. Although the category of conflict most commonly associated with conflict diamonds is armed violence that is intended to undermine legitimate government, other types of conflict—of which the kimberlite riot is an example—can pose grave threats to mining communities.

THE KIMBERLITE RIOT

On December 13, 2007, a clash between Koidu Holdings, a kimberlite mining venture, and residents of the nearby communities left two dead.[28] Had both sides been armed, there would have been many more casualties. As noted earlier, such conflicts can undermine long-term peace in Sierra Leone; it is therefore important to understand the origins and aftermath of the clash.

---

[27] Total diamond-export values for 2001 through 2006 were as follows: 2001, US$26 million; 2002, US$41.7 million; 2003, US$76 million; 2004, US$126.7 million; 2005, US$142 million; and 2006, US$125 million. In 2008 and 2009, exports declined to US$99 million and US$80 million, respectively (MMR 2010). Though diamond smuggling has allegedly increased (*Global Times* 2011), there has been a drop in diamond mining in general. The decline has been attributed to (1) lower market prices, (2) a drop in local investment (which had been largely supported by Lebanese diamond traders, many of whom closed down their businesses), and (3) increased export taxes (a November 2009 law increased export taxes on all diamonds to 6.5 percent, and taxed individual stones worth more than US$500,000 at 15 percent) (Reuters 2010a, 2010b).

[28] The Koidu kimberlite mining-lease area includes three towns in Tankoro Chiefdom (Swarray, Sokogbeh, and Saquee), as well as Manjamadu Town, which is located at the project boundary (Digby Wells & Associates and CEMMATS 2003).

Background

Originally created in September 2003, through a joint venture agreement between Diamond Works, Branch Energy Ltd.,[29] and Magma Diamond Resource Ltd., Koidu Holdings is now owned by BSGR Diamonds Ltd., a wholly owned subsidiary of BSG Resources Ltd. (Koidu Holdings S.A. n.d.a).[30] The company operates primarily in the Kono district under a twenty-five-year mining lease signed in 1995 (MMR 2008b). Under the Profit-Sharing Agreement between Koidu Holdings and the government of Sierra Leone, Koidu Holdings pays out 20 percent of its net profit: 10 percent to the government and 10 percent to the Koidu Community Trust (Jenkins-Johnston Commission of Inquiry 2008; Koidu Holdings S.A. n.d.b.).[31]

Before the mining started, an environmental and social impact assessment had identified a number of anticipated positive impacts: regional development, economic opportunities, increased household income and social welfare, and greater political representation for the affected communities at the national level. But the assessment also anticipated a number of negative impacts, including forced relocation from the mining sites, an influx of people into the area, land degradation (through erosion and loss of vegetation), a decrease in biodiversity, an overall reduction in water quality, and air and noise pollution (Digby Wells & Associates and CEMMATS 2003).

Discontent among community residents ultimately led to the clash in December 2007.[32] On November 15 of that year, the Affected Property Owners Association (APOA) had submitted a fourteen-point resolution listing its grievances and concerns to a number of parties, including the Ministry of Mineral Resources (MMR), the president and vice president of Sierra Leone, the paramount chief of Tankoro Chiefdom, the local unit commander for the Tankoro Chiefdom

---

[29] In 1996, Diamond Works, a company listed on the Toronto Stock Exchange, acquired Branch Energy Ltd. and its entire mineral rights. But in May 1997, after a coup in Sierra Leone, Diamond Works was forced to halt its activities. Over the ensuing five years of conflict, the company's assets at Koidu were completely destroyed, and no further exploration could be undertaken. In 2002, after the war had ended, Diamond Works returned to Sierra Leone and began to restore facilities that had been damaged during the war (Koidu Holdings S.A. n.d.a).

[30] BSG Resources Ltd. is a resource arm of the Beny Steinmetz Group (BSG), a privately owned holding company based in Geneva.

[31] The precise numbers are difficult to confirm. The Profit-Sharing Agreement does not appear to be publicly available. Moreover, as will be noted later in the chapter, Jan Joubert, the CEO of Koidu Holdings, testified to the Jenkins-Johnston Commission of Inquiry that the company paid US$10.2 million, out of US$108 million, of "revenue" to the Koidu Community Trust, which is not 10 percent. The commission report also found that Koidu Holdings had paid US$9.5 million, out of US$86 million, of "income" to the government, which is 11 percent, not 10 percent.

[32] Unless otherwise specified, the description of the events is based on the author's August 2008 interviews with representatives of the Affected Property Owners Association.

police, and the chief executive officer of Koidu Holdings. On November 23, 2007, the APOA notified the recipients of the resolution of its intent to stage a peaceful demonstration in twenty-one days (that is, on December 14) if the government and other parties failed to address the resettlement action plan proposed by the APOA. The APOA further stated that it wished to negotiate with the company as soon as possible (Jenkins-Johnston Commission of Inquiry 2008).

Not only did the company ignore the APOA's request for negotiations, but it also announced its intention to carry out blasting on December 13. In response, the APOA staged a peaceful demonstration on that day, outside the company grounds. At about 2:30 in the afternoon, the company sounded a siren; at 3:45, it began blasting, before the demonstrators had been evacuated. When the demonstrators began stoning the company premises, the police responded with tear gas and rifle bullets, killing two and injuring dozens. The crowd then burned two police posts to the ground (Jenkins-Johnston Commission of Inquiry 2008). On December 17, representatives from the company and the affected communities were invited to attend a meeting of the Jenkins-Johnston Commission of Inquiry, which was held at the statehouse in Freetown. That same day, the government ordered the company to suspend operations.

In March 2008, the commission of inquiry released a report with recommendations, most of which the government accepted in a subsequent white paper (GOSL 2008). The MMR set up a committee—consisting of the director of the Mines Division of the MMR, the paramount chief, and representatives of the APOA and civil society, among others—to focus on (1) the reopening of the mining operation and (2) compensation for those who had been injured and for the families of those who had been killed. On July 31, 2009,

> a Resettlement Action Plan was signed between the government, Koidu Holdings, CEMMATS and the APOA after crop compensation of over $700,000 was paid to the affected crop owners.... There is now a standing village resettlement committee, which includes all stakeholders, working with CEMMATS to implement the Resettlement Action Plan and to address issues on the ground (Koroma 2009).[33]

The causes of the riot

The commission of inquiry identified two immediate and proximate causes for the riot: (1) the blasting and (2) poor organization and deployment on the part of the police. But the commission identified tension between the company and the communities as the root cause.

---

[33] CEMMATS is a multidisciplinary engineering and project management firm based in Sierra Leone.

Immediate causes

The commission of inquiry found that the company had conducted blasting despite the presence of a crowd of people immediately outside its premises.[34] With respect to the behavior of the police, the situation was more complicated. According to witness testimony, all staff of the Tankoro police station are under the control of the local unit commander. But there is a second police presence in the area: an operational support division (OSD), based in Freetown, whose area of operation includes Tankoro Chiefdom. The local unit commander of the Tankoro police testified that the OSD is deployed at Koidu Holdings and is under the operational control of the company, not that of the local police commander. On the day of the riot, officers from both the Tankoro police and the OSD were on site, along with the local unit commander and two OSD commanders. The OSD officers were armed; the Tankoro police were not (Jenkins-Johnston Commission of Inquiry 2008).

After the local unit commander and one OSD commander had left the site, an OSD officer opened fire, and other officers also started shooting. The OSD commander who had remained at the site testified that the officers were shooting in order to "stop" the riot, but he also stated that "there is no difference between shooting to stop and shooting to kill" (Jenkins-Johnston Commission of Inquiry 2008, 56). Thus, the main factor that led to the two deaths was the failure of the OSD officers to adhere to their rules of engagement—that is, the fact that they shot without orders.[35]

Root causes

With respect to root causes, the commission raised a number of issues, four of which will be examined here:

- Relocation and resettlement.
- Forced evacuation before blasting.

---

[34] Regarding this point, the commission's report states that "the untimely death... could have been avoided if the Koidu Holdings Company had shown a little bit of restraint and sensitivity towards the Demonstrators and Evacuees by not proceeding with the blasting on 13/12/07" (Jenkins-Johnston Commission of Inquiry 2008, 88–89).

[35] According to the director of the OSD, Sierra Leone police provided security for a number of mining companies, including Koidu Holdings, Sierra Rutile, and Sierra Leone Diamond Company (Jenkins-Johnston Commission of Inquiry 2008)—which means that poor coordination between local police and the OSD could potentially have the same results witnessed at Koidu Holdings. (As of this writing, the OSD is no longer deployed at the Sierra Leone Diamond Company.)

- Lack of community benefits (including revenue sharing).[36]
- Lack of community participation.[37]

All four issues were addressed by the commission's recommendations, but implementation of the recommendations did not begin until July 2009, when the new resettlement action plan was signed.

The stage was set for relocation issues as far back as the 1960s, when the SLST had undertaken exploration to determine the exact location of the Kono kimberlite pipes (PAC and Network Movement for Justice and Development 2005).[38] In the wake of the exploration, residential dwellings were prohibited in the kimberlite deposit area, but the SLST failed to enclose the area; as a consequence, by 1995, when Branch Energy was granted a twenty-five-year mining lease, there were more houses in the prohibited zones than there would have been if SLST had effectively closed off the area. The situation was further complicated by the lack of explicit legal procedures for relocation. Although the 1994 Mines and Minerals Decree allows for relocation, it includes no formal procedures; companies and communities are left on their own to decide how relocation will occur (NPRC 1994).

By 2003, about 4,500 people (284 households) were living in the mining-lease area of Koidu Holdings (Digby Wells & Associates and CEMMATS 2003). Though these dwellings could have been regarded as illegal (PAC and Network Movement for Justice and Development 2005), Digby Wells & Associates and CEMMATS—the consulting firms that had conducted the environmental impact assessment, created the resettlement action plan, and conducted the public disclosure and consultation process for the project—had concluded that "all households that own/occupy a household plot, have formal and legal rights to land and assets, and who are affected by mining activities requiring resettlement,

---

[36] Both the Commission of Inquiry and the Kono residents interviewed by the author were inconsistent in their use of "revenue" versus "profit." To maintain the coherence of the discussion, the chapter will use "revenue" except in the case of direct references to the Profit-Sharing Agreement signed on August 28, 2006.

[37] The commission of inquiry also criticized the MMR and the Ministry of the Environment for not having known (1) that Koidu Holdings' engineers did not have a valid blasting certificate or (2) that the company was using an environmental impact assessment license issued in the name of Branch Energy. The commission also claimed that the fiscal regime was unsatisfactory, in that it failed to provide an appropriate income for either the government or the communities (Jenkins-Johnston Commission of Inquiry 2008). Because the relevant exhibits were unavailable for review, the author could not confirm that the commission's statements were justified by the facts.

[38] Diamonds form more than 150 kilometers below the earth's surface and are then pushed upward by volcanic activity; during this process, underground pipes (known as *kimberlite* or *kimberlite pipes*) form. The pipes are shaped like champagne flutes and are composed of magma, minerals, and rock fragments.

will be eligible for full assistance and compensation" (Digby Wells & Associates and CEMMATS 2003, 13).

One reason that the company decided to use vertical, rather than open-pit mining, was to reduce environmental and social impacts, including relocation and resettlement issues (Koidu Holdings S.A. 2006).[39] Nevertheless, residents remained deeply discontented with the relocation arrangements. For example, among the findings of the commission of inquiry were the following:

- Koidu Holdings had failed to relocate and resettle all 284 of the affected households before the blasting started.
- The company should have constructed as many as 360 houses for the resettlement of affected residents but had built only 70 houses—all of which were of substandard quality, and none of which had a kitchen, bathroom, toilet, or running water.
- The resettlement village that the company built had no social amenities such as a market, school, church, or mosque (Jenkins-Johnston Commission of Inquiry 2008).[40]

The second problem identified by the commission of inquiry, forced evacuation before blasting, was related to the lack of proper resettlement arrangements. Since most of the 284 affected households had not been relocated, they had been evacuated by company security and police—who had in some cases used harsh methods—before December 13, 2007. This treatment intensified residents' resentment of both the company and the police (Jenkins-Johnston Commission of Inquiry 2008).

The third problem identified by the commission of inquiry was that local residents had seen few benefits from mining. Jan Joubert, the chief executive officer of Koidu Holdings, testified that the company paid US$10.2 million out of US$108 million of revenue to the Koidu Community Trust;[41] he also noted that the company had provided employment for six hundred people; supported an agricultural development fund; helped provide scholarships for children to attend school; sent two community members to be trained as agriculturalists; and provided clean drinking water (Jenkins-Johnston Commission of Inquiry 2008). Nevertheless, as one APOA member said, "the company does not do enough to the community. . . . we have not seen much development." With respect to revenue sharing, another APOA member noted that the company's operations are "not

---

[39] Vertical mining requires much less land area (in the case of Koidu Holdings, approximately 4,388 square meters, just over half the size of a soccer field), thus reducing environmental and social impacts (Koidu Holdings n.d.c.).

[40] The commission's findings were confirmed by the author's interviews with representatives of the APOA.

[41] The report also found that Koidu Holdings paid US$9.5 million out of US$86 million of "income" to the government.

transparent.... There is too much secrecy in the company. We have no choice but to guess. We need more transparent and accurate information." There was thus concern not only about insufficient benefits, but also about the lack of transparency regarding revenue sharing and expenditures on community benefits.

As the fourth root cause of the riot, the commission of inquiry pointed to the government's failure to obtain the legitimate participation of the local community: neither the paramount chief nor any resident of the chiefdom had been involved in the negotiation or signing of the agreements with Koidu Holdings (Jenkins-Johnston Commission of Inquiry 2008).[42] According to one chiefdom resident, "The negotiation with the company was dealt with by the central government without consultation of the local community. The government allocated land to the company without approval of the community."[43] Before the agreement was signed, the government threatened the community, in order to compel it to accept the mining (Jenkins-Johnston Commission of Inquiry 2008). One resident stated, for example, that he had been arrested after having publicly expressed his refusal to accept the mining (Jenkins-Johnston Commission of Inquiry 2008). In the end, it was not the local community or a local authority but the MMR that approved the transfer of the mining lease from Branch Energy to Koidu Holdings and that signed as a party in the Profit-Sharing Agreement (Jenkins-Johnston Commission of Inquiry 2008).

LESSONS LEARNED

What can be learned from Sierra Leone's efforts to manage its diamond resources in ways that will support peace? Overall, the DACDF and the KPCS have contributed to peacebuilding: the first by alleviating grievances, and the second by dramatically boosting legitimate exports. In the years leading up to the war, diamond-mining communities were among the poorest in the country, and marginalized youth in those areas offered fertile ground for RUF recruiters. The DACDF has transferred a substantial amount of diamond revenues to local communities; though grievances remain, infrastructure has been constructed, and educational and job opportunities for youth have increased. The KPCS has considerably reduced diamond smuggling from Sierra Leone, increasing the government's revenues from diamond exports and undermining the shadow state.

Although kimberlite mining has the potential to increase government revenues and thereby support peace, it can also destabilize local communities, as the riot of December 2007 attests. Such problems are not unique to Sierra Leone.

---

[42] The commission was referring to three agreements: the Koidu Kimberlite Project Mining Lease Agreement (Mining Lease No. ML 6/95), the Transfer of the Mining Lease Agreement (October 20, 2003), and the Profit-Sharing Agreement (August 28, 2006).
[43] Interview with the author, Kono, Sierra Leone, August 21, 2008.

In Botswana, for example, which is often cited as an example of successful economic development through kimberlite mining, the government allegedly coerced the San (Basarwa), an indigenous minority tribe, to relocate by halting public services for those who refused (Mokhawa 2005).

The kimberlite riot offers several lessons for the mitigation of potential conflict.

- To support relocation, companies must provide a sufficient number of houses whose quality and design are acceptable to the relocated households. The resettlement community must also be far enough away from the mining operation to minimize the effects of blasting.
- The resettlement community should include amenities such as schools and clinics. Although the provision of such amenities is ultimately the government's responsibility, the government would not have to construct additional schools and clinics if it were not for the presence of the mine, so the company should provide some degree of financial support.
- Arrangements for revenue sharing and for the use of revenues to benefit the community must be transparent: specifically, communities should be told what the total revenues are; what percentage of revenues will be transferred to the central government, to the local government, and directly to communities; and how the central and local governments will spend funds on behalf of the communities.
- Local residents must participate in planning, implementing, and monitoring mining projects (Ajei 2008); this includes direct involvement in negotiations and in the execution of both the mining lease and revenue-sharing agreements. No legal agreements should be made without community consensus.

Recognizing the significance of these lessons, the government of Sierra Leone accepted most of the recommendations of the commission of inquiry and established a stakeholder committee to determine compensation for injuries and deaths and to develop a new resettlement plan.

The development community has also taken note of what occurred in Sierra Leone. By commissioning a report on relocation policy, the World Bank has supported capacity building within Sierra Leone's government and mining sector (Ajei 2008).[44] In February 2008, Sierra Leone became an Extractive Industries Transparency Initiative (EITI) candidate; as a consequence, large-scale mining companies will have to meet higher standards of accountability. On March 25, 2010, Sierra Leone published its first EITI reconciliation report, which covers payments made between January 2006 and December 2007 to the central and

---

[44] The findings of the World Bank report on relocation policy in Sierra Leone were in keeping with those of the commission of inquiry: local residents should be involved from the beginning in planning, implementation, monitoring, and evaluation of projects (Ajei 2008).

local governments by six industrial mining companies (including Koidu Holdings) and three "exporters/dealers" (Verdi Consulting 2010).[45]

The lessons of the kimberlite riot are also applicable to the large-scale extraction of other mineral resources. Sierra Leone is expanding industrial mining to include rutile, bauxite, and iron ore, and will need to ensure that the kimberlite lessons are applied in those settings as well.

CONCLUSION

It remains to be seen whether and how diamonds will help build peace in Sierra Leone. All three approaches—the DACDF, the KPCS, and kimberlite mining—have potential problems: for example, if the DACDF benefits a handful of elites, if the KPCS overlooks loopholes, and if communities' grievances against kimberlite mining companies are not resolved, diamonds will not help achieve a lasting peace. The government of Sierra Leone, national and international NGOs, donor nations and agencies, and international organizations are well aware of the lessons of the DACDF, the KPCS, and kimberlite mining. What matters most is how those lessons will be put into practice in the future.

REFERENCES

Abdullah, I. 1998. Bush path to destruction: The origin and character of the Revolutionary United Front/Sierra Leone. *Journal of Modern African Studies* 36 (2): 203–235.

Ajei, M. O. 2008. Government of Sierra Leone/World Bank mining sector technical assistance project: Resettlement policy framework final draft. Nimba Research & Consultancy Co. Ltd. www.slmineralresources.org/int_perspective/WB_resettlement_framework.pdf.

Amnesty International USA. 2002. 2002 *Annual report for Sierra Leone*. www.amnestyusa.org/annualreport.php?id=ar&yr=2002&c=SLE.

Diamond High Council and Antwerp World Diamond Center. 2000. *Progress report*. Conflict diamonds: Analyses, actions, solutions. www.conflictdiamonds.com/pages/Interface/reportframe.html.

Digby Wells & Associates and CEMMATS. 2003. *Summary document for the environmental and social studies for the Koidu kimberlite project Sierra Leone Koidu Holdings S.A.* Vol. 3. October. Randburg, South Africa: Digby Wells & Associates; Freetown, Sierra Leone: CEMMATS.

---

[45] The report found discrepancies between government revenues and payments from companies to the government of US$220,155 in 2006 and US$235,151 in 2007. The report further noted that these discrepancies represented 5.15 percent and 2.62 percent of total payments reported for 2006 and 2007, respectively. The discrepancies were attributed to the failure of government entities to accurately report revenue, companies' failure to substantiate their reports, and insufficient documentation for reported payments (Verdi Consulting 2010). The report concluded that the process of engaging the government, the companies, and the people in the EITI process was a successful first step in promoting transparency and accountability in the government of Sierra Leone.

Eisenstein, A., and P. Temple. 2008. Sierra Leone integrated diamond management program: Final program report. http://pdf.usaid.gov/pdf_docs/PDACL735.pdf.

Fanthorpe, R. 2001. Neither citizen nor subject? "Lumpen" agency and the legacy of native administration in Sierra Leone. *African Affairs* 100 (400): 363–386.

Farah, D. 2001. Al Qaeda cash tied to diamond trade: Sale of gems from Sierra Leone rebels raised millions, sources say. *Washington Post*, November 2. www.washingtonpost.com/ac2/wp-dyn/A27281-2001Nov1.

Francis, D. 2005. *Civil militia: Africa's intractable security menace?* Aldershot, UK: Ashgate Publishing.

Gberie, L. 2002. *War and peace in Sierra Leone: Diamonds, corruption, and the Lebanese connection.* Ottawa: Partnership Africa Canada. www.pacweb.org/Documents/diamonds_KP/6_War-Peace_sierraleone_Eng-Nov2002.pdf.

Gibrill, H. 2007. The disintegration and restoration of state authority in Sierra Leone. In *Beyond state failure and collapse: Making the state relevant in Africa*, ed. G. K. Kieh. Lanham, MD: Lexington Books.

Global Times. 2011. Diamond smuggling intensifies. www.globaltimes-sl.org/news1337.html.

Global Witness. 1998. *A rough trade: The role of companies and governments in the Angolan conflict.* www.globalwitness.org/media_library_detail.php/90/en/a_rough_trade.

———. 2003. *For a few dollars more: How al Qaeda moved into the diamond trade.* www.globalwitness.org/media_library_detail.php/109/en/for_a_few_dollars_more.

———. 2005. *Timber, Taylor, soldier, spy: How Liberia's uncontrolled resource exploitation, Charles Taylor's manipulation and the re-recruitment of ex-combatants are threatening regional peace.* A report submitted to the UN Security Council by Global Witness. June. www.globalwitness.org/media_library_get.php/237/1257352721/TimberTaylorSoldierSpy.pdf.

Global Witness and PAC (Partnership Africa Canada). 2004. *Rich man, poor man: Development diamonds and poverty diamonds; The potential for change in the artisanal alluvial diamond fields of Africa.* www.globalwitness.org/media_library_get.php/223/1257353826/RichManPoorManenglish.pdf.

GOSL (Government of Sierra Leone). 2008. *The government white paper on the report of the Jenkins-Johnston Commission of Inquiry into the events leading to the disturbances in Koidu City on the 13th December 2007, which resulted in the death of two persons and injuries to a number of other reasons under the chairmanship of Mr. Blyden Jenkins-Johnston, Mr. Ivan C.A. (Member), and Brigadier (RTD) M.K. Dumbuya (Member).* Freetown: GOSL.

GOSL (Government of Sierra Leone) and RUF (Revolutionary United Front of Sierra Leone). 1999. Peace agreement between the government of Sierra Leone and the Revolutionary Front of Sierra Leone. July 7, Lomé, Togo.

Government Gold and Diamond Office. 2008. Diamond exports 2000 to 2008. (On file with author.)

Hirsch, J. L. 2001. *Sierra Leone: Diamonds and the struggle for democracy.* Boulder, CO: Lynne Rienner.

Human Rights Watch. 1998. Sowing terror: Atrocities against civilians in Sierra Leone. *Human Rights Watch Reports* 10 (3)(A). www.hrw.org/legacy/reports98/sierra/.

ICG (International Crisis Group). 2001a. Sierra Leone: Managing uncertainty. *ICG Africa Report* No. 35. October. www.crisisgroup.org/~/media/Files/africa/west-africa/sierra-leone/Sierra%20Leone%20Managing%20Uncertainty.ashx.

———. 2001b. Sierra Leone: Time for a new military and political strategy. *ICG Africa Report* No. 28. April. www.crisisgroup.org/en/regions/africa/west-africa/sierra-leone/028-sierra-leone-time-for-a-new-military-and-political-strategy.aspx.

———. 2002. Liberia: The key to ending regional instability. *ICG Africa Report* No. 43. April. www.crisisgroup.org/~/media/Files/africa/west-africa/liberia/Liberia%20The%20Key%20to%20Ending%20Regional%20Instability.ashx.

IRBC (Immigration and Refugee Board of Canada). 1999. Sierra Leone: Forcible recruitment of members of the Mende tribe. sle32530.E. August 5. www.unhcr.org/refworld/docid/3ae6ad7658.html.

Jenkins-Johnston Commission of Inquiry. 2008. *Report of the Jenkins-Johnston Commission of Inquiry into the events leading to the disturbance at Koidu on the 13th December 2007 which resulted in the death of two (2) persons and injuries to a number of other persons; and the causes of discontent between Koidu Holdings Mining Company and the people of the Tankoro Chiefdom and the surrounding communities wherein they work.* (On file with author.)

Keen, D., 2000. Incentives and disincentives for violence. In *Greed and grievance: Economic agendas in civil wars*, ed. M. Berdal and D. M. Malone. Boulder, CO: Lynne Rienner.

Kimberley Process. n.d. What is the Kimberley Process? www.kimberleyprocess.com/.

Koidu Holdings S.A. 2006. Sierra Leone. *New York Times* special advertising supplement. March 6. www.koiduholdings.com/images/press_releases/2%20Supplement%20to%20the%20New%20York%20Times%206%20March%202006.pdf.

———. n.d.a. Company history. www.koiduholdings.com/about_company_history.html.

———. n.d.b. Profit sharing agreement. www.koiduholdings.com/mining_koidu_profit_sharing.html.

———. n.d.c. Vertical pit development. www.koiduholdings.com/mining_koidu_no1pipe_vertical_pit.html.

Koroma, A. 2009. Some notes and observations. Correspondence with Usman Boie Kamara, director of mines, Sierra Leone. August 18. (On file with author.)

Le Billon, P. 2001. The political ecology of war: Natural resources and armed conflicts. *Political Geography* 20 (5): 561–584.

Maconachie, R. 2008. Diamond mining, governance initiatives and post-conflict development in Sierra Leone. Brooks World Poverty Institute Working Paper No. 50. University of Manchester.

———. 2009. Diamonds, governance and "local" development in post-conflict in Sierra Leone: Lessons for artisanal and small-scale mining in sub-Saharan Africa? *Resources Policy* 34 (1–2): 71–79.

Maconachie, R., and T. Binns. 2007a. Beyond the resource curse? Diamond mining, development and post-conflict reconstruction in Sierra Leone. *Resources Policy* 32 (3): 104–115.

———. 2007b. "Farming miners" or "mining farmers"? Diamond mining and rural development in post-conflict Sierra Leone. *Journal of Rural Studies* 23 (3): 367–380.

M'cleod, H. 2008. Minerals sector reform: Context and economic potential. Presidential workshop: Minerals sector reform. www.slmineralresources.org/docs/pres_wksp_presentations.pdf.

MMR (Ministry of Mineral Resources, Sierra Leone). 2008a. Diamond area community development fund: Stakeholder consultation meeting. July 16. www.slmineralresources.org/docs/DACDF_Presentation_07_2008.ppt.

———. 2008b. *Sierra Leone—Yours to Discover* 1 (1). www.slmineralresources.org/docs/MMR_newsletter_July%202008.pdf.

———. 2010. Sector transparency: Stemming the flow of conflict diamonds—The Kimberley Process. www.slminerals.org/content/index.php?option=com_content&view=article&id=11&Itemid=15.

———. n.d. Allocation disbursed from Jan 2001–Dec 2006 (Le). www.slmineralresources.org/docs/DACDF%20payments%20and%20No%20AM%20Licences.pdf.

Mokhawa, G. 2005. All that glitters is not diamond: The politics of diamond dependence and abundance in Botswana. In *Resource politics in sub-Saharan Africa*, ed. M. Basedau and A. Mehler. Hamburg: Institute of African Affairs.

Ndumbe, J. A., and B. Cole. 2005. The illicit diamond trade, civil conflicts, and terrorism in Africa. *Mediterranean Quarterly* 16 (2): 52–65.

NPRC (National Provisional Ruling Council), Sierra Leone. 1994. The mines and minerals decree, 1994. NPRC Decree No. 5. www.slmineralresources.org/mining_government/sl_mineral_degree94.pdf.

PAC (Partnership Africa Canada) and Global Witness. 2005. Implementing the Kimberley Process: 5 years on—How effective is the Kimberley Process and what more needs to be done? June. www.pacweb.org/e/images/stories/documents/implementing%20kp-5years%20on-june%202005.pdf.

PAC (Partnership Africa Canada) and Network Movement for Justice and Development. 2005. *Diamond industry annual review: Sierra Leone 2005*. Ottawa: Partnership Africa Canada; Freetown: Network Movement for Justice and Development. www.pacweb.org/Documents/annual-reviews-diamonds/SierraLeone_AR_2005-eng.pdf.

———. 2006. *Diamond industry annual review: Sierra Leone 2006*. Ottawa: Partnership Africa Canada; Freetown: Network Movement for Justice and Development. www.pacweb.org/Documents/annual-reviews-diamonds/SierraLeone_AR_2006-eng.pdf.

Polgreen, L. 2006. A master plan drawn in blood. *New York Times*, April 2. www.nytimes.com/2006/04/02/weekinreview/02polgreen.html?pagewanted=print.

Reno, W. 1997. Humanitarian emergencies and warlord economies in Liberia and Sierra Leone. UNU/WIDER Working Papers No. 140. August. Helsinki: United Nations University/World Institute for Development Economics Research. www.wider.unu.edu/publications/working-papers/previous/en_GB/wp-140/_files/82530852723302161/default/WP140.pdf.

———. 2000. Shadow states and the political economy of civil wars. In *Greed and grievance: Economic agendas in civil wars*, ed. M. Berdal and D. M. Malone. Boulder, CO: Lynne Rienner.

———. 2003. Political networks in a failing state: The root and future of violent conflict in Sierra Leone. *Internationale Politik und Gesellschaft* 2 (2003): 44–66.

Reuters. 2010a. Sierra Leone 09 diamond exports drop 20 pct in value. January 26. http://uk.reuters.com/article/idUKLDE60P1YW20100126.

———. 2010b. S. Leone levies 15 pct on high-value diamonds. *Reuters Africa*, January 5. http://af.reuters.com/article/investingNews/idAFJOE6040KQ20100105.

Ross, M. L. 2004. What do we know about natural resources and civil war? *Journal of Peace Research* 41 (3): 337–356.

SIPRI (Stockholm International Peace Research Institute). 2010. UN arms embargo on Liberia. March 8. www.sipri.org/databases/embargoes/un_arms_embargoes/liberia.

Smillie, I., L. Gberie, and R. Hazleton. 2000. *The heart of the matter: Sierra Leone, diamonds & human security (complete report)*. Ottawa: Partnership Africa Canada. www.pacweb.org/Documents/diamonds_KP/heart_of_the_matter-full-2000-01-eng.pdf.

Special Court for Sierra Leone. n.d. The Prosecutor vs. Charles Ghankay Taylor. www.sc-sl.org/CASES/ProsecutorvsCharlesTaylor/tabid/107/Default.aspx.
UNDDR (United Nations Disarmament, Demobilization and Reintegration) Resource Center. n.d. Country programme: Sierra Leone. www.unddr.org/countryprogrammes.php?c=60.
UNSC (United Nations Security Council). 1992. Resolution 788. S/RES/788 (1992). November 19.
———. 2000a. Report of the panel of experts appointed pursuant to Security Council Resolution 1306 (2000), paragraph 19, in relation to Sierra Leone. S/2000/1195. www.un.org/Docs/sc/committees/SierraLeone/sclet11951e.pdf.
———. 2000b. Resolution 1306. S/RES/1306 (2000). July 5. www.undemocracy.com/S-RES-1306(2000).pdf.
———. 2001. Resolution 1343. S/RES/1343 (2001). March 7. www.undemocracy.com/S-RES-1343(2001).pdf.
———. 2002. Resolution 1408. S/RES/1408 (2002). May 6. www.undemocracy.com/S-RES-1408(2002).pdf.
———. 2003. Resolution 1478. S/RES/1478 (2003). May 6. www.undemocracy.com/S-RES-1478(2003).pdf.
———. 2005. Resolution 1620. S/RES/1620 (2005). August 31. www.undemocracy.com/S-RES-1620(2005).pdf.
———. 2008. Resolution 1829. S/RES/1829 (2008). August 4. www.undemocracy.com/S-RES-1829(2008).pdf.
U.S. Department of State, Bureau of African Affairs. 2010. Background note: Sierra Leone. www.state.gov/r/pa/ei/bgn/5475.htm.
Verdi Consulting. 2010. *First Sierra Leone EITI reconciliation report: Final report.* Sierra Leone Extractive Industries Transparency Initiative (SLEITI). March 8. www.sleiti.org/reporting/SLEITI_FIRST_DATA_RECONCILIATION_REPORT.pdf.

Assigned corporate social responsibility in a rentier state: The case of Angola

Arne Wiig and Ivar Kolstad

What responsibilities do oil companies in Angola have to improve the situation of the Angolan population? Standard corporate social responsibility (CSR) projects have little effect where the rents from natural resources entrench the lack of democratic accountability. Since corporations help fuel the Angolan patronage system, this raises the question of whether companies also have a responsibility to address governance in the country. This chapter argues, on the basis of the assigned-responsibility model, that companies do have a responsibility to act to improve governance in Angola. The chapter also argues, however, that because oil companies gain from dysfunctional institutions, they do not adopt this kind of responsibility. Accordingly, incentives will be necessary to change corporate behavior.

Angola is the second-largest producer of oil in sub-Saharan Africa. But despite the country's substantial revenues from oil production, the majority of the Angolan population remains poor. Almost 70 percent of the population lives on less than US$2 a day, and inequality is rampant.[1] Most Angolans lack access to basic health care; primary-school enrollment is at 56 percent; the illiteracy rate is 50 percent in rural areas; and life expectancy at birth is forty-one years (World Bank 2006). In other words, if you were born in Angola, you would probably be poor, lack access to basic health care, have only a one-in-two chance of attending primary school, and expect to die young, despite the country's substantial natural resource revenues.

Angola clearly exhibits the characteristics of the so-called resource curse, in which resources hinder development instead of spurring it. Political economy

---

Arne Wiig is a senior researcher at the Chr. Michelsen Institute (CMI). Ivar Kolstad is research director for the Poverty Reduction Group at CMI.

[1] Angola has a Gini coefficient of 0.62. The Gini coefficient is a measure of the inequality of income distribution in a country. In theory, it ranges from 0 to 1, but in practice it ranges from 0.25 to 0.75. It would be 0 in a country in which everyone's income was precisely equal, and 1 where one person earned everything and everyone else nothing.

models suggest that two kinds of dysfunctional behavior underlie the resource curse: patronage and rent seeking.[2] Empirical results support these models and suggest that the resource curse depends on the condition of institutions: where democratic accountability and the rule of law are weak, resources will have a negative impact; where democratic accountability and the rule of law are strong, resources will have a positive impact (Damania and Bulte 2003; Mehlum, Moene, and Torvik 2006; Kolstad 2009a). Accordingly, lifting the resource curse requires an emphasis on governance—on improving the country's institutions.

Institutions in Angola are extremely weak, partly as the result of more than thirty years of civil war. Angola scores low on indicators of democratic accountability; on the Polity measure of democracy, for example, Angola scores only 2 on a scale of 0 to 10 (Center for Systemic Peace 2007).[3] Before the parliamentary elections held in 2008, the last parliamentary and presidential elections took place in 1992. Patronage is widespread (Hodges 2007), and Angola places 158th out of 180 countries on the 2008 Transparency International Corruption Perceptions Index (Transparency International 2008). Public budgets are nontransparent (Isaksen et al. 2007; International Budget Partnership 2008)—and, apart from political stability, there are few if any political or social indicators that show improvement in the aftermath of the war.

The importance of better institutions is underscored by the fact that access to resources fuelled the civil war and exempted the leadership of the fighting organizations from demands for public legitimacy and accountability (Le Billon 2001).[4] Democratic accountability is vital for a successful peace process, as it not only restricts capture of resource rents—or *greed*, to use the terminology of Paul Collier and Anke Hoeffler (2004)—but also reduces grievance, by affording more people a say in public policies. But the Angolan government does not appear inclined to improve the relevant institutions, and international initiatives

---

[2] See, for example, Robinson, Torvik, and Verdier (2006); Mehlum, Moene, and Torvik (2006); and Kolstad and Wiig (2009b). *Patronage* means that government officials use resource revenues to secure their hold on power. *Rent seeking* occurs when groups or individuals attempt to obtain access to economic benefits without contributing to overall income production. For additional information on rent seeking, see Paul Collier and Anke Hoeffler, "High-Value Natural Resources, Development, and Conflict: Channels of Causation," in this volume.

[3] The Polity Project codes all countries according their state-authority characteristics along two axes: democracy (0–10) and autocracy (0–10); often, the two are combined by subtracting the autocracy score from the democracy score, creating the so-called Polity Score, which has a scale from −10 to 10.

[4] The União Nacional para a Independência Total de Angola (UNITA) and the Movimento Popular para a Libertação de Angola (MPLA) were the two armed groups that controlled diamonds and oil, respectively. Governments that have an alternative revenue source, and therefore do not need to tax the population, do not need to be accountable to it. For additional information on this phenomenon, see Paul Collier and Anke Hoeffler, "High-Value Natural Resources, Development, and Conflict: Channels of Causation," in this volume.

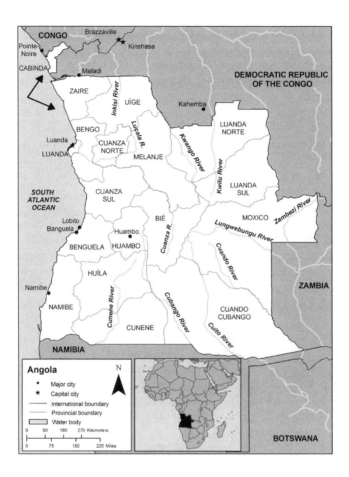

in resource-rich countries have failed to address the key governance issues.[5] The absence of government or other commitment in this area raises the question of whether multinational oil companies have a responsibility to address governance problems. The sections that follow present an ethical argument that multinational corporations have such a responsibility.

THE ASSIGNED-RESPONSIBILITY MODEL

The assigned-responsibility framework proposed by Goodin (1985, 1988) provides a model for delineating the ethical responsibilities of multinational companies in

---

[5] For further elaboration of this point, see Kolstad and Wiig (2009a) and Kolstad, Wiig, and Williams (2009).

addressing institutional and governance failures in countries where they operate.[6] Goodin takes utilitarianism as his point of departure, which states that an action is ethically justified if it maximizes the sum of happiness or utility for all individuals, but the general approach is also amenable to other ethical perspectives (Kolstad 2009b).

The main point is that everyone has general obligations toward everyone else. The best possible state of affairs in terms of total happiness or utility is unlikely to occur, however, if everyone went about thinking about the happiness of everyone else. Some form of specialization is required, where each agent is given a limited set of tasks for which that agent is responsible or a limited number of people to take into account when acting. Our general responsibilities toward everyone else are thus more effectively pursued if we are assigned more limited special responsibilities for certain tasks or people. In other words, ethical theories of this kind imply a division of moral labor.

This raises the question of which responsibilities to allocate to which agents. To have a division of moral labor—that is, an assignment of special responsibilities—that produces the best possible state of affairs, each task should be allocated to the agent who is in the best position to carry out that task. One argument holds that an appropriate division of labor in a society is for public institutions to have responsibility for redistribution and for creating and enforcing the basic rules under which a society operates, and for companies to have responsibility for generating wealth (Kolstad 2006). The state thus has the primary responsibility for alleviating poverty, reducing inequality, providing schooling and health services, and so on. In societies in which this division of moral labor works well, where each party fulfills its assigned responsibilities, there is no reason for companies to pursue redistributive or social tasks.

However, as the case of Angola illustrates, the state does not always shoulder the responsibilities assigned to it under the ideal division of moral labor. In this case, as Robert Goodin argues, these tasks become the "residual responsibility of all," and other agents will then have secondary responsibilities for the task in question (Goodin 1988, 684). This is necessary for the general responsibilities to be met, since if no one stepped in when others defaulted on their obligations, the welfare interests of some individuals would not be adequately protected. In short, if no one addresses the issue of poverty, the poor are in effect not counted in our moral decisions.

When the Angolan state defaults on its responsibilities, it is not immediately apparent that the secondary responsibilities fall on oil companies. More likely candidates are the international community (that is, other states) or civil society. But where these other agents also fail to address these responsibilities, they will eventually fall on corporations. In Angola, the influence of the international donor community is weak and civil society fledgling, which implies that secondary

---

[6] It is beyond the scope of this chapter to give a full exposition of this perspective. For details, see Goodin (1985, 1988).

responsibilities for improving the socioeconomic situation will fall on the multinational oil companies operating in the country. An unwillingness to take on this kind of responsibility means, in effect, that companies attribute no moral weight to poor Angolans.

THE ROLE OF THE OIL COMPANIES

The government's lack of commitment to improving governance has not been met by an increasing eagerness on the part of the oil companies to do so. Oil companies operating in Angola do provide support to education and health initiatives but do not support initiatives related to governance. This is problematic, because in order to have a significant and substantial effect on the socioeconomic situation in Angola, companies would have to address the cause of the problems, which are the dysfunctional institutions. Such an effort would require the oil companies to address the country's governance problems and intervene in its politics.

A 2005 study by John McMillan found that companies have traditionally played a reactive role in making contracts and payments transparent in Angola. And a 2010 study showed that governance is not a priority in oil company CSR policies (Wiig and Kolstad 2010). Instead, companies use CSR strategically to obtain licenses from the Angolan government: that is, CSR is designed to improve the bottom line or to reduce company risk, rather than to improve conditions in the host countries. By using CSR strategically to get licenses and contracts, multinational corporations risk facilitating patronage in resource-rich countries, exacerbating the resource curse (Wiig and Kolstad 2010).

Clearly, the application of the assigned-responsibility argument assumes that multinational oil companies have the capacity to influence governance in a country like Angola. Corporations commonly object that they do not have this type of influence, but this objection is questionable. Large multinational corporations are clearly powerful players in the Angolan economy: they have the technology and expertise on which the extraction of oil depends, and their negotiating skills are often superior to those of their counterparts in the national oil bureaucracy. Moreover, in a number of resource-rich developing countries, large multinationals have been able to bargain for highly favorable terms, and some have also wrought substantial harm on the host country's institutional environment. Thus, corporations should also have the capacity to influence institutions in a more benign way. More importantly, multinational oil companies have considerable collective influence; acting in concert, oil companies could effectively address governance issues. Oil companies already cooperate in other areas—for example, to reduce gas flaring and as license partners.[7] There is hence little doubt that multinational oil companies could have a positive impact on governance in Angola.

---

[7] When oil is produced, gas is often a byproduct. Burning the gas (as waste) causes environmental problems.

As noted earlier, CSR policies are largely dictated by profitability. But what companies profit from is not always in the best interest of society. In Angola, the CSR activities that companies pursue to acquire contracts and licenses are at best irrelevant and at worst counterproductive to inducing the kind of institutional change that would permit Angola to escape the resource curse.

CORPORATIONS, INSTITUTIONS, AND INCENTIVES

The case of Angola calls into question the standard assumption that good institutions are in the interest of corporations—an assumption that ignores the distributive consequences of institutional reform, which are highlighted by a resource-rich context. Institutional reform that shifts resource rents from oil companies to host-country populations may not be in the interest of corporations, individually or collectively. A study by Massimo Guidolin and Eliana La Ferrara (2007) found that as the war in Angola ended, diamond companies active in Angola suffered a decline in their relative stock performance. One possible reason is that ongoing war weakens transparency standards, permitting profitable unofficial dealings. Thus, one might wonder whether corporate inaction on governance reflects the difficulty of engaging in collective action or merely the collective complacency of multinational oil companies.[8]

A durable peace that benefits the Angolan population requires more of a focus on the basic institutional problems of the country—in particular, the lack of democratic accountability. Where the Angolan government and other agents fail to address institutional deficiencies, there is an ethical argument that multinational oil companies are responsible for addressing governance. However, as it is not in the interest of corporations to pursue these kinds of questions, incentives will be needed to persuade the companies to act differently, and to align their interests more closely with those of the population of the countries in which they operate. Current voluntary efforts—such as the Extractive Industries Transparency Initiative, which tracks and publicizes revenue flows between companies and states—are unlikely to change the behavior of companies or governments because they do not raise the costs of maintaining current institutional deficiencies. Hard incentives—of the sort that affect the bottom line of corporations and the take of corrupt government officials—are needed. One option is to implement licensing or procurement requirements in industrialized countries that would put irresponsible companies at a disadvantage; another is to adjust the rules of international oil markets so that dubiously extracted oil is costlier to shift.

The argument that companies are complacent (i.e., that it is in their interest to keep things as they are) casts doubt on companies' claims that they are reluctant to address governance problems because of the risk that they will simply be replaced by less scrupulous companies (from China, for example). If institutional

---

[8] See Wiig and Kolstad (2010) for an elaboration of this point.

improvement is not in the interest of corporations generally, this "competition" argument is nothing more than an attempt to put a respectable front on murkier corporate objectives. At any rate, the presence of less scrupulous corporations would not undermine the case for corporate action in addressing governance; it would simply mean that incentives would have to be extended to these agents.

Like the Kimberley Process Certification Scheme, which is designed to reduce the trade in conflict diamonds, a change in the rules of the international oil market—so that trading would be more costly for companies that exploit weak institutions in developing countries—would affect all companies. Leif Wenar (2008) refers to the oil extracted in undemocratic countries as "stolen goods," since the government pockets profits that rightly belong to the populace. Accordingly, he recommends the imposition of tariffs on countries whose companies exploit weak institutions in oil-rich countries; such an approach would give the home countries of multinational corporations an incentive to monitor and improve the activities of their companies. Future research in the area of corporate social responsibility should focus on finding additional effective means of making multinational corporations behave more responsibly in oil-rich countries like Angola.

REFERENCES

Center for Systemic Peace. 2007. Polity IV country report 2007: Angola. www.systemicpeace.org/polity/Angola2008.pdf.

Collier, P., and A. Hoeffler. 2004. Greed and grievance in civil war. *Oxford Economic Papers* 56 (4): 563–595.

Damania, R., and E. Bulte. 2003. Resources for sale: Corruption, democracy and the natural resource curse. Discussion Paper No. 0320, Centre for International Economic Studies, University of Adelaide.

Goodin, R. E. 1985. *Protecting the vulnerable: A reanalysis of our social responsibilities.* Chicago: University of Chicago Press.

———. 1988. What is so special about our fellow countrymen? *Ethics* 98:663–686.

Guidolin, M., and E. La Ferrara. 2007. Diamonds are forever, wars are not: Is conflict bad for private firms? *American Economic Review* 97 (5): 1978–1993.

Hodges, T. 2007. The economic foundations of the patrimonial state. In *Angola: The weight of history*, ed. P. Chabal and N. Vidal. London: Hurst & Company.

International Budget Partnership. 2008. http://openbudgetindex.org/files/Rankings2008-Revised.pdf.

Isaksen, J., I. Amundsen, and A. Wiig, with C. Abreu. 2007. Budget, state and people: Budget process, civil society and transparency in Angola. CMI Report R 2007:7. Bergen, Norway: Chr. Michelsen Institute.

Kolstad, I. 2006. What's so special about poor countries? Mimeograph. Bergen, Norway: Chr. Michelsen Institute.

Kolstad, I. 2009a. The resource curse: Which institutions matter? *Applied Economics Letters* 16 (4): 439–442.

———. 2009b. Human rights and assigned duties: Implications for corporations. *Human Rights Review* 10 (4): 569–582.

Kolstad, I., and A. Wiig. 2009a. Is transparency the key to reducing corruption in resource-rich countries? *World Development* 37 (3): 521–532.

———. 2009b. It's the rents, stupid! The political economy of the resource curse. *Energy Policy* 37 (12): 5317–5325.

Kolstad, I., A. Wiig, and A. Williams. 2009. Mission improbable: Does petroleum-related aid address the resource curse? *Energy Policy* 37 (3): 954–965.

Le Billon, P. 2001. Angola's political economy of war: The role of oil and diamonds, 1975–2000. *African Affairs* 100 (398): 55–80.

McMillan, J. 2005. Promoting transparency in Angola. *Journal of Democracy* 16 (3): 155–168.

Mehlum, H., K. Moene, and R. Torvik. 2006. Institutions and the resource curse. *Economic Journal* 116:1–20.

PAC (Partnership Africa Canada). 2009. Diamonds and Security: Annual Review 2009. Ottawa.

Robinson, J. A., R. Torvik, and T. Verdier. 2006. Political foundations of the resource curse. *Journal of Development Economics* 79:447–468.

Transparency International. 2008. 2008 corruption perceptions index. www.transparency.org/news_room/in_focus/2008/cpi2008/cpi_2008_table.

Wenar, L. 2008. Property rights and the resource curse. *Philosophy & Public Affairs* 36 (1): 2–32.

Wiig, A., and I. Kolstad. 2010. Multinational corporations and host country institutions: A case study of CSR activities in Angola. *International Business Review* 19 (2): 178–190.

World Bank. 2006. Angola: Oil, broad-based growth, and equity—Country economic memorandum. Report Number 35362. http://go.worldbank.org/4B6PM2P190.

PART 2

Commodity and revenue tracking

Introduction

Unofficial and illegal resource extraction and trade should be formalized to curb peace spoilers' access to resources and to maximize state revenues. Although commodity- and revenue-tracking systems can be useful in this regard, tracking is only a part of the picture: it is also essential to publicly disseminate information about resource and revenue flows. Transparency can help limit opportunities for corruption, and the ability to compare the revenues that the government receives to the services it provides can increase demands for public scrutiny of expenditures.

Four chapters in part 2 take a close look at the Kimberley Process Certification Scheme (KPCS), a methodology used to track the origins and global movement of rough diamonds, and the process that led to its development. The chapters offer the viewpoints of a researcher, an industry representative, a practitioner, and a government official who was closely involved in developing the scheme and in the early phase of its implementation. Part 2 also includes chapters on the Extractive Industries Transparency Initiative (EITI), which supports transparency in the management of oil, gas, and mining revenues, and the Forest Law Enforcement, Governance and Trade (FLEGT) initiative of the European Union (EU), which is designed to curb the trade in illegal timber.

The KPCS, currently the most advanced commodity-tracking system in use, was developed to break the link between rough diamonds and conflict. Diamond-exporting countries that participate in the Kimberley Process (KP), the organizational entity that originated and oversees the KPCS, must certify that rough diamonds come from legitimate sources that do not contribute to conflict. Importing KP members allow only certified diamonds to cross their borders.

"The Kimberley Process at Ten: Reflections on a Decade of Efforts to End the Trade in Conflict Diamonds," by J. Andrew Grant, outlines the workings of the KPCS and the principal achievements of the KP: the formalization of mining and trade, increased government revenues in diamond-rich countries, the creation of national and international platforms for discussion of issues related to the diamond trade, and increased transparency in the diamond sector. Grant also traces the history of diamonds in conflict, particularly in Sierra Leone and Angola, and briefly summarizes how the KPCS was implemented in these two countries.

The KPCS was the first serious attempt to curb exploitation of a conflict resource at the global level. One of the cornerstones of its success was that it brought together governments, civil society, and industry in an effort to achieve a common goal. In "The Kimberley Process Certification Scheme: A Model Negotiation?" Clive Wright traces the history of the KP from 2000, when it was established, until the KPCS was signed three years later, after difficult negotiations between the three principal stakeholder groups. Wright identifies three key ingredients that secured the success of the KP in its early years: decision making based on consensus, mutual interest, and respect for the unique experience and expertise of other members. In "The Kimberley Process Certification Scheme:

The Primary Safeguard for the Diamond Industry," Andrew Bone outlines the industry's role in the KP and in the development of the KPCS, and highlights what the diamond industry expects from the KP and the KPCS in the future.

Despite the KP's demonstrable achievements, the success of the process is debated. Smuggling continues in some participating countries; diamonds have financed conflict in Côte d'Ivoire; and diamonds have been linked to violence and human rights abuses in the Democratic Republic of the Congo (DRC) and Zimbabwe. In "A More Formal Engagement: A Constructive Critique of Certification as a Means of Preventing Conflict and Building Peace," Harrison Mitchell argues that although a growing number of mining sites and a larger share of exports are now registered officially, and many diamond-exporting countries have experienced an increase in revenues, it is difficult to prove that the KPCS has had a direct effect on peacebuilding.

"Addressing the Roots of Liberia's Conflict through the Extractive Industries Transparency Initiative," by Eddie Rich and T. Negbalee Warner, describes how the Liberia EITI (LEITI) has helped to address the causes of the Liberian civil war. By providing civil society with a source of credible data on revenue flows between extractive companies and the government, the LEITI has increased public awareness of revenue flows, provided a platform for the discussion of governance issues related to the extractive sector, and alleviated mistrust and suspicion among the population. The authors underline, however, that improving transparency is only a first step in addressing a more fundamental issue: how resource revenues are spent.

The FLEGT initiative is designed to increase the transparency of forest management and to exclude illegal timber from the EU. Partially modeled on the KPCS, the FLEGT initiative is based on voluntary partnership agreements (VPAs) between the EU and timber-producing countries. Although the licensing system was not designed for conflict-affected countries in particular, many such countries are likely to adopt it. Because the FLEGT initiative focuses on improving forest governance, it has the potential to contribute to peacebuilding. In "Excluding Illegal Timber and Improving Forest Governance: The European Union's Forest Law Enforcement, Governance and Trade Initiative," Duncan Brack describes the purpose of the FLEGT and the VPAs, and explains how the VPAs work. Brack also considers the relevance of the FLEGT initiative for post-conflict Liberia.

The chapters in part 2 describe specific commodity- and revenue-tracking regimes currently in operation. Of these, the KP is unique: it focuses on one specific commodity; has global coverage; and includes national governments, industry, and civil society among its members. Although it may not be possible (or necessary) to set up similar global arrangements for other conflict commodities, the KP and the KPCS can usefully inform other initiatives that target different commodities and smaller regions; the current efforts to rein in commodity mining and trade in the eastern DRC are an example. In order to enhance public participation and strengthen demands for improved management of resources revenues, however, all these initiatives need to be accompanied by transparency of revenue flows between extractive industries and government.

The Kimberley Process at ten: Reflections on a decade of efforts to end the trade in conflict diamonds

J. Andrew Grant

Rough diamonds are not the only natural resource linked to violent conflict, but they have gained much notoriety through their association with civil wars in Sierra Leone and Angola, among other countries. Although diamonds did not cause these wars, they were a major funding source, allowing the fighting to continue. In the late 1990s, an intense international outcry against these "blood diamonds" led to the creation of an international governance framework to sever the link between the gems and the violence they facilitated.

Since its inception in 2000, the Kimberley Process (KP) has sought to end the trade in conflict diamonds. The KP has carried out this objective by imposing a set of verification and trade procedures. These procedures, known collectively as the Kimberley Process Certification Scheme (KPCS), were implemented in 2003. The implementation of the KPCS has been facilitated by the collaboration of both governments and nonstate actors, including diamond firms, industry associations, and nongovernmental organizations (NGOs).

Nearly all diamond-producing and diamond-trading countries are members of the KP—which, at the time of writing, had seventy-nine participating nations, including Australia, Botswana, Canada, China, India, Israel, Japan, Russia, South Africa, and the United States.[1] The KP also relies on the participation of industry, through the World Diamond Council (which includes De Beers, the leading

---

J. Andrew Grant is an assistant professor in the Department of Political Studies at Queen's University in Kingston, Ontario. The research on which this chapter is based was funded by the Social Sciences and Humanities Research Council of Canada and an Advisory Research Committee grant from Queen's University. The author wishes to thank Daniel Bach for his helpful comments and suggestions. The views presented in this chapter are the author's own and do not represent those of the aforementioned institutions.

[1] The figure of seventy-nine participants includes all members of the European Union as well as Venezuela and Côte d'Ivoire. Although Venezuela and Côte d'Ivoire are still considered KP participants, both nations have suspended the importing and exporting of rough diamonds, and neither is issuing KP certificates. Chinese Taipei has also conformed to the minimum requirements of the KPCS and is recognized by the KP as an importer and exporter of rough diamonds.

160   High-value natural resources and post-conflict peacebuilding

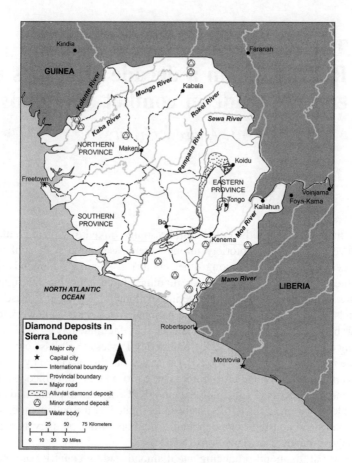

Figure 1.   Diamond deposits in Sierra Leone
Source: Based on original map from Aureus Mining.

rough-diamond wholesaler) and NGOs—such as Global Witness and Partnership Africa Canada (PAC)—that focus on the links between violent conflict and natural resources. This multi-stakeholder governance has made it more difficult for conflict diamonds to make their way into the global market; by removing the gems as a funding source for violent conflict, the KP has supported peacebuilding. The KP has also made a positive contribution to the management of this valuable natural resource by strengthening governance capacity in member states.

The chapter is divided into five major parts: (1) a review of the emergence of conflict diamonds and the subsequent international response; (2) a description of the workings of the KPCS; (3) a comparison of Sierra Leone and Angola (see figures 1 and 2) particularly with respect to their implementation of the KPCS; (4) a discussion of the implications of involving former combatants in post-conflict natural resource schemes; and (5) a brief conclusion.

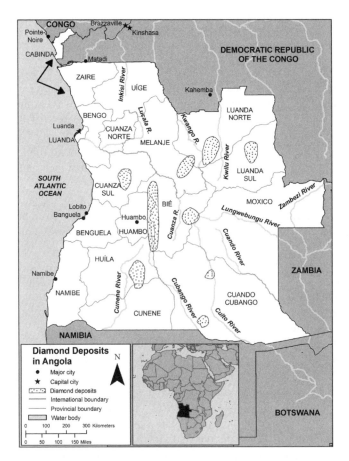

Figure 2. Diamond deposits in Angola
Source: PAC (2009b).

CONFLICT DIAMONDS AND INTERNATIONAL CONTROLS

Conflict diamonds are not a new phenomenon. Rough diamonds have sparked violence since the 1950s, often in connection with efforts to punish or deter diamond smugglers in artisanal mining areas. In Sierra Leone in the 1950s, security forces shot diamond smugglers attempting to transport diamonds into neighboring Liberia (Smillie, Gberie, and Hazelton 2000). In Brazil in 2004, members of the Cinta Larga tribe killed as many as twenty-nine diamond miners who were engaged in illicit mining on tribal land (Blore 2005).

In the late 1980s and early 1990s, conflict diamonds began to trickle out of Angola and Sierra Leone, which would become the most notorious examples of diamond-funded armed violence. According to Jean-Philippe Ceppi (2000), by the late 1980s, several multinational diamond firms were purchasing rough diamonds from parts of Angola that were under the control of the União Nacional para a

Independência Total de Angola (UNITA). Because the pro-West UNITA rebels were fighting against the Soviet-allied Movimento Popular de Libertação de Angola (MPLA) government, and the trade was occurring during the waning years of the Cold War, countries such as the United States and South Africa turned a blind eye to the trade in conflict diamonds. By the mid-1990s, however, the trickle of conflict diamonds had become a sizable stream: in Angola, UNITA was earning as much as US$700 million per year from rough diamonds (Global Witness 1998; Cortright, Lopez, and Conroy 2000); and in Sierra Leone, the Revolutionary United Front (RUF) had gained control of the vast majority of the diamond-mining areas in the eastern part of the country. At its peak, the RUF's annual income from rough diamonds was estimated at US$125 million (UNSC 2000a).

By the late 1990s, the growing trade in conflict diamonds had drawn the attention of several human rights organizations, including heavyweights Amnesty International and Human Rights Watch. But it was Global Witness, a modest-sized NGO at the time, that captured the attention of the mainstream media—by publishing, in December 1998, *A Rough Trade: The Role of Companies and Governments in the Angolan Conflict*, a report that shed an uncomfortably bright light on diamond firms' dealings with UNITA and on De Beers' dealings with the notoriously corrupt Angolan government parastatals (government-owned enterprises). In January 2000, PAC published an equally damning report on conflict diamonds in Sierra Leone (Smillie, Gberie, and Hazelton 2000). Through the work of Global Witness and PAC, conflict diamonds quickly gained worldwide attention. The BBC, the *New York Times*, the *Washington Post*, and other media outlets began to run articles on the role of diamonds in several African civil wars, including those in Liberia and the Democratic Republic of the Congo (DRC).[2] Even *Vanity Fair*, a self-described "cultural catalyst" based in the United States, published an article (Junger 2000) detailing the link between diamonds and violence in Sierra Leone. Scholars also began to weigh in on the threat that conflict diamonds posed to regional security and stability.[3]

By 2000, it had become impossible for the diamond industry and for diamond-producing and trading countries to deny the existence of conflict diamonds (Grant and Taylor 2004; Hughes 2006; Grant 2009b). Over the subsequent decade, Global Witness and PAC continued to publish detailed reports and press releases on conflict diamonds. Although exact numbers are difficult to establish, Amnesty

---

[2] See, for example, *New York Times* (2000), *BBC News* (2001), and Farah (2001).
[3] For research on conflict diamonds in Sierra Leone, see Reno (1995, 1997), Abiodun (1999), Zack-Williams (1999), Grant (2005a, 2005b, 2008, 2009a), Gberie (2005), Keen (2005), Davies (2006), and Kabia (2008). On Angola, see Sherman (2000), Dietrich (2000a), Malaquias (2001), Le Billon (2001), Hodges (2001), and Grant (2002). On the Democratic Republic of the Congo, see Dietrich (2000b, 2002), MacLean (2003), Pugh, Cooper, and Goodhand (2004), and Reno (2006). On Liberia, see Reno (1998), Bøås (2001), Adebajo (2002), and Sawyer (2004). And on Côte d'Ivoire, see Grant (2010). For large-number analyses of conflict diamonds, see, for example, Le Billon (2008) and Lujala (2009, 2010).

International has estimated that 3.7 million deaths were linked, either directly or indirectly, to the proceeds from conflict diamonds (Amnesty International n.d.).

In the late 1990s, the United Nations took an interest in conflict diamonds. The UN Security Council (UNSC) imposed sanctions on diamond exports from Angola in June 1998, from Sierra Leone in July 2000, from Liberia in March 2001, and from Côte d'Ivoire in December 2005. The UNSC also established UN expert panels on these countries, and one of the panels' many duties was to track and report on the illicit diamond trade.[4]

As the threat of a consumer boycott emerged, the South African government—concerned about the potential economic impact—invited representatives from industry, NGOs, and other diamond-producing and -trading states to meet in Kimberley, in May 2000. The objective of the meeting was to develop a mechanism that would prevent trade in conflict diamonds. After more than a dozen meetings over the next two-and-a-half years, the KPCS—an overarching regulatory agreement that would oversee the international trade in rough diamonds—was developed. Since December 2000, the UN General Assembly has issued a number of resolutions in support of the KP's efforts.[5]

THE KIMBERLEY PROCESS CERTIFICATION SCHEME

The KPCS is a global regulatory framework that is supported by stringent national legislation governing the export and import of rough diamonds.[6] To gain entry to the KPCS (and hence become an official member of the KP), a country must provide evidence that its legislation includes strong regulations, rules, procedures, and practices to control the production and trade of rough diamonds. Countries that are admitted to the KPCS pledge to monitor internal mining and trading of rough diamonds; to submit to the KP secretariat, on a quarterly basis, statistics on diamond production, exports, imports, and the number of KP certificates issued and collected; and to adhere to the various requirements and responsibilities set out in the KPCS.

The KP secretariat is hosted and staffed by the government of the country that is the current KP chair. Each member state designs and issues its own KP certificate, a process that is overseen by the government agency responsible for KP matters. Although the government agencies vary from country to country, KP certificates are typically overseen by ministries responsible for customs and trade, mineral resources, or finance.

---

[4] See, for example, UNSC (2000a, 2000b, 2001, 2005a, and 2005b).
[5] See, for example, UN General Assembly resolutions 55/56 (December 2000), 56/263 (March 2002), 57/302 (April 2003), 58/290 (April 2004), 59/144 (December 2004), and 60/182 (December 2005). For further information about the KP, see Clive Wright, "The Kimberley Process Certification Scheme: A Model Negotiation?" in this volume.
[6] The KPCS is available for download at www.kimberleyprocess.com/download/getfile/4.

Rough diamonds are usually traded in parcels (or shipments) containing any number of individual stones, ranging from one to several hundred. Before a parcel can be exported from its country of origin, it must have a KP certificate attached to it.[7] If the parcel is somehow exported without a KP certificate, customs officials of the receiving member state must confiscate it. If the absence of the certificate is judged to be an honest mistake, the shipment may be returned to the exporter. Otherwise, both the importer and the exporter of the confiscated diamond shipment may be fined, face criminal charges, or both, in accordance with the national legislation of the receiving country. According to a 2006 survey of KP participants, half of all members had recorded at least one case of KPCS infringement since 2003. The leaders in terms of reported cases of KPCS infringement were as follows: the European Union, 26;[8] Sierra Leone, 16; Australia, 8; and Canada, 5.[9]

The most common outcome of confiscation is seizure (that is, forfeiture) of the diamond shipment. From 2003 to 2006, the European Union seized rough diamond shipments worth about US$1.5 million; several convictions were also recorded.[10] Since KPCS infringement (and subsequent criminal charges) are domestic issues, few cases are publicized within KP circles. In 2008, however, the KP Working Group on Monitoring began discussing having member states report all KPCS infringements to the KP secretariat. As of this writing, these discussions had yet to yield a formal recommendation for consideration by the KP membership.

In addition to monitoring the production and trade of rough diamonds and submitting quarterly statistics to the KP secretariat, member states must allow the KP to periodically send a review team—consisting of representatives from government, industry, and NGOs—to assess the member state's implementation of the KPCS. All KP members have hosted a review team at least once since 2004. In 2009, Angola, the DRC, the European Union, Liberia, Sierra Leone, and Turkey all hosted review teams. Several countries, including Sierra Leone, have hosted two visits. Canada and the United States have indicated that they are ready for the KP to send review teams for a second visit during 2010.

The KP—through its rotating chair, its various working groups and committees, and its intersessional and plenary meetings—governs the implementation of the KPCS.[11] The purpose of the annual intersessional and plenary meetings is

---

[7] In 2006, KP participants issued approximately 55,000 KP certificates, which were attached to rough diamond exports worth about US$35.7 billion. As of 2006, KP diamonds represented approximately 94 percent of the official trade in rough diamonds—a figure that has increased as the KP has added new members to its roster (Kimberley Process 2007).
[8] Under the auspices of the European Commission, which serves as the executive branch of the European Union.
[9] According to documents in the author's possession.
[10] According to documents in the author's possession.
[11] The KP working groups and committees report to the KP chair; the KP chair provides information and updates to all KP members via teleconferences and electronic communications.

to address all issues relating to the KP—from reports of noncompliance, to problems with statistical reporting, to proposed improvements to the KPCS.

All KP activities depend on cooperation between states, industry, and NGOs. Since 2000, the relationship between these three groups of stakeholders has ranged from supportive to cordial to hostile, depending on the issue. Since 2004, participants found to be noncompliant with the KPCS have sparked the most heated debates. One reason for the contention concerning noncompliance may be that the KPCS does not provide explicit directives concerning sanctions or penalties in such cases. Moreover, because all KP decisions are made by consensus, each member state has effective veto power. Nevertheless, the KP has imposed suspensions, and some countries have opted for "self-suspension."

In 2004, the Republic of the Congo was suspended after a KP review found that the government's ministries of revenue and mineral resources could not provide details about the location of diamond-mining areas or other sources for their rough diamond exports. In addition, industry experts knew that the Republic of the Congo had very little of its own diamondiferous land, and that it had been suspected, for several decades, of serving as a smuggling route for gems from neighboring Angola and the DRC. The Republic of the Congo accepted the suspension; it was reinstated in November 2007, after demonstrating that it had addressed governance problems in its diamond export sector.

In late 2008, Venezuela announced that it would suspend rough diamond exports until it could better organize the government agency responsible for governing its diamond sector. The move was in response to informal pressure from other KP members, who were concerned about Venezuela's failure to submit statistical information and to take adequate steps to curb diamond smuggling to Guyana and Brazil. During the 2009 KP plenary meetings, the Participation Committee announced that it would assist Venezuela in its efforts to meet minimum KPCS standards and rejoin the KP as an active member. Venezuela's self-suspension has frustrated NGOs within the KP because reports of cross-border smuggling to Guyana and Brazil continue to emerge.

Since legal rough diamond shipments must now possess a KP certificate issued by a recognized government, it has become much more difficult for conflict diamonds to gain entry to the world market. But the capacity to fully implement the national regulatory controls called for by the KPCS varies from country to country. Similarly, some KP participants have been more willing to accept technical and other assistance under the auspices of the KP than others.

Capacity building—the transfer of logistical and technical knowledge—is one of the most important benefits of the KP. Canada, China, the European Union, and the United States, among other KP members, have provided fellow KP participants with technical assistance in several areas, including the collection of statistics and the registration of diamond miners and traders, and have run training workshops on database operations, diamond evaluation, and internal controls. The World Diamond Council, which represents the industry as an official KP observer, has also provided technical assistance and training workshops for various KP participants. In addition to Sierra Leone and Angola, other countries—most notably the DRC, Ghana, and Liberia—have also benefited from such assistance.

GOVERNING DIAMOND RESOURCES IN SIERRA LEONE AND ANGOLA

Conflict diamonds played a significant role in the Sierra Leonean and Angolan civil wars, and served as part of the impetus for establishing the KP in 2000. It therefore makes sense to delve into these two prominent cases in greater detail.

Sierra Leone

The existence of rough diamond reserves did not cause Sierra Leone's civil war; the roots of the violent conflict that broke out in March 1991 can be traced to two decades of corrupt and venal governance, and to the grievances that naturally resulted.[12] Diamond-related corruption did, however, contribute to the contempt with which many people viewed the government. More importantly, control over diamond resources fueled the continuation of conflict once civil war had broken out.

Diamonds and civil war in Sierra Leone

The National Provisional Ruling Council (NPRC), the military junta that assumed power after a coup deposed President Joseph Saidu Momoh in April 1992, claimed that it would defeat the RUF rebel group and root out government corruption, but it quietly operated its own diamond-laundering schemes in the meantime (Keen 2005). As the midpoint of the decade approached, the focus of the conflict shifted to gaining control of the diamond-mining areas for private profit. In May 1995, the cash-strapped NPRC sold a twenty-five-year diamond-mining lease to Branch Energy, The mining arem of a private military company, Executive Outcomes; in return, the company defended the region outside Freetown (the capital) and ejected the RUF from the diamond-producing regions of the country (Smillie, Gberie, and Hazelton 2000). But by mid-1997, Executive Outcomes had completed its original mandate and had left the country, and the RUF had begun to take advantage of its departure—and of the fact that government forces had limited operational capabilities—to resume looting rough diamonds in Kono

---

[12] For additional information on diamonds in Sierra Leone, see Roy Maconachie, "The Diamond Area Community Development Fund: Micropolitics and Community-led Development in Post-war Sierra Leone," and Kazumi Kawamoto, "Diamonds in War, Diamonds for Peace: Diamond Sector Management and Kimberlite Mining in Sierra Leone," both in this volume.

and Kenema districts and exchanging them for money, weapons, narcotics, and other goods (Gberie 2002).[13]

The civil war officially ended in January 2002, after nearly eleven years of fighting that had left 75,000 dead and roughly 2 million displaced, and had included acts of extraordinary brutality. As noted earlier in the chapter, diamonds had played an important role in the civil war. Nonetheless, the post-war government excluded former combatants from the evolving governance frameworks for natural resource management. Although the logic of this decision is understandable, it did carry some risk: aggrieved former combatants could have taken up arms against the government.

After the signing of the Lomé Peace Accord, in 1999, the UN established a peacekeeping mission in Sierra Leone. When the war ended, Sierra Leoneans understood that the UN peacekeepers would depart sooner rather than later, and that the stability they had provided would be difficult for the new government to replace. Although former combatants could have attempted to spoil the fragile peace, they did not. Some members of the RUF attempted to take a legitimate stake in the government by transforming the rebel group into a political party. Other members demobilized, through the program created by the National Committee for Disarmament, Demobilization and Reintegration (NCDDR). Still others either attempted to blend into the civilian population without the assistance of the NCDDR or fled to neighboring Côte d'Ivoire, Guinea, or Liberia (Keen 2005; Grant 2008).

Not long after the war, international financial institutions and NGOs, including the World Bank and the Network Movement for Justice and Development (NMJD), sought to influence the development of reforms in the natural resource sector. But because of the atrocities committed by the RUF during the war, neither the World Bank nor the NMJD had much sympathy for former combatants or much inclination to press the Sierra Leonean government to include ex-combatants in resource governance structures. Nor would the government have been likely to agree in any case: under the 1999 Lomé Peace Accord, the rebel leader Foday Sankoh had been placed at the head of the Commission for the Management of Strategic Mineral Resources—a position that he used to reap personal profits from diamond exports by signing deals with mining firms. As a consequence of this past experience, former combatants were excluded from Sierra Leone's governance schemes for natural resource management.

Implementing the KPCS in Sierra Leone

Despite its limited resources and its need to rely on the UN for security, the Ministry of Mineral Resources wanted to demonstrate to donor states and international

---

[13] Much of Sierra Leone's diamond reserves can be extracted though artisanal mining techniques that require very little skill, capital investment, or infrastructure, enabling rebel commanders to organize and control production with little effort.

aid agencies that the government of Sierra Leone was committed to strengthening overall governance, especially in the diamond sector. Membership in the KP allowed Sierra Leone to achieve this objective. Beginning in 2003, Usman Boie Kamara served as the point person for Sierra Leone's participation in the KP. Kamara is well respected in KP circles and has worked tirelessly to ensure Sierra Leone's compliance with the KPCS.[14] He has also worked with other KP members to improve Sierra Leone's capacity to submit statistical information and to oversee the implementation of miner registration programs.

In 2001, as the civil war was winding down, Sierra Leone exported 222,521 carats of rough diamonds (PAC 2004). In 2003, which marked the first year of Sierra Leone's participation in the KPCS, diamond exports more than doubled, totaling 506,674 carats. From 2004 to 2007, the country's annual diamond exports rose to the 600,000- to 700,000-carat range, with a value between US$125 million and US$142 million (PAC 2009b). Beginning in early 2008 and extending through 2009, the global recession reduced the demand for gem-quality diamonds; as a result, diamond exports declined during that period. Sierra Leone was not immune to the drop in demand. Moreover, Koidu Holdings Limited, the country's largest diamond producer, stopped mining in December 2007. In 2008, Sierra Leone's rough diamond exports dropped to 371,260 carats, valued at US$98,772,170 (PAC 2009b).

In the decade before the outbreak of the civil war, as much as 90 percent of Sierra Leone's diamond production was being smuggled out of the country, circumventing government channels—and hence government coffers. Although the overall increase in export volume can be largely attributed to the war's end, the regulatory regime required by the KPCS substantially increased the proportion of rough diamonds exported through government channels (GOSL 2008). Diamond production provides about US$5 million to US$7 million in export duties and fees, and generates indirect economic benefits in the form of investment and employment (GOSL 2008).

In 2007, the All People's Congress (APC) defeated the Sierra Leone People's Party (SLPP) in a narrow and hotly contested election. Among the APC's campaign promises was a pledge to review all mining contracts. Although the APC did conduct the review, it had failed to yield any significant changes by the time of writing. Nevertheless, the review did highlight the fact that diamond mining remains a sensitive issue in Sierra Leone.[15]

Angola

Like Sierra Leone's civil war, Angola's was not caused by diamonds—but again, diamonds did play an important role. Interestingly, the gems had little impact on

---

[14] This statement is based on conversations and interviews with KP participants and observers between 2005 and 2009.
[15] Although he was a holdover from the previous SLPP administration, Kamara was retained by the new APC government, thanks largely to his valuable technical and governance skills. However, at the 2009 KP plenary meeting, Kamara announced that he would retire at the end of the year.

the country's armed struggle for independence (1961–1974). After the Portuguese were ousted, the new nation's transitional government lasted for about a year before crumbling into three warring factions: UNITA, the MPLA, and the Frente Nacional de Libertação de Angola.

Diamonds and the civil war in Angola

The 1975–2002 civil war was not caused by a power struggle over diamond resources. Rather, as one scholar correctly asserts, the war was ignited by the combination of "mutual suspicion among the movements and the personal ambitions of their leaders" (Tvedten 1997, 36). Because the Cold War was still raging, Angola's combatants found funding through strategic alliances: the MPLA attracted Soviet weapons and Cuban soldiers, while UNITA was supported by South Africa and the United States.[16] From 1976 to 1991, the South African Defence Force flew numerous sorties, provided sustained military assistance, and engaged in a wide range of covert operations. From 1986 to 1991, the United States provided UNITA with weapons and funds, to the tune of US$15 million to US$50 million a year (de Beer and Gamba 2000). The signing of the Bicesse Accords, in May 1991, led to a respite in the violence. But the war resumed after Jonas Savimbi, UNITA's presidential candidate, declared that the country's first democratic elections, which had been held in September 1992, were rigged. By this time, however, the Cold War was over. Unable to rely on assistance from the United States and South Africa, UNITA had to find another means of financial support: rough diamonds.

Under Savimbi's centralized leadership, UNITA had been smuggling rough diamonds to buyers in the DRC (then Zaïre) and South Africa since the late 1980s. This activity was stepped up in 1990 and 1991, when UNITA smuggled out US$100 million and US$300 million worth of rough diamonds, respectively (Dietrich 2002). Like the RUF in Sierra Leone, UNITA was able to take control of artisanal extraction in Angola's alluvial diamond-mining regions, which included the Cuango River floodplains in Lunda Norte and Lunda Sud. The challenge was to maintain military control over the diamond-mining areas in the northeast—a not inconsiderable problem, given Angola's size and the distance between the mines and UNITA's traditional strongholds in southern Angola.

Over the next decade, UNITA's military fortunes rose and fell in tandem with its ability to repel government forces from the diamond territories. From 1992

---

[16] The Cold War was not the only reason for South Africa's support for UNITA: the South African government knew that as long as the MPLA remained weak, it would be unable to pursue anti-apartheid policies. Generally speaking, regional instability was in South Africa's interest, because it would prevent other African governments from mounting pressure against apartheid. By the early 1990s, however, aware that apartheid would come to an end within a few years, the South African government had less reason to continue to support UNITA.

to 1994, UNITA earned between US$600 million and US$700 million per year in diamond proceeds. In 1995, UNITA lost control over parts of the diamond-producing areas in the Cuango Valley, Lunda Norte, and Lunda Sud, halving diamond revenues for that year. In 1996 and 1997, after UNITA had regained control of these areas, revenues returned to the US$700 million range. In 1998, however, UNITA again lost control of much of the territory to government forces. The rapid decline in UNITA's rough-diamond proceeds from 1998 to 2001—from US$300 million to US$50 million annually—also coincided with UN Resolution 1173 which imposed sanctions that came into effect on June 12, 1998 (UNSC 1997, 1998; Global Witness 1998; Shaxson 1999; Cortright, Lopez, and Conroy 2000).

The UNSC sanctions banned the purchase of diamonds from UNITA and froze the rebel movement's financial assets—and hence the group's ability to conduct financial transactions. While the sanctions reduced the outflow of diamonds from UNITA, political and business elites in Burkina Faso, the DRC, and Togo still managed to purchase UNITA-produced diamonds and to serve as weapons brokers to the rebels. Throughout the 1990s, diamond revenues had allowed UNITA to purchase Bulgarian- and Ukrainian-made heavy weaponry, which enabled the rebel group to move away from guerrilla tactics and to fight a conventional war against government forces in and around Angola's cities. But the tactical shift to conventional warfare proved to be an error. Using offshore oil revenues, the MPLA government had bolstered its armed forces, which were trained in conventional warfare. As Assis Malaquias has noted, UNITA's decision to opt for "conventional tactics of warfare—including the deployment of large infantry units, mechanized units, and heavy artillery—to face government forces proved fatal for the rebels" (2007, 110). The civil war ended in April 2002, less than two months after Savimbi's death at the hands of government forces.

Savimbi had maintained a firm grip on the rebel group, making the vast majority of its military and political decisions; the death of its leader left UNITA in disarray. In the absence of a leader who could claim to speak for UNITA as a whole, the MPLA government was in a position to dictate the terms of UNITA's disarmament and reintegration. Although UNITA was a shadow of its former self, the MPLA government wanted to ensure that the former combatants lacked the financial means to resume a civil war. Moreover, government elites were eager to consolidate control of the diamond-mining areas and establish the kinds of opaque joint ventures they already enjoyed in the country's petroleum sector. Slowly, and without much in the way of assistance from the Angolan government or the international community, UNITA members returned to their original communities or migrated to larger urban centers such as Luanda. As they had been in Sierra Leone, former combatants were excluded from governance schemes for natural resources.

Implementing the KPCS in Angola

The KPCS in Angola is implemented through existing legislation. The legislative document that forms the basis for the governance of Angola's diamond sector is Law

No. 16/94—more commonly known as the "diamond law"—which was established on October 7, 1994. Under this law, a government-owned company, Endiama (Empresa Nacional de Diamantes de Angola), enjoys exclusive rights to prospect for, extract, purchase, and trade diamonds within Angola. In February 2000, Executive Decree No. 7-B/00 established Sodiam (Sociedade de Commercialização de Diamantes de Angola), which is a subsidiary of Endiama and is responsible for all exports of Angolan diamonds. Although the Angolan Ministry of Geology and Mines collects export data and KP certificates (and related statistics, which it submits to the KP secretariat), Sodiam is responsible for implementing the KPCS (Blore 2007) and is therefore responsible for Angola's "diamond pipeline"—ranging from inspecting diamond parcels from the mining areas to preparing shipments for valuation and export.

In 2001 and 2002, Angola exported approximately 5 million carats each year. In 2003, with the implementation of the KPCS, exports rose to 6 million carats, and in 2004 to just over 6 million carats. In 2005, exports were 7 million carats; in 2006, 9.5 million carats; in 2007, 8.5 million carats; and in 2008, 7.4 million carats (Blore 2007; Kimberley Process n.d.). As in Sierra Leone, the increases were due, in part, to the end of the civil war, but they were also bolstered by the KPCS.

For investors engaged in industrial-scale extraction, stronger domestic and global regulations have reduced the perception of risk associated with Angola's diamond sector, assuaging fears that rebel groups would seize diamond-mining areas or that consumers would boycott blood diamonds. In the artisanal diamond sector, however, the Angolan government is still struggling to implement the stronger controls that were recommended after a 2005 KP review. In 2009, the government implemented new legislation to strengthen the governance of artisanal diamond mining, but it remains unclear whether the legislation will allow verifiable tracking of artisanal production from mining areas to export points in Luanda.

Sierra Leone and Angola in the KP: A comparison

Since 2005, diamond production in Angola has yielded approximately US$1 billion in annual exports, depending on the quality of the rough diamonds, allowing the government to earn about US$150 million each year in royalties and export duties (Blore 2007).[17] Although impressive in absolute terms, Angola's diamond revenues represent only one-tenth of those earned from oil exports. Sierra Leone's annual diamond revenues, of US$5 million to US$7 million, are much smaller, but represent about half of all government income from export duties, taxes, and fees (GOSL 2008). The more telling difference between the two countries, however, is the level and quality of participation in the KP.

---

[17] The quality of diamond exports depends on the shape, color, clarity, and flaws of each rough diamond. The higher the overall quality, the higher the value (price per carat).

Sierra Leone and Angola share many common traits with respect to the KP. Both countries are long-standing members, and both established their own certificates of origin for rough diamonds three years before the KPCS began operating. After their wars had ended, both countries excluded former combatants from participating in the governance of natural resources. Through their membership in the KP, both Sierra Leone and Angola (although the latter to a lesser extent) have benefited from logistical assistance and technical knowledge provided by other KP members, which has not only strengthened their capacity to capture a greater portion of revenues from rough diamond production but has also enabled the countries to implement safeguards designed to help curb the threat of conflict diamonds. Finally, both countries have benefited economically from membership in the KP.

In Sierra Leone, governance has improved throughout the nation's decade-long association with the KP. Under the auspices of the KP, civil servants in Sierra Leone's Ministry of Mineral Resources (particularly in the Gold and Diamond Department) have received specialized training in a number of areas, including diamond valuation, governance logistics, and the development and use of production and export databases. Sierra Leone has also been an active member of the KP Working Group on Artisanal Alluvial Diamond Producers, which is a collective effort to address the governance challenges associated with artisanal diamond mining. And from 2007 to 2008, Sierra Leone received advice from the KP Working Group on Statistics on how to improve the collection and reporting of KP certificates.

Whereas Sierra Leone's association with the KP has yielded logistical and technical improvements, along with some modest increases in transparency,[18] very little has changed in Angola. During the early years of the KP, the Angolan delegation attended KP meetings but was more observant than active—although, when Global Witness and PAC criticized Angola's governance of diamond resources (for, among other things, lack of transparency and the heavy-handed expulsions of foreign *garimpeiros*—artisanal miners), the Angolan delegation would occasionally respond by disputing the accuracy of the reports.[19]

In recent years, however, Angola has begun to participate in various KP working groups and committees, largely because of its desire to become chair of the KP—a development that is consistent with the country's wish to increase its diplomatic power, not only in Southern Africa but across the continent. During the November 2005 KP plenary meetings in Moscow, Angola's representatives quietly let it be known that Angola wanted to serve as vice-chair of the KP.[20] The convention in the KP

---

[18] The increases in transparency occurred indirectly, through KP membership, and were made at the behest of international donors, NGOs, and the media.

[19] This information is based on the author's in-person observations of KP plenary meetings held between 2004 and 2009.

[20] Although the vice-chair is chosen by consensus, much politicking occurs behind the scenes, so that by the end of the plenary session, only one name is usually put forward for the position.

is that after serving one year as vice-chair—learning the ropes, sitting on the various KP working groups and committees, and generally assisting the KP chair—the vice-chair assumes the role of KP chair. Thus, by expressing interest in the position of vice-chair, Angola was actually expressing a desire to be chair.

Given that Angola would be expected to allocate much time, effort, and funding to serving as KP chair, its interest in the position is laudable. Nevertheless, having Angola serve as KP chair would be perceived as problematic in some quarters, given its poor track record in the realm of natural resource governance. For decades, the oil and diamond sectors have been under the control of joint ventures between the Angolan government and private individuals who have close political ties to the government or the army. Reports abound of proceeds from oil and diamond projects being siphoned off into private bank accounts—much to the chagrin of foreign investors and the International Monetary Fund (Global Witness 1999; Hodges 2001, 2004). Whereas Sierra Leone has usually been eager to receive logistical and technical assistance from the KP, the attitude of the Angolan delegation has been that it knows best and that no help is needed.[21] Angola's membership in the KP has led to some tangential governance improvements, but the Angolan government has resisted efforts to improve transparency in the diamond sector. Finally, the Angolan government is notorious for its restriction of the media and civil society groups, including both Angolan and transnational NGOs.[22] In view of the selection of the DRC as incoming KP vice-chair for 2010, the concerns about Angola's suitability to serve as KP chair have been placed on hold for another year.

THE INCLUSION OF FORMER COMBATANTS IN POST-CONFLICT RESOURCE MANAGEMENT

Inclusiveness—generally understood to mean as high a degree of participation among as many stakeholders as is feasible—is one indicator of good governance in a natural resource sector. This is not to say, however, that all stakeholders must be involved in all natural resource governance schemes at all times. In natural resource governance—the mining sector, for example—inclusiveness can take many forms; the following are all examples of inclusiveness:

- Public disclosure of government revenues from mineral exports, and of the details of mining agreements with firms.
- Consultations with stakeholders, such as representatives of civil society groups.
- The creation of legislation that (1) assigns responsibility for the mining sector to specific individuals or groups or (2) includes mining-employment provisions that apply to specific individuals or groups. Examples include the appointment

---

[21] This information is based on the author's in-person observations of KP plenary meetings held between 2004 and 2009.
[22] See, for example, Grant (2002), Vesely (2004), and Malaquias (2007).

of a former rebel leader as the head of a ministerial portfolio responsible for mining, and the allocation of land to former combatants for mining purposes.

Inclusiveness is an admirable goal and an important means of preventing the recurrence of the kinds of grievances that may have led to conflict in the first place. In a post-conflict context, however, inclusiveness must be balanced against other priorities.

On the one hand, natural resource management offers an opportunity to bring together former combatants and to insulate fragile post-conflict conditions from potential peace spoilers: structuring a new resource governance scheme so as to provide all former belligerents with some form of access to natural resources lessens the motivation to engage in conflict for economic reasons. On the other hand, the inclusion of former combatants in natural resource management schemes may be neither practical nor prudent. Mining firms, for example, would likely balk at being required to hire former combatants. And appointing a former rebel leader to a ministerial post that is responsible for mining, or allocating land for former combatants to mine, would provide access to the financial means to resume hostilities. If combatants previously used natural resources to fund armed campaigns, the chances are great that they will do so again. While certain natural resources, such as land or water for agricultural use, might appropriately be allocated to former combatants, resources such as diamonds and gold can be readily (and quickly) extracted and traded for cash, weapons, and other means to wage war.

In Sierra Leone and Angola, former rebels were excluded from natural resource management schemes during the post-conflict period. The governments of both countries were mindful of past problems: the 1999 Lomé Peace Accord, in Sierra Leone, and the 1994 Lusaka Protocol, in Angola,[23] had placed former rebel leaders in charge of natural resource ministries, and in both cases, the former rebels used the government portfolios to continue trading in conflict diamonds.

The KPCS was specifically designed to keep rough diamonds out of the hands of rebel groups; thus, the KPCS does not require members to include former combatants in their diamond sectors. When KP members discuss former combatant groups, the conversation tends to focus on how to restrict their access to diamond sectors, not on finding opportunities to be inclusive. Diamonds had played a smaller role in Liberia's civil war than in those of Sierra Leone and Angola; nevertheless, Liberia was scrutinized at length by the KP before its admittance in 2007, out of concern that access to diamond proceeds might provide the means to resume fighting. Furthermore, former rebels and militia groups were excluded from the process of revising Liberia's diamond legislation.

---

[23] The Lusaka Protocol contained provisions for a cease-fire and a disarmament process, and provided UNITA with key ministerial posts, including those responsible for mining and commerce. The terms of the agreement were repeatedly violated, however, which led to its eventual collapse, in December 1998.

The experiences of Sierra Leone, Angola, and Liberia will be instructive for Côte d'Ivoire, which will be admitted to the KP after its low-intensity civil war ends. Although Côte d'Ivoire was one of the original members of the KP, it suspended its membership in 2003, when the KPCS requirements were introduced. In Côte d'Ivoire, the Forces Nouvelles (FN) rebel group earns as much as US$12 million per year by "taxing" the rough diamonds mined in the fields under its control. Given the history of regional disparities in the country, national and international actors (such as France and the United Nations) participating in Côte d'Ivoire's peacebuilding initiatives would be wise to lean in the direction of inclusiveness when it comes to natural resource governance schemes. Though it is doubtful that the FN rebels will be offered control over Côte d'Ivoire's Ministry of Mines as part of a peace deal, elements of the civilian population harbor significant grievances, and a governance scheme that rendered the agricultural (e.g., cocoa) and mineral (e.g., diamond) sectors more inclusive would foster reconciliation among civilian groups.

CONCLUSION

Even though neither the KP nor the KPCS was devised with post-conflict objectives in mind, both have contributed to post-conflict peacebuilding in practice. Since 2003, when the KPCS was implemented, Sierra Leone and Angola, the two countries most notorious for conflict diamonds, have remained free of civil war. The KPCS makes it more difficult, and hence more costly, to trade conflict diamonds. Rough diamond parcels that do not have a KP certificate may be seized, and the exporters and importers may be subject to fines, criminal charges, or both. Because more than 99 percent of all diamond-producing and -trading countries are KP members, it is difficult to find buyers for non-KPCS diamonds.

The lessons of Sierra Leone and Angola are instructive for future efforts to curb conflict commodities through certification. Diamonds are a unique case in many ways, but not so unique that the KP "recipe" cannot inform other initiatives. The crucial first step for success in similar efforts is to include government, industry, and civil society in all phases of national and international negotiations to devise the natural resource governance framework. The second step is to incorporate all three stakeholder groups into the subsequent (and much longer) implementation phase of the governance scheme.

The number and diplomatic power of the states that are involved are crucial elements in the success of global governance initiatives. Involving as many states as possible is important because it limits the number of potential destinations for noncertified natural resources. But gaining the support of diplomatic heavyweights—such as China, the European Union, India, Russia, and the United States, all of whom are members of the KP—helps increase the legitimacy and clout of any global governance initiative.

Bringing industry within the global governance framework is vital, and should not be difficult: firms profit from stable domestic settings and the reliable management of natural resources, while instability and uncertainty hamper investment. At the KP, in addition to having been given a seat at the table (as opposed to having been cast as the villain), industry has contributed specialized technical knowledge to bolster natural resource governance. Similarly, national and transnational civil society groups have a great deal to offer any global governance initiative, including their research proficiency and their ability to serve as watchdogs. Global Witness and PAC, both part of the KP from the very beginning, influenced the direction of the KP and helped mold the KPCS.

Although the KP has experienced a great deal of success over the past decade, it faces a number of challenges. Because it operates by consensus, the KP has been unable to act swiftly when the need arose—specifically when dealing with noncompliance on the part of Venezuela and Zimbabwe. As noted earlier, the KP's civil society members are frustrated by Venezuela's self-suspension because it prevents any action from being taken against cross-border smuggling of Venezuelan rough diamonds to Guyana and Brazil. In 2009, the KP's civil society members, along with some industry representatives and several countries, pushed for more resolute action toward the Zimbabwean government, but Bernhard Esau, the KP chair, was reluctant to act too harshly because he wanted to preserve diplomatic ties between Zimbabwe and his home country, Namibia. Although a compromise was finally hammered out during the November 2009 plenary meetings, the delays have given the appearance that the KP is equivocal about human rights abuses occurring in and around the diamond-mining areas of Marange, Zimbabwe.[24]

If the KP is to continue to enjoy credibility and legitimacy in the eyes of the international community, then it must make progress in dealing with Venezuela and Zimbabwe.[25] In essence, the KP needs to implement more rapid and more powerful mechanisms for dealing with noncompliance. In the meantime, instead of engaging in perfunctory consultations with the two nations during intersessional and plenary meetings, the KP chair and members of the KP working groups and committees must engage with these countries on a continuous basis. Otherwise, a protracted period of noncompliance by Venezuela and Zimbabwe will place the KP and all of its accomplishments in jeopardy, and potentially lead this unique global governance initiative toward irrelevance.

REFERENCES

Abiodun, A. 1999. Diamonds are forever . . . but so also are the controversies: Diamonds and the actors in Sierra Leone's civil war. *Civil Wars* 3 (2): 43–64.

---

[24] The compromise is detailed in a six-page KP administrative decision known as the 2009 Joint Work Plan on Zimbabwe. For more information on the situation in Zimbabwe's mining areas, see Partnership Africa Canada (2009a).

[25] For an additional perspective on the KPCS, see Harrison Mitchell, "A More Formal Engagement: A Constructive Critique of Certification as a Means of Preventing Conflict and Building Peace," in this volume.

Adebajo, A. 2002. *Liberia's civil war: Nigeria, ECOMOG, and regional security in West Africa*. Boulder, CO: Lynne Rienner.

Amnesty International n.d. *Conflict diamonds*. www.amnestyusa.org/business-and-human-rights/conflict-diamonds/page.do?id=1051176.

BBC News. 2001. Liberia blasts sanctions. May 7. http://news.bbc.co.uk/2/hi/africa/1318232.stm.

Blore, S. G., ed. 2005. *The failure of good intentions: Fraud, theft and murder in the Brazilian diamond industry*. Ottawa: Partnership Africa Canada.

———, ed. 2007. *Diamond industry annual review: Republic of Angola 2007*. Ottawa: Partnership Africa Canada.

Bøås, M. 2001. Liberia and Sierra Leone—dead ringers? The logic of neopatrimonial rule. *Third World Quarterly* 22 (5): 697–723.

Ceppi, J.-P. 2000. Conducting business in war-prone areas. In *War, money and survival*, ed. G. Carbonnier and S. Fleming. Geneva: International Committee of the Red Cross.

Cortright, D., G. A. Lopez, and R. W. Conroy. 2000. Angola's agony. In *The sanctions decade: Assessing UN strategies in the 1990s*, ed. D. Cortright and G. A. Lopez. Boulder, CO: Lynne Rienner.

Davies, V. A. B. 2006. Diamonds, poverty and war in Sierra Leone. In *Small-scale mining, rural subsistence and poverty in West Africa*, ed. G. Hilson. Rugby, UK: Intermediate Technology Publications.

de Beer, H., and V. Gamba. 2000. The arms dilemma: Resources for arms or arms for resources? In *Angola's war economy: The role of oil and diamonds*, ed. J. Cilliers and C. Dietrich. Pretoria: Institute for Security Studies.

Dietrich, C. 2000a. UNITA's diamond mining and exporting capacity. In *Angola's war economy: The role of oil and diamonds*, ed. J. Cilliers and C. Dietrich. Pretoria: Institute for Security Studies.

———. 2000b. Porous borders and diamonds. In *Angola's war economy: The role of oil and diamonds*, ed. J. Cilliers and C. Dietrich. Pretoria: Institute for Security Studies.

———. 2002. *Hard currency: The criminalized diamond economy of the Democratic Republic of the Congo and its neighbours*. Ottawa: Partnership Africa Canada.

Farah, D. 2001. Digging up Congo's dirty gems. *Washington Post*. December 30.

Gberie, L. 2002. *War and peace in Sierra Leone: Diamonds, corruption and the Lebanese connection*. Ottawa: Partnership Africa Canada.

———. 2005. *A dirty war in West Africa: The RUF and the destruction of Sierra Leone*. London: C. Hurst and Company.

Global Witness. 1998. *A rough trade: The role of companies and governments in the Angolan conflict*. London.

———. 1999. *A crude awakening: The role of oil and banking industries in Angola's civil war and the plunder of state assets*. London: Global Witness.

GOSL (Government of Sierra Leone). 2008. Official, Gold and Diamond Department, interview with author. June 2. Freetown, Sierra Leone.

Grant, J. A. 2002. Angola's ashes: The legacy of dirty oil, blood diamonds, and government graft. In *Advancing human security and development in Africa: Reflections on NEPAD*, ed. S. J. MacLean, H. J. Harker, and T. M. Shaw. Halifax: Centre for Foreign Policy Studies.

———. 2005a. Diamonds, foreign aid, and the uncertain prospects for post-conflict reconstruction in Sierra Leone. *Round Table* 94 (381): 443–457.

———. 2005b. Salone's sorrow: The ominous legacy of diamonds in Sierra Leone. In *Resource politics in sub-Saharan Africa*, ed. A. Mehler and M. Basedau. Hamburg: Institute of African Affairs.

———. 2008. Informal cross-border micro-regionalism in West Africa: The case of the Parrot's Beak. In *Afro-regions: The dynamics of cross-border micro-regionalism in Africa*, ed. F. Söderbaum and I. Taylor. Uppsala, Sweden: Nordic Africa Institute.

———. 2009a. Cracks, shadows, and other flaws: Examining the impact of dirty diamonds on regional security in West Africa. Paper presented at the twenty-first International Political Science Association World Congress, July 15, Santiago, Chile.

———. 2009b. *Digging deep for profits and development? Reflections on enhancing the governance of Africa's mining sector*. SAIIA Occasional Paper 49. Johannesburg: South African Institute of International Affairs.

———. 2010. Natural resources, international regimes and state-building: Diamonds in West Africa. *Comparative Social Research* 27 (1): 223–248.

Grant, J. A., and I. Taylor. 2004. Global governance and conflict diamonds: The Kimberley Process and the quest for clean gems. *Round Table* 93 (375): 385–401.

Hodges, T. 2001. *Angola from Afro-Stalinism to petro-diamond capitalism*. Oxford, UK: James Currey; Bloomington: Indiana University Press.

———. 2004. *Angola: Anatomy of an oil state*. Oxford, UK: James Currey; Bloomington: Indiana University Press.

Hughes, T. 2006. Conflict diamonds and the Kimberley Process: Mission accomplished or mission impossible? *South African Journal of International Affairs* 13 (2): 115–130.

Junger, S. 2000. The terror of Sierra Leone. *Vanity Fair,* August.

Kabia, J. M. 2008. Greed or grievance? Diamonds, rent-seeking and the civil war in Sierra Leone. In *Extractive economies and conflicts in the Global South*, ed. K. Omeje. Aldershot, UK: Ashgate.

Keen, D. 2005. *Conflict and collusion in Sierra Leone*. Basingstoke, UK: Palgrave Macmillan.

Kimberley Process. 2007. *Kimberley Process communiqué 2007*. Brussels.

———. n.d. Kimberley Process rough diamond statistics. https://kimberleyprocessstatistics.org/.

Le Billon, P. 2001. Angola's political economy of war: The role of oil and diamonds, 1975–2000. *African Affairs* 100 (398): 55–80.

———. 2008. Diamond wars? Conflict diamonds and geographies of resource wars. *Annals of the Association of American Geographers* 98 (2): 345–372.

Lujala, P. 2009. Deadly combat over natural resources: Gems, petroleum, drugs, and the severity of armed civil conflict. *Journal of Conflict Resolution* 53 (1): 50–71.

———. 2010. The spoils of nature: Armed civil conflict and rebel access to natural resources. *Journal of Peace Research* 47 (1): 15–28.

MacLean, S. J. 2003. New regionalism and conflict in the Democratic Republic of Congo: Networks of plunder and networks for peace. In *The new regionalism in Africa*, ed. J. A. Grant and F. Söderbaum. Aldershot, UK: Ashgate.

Malaquias, A. 2001. Diamonds are a guerrilla's best friend: The impact of illicit wealth on insurgency strategy. *Third World Quarterly* 22 (3): 311–325.

———. 2007. *Rebels and robbers: Violence in post-colonial Angola*. Uppsala, Sweden: Nordic Africa Institute.

New York Times. 2000. Diamond traders act on Africa war issue. September 8. www.nytimes.com/2000/09/08/business/diamond-traders-act-on-africa-war-issue.html.

PAC (Partnership Africa Canada). 2004. *Diamond industry annual review: Sierra Leone 2004*. Ottawa.

———. 2009a. *Zimbabwe, diamonds and the wrong side of history*. Ottawa.

———. 2009b. *Diamonds and human security: Annual review 2009*. Ottawa.

Pugh, M., and N. Cooper, with J. Goodhand. 2004. *War economies in a regional context: Challenges of transformation.* Boulder, CO: Lynne Rienner.

Reno, W. 1995. *Corruption and state politics in Sierra Leone.* Cambridge, UK: Cambridge University Press.

———. 1997. War, markets, and the reconfiguration of West Africa's weak states. *Comparative Politics* 29 (4): 493–510.

———. 1998. *Warlord politics and African states.* Boulder, CO: Lynne Rienner.

———. 2006. Congo: From state collapse to "absolutism," to state failure. *Third World Quarterly* 27 (1): 43–46.

Sawyer, A. 2004. Violent conflicts and governance challenges in West Africa: The case of the Mano River Basin area. *Journal of Modern African Studies* 42 (3): 437–463.

Shaxson, N. 1999. Fuelling the war: Diamonds and oil. *BBC News*, January 28. http://news.bbc.co.uk/hi/english/special_report/1999/01/99/angola/newsid_264000/264228.stm.

Sherman, J. H. 2000. Profit vs. peace: The clandestine diamond trade in Angola. *Journal of International Affairs* 53 (2): 699–719.

Smillie, I., L. Gberie, and R. Hazleton. 2000. *The heart of the matter: Sierra Leone, diamonds and human security.* Ottawa: Partnership Africa Canada.

Tvedten, I. 1997. *Angola: Struggle for peace and reconstruction.* Boulder, CO: Westview Press.

UNSC (United Nations Security Council). 1997. Resolution 1127. S/RES/1127 (1997). August 28.

———. 1998. Resolution 1173. S/RES/1173 (1998). June 12.

———. 2000a. Report of the panel of experts appointed pursuant to UN Security Council Resolution 1306 (2000), paragraph 19, in relation to Sierra Leone. S/2000/1195. New York: United Nations.

———. 2000b. Report of the panel of experts on violations of Security Council sanctions against UNITA. S/2000/203. New York: United Nations.

———. 2001. Report of the panel of experts on the illegal exploitation of natural resources and other forms of wealth of the Democratic Republic of the Congo. S/2001/357. New York: United Nations.

———. 2005a. Report of the panel of experts submitted pursuant to paragraph 8 (e) of Security Council Resolution 1579 (2004) concerning Liberia. S/2005/360. New York: United Nations.

———. 2005b. Report of the group of experts submitted pursuant to paragraph 7 of Security Council Resolution 1584 (2005) concerning Côte d'Ivoire. S/2005/699. New York: United Nations.

Vesely, M. 2004. Angola battles human rights groups. *African Business* 299 (June): 54.

Zack-Williams, A. B. 1999. Sierra Leone: The political economy of civil war, 1991–98. *Third World Quarterly* 20 (1): 143–162.

The Kimberley Process Certification Scheme: A model negotiation?

Clive Wright

In the late 1990s, a series of alarming reports from civil society groups set out the clear link between the global trade in rough diamonds and the prosecution and perpetuation of brutal civil wars in countries such as Angola, the Democratic Republic of the Congo (DRC), and Sierra Leone (Global Witness 1998). In 1999, several governments—led by the three main diamond-producing countries in Africa (Botswana, Namibia, and South Africa) and the three leading consumers and marketers of diamonds (Belgium, the United Kingdom, and the United States)—came together to craft a response. One of the first meetings was held in the South African diamond-mining town of Kimberley; what became known as the Kimberley Process (KP) eventually embraced many more governments, as well as industry and civil society. The objective of the KP was to break the link between diamonds and civil war, and the model that was chosen—the Kimberley Process Certification Scheme (KPCS)—was signed in 2003, after three years of negotiation.[1]

Under the KPCS, the seventy-five participating countries must certify that all rough diamonds exported from their territory have come from legitimate sources that were not involved in supporting civil war.[2] Participants are also required to regulate the import of rough diamonds to ensure that they, too, have come from a legitimate source (as testified by the exporting participant), and to ensure transparency by exchanging information with all participants. The KPCS is the formal method that each participating country uses to assure all other participating countries that rough diamonds exported from its territory comply

---

Clive Wright, a member of the United Kingdom's Foreign and Commonwealth Office, led the UK delegation to the Kimberley Process Certification Scheme from October 2000 to December 2004. The views expressed here are those of the author alone and not necessarily those of the British government.

[1] See, for example, Grant and Taylor (2004), Paes (2005), and Wright (2004).
[2] For the full list of participating countries, see www.kimberleyprocess.com/structure/participants_world_map_en.html.

with the requirements of the scheme;[3] the implementation of the KPCS in each country must be fully transparent and is subject to peer review.

This chapter focuses on the roles played by the key actors during a negotiation that produced a unique agreement: the first to make a serious attempt, on a global basis, to end the illegal exploitation of a natural resource and break the link with armed conflict. The negotiation was also the first in which governments, industry, and civil society interacted on an equal footing. This may be the most important legacy of the KPCS: demonstrating that governments, industry, and civil society could put aside their differences and work closely to reach a common understanding on key international issues. Perhaps equally important, the participants took a vital decision early on: that they would act only by consensus, and on the basis of views expressed by any of the participants—views that carried equal weight, regardless of the author.

In the early stages of the negotiation, disagreements and preconceptions were commonplace. Outside of command economies such as the Soviet Union's, the diamond trade had enjoyed a nonregulated environment for as long as anyone could remember. Hence, industry viewed government "interference" with suspicion and alarm: allowing bureaucrats access to insider information and giving them a role in policing the industry was anathema. But behind the bluster was a more fundamental fear that elements within the industry had at best turned a blind eye to—and had at worst colluded in—some of the most brutal conflicts since the Second World War. The prospect of close government examination of the diamond industry was hardly palatable.

At the same time, many participating governments regarded industry as having ducked the corporate social responsibility (CSR) standards they had exhorted their business sectors to adopt. One such effort was the Global Compact, a policy initiative that the United Nations had launched in 1999. The compact, which incorporated ten basic principles in the areas of human rights, labor standards, and the environment, evoked only patchy participation in the early days of the initiative; but in any event, the governments engaged in the KP ultimately regarded the voluntary principles as not the best means of meeting the unique challenge posed by conflict diamonds.

Meanwhile, certain governments, particularly those functioning under more authoritarian models of governance, found it difficult to accept the participation of civil society groups, whom they viewed as interfering and intrusive, and as lacking a popular mandate or base of support. Nor were these governments keen to have a spotlight cast on their state-run diamond sectors, for the viewing pleasure of competitors from other states and private industry.

---

[3] For additional views of the KPCS, see J. Andrew Grant, "The Kimberley Process at Ten: Reflections on a Decade of Efforts to End the Trade in Conflict Diamonds," and Harrison Mitchell, "A More Formal Engagement: A Constructive Critique of Certification as a Means of Preventing Conflict and Building Peace," in this volume.

Finally, the civil society groups that were involved in the KPCS were skeptical about industry's commitment to reform and reluctant to believe that governments would make any more than a halfhearted attempt to take on the industry, regulate it, and open it up to external scrutiny. At the same time, the civil society groups that had been invited to participate in the negotiations had to contend with accusations, from fellow organizations that were not directly involved and were frustrated at having been excluded, that they had "sold out."[4]

STAKEHOLDERS AND PARTICIPANTS

With all the baggage that the three groups brought to the table, how were they supposed to cooperate and produce a unique international agreement? The answer was, primarily and initially, mutual interest. Industry saw the threat of a consumer backlash as very real; movement in that direction was being stirred up in the U.S. Congress and elsewhere. Governments were alarmed about the threat to an industry worth US$50 billion per year—and equally intrigued by the prospect of, for once, breaking the link between natural resources and conflict. Nongovernmental organizations (NGOs) saw an opportunity to influence the outcome of a debate that they, more than anyone else, had framed, as well as the opportunity to exploit the high-profile "blood diamond" issue and to secure future funding for this and other campaigns.

But beyond those early objectives that converged on a common goal, albeit from different directions, each party quickly found that it admired the expertise and earnestness of the other two. The conscious decision by many of the participating delegations to retain the core membership throughout the three years of a highly technical and specialized negotiation (and beyond, during the implementation phase), helped the participants develop a level of confidence in each other that often transcended the politics of the moment.

Perhaps above all, the participants felt genuine ownership in the process, and believed that direct negotiations would allow a degree of focus and a sense of urgency that others, lacking intimate knowledge of the issue, could never achieve. So, for example, early attempts to have the UN run the negotiations were rejected with equal enthusiasm by government, industry, and NGOs alike. This was no time for diplomats to languish over a bureaucratic exercise: the wrangling and horse-trading in which the UN traditionally engages would only generate complications and delays. Thus, apart from being brought in periodically to bless and legitimize the progress made to date and to encourage further efforts through official resolutions, the UN was excluded.

---

[4] Those civil society groups that had been involved in the earliest meetings—in particular, Global Witness and Partnership Africa Canada—agreed with the other groups to represent all civil society. During the first rounds of negotiation, mining unions from Southern Africa were among the civil society groups, but they dropped out early on, as they lacked sufficient funds to continue to participate.

In sum, a common purpose, shared experiences and expertise, a sense of ownership, and the assurance of being heard were the key ingredients that made the KPCS a success. Which is not to say that the process was entirely straightforward. The first group, sovereign governments, sat as individuals or were grouped as economic blocs. That arrangement ought to have been simple enough—but the European Union (EU), a single economic bloc, included two countries, Belgium and the United Kingdom, that felt they had a lot at stake, given the importance of the diamond industry in both countries. Interactions within the EU contingent were often fractious as a result, but at least the bloc appeared cooperative in public. Another issue was the presence of Taiwan, which plays an active role in the diamond industry and is an important trading partner for Shanghai, for example. Persuading an almost implacably hostile China to share the table with Taiwan (particularly when Beijing was already unhappy about Hong Kong's semi-independent role in the process) took a great deal of political effort.

Life among the NGOs also had its more difficult moments. It would have been impossible for all NGOs with an interest in the KPCS to be at the table. Ultimately, two were selected to represent the wider group: Global Witness and Partnership Africa Canada, the two organizations that had done the most to bring to the world's attention the relationship between conflict and diamonds. A much wider group of civil society organizations met on the sidelines during negotiations, as well as between negotiations, to agree on a way forward. Among the NGOs that had been left out, including Amnesty International and Oxfam, there was initially respect for the two chosen representatives. But relations occasionally soured during negotiations, when some NGOs viewed the inevitable compromises needed to achieve consensus—on the issue of the inspection and audit of industry's books, for example—as "selling out." Eventually, however, the other NGOs were persuaded to go along with the result.

Nor was industry free of internal bickering. There was never any question that De Beers would call the shots for industry: its dominance was total.[5] The establishment of the World Diamond Council, in 2001, created the fig leaf of wider representation, bringing together traders, cutters, and polishers. The council's elected officeholders negotiated on behalf of industry, while De Beers sat quietly in the second row of seats and decided matters during the breaks in the negotiation. Not that the company's influence was negative: far from it. De Beers had clearly decided early on to make the KPCS happen, and senior staff members spent a great deal of time and effort—and engaged in a lot of arm-twisting—to persuade industry to go with the flow.

The three main players came to the table not only with preconceived views of each other, but also with disparate visions of the shape and content of an

---

[5] Almost two-thirds of the world's diamonds are channeled through De Beers' head office in London. Although far from being a monopoly or a cartel, as some claim, De Beers still exercises huge influence through its substantive holdings, mining operations, and marketing arm.

agreement. At times, fundamental conflicts about the details of the certification system, including participation, degree of transparency, and inspection by fellow participants (and even by outside third parties), almost derailed the process. But the key ingredients always ensured that such difficulties could be resolved to the satisfaction of all participants.

The negotiations also yielded spin-off benefits. Through repeated dealings with civil society groups over a three-year period, some governments' previously hostile attitude toward the participation of such groups in debates at the UN, and other similar forums, changed almost beyond recognition. The bureaucratic rigidity that might otherwise have stifled nimble responses to sudden political developments affecting the KPCS fell away, as phone lines hummed between London and Moscow, Luanda and Tel Aviv. For diplomats, the ability to fix problems with a single phone call to another capital was an exhilarating change from the more traditional course of diplomatic notes and protracted negotiations. Simply knowing the person on the other end of the line—as someone whose word could be trusted, and with whom you had worked closely during many days and nights, in different parts of the world, as the KPCS unfolded—allowed swift and effective progress on a variety of issues.

BUILDING CONSENSUS

One area of agreement among all three of the major stakeholder groups was the need to discipline errant participants. For the certification scheme to be respected both by the participants and the wider international community, the collective membership had to demonstrate that it would not tolerate failure to fulfill the membership requirements. It was therefore something of a shock for officials from Lebanon, as well as for those from more than half a dozen other countries, to find that they had been suspended from the KP for failing to enact local legislation implementing the KPCS.[6] And the suspensions had further implications. In the case of the Republic of the Congo, for example, the repeated failure to be transparent about the movement of rough diamonds through its territory got the attention of international financial institutions, whose displeasure and threats of punitive economic and financial sanctions forced the country quickly back to the straight and narrow.

A MODEL NEGOTIATION?

Was the KPCS a model negotiation? In many respects, yes. It brought together some highly disparate groups in a way that enabled them to find common cause; it also bound them together in a collaborative effort to deliver an outcome

---

[6] For reasons that were unconnected to the KPCS and had far more to do with internal politics, the Lebanese parliament was dragging its feet over the introduction of regulations.

that has been highlighted by the UN and other bodies as an example of cooperation and practical endeavor, and that has gone a long way toward ending the scourge of the so-called blood diamond. The KPCS is not a perfect agreement. One does not exist. Yet it stands out as having arisen from a negotiating model that set consensus as its highest goal, and that cast aside any sense of hierarchy among negotiators, no matter what their affiliation.

The KP cannot necessarily be transplanted successfully into other sectors or deployed for different issues. The ingredients for success will always depend on circumstances, players, and other influences, both internal and external. In addition, and most critically, the technical elements of the certification scheme were developed by people with an intimate knowledge of an opaque and quirky industry that, over the centuries, had developed its own unique way of doing business. Industry was able to embrace a far higher degree of transparency, as well as government regulation and oversight, only because the elements of the certification scheme were tailor-made. So the KPCS is not a case of "one size fits all": far from it. But the core elements are essential if the success of the certification scheme is to be emulated by others.

The KPCS made a difference. Brutal civil wars in Angola, the DRC, and Sierra Leone may have stopped for reasons other than the successful negotiation of a global regulatory regime for rough diamonds. But the fact that one now exists makes future prosecution of similar wars much more difficult, as long as the KP continues to forcefully defend its integrity.

And today, that is the rub. In October 2009, Zimbabwe's government stood accused, with good reason, of mass murder in connection with the ownership and operation of certain diamond deposits in that country—but the KP had not yet taken action. To many who had built the KP from the ground up and who continued to believe in it, this position was anathema. The organization may yet do the right thing, although there is clearly dissent as to the best course of action. If it does not, it will have severely undermined its credibility—as well as the argument that war sustained by natural resources need not be part of our future.

That said, the KP has vividly demonstrated that it is possible to directly and effectively address the poisonous connection between natural resources and conflict. And the transparency that the certification scheme brought to so many governments, in Africa and elsewhere, has allowed those governments to benefit from larger, more predictable revenue streams, which are vital to post-conflict nation building. Finally, the KP has allowed countries like Sierra Leone to see, at first hand, in places like Botswana and South Africa, that diamonds can be a blessing rather than a curse, and can strengthen development instead of undermining peace.

REFERENCES

Global Witness. 1998. *A rough trade: The role of diamond companies and governments in the Angolan conflict.* www.globalwitness.org/media_library_detail.php/90/en/a_rough_trade.

Grant, J. A., and I. Taylor. 2004. Global governance and conflict diamonds: The Kimberley Process and the quest for clean gems. *Round Table* 93 (375): 385–401.

Paes, W.-C., 2005. "Conflict diamonds" to "clean diamonds": The development of the Kimberley Process Certification Scheme. In *Resource politics in Sub-Saharan Africa*, ed. A. Mehle, and M. Basedau. Hamburg: Institute of African Affairs.

Wright, C. 2004. Tackling conflict diamonds: The Kimberley Process Certification Scheme. *International Peacekeeping* 11 (4): 697–708.

The Kimberley Process Certification Scheme: The primary safeguard for the diamond industry

Andrew Bone

Diamonds evoke emotions—and for decades, the international diamond industry has relied on positive emotional messages to promote the gems. Recently, however, the industry has learned that emotional messages can also be used to put diamonds in a negative light. Love and commitment—or war and misery? The emotional value of a diamond is only what the consumer believes it to be.

Clearly, a product that aspires to be associated with the highest human values should not be associated with the misery and destruction of armed conflict. To the consumer, a diamond is a symbol of love, commitment, and self-esteem—qualities that the consumer understands and desires. And what the industry desires is to safeguard this proposition.

Without question, industry leaders have a central role to play in ensuring that diamonds are mined and traded in ways that Nicky Oppenheimer, chairman of De Beers,[1] describes as "living up to diamonds." In practical terms, living up to diamonds means taking personal responsibility for ensuring that every gem that passes through the diamond value chain comes from ethical and properly managed sources.

From the deserts of Botswana to the frozen tundra of Canada, the vast majority of diamonds are mined under secure and well-managed conditions, and provide economic development and other benefits to the countries and communities where they are extracted. But a significant percentage of diamonds originate in areas that are subject to poor governance and lack the capacity or political will to manage the trade. Although this segment makes up a minority of the trade, it is here that governments, the diamond industry, and civil society focus their attention and resources, through various organizations and initiatives, the most prominent of which is the Kimberley Process Certification Scheme (KPCS).[2]

Andrew Bone is director of international relations for the De Beers Group.
[1] De Beers, established in 1888, is the world's largest diamond producer; it has mining operations across Botswana, Namibia, South Africa, and Canada.
[2] For additional perspectives on the KPCS, see J. Andrew Grant, "The Kimberley Process at Ten: Reflections on a Decade of Efforts to End the Trade in Conflict Diamonds"; Clive Wright, "The Kimberley Process Certification Scheme: A Model Negotiation?"; and Harrison Mitchell, "A More Formal Engagement: A Constructive Critique of Certification as a Means of Preventing Conflict and Building Peace," all in this volume.

The first thing to say about the KPCS is that it is not a perfect construct—but then, few international arrangements are. It is a work in progress, evolutionary by its very nature. It is for that reason that this unique partnership between governments, the international diamond industry, and civil society meets twice each year: to improve and refine the systems that have led diamonds to be one of the most monitored and audited natural resources in the world.

THE INDUSTRY'S PRIMARY SAFEGUARD

The diamond industry, from mining companies to jewelry stores, participates in the Kimberley Process (KP) through representation on the World Diamond Council (WDC). Given such a wide and disparate constituency, each sector of the industry that is represented on the council's board must take a pragmatic approach. Discussions are occasionally spirited—but, ultimately, the focus remains on securing credible and enduring solutions to the challenges that confront the KPCS.

Although the diamond industry participates in the KP and provides it with financial and logistical support and expertise, the WDC does not "run" the KP, nor does it act as an apologist for it. Rather, it is the government members who are responsible for implementing and enforcing the requirements to which they have committed themselves by enacting national legislation. The industry's responsibility is to ensure its own compliance with the standards of the KPCS, to remain vigilantly on guard against illegal activity, and to work with member governments and civil society to highlight issues that threaten the security and credibility of the process.

In fact, the WDC often sides with civil society in challenging the governments and calling for improvements. The reason is simple: the WDC regards the KPCS as its primary safeguard against criminal infiltration or abuse during armed conflict, and as a bulwark in its efforts to provide assurance to consumers. Where differences arise between the WDC and civil society, attempts are made to resolve them, usually through informal engagement—meetings and teleconferences—at which issues are discussed, divergences addressed, and solutions sought. There is often agreement on strategy and objectives, although there may be disagreement on precisely which tactics to deploy.

It is the diamond industry that has most to gain from an effective and credible KPCS; it is thus in the interests of the industry to seek common ground with both government and civil society. In his address to the 2006 KP plenary, in Gaborone, Botswana, Eli Izhakoff, chairman of the WDC, said,

> Let me make this absolutely clear. The international diamond industry believes that a workable and effective Kimberley Process is absolutely essential if we, and the millions of people who depend on this industry, are to be properly protected from criminal activity and rebel or terrorist organizations that have no interest whatsoever in protecting the lives of innocents, in business ethics or in sustainable development in Africa (Izhakoff 2006).

WHAT THE KPCS IS—AND WHAT IT IS NOT

Although the WDC acknowledges that the scheme is not perfect and that there remains much work to be done, the council also believes that it is counterproductive and ineffectual to attack the KP as if it were an independent organization with its own exclusive resources, such as police and dedicated monitors. The KP depends on its member governments to provide political will and the resources of the state—border control, customs, etc.—that will enable the KPCS to realize its objectives and reach its full potential. Without the government support that is its lifeblood, neither the KPCS, nor any other initiative of its kind, will work as effectively as it could or should.

The KPCS is primarily designed to shine a light on noncompliance and illegal activity; in doing so, it relies on government agencies to act in harmony. For example, customs officials in each importing and exporting country are responsible for ensuring that diamond parcels are accompanied by the correct documentation and transported in the proper containers. Every KP member state has laws on smuggling that have been on the books for decades—and police and border control agencies are responsible for ensuring that those laws are enforced, with or without the existence of the KPCS. Similarly, domestic and international laws and treaties prohibiting human rights abuses have been in place for some time, and are subject to enforcement regardless of the activity with which those abuses may be associated or by whom they may be perpetrated. It is incumbent upon governments and the international community to act on these violations.

Clearly, the KPCS has an important and high-profile role—but what is needed, to achieve lasting success, is more effective cooperation and collaboration within and between governments. Although cooperation is not entirely lacking, it is not yet at the level necessary to achieve significant progress. Indeed, intra- and intergovernmental cooperation is the foundation for addressing current and future risks to the credibility of the KPCS. Without it, the KP's ability to resolve clear examples of noncompliance—and even capriciousness—is limited.[3] Neither outright noncompliance nor lesser offenses, however, are failures of the KP; instead, they stem from insufficient resources and political support on the part of member nations.

The industry has called for a higher level of cooperation and continues to do so. Although recognizing that there have been many achievements since implementation in 2003, such as the creation of the review missions and the implementation of greater transparency in the collection and sharing of trading data, the WDC is currently pressing for the following reforms:

---

[3] Too many issues have remained outstanding for too long. Although Zimbabwe continues to secure the headlines and occupy much of the KP's time, noncompliance in Venezuela and serious challenges in Côte d'Ivoire, Guinea, and Lebanon linger on (Global Witness 2007, 2009; KPA 2005a, 2005b, 2006, 2008).

- *The creation of a small, permanent secretariat.* The industry believes that the KP's operations are compromised by the lack of full-time professional support. Particularly in light of the fact that the chair changes annually, ongoing support is needed to provide continuity, arrange logistics, coordinate the working groups, and carry out rudimentary research, among other tasks.
- *A move away from consensus to a system of majority voting.* Consensus among government participants was essential to the early development of the KPCS and was instrumental in bringing together a large number of diverse governments, with differing agendas and political cultures. Seven years later, however, it is no longer the most effective method of decision making. Although consensus may be necessary for some issues, many decisions these days are technical and operational, and a simple majority vote would suffice. Relying solely on consensus as the decision-making mechanism leads to inertia and politicization: there is a temptation to delay the simplest decisions in order to engage in horse-trading on other, unrelated agenda items.
- *Greater transparency with regard to reports and decision making.* Clearly, there is a need for a certain level of confidentiality regarding the reports and decisions of the KP. But it is important to recognize that in addition to its primary function—preventing trade in conflict diamonds—the KPCS is also a process that is of legitimate interest to the public, including consumers of diamond jewelry.

The WDC also supports the efforts of civil society participants to include specific wording in the KPCS that will address human rights in the diamond mining sector (including the artisanal sector); in particular, the WDC believes that security measures should be consistent with international human rights obligations, and should apply to both diamond miners and local communities. Although several governments—including the United Kingdom, the United States, and Canada—have joined the call for the inclusion of such wording in the KPCS, some participating governments believe that human rights issues are outside the purview of the KPCS. But in fact, the KPCS was largely born out of the need to address human rights abuses in central and western Africa—an origin that is explicitly reflected the preamble to the KPCS: "recognising the devastating impact of conflicts fuelled by the trade in conflict diamonds on the peace, safety and security of people in affected countries and the systematic and gross human rights violations that have been perpetrated in such conflicts" (KPA 2002).

THE NEED FOR A MULTILATERAL APPROACH

At the time of the KPCS's implementation, in 2003, Secretary-General of the United Nations Kofi Annan said,

> It is time for a fundamental reassessment of how the world body [United Nations] works. We are living through a crisis of the international system, and the

emergence of new and non-conventional threats forces us to ask whether the institutions and methods to which we are accustomed are really adequate (Turner 2003, 3).

The KPCS is a new methodology and a relatively new institution that has demonstrated the potential to reconcile differing and occasionally entrenched positions. It is an opportunity to be seized and embraced, but political will and adequate support will be required to bring it to its full potential.

The KPCS should also be regarded as one of several instruments capable of addressing the many socioeconomic challenges facing developing nations, where governance is often the overarching issue. Addressing a KP meeting in Johannesburg in November 2003, Nicky Oppenheimer highlighted the role of the KPCS in supporting good governance:

> We—industry and governments together—need to provide assistance to those countries where the logistics of control are more complicated to ensure that diamond revenues are retained by local communities and for redevelopment post-conflict. Failure to secure these productions will leave them, large number of diggers and many needy communities vulnerable to unscrupulous buyers seeking to circumvent the Kimberley provisions.
>
> To achieve this goal we need to engage with these countries, encouraging a return to good governance, the rule of law, and sound fiscal policy in exchange for benign investment. Security of tenure, legal protection of property rights and contracts, courts immune to political whim, and bureaucrats free of corruption are essential pre-conditions. Industry, in turn, must ensure that profits gained make a real and lasting contribution to the countries and communities in which it operates, and this should be done in tandem with local and international NGOs (Oppenheimer 2003).

Oppenheimer's comments underline a point made earlier: namely, that viewing the KP as solely responsible for governance issues related to mining and trading—much less as having the wherewithal to address such issues unilaterally—is a distraction from the legitimate debate about how best to address the challenges facing many communities today. Instead of focusing on the presumed shortcomings of the KP, all parties concerned should use the experience that they have acquired through the KPCS to turn a spotlight on issues that are associated with, but not exclusive to, the diamond business. After all, smuggling, poor working conditions, human rights, and corruption are problems that face not just mining, but all extractive industries—not to mention other industries as well. These problems can and should be dealt with through collaboration across sectors and borders; the KPCS has an important contribution to make to this effort, but it is not the silver bullet.

CONCLUSION

The KPCS is a unique, world-class example of cross-sector collaboration. In spite of the challenges it faces, it is making progress. But the diamond industry is the first to acknowledge that a thing is only well done when it *is* done—and the work of the KPCS is not yet done.

Through the KPCS, the industry has learned that positive engagement with all stakeholders not only benefits the industry—by allowing it to be part of the solution—but is also the most effective way to develop solutions that are sustainable because they involve all interested parties. A multi-stakeholder approach creates a sense of universal ownership and accountability, enabling all participants—from industry and nongovernmental organizations to governments and communities—to feel that they have made an investment in something important and lasting.

REFERENCES

Global Witness. 2007. Kimberley Process must expel Venezuela. Press release. www.globalwitness.org/media_library_detail.php/606/en/kimberley_process_must_expel_venezuela.

———. 2009. Blood diamonds—Time to plug the gaps. www.globalwitness.org/media_library_detail.php/774/en/blood_diamonds_time_to_plug_the_gaps_.

Izhakoff, E. 2006. Address to Kimberley Process plenary, November 6, Gaborone, Botswana. www.worlddiamondcouncil.com/press/wdc_110606.htm.

KPA (Kimberley Process Authority). 2002. Kimberley Process Certification Scheme. www.kimberleyprocess.com/documents/basic_core_documents_en.html.

———. 2005a. Participants world map. www.kimberleyprocess.com/structure/participants_world_map_en.html.

———. 2005b. Summary of the Kimberley Process review visit to Guinea. www.kimberleyprocess.com/download/getfile/64.

———. 2006. Annual report on the implementation of KPCS in accordance with section VI, paragraph 11 of the KPCS document, Lebanon. www.kimberleyprocess.com/structure/participants_world_map_en.html.

———. 2008. Kimberley Process Chair letter on Venezuela. www.kimberleyprocess.com/download/getfile/788.

Oppenheimer, N. 2003. Royalty bill could jeopardize KP. www.diamonds.net/news/NewsItem.aspx?ArticleID=8003.

Turner, M. 2003. New challenges mean time for change at the UN. *Financial Times* (weekend edition). September 6/7.

A more formal engagement: A constructive critique of certification as a means of preventing conflict and building peace

Harrison Mitchell

For policy makers who wish to prevent military groups from benefiting from mineral resources, a certification process that ensures a "conflict-free" mineral-trading chain is an attractive proposition. The most well-established certification system for the mineral trade, the Kimberley Process Certification Scheme (KPCS), has been in effect since 2003.[1] Supporters of the KPCS point to the scheme's success in stemming the flow of "conflict diamonds" by verifying the origin of the gems.[2] This chapter argues, however, that the true success of the KPCS lies in two achievements: (1) helping to formalize the international diamond trade at the point of export and (2) providing some rationalization of the sector. By increasing their ability to tax formal trade and exports, formalization and rationalization have assisted the governments of producing countries to strengthen their fiscal link to the diamond trade. Because the achievements associated with the KPCS provide income (and foreign exchange) for often impoverished states, they are important in the context of peacebuilding; but the ability of the KPCS (or similar certificate-of-origin schemes) to prevent armed groups from benefiting from resources remains largely untested.

Although the KPCS requires producing countries to establish internal control systems to verify that diamonds are conflict free, full and genuine assurance of origin is difficult to obtain, particularly in developing countries with large artisanal mining communities, where the informality, size, and geography of the sector combine with a lack of resources, capacity, and political will (Kimberley Process 2002, sec. IV). Recent studies have confirmed that, particularly in developing states with large and informal artisanal sectors, the informal trade in diamonds

---

Harrison Mitchell is a director of Resource Consulting Services and has performed country audits of China and Lebanon for the Kimberley Process Certification Scheme.

[1] For additional perspectives on the KPCS, see J. Andrew Grant, "The Kimberley Process at Ten: Reflections on a Decade of Efforts to End the Trade in Conflict Diamonds"; Andrew Bone, "The Kimberley Process Certification Scheme: The Primary Safeguard for the Diamond Industry"; and Clive Wright, "The Kimberley Process Certification Scheme: A Model Negotiation?" all in this volume.

[2] For more information on the KPCS, see www.kimberleyprocess.com.

and other precious minerals within and between producer countries remains largely unmonitored (Garrett, Mitchell, and Levin 2008). In Côte d'Ivoire, for example, small quantities of conflict diamonds continue to be laundered through well-established informal trading networks whose size and effectiveness place them well beyond the control of local and international authorities.

Artisanally mined diamonds, which are produced in small mines that are often far from town centers, can easily be carried out of the country—from Sierra Leone to Ghana, for example, or from the Congo to Angola—by traders who use the gems as a lightweight and concealable form of currency, exchanging them for cash once they reach their destination. After obtaining a fraudulent origin along the way, many of these informally traded diamonds enter the formal trade in other KPCS member countries.[3] This process—by which informally traded diamonds of uncertain origin enter the formal diamond trade—poses a threat to the integrity of a system that claims to offer assurance that its diamonds are conflict-free.

The realities of the informal diamond trade in Central and West Africa, where Angolan diamonds are certified in the Democratic Republic of the Congo and Sierra Leonean diamonds in Liberia, make it difficult to believe in the KPCS label of origin; they also call into question one of the primary goals of the KPCS, which is to support peacebuilding by depriving rebel groups of access to diamonds. The ease with which diamonds can be laundered through KPCS member nations (or even bypass such nations, by following an entirely informal route to trading centers such as Dubai), suggests that it remains difficult for certificate-of-origin schemes to verify their own integrity, let alone affect the vibrant and ongoing informal trade.[4]

Although this is not an argument against certification per se, it does apppear that attempting to establish certification before traditionally informal sectors have been formalized is likely to undercut the ability to enforce certain tenets, such as origin, on a significant scale. In order to provide meaningful assurance of origin, national and international agencies and organizations must engage with the informal sector on two levels: first by helping to formalize exploitation and trade, and second by providing the informal sector with both the will and the means (that is, with incentives and capacity) to support assurance of origin that meets Western consumers' standards for origin and quality control.

---

[3] For a description of the artisanal mining trade, see Garrett, Mitchell, and Levin (2008).
[4] When measures such as sanctions are imposed on a mineral trade, severe consequences for the local population have the potential to negate the security aims of the certification scheme. Gavin Hilson (2008) describes the serious disruption and loss of income for the local population that occurred after a temporary suspension of the trade in diamonds from Ghana, which was suggested by the Kimberley Process when Ivorian conflict diamonds were allegedly being laundered through Ghana. In late 2008, when the price of minerals dropped in Katanga Province, in the Democratic Republic of the Congo, miners joined armed groups, and there was an increase in petty crime because miners were unable to find work elsewhere.

A series of studies published by the World Bank in 2003, around the time that the KPCS was established, shows that for some observers the jury was still out on whether certification schemes were truly effective mechanisms for preventing natural resource revenues from perpetuating conflict (Crossin, Hayman, and Taylor 2003). Some of the KPCS's initial proponents viewed the scheme as one of many possible means of breaking the link between natural resources and the funding of conflict, but not as a solution in and of itself (Bannon and Collier 2003). Ian Bannon and Paul Collier (2003), for example, viewed the KPCS as one of a set of actions—ranging from econonomic development to greater transparency—that the international community could support.[5]

Indeed, given that the KPCS was established in 2003, after the diamond-fuelled wars of Sierra Leone and Angola had already ended, the scheme's ability to prevent natural resource sales from funding rebel groups remains largely untested. The KPCS has imposed only one conflict-related sanction: a ban on diamond exports from the north of Côte d'Ivoire, which has been in place since 2005 without apparent effect on the trade in Ivorian diamonds; as noted earlier, these gems are traded through informal networks and may be brought into the formal economy through KPCS-certified trading chains (Global Witness 2006). The Ivorian example raises questions about the ability of certificate-of-origin schemes such as the KPCS to effectively prevent military groups from benefiting from supply chains, particularly where production is small enough to be absorbed into informal trading networks. That the KPCS remains largely untested in this respect should serve as a warning for proponents of similar schemes involving other minerals.

The successes to which the KPCS can point are not in preventing conflict but in boosting the benefits of diamond resources to post-conflict states. First and foremost, by providing an administrative bottleneck between international sellers and buyers, the KPCS has helped increase export tax revenues for producing countries. This has helped formalize the international trade in rough diamonds and strengthened the overall fiscal link between natural resources and the state, an important factor in peacebuilding. It has also led to some rationalization of the sector, as countries such as Sierra Leone adjusted their mining laws to limit the number of possible actors in a trading chain (in particular, by limiting the number of exporters, who operate at the point where the government can have the most control). Large private sector actors have also used the KPCS to increase the transparency of their diamond supply chains, and thereby helped manage public perceptions of their potential association with conflict diamonds. Finally, the

---

[5] Bannon and Collier (2003) are supportive of the KPCS, going so far as to suggest that the scheme might be judged a success even if the most it did was to force rebels to sell at a deep discount. Though the evidence is anecdotal, one industry expert formerly associated with De Beers has suggested that after the KPCS was instituted and rebel goods became more difficult to sell, people got scared—and the price of certain rough diamonds on the Antwerp Diamond Bourse dropped (Gilbert 2010).

Table 1. Effects of a top-down mineral certificate-of-origin scheme

Likely	Unlikely
Increase transparency and traceability in the context of formal international trade.	Eliminate avenues for the laundering of "conflict" or corruption minerals at subnational levels. Eliminate informal international trade.
Foster formalization, including taxation, at the point of export.	Foster formalization of artisanal, small-scale, and other informal forms of mining and trading.
Encourage legal (or mostly legal) actors to comply.	Remove illegal actors and military groups from the supply chain.
Increase scrutiny of the downstream mineral chain, which may lead to greater focus on upstream labor rights and environmental issues.	Eliminate upstream human rights abuses, inequality, poverty, insecurity, etc.
Place a significant monitoring burden on states, albeit while enhancing the state's technical expertise; create new opportunities for state corruption, rent seeking, and deliberate misclassification of minerals.	Eliminate corruption, rent seeking, and deliberate misclassification by state institutions.

Source: Adapted from Garrett and Mitchell (2009).

KPCS has created a forum for expanding the debate about diamonds beyond the issue of conflict to include matters such as labor practices, the environment, and human rights.[6]

Table 1, which is based on field research conducted by Nicholas Garrett and Harrison Mitchell (2009), summarizes the likely and unlikely effects of a top-down certificate-of-origin scheme such as the KPCS. For development and peacebuilding policy makers, the outcomes enumerated in the table suggest that the role of certificate-of-origin schemes should be reevaluated. Specifically, one must ask whether the emphasis on assurance of origin is misplaced, given that such initiatives exist in parallel with well-established informal networks. Where resources are limited, should they be directed to such schemes, or would they be better allocated to other mechanisms or policy approaches? This question is particularly pertinent in light of the difficulty of effectively implementing such schemes under conditions of limited capacity.

Given that armed groups benefit from the mineral sector—and that, by operating through informal channels, they will continue to do so—the lessons of the KPCS suggest that the international community should assist countries to formalize their informal and artisanal extractive sectors, rather than compel

---

[6] For expanded discussions of diamond-related human rights and labor rights issues, see the web sites of the Madison Dialogue (www.madisondialogue.org) and the Diamond Development Initiative (www.ddiglobal.org), both of which were established after the KPCS.

them to provide an assurance of origin that means little where informal mining and trading networks remain dominant.[7] Certificate-of-origin schemes can be costly to establish and monitor over the long term, especially in developing countries characterized by low administrative capacity, lack of resources, vested interests, and well-established informal networks. In addition, if border controls and export procedures are sufficiently sophisticated to obtain the appropriate tax, assurance of origin will not even be necessary to support the fiscal link between the mineral trade and the government.

Finally, it is worth noting that many assurance initiatives are designed to meet the demands of consumers or governments in Western markets, rather than to meet the needs of artisanal mining communities and local traders. Given the right incentives and assistance, these miners and traders could work toward formalizing and professionalizing their operations, but they have been largely ignored by the international community in favor of certificate schemes that, by assuring origin, purport to serve a security function. Given that assistance with formalization could potentially pay a far greater development dividend for local mining communities over the medium to long term, the question remains whether this assistance might in fact have a far greater impact on building peace than would an uncertain promise of origin.

REFERENCES

Bannon, I., and P. Collier. 2003. Natural resources and conflict: What can we do? In *Natural resources and violent conflict: Options and actions*, ed. I. Bannon and P. Collier. Washington, D.C.: World Bank.

Crossin, C., G. Hayman, and S. Taylor. 2003. Where did it come from? Commodity tracking systems. In *Natural resources and violent conflict: Options and actions*, ed. I. Bannon and P. Collier. Washington, D.C.: World Bank.

Garrett, N., and H. Mitchell. 2009. *Trading conflict for development: Utilising the trade in minerals from eastern DR Congo for development*. London: Department for International Development / Crisis States Research Centre / London School of Economics and Political Science / Conflict Research Group, University of Ghent.

Garrett, N., H. Mitchell, and E. Levin. 2008. Regulating reality: Reconfiguring approaches to the regulation of trading artisanally mined diamonds. In *Artisanal diamond mining: Perspectives and challenges*, ed. K. Vlassenroot and S. Van Bockstael. Brussels: Egmont Royal Institute for International Relations.

Gilbert, S. 2010. Former manager, external relations, De Beers Group. Interviews with author. March.

Global Witness. 2006. The truth about diamonds. www.globalwitness.org/data/files/media_library/7/en/the_truth_about_diamonds.pdf.

---

[7] Formal trade is regulated by the institutions of society and taxed and monitored by government. The formalization of informal and unregulated production and trade encompasses many reforms, including providing artisanal miners with legal rights, registering miners and traders, and imposing taxes. For a broader discussion of formalization, see Mitchell and Garrett (2009).

Hilson, G. 2008. Mining and rural development: The trajectory of diamond production in Ghana. In *Artisanal diamond mining: Perspectives and challenges*, ed. K. Vlassenroot and S. Van Bockstael. Brussels: Egmont Royal Institute for International Relations.

Kimberley Process. 2002. Kimberley Process Certification Scheme. www.kimberleyprocess.com/download/getfile/4.

Mitchell, H., and N. Garrett. 2009. *Beyond conflict: Reconfiguring approaches to the regional trade in minerals from eastern DRC*. Washington, D.C.: Communities and Small-Scale Mining (CASM), World Bank. www.artisanalmining.org/UserFiles/file/Beyond_Conflict_RCS_CASM.pdf.

Addressing the roots of Liberia's conflict through the Extractive Industries Transparency Initiative

Eddie Rich and T. Negbalee Warner

The Extractive Industries Transparency Initiative (EITI) sets a global standard for transparency in the management of oil, gas, and mining revenues. Launched in 2002 and now endorsed by many international bodies and institutions, including the United Nations General Assembly, the World Bank, and the Group of Twenty,[1] the EITI is designed to strengthen governance by improving transparency and accountability in the extractive sector through the full publication of company payments and government revenues from oil, gas, and mining.

Compliance with the EITI standard is overseen by a coalition of governments, companies, and civil society groups, both at the international level and within each of the countries in which it is being implemented. The EITI has a robust yet flexible methodology that ensures that the standard is maintained throughout all participating countries.[2] The EITI board, which is made up of representatives from government, the private sector, and civil society, is the guardian of that methodology. Implementation itself, however, is the responsibility of the individual countries.

In many resource-rich countries, especially those that are recovering from civil war, opacity and silence have created mistrust and suspicion. Citizens often assume that the government and the extractive companies are in cahoots to keep the wealth for themselves, and companies sometimes feel that governments and citizens are ganging up on them to reset the rules and renegotiate contracts. The

---

Eddie Rich is deputy head of the Extractive Industries Transparency Initiative (EITI) International Secretariat, which is based in Oslo. T. Negbalee Warner practices and teaches law in Liberia, and was the head of the Liberian EITI Secretariat from 2007 to 2010.

[1] The Group of Twenty (also known as the G-20) is an international forum for economic development "that promotes open and constructive discussion between industrial and emerging-market countries on key issues related to global economic stability" (G-20 n.d.).

[2] The validation methodology assesses a country's meaningful and compliant implementation of the EITI on the basis of a number of indicators, including the country's overall work plan and the dissemination of information to the public. For the full methodology, see EITI (n.d.a).

EITI has been held up as a shining example of how multi-stakeholder initiatives can address these kinds of challenges. But the initiative is still young, and much of this praise has been premature.

Although the number of countries participating in the EITI has expanded rapidly to thirty, only half of the countries have produced EITI reports detailing what companies claim to have paid to the government in taxes and royalties, and what the government claims to have received. As these countries approach validation—the quality assurance test that determines whether they have met all the requirements of the EITI governance standard—the first clear picture of the relationship between transparency, multi-stakeholder approaches, and reconciliation is emerging.[3] In October 2009, Liberia became the first African country to pass validation, and thus be designated EITI compliant. Liberia is therefore a test case.

LIBERIA AND THE EITI

Liberia's natural resource wealth has long been at the center of the country's tumultuous history, as well as at the root of much of its corruption.[4] Despite an abundance of iron ore, diamonds, gold, timber, and rubber, Liberia was ravaged by a fourteen-year civil war (1989–2003) that devastated the nation. By 2007, the country was still at the bottom of the UN's Human Development Index, ranking 169 out of 182 (UNDP 2009). After general elections were held in 2005, the new government led by President Ellen Johnson Sirleaf vowed to ensure growth, development, and reconciliation by improving transparency in the extractive sectors. In accordance with Johnson Sirleaf's priorities, Liberia joined the EITI and established the Liberia EITI (LEITI), a multi-stakeholder body responsible for implementing the EITI.

Recognizing the role that corruption, mismanagement, and distrust had played in fueling the war, the LEITI has made a special effort to be inclusive; for example, Liberia was the first EITI participant to incorporate rubber and forestry into the extractive industries initiative. The LEITI has also made extensive efforts to raise awareness of the initiative throughout the nation. The first LEITI report (Crane et al. 2009), which was published in February 2009 and covered July 2007 through June 2008, generated contagious interest among Liberians both within and outside the country; that interest was intensified by LEITI's outreach efforts, which publicized the results of the report through town hall meetings, radio programs, newspaper articles, street theater, and posters displayed in every

---

[3] For more details on the validation process, see EITI (n.d.b).
[4] For more details on the conflict, see Stephanie L. Altman, Sandra S. Nichols, and John T. Woods, "Leveraging High-Value Natural Resources to Restore the Rule of Law: The Role of Liberia Forest Initiative in Liberia's Transition to Stability," and Michael D. Beevers, "Forest Resources and Peacebuilding: Preliminary Lessons from Liberia and Sierra Leone," both in this volume.

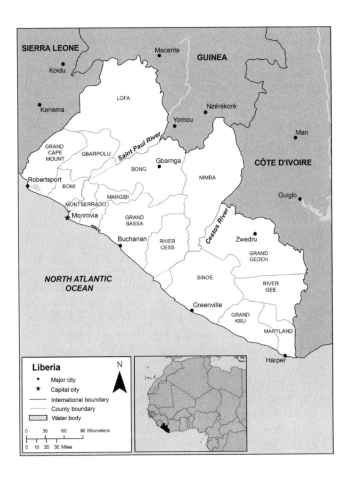

public building in Liberia.[5] The value of discussions about the report cannot be overemphasized, especially in Liberia, where information of this sort is hardly ever in the public domain.

The LEITI report

But what did Liberia's first LEITI report actually reveal? The report detailed, on a company-by-company basis, what mineral and forestry companies had paid to the government, in the form of taxes and other contributions. Because reported payments were matched to reported receipts, any discrepancy between what a company claimed to have paid and what the government claimed to have received was clearly revealed. The report, which covered almost thirty companies from

---

[5] The second LEITI report was published in February 2010. LEITI reports and related documents are available at www.leiti.org.lr/content.php?sub=48&related=62&third=48.

the oil, gas, and mining sectors, showed that the government received about US$30 million in taxes and royalties from July 2007 through June 2008.

The report brought to light three key points. First, although taxes and other payments made to the government contribute to stability and sustainable development, the extent of this contribution has not always been recognized, even in the communities in which the extractive industries operate: the communities simply did not know what the companies paid or where the payments went. The report thus increases citizens' immediate understanding of the contributions made by extractive companies. It is little wonder that the LEITI is strongly backed by companies that are seeking a level playing field on which to compete.

In 2005, for example, ArcelorMittal, a Luxembourg-based multinational mining giant, signed a billion-dollar mineral development agreement with the transitional government of Liberia. When the current government rejected the agreement, holding that it was not in the interest of Liberia, the firm became the subject of criticism, negative publicity, and suspicion. The agreement was renegotiated in 2007—and, as the LEITI report shows, the nearly US$24 million that the government received from ArcelorMittal constituted three-quarters of all taxes and royalties from the oil, gas, mining, and forestry sectors for the period covered by the report. In accordance with the terms of the renegotiated agreement, about US$7 million of all taxes and royalties was for the direct benefit of the municipalities and counties where the company has its operations.[6]

The LEITI report thus represents an independent confirmation that ArcelorMittal paid the agreed-upon benefits and that the government of Liberia received the payments on behalf of the communities. As part of its efforts to rebuild trust with communities, ArcelorMittal has pointed to its contributions to the central government and to communities. Referring to the first report, Joe Mathews, chief executive officer of ArcelorMittal-Liberia, said that

> the EITI is playing a key role in our relations with stakeholders, helping us to connect with the communities where we operate and with the government. Participation in the EITI also helps us to uphold the strong principles of corporate responsibility we believe in through supporting fair and transparent business practices and ensuring that proper accounting is made of all payments in our operations in Liberia (EITI 2010, 15).

Second, as previously noted, the report identified discrepancies between what the companies claim to have paid and what the government claims to have received. Most of these were minor, and were likely to have arisen because of differences in accounting classifications. One significant discrepancy concerned an income tax payment of over US$100,000 from a precious metals and minerals company, AmLib United Materials, which the government denied having received—

---

[6] For more details, see EITI (2009).

a position that was confirmed by a subsequent investigation. AmLib traced the discrepancy and found a clear-cut matter of internal fraud. The firm has since paid the government and taken appropriate legal action; it is also shoring up its financial systems. AmLib representatives have attended many of LEITI's town hall and public meetings, where they explained the matter directly to community residents and described the steps being taken to prevent such a thing from happening again.

Third, the report highlighted a number of suspicious, unexplained payments that had been made by some companies but had not been received by the government, and revealed that other companies that had failed to report at all—creating significant discussion within communities. Who is operating the mine down the road? Why was this payment made, and to whom? How can we raise our concerns with the government and with the companies themselves?

Although the report itself does not provide full answers to these questions, the LEITI has created a forum in which these and other questions can be discussed with both the companies and the government: openly, frankly, and in a safe and noncombative environment. The communities—and indeed all Liberians—have also used the opportunity to raise questions about how money is being allocated and used, and whether communities are receiving a fair return for their resources.

The LEITI Act

In July 2009, following the publication of the first EITI report, the LEITI Act came into force (GOL 2009). The act requires all government agencies and extractive companies to comply with the LEITI process. The LEITI Act goes far beyond the core EITI requirements; in addition to obligating each company to document its payments to the government, it calls for all operating contracts and licenses to be reviewed, archived, and made available to the public.[7] This provision assures citizens and companies alike that all extractive companies operating in Liberia—whether from China, Malaysia, Europe, or elsewhere—are on an open and level playing field, and that there is a forum in which stakeholders can voice their concerns. Under the LEITI Act, any company that refuses to publish its contract is subject to sanctions.

LESSONS AND CHALLENGES

The story of the LEITI demonstrates the power of the EITI process to create a platform for dialogue. The results achieved by the LEITI process were made possible through the personal commitment of the president; the dedication of the LEITI Multi-Stakeholder Steering Group, which is the governing body of the

---

[7] See GOL (2009), sec. 4.1(d)(ii), (e), and (f).

LEITI; and the shared commitment of all stakeholders, including the extractive companies.[8]

But Liberia's experience is also a reminder of another key fact about the EITI: it is only a start. The EITI is one component in the resource-governance value chain that begins with the award of a contract and continues through contract monitoring, documentation of payments and revenues, use of revenues, and the development of policies to support sustainable resource use. The EITI is therefore a necessary, but not sufficient, condition for peace, stability, and improved resource governance—as is evident in Liberia, where, despite successful implementation of the EITI, no one is yet better fed, or in school, or receiving medicines because of the EITI. It is even difficult to argue that the EITI has contributed to peacebuilding in Liberia. Nevertheless, Liberia now has a platform for the discussion of governance issues related to the extractive sector—which, in itself, has the potential to consolidate the EITI's achievements and deliver real impact. Not to mention the fact that the first report identified a clear-cut case of fraud.

Several further challenges face the LEITI in particular and Liberia's natural resource sector in general. Liberian civil society groups have developed a dossier of what they perceive as dubious contracts; donors and international observers still complain about ongoing graft in concessions; and communities still contend that extractive firms and local politicians are colluding to steal mine proceeds. In addition, reports from Global Witness, a nongovernmental organization that researches and campaigns against corrupt exploitation of natural resources, have warned against an overconcentration of particular companies in the forestry sector, and a UN panel of experts has filed a report about inadequate contracting procedures (UNSC 2008). Some ministers and government officials continue to be the focus of suspicion and innuendo. And finally, the expected returns on resource investments, particularly in forestry, have been slow to materialize.

On taking power, President Johnson Sirleaf arranged for a international panel of independent experts to undertake a full review of all resource contracts. Yet in the eyes of many observers, even this step failed to ensure maximum benefits for the Liberian people.[9] There are five principal reasons:

- After years of civil war, personal agendas, vested interests, and suspicion still remain. As a consequence, the advice of independent experts was not always followed.
- Once the international technical advisers had completed their review of existing contracts, the Forestry Development Authority and the relevant ministries lacked the capacity, and in some cases were reluctant, to negotiate new contracts.

---

[8] The Multi-Stakeholder Steering Group is made up of fifteen members from government, civil society, and the private sector.
[9] Among the entities that have expressed such concerns are Publish What You Pay; the Energy, Environment and Development Programme; and Global Witness. See Friends of the Earth (2006), illegal-logging.info (n.d.), and Global Witness (2006).

- Systemic corruption continues to thrive, compromising many governmental institutions and processes. The Liberian media is rife with reports of corruption involving senior government officials, and President Johnson Sirleaf has acknowledged that corruption is a crucial problem. Although successful implementation of the EITI is no guarantee against corruption, it should help combat it. The EITI has helped to create a civil society that, empowered and emboldened by credible data, can demand greater accountability and transparency. It is still too early to assess the impact of the LEITI data on efforts to strengthen governance and eliminate corruption.
- Extractive contracts have not always been fully monitored and enforced. Although monitoring and enforcement are beyond the scope of the EITI, Liberia has fortunately chosen to incorporate contract transparency into the LEITI, which may help improve the integrity of the sector. But this will take time.
- A collapse in the global price of commodities led to massive delays in mining and forestry contracts.

In sum, there is no room for complacency with regard to natural resource management in Liberia. The battle against corruption and for reconciliation goes on, within and outside the LEITI arena.

CONCLUSION

Building trust in a resource-rich, post-conflict environment like Liberia's may take years, and will depend largely on sustained, interlocking, and self-reinforcing interventions in many areas of governance, including the judiciary, the civil service, and auditing institutions. There is a need for the president to provide exemplary leadership to all senior government officials by establishing and strengthening a culture of transparency and accountability.

The EITI focuses on just one area. Its contribution should therefore be recognized as the first bold step in creating an environment for reconciliation—that is, as a necessary, but not sufficient, framework for change. As President Johnson Sirleaf has said, "Trust is the greatest asset a country can have. . . . [LEITI] represents an important step in advancing our efforts to engage with stakeholders, to talk about our resources, and to build trust in our communities" (Johnson Sirleaf 2008).

EPILOGUE

In October 2009, after the first LEITI report, Liberia became the first country in Africa (and the second country in the world, after Azerbaijan) to achieve EITI compliance.[10] Liberia's second LEITI report, produced in February 2010, represented

---

[10] This epilogue draws from LEITI (2010).

a significant improvement over the first: it covered more sectors and companies, reported more payments and revenues, and contained fewer discrepancies.

According to the second report, before reconciliation, total payments amounted to US$32,391,137, and total revenues amounted to US$50,300,746. Using source documents, including actual receipts, the reconciler confirmed that oil, forestry, agriculture, and mining companies (including a few diamond and gold dealers and brokers) had paid the government US$35,280,234 in the form of taxes, royalties, rental and administrative fees, and other contributions, and that the government had received US$35,425,230. The difference (US$144,955, or 0.04 percent of the total declared by government agencies) resulted from two main causes: first, four companies claimed to have paid certain amounts to the government but failed to substantiate their payments; second, seven companies failed to submit payment data to the LEITI independent administrator, although the government proved that it had indeed received payments from those seven companies. Hence, the report reflected the proved revenues declared by the government, even where no corresponding data for payments were received. The LEITI subsequently fined the companies that had failed to report.

Moore Stephens LLP, the independent administrator, worked to resolve all discrepancies between payment and revenue data. Nevertheless, like the first LEITI report, the second report contains a few minor, unresolved discrepancies and two significant unresolved discrepancies.

The first significant unresolved discrepancy concerns the amount of US$95,253, which Cocopa Rubber Company declared, but failed to substantiate—despite several reported requests for proof. The second material unresolved discrepancy involves Subseas Resources DMCC, which transferred its mineral rights to Ocean Bottom Resources West Africa, Inc., on November 26, 2008. Before transferring its mineral rights to Ocean Bottom Resources, Subseas made payments of US$127,235 to the government of Liberia. The government reported and substantiated receipt of the Subseas payments, but Subseas did not report any data to the reconciler. Hence, the proved revenues received and reported by the government lacked corresponding reported payments from Subseas.

Despite the presence of unresolved discrepancies, the second LEITI report was widely disseminated and positively received by communities, civil society organizations, and other individuals and groups. This positive reception may be explained by three factors: First, the publication of unresolved discrepancies is viewed as evidence of a new spirit of transparency, in which the government is not concealing weaknesses or inconvenient facts. Second, because the payment and revenues data are published separately, it is easy to see the specific causes of the discrepancies. Third, it has emerged that many reports published by other EITI countries also contain discrepancies—and, as in the case of Liberia, some of the discrepancies are attributable to accounting and reporting weaknesses and are not necessarily the result of corruption or theft. Hence, the implementation of the EITI and the attending publication of payments and revenues data is helping to build confidence and trust, and thereby reduce suspicion and conflict in Liberia.

REFERENCES

Crane, D., C. White, P. Jefferson, and S. Ponsonby. 2009. Final report of the administrators of the first LEITI reconciliation. www.leiti.org.lr/doc/LEITIADMINISTRATORSREPORT01.pdf.

EITI (Extractive Industries Transparency Initiative). 2009. Advancing the EITI in the mining sector: A consultation with stakeholders. http://eiti.org/files/MINING%20Compressed.pdf.

———. 2010. Impact of EITI in Africa: Stories from the ground. http://eitransparency.org/files/EITI%20Impact%20in%20Africa.pdf.

———. n.d.a. EITI rules including the validation guide. http://eiti.org/document/rules.

———. n.d.b. Extractive Industries Transparency Initiative validation guide. http://eiti.org/files/document/validationguide.pdf.

Friends of the Earth. 2006. Governance and Economic Management Assistance Program (GEMAP): An update on GEMAP by Friends of the Earth, with contributions from the Sustainable Development Institute. www.publishwhatyoupay.org/en/resources/gemap-update-liberia's-progress-gemap.

G-20. n.d. What is the G-20. www.g20.org/about_what_is_g20.aspx.

Global Witness. 2006. Heavy Mittal? A state within a state: The inequitable mineral development agreement between the government of Liberia and Mittal Steel Holdings NV. www.globalwitness.org/media_library_detail.php/156/en/heavy_mittal.

GOL (Government of Liberia), Ministry of Foreign Affairs. 2009. An act establishing the Liberia Extractive Industries Transparency Initiative (LEITI). Monrovia: Ministry of Foreign Affairs.

illegal-logging.info. n.d. Liberia. www.illegal-logging.info/approach.php?a_id=65.

Johnson Sirleaf, E. 2008. Foreword. In *Talking transparency: A guide for communicating the Extractive Industries Transparency Initiative*. Extractive Industries Transparency Initiative. http://eiti.org/files/EITI%20Communications%20Guide.pdf.

LEITI (Liberia Extractive Industries Transparency Initiative). 2010. Summary of LEITI second report: 1 July 2008–30 June 2009. www.leiti.org.lr/doc/leiti_report_forweb.pdf.

UNDP (United Nations Development Programme). 2009. *Overcoming barriers: Human mobility and development*. Human development report 2009. http://hdr.undp.org/en/media/HDR_2009_EN_Complete.pdf.

UNSC (United Nations Security Council). 2008. Report of the panel of experts submitted pursuant to paragraph 1 of Security Council Resolution 1819 (2008) concerning Liberia. S/2008/785. www.securitycouncilreport.org/atf/cf/%7B65BFCF9B-6D27-4E9C-8CD3-CF6E4FF96FF9%7D/Liberia%20S%202008%20785.pdf.

Excluding illegal timber and improving forest governance: The European Union's Forest Law Enforcement, Governance and Trade initiative

Duncan Brack

In many timber-producing countries in the developing world, illegal logging and the trade in illegally logged timber cause environmental damage, hinder sustainable development, cost governments billions of dollars in lost revenue, promote corruption, and undermine governance and the rule of law. Consumer countries contribute to these problems by importing timber and other forest products without ensuring that they are legally sourced.

Illegal logging and the trade in illegally logged timber first came to international attention in the late 1990s. The event that was largely responsible for triggering international discussion of the issue was the inclusion of illegal logging in the 1998–2002 G8 Action Programme on Forests—which, in recognition of the importance of forestry to development and the environment, was intended to accelerate implementation of the actions that had been proposed in 1997 by the United Nations Intergovernmental Panel on Forests. The Action Programme covered five areas: monitoring and assessment; national forest programs; protected areas; the private sector; and illegal logging. In most of these areas, the G8 countries simply lent support to national initiatives that were already under way; under the heading of illegal logging, however, the United Kingdom took the lead, initiating a wide range of studies, discussions, and meetings—including ministerial-level conferences on forest law enforcement and governance in (1) East Asia, (2) Africa, and (3) Europe and North Asia (G8 Action Programme on Forests 2002). These efforts are still bearing fruit today.

Since the early 2000s, producer and consumer countries alike have increased their efforts to curb illegal logging and the trade in illegal timber. In 2003, the European Union (EU) published the Forest Law Enforcement, Governance and Trade (FLEGT) action plan, the most ambitious set of measures

---

Duncan Brack was a senior research fellow in the Energy, Environment and Development Programme at Chatham House (Royal Institute of International Affairs), United Kingdom. The author would like to thank Stephanie Altman, Art Blundell, Jade Saunders, and Hugh Speechly for their comments and helpful observations.

adopted by any consumer country or bloc to date. The FLEGT action plan includes the following components:

- The negotiation of voluntary partnership agreements (VPAs) between the EU and timber-producing countries. Each VPA includes a licensing system designed to identify legal products and license them for import to the EU (unlicensed products are denied entry) and capacity-building assistance to help partner countries set up the licensing scheme, improve enforcement, and, where necessary, reform their laws.
- Consideration of additional legislative options to facilitate broader control of the import of illegal timber to the EU—specifically, controls on products that originate in countries that do not have VPAs and are therefore not covered by the licensing scheme.[1]
- Encouragement of voluntary industry initiatives and government procurement policies that would limit purchases to legal sources.
- Encouragement for financial institutions to more closely scrutinize investments in the forestry industry, to help ensure that they are not helping to fund illegal activities.

The VPAs are at the core of the FLEGT approach. Within the EU, the regulation limiting timber imports from VPA countries to licensed products was adopted in December 2005 (European Council 2005). The first countries to enter into VPAs were Ghana (September 2008) and the Republic of Congo (March 2009).[2] Implementation of the VPAs is anticipated to take at least two years, so the first FLEGT-licensed timber could be entering trade in 2011. As of this writing, negotiations were complete with Cameroon and were still under way with the Central African Republic, the Democratic Republic of the Congo, Indonesia, Liberia, Malaysia, and Vietnam; many other countries, particularly in Africa and Southeast Asia, have expressed an interest in entering negotiations.

The FLEGT action plan contained a short section on "conflict timber," which it defined as "timber traded by armed groups, the proceeds of which are used to fund armed conflicts" (Commission of the European Communities 2003, 4). In some countries, most notably Cambodia, the Democratic Republic of the Congo, and Liberia, revenues from illegal logging have funded fighting. Regardless of whether timber that meets the definition of conflict timber is being extracted illegally,[3] efforts to control the trade in illegal products and the trade in conflict

---

[1] This aspect of the action plan eventually led to the timber regulation explained later in the chapter.

[2] The only VPA text that is currently available publicly is that of Ghana; see www.illegal-logging.info/item_single.php?it_id=843&it=document.

[3] In some circumstances, conflict timber may not be illegal; in Liberia, for example, President Charles Taylor legally asserted control over the country's forests, then used revenues from the sale of timber to fund armed intervention in Sierra Leone.

products overlap; in fact, the VPA licensing system is modeled, to an extent, on the Kimberley Process Certification Scheme for conflict diamonds.[4]

The FLEGT action plan is not explicitly designed to support post-conflict peacebuilding, but in forest-rich countries recovering from war, it could make a contribution. This chapter describes the FLEGT initiative in more detail—with a particular focus on the VPAs—and considers to what extent it may contribute to peacebuilding in Liberia, where a VPA is currently being negotiated, and in broader contexts.

EXCLUDING ILLEGAL TIMBER

Assuming that it works properly, the licensing system established under the VPAs will prevent partner countries from exporting illegally produced timber products to the EU. "Illegal" timber is defined by the laws of the country in which the timber is being harvested; there is no international agreement on forest management or the timber trade that sets a global framework. Even within a single country, however, determining legality is not always straightforward; in developing countries in particular, the laws governing forests may be unclear, or those at the national level may conflict with those at regional or local levels. And even where the laws are clear, there is the question of which are central to definition of legality. Those that relate to timber harvesting or to the payment of royalties or export duties, for example, are clearly important, but laws that regulate the working conditions of the truckers who transport the timber, for instance, may be more tangential. It is possible to define illegal logging so broadly that no country could avoid it. To avoid that, Cameroon and Indonesia have engaged in multi-stakeholder processes to develop working definitions; in Ghana and the Republic of Congo, the VPAs include commitments to reforms that will clarify relevant laws.

In each country, the VPA will define the scope of the applicable legislation, which is expected to include laws relating to the following (Falconer 2009):

- Access rights.
- Company registration requirements.
- Social obligations, including labor laws.
- Rights of local communities and indigenous populations.
- Environmental safeguards, forest management, timber harvesting, processing operations, and associated financial obligations.
- The transport and commercialization of timber.

---

[4] For additional perspectives on the Kimberley Process, see J. Andrew Grant, "The Kimberley Process at Ten: Reflections on a Decade of Efforts to End the Trade in Conflict Diamonds"; Harrison Mitchell, "A More Formal Engagement: A Constructive Critique of Certification as a Means of Preventing Conflict and Building Peace"; and Clive Wright, "The Kimberley Process Certification Scheme: A Model Negotiation?" in this volume.

For each element, the VPA will list the criteria, indicators, and means of verification (such as the documents that timber companies will need in order to prove compliance) that will form the basis for enforcement (Falconer 2009). The designated licensing authority in the partner country will issue FLEGT licenses on the basis of proof of legality, which will be provided by the timber operator.[5]

To ensure the system's integrity, the VPAs will include provisions for independent third-party monitoring, which will specify the responsibilities of the monitoring organizations and the extent to which their findings will be made public. Any major compliance problems will be discussed by a joint oversight committee made up of representatives from both the partner country and the EU. The ultimate sanction is suspension of the agreement, which either party can do.

The VPAs will also include provisions that allow the timber to be tracked through the supply chain. The partner country's timber-tracking system obviously cannot extend outside its borders to cover timber produced elsewhere, which may be imported into the partner country and then exported to the EU. However, under the VPA, the FLEGT license will indicate the country in which the product was harvested, and partner countries will be prohibited from issuing licenses to products that include timber that has been illegally produced in any other country. The Cameroon VPA restricts imports to products that already have a FLEGT or "other authorized" license; and in both Cameroon and the Republic of Congo, mills will be required to use only legal timber, whether domestic or imported. How readily such provisions will be implemented in practice remains to be seen.

The licensing system will apply only to timber products traded between the VPA partner countries and the EU; partner countries are not required to attach FLEGT licenses to products exported to other countries (for example, timber produced in Ghana, processed in China, and ultimately exported to the EU would not need to show a licence at the EU border). But since all the partner countries that have so far entered into VPAs intend to license all their timber exports, regardless of destination, the system may begin to extend beyond the direct trade between the partner countries and the EU.

The potential result—a multilateral timber-licensing system—could help to address an obvious problem with the FLEGT licensing scheme. Since the system is built on agreements with individual countries, it is vulnerable to evasion: illegal products could simply be shipped through nonpartner countries to the EU, thereby avoiding the need for a license. The FLEGT action plan recognized this problem but did not specify precisely how it should be addressed. In 2010, a new timber regulation was agreed on that is designed to counter the risk of

---

[5] In many ways, this approach resembles the voluntary forest-certification schemes of the Forest Stewardship Council and the Programme for the Endorsement of Forest Certification, but with the important difference that it applies nationwide. For more details on forest certification, see www.illegal-logging.info/certification.

evasion; the regulation is scheduled to enter into force in March 2013 (European Parliament and Council of the European Union 2010).

Under the regulation—which will apply to all timber imports, including those from non-VPA countries, as well as to timber harvested in the EU—timber producers and importers who place timber products on the EU market must possess due diligence systems designed to minimize their chances of handling illegal timber; moreover, the handling of illegal products will be classified as an offense. VPA-licensed timber will automatically qualify without any further checks, thus providing an additional incentive for countries to enter into VPAs. The system has been criticized for applying to imports only at the first point of entry to the EU and not further down the supply chain (there is doubt that some EU member states will be able to effectively control imports); however, this problem may be mitigated by the requirement that traders along the supply chain within the EU keep records showing who their timber or timber product was bought from and to whom it was sold.[6]

IMPROVING GOVERNANCE

Illegal logging can be seen, at its base, as a failure of governance, law enforcement, or both. The legal and regulatory regime that should control timber exploitation may be inadequately designed, poorly enforced, undermined by corruption—or all three. Although the licensing system established by the VPAs is designed mainly to exclude illegal timber from the EU market, the FLEGT initiative may have long-lasting effects on governance in the partner countries.[7]

The VPAs for both Ghana and the Republic of Congo include the following:

- A definition of legal timber, an analysis of existing legislation and its shortcomings, and commitment to reforms where necessary.
- A provision for independent monitoring of the licensing system, with outcomes available to the public.
- A commitment to national stakeholder involvement in the committees established to oversee the process.
- Improvements in transparency, including annual reporting on the functioning of the licensing system and agreement to make more information available on forest sector management (e.g., information on production, rights allocation, finances, and audits).

---

[6] The regulation is similar in principle to, though somewhat different in operation from, the Lacey Act, a U.S. law that makes it illegal to import or handle timber products that have been produced illegally in other countries; for more information, see www.illegal-logging.info/approach.php?a_id=202.

[7] For more details, see Falconer (2009).

The negotiation process itself has also helped to improve transparency, primarily because partner-country civil society groups have been included.

Many governance problems are caused by lack of capacity, and it was always recognized that the VPAs would need to be accompanied by capacity building to support the establishment of the licensing system and improve governance and enforcement. Although the partner countries will meet the costs of operating the licensing systems (which should be somewhat offset by a reduction in illegal behavior and an increase in revenues from taxes and royalties), in most cases the EU will need to help establish the systems. Although such support is not a formal part of the VPAs, where necessary it is being agreed to in the course of the VPA negotiations.

THE FLEGT INITIATIVE IN A POST-CONFLICT SETTING: LIBERIA

As noted earlier, illegal logging has funded conflict in Liberia and the Democratic Republic of the Congo, among other places. To date, Liberia is the only post-conflict country engaged in the VPA process, though the Democratic Republic of the Congo has expressed interest in the process.

In 2003, in an effort to eliminate the trade in conflict timber that had helped fund both the Liberian civil war and Charles Taylor's destabilizing forays into neighboring Sierra Leone, the UN imposed sanctions on Liberian timber exports. The sanctions were provisionally lifted in June 2006, in the wake of the peaceful presidential elections of November 2005; the lifting was confirmed in October 2006, after the enactment of the National Forestry Reform Law.[8] Entering into a VPA was viewed as means of reinforcing the forestry reform process, and negotiations opened in March 2009.[9] As forestry minister Chris Toe observed at the start of the negotiations,

> the launching of the VPA is a notable mark in Liberia's history. Forests cover almost half of the land area of Liberia and are a significant factor in the wealth, and thus political power, of the country. It is well known that Liberia's wealth of timber resources contributed to and supported the protracted and devastating civil conflict, not in small part due to power given by international market forces and economic agendas. The VPA process represents an opportunity for Liberia to further combat illegal logging and strengthen its reform process by reinforcing the notable systems already in place (illegal-logging.info 2009).

---

[8] For additional information on the reform, see Stephanie L. Altman, Sandra S. Nichols, and John T. Woods, "Leveraging High-Value Natural Resources to Restore the Rule of Law: The Role of the Liberia Forest Initiative in Liberia's Transition to Stability," and Michael D. Beevers, "Forest Resources and Peacebuilding: Preliminary Lessons from Liberia and Sierra Leone," in this volume.

[9] For more information on Liberia and the FLEGT initiative, see www.illegal-logging.info/approach.php?a_id=309.

The European Union's FLEGT initiative 217

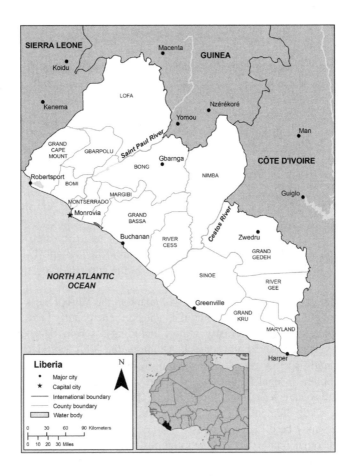

Unfortunately, the reform process has not proceeded as smoothly as was hoped. In December 2008, for instance, the UN panel of experts on Liberia reported that "the actions of the Forestry Development Authority do not appear to be in compliance with some important requirements of the National Forestry Reform Law and its regulations regarding the process of awarding contracts for commercial timber concessions" (UNSC 2008b, 3). Nongovernmental organizations have raised concerns about violations of the law by bidding companies, and about the failure of government-appointed due diligence teams to undertake full background checks of the bidders.[10] Finally, the community forest law passed in October 2009 explicitly rules out awarding small- and medium-scale contracts (up to 50,000 hectares) on a competitive basis—hardly an encouragement to transparency (GOL 2009).

---

[10] See, for example, Global Witness (2009).

Given the record of other VPA negotiations, it seems unlikely that the EU would agree to a VPA that did not convincingly deal with the weaknesses in the reform process and in Liberia's forestry laws. As the UN panel of experts commented in June 2009, "the Panel notes that Liberia has entered into formal negotiations with the European Union. The Panel will monitor this development as it could have very positive implications for the functioning of Liberia's internal controls on the timber sector" (Panel of Experts on Liberia 2008a, 23).

One advantage of the VPA process is the potential to provide a forum in which such problems can be raised and addressed by a variety of stakeholders, including Liberian civil society. There are also indications that the Liberian government plans to use the VPA as a broader opportunity to discuss the forestry reform efforts of the past five years—including the extent to which the reforms realistically reflect the country's institutional capacity. The working group that is developing the definition of legality has expressed interest in carrying out a wholesale review of the forestry reform law and its associated regulations, including the legislation's effects on the contract allocation process to date.

Another possibility is that Liberia will abandon the VPA process altogether, or that negotiations will proceed without conclusion. The country faces substantial problems in reforming its forestry sector, including a serious lack of capacity in both government and civil society. Although the VPA would certainly be beneficial, and possibly essential, in helping Liberia establish a reputation as a reliable supplier of legal timber, export markets other than the EU—China, for example—may care less about such matters. The reconstruction of the timber industry is a key element in the country's economic recovery, and the lure of easy exports may be difficult to resist.

On the other hand, the VPA negotiations have already been accompanied by capacity-building assistance from the EU to establish a timber-tracking system, and the promise of further support should be attractive. The EU market is likely to be more reliable and of higher value than other export destinations (public procurement policies in some EU member states, for example, have already led to price premiums for certified tropical timber products). While the VPA certainly has the potential to reinforce the post-conflict reform process, it will not be enough by itself. Political will and commitment on the part of the Liberian government, the EU, and international donors will be more important.

CONCLUSION: VPAS AND PEACEBUILDING

Liberia's VPA negotiations will offer useful lessons in the extent to which the FLEGT initiative can contribute to peacebuilding. The FLEGT initiative was never, of course, designed to do so, and the issue has never been discussed systematically, within the EU or elsewhere. Furthermore, the number of countries that export possibly illegal timber to the EU (and that are therefore potential VPA partners) substantially exceeds the number of timber-rich countries that are emerging from conflict. It would therefore be a mistake to view the VPAs as a principal means of contributing to post-conflict recovery.[11]

Nevertheless, VPAs have the potential to help. A VPA provides a framework that should reinforce any forestry reform process that is already under way, and can also help to create forums in which representatives from government, industry, and civil society can discuss forest reform and related matters; such forums are commonly viewed as valuable in peacebuilding efforts related to extractive sectors. Once the timber regulation comes into force in the EU, a VPA may offer the easiest means of demonstrating the legality of timber exports, which will be needed for access to the EU market. (Similar, though arguably more effective, legislation is already in place in the United States, in the shape of the Lacey Act, so any timber exports to the United States will also come under increasing scrutiny.)[12]

What remains unclear is whether a country emerging from conflict will have the capacity to negotiate or implement a VPA. Given the political will, the negotiation process can be quite fast—less than a year for the Republic of Congo, for example. But implementation poses significant challenges (particularly in the establishment of a nationwide timber-tracking system), even in countries where the standards of governance are high; post-conflict countries, where both governance and capacity are likely to be weak, will face even bigger problems, and the EU may be called on to expend much greater resources for capacity building in post-conflict nations than in other countries. The progress of the Liberia VPA will suggest to what degree the benefits of the system can be extended to other forest-rich post-conflict countries.

REFERENCES

Commission of the European Communities. 2003. Communication from the Commission to the Council and the European Parliament: Forest law enforcement, governance and trade (FLEGT)—Proposal for an EU action plan. COM (2003) 251 final. www.illegal-logging.info/item_single.php?it_id=49&it=document.

European Council. 2005. Regulation no. 2173/2005 on the establishment of a FLEGT licensing scheme for imports of timber into the European community. *Official Journal of the European Union* L series (347): 1.

European Parliament and Council of the European Union. 2010. Regulation (EU) No 995/2010 of the European Parliament and of the Council of 20 October 2010 laying down the obligations of operators who place timber and timber products on the market. *Official Journal of the European Union*. I. 295/23. http://illegal-logging.info/uploads/l29520101112en00230034.pdf.

---

[11] This is particularly the case for countries with a limited or nonexistent history of exporting timber to the EU, where the current model of the VPA, which is built primarily on regulating trade, is largely irrelevant.

[12] Lacey Act of 1900. 16 U.S.C. ch. 53, secs. 3371–3378.

Falconer, J. 2009. FLEGT VPA update. Presentation at the illegal logging update meeting of the European Commission. Chatham House, London. www.illegal-logging.info/item_single.php?it_id=369&it=presentation.

G8 Action Programme on Forests. 2002. *G8 action programme on forests—Final report*. www.illegal-logging.info/item_single.php?it_id=38&it=document.

Global Witness. 2009. Brief on problems with Liberian forest management contracts (FMC) process. October 2.

GOL (Government of Liberia), Ministry of Foreign Affairs. 2009. An act to establish the community rights law of 2008 with respect to forest lands. www.loggingoff.info/media/articles/article_678.pdf.

illegal-logging.info. 2009. Launch of voluntary partnership agreement between government of Liberia and EU: Minister Chris Toe's opening statement at the launch of negotiations. March 26. www.illegal-logging.info/item_single.php?it_id=3355&it=news.

UNSC (United Nations Security Council). 2008a. Mid-term report of the panel of experts on Liberia submitted pursuant to paragraph 4 of Security Council Resolution 1854 (2008). S/2009/90.

———. 2008b. Report of the panel of experts submitted pursuant to paragraph 1 of Security Council Resolution 1819 (2008) concerning Liberia. S/2008/785.

PART 3

Revenue distribution

Introduction

Post-conflict countries often have to navigate between incompatible needs. On the one hand, they need to rapidly increase revenue flows from natural resources, in order to recover from conflict. On the other hand, they need to develop or strengthen the capacity to properly manage resource revenues—a process that can take considerable time. It is thus important to consider strategies for revenue distribution while institutions are still developing.

In this regard, the transfer of revenues from the central government to subnational entities is an important issue. Distribution schemes must balance the needs of the nation as a whole against what is considered fair by certain groups, particularly those in producing regions. It is also important to provide safeguards to ensure that revenues reach the general population, instead of being siphoned off by corruption.

No matter what principles are used to distribute revenues, there will always be disputes over who gets what. For example, should revenues be distributed equally among all subnational entities, or should the producing regions get a larger share? If so, how much more should the producing regions get? Should ethnic or religious groups get a larger share, as reparation for past harms? However difficult it may be to find a formula that satisfies all groups or regions, the effort must be made: if some groups feel that they have been unfairly treated, there is a risk of conflict relapse.

In "Sharing Natural Resource Wealth during War-to-Peace Transitions," Achim Wennmann argues that wealth sharing plays a dual role in post-conflict societies—simultaneously helping to end and ameliorate old disputes while laying the foundation for a new economic future. Wennmann describes several wealth-sharing mechanisms, including vertical and horizontal distribution, direct distribution, and tax base adjustments; compares centralized and decentralized distribution of resource revenues; and analyzes wealth-sharing strategies in Sudan and Aceh.

In "Horizontal Inequality, Decentralizing the Distribution of Natural Resource Revenues, and Peace," Michael L. Ross, Päivi Lujala, and Siri Aas Rustad further explore centralized versus decentralized revenue distribution, focusing particularly on cases in which resources are distributed along ethnic, religious, or other lines. Ross, Lujala, and Rustad argue that because local institutions often lack both policy-making and administrative capacity, a fairly centralized approach may be more practicable and efficient. More decentralized strategies, on the other hand, can better addresses demands for self-determination and regional compensation, which may be politically important in settings where there are potential peace spoilers, or where producing regions are dominated by particular religious or ethnic groups.

In "The Diamond Area Community Development Fund: Micropolitics and Community-led Development in Post-war Sierra Leone," Roy Maconachie examines a wealth-sharing strategy that engages local communities in decision making about the expenditure of resource revenues. Since 2001, 25 percent of the 3 percent diamond industry export tax (i.e., 0.75 percent of the total export value) levied by Sierra Leone has flowed into a fund that was designed to support locally driven development projects in diamond-producing regions. When the funds were initially distributed to the communities, however, expenditures were heavily influenced by local power relationships and prewar patronage structures; as a result, the funds were not used efficiently, and distribution was temporarily suspended. Although community-led decision making does create a new space for public participation, Maconachie argues that to continue to successfully engage the public, the government must carefully design a participation strategy that takes existing power relationships into account.

In the final chapter of part 3, "Direct Distribution of Natural Resource Revenues as a Policy for Peacebuilding," Martin E. Sandbu highlights a more controversial strategy: direct distribution, in which resource revenues are distributed directly to the public. Sandbu argues that direct distribution could address many of the concerns raised by Wennmann and by Ross, Lujala, and Rustad. For example, it can be a particularly effective means of bypassing corruption at both the central and subnational levels. Despite the potential advantages noted by Sandbu, direct distribution has been fully implemented only in Alaska, although it has been discussed as a possible solution in some post-conflict countries.

The chapters in part 3 highlight various aspects of post-conflict distribution of natural resource revenues. The chapters do not offer a single solution but discuss the advantages and disadvantages of various strategies. Two themes that all the chapters share, however, are the challenge of curbing corruption and the importance of ensuring that revenues are used as a peace dividend.

Sharing natural resource wealth during war-to-peace transitions

Achim Wennmann

Since the early 1990s, the relationship between natural resources and armed conflict has been a recurring topic in the policy and scholarly worlds. "Conflict diamonds" and the complicity of companies in conflict economies have made headline-grabbing news, and the role of resources in financing belligerents has placed natural resources at the heart of discussions at the United Nations Security Council (UNSC). In academia, natural resources have come to occupy a central place in explaining conflict dynamics, as a source of both means and motives in the use of armed violence. While natural resource wealth has found its way onto the political and research agendas for different reasons, all the reasons converge on a single point: natural resource wealth is a problem because it allows and sustains armed conflict, and thereby creates an obstacle to peacemaking.

This chapter reverses this perspective. The goals here are (1) to explore the opportunities that natural resource wealth creates for peacemaking, and (2) to ask whether, by addressing resource wealth during peace processes, it is possible to strengthen post-conflict economic recovery and help establish a lasting peace. Wealth sharing can be said to play a dual role in war-to-peace transitions: it looks backward, to address the ends or means of past disputes; and it looks forward, to shape the vision of a new society and economy (Zartman 2005).

As used in this chapter, *wealth sharing* refers to a negotiated agreement about the distribution of income derived from natural resources. The two types

---

Achim Wennmann is a researcher at the Centre on Conflict, Development and Peacebuilding (CCDP) of the Graduate Institute of International and Development Studies in Geneva. The author wishes to thank Gilles Carbonnier, Simon Mason, and Axel Wennmann for their constructive comments. An earlier version of this chapter was presented at the Thirteenth Annual International Conference on Economics and Security, Thessaloniki, Greece, June 24–26, 2009. The research for this chapter was conducted as part of a project entitled Economic Issues and Tools in Peace Processes, which was supported by the Swiss Federal Department of Foreign Affairs. This chapter also draws from a guidance note for mediators on income sharing from natural resources and the author's book *The Political Ecomomy of Peacemaking* (Routledge 2011).

of distribution are (1) company-to-government transfers and (2) special sharing schemes between the central government and subnational entities.[1]

The chapter is divided into five major parts: (1) a review of the relationship between development, conflict, and natural resource wealth; (2) a discussion of the role of natural resources in peace processes; (3) a description of various forms of, and approaches to, wealth sharing; (4) an evaluation of wealth-sharing schemes in Sudan and Indonesia, where natural resources had contributed to armed conflict in Southern Sudan and Aceh, respectively; and (5) concluding thoughts on the effective integration of wealth sharing into war-to-peace transitions.

DEVELOPMENT, CONFLICT, AND NATURAL RESOURCE WEALTH

Natural resources, whether renewable or nonrenewable, are actual or potential sources of wealth; examples include timber, water, land, wildlife, minerals, metals, stones, and hydrocarbons, such as petroleum and natural gas (UNEP 2009). Revenue from natural resources is particularly important for many developing countries, half of which rely on four commodities for more than 50 percent of their export earnings, and one-third of which rely on four commodities for more than 75 percent of their export earnings. The principal commodities exported by developing nations are oil and oil products, fish, natural gas, forestry products, sugar, cocoa, and coffee (UNCTAD 2008). Some natural resources, such as oil and minerals, yield unearned income, or "rents"—the excess of revenues over all costs, including normal profit margins (Collier 2009).

But many countries with an abundance of certain natural resources—particularly oil, gas, and valuable minerals—experience lower economic growth and human development than countries where such resources are scarce (Auty 1993; Karl 1997). One explanation for this phenomenon is that natural resources are not revenues but assets. Oil, for example, is part of a country's natural endowment; when it is commercialized—that is, extracted from the ground and sold—it is converted into a liquid asset (Radon 2007). But this transaction does not represent income; it is simply a change in the denomination of the asset from barrels of oil to U.S. dollars.

Thus, the challenge for developing countries is to transform natural resource assets into lasting development benefits without depreciating the assets themselves. Such efforts are often complicated by the self-destructive incentives created by natural resources: first, they tempt leaders to overspend for current needs; second, they are perceived as prizes that various parties attempt to capture, either through

---

[1] For additional perspectives on resource sharing, see Michael L. Ross, Päivi Lujala, and Siri Aas Rustad, "Horizontal Inequality, Decentralizing the Distribution of Natural Resource Revenues, and Peace," and Roy Maconachie, "The Diamond Area Community Development Fund: Micropolitics and Community-led Development in Post-war Sierra Leone," both in this volume.

corruption or armed force (Humphreys, Sachs, and Stiglitz 2007);[2] third, they can foster "rentier states," which rely on rents from natural resources, rather than on the productive activities of the population, for their revenue base. Rentier states are marked by weak state-society relations and by semiauthoritarian governments in which the capture of natural resource rents accords disproportionate power to government elites (Beblawi and Luciano 1987; Ottaway 2003).[3]

After the end of the cold war, a number of the conflicts in Africa placed the spotlight on the relationship between natural resources and armed conflict. The issue gained prominence (1) through detailed reports filed by the UNSC sanctions-monitoring mechanisms for Angola, the Democratic Republic of the Congo (DRC), Liberia, and Sierra Leone, and (2) through multi-stakeholder initiatives undertaken to curtail trafficking in conflict diamonds and the abusive and illegal behavior of companies in conflict zones (Banfield, Lilly, and Haufler 2003; Smillie 2005; Ballentine and Haufler 2005). In addition, in 2003, the World Bank identified armed conflict as an obstacle to development and opened an entire research stream on the economics of political and criminal violence (Collier et al. 2003; Bannon and Collier 2003; Collier and Sambanis 2005). The resulting findings emphasized the role of natural resources in the development of a "conflict trap" in which "war wrecks the economy and increases the risk of future war" (Collier et al. 2003, 1). Specifically, natural resources provide insurgents with the means and motives to secede from or challenge the state; the state's lack of institutional and military capacity, in turn, increases the incentive for insurgents to make the effort (Herbst 2004).[4]

In sum, natural resource wealth can have a range of adverse effects on a country: it can weaken the economy and state-society relations, provide belligerents with both the means and motives to continue armed conflict, and influence the dynamics of armed conflicts. Thus, it can be said that natural resources facilitate conflict and undermine the transition to peace. The rest of this chapter looks at the other side of the coin: how, and to what extent, can natural resource wealth end armed conflict and support lasting peace?

NATURAL RESOURCES AND PEACE PROCESSES

Armed conflict originates in the perception of irreconcilable differences on particular issues; violence is the chosen means of resolving these differences

---

[2] For further discussion of the resource curse, see Paul Collier and Anke Hoeffler, "High-Value Natural Resources, Development, and Conflict: Channels of Causation," in this volume.

[3] State-society relations tend to be weaker in rentier states because they have fewer incentives to nurture relations with their citizens than do states that depend on taxation for governmental revenues.

[4] For further discussion of the link between natural resources and armed conflict, see Paul Collier and Anke Hoeffler, "High-Value Natural Resources, Development, and Conflict: Channels of Causation," in this volume.

(Holsti 1991). Thus, one of the main objectives of a peace process is to change perceptions by focusing on the issues that underlie the conflict; using an issues-based approach, mediators and negotiators can reframe disagreements, allowing compromises to be forged and future disputes to be resolved without recourse to armed violence (Zartman 1995).

Although economics and political economy are standard approaches to conflict analysis, the economic dimensions of peace processes have received little attention. A comparison of provisions in twenty-seven peace agreements, for example, showed that most focus on security and political power; economic provisions are marginal (Suhrke, Wimplemann, and Dawes 2007). It is not clear why natural resources and other economic issues are often omitted. One possibility is that the parties may be more concerned with other issues; another is that mediators, preferring to keep the focus on ending armed violence and getting a signed agreement, may be reluctant to overload the agenda (Wennmann 2009a). Moreover, armed groups who are financed by natural resources may be disinclined to discuss them, and may even reject the entire peace process if they feel that their ability to mobilize is threatened (Dwan and Bailey 2006).

Nevertheless, a focus on economic issues opens new opportunities for conflict resolution. For one thing, disagreements over economic issues should be easier to solve (at least in principle) than, for example, identity disputes. Unlike the emotions associated with ethnic conflict, the control of mines, markets, and economic infrastructure can be quantified and divided. Certainly, economic issues are often intricately connected to cultural and identity disputes, but addressing economic issues in peace processes as a "rational" rather than as an "emotional" topic may facilitate a negotiated exit from armed conflict. Moreover, if an armed conflict is actually about greed, belligerents may be responsive to the argument that they stand to make more money through private sector investment—within the bounds of a functioning state and a lasting peace. More broadly, the inclusion of wealth-sharing arrangements in peace processes may strengthen the belief among the parties and their constituencies that agreeing to stop fighting offers the prospect of a better life. Thus, wealth sharing creates an economic incentive on two levels: by providing direct benefits to all parties, and by attaching an opportunity cost to continued conflict.

In the relatively few instances in which natural resources have been meaningfully addressed in peace processes, it has primarily been through wealth-sharing arrangements, which have three specific functions:

- If disputes over the control of natural resources were a factor in the outbreak of a conflict, wealth-sharing arrangements directly address such disputes.
- If natural resources were used to pay for the initiation and perpetuation of a conflict, wealth-sharing arrangements target the means of financing armed groups.
- If the parties agree to enter into a transitional agreement to lead their country or community out of armed conflict, wealth sharing can shape new governance arrangements and help ensure a speedy economic recovery.

Ensuring that the violence stops is important, but unless combatants and civilians have a vision of what comes next, some may believe that their life during the conflict was more profitable and may return to violent appropriation as a means of achieving a livelihood. Talking about wealth sharing can help craft a shared vision of a new economic future in which former combatants and conflict-affected populations can start believing. Developing such a vision entails, among other strategies, creating opportunities for employment and vocational training, and stimulating private investment in support of demobilization, disarmament, and reintegration (DDR). Ultimately, failure to persuade the parties that peace offers the chance of a better life may lead to criminal parallel economies, the collapse of DDR initiatives, or even a full-scale renewal of fighting (Reno 1997).

Wealth sharing can also be an element in power-sharing negotiations, which are part of forging a political future in which the benefits of participating in a government or in an autonomous entity are greater than those of challenging or overthrowing the state (Hartzell 1999). Like peace agreements, constitutions and constitutional reform processes can play an important role in formalizing agreed-upon revenue assignments, sharing principles, and modes of transfer (Haysom and Kane 2009). The trend toward addressing power sharing (including wealth/sharing) in peace agreements and constitutional reforms may stem from the fact that such arrangements can be amended only through special procedures (i.e., not simply by a majority vote) and are therefore perceived as more permanent.

Addressing wealth sharing effectively in peace processes also implies preparing the groundwork for the prevention of future armed conflict. Wealth sharing addresses security concerns by (1) balancing the relative gains that each party receives from natural resources and (2) regulating access to funds that could potentially be used for another round of conflict, and thereby ensuring that no party has the means to impose itself militarily in the future (Siriam 2008).

In sum, wealth sharing addresses key elements of peacemaking:

- Ending or transforming a past armed conflict.
- Setting out a vision of a future society and economy that both former combatants and civilians can believe in.
- Preventing the resumption of renewed armed conflict over natural resources.

Accordingly, wealth-sharing arrangements seek to reduce access to revenue sources that might otherwise enable spoilers to restart a war, nurture an indigenous revenue base for economic recovery, and support a viable peace that increases the opportunity costs of renewed conflict. Thus, getting wealth sharing right in the peace process can help protect against future losses in the realms of peacebuilding and development investment.

APPROACHES TO WEALTH SHARING

Wealth sharing takes two forms: the first occurs between companies and the central government, and the second occurs between the central government and subnational entities. This section describes the characteristics of these two types of wealth sharing; it also discusses the practicalities of wealth-sharing schemes: vertical and horizontal sharing, direct distribution, tax base adjustments, and centralized versus decentralized sharing. Finally, the section explores how wealth-sharing arrangements have been used to strengthen economic development, and the potential role of such arrangements in supporting the transition from conflict to peace.

Company-to-government transfers

Extractive industries are central to wealth sharing: they explore, exploit, produce, and market natural resources and derivative products, and negotiate with governments on the basis of costs and risks, return on investments, and profit margins. Wealth sharing between companies and governments occurs in accordance with contractual obligations. Once funds are transferred, whatever happens to them is a matter of national policy and depends on the host government's development priorities. Thus, this type of wealth sharing does not guarantee that funds will be spent in a particular way or even in a sound way: it only means that companies transfer wealth to the government.

Decisions about how company-to-government transfers will occur are typically made in the context of larger negotiations about the structure of a contract between a company and a state. Among the typical arrangements are license agreements, production sharing, joint ventures, and service agreements.

A license agreement is perhaps the most common contractual arrangement.[5] License agreements are particularly attractive for governments that have little or no capacity to extract or exploit a particular resource (e.g., oil or kimberlite diamonds), but licenses are also granted for other resources, such as timber. Under a license agreement, the government grants a company exclusive development and production rights in a particular area for a specific period of time; in return, the government receives a license fee, royalties,[6] and (if production occurs) income tax payments. Licenses are usually granted by national governments but may be granted by subnational entities that have the authority to do so. Arrangements for income taxes may include a windfall profit tax to ensure that the government receives its fair share, especially if prices for a particular natural resource are high (Radon 2007).[7]

---

[5] Generally, there are few differences between license agreements, licenses, permits, extraction contracts, and concessions. In some instances, different terms may be applied to larger areas and to more specific sites, but there is no consistent usage.

[6] Unlike license fees, which are usually one-time, up-front payments, royalties are paid as the resource is extracted. A royalty may be a fixed percentage of the value of the extracted resource, a graduated percentage (e.g., X percent for the first Y barrels of oil, Z percent for all oil above that amount), a fixed fee (e.g., US$X per barrel), a graduated fee, or some combination.

[7] Windfall revenues usually reflect temporary booms in income caused by higher commodity prices. When resource prices are within the normal range, there are no windfall profits.

Because some governments, under license agreements, have lost control of natural resources to private companies, many governments use production-sharing contracts, which recognize that the host country has sole ownership rights to the resource in question. Under a production-sharing contract, the company bears all risk and all exploration, development, and production costs; in return, the company receives a stipulated share of whatever is produced (Humphreys, Sachs, and Stiglitz 2007).

Through a joint venture, two or more companies work together to exploit natural resources. In the case of natural resource extraction, joint ventures often include a national resource company: in one region of Algeria, for example, Statoil (the Norwegian state oil company), British Petroleum, and Sonatrach (the Algerian state oil company) jointly operate a large oil field. Joint ventures allow companies to share risks, which makes it easier for local firms to engage in capital-intensive natural resource extraction. Where a national resource company is part of a joint venture, such involvement may increase the government's role in decision making.

In service agreements, the host government contracts with a company to perform specific tasks related to natural resource extraction (Radon 2007). These tasks may include, for example, renting exploration or production rigs. In such arrangements, the government retains more control, assumes more responsibility, and usually receives more revenues from the resources.

Negotiating company-to-government transfers is usually a hard-fought battle. Governments, for example, generally like royalty arrangements because they provide immediate compensation. Companies, for their part, want to keep the size of the royalty as manageable as possible to avoid slowing the recovery of capital investment and increasing commercial uncertainty (Radon 2007). Another area of contention involves the balance between the company's profit margin and the government's share of revenues.[8] What makes this issue particularly complex is that most companies are reluctant to disclose contractual details, because they wish to avoid compromising their negotiations or contracts in other countries.

Historically, it has been difficult for governments to negotiate a fair share: companies generally have better information, more highly skilled negotiators, and the resources to outlast the government during long-term negotiations (Radon 2007). Nevertheless, as new multinational companies based in emerging economies have intensified the competition for natural resources, governments have gained negotiating power. With more companies fighting for contracts, governments can insist on better contractual terms and exploit the willingness of Chinese state companies, for example, to link mining contracts to investments in infrastructure, telecommunications, public buildings, and sports stadiums (Ford 2007).

---

[8] Governments fare best if they reach agreements with companies before production begins; once production has started, it is more difficult to make claims for a fair share of revenues. Governments should also require companies to justify their claims for compensation for production costs.

Nongovernmental organizations (NGOs) also play an increasingly important role in company-to-government transfers. Local, national, and international NGOs lobby for transparency in payments and contracts, and for public accountability for revenues and disbursements; they have also become increasingly integrated into global campaigns such as Publish What You Pay and the Extractive Industries Transparency Initiative (EITI) (Carbonnier 2008).[9] Nevertheless, local, national, and international NGOs sometimes have different attitudes toward natural resource ventures. Local and national NGOs may be more open to compromise on the potentially harmful effects of natural resource ventures—such as pollution and disease—in exchange for investments, jobs, and infrastructure, whereas international NGOs often insist on standards that reflect policy concerns in developed countries, rather than local economic needs.

National wealth-sharing schemes

The distribution of natural resource wealth to subnational units can involve a number of schemes, including vertical sharing, horizontal sharing, direct distribution, and tax base adjustment (see table 1). Vertical sharing refers to the distribution of revenues between central and subnational governments; horizontal sharing refers to the distribution of revenues among subnational units (Bahl and Tumennasan 2002). Under one approach to horizontal sharing, known as the derivation principle, the share accorded to each subnational entity depends on the portion of revenue that originated in its territory (Ahmad and Mottu 2002). But because natural resource wealth is usually unevenly distributed within a country, relying on the derivation principle alone can create significant inequity between producing and nonproducing regions. Thus, governments also employ other sharing principles that depend, for example, on the size of a region's population or its development needs (Bahl and Tumennasan 2002). Taxes, grants, and other means can also be used to transfer revenue to subnational entities (Haysom and Kane 2009; Iff and Töpperwien 2008).

Wealth sharing may also involve the direct distribution of natural resource income to citizens, as is the case in Alaska (United States) and Alberta (Canada).[10] Direct sharing of natural resource wealth is difficult in fragile or conflict-affected settings because state institutions are weak and citizen registries are either incomplete or nonexistent (Ross 2007). In many instances, companies share revenue with local communities through investments in social, health, education, or transport infrastructure. Central governments may, however, have reservations about these

---

[9] For further discussion of the EITI, see Eddie Rich and T. Negbalee Warner, "Addressing the Roots of Liberia's Conflict through the Extractive Industries Transparency Initiative," in this volume.

[10] For a more detailed discussion of direct distribution, see Martin E. Sandbu, "Direct Distribution of Natural Resource Revenues as a Policy for Peacebuilding," in this volume.

Table 1. Income-sharing schemes

Scheme	Description
Vertical sharing	Revenue from natural resources is shared between the central government and subnational governments; arrangements specify how much is allotted to the central government and how much is allotted to subnational entities.
Horizontal sharing	Income is shared among subnational entities, both natural-resource-rich and natural-resource-poor. This often involves revenue equalization schemes, in which the federal government collects and redistributes income from natural resources to subnational entities according to an agreed-upon formula.
Direct distribution	Direct payments are made to citizens.
Tax-base adjustment	Income sharing from natural resources is converted to authority for subnational entities over tax bases. Subnational entities retain a greater share of their tax receipts; the share corresponds to the amount of revenue that they would otherwise have received as income from natural resources.

Sources: Ahmad and Mottu (2002); Bahl and Tumennasan (2002); Ross (2007).

investments, because they prefer to monopolize relations with extractive companies (Batruch 2009).

Under the wealth-sharing scheme known as tax base adjustment, the central government allows regional or local governments to retain a greater share of their tax receipts; the extra share represents the amount of revenue that they would otherwise have received as income from natural resource exploitation. In return, the central government retains all income from natural resources, which allows it to maintain maximum control over macroeconomic policy and development planning. Economically, tax base adjustments are the least distorting form of income sharing because they are not as volatile as direct revenue sharing, which is susceptible to changes in commodity prices and production quantities. Tax base adjustments are more effective if resource deposits are located in areas that have strong economies that are not based on natural resources. Where the economic base is less strong or where windfall revenues are high, wealth can be shared through a mix of tax base adjustments and vertical sharing. Tax base adjustments also help diversify regional and local economies (Ahmad and Mottu 2002).

Centralized versus decentralized wealth sharing

Central and subnational governments often have differing views of centralization and decentralization in wealth-sharing schemes. To justify centralized wealth sharing, central governments invoke both the state's sovereignty over surface and subterranean resources and its custodial obligation to manage natural resources that are owned collectively by all citizens (Collier 2009). It is this ownership claim that makes central governments the main contractual partners for extractive industries and entitles them to receive the cash flows from natural resource ventures. Some governments also maintain that the income from natural resources has to be centralized first, before being distributed, in order to strengthen national unity and ensure equal treatment for subnational entities. In small or fragile states, centralization may be the only feasible option when subnational governments lack the institutions or expertise to manage large revenue flows.

Producing regions and communities make a number of arguments to justify decentralized wealth sharing:

- Since they live on the land where the natural resources are located, they have an ownership claim on the resources.
- Local communities view natural resource wealth as a heritage that must be preserved; thus, those who are selling off their heritage deserve a fair share of the revenues (Bennett 2002).
- Producing entities deserve to be compensated for the negative effects of resource extraction, including pollution and disease.

When central governments resort to wealth-sharing schemes, they often do so out of political expediency: to improve relations with subnational entities or to appease secessionist factions (Bahl and Tumennasan 2002). Another advantage of wealth sharing is that it may prevent local authorities from approaching extractive industries directly, in order to obtain direct payments through local taxes or community investments. Such initiatives may directly benefit local communities, but if they become excessive they may result in economic distortions, worsen relations with the extractive industries, and weaken investment conditions in the long term (Bahl and Tumennasan 2002).

A review of twenty-five countries showed that natural resource revenue management was centralized in fourteen and partially decentralized in ten; in only one instance was it fully decentralized (Ahmad and Mottu 2002). The tendency toward centralization can be explained by the fact that windfall revenues have to be administered centrally, in order to manage price and market volatilities, strengthen macroeconomic policy, and support national development plans. Centralized wealth sharing also prevents subnational governments from engaging in debt financing.

Wealth sharing and development prospects

A poorly conceived wealth-sharing arrangement can have tremendous political costs. At worst, excessive centralization and the perception that revenues from natural resources have been distributed unfairly can foster the mobilization of armed groups, as evidenced in Angola (Cabinda), the DRC (Katanga), Morocco (Western Sahara), Nigeria (Biafra), and Papua New Guinea (Bougainville) (Ross 2007). In the mid-1970s, rebels succeeded in mobilizing in Aceh even though the local populace had initially welcomed gas exploration in the belief that it would bring jobs, roads, schools, medical facilities, and housing. The separatists gained local support by focusing public attention on the Indonesian government's appropriation of the region's natural resources and by raising expectations that natural resources could be the basis for an independent state. When the central government responded with armed reprisals and further centralization, it lost legitimacy in the eyes of the Acehnese, which further strengthened the rebel movement. Thus, by failing to share wealth from natural resources, the central government lost an opportunity to defuse tensions (Ross 2005).

The case of Aceh illustrates that disputes over natural resources are intricately linked to the ways in which communities, ethnic groups, and subnational areas think about their economic future. The discovery of natural resources often raises expectations for a better life; by the same token, if those expectations remain unmet after several years of production, frustration results.

To use natural resource wealth to stimulate economic development, many governments create natural resource funds (NRFs), which accumulate financial flows from natural resource ventures, manage market and price volatility, and meet national development needs (Bell and Faria 2007).[11] Experience with NRFs offers some lessons about effective practice in the realm of economic development.

NRFs tend to be more effective if they specify what types of revenue sources (e.g., royalties, signing bonuses, income taxes from extractive industries, windfall profit taxes) will make up the inflow into the NRF, and which commercial projects (e.g., specific oil fields or mines) inflow will be drawn from. To avoid abuse and corruption, detailed records must be kept on payments into and withdrawals from the NRF. Furthermore, to ensure effective oversight, these records should be made public. To reduce the risk of wasteful disbursement, the entities that decide how much is spent should be separate from those that decide what it is spent on. To remove resource wealth from domestic political pressures and prevent Dutch disease,[12] it may be best to have the NRF administered abroad; the oil fund of São Tomé and Principe, for example, is administered by the New York Federal Reserve (Bell and Faria 2007; Radon 2007).

---

[11] Examples include Kiribati's Revenue Equalisation Reserve Fund (1956), Kuwait's General Resource Fund (1960), the Alaska Permanent Fund (1976), and the Norwegian State Petroleum Fund (1990). More recently, NRFs were established in Azerbaijan (1999), Kazakhstan (2001), São Tomé and Principe (2004), and Timor-Leste (2005). In Timor-Leste and Sudan, NRFs were part of the transition to peace and directly contributed to the revenue of the respective governments (Bell and Faria 2007).

[12] Dutch disease is a phenomenon in which the discovery of substantial natural resource wealth negatively affects a nation's economy. The discovery often causes sudden appreciation in the value of the nation's currency—which, in turn, decreases the nation's competitiveness in the international commodity markets. This reduces the country's exports of manufactured and agricultural commodities and increases its imports. At the same time, the natural resource sector draws a substantial share of domestic resources such as labor and materials, increasing their cost to other sectors. Moreover, when the initially booming resource sector eventually declines, the non-resource-based sectors may find it difficult to recover.

These lessons are relevant for transitions from conflict to peace because they underline some of the technical implications of transforming revenues from natural resources into long-term development benefits. During a peace process, NRFs and wealth-sharing schemes can be used to forge new visions for the future and persuade negotiators and their constituents that a better life after war is a real possibility. The section that follows illustrates the opportunities and limitations of sharing natural resource wealth and the role of wealth sharing in the transition to peace.

THE WEALTH-SHARING EVIDENCE: SUDAN AND INDONESIA

In Sudan and Indonesia, natural resources (oil, and in the case of Indonesia, natural gas as well) were important elements in long-lasting armed conflict.[13] In both cases, natural resource wealth was addressed in peace negotiations, although very differently: in Sudan, the parties agreed to a detailed wealth-sharing agreement that included a wealth-sharing formula and the establishment of new institutions; in Indonesia, wealth sharing was part of a broader offer of autonomy from the central government.

Wealth sharing in Sudan

Sudan's North-South conflict (1983–2005) stemmed from clashes over political power; cultural identity; and natural resources, including land, water, and oil. A number of structural issues fueled the dispute: weak state institutions; a history of governance by elites; and attempts, in a country where citizens belonged to many different cultures and many different religions, to build a national identity based on Arab culture and Islam (Prunier and Gisselquist 2003; Simmons and Dixon 2006).

Oil has been one of the drivers of the North-South conflict, particularly since 1999, when production first began. The location of oil in the border area between northern and southern Sudan elevated the oil's strategic significance; hence, much of the fighting was concentrated in that area (see figure 1). Moreover, the government's exploitation of oil brought no tangible benefits to the South, which fostered grievances in the region and made oil a rallying point for the mobilization of the Sudan People's Liberation Movement/Army (SPLM/A), especially between 1999 and 2005. Over time, oil also shifted the military balance in favor of the government and entrenched the rule of the National Congress Party (NCP) (Johnson 2003; Jok 2007).

---

[13] The case studies on Sudan and Aceh are elaborated more fully in Wennmann (2009b) and Wennmann and Krause (2009). See also Luke A. Patey, "Lurking Beneath the Surface: Oil, Environmental Degradation, and Armed Conflict in Sudan," in this volume.

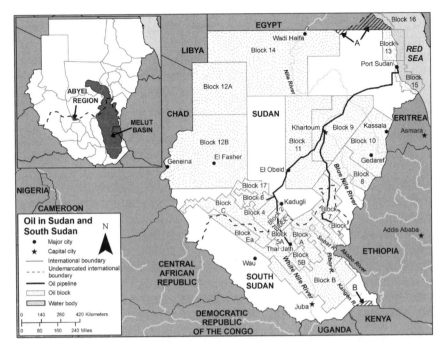

Figure 1. Oil in Sudan and South Sudan
Source: IHS (1998).
Notes:
A – The Hala'ib Triangle, claimed by Sudan and de facto administered by Egypt.
B – The Ilemi Triangle, claimed by Ethiopia, Sudan, and Kenya and de facto controlled by Kenya.
For information on ownership of specific concession blocks, see page 570.

The Sudan Comprehensive Peace Agreement and the Agreement on Wealth Sharing

The Sudan Comprehensive Peace Agreement (CPA) of January 9, 2005, was a landmark settlement of one of Africa's longest civil wars. The CPA included provisions for an interim period (2005–2011) that addressed security, wealth sharing, power sharing, and the future of three regions: Abyei, Southern Kordofan, and Blue Nile. It also called for general elections in 2010 and a referendum on the status of southern Sudan in 2011.

The Agreement on Wealth Sharing (AWS) of January 7, 2004, one of the six protocols that make up the CPA, was a major achievement of the North-South peace process. In addition to having been a major factor in the onset and dynamics of the conflict, oil represented an indigenous source for financing post-conflict recovery. Wealth sharing was an issue in the peace process mainly because of the high-value oil wells located in the border region between Northern and Southern Sudan. The war had made it difficult to attract additional capital investment and had prevented oil companies from continuing to operate in the region; oil was therefore an incentive for peace (Batruch 2004). Oil was also an element

238 High-value natural resources and post-conflict peacebuilding

in the tactically informed choices of the belligerents to relocate the fighting from the battlefield to the negotiating table (Wennmann 2009b).

The AWS describes resource-sharing arrangements for Sudan's post-conflict economy during the interim period. The agreement covers the division of oil and nonoil revenues, the management of the oil sector, monetary authority, and the reconstruction of war-affected areas; it also establishes new institutions for economic governance, including the National Land Commission, the National Petroleum Commission, the Bank of Southern Sudan, the Southern Sudan Reconstruction and Development Fund, the National Reconstruction and Development Fund, and the multi-donor trust funds (MDTFs). The AWS does not address ownership of natural resources, but it does specify that the parties have agreed to resolve that issue at a later date (AWS 2004).

One of the main provisions in the AWS calls for net oil revenue from wells in Southern Sudan to be divided equally between the Government of Southern Sudan (GOSS) and the Government of Sudan (GOS).[14] With respect to nonoil revenue, the agreement specifies various revenue sources for the GOS and the GOSS, including taxes and fees.

Forging and implementing the AWS

During negotiations on the AWS, the parties managed to solve a number of critical problems. First, the decoupling of resource management and ownership prevented an early collapse of the negotiations. Second, the GOS became more open to wealth sharing once it became clear that the 50/50 sharing formula would only apply to wells in Southern Sudan, and not to all oil wells in Sudan (Wennmann 2009b). Agreement on wealth sharing was further facilitated by four factors:

- The decision to work from a single document, which made it easier to develop trade-offs to address outstanding issues.
- The use of resource experts, which enabled negotiators to address complex issues and to develop an understanding on oil reserves and potential.
- Compromise between obligations to service outstanding debt and economic development needs.
- Changes in the modes of payment for oil exports, such as the shift from accepting payment in the form of consumer goods to payment in the form of financial transfers (Wennmann 2009b).

The AWS was accompanied, however, by implementation problems that complicated the peace process in the South. These problems were associated

---

[14] Under article 5.6 of the AWS, the 50/50 sharing formula applies after (1) payments have been made to the Oil Revenue Stabilization Account and (2) at least 2 percent of net oil revenues have been allocated to producing states or regions, in proportion to their contribution to total production (AWS 2004).

with a lack of transparency about oil exploitation on the part of the GOS; a lack of trust between the NCP and the SPLM/A; absence of any formal meetings other than those of the joint technical committee; and concerns about the social and environmental consequences of exploitation (UNSC 2007). Nevertheless, in February 2006, more than one year after the CPA was signed, the GOS reportedly transferred US$800 million to the GOSS. There was no indication, however, what time period this payment corresponded to, or whether it reflected a 50/50 distribution (ICG 2007).

By 2008, wealth sharing between the GOS and GOSS had improved, and the GOS had paid arrears for 2005 through 2007 (UNSC 2008). In 2007, the GOSS received US$1,458 million in revenues (SMF 2008). Despite the transfer of considerable sums, suspicions remain in the South as to whether the transfers did indeed comply with the AWS sharing formula; Global Witness, an international NGO, has even claimed that the GOSS has received only half of what it is due under the AWS (Global Witness 2009). Assessing the GOS's compliance will remain difficult as long as oil contracts, exports, and price arrangements are not subject to independent verification (ICG 2008).

Failure to achieve a peace dividend

Despite the transfer of funds from the GOS to the GOSS, the AWS has yet to yield a substantial peace dividend. There are a number of reasons for this failure. First, the GOSS lacks the capacity to systematically collect, store, manage, and allocate oil and nonoil revenues (ICG 2007); there have also been allegations that this lack of capacity created an environment within the SPLM/A that was ripe for corruption (Jooma 2007). Second, the relative lack of prewar development and the duration and impact of the armed conflict have probably inhibited economic growth—a problem that Benaiah Yongo Bure identified as early as 2005 (Bude 2005). Third, the promised international assistance for the GOSS—through multi-donor trust funds and other aid instruments—was delayed; for example, the first MDTF disbursement occurred in March 2006, over one year after the CPA had been signed (Scanteam 2007).

The limited treatment of water and land in the AWS has also hobbled its contribution to economic recovery. Water issues were not a primary interest for either the GOS or the GOSS; moreover, addressing them would have drawn Sudan's neighbors into the peace process, further complicating the effort (Rogier 2005; Schafer 2007). The AWS addresses land issues only in vague terms, in relation to the National Land Commission (Jooma 2005). The failure to systematically address land rights has prevented the resolution of long-simmering local conflicts that have been exacerbated by population movements (IISS 2007).

Contextual factors must also be taken into account. Sudan's political and security conditions hardly created a conducive environment for the AWS to make a constructive contribution to post-conflict economic recovery. Although the CPA stopped the conflict between the GOS and the SPLM/A, fighting escalated in

Darfur, in western Sudan, and between Sudan and Chad; meanwhile, armed groups have continued to proliferate in Southern Sudan, forming constantly shifting alliances (SAS 2007). In addition, despite the signing of the CPA, both northern and southern Sudan have become increasingly militarized, receiving large-scale military assistance from China; expanding their weapons imports; and developing indigenous arms-manufacturing industries (HSBA 2007a, 2007b). The monumental task of demobilizing and reintegrating about 180,000 former combatants has yet to be completed (IRIN 2008). Finally, as the United Nations Security Council has observed, "the lack of mutual trust and confidence between the NCP and SPLM/A remains the main challenge for the implementation of the [CPA]" (UNSC 2008, 15). In October 2007, the SPLM/A even temporarily withdrew from the Government of National Unity.[15]

Oil reserves and Sudan's economic future

Declining deposits of high-quality oil in the South pose a challenge to the future viability of Southern Sudan. Because oil—in particular, high-quality oil—is concentrated in the Abyei region and in the Melut Basin, in eastern Sudan, border demarcation between Northern and Southern Sudan and the status of Southern Sudan (particularly its independence) have significant commercial implications. Thus far, production and pipeline construction have focused on these two areas; after years of intensive exploitation, however, production in the Abyei oil fields has declined. It is estimated that more than half the reserves in Abyei have been exploited, whereas the Melut Basin remained largely untapped as of 2006 (ECOS 2008; ICG 2007). The decline in production in Abyei may have been caused by a GOS policy to extract as much as possible before the referendum in 2011; because of the lack of transparency in Sudan's oil sector, however, it is impossible to verify these allegations (ICG 2008). In any case, fewer resources are available for wealth sharing in 2011 than there were in 2005—which, in turn, has implications for the significance and function of wealth sharing in a future peace process.

Lessons learned

The inability of the AWS to foster immediate post-agreement peace dividends is a potent reminder that money alone is not the key to successful economic development. Governance capacity, the implementation environment, and weaknesses in the content of an agreement all have potential bearing on economic recovery. Moreover, the lack of development progress must be set against the objectives of the peace process. Ultimately, the CPA reflected an agreement, on the part of the GOS and the SPLM/A, to continue fighting by other means. In

---

[15] The Government of National Unity was the transitional government stipulated by the 2005 peace agreement; elections held in April 2010 replaced the transitional government with an elected one.

other words, the CPA embodied short-term military, political, and economic interests, and is thus more a reflection of the parties' self-interest and mutual mistrust than a "shared commitment to addressing the country's key problems and building a common future" (Rogier 2005, xiv). Viewed from this perspective, the AWS was an acceptable interim compromise on oil revenues and part of a larger peace process that was neither designed, nor required, to address any issues that were outside the bounds deemed acceptable by the parties.

Wealth sharing in Aceh, Indonesia

The discovery of natural gas in northeastern Aceh, in 1974, was central to the origin and evolution of Aceh's civil war. The military presence in Aceh dates back to the discovery of natural gas, when the Indonesian armed forces (*Tentara Nasoinal Indonesia*, or TNI) were deployed to protect the gas production

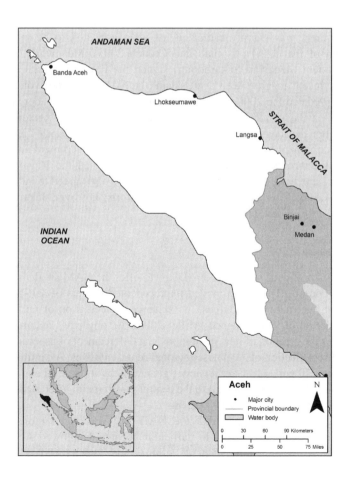

facilities (Mietzner 2006). In 2000, TNI forces in Aceh numbered about 30,000; by 2003, between 13,000 and 15,000 police and special forces had been deployed (Schulze 2006). The civil war can largely be explained as a reaction to the TNI's presence.

Three decades of armed conflict ended in 2005, after Aceh had been severely affected by a tsunami. Before the natural disaster, the Indonesian central government and the Free Aceh Movement (Gerakan Aceh Merdeka, or GAM) had begun to explore a negotiated settlement. The memorandum of understanding (MOU) of August 15, 2005, closed one of Asia's longest civil wars and framed Aceh's post-conflict and tsunami recovery.

Peace negotiations

The first attempts at a negotiated settlement began only after the fall of President Suharto, who ruled Indonesia from 1967 to 1998. In 2000, the Geneva-based Centre for Humanitarian Dialogue led a peace initiative that culminated in a humanitarian pause in fighting in 2000, and a cease-fire agreement in 2002. But the government was sharply criticized for what appeared to be international recognition of the GAM (Aspinall and Crouch 2003). Meanwhile, in August 2001, President Megawati Sukarnoputri signed the Law on Special Autonomy for the Province Nanggroe Aceh Darussalam (the NAD law). The evolution of the NAD law predated the 2000 peace process and was part of a broader attempt by then-president Bacharuddin Jusuf Habibie to address Indonesia's center-periphery relations after decades of centralized authoritarian rule. On April 23, 1999, for example, parliament had passed the Law on Regional Government and the Law on Fiscal Balance between the Central Government and the Regions (Miller 2006); that same year, the Indonesian government had also agreed to independence for Timor-Leste. After these decentralization efforts, however, Jakarta became resistant to further devolution of powers.

The NAD law

President Sukarnoputri signed the NAD law to offer the GAM an alternative way out of the conflict. The law provided unprecedented powers of self-governance and control over natural resources, in exchange for cessation of hostilities and the renunciation of independence (Miller 2006). Among other features, the law provided for the creation of new institutions, the enforcement of aspects of Islamic law, and direct election of Acehnese regional representatives. A central provision granted Aceh 70 percent of the revenues generated by its rich oil and gas fields; the remaining 30 percent would go to the central government. After eight years, the shares would be equalized to 50 percent.

The government claimed that the NAD law was much more generous than previous legal provisions—in particular because it allowed Aceh also to retain revenues from fishing, general mining, and forestry (NAD law 2001;

ICG 2001). As a wealth-sharing instrument, however, the NAD law had a number of limitations:

- It failed to realistically address Aceh's economic grievances and prospects; even more important, it failed to build confidence among the Acehnese that the central government was committed to the implementation of the law.
- The law did not include baseline assessments of economic reserves or indicate the specific mechanisms by which revenues would be shared.
- No consideration was given to Aceh's economic prospects once oil and gas reserves had been depleted (ICG 2001).
- The law made it unclear whether the oil and gas revenues that were to be shared with the central government would be based on production throughout the province or only in a part of it (Martin 2006).
- The fact that revenue would first be collected by Jakarta, then disbursed to local officials, fuelled suspicions among the Acehnese that disbursements would become a means of exerting political leverage (ICG 2001).

As a result of these issues, among others, the NAD law was received unfavorably in Aceh. In particular, the revenue-sharing provisions were perceived as an avenue for providing incumbent political elites with additional opportunities for corruption. And even though some government officials presented the NAD law as a flexible starting point for further negotiation, a number of important omissions—including any mention of the reduction of Jakarta's military presence and investigations into past atrocities—fanned the perception that the NAD law was a ploy (Aspinall and Crouch 2003). Finally, because the law was conceived without any input from the GAM or Acehnese civil society, the Acehnese had no sense of ownership in the law. Consequently, the GAM rejected the legitimacy of the NAD law, a decision that reflected widespread lack of support among the Acehnese for the law and a prevailing mistrust of Jakarta (Miller 2006).

Nevertheless, the government remained convinced that the NAD law was a generous offer—a conviction that made it unwilling to agree to any other concessions and provided further scope for both parliament and the TNI to pressure the government (namely, the executive branch) to resist any further compromises (Huber 2004). The government's commitment to the NAD law thus limited its room to maneuver and complicated its negotiating position.

New strategies

In 2003, President Sukarnoputri initiated a multi-pronged strategy that included the NAD law, diplomatic efforts to undermine the GAM's international standing, back-channel contacts with the GAM, and continued military activities (Schulze 2006). This approach enabled her to manage various constituencies, especially her backers in the military and in the international community. The Indonesian military continued to support the NAD law, but only as a final offer, not as a basis for further negotiations with the GAM. Six months after the president had initiated the multi-pronged strategy, the military persuaded her to adopt a purely military strategy, which included the creation of a special military command for Aceh (Jemadu 2006); this was the death knell for the NAD law and its wealth-sharing provisions. The resulting escalation of armed conflict effectively abolished any belief, on the GAM's part, that the offers of wealth sharing and autonomy embodied in the NAD law had been made in good faith (Aspinall 2005; Wennmann and Krause 2009).

The MOU, resource deposits, and Aceh's economic future

The memorandum of understanding of August 2005 refers to wealth sharing only in principle: "Aceh is entitled to retain seventy (70) per cent of the revenues from all current and future hydrocarbon deposits and other natural resources in the territory of Aceh as well as in the territorial sea surrounding Aceh" (MOU 2005). Although the destruction wrought by the tsunami and the subsequent humanitarian and development investments make it difficult to isolate the effect of the MOU's limited treatment of wealth sharing, the MOU's lack of precision about wealth sharing has complicated its implementation (Yusuf 2007). According to Irwandi Yusuf, the governor of Aceh, the MOU does not "mention who will regulate and govern [hydrocarbon revenue sources], or who has the authority to give licences for new explorations. The LOGA [Law on the Governing of Aceh] says only that the central and Aceh governments will manage the resources jointly. We should have made it right in the MoU" (Yusuf 2008, 82).

The overall significance of wealth sharing in Aceh's peace process, post-conflict transition, and recovery from the tsunami has been lessened by the gradual depletion of resource deposits. Production peaked during the 1990s, and by 2007, oil and gas were "almost finished" (Yusuf 2007). In April 2000, because of declining reserves, ExxonMobil and Pertamina closed two of the Arun gas fields (Tse 2000). According to ExxonMobil, oil production in Aceh will end by 2011; 90 percent of recoverable gas reserves are already depleted, and the gas fields are expected to close in 2016 (Indonesia Relief 2005; EIA n.d.; World Bank 2008).

The rapid depletion of oil and gas reserves led Aceh's economy to contract by 5.8 percent in the first half of 2008, a trend that is expected to continue (World Bank 2008). Thus, the role of wealth sharing in Aceh must be placed in the context of the relative economic importance of oil and gas. In the 1970s, these two resources were drivers of conflict, but the exhaustion of the reserves substantially reduces their relative importance.

Lessons learned

The Indonesian government's efforts to integrate wealth sharing into the peace process failed on a number of counts; in particular, wealth sharing was not presented as a credible element of conflict resolution or as the basis for a new economic vision for Aceh, and the wealth-sharing provisions of the NAD law failed to clarify ownership or to specify precisely how revenues would be shared. Thus, the government missed an opportunity to use wealth sharing to advance and strengthen the peace process.

CONCLUSION

Wealth sharing is not a magical solution to the difficulties of post-conflict transitions. As the examples of Southern Sudan and Aceh illustrate, so many factors are in play during post-conflict transitions that a good wealth-sharing agreement does not necessarily guarantee long-term development benefits. Any effort to address natural resource wealth in the course of peace processes must be undertaken with an awareness that resources are inevitably connected to broader political, military, and social realities, and that these realities define the bounds of negotiations and expectations in transitions to peace.

Despite the complexities associated with implementation, it is important to address wealth sharing in the peace process: wealth-sharing arrangements can help end or transform armed conflict over natural resources; create a vision for the future; provide the prospect of a better life after armed conflict; and prevent a renewal of hostilities. But to have the desired effect, wealth-sharing arrangements must be thoughtfully constructed. The five strategies that follow can increase their effectiveness.

1. *Define what is to be shared, and how.* A clear understanding of which resources are involved and the precise mechanisms by which wealth will be shared can prevent difficulties during both the peace process and the post-conflict implementation. In Sudan, the AWS featured institutional, management, and oversight provisions that facilitated the management of the oil sector, including wealth sharing. In Aceh, the lack of precision in the MOU about who would regulate and govern the resources appears to have complicated the post-conflict transition. General experience with natural resource funds also suggests how important it is to clearly identify the resources and commercial projects whose revenues will flow into the fund, and for what time period.

2. *Generate and share information.* Creating information on the value and future prospects of natural resources is important to managing expectations and ensuring that all parties are equally well-informed. In fragile and conflict-affected situations, information is often unreliable: vested interests, insecurity, and the weakness of state institutions may undermine data collection and analysis or cause information to be shielded from public scrutiny. Sharing information can also help bridge the gap when parties have differing levels of knowledge or different views of resources and their value. In Sudan, for example, seminars conducted by outside experts helped to bridge such differences and made it possible to draft a proposal on wealth sharing that would later serve as a basis for trade-offs. One challenge, however, is to manage disagreements about the real and imagined value of resources—and the associated disappointments—so

that a pragmatic understanding of economic reality can become the basis for a transitional pact.

3. *Allow ownership of resources to remain unresolved.* The example of Sudan suggests that to maintain momentum in negotiations, it may be desirable to allow resource ownership to remain unresolved and to focus instead on wealth sharing. In Sudan, this approach prevented an early collapse of the talks, allowed both parties to achieve their central economic interests, and enabled the negotiators to avoid losing face in the eyes of their constituencies.

4. *Be inclusive—but do not allow negotiations to be undermined by spoilers.* Wealth-sharing negotiations may make a more lasting contribution to peace if they are as inclusive as possible—that is, if the negotiators and their constituencies feel ownership of the agreements. In Aceh, for example, because the NAD law was conceived without any input from the GAM or Acehnese civil society, the legitimacy of the law—including the notion of wealth sharing—was rejected. At the same time, mediators must ensure that the members of the negotiating teams generally support the peace process and that spoilers are marginalized (Darby 2001).

5. *Present wealth sharing as an incentive for peace.* By ensuring that all parties enjoy equivalent gains from natural resources, wealth-sharing agreements can override animosities and increase security. In Sudan, oil created an incentive for peace because investment and exploitation could not occur in the midst of a war. Oil also increased the government's military power, which made the SPLM/A realize that peace talks were in its own best interest. Oil revenues thus shaped tactically informed choices to relocate the fighting from the battlefield to the negotiating table.

The experiences of Southern Sudan and Aceh illustrate that peace processes do not end with a peace agreement. A negotiated exit from armed conflict requires a strong transitional pact that must be nurtured and supported as the parties implement the agreement that ends their past conflict and prepares them for what is next. Transitions from conflict to peace require constant human effort to succeed, as well as ongoing support mechanisms and the requisite capacity to facilitate peace processes. While the necessary infrastructure for mediation support is growing at the bilateral, multilateral, and civil society levels, most efforts are focused on ending conflict. Unless they are offered credible new futures, some groups and individuals will conclude that life will be better for them if they continue to use guns. Wealth sharing from natural resources has the potential to shape new visions for the future and to strengthen the transitional pacts—between belligerents, local communities, the international community, and the private sector—that are necessary to successfully manage the transition to peace.

REFERENCES

Ahmad, E., and E. Mottu. 2002. Oil revenue assignments: Experiences and issues. IMF Working Paper 02/203. Washington, D.C.: International Monetary Fund.

Aspinall, E. 2005. *The Helsinki agreement: A more promising basis for peace in Aceh?* Washington, D.C.: East-West Center.

Aspinall, E., and H. Crouch. 2003. *The Aceh peace process: Why it failed.* Washington, D.C.: East-West Center.

Auty, R. 1993. *Sustaining development in mineral economies: The resource curse thesis.* London: Routledge.

AWS (Agreement on Wealth Sharing during the Pre-Interim and Interim Period). 2004. www.reliefweb.int/rw/RWB.NSF/db900SID/SZIE-5ZJSKB?OpenDocument.

Bahl, R., and B. Tumennasan. 2002. How should revenues from natural resources be shared in Indonesia? International Studies Program Working Paper 02-14. Atlanta: Georgia State University.

Ballentine, K., and V. Haufler. 2005. *Enabling economies of peace: Public policy for conflict-sensitive business.* New York: United Nations Global Compact.

Banfield, J., D. Lilly, and V. Haufler. 2003. *Transnational corporations in conflict-prone zones: Public policy responses and a framework for action.* London: International Alert.

Bannon, I., and P. Collier, eds. 2003. *Natural resources and violent conflict: Options and actions.* Washington, D.C.: World Bank.

Batruch, C. 2004. Oil and conflict: Lundin Petroleum's experience in Sudan. In *Business and security: Public-private sector relationships in a new security environment*, ed. A. J. K. Bailes and I. Frommelt. Oxford, UK: Oxford University Press.

———. 2009. Lundin Petroleum's experience in East Africa: The role of the private sector in conflict-prone countries. Paper presented at the 13th Annual International Conference on Economics and Security, Thessaloniki, Greece, June 24–26.

Beblawi, H., and G. Luciano. 1987. *The rentier state.* London: Routledge.

Bell, J. C., and T. M. Faria. 2007. Critical issues for a revenue management law. In *Escaping the resource curse*, ed. M. Humphreys, J. D. Sachs, and J. E. Stiglitz. New York: Columbia University Press.

Bennett, J. 2002. *Conflict prevention and revenue-sharing regimes.* New York: United Nations Global Compact.

Bure, B. Y. 2005. Peace dividend and the Millennium Development Goals in Southern Sudan. Sudan Economy Research Group Discussion Paper No. 36. Bremen: University of Bremen.

Carbonnier, G. 2008. Les négociations multi-parties prenantes: L'exemple de l'Initiative de Transparence des Industries Extractives. *Relations Internationales* 136:101–113.

Collier, P. 2009. The political economy of natural resources. Paper presented at the 10th annual conference of the Global Development Network, Kuwait.

Collier, P., L. Elliott, H. Hegre, A. Hoeffler, M. Reynal-Querol, and N. Sambanis. 2003. *Breaking the conflict trap: Civil war and development policy.* Washington, D.C.: World Bank.

Collier, P., and N. Sambanis, eds. 2005. *Understanding civil war: Evidence and analysis.* Washington, D.C.: World Bank.

Darby, J. 2001. *The effects of violence on peace processes.* Washington, D.C.: United States Institute of Peace Press.

Dwan, R., and L. Bailey. 2006. *Liberia's Governance and Economic Management Assistance Programme (GEMAP): A joint review by the Department of Peacekeeping Operations' Peacekeeping Best Practices Section and the World Bank's Fragile States Group.* New York: United Nations; Washington, D.C.: World Bank.

ECOS (European Coalition on Oil in Sudan). 2008. *Whose oil? Sudan's oil industry.* Utrecht: IKV Pax Christi.
EIA (U.S. Energy Information Administration). n.d. Country analysis brief: Indonesia—natural gas. www.eia.doe.gov/emeu/cabs/Indonesia/NaturalGas.html.
Ford, N. 2007. Power struggle: Boosting competition for African energy. *Jane's Intelligence Review* 19 (1): 64–65.
Global Witness. 2009. *Fuelling mistrust: The need for transparency in Sudan's oil industry.* London.
Hartzell, C. A. 1999. Explaining the stability of negotiated settlements to intrastate wars. *Journal of Conflict Resolution* 43 (1): 3–44.
Haysom, N., and S. Kane. 2009. *Negotiating natural resources for peace: Ownership, control and wealth sharing.* Geneva: Centre for Humanitarian Dialogue.
Herbst, J. 2004. African militaries and rebellion: The political economy of threat and combat effectiveness. *Journal of Peace Research* 41 (3): 357–369.
Holsti, K. J. 1991. *Peace and war: Armed conflicts and international order, 1648–1989.* Cambridge, UK: Cambridge University Press.
HSBA (Human Security Baseline Assessment). 2007a. The militarization of Sudan: A preliminary review of arms flows and holdings. Sudan Issue Brief No. 6. Geneva: SAS.
———. 2007b. Arms, oil and Darfur: The evolution of relations between China and Sudan. Sudan Issue Brief No. 7. Geneva: SAS.
Huber, K. 2004. *The HDC in Aceh: Promises and pitfalls of NGO mediation and implementation.* Washington, D.C.: East-West Center.
Humphreys, M., J. D. Sachs, and J. E. Stiglitz. 2007. Introduction: What is the problem with natural resources? In *Escaping the resource curse*, ed. M. Humphreys, J. D. Sachs, and J. E. Stiglitz. New York: Columbia University Press.
ICG (International Crisis Group). 2001. *Aceh: Can autonomy stem the conflict?* Jakarta and Brussels.
———. 2007. *Sudan: Breaking the Abyei deadlock.* Nairobi and Brussels.
———. 2008. *Sudan's comprehensive peace agreement: Beyond the crisis.* Nairobi and Brussels.
Iff, A., and N. Töpperwien. 2008. Power sharing: The Swiss experience. *Politorbis* No. 45. Bern: Federal Department of Foreign Affairs.
IHS. 1998. Melt Basin monitor report. http://maps.ihs.com/basin-monitor-ordering-service/africa/melut-basin-monitor-report.html.
IISS (International Institute for Strategic Studies). 2007. *Strategic survey 2007.* London.
Indonesia Relief. 2005. World Bank: Bye-bye Aceh oil. August 26. www.indonesia-relief.org/mod.php?mod=publisher&op=viewarticle&cid=29&artid=1569.
IRIN (Integrated Regional Information Networks). 2008. Sudan: Preparing for massive demobilisation. *IRIN Humanitarian News and Analysis,* 21 October. www.irinnews.org/report.aspx?ReportId=81014.
Jemadu, A. 2006. Democratisation, the Indonesian armed forces, and resolving the Aceh conflict. In *Verandah of violence: The background to the Aceh problem*, ed. A. Reid. Singapore: Singapore University Press.
Johnson, D. H. 2003. *The root causes of Sudan's civil wars.* Bloomington: Indiana University Press.
Jok, J. M. 2007. *Sudan: Race, religion, and violence.* Oxford, UK: Oneworld.
Jooma, M. 2005. Feeding the peace: Challenges facing human security in post-Garang South Sudan. Institute for Security Studies. August 23. www.issafrica.org/uploads/050823SUDAN.PDF.

———. 2007. Dual realities: Peace and war in the Sudan—An update on the implementation of the CPA. Institute for Security Studies. www.issafrica.org/uploads/SUDANSITREPMAY07.PDF.
Karl, T. L. 1997. *The paradox of plenty: Oil booms and petro states*. Berkeley: University of California Press.
Martin, H. 2006. *Kings of peace, pawns of war: The untold story of peace-making*. London: Continuum.
Mietzner, M. 2006. *The politics of military reform in post-Suharto Indonesia: Elite conflict, nationalism, and institutional resistance*. Washington, D.C.: East-West Center.
Miller, M. A. 2006. What's special about special autonomy in Aceh? In *Verandah of violence: The background to the Aceh problem*, ed. A. Reid. Singapore: Singapore University Press.
MOU (Memorandum of Understanding between the Government of the Republic of Indonesia and the Free Aceh Movement). 2005. www.aceh-mm.org/download/english/Helsinki%20MoU.pdf.
NAD law (Special autonomy law in Nanggroe Aceh Darussalam (NAD) Law No. 18 of 2001). 2001. www.kbri-canberra.org.au/s_issues/aceh/aceh_specautonomy.htm.
Ottaway, M. 2003. *Democracy challenged: The rise of semi-authoritarianism*. New York: Carnegie Endowment for International Peace.
Prunier, G., and R. Gisselquist. 2003. The Sudan: A successfully failed state. In *State failure and state weakness in a time of terror*, ed. R. I. Rotberg. Washington, D.C.: Brookings Institution Press.
Radon, J. 2007. How to negotiate an oil agreement. In *Escaping the resource curse*, ed. M. Humphreys, J. D. Sachs, and J. E. Stiglitz. New York: Columbia University Press.
Reno, W. 1997. War, markets, and the reconfiguration of West Africa's weak states. *Comparative Politics* 29 (4): 493–510.
Rogier, E. 2005. *Designing an integrated strategy for peace, security and development in post-agreement Sudan*. The Hague: Netherlands Institute of International Relations Clingendael. www.clingendael.nl/publications/2005/20050400_cru_paper_rogier.pdf.
Ross, M. 2005. Resources and rebellion in Aceh, Indonesia. In *Understanding civil war. Volume II: Europe, Central Asia, and other regions*, ed. P. Collier and N. Sambanis. Washington, D.C.: World Bank.
———. 2007. How mineral-rich states can reduce inequality. In *Escaping the resource curse*, ed. M. Humphreys, J. D. Sachs, and J. E. Stiglitz. New York: Columbia University Press.
SAS (Small Arms Survey). 2007. *Small arms survey 2007: Guns in the city*. Cambridge, UK: Cambridge University Press.
Scanteam. 2007. *Review of post-crisis multi-donor trust funds: Country study annexes*. Oslo: World Bank, Norwegian Ministry of Foreign Affairs, and Norwegian Agency for Development Cooperation.
Schafer, L. A. 2007. Negotiating the North/South conflict: Sudan's comprehensive peace agreement. ISS Paper 148. Institute for Security Studies. www.humansecuritygateway.com/showRecord.php?RecordId=28903.
Schulze, K. E. 2006. Insurgency and counter-insurgency: Strategy and the Aceh conflict, October 1976–May 2004. In *Verandah of violence: The background to the Aceh problem*, ed. A. Reid. Singapore: Singapore University Press.
Simmons, M., and P. Dixon. 2006. Introduction. In *Peace by pieces: Addressing Sudan's conflict*, ed. M. Simmons and P. Dixon. London: Conciliation Resources.

Siriam, C. L. 2008. *Peace as governance: Power sharing, armed groups, and contemporary peace negotiations*. Houndmills, UK: Palgrave Macmillan.

SMF (Sudan Ministry of Finance). 2008. Template for publication of Sudan oil sector data 2007. www.ecosonline.org/news/2008/Sudan%20production%20and%20exports%20 by%20blend_2007_MOF.pdf.

Smillie, I. 2005. What lessons from the Kimberley Process Certification Scheme? In *Profiting from peace: Managing the resource dimension of civil war*, ed. K. Ballentine and H. Nitzschke. Boulder, CO: Lynne Rienner.

Suhrke, A., T. Wimpelmann, and M. Dawes. 2007. *Peace processes and statebuilding: Economic and institutional provisions of peace agreements*. Bergen: Chr. Michelsen Institute.

Tse, P.-K. 2000. *The mineral industry of Indonesia*. http://minerals.er.usgs.gov/minerals/pubs/country/2000/9313000.pdf.

UNCTAD (United Nations Conference on Trade and Development). 2008. *Development and globalisation: Facts and figures*. Geneva: United Nations.

UNEP (United Nations Environment Programme). 2009. *From conflict to peacebuilding: The role of natural resources and the environment*. Nairobi.

UNSC (United Nations Security Council). 2007. Report of the Secretary-General on the Sudan. S/2007/213. New York.

———. 2008. Report of the Secretary-General on the Sudan. S/2008/662. New York.

Wennmann, A. 2009a. Economic provisions in peace agreements and sustainable peacebuilding. *Négociations* 11 (1): 43–61.

———. 2009b. Wealth sharing beyond 2011: Economic issues in Sudan's North-South peace process. CCDP Working Paper 1. Geneva: Graduate Institute of International and Development Studies.

Wennmann, A., and J. Krause. 2009. Managing the economic dimensions of peace processes: Resource wealth, autonomy, and peace in Aceh. CCDP Working Paper 3. Geneva: Graduate Institute of International and Development Studies.

World Bank. 2008. Aceh conflict monitoring update, 1st–30th September 2008. Jakarta.

Yusuf, I. 2007. Q&A with Aceh's Governor Irwandi Yusuf. *AsiaSource*, 13 September.

———. 2008. Aceh's new era: An interview with Irwandi Yusuf. In *Reconfiguring politics: The Indonesia-Aceh peace process*, ed. Aguswandi and Judith Large. *Accord* 20. www.aceh-eye.org/data_files/english_format/peace_process/peace_process_augmou/augmou_analysis/augmou_analysis_2008_00_00.pdf.

Zartman, I. W. 1995. Dynamics and constraints in negotiations in internal conflict. In *Elusive peace: Negotiating an end to civil wars*, ed. I. W. Zartman. Washington, D.C.: Brookings Institution.

———. 2005. Looking forward and looking backward on negotiation theory. In *Peace versus justice: Negotiation forward- and backward-looking outcomes*, ed. I. W. Zartman and V. Kremenyuk. Lanham, MD: Rowman and Littlefield.

Horizontal inequality, decentralizing the distribution of natural resource revenues, and peace

Michael L. Ross, Päivi Lujala, and Siri Aas Rustad

High-value resources such as oil and minerals are often unequally distributed within countries. When the distribution happens to coincide with ethnic, religious, or other divisions between groups, real or perceived inequality—known as *horizontal inequality*—may result, creating potential grounds for grievances. In Niger, for example, mineral revenues are siphoned to the capital, and little is invested in the region from which the revenues originate. This practice has created grievances among the Tuareg, the nomadic people whose ancestral lands encompass the mining areas. In other cases, the "aggrieved" parties are privileged groups. For example, Santa Cruz Department—one of the wealthiest states in Bolivia—has sought greater autonomy, out of a growing reluctance to share gas revenues with the poorer states. Unsurprisingly, many resource-rich countries are plagued by secessionist movements pursuing a radical approach to decreasing (or increasing) horizontal inequality.

Decentralization of natural resource revenues has become a common means of easing and preventing horizontal inequality, both within and outside the post-conflict context. In the case of oil and other mineral rents, there appears to be a global trend toward decentralization (Brosio 2003). Decentralization has also gained some momentum in peacebuilding processes, where it is a popular option among policy makers because it is politically feasible and helps to manage regional grievances. In the processes that led to the signing of peace agreements in Sudan, for example, decentralization of revenues played a central role.[1] Nevertheless,

---

Michael L. Ross is a professor of political science at the University of California, Los Angeles (UCLA), and director of the UCLA Center for Southeast Asian Studies. Päivi Lujala is an associate professor of geography at the Norwegian University of Science and Technology and a senior researcher at the Centre for the Study of Civil War at the Peace Research Institute Oslo. Siri Aas Rustad is a researcher at the Centre for the Study of Civil War at the Peace Research Institute Oslo. This chapter was adapted from Michael L. Ross, "How Can Mineral Rich States Reduce Inequality?" in *Reversing the Resource Curse*, ed. Macartan Humphreys, Jeffrey Sachs, and Joseph Stiglitz (New York: Columbia University Press, 2007). The authors would like to acknowledge the assistance of Heather Croshaw of the Environmental Law Institute.

[1] For a description of these two processes, see Achim Wennmann, "Sharing Natural Resource Wealth during War-to-Peace Transitions," in this volume.

decentralization can also have serious drawbacks, which should be carefully assessed beforehand.

This chapter focuses on the role of decentralizing natural resource revenues in promoting peacebuilding, particularly where horizontal inequality has played a role in the conflict.[2] Although decentralization can take a number of different forms, the focus in this chapter is on distributing the revenues to the regions from which the resources were extracted. The chapter is divided into three main sections: (1) a consideration of the links between mineral wealth, horizontal inequality, conflict, and peacebuilding; (2) a discussion of the benefits and obstacles associated with various approaches to decentralization; and (3) a brief conclusion.

RESOURCE WEALTH, HORIZONTAL INEQUALITY, CONFLICT, AND PEACEBUILDING

If producing areas are onshore and concentrated in one or a few parts of the country, a booming natural resource sector may affect the geographical distribution of income. The strength and direction of this effect will depend on three factors:

- Initial incomes in the extractive region.
- The strength of the connections between the resource sector and other economic activities.
- The ability of the subnational government to capture income from the resource sector.

If the producing region is poor, resource wealth can help to close any gaps between that region and the rest of the country; if it is relatively rich, resource wealth can widen gaps. If extraction facilities operate as enclaves and the regional government has no taxing authority, then a booming resource sector may have little or no impact on regional living standards. But if the extractive sector is strongly connected to the local economy or if the local government can tax resource revenues (either directly or indirectly), resource wealth can sharply boost regional employment and wages and increase local revenues.

While an increase in the region's actual income may be good, a disproportionate rise in income *expectations* may pose problems. People are dissatisfied with their income, no matter how large it is, if it falls short of their aspirations (Frey and Stützer 2002); a large gap between real and expected income can thus lead to political and social unrest. Such gaps are exceptionally risky in areas where revenues accrue to the central state rather than to the local government, and the producing regions are geographically peripheral, have little influence over the central government, and are populated by people with a distinct ethnic

---

[2] In a completely centralized system, natural resource revenues are distributed strictly on the basis of various criteria, including needs and national development plans, and producing regions receive no preferential treatment.

or religious identity, as in Niger. In these cases, the discovery and exploitation of natural resources can lead to frustration over unrealized expectations, even if no measurable adverse effects on income or income distribution occur (Østby, Nordås, and Rød 2009; Stewart 2000). As Paul Collier and Anke Hoeffler have noted, the "allure of claiming ownership of a natural resource discovery" can encourage populations in peripheral regions to favor independence (2006, 39).

The notion that frustration over unrealized expectations may spark or facilitate conflict is supported by statistical studies that have found a relationship between the production or export of oil, gas, and precious stones and armed civil conflict.[3] In many cases, such conflicts concern the autonomy of a resource-rich region. Table 1 lists ten examples of violent separatist movements in regions with significant oil, gas, or other natural resource wealth. Although none of the movements developed solely in response to the presence of resource wealth, in each case separatists appeared to believe that resource revenues would increase the benefits, or lower the costs, of independence.

Table 1. Oil, gas, and mineral resources and secessionist movements

Country	Region	Duration of secessionist movement	Resources
Angola	Cabinda	1975–2002	Oil
Myanmar	[Hill tribes][a]	1983–1995	Tin, gems
Democratic Republic of the Congo	Katanga	1960–1965	Copper
Indonesia	West Papua	1969–present	Copper, gold
Indonesia	Aceh	1975–2005	Natural gas
Nigeria	Biafra	1967–1970	Oil
Papua New Guinea	Bougainville	1988–1997	Copper, gold
Sudan	South	1983–2005	Oil
Yemen	East and south	1994	Oil
———	Western Sahara[b]	1975–1988	Phosphates, oil

a. The Hill tribes are concentrated in the states of Kachin, Rakhine, and Shan, and the district of Sagaing.
b. Western Sahara is a disputed territory in North Africa. Parts of it have been or currently are recognized by different political entities as (1) the sovereign state of the Sahrawi Arab Democratic Republic, (2) part of the state of Morocco, or (3) a non-self-governed territory.

Just as horizontal inequalities and group expectations regarding "fair" shares of resource revenues motivate and facilitate conflicts, they also play a central role in peace negotiations. Some expectations are unrealistic and cannot be met; others are fair but are not (or cannot be) addressed by the state because of corruption, lack of institutional capacity, or lack of political will. Given the risks associated with horizontal inequality, addressing such inequality, whether real or perceived, is vital for preventing new outbreaks of conflict, particularly where the distribution of natural resource revenues has been one of the driving forces

---

[3] See, for example, Collier and Hoeffler (2006), Lujala (2010), and Ross (2004).

of previous conflict. One strategy for offsetting expected increases in horizontal inequality or mitigating existing inequality is to decentralize resource revenues.[4]

APPROACHES TO REVENUE DECENTRALIZATION

Subnational governments may receive decentralized mineral revenues in three ways:

- They may levy taxes directly on the resource industry.
- They may receive a direct transfer from the central government that is a defined share of the revenues originating in the region. Each oil-producing state in Nigeria, for example, receives 13 percent of the oil revenues generated in that region.
- They may receive indirect transfers—through the national budgeting process—that reflect preferential treatment for producing regions.

Although all three approaches have decentralizing effects, they vary in the degree of decentralization. In the least decentralized approach, in which the region receives transfers from the central government after the revenues have passed through the national budgeting process, distribution is based on criteria such as population, equity, needs, and the national interest, although the producing area is given preferential treatment. One of the countries in which this approach has been used is Indonesia, which eventually adopted a more direct approach to decentralization. In the more decentralized approaches, local governments may directly tax the mineral industry or may receive transfers of defined shares of the central government's resource revenues, on the basis of a set formula.

The two most decentralized approaches have a number of serious drawbacks:

- If the local economy is overly dependent on its resource base, it may simply be too small to be insulated from the economic impact of sharp and sudden changes in the international prices of raw materials.
- Post-conflict countries often suffer from weak institutions and state capacity. Local institutions in conflict-ridden areas are particularly likely to be weak, which exacerbates the potential risk associated with volatile resource revenues. Specifically, local governments may lack the capacity (1) to implement countercyclical fiscal policies—that is, to adjust their economic policies to protect

---

[4] In addition to decentralization, governments can use many other approaches to narrow the gap between actual and expected incomes in resource-rich regions, including creating incentives to hire local workers, restricting the migration of workers to extractive regions, investing in local development, using nongovernmental organizations to mediate between local communities and extractive companies, promoting transparency, and distributing revenues directly to the population. For more information on direct distribution, see Martin E. Sandbu, "Direct Distribution of Natural Resource Revenues as a Policy for Peacebuilding," in this volume.

themselves from boom and bust cycles—and (2) to balance the budget, so that income equals expenditures over time.[5]
- Subnational governments have a lower capacity than national institutions to efficiently absorb the new investments made possible by resource revenues.
- Subnational governments rarely have the administrative capacity to impose taxes and are less able to administer complex types of taxes or to tax large foreign firms.
- When subnational governments impose their own taxes or royalties, they may create inefficiencies by overlapping with national levies.

The least decentralized approach—indirect transfers from the central government—has several advantages:

- The job of handling the transfers could be delegated to a specific ministry whose capacity for dealing with this particular task could be built up.
- Local governments would not have to engage in budgeting, manage spending, or create or strengthen local taxation capability.
- Payments would be stable and able to withstand fluctuations in commodity prices. (For example, the payment could be a fixed annual fee that is corrected for inflation.)
- Particularly in post-conflict settings, transfers could take the form of schools or other infrastructure projects, thus serving as peace dividends.

Nonetheless, a case can be made for the two most decentralized approaches to revenue distribution, particularly in the post-conflict context. Subnational governments are clearly entitled to revenues that would provide compensation for the social, environmental, and infrastructure costs associated with extraction—and in some cases they may even be entitled to compensation for damage caused by conflicts over resources. Moreover, decentralized distribution addresses the issues of self-determination and resource control that concern the inhabitants of some regions, such as Nigeria's Niger Delta.[6] In the short run, the more decentralized approaches may have a political advantage in helping to sustain a peace agreement, as is the case in Sudan. Secessionist movements in particular, which are typically mistrustful of the central government, need reassurance that they will receive the revenues that were promised during peace talks. Granting taxation rights or allowing direct transfers—neither of which have the opacity associated with funds that have been first circulated through the central government budget—may help create such reassurance. In fact, the most centralized option

---

[5] On these points, see Ahmad and Mottu (2003), Bahl (2001), Brosio (2003), and McLure (2003).
[6] For more information on the conflict in the Niger Delta, see Annegret Mähler, "An Inescapable Curse? Resource Management, Violent Conflict, and Peacebuilding in the Niger Delta," in this volume.

is likely to work only where there is a high degree of trust, which is in short supply in many post-conflict situations.

Of course, establishing a distribution system that is based on a specific revenue-sharing formula or on the right to levy taxes does not guarantee its success. In the years following the 2005 peace agreement in Sudan, southern Sudan was entitled to 50 percent of revenues from oil wells located in southern Sudan; suspicions remain, however, that the sums allocated to the region have not followed the formula laid out in the peace agreement (Global Witness 2009). Nor does decentralization guarantee peacebuilding success: according to Binningsbø and Rustad (2010), wealth-sharing arrangements do not increase the likelihood of long-term peace.

Bargaining with subnational governments about the size of transfers can also be an arduous process. The division of oil revenues is a zero-sum game in which every state and local government wants as much as it can get: there is no allocation formula that everyone will think is just. Accommodating the claims of some groups may increase the inequality of distribution between groups or strengthen group identities, sowing the seeds of new or renewed conflict. Finally, if it becomes clear that pressing a claim is effective, other groups in other regions may be encouraged to press theirs as well, in order to gain a higher share of the resource revenues originating in their area.

Ahmad and Mottu (2003) have argued that in the case of oil, the best arrangement is centralization of all revenues, with carefully designed transfers to subnational governments. Recognizing that this arrangement is often politically unattainable, their second-best alternative is to allow subnational governments to levy relatively small, stable types of petroleum taxes—such as production excise taxes—while the national government levies taxes and royalties that capture more volatile forms of revenue.[7] Ahmad and Mottu prefer this approach to direct transfers—which, in their view, allow subnational governments to avoid accountability, complicate macroeconomic planning, and fail to provide subnational governments with stable financing for local public services, all of which are relevant concerns in the peacebuilding context.

Brosio (2003), in contrast, views direct transfers as the second-best alternative to centralization of oil revenues, arguing that the process of collecting and administering taxes makes it more difficult to equalize revenues across subnational jurisdictions; impinges on national energy policy by affecting production decisions; and is too complex for most subnational governments to carry out, at least in developing states. And since the taxation capacity of local governments in a war-torn region may be nearly nil, taxation may not be an option at all.

Although centralized distribution may be the best choice, particularly over the long term, it may be untenable in post-conflict settings because of lack of trust and willingness on the part of producing regions. In such cases, the government

---

[7] Production excise taxes are based on the volume of production, rather than on profits or level of exports—and are hence easier to calculate and to collect.

should try to adopt a more decentralized distribution system that addresses the challenges discussed earlier in the chapter. Specifically,

- The system should be designed to minimize the volatility of subnational revenues and should be based on a formula that is stable over time, so that the issue of distribution will not be constantly revisited.
- The revenues should be accompanied by expenditure responsibilities, so that the additional revenues are directed toward public goods.
- Measures should be taken to limit inefficiencies created by overlapping tax bases.
- The revenue flows should be publicly announced, fully transparent, and regularly audited to increase scrutiny and reduce opportunities for corruption.
- To build trust and avoid disillusionment, both the national and local governments should be held accountable for the receipt and use of the funds.
- The system should not exacerbate existing regional inequalities.

Whichever decentralization method is chosen, it is important to ensure that the agreed-upon sums are in fact transferred and that the receiving local government is accountable for their use. All stakeholders can play a role in making the revenue distribution successful, particularly in the areas of transparency and trust building. In particular, national and international NGOs can serve as monitors, as pressure groups, and as sources of independent statistics on transfers that may inspire greater confidence, among members of local communities, than the data generated by the government. Extractive firms, for their part, can promote transparency by publicly releasing the amounts they pay to the government. Finally, humanitarian and development agencies, international financial institutions, multinational corporations, and UN peacekeeping missions can also help promote transparency and accountability.

Lack of trust between national and subnational governments can undermine the negotiation and implementation of revenue decentralization. At the local level, the national government can build trust by addressing the concerns of local stakeholders. Mining communities, in particular, are deeply affected by mineral extraction and, in some cases, by associated violent conflict. All stakeholders should be compensated for the social and environmental costs of mineral extraction, and possibly for damage caused by conflicts over resources. Local and indigenous peoples, who live on the land where extraction is occurring, deserve consideration—beginning with full recognition as stakeholders whose concerns must be addressed. Ensuring that the negotiation and design of the revenue-sharing plan take account of the needs of both subnational governments and local communities is a step toward building trust.

CONCLUSION

This chapter argues that one key to success in post-conflict settings is the careful management of the impact of natural resource revenues distribution. Of the three approaches to distributing such revenues, the two most decentralized approaches—granting taxing authority to subnational governments and transferring an appropriate share of resource revenues to local governments—have serious drawbacks; nevertheless, these approaches may be necessary to address conflict-related issues (particularly if the conflict was partially caused by perceived or real inequality in revenue or income distribution). Although the best approach is for the central government to collect all revenues and make allocation decisions, this strategy is effective only if local and regional authorities have the opportunity provide input, in order to increase accountability, transparency, and trust between institutions. In many cases, however, local communities and rebel movements are reluctant to agree to central collection and allocation of revenues, leaving the more direct approaches as the only viable alternatives.

In resource-rich regions such as Aceh, Indonesia, revenue-sharing arrangements have sometimes been important components of broader policies to reduce secessionist pressures. In such cases, some degree of decentralization may be politically necessary and desirable, but it must be accompanied by checks and balances that address the accompanying drawbacks. A less risky approach would be to adopt policies that narrow the income gap between the extractive region and the rest of the country, in conjunction with policies that reduce the gap between real and expected incomes within the extractive region. Such measures include full revenue transparency, the promotion of good corporate citizenship, restriction of migration to the extractive region, fostering the role of NGOs, and curtailing predation.

The case for giving subnational governments taxing authority or a direct share of resource revenues would be strengthened if there were evidence that these measures could help avert secessionist movements or prevent relapse into conflict, but few systematic analyses of this issue have been undertaken.[8] Clearly, the decentralization of natural resource revenues is a contentious and challenging issue that deserves more scholarly attention, particularly in the post-conflict setting.

REFERENCES

Ahmad, E., and E. Mottu. 2003. Oil revenue assignments: Country experiences and issues. In *Fiscal policy formulation and implementation in oil-producing countries*, ed. J. Davis, R. Ossowski, and A. Fedelino. Washington, D.C.: International Monetary Fund.

Bahl, R. 2001. Equitable vertical sharing and decentralizing government finance in South Africa. Georgia State University International Studies Program Working Paper 01-6. Atlanta: Georgia State University. http://aysps.gsu.edu/isp/files/ispwp0106.pdf.

Binningsbø, H., and S. A. Rustad. 2010. Sharing the wealth: A pathway to peace or a blind alley? Working Paper. Oslo: Centre for the Study of Civil War, Peace Research Institute Oslo.

---

[8] The few exceptions include Binningsbø and Rustad (2010); Hartzell and Hoddie (2007); and Mattes and Savun (2009).

Brosio, G. 2003. Oil revenue and fiscal federalism. In *Fiscal policy formulation and implementation in oil-producing countries*, ed. J. Davis, R. Ossowski, and A. Fedelino. Washington, D.C.: International Monetary Fund.

Collier, P., and A. Hoeffler. 2006. The political economy of secession. In *Negotiating self-determination*, ed. H. Hannum and E. F. Babbitt. Lanham, MD: Lexington Books.

Frey, B. S., and A. Stützer. 2002. *Happiness and economics: How the economy and institutions affect well-being*. Princeton, NJ: Princeton University Press.

Global Witness. 2009. *Fuelling mistrust: The need for transparency in Sudan's oil industry*. London: Global Witness.

Hartzell, C., and M. Hoddie. 2007. *Crafting peace: Power-sharing institutions and the negotiated settlement of civil wars*. University Park: Pennsylvania State University Press.

Lujala, P. 2010. The spoils of nature: Armed civil conflict and rebel access to natural resources. *Journal of Peace Research* 47 (1): 15–28.

Mattes, M., and B. Savun. 2009. Fostering peace after civil war: Commitment problems and agreement design. *International Studies Quarterly* 53 (3): 737–759.

McLure, C. E. 2003. The assignment of oil tax revenue. In *Fiscal policy formulation and implementation in oil-producing countries*, ed. J. Davis, R. Ossowski, and A. Fedelino. Washington, D.C.: International Monetary Fund.

Østby, G., R. Nordås, and J. K. Rød. 2009. Regional inequalities and civil conflict in 21 sub-Saharan countries, 1986–2004. *International Studies Quarterly* 53 (2): 301–324.

Ross, M. 2004. What do we know about natural resources and civil war? *Journal of Peace Research* 41(3): 337–356.

Stewart, F. 2000. Crisis prevention: Tackling horizontal inequalities. *Oxford Development Studies* 28 (3): 245–262.

The Diamond Area Community Development Fund: Micropolitics and community-led development in post-war Sierra Leone

Roy Maconachie

The Diamond Area Community Development Fund (DACDF), an initiative of the central government in Sierra Leone, was designed to strengthen citizen participation in decision making about natural resource management.[1] Like other community-based natural resource management initiatives in Africa,[2] the DACDF embraces community-led decision making as a means of ensuring that more benefits accrue to impoverished and vulnerable communities than has historically been the case.[3] Among the major goals of the DACDF are to redress unequal power relationships within the diamond industry and to make local decision making about diamond resources more equitable. But the DACDF has largely failed to address many of the underlying power issues that shape decision making at the local level. The endurance of prewar patrimonial relationships subverts fair access to, and control of, the nation's diamond resources and threatens prospects for peacebuilding and post-conflict reconstruction. Although the Sierra Leone Ministry of Mineral Resources has developed a new set of procedures and guidelines to address the shortcomings of the DACDF, it remains unclear whether these guidelines will address the fundamental issue: namely, how community members participate in decision making about natural resources.

This chapter argues that there is a pressing need to view community participation in natural resource management within the broader political, cultural, and historical contexts in which it occurs, rather than to treat it as occurring

---

Roy Maconachie is a lecturer in international development at the University of Bath.
[1] The fieldwork on which this chapter is based was undertaken in two communities in Kono District—Koidu and Kayima—between September and December 2008.
[2] Examples include CAMPFIRE, in Zimbabwe (see Hulme and Murphree 2001), and Gestion des Terroirs, in Mali (see Batterbury 1998).
[3] In addition, because the DACDF returns a percentage of mining revenue to the producing chiefdoms, it has been widely heralded as providing considerable incentive for both miners and diamond-rich chiefdoms to report revenues and to engage in legal diamond mining, thereby enhancing the Kimberley Process Certification Scheme (KPCS) for rough diamonds. See Maconachie (2009) for further discussion of the relationship between the KPCS and the DACDF.

within a romanticized notion of democratic space that is isolated from and unaffected by the real world. The chapter is divided into four sections: (1) a description of the background against which the DACDF came into being; (2) an exploration of the problems and prospects associated with the DACDF; (3) a list of lessons learned; and (4) brief concluding remarks.

BACKGROUND

Sierra Leone is a constitutional republic with an elected president who serves as head of state and head of the central government. The country is divided into thirteen districts (twelve districts plus the Western Area). Each district is subdivided into chiefdoms, which have traditionally been the basic unit of local government outside the capital, Freetown. Each chiefdom is headed by a paramount chief, who is the head of a native administration. Since 2004, however, with the reinstatement of the Local Government Act, all thirteen districts and six major cities have elected local councils (GOSL 2004).[4] The model of decentralization adopted in Sierra Leone assumes that traditional leaders at the chiefdom level (that is, the chiefs and the native administrations) will work alongside elected councilors, with the chiefs taking responsibility for rural security, justice, and land issues, and the local councils taking responsibility for service delivery and rural development.

A great deal of academic attention has focused on the political economy of the decade-long civil war that Sierra Leone endured during the 1990s—and on the role of diamonds in fuelling what some regard as a "greed-based" insurgency and others regard as a "grievance-based" rebellion.[5] The causes of the country's protracted conflict were complex, and an extended discussion of the events leading up to the war is beyond the scope of this chapter.[6] Despite controversy about the specific causes of the war, there appears to be consensus that diamonds were a central feature of the conflict, principally because they allowed the various fighting factions to fund their warring activities. It has been argued that poor governance, overcentralization, and the development of an underclass were prime factors in creating the preconditions for war. The final report of the Sierra Leone Truth and Reconciliation Commission broadly endorses this position, blaming "the political elite of successive regimes in the post-independence era" for the country's descent into chaos and destruction. The "greed, corruption and nepotism" of this group, the report argues, deprived the nation of its dignity, undermined the rule of law,

---

[4] Local governments were abolished under President Siaka Stevens in the early 1970s. In May 2004, Sierra Leone successfully conducted its first local government elections in thirty-two years.

[5] On greed-based insurgency, see, for example, Keen (2005), Richards (2003), and Smillie, Gberie, and Hazelton (2000). On grievance-based insurgency, see Richards (1996).

[6] For further background on the conflict, see Kazumi Kawamoto, "Diamonds in War, Diamonds for Peace: Diamond Sector Management and Kimberlite Mining in Sierra Leone," in this volume.

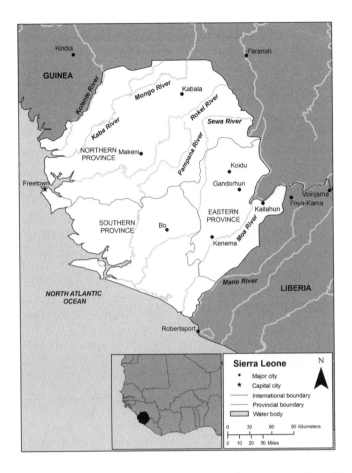

and reduced the people to a state of poverty. Youths in particular "lost all sense of hope for the future" (Sierra Leone TRC 2004, para. 95–97).

Local and national politics in Sierra Leone have long been shaped by diamonds. Most notably, in 1978, when the All People's Congress government was in power, Siaka Stevens, the president of Sierra Leone, created a one-party state, and diamonds became a key strategic resource for upholding the dictatorial regime. Stevens's strategy of using state power as an instrument of patronage was central to the creation of a "shadow state" (Reno 1995) in which diamond wealth was controlled by a small group of elites, while the majority of Sierra Leoneans remained poor and marginalized, and had little opportunity to participate in public decision making.[7]

---

[7] Patronage, or patron-client relationships, involves reciprocal obligations and exchanges between different actors. As noted by Edward Gonzalez-Acosta, they are "compulsory pact[s], tacit or explicit, between the patron, an actor who has authority based on social capital, financial power, or some other resource, and the client, another actor that benefits from supporting or showing deference to the patron" (Gonzalez-Acosta 2007).

Patron-client relationships have had a long history of mediating access to resources in Sierra Leone, and the networks of power associated with diamond mining, in particular, have also shaped rural politics and identity, especially the relationships between youth and the so-called gerontocracy. One argument put forward by proponents of the "grievance thesis" is that customary institutions regulated by chiefs, particularly those that exercise power over marriage systems and youth labor, have long been the cause of great inequality and division in rural areas.[8] In the diamondiferous regions of the country, the chiefs' power and privilege have been strengthened by their patrimonial relationships with politicians and by their strong brokerage role in the artisanal diamond industry, where they have been central to maintaining the "tributor-supporter" system of mining governance (Zack-Williams 1995).[9] Critics have suggested that these conditions provide little opportunity for rural subjects to participate in local decision making about resources or to make meaningful choices in their lives. On this basis, it has been argued that many Sierra Leoneans who were forced to endure years of injustice and oppression under a rural gerontocracy joined the rebel Revolutionary United Front during the war in order to exact revenge on the rural elite and sever their ties to customary obligations (Archibald and Richards 2002; Richards 2005; Peters 2006).

While elite capture in the diamond sector—whether initiated by politicians or chiefs—has a well-established history in Sierra Leone, efforts are currently being made to address such practices and to more equitably distribute the benefits of diamond resources.[10] Recognizing that the sustainable development of the country's valuable mineral resources—which include not only diamonds but also gold, rutile, bauxite, and iron ore—is a national priority, the government has made resources a central focus of participatory development plans such as the National Recovery Strategy and the Poverty Reduction Strategy Paper (GOSL 2002, 2005). Across all sectors of the government, donor-driven policies and programs have proliferated that are designed to strengthen civil society and to create new democratic spaces for citizen engagement; many of these policies and programs originated in the decentralization program that began in 2004. In 2008, the government set up a presidential task force to reevaluate all mining policies, laws, and contracts; as of fall 2009, the review was still ongoing.

The current emphasis on decentralizing the government's management of resources has added a layer of institutional complexity to an increasingly

---

[8] On the grievance thesis, see especially the work of Paul Richards.

[9] The tributor-supporter system of labor organization is essentially a form of modern-day slavery. Under this system, miners (tributors) are hired by a supporter (a mining license holder) and are provided with rice and the rudimentary tools needed for alluvial mining. The miners must then sell their diamonds back to the supporter, who usually pays below-market prices for them, ensuring that he recovers all the costs of his investment.

[10] In the context of this chapter, elite capture occurs when high-status individuals use their prestige and power to manipulate decision-making processes and development agendas to obtain personal benefit.

complicated local governance system, in which new, formally defined spaces for citizen participation overlap with the traditional structures of native administrations. In the case of diamond management, some of the main conflicts have concerned revenue generation and collection—specifically, the collection of surface rents and license fees for diamond mining. However, as this chapter will demonstrate, there have also been disputes over how locally generated diamond revenue should be spent, and concerns about lack of clarity in the roles and responsibilities of the various local authorities involved in decision making.

COMMUNITY-LED DEVELOPMENT AND THE DACDF

The DACDF was formally approved by Sierra Leone's Ministry of Mineral Resources in December 2001, as part of a broader reform program for the diamond sector initiated after the end of the civil war. The DACDF is funded by a small portion of the government's 3 percent diamond export tax (amounting to 0.75 percent of the total export value), which is put into the DACDF to support small-scale community-managed development projects in diamondiferous regions.[11] To further strengthen social and infrastructural development, donors have been asked to match funding to the DACDF, although the likelihood of follow-through on this arrangement remains unclear (Temple 2005).

Under the DACDF, an unprecedented amount of diamond revenue has been returned to diamond-mining communities. The first tranche was made for January through June of 2001, and disbursements were made every six months thereafter until the end of 2006. The fund has accumulated more than US$4.25 million in revenue, of which US$3.5 million had been disbursed to diamondiferous communities by the end of 2006 (Temple 2008). Much evidence suggests that some chiefdoms and local councils have used the fund wisely, financing local infrastructure, education, health services, and vocational-skills training centers (Temple 2005). But considerable number of constraints—particularly in the early days of the initiative—have made it a challenge to implement the goals of the fund.

Challenges and shortcomings

Concerns about the DACDF focus primarily on three areas: effective use of funds, transparency and accountability in the use of funds, and citizen participation in decision making. Chiefdoms benefit from the DACDF in accordance with the number of mining licenses issued and the value of the diamonds recovered

---

[11] For example, in 2007, total collections for the DACDF amounted to Le2,513,614,868.59 (approximately US$852,618). At the time of writing, DACDF figures were not available for 2008, but discussions with mining advisors at the Ministry of Mining Resources, in Freetown, revealed that 2008 collections were approximately 40 percent lower than those in 2007, because of decreased exports (thus, the 2008 total would be approximately US$511,571).

from their territory. In 2002, a series of ad hoc reports revealed that a number of chiefdoms were not making competent decisions about the use of the fund (see Temple 2005). Consequently, in 2003, the DACDF Coalition—which consists of representatives from the Ministry of Mineral Resources, the Ministry of Local Government, national and international nongovernmental organizations (NGOs), the Anti-Corruption Commission, and the Miners' Union—was set up to ensure that the fund was used more effectively. Evidence suggests that since its creation, the coalition has helped chiefs improve their accountability for funds and their responsiveness to community interests. A report by Management Systems International, a development consulting firm based in Washington, D.C., notes, for example, that

> constant sensitization, reporting on mis-spending, and refusal by central government to accept mismanagement of DACDF funds, has resulted in a remarkable turnaround in fiscal responsibility. Whereas fully sixty percent of the first tranche of DACDF funds disappeared, by the most recent tranche almost ninety percent of all funds were accounted for—including recovery of some of those funds missing initially (MSI 2004, 4).

Nevertheless, the government's High Level Diamond Steering Committee (HLDSC) raised concerns about the misuse of the DACDF, which eventually led to the suspension of disbursements after the July–December 2006 tranche was released (MMR 2009). Some of the primary concerns involved a continuing lack of transparency in the use of the fund; poor community awareness of the fund and its intended uses; and poor local participation in decision making about the use of the fund. These observations echoed the findings of a January 2003 study carried out by Search for Common Ground (SFCG), an NGO that assessed the status of DACDF projects undertaken in five chiefdoms and explored the levels of community participation in each project (SFCG 2003). Like the HLDSC, SFCG raised a number of concerns about transparency, accountability, and community involvement in decision making—in particular, consultations with youth and women. The project report notes that

> cheques [from the DACDF] were received, but in most cases however, the signatories to the accounts were the Paramount Chief and his/her cronies (wife, District Officers and Treasury Clerks). The withdrawal of the funds as well as its use was questionable as community people were not represented in the process. The people knew about the fund but nothing about subsequent actions as they were not part of the process (SFCG 2003, 5).

In an effort to ensure that decision making about DACDF projects was carried out more equitably and accountably, a number of civil society organizations—including the National Advocacy Coalition on Extractives, an alliance of eighteen national and international NGOs whose work focuses on mining and other extractive industries—lobbied for the creation of chiefdom development committees (CDCs). To ensure representation of a broad range of community interests, each

CDC was to be composed of a wide cross-section of elected chiefdom residents. Reports suggest, however, that the CDCs have more often been composed entirely of members of the rural elite, such as section chiefs—stifling the notion of local ownership of the fund and further alienating many stakeholders, such as women and youth (Temple 2005).[12] The situation is vividly described by Daniel Moiwo, the director of GTZ in Kono District:[13]

> The chief appoints the members of the CDC, and they are basically his group of "yes men." The committee's loyalty must be directed towards the chief, there is an understanding that the members will be given instructions on what to do, and that they will dance to the chief's tune. But it is not supposed to be like that.... [The committee] should be made up of people who are elected because they are reliable, hardworking, truthful and willing to represent the community's affairs honestly (Moiwo 2008).

A 2006 study of nineteen diamond-producing communities found that local governance factors have greatly inhibited transparency and accountability (NMJD 2006). The study noted that a "consistent trend of poor participation by grassroots stakeholders in project decision-making" explains why most DACDF projects are concentrated around chiefdoms or district headquarters towns (2006, 11). With few exceptions, the most important implication of poor participation is that the majority of local people do not readily identify with DACDF projects.

In short, while some chiefdoms have demonstrated the capacity to use the DACDF effectively, many have not. A 2007 article by Paul Jackson highlights the continuing misuse of the fund: "There is no accountability mechanism for ensuring that this cash is used for development, and it is extremely common to hear that local people complain of the chief's abuse of the system in pocketing this money" (Jackson 2007, 100). The report produced by NMJD argues that because the CDCs have handled the funds at the local level, without any reporting mechanisms or systematic oversight from the Ministry of Mineral Resources, local abuses of power have flourished (NMJD 2006). One solution, the report suggests, is to establish a technical team with experience and skills in participatory community programming. The team could provide technical assistance to strengthen

---

[12] In Sierra Leone, the native administration of a chiefdom is composed of a hierarchy of chiefs, of which the paramount chief is the highest ranking. The rest of the hierarchy consists of lower-ranking chiefs and officials—the regent chief, chiefdom speaker, section chiefs, town chiefs, and village chiefs—all of whom have different responsibilities and functions. For a good overview of the chieftaincy system in Sierra Leone, see Campaign for Good Governance, Methodist Church of Sierra Leone, and Network Movement for Justice and Development (2009).

[13] GTZ (Deutsche Gesellschaft für Technische Zusammenarbeit) was a federally owned German corporation that focused on international cooperation for sustainable development. GTZ is now GIZ (Deutsche Gesellschaft für Internationale Zusammenarbeit).

community capacity and ensure that the CDC represents a genuine cross-section of the community; help communities identify their needs; and review proposals for development projects.

That such a team could successfully circumvent the hierarchical power structures within Sierra Leonean society and facilitate more equitable community participation remains unlikely, however. The power structures are deeply entrenched; in fact, a number of observers have pointed out that since the end of the war, power imbalances have continued to fuel a rift between youths and chiefs in the countryside. Paul Richards (2005), for example, suggests that the war itself was largely a product of this division. Glyn Williams notes that uncritical acceptance of the notion that the community is where development should take place runs the risk of depoliticizing development—that is, directing attention away from the wider power relationships within which local development occurs (Williams 2004).

Current status and future prospects

Unequal power relationships have always been prevalent in rural communities in Sierra Leone, but a recurrent theme in the history of diamond-mining regions, particularly in Kono District, has been tension between two groups: elites seeking greater control over diamond production, and indigenous communities seeking to maximize their own returns from the industry and to defend their putative rights and entitlements (Fanthorpe and Maconachie 2010). At various points in history, from the colonial era to the present, the government has become involved in mediating these relationships, and diamonds have been an important strategic resource in such efforts. This was particularly the case for the Siaka Stevens' government, which took direct control of mining rights for Yengema and Tongo Field and used the authorization of mining licenses to build a strong alliance of political networks in Kono District. Since the end of the civil war, however, as mining has shifted toward more capital-intensive modes of extraction and has become increasingly attractive to larger companies that plan to pursue mechanized production, tensions between elites, local communities, and the government have reportedly become exacerbated. Discussions with the NMJD director for Kono District underscore this development:

> What is very clear is that since the late 1980s, the influx of corporate entities into Kono has increased the tendency for conflict between chiefs, community landholders and the government. Before the companies started to arrive, the situation was not nearly as bad. The chiefs are influential, so the companies want them on their side. They [the chiefs] are supposed to act on behalf of the people, but they are part of the deal and they are benefiting financially, so their hands are tied. And nobody questions the chief because they are afraid they will be victimized— the chief can use his power to make life difficult for you (Tongu 2008).

These tensions appear to extend to the CDCs, and have provoked significant controversy. Although the CDC is intended as a mechanism to allow participation on the part of a wide range of community stakeholders—including marginalized groups, such as women and youth—the reality is that the chiefs and their confederates control decision making in the group.

Recognizing that the DACDF was not producing the intended development results, the Ministry of Mineral Resources froze the fund at the end of 2006; nevertheless, revenue allocations have continued to accrue, and four undisbursed deposits had accumulated by the end of 2008. In August 2008, with the hope of addressing many of the shortcomings previously noted, the Ministry of Mineral Resources developed a new set of procedures and guidelines. The new system features rigorous monitoring and an extensive paper trail: communities are now required to elect chiefdom project committees, which then submit a project proposal form for approval to a local review committee made up of the district administrator, the provincial administrator, and the government mines engineer, from the Ministry of Mineral Resources. If the local review committee accepts the community proposal, the work is put out to bid to local contractors in the chiefdom; this phase is followed by monitoring and evaluation to ensure that the funds are being spent properly.

In February 2009, to get the ball rolling, the government released the first of four backdated allocations (January–June 2007) without having received any community proposals. Communities that wish to access the remaining three allocations, however, must submit proposals. The strict new monitoring procedures are intended to improve the use and management of the fund and to increase accountability. But the underlying issue of how community members participate in decision making remains largely unaddressed. Whether communication between the CDCs and the community will improve—allowing for greater transparency in the selection of projects, the hiring of contractors, and payments to suppliers—remains to be seen.

LESSONS LEARNED

A number of useful lessons have emerged about two matters: the administration of the fund and the involvement of local communities in the fund's management.

Administration of the fund

The first disbursements from the DACDF were made directly to the paramount chiefs by the central government in the form of a check, which was often presented publicly in the local Court Barrie (the community town hall), with the entire community present. There was little effort to prepare the community for the arrival of the disbursements or to explain the origins of the revenue; a number of chiefs, as well as community members, were confused about the intended use of the fund. During these initial years, accountability was poor, and many chiefs were unable to explain how their DACDF allocations had been spent.

Nor was there sufficient transparency or accountability at the central government level, where the DACDF revenues were collected and controlled. Even today, there is concern about the lack of transparency within the central government, where large amounts of diamond revenue continue to accrue. Such concerns echo a 2007 Human Development Report undertaken by the United Nations Development Programme, which points to accountability, transparency, and corruption as the key challenges of post-conflict governance (UNDP 2007). For decentralized resource management to be effective, there must be a clear line of accountability, both at the local and at the central government level. As Jesse Ribot (2002) has pointed out in other contexts, decentralization is more successful if there is a strong and accountable central government to guide and oversee it.

At the time the DACDF was initially proposed, in 2001, the Local Government Act had not been ratified; thus, the local councils, which were reinstated by the act and are now beneficiaries of the DACDF (receiving 20 percent of the disbursements for development projects), were not initially involved in the fund's implementation.[14] Although it could be argued that the addition of another layer of governance, in the form of the local councils, should improve accountability and fund management, the reinstatement of the councils may actually have caused further conflict and confusion, which could have had an impact on the rational use of funds.[15] Indeed, studies carried out elsewhere in Africa suggest that decentralized natural resource management initiatives do not always yield the intended social and economic benefits or the hoped-for participation of all members of society in decision making (Ribot 2004).

Community involvement in decision making

Invitations to participate in formally defined decision-making initiatives—such as the DACDF—do not always yield results that are consonant with idealized notions of democratic space. Consequently, one of the most important lessons is that citizen engagement is always mediated by existing power relationships,

---

[14] Since the DACDF is not designed to share diamond revenue with all parts of the country, only local councils in diamondiferous districts get a share of the DACDF revenues.

[15] In November 2008, a joint Ministry of Mineral Resources and local government "road show" was used to introduce the new DACDF guidelines to communities, chiefs, and district officials in all diamondiferous regions. Reports from the Ministry of Mineral Resources indicate that the amendments for the proposed use of the fund were the most contentious aspect of the guidelines. Historically, a portion of the DACDF had been used to pay administrative salaries (e.g., in the chiefdom administration, district councils, and town councils), but this is not permitted under the new regulations—a change that has been met with some resistance from those who had previously received part of their compensation through the DACDF.

including the modes of influence that participants exercise.[16] As Andrea Cornwall rightly suggests, community participation may best be treated as a "situated practice"—one that is shaped and defined by political, social, cultural, and historical determinants (2002, 51).

On a positive note, Taylor Brown et al. (2006) argue that for all the destruction and disruption caused by Sierra Leone's civil war, its resolution may have opened up new spaces for participation that could potentially change social rules and institutional practices. On the other hand, they also note that in many respects, Sierra Leonean society and politics have proven to be much less malleable than many observers had initially assumed. They suggest that many of the patrimonial institutions and practices that shaped natural resource access during the pre-conflict era may have been preserved, and in some cases even strengthened, in the post-conflict period. In such situations, where prewar power structures continue to endure, Frances Cleaver warns that there is a danger of participation being based on "over-optimistic notions of agency . . . combined with romantic ideas about groups and institutions" (2004, 271). In the case of Sierra Leone, the exercise of agency and citizenship rights is embedded in social relations that are defined by a highly unequal distribution of power and located within a messy web of micropolitics.

CONCLUSION

While this chapter focuses on just one initiative, the DACDF, the implications for future natural resource management and development in the diamond-bearing regions of Sierra Leone are far broader. Security concerns remain high in diamondiferous areas, where large numbers of uneducated, unemployed, and potentially volatile youth have little ability to make meaningful choices in their lives. The legacy of economic oppression and political exclusion from public decision making continues to be a source of considerable concern: history has shown that identity- and interest-based inclusion in public decision making can fragment communities and ignite conflict (Ribot 2004), and a number of observers have warned that, in the case of Sierra Leone, limiting or shutting down spaces of public participation risks recreating the inequalities that led to the country's protracted civil war.[17] Thus, if the government has indeed given priority to the sustainable development of mineral resources as a key part of its reconstruction program, while at the same time recognizing the need for increased public participation in resource governance, it must rethink how its policies and programs are playing out in practice. Even where citizens are invited to participate in intentionally designed institutional spaces, local actors' full and fair participation in the decision-making process cannot be assumed.

---

[16] This observation, of course, has relevance for community-led revenue-sharing programs for a wide range of natural resources, across sub-Saharan Africa and beyond.

[17] See, for example, Hanlon (2005).

In the diamondiferous regions of Sierra Leone, unequal power relationships continue to shape resource use, livelihood options, participation in decision making, and development outcomes. Ultimately, these enduring political and economic struggles over resource access and control remain the greatest threats to the potential benefits of diamond-sector reforms, and to Sierra Leone's post-war transition to sustainable peace.

REFERENCES

Archibald, S., and P. Richards. 2002. Conversion to human rights? Popular debate about war and justice in rural central Sierra Leone. *Africa* 72 (3): 339–367.

Batterbury, S. 1998. Local environment, land degradation and the "*gestion des terroirs*" approach in West Africa: Policies and pitfalls. *Journal of International Development* 10 (7): 871–898.

Brown, T., R. Fanthorpe, J. Gardener, L. Gberie, and M. Gibril Sesay. 2006. *Sierra Leone: Drivers of change.* Bristol, UK: IDL Group.

Campaign for Good Governance, Methodist Church of Sierra Leone, and Network Movement for Justice and Development. 2009. Reform is not against tradition: Making chieftaincy relevant in 21st century Sierra Leone. www.scribd.com/doc/23045685/Chieftancy-Report-vis3-15-Oct.

Cleaver, F. 2004. The social embeddedness of agency and decision-making. In *Participation: From tyranny to transformation? Exploring new approaches to participation in development,* ed. S. Hickey and G. Mohan. London: Zed Books.

Cornwall, A. 2002. Locating citizen participation. *IDS Bulletin* 33 (2): 49–58.

Fanthorpe, R., and R. Maconachie. 2010. Beyond the "crisis of youth"? Mining, farming, and civil society in post-war Sierra Leone. *African Affairs* 109 (435): 251–272.

Gonzalez-Acosta, E. 2007. Central America—CAFTA and the U.S. patron-client relationship with Dominican Republic and Central America. May 24. www.alterinfos.org/spip.php?article1385.

GOSL (Government of Sierra Leone). 2002. National recovery strategy: Sierra Leone 2002–2003. Freetown, Sierra Leone.

———. 2004. Local government act. Freetown, Sierra Leone.

———. 2005. Sierra Leone poverty reduction strategy paper, 2005–2007. Freetown, Sierra Leone.

Hanlon, J. 2005. Is the international community helping to recreate the pre-conditions for war in Sierra Leone? *Round Table* 94 (381): 459–472.

Hulme, D., and M. Murphree. 2001. *African wildlife and livelihoods: The promise and performance of community conservation.* Oxford, UK: James Currey.

Jackson, P. 2007. Reshuffling an old deck of cards? The politics of local government reform in Sierra Leone. *African Affairs* 106 (422): 95–111.

Keen, D. 2005. *Conflict and collusion in Sierra Leone.* Oxford, UK: James Currey.

Maconachie, R. 2009. Diamonds, governance and "local" development in post-conflict Sierra Leone: Lessons for artisanal and small-scale mining in sub-Saharan Africa? *Resources Policy* 34 (1–2): 71–79.

MMR (Ministry of Mineral Resources, Government of Sierra Leone). 2009. Personal communication, technical mining advisor. March 11.

Moiwo, D. 2008. Interview by author of the director of GTZ (Deutsche Gesellschaft für Technische Zusammenarbeit). September 25, Koidu, Kono District, Sierra Leone.

MSI (Management Systems International). 2004. *Integrated diamond management in Sierra Leone: A two-year pilot project.* Report prepared for the U.S. Agency for International Development. Washington, D.C. April.

NMJD (Network Movement for Justice and Development). 2006. *An impact audit study on the Diamond Area Community Development Fund (DACDF).* Freetown, Sierra Leone.

Peters, K. 2006. Footpaths to reintegration: Armed conflict, youth and the rural crisis in Sierra Leone. Ph.D. diss., Wageningen University, Netherlands.

Reno, W. 1995. *Corruption and state politics in Sierra Leone.* Cambridge, UK: Cambridge University Press.

Ribot, J. 2002. *Democratic decentralization of natural resources: Institutionalizing popular participation.* Washington, D.C.: World Resources Institute.

———. 2004. *Waiting for democracy: The politics of choice in natural resource decentralizations.* Washington, D.C.: World Resources Institute.

Richards, P. 1996. *Fighting for the rainforest: War, youth and resources in Sierra Leone.* Oxford, UK: James Currey.

———. 2003. The political economy of internal conflict in Sierra Leone. Working Paper 21. Conflict Research Unit, Netherlands Institute of International Relations Clingendael. August.

———. 2005. To fight or to farm? Agrarian dimensions of the Mano River conflicts (Liberia and Sierra Leone). *African Affairs* 104 (417): 571–590.

SFCG (Search for Common Ground). 2003. Sierra Leone diamond policy and training activity. Unpublished internal report.

Sierra Leone TRC (Sierra Leone Truth & Reconciliation Commission). 2004. *The Final Report of the Truth & Reconciliation Commission of Sierra Leone.* Vol. 2.

Smillie, I., L. Gberie, and R. Hazleton. 2000. *The heart of the matter: Sierra Leone, diamonds and human security.* Ottawa: Partnership Africa Canada.

Temple, P. 2005. *Improving the effective use of the Diamond Area Community Development Fund (DACDF).* Report by the Integrated Diamond Management Program (IDMP) for submission to the Government of Sierra Leone High Level Diamond Steering Committee (HLDSC). Washington, D.C.: Management Systems International.

———. 2008. Diamond sector reform in Sierra Leone: A program perspective. In *Artisanal diamond mining: Perspectives and challenges,* ed. K. Vlassenroot and S. Van Bockstael. Brussels: Egmont.

Tongu, P. 2008. Interview by author of the director of the Network Movement for Justice and Development. September 19. Koidu, Kono District, Sierra Leone.

UNDP (United Nations Development Programme). 2007. *Sierra Leone human development report 2007.* Freetown, Sierra Leone.

Williams, G. 2004. Evaluating participatory development: Tyranny, power and (re)politicisation. *Third World Quarterly* 25 (3): 557–578.

Zack-Williams, A. 1995. *Tributors, supporters and merchant capital: Mining and underdevelopment in Sierra Leone.* London: Edwin Mellen Press.

Direct distribution of natural resource revenues as a policy for peacebuilding

Martin E. Sandbu

This chapter examines direct distribution of natural resource revenues as an element in post-conflict peacebuilding. Direct distribution, a radical proposal that has been put fully into practice in only one place—the U.S. state of Alaska—represents a fundamental shift in the management of revenues from natural resources: from financing government spending (or the enrichment of government officials) to funding regular cash payments to the population at large. Nevertheless, it is gaining increasing attention as a possible means of addressing the negative consequences of extractive resource dependence. The question is whether such a policy should be included among the tools used to establish and maintain peace in post-conflict societies.

Whether, to what extent, and how dependence on extractive resources puts a country at risk of violent conflict remains an actively debated topic. That resources have *some* nefarious effect in relation to war is difficult to doubt; it is also borne out by a great deal of statistical evidence.[1] The facilitation of conflict is but the worst manifestation of the "natural resource curse," whose other effects can include economic stagnation in the form of "Dutch disease," endemic corruption, and political underdevelopment.[2]

Martin E. Sandbu is an editorial writer for the *Financial Times* and a senior fellow at the Zicklin Center for Business Ethics Research, the Wharton School.

[1] See, for example, Collier and Hoeffler (1998) and Fearon and Laitin (2003).

[2] *Dutch disease* is a phenomenon in which the discovery of substantial natural resource wealth negatively affects a nation's economy. The discovery often causes sudden appreciation in the value of the nation's currency—which, in turn, decreases the nation's competitiveness in the international commodity markets. This reduces the country's exports of manufactured and agricultural commodities and increases its imports. At the same time, the natural resource sector draws a substantial share of domestic resources such as labor and materials, increasing their cost to other sectors. Moreover, when the initially booming resource sector eventually declines, the non-resource-based sectors may find it difficult to recover. On Dutch disease, see Krugman (1987) and Sachs and Warner (1995); on corruption, see Leite and Weidmann (1999), Gary and Karl (2003), and Global Witness (2004); and on political underdevelopment, see Karl (1997), Auty (2001), and Isham et al. (2002).

Direct distribution is being proposed with increasing frequency—so far, to unenthusiastic reception—as a broad means of addressing the resource curse.[3] This chapter examines the arguments for and against the idea that direct distribution may be a valuable tool for peacebuilding in resource-rich post-conflict countries.[4]

The chapter is divided into five main parts: (1) a description of the policy of direct distribution; (2) an analysis of the ways in which direct distribution might help to strengthen peace; (3) a discussion of the objections to direct distribution; (4) a consideration of past experience with direct distribution; and (5) a brief conclusion.

THE PROPOSAL

The common theme of all direct distribution proposals is to distribute some or all of the revenues a nation receives from natural resource exploitation directly (in cash) and unconditionally (or with only minimal conditions) to the population. Beyond that basic approach, direct distribution schemes can be designed to vary along a number of dimensions:

- The proportion of extractive revenues to be directly distributed.
- Whether the amount to be distributed—known as the *resource dividend*—is taxable. (This dimension clearly interacts with the previous one.)
- Whether the resource dividend for a given period is calculated on the basis of actual revenues or is smoothed out by means of a stabilization fund or similar mechanism.[5]
- The definition of eligibility in relation to demographic characteristics (e.g., whether the resource dividend is payable to everyone, to adults only, or to heads of households only).

---

[3] Recent proponents include Sala-i-Martin and Subramanian (2003), Palley (2003), Birdsall and Subramanian (2004), Sandbu (2006), Shaxson (2007), Shaxson and Sandbu (2009), Moss and Young (2009), *La Razón* (2009), and Morales (2007). Among politicians, U.S. senators Hillary Clinton and John Ensign sponsored a resolution, in 2008, in favor of direct distribution in Iraq (S. 3470: Support for Iraq Oil Trust Act of 2008), and presidential candidates in Venezuela and Iran included direct distribution in their electoral platforms in 2006 and 2009, respectively (*BBC News* 2006; *Economist* 2009).

[4] Many of the arguments in this chapter are set out in greater detail in Sandbu (2006).

[5] Stabilization funds are used to build up reserves when resource prices are high; when prices fall, the funds can then be drawn down, allowing spending to be stable from year to year.

- The definition of eligibility in relation to citizenship or residency (e.g., whether the resource dividend is payable to all citizens, to resident citizens, or to all residents of a certain tenure).
- The conditions, if any, to be placed on recipients.[6]

Two further dimensions may be particularly relevant for post-conflict societies, especially where conflict has been waged along regional lines:

- Whether the resource dividend will vary by region—in particular, between producing and nonproducing regions.
- The relationship between the resource dividend and the claim on extractive revenues made by various levels of government and by different jurisdictions at each level.

Subject to choices along these dimensions, a certain part of a nation's extractive revenues would circumvent governmental budgets and instead be available for individuals as part of their disposable income. If the resource dividend is taxable, then some of it would be returned to the public treasury, but through individual income taxes rather than through (1) royalties or taxes on extractive companies or (2) profits from government ownership of or stakes in resource ventures.[7] In other words, royalties, corporation taxes, and profit sharing with resource companies would not cease, but the revenues raised thereby would be directly distributed to the population.

The question of how much to distribute is conceptually separate from the question of how the purchasing power derived from resource rents should be divided between the public and private sectors. In the discussion that follows, it is assumed that cash distributions are taxable but leave a noticeable (say, at least a quarter) share of resource rents in widely dispersed private hands.

---

[6] Most advocates of direct distribution oppose means testing for potential recipients of the resource dividend, preferring instead that the distributions count as taxable income. As long as the tax structure is progressive, this approach will take care of concerns about vertical equity. (Vertical equity refers to inequalities between the rich and the poor, as opposed to inequalities between groups defined along ethnic, gender, regional, or other dimensions.)

[7] If the resource dividend is taxable, the revenues could be distributed in their entirety, without affecting the desired split between public and private control over how the resource rent is spent. In the extreme case, full direct distribution would be subject to 100 percent taxation: the final allocation of purchasing power would then be the same as it is in most resource-producing countries, where 100 percent of resource revenues go directly to the government (once the private companies engaged in extraction have been paid). Nevertheless, channeling the funds through the private sector would significantly improve the political economy, for the reasons outlined in the next section; see also Sandbu (2006).

HOW DIRECT DISTRIBUTION COULD STRENGTHEN PEACE

This section of the chapter surveys two potential advantages of direct distribution in post-conflict environments: (1) improving incentives to keep the peace and (2) removing the spurs of conflict.

Improving incentives to keep the peace

Post-conflict environments are characterized by three principal needs: to invest in infrastructure destroyed by violent conflict; to prevent civilians from becoming disillusioned by peace; and to channel the demands of former belligerents in the direction of political competition and cooperation, in order to protect against the temptation of returning to arms. How can direct distribution contribute to these needs?

One factor often underlying the resource curse is the state's inability to invest without waste or corruption; this difficulty is likely to be at least as severe—if not worse—in a post-conflict situation, where crucial human and organizational capacity may have been lost, and time may be needed to reestablish effective checks and balances. As is discussed later in the chapter, direct distribution may tamp down the forces that fuel waste and corruption in resource-rich states, and strengthen the incentives for post-conflict leaders to act in ways that benefit the population at large. But the most immediate significance of direct distribution in a post-conflict setting is this: by putting cash in the hands of the population, it fosters an immediate surge of investment in private goods, with no need to wait for state capacity to improve sufficiently to provide public goods. In particular, cash payments can enable even the poor to invest by constructing or purchasing homes, and can also finance the inputs needed for small-scale production. More generally, the payments can kick-start a private economy that can meet the material needs of individuals even if public investment is lagging.

To prevent post-conflict frustration from growing into deeper grievances that can foster a return to violence, the population must experience the end of conflict as something that benefits them. Philippe Le Billon argues that

> direct revenue allocation provides tangible evidence of a "peace dividend" for the population. Recent studies show that direct cash payments contribute positively to poverty alleviation and disaster recovery, including in conflict-affected environments (2008, 9).

Finally, direct distribution may give policy makers—who are likely to be excombatants—more constructive incentives than they would otherwise have. Sandbu (2006) argues that by redefining the claims of citizens in relation to the state and bringing transparency to the extent and value of the nation's natural resources, direct distribution can affect the way the social contract is perceived. If this is the case, then the policy may subject post-conflict rulers to greater public scrutiny, forcing them to pay more attention to what they provide to the population—rather than to, say, personal enrichment or the pursuit of wartime grudges. This is particularly important when a conflict has been fought over control of resources, either as a prize or as a source of support for violence.[8]

The most intriguing outcome for the incentive effects of direct distribution is the possibility of altering the politics of regional or ethnic conflict. If a conflict was fought between regionally or ethnically defined groups, the end of the conflict may cover a still-simmering resentment; if one group has defeated the other, victory may be taken as a license for abuse or discrimination. By creating a symbol of unity, a universal resource dividend can redirect political focus away from the fragmentation of the past and toward a unified future. Le Billon, for example, suggests that if "the choice is made to distribute the revenue equally across the entire population, this can contribute to a sense of national identity and common destiny" (2008, 9).

There is a second reason that direct distribution could defuse regional or ethnic tensions: although such resentments may be genuine, they are often manipulated by elites, who take advantage of grievances that are ultimately rooted in poverty, marginalization, and corruption. Poor people who live in a resource-producing region can easily be persuaded that other parts of the country are stealing "their" resources. For example, although the states that make up the Niger Delta should theoretically be flush with cash because of a derivation formula that allocates an extra 13 percent of national oil revenues to producing states (beyond what all states get from revenue sharing between central and state governments), much of this money has been wasted or stolen. Nevertheless, Niger Delta insurgents continue to demand even more revenue from "their" oil.

One possible response to such misdirected grievances is to fully distribute resource rents, then render them taxable not only at the central but also at the regional level, in order to focus on the political relationship between regional governments and the population of each region (Sandbu 2006). The idea is that if the division of resources between private individuals and public authorities *within each region* becomes politically salient, people's focus will shift to how well regional (and local) officials manage whatever resource revenue the region disposes of, rather than on how much more the region could get if other regions got less. In a post-conflict situation, the hope would be that attention can be shifted from an earlier "frame," which is focused on the allocation of benefits to different regional or ethnic groups, to a different frame, which is focused on

---

[8] In the "greed" explanation of conflict over natural resources, control of resources is a prize: the goal is to capture the state in order to capture the resource rents. In the "grievance" explanation of conflict over natural resources, resource rents give rebels access to funding, even if the rebellion is motivated by other factors. In either case, the issue is not low-level looting, but the criminal enrichment at a grand scale afforded by controlling at least part of the state territory.

how those in power use common resources for the benefit of those without it. As is discussed later in the chapter, current events in the Niger Delta may well shed light on whether this is a realistic possibility.

Removing the spurs of conflict

The details of why dependence on natural resources seems to cause conflict are beyond the scope of this chapter, but most such mechanisms can be divided into *economic* and *political economy* effects.[9]

Economic effects

The evidence that natural resource dependence retards economic growth is overwhelming.[10] The exception is when resource booms occur within the context of strong governing institutions (Mehlum, Moene, and Torvik 2006), which is rarely the case. When disagreements are dealt with through violence, governing institutions are, by definition, failing. It also seems clear that drops in income increase the risk of conflict (Miguel, Satyanath, and Sergenti 2004).

Insofar as direct distribution can remedy the negative effects of resource wealth on growth, it will also blunt the economic causes of conflict. There are three reasons why direct distribution schemes may do this:

- *States are bad at allocating spending over time.* Despite the recent flurry of savings and stabilization funds, resource-rich countries find it extraordinarily hard to smooth out their spending of resource-derived revenues, which are rendered highly volatile by fluctuating commodity prices and eventual depletion.[11] Evidence from commodity booms that have benefited households and businesses, in contrast, indicate that the private sector does a better job of managing windfall revenues than the public sector: households and businesses save more, and therefore have larger buffers with which to smooth out consumption patterns (Collier and Gunning 1999). Studies of cash distribution schemes in nonresource settings also suggest that, contrary to stereotype, poor households are good stewards of unearned income, some of which they put toward investment goods such as household animals; nor does unearned income make poor people less likely to work (Skoufias and McClafferty 2001; Gertler, Martinez, and Rubio 2005).

---

[9] For a more detailed treatment of the relationship between conflict and natural resources, see Paul Collier and Anke Hoeffler, "High-Value Natural Resources, Development, and Conflict: Channels of Causation" in this volume.
[10] See, for example, Sachs and Warner (1995) and the many studies cited in Sandbu (2006).
[11] See Humphreys and Sandbu (2007) for an analysis of what savings and stabilization funds can and cannot do.

- *At any one point in time, states are bad at allocating spending between different uses.* Even if the private and public sectors made equally poor spending choices over time, weak states would likely be less competent at efficiently allocating spending for any given period. Although poor countries are often in dire need of investment in public goods, in practical terms, corruption or simple incapacity may lead to the waste of public funds (Robinson and Torvik 2005). Thus, public allocation of funds may be worse than what could be achieved by market allocation of private funds—even accounting for the fact that some public goods would then be unavailable. (Of course, if the government does not have the wherewithal to supply public goods, they would not be available in any case.)[12]
- *Universal cash distribution is one of the most effective policies for alleviating poverty.* "Relative deprivation" accounts suggest that even if incomes *on average* are not so low as to increase the risk of conflict, severe inequality around a given average can trigger conflict (Gurr 1970). Widely distributed cash payments are by far the quickest way of alleviating poverty and inequality—and may even, in the long run, be as effective as targeted (means-tested) poverty alleviation schemes, which typically suffer from "take-up" problems: that is, many of those entitled to benefits do not make use of them (Atkinson 1995). As noted later in the chapter, Alaska's direct distribution scheme probably accounts for the fact that during the 1990s, the state bucked the national trend toward increasing income inequality.

Political economy effects

The political economy effects of natural resources can be briefly summarized as follows: states that are financed mostly by resource rents rather than by broad-based taxes tend to be (1) insulated from public pressure to deliver public goods to their constituents and (2) capable of (indeed, reliant on) buying political support, which further entrenches patronage systems (Ross 2001b; Isham et al. 2002).[13] These circumstances have institutional effects: such states become bloated, corrupt (or more corrupt), and remain underdeveloped in terms of administrative capacity and responsiveness to the public (Karl 1997; Auty 2001; Ross 2001a, 2004; Herb 2003). But there are indirect economic effects as well:

---

[12] The reasons that decentralized market allocation can be more efficient than public planning (despite the fact that only the government can supply public goods) are well-known and much rehearsed; one of the less frequently emphasized reasons is the information-providing function of markets. As Hayek (1945) explained, decentralized markets are good at efficiently allocating resources because they compel local decision makers to use information that is locally available to them; central planning, in contrast, requires an impossible centralization of dispersed information about how resources are best deployed in circumstances that differ from place to place.

[13] For further discussion of this point, see Sandbu (2006).

bad institutions increase risks for private enterprise, which tends to be crowded out by rent-seeking activities that offer higher private returns (but lower social returns) than genuine value creation (Ross 2001b).

It has been argued, on the basis of the political economy effects of the natural resource curse, that direct distribution policies offer a particularly promising cure (Sandbu 2006; Shaxson 2007). The simple version of this argument holds that direct distribution can improve the deleterious effect of natural resource rents on governing institutions through two mechanisms. The first mechanism is simple circumvention: by leaving a smaller proportion of total resource rents in the hands of government officials, direct distribution reduces both (1) the damage the rents can do to the public sector and (2) the damage the public sector can do with the resources. With less "free money" flowing through the government, the rewards of corruption are smaller—and the number of wasteful projects or patronage positions that can be financed are fewer.

The second mechanism involves a more intricate claim about political psychology (Sandbu 2006). Paying resource rents to individuals has a cognitive effect: it informs individual citizens of the magnitude and volatility of resource revenues, both by eliminating secrecy and by expressing numbers in an easy-to-grasp way—that is, in per capita terms. It also has a motivational effect: once private individuals receive *some* share of resource rents, the question of *how much* they get is opened to political debate. That openness, in turn, gives citizens an incentive to pressure officials either to do a better job of spending the money that remains in the public sector, or to increase the share that is distributed. At the same time, putting a direct distribution policy on the table gives politicians an incentive to draw citizens into the political process by offering them meaningful and easy-to-grasp choices between competing versions of the policy. The incentives that affect private individuals and politicians are likely to be mutually reinforcing.

Under one scheme that has been proposed for direct distribution, "natural wealth accounts," all resource rents are distributed but are then taxed (Sandbu 2006). This approach would further strengthen the public's incentive to hold rulers to account: psychologically, people are inclined to care much more about money they consider their own and then have to give up (such as taxes on a resource dividend) than about money they had never had the opportunity to consider theirs (such as resource rents funnelled directly into the public treasury).

But all versions of direct distribution will increase pressure for government accountability—which, in turn, is likely to increase the likelihood that the government will perform better than resource-rich states typically have, particularly in the realms of institutional development and ensuring that economic growth benefits the population. This shift, in turn, should temper both the politico-institutional and economic causes of conflict. Thus, in a post-conflict setting, direct distribution may contribute to peacebuilding by reducing two risks—disenchantment with peace and a reignition of the conflict—and by helping citizens to see that peace works: that is, that those who are in power are producing benefits for them.

OBJECTIONS

The objections to direct distribution come in three forms. The first concerns practical feasibility: universal cash distributions may seem unrealistic in poor (especially war-torn) societies. There are three answers to this objection:

- Direct distribution need not be complicated: it can be carried out through simple accounts held at rural post offices with check-cashing facilities; fraud can be prevented through the same techniques that are used to prevent double voting in elections.[14] Naturally, the system would still require a huge logistical effort, but one that should be possible to overcome in all but the worst situations. (The initial establishment of the system would of course require adequate resources, and would likely have to be contracted out to an international organization—perhaps to a private company with logistics expertise.)
- The organization required for direct distribution is complementary to other infrastructural needs in post-conflict settings—such as a census, electoral rolls, and basic transportation and communication networks. Since these needs have to be met in any case, the additional cost of implementing direct distribution is small.
- The take-up problem referred to earlier would probably be minimal, as the incentives for getting registered and obtaining the allotted cash would be huge.

A second category of objection is that even if direct distribution were feasible, it would be politically impossible to implement. If direct distribution will, in effect, force government to implement better policies than it otherwise would, why would political leaders want to establish a system that will reduce their room for maneuver or their ability to divert money for personal gain? This concern has been addressed in normal (nonconflict) situations with the following argument: although the problem is a serious one, it is important to acknowledge political circumstances that could encourage the adoption of direct distribution (Sandbu 2006):

- A state with newly discovered natural resource wealth, which has not yet been trapped by the political economy of the resource curse.
- The presence of political outsiders who can challenge entrenched elites and who may have an interest in a populist policy (which direct distribution no doubt is) as a means of shoring up popular support.

---

[14] A first round of cash distributions could be made to all those who are physically present in the country, which would be documented through the indelible ink marks used in elections in Iraq and Afghanistan. As the distributions are made, handheld biometric scanners could be used to register the recipients so that they could simultaneously be added to a census and have an account opened, on their behalf, to receive subsequent annual distributions. Moss and Young (2009) give a convincing overview of what is possible using modern identification technology.

- Moments of upheaval (such as wars or other sources of regime change), which present windows of opportunity during which institutional structure may be "up for grabs."

Upheaval is of particular relevance in post-conflict societies. The principal question is whether the open-ended situation that prevails for some time in the immediate aftermath of a conflict is particularly conducive to, or particularly likely to inhibit, the establishment of a direct distribution system. The answer depends, in part, on how the conflict ended—in particular, on whose support the new leaders rely. If the conflict did not culminate in a decisive victory for one side, direct distribution may be an attractive means of defusing distrust between power-sharing elites, precisely because it reduces the scope for foul play. But if one side completely dominates the post-conflict political landscape (especially if the war was between regionally or ethnically defined groups with little sense of common identity), this incentive is clearly missing. Nevertheless, even in this case, new leaders may see a need to win over the vanquished population, at least if they are not perceived by the vast majority as liberators who deserve a long honeymoon of unquestioned legitimacy (as could be the case, for example, for exiled leaders returning after the end of foreign occupation). When legitimacy is questioned, direct distribution may be an attractive way to obtain it; indeed, it could be justified in much the same way as patronage, with the crucial difference that it would cover the entire population.

Even if new leaders do not need (or worse, do not care) to win over the population, the international community is likely to have its greatest influence on local politics in the year or two after a conflict ends. This is when the demand for donor funds is highest, especially in resource-rich states, where the conflict may have debilitated the state's institutional and physical capacity to obtain or control the revenues from resource exploitation. It is therefore imaginable that a coalition of donors might require, as a condition for funds, the establishment of a direct distribution system once resource revenues start to flow. Donor governments could even channel their own aid wholly or partly through a direct distribution system, on the publicly declared understanding that within a few years, the country's own government will replace donor funds with those from extractive resources. This approach would have a significant advantage: the establishment of the system would not have to depend on the weakened capacity of the war-torn state itself.

None of this is intended to minimize the political challenges associated with getting direct distribution off the ground in a post-conflict environment. But the potential benefits of such a system make it worth the effort to identify opportunities for making the attempt. Moreover, the political incentives for keeping the system in place once it is established are much less in doubt: once a population becomes accustomed to regular cash payments, it would be extremely politically costly to stop them. The example of Alaska, reviewed later in the chapter, bears this out.

A final category of concern is that direct distribution will create perverse effects. For example, an approach in which different resource dividends are paid to different regions or only to selected regions may not only create grievances, but may also generate a tremendous incentive for migration, which can stir up tensions in a fragile post-conflict environment. This concern justifies making direct distribution as universal as possible. Also in the category of potential perverse effects are new problems that may upset the equilibrium required for peace. For example:

- Recipients may waste the money on unproductive consumption.
- Direct distribution may lead to inflation rather than to development.
- A system in which people receive cash at regular intervals may encourage criminality, such as extortion by gangs on "payday."
- The distribution system itself may attract corrupt individuals, just as normal fiscal processes do when institutional controls are weak.

The answer to these objections is that the correct comparison is not between the behavior of an ideal government and the behavior of private individuals or public officials under a direct distribution system, but between direct distribution and business as usual—that is, channeling resource revenues to the public treasury, despite the governance failures exhibited by most resource-rich countries. Using the appropriate comparison, there seems little reason to fear that the results of direct distribution would be any worse than those of the usual scenario. So entrenched are the criminality and corruption that distort the public use of resource revenues in most countries—especially conflict-torn countries—that even a widely flawed direct distribution system (which is likely to be the case, at least in the early phases) may well be an improvement. As for concerns that the private sector will waste the resource dividends, as the next section will demonstrate, evidence suggests that the private sector, on the whole, does a better job of managing windfalls than the public sector.

EXAMPLES AND EVIDENCE

This section considers evidence of the outcomes of direct distribution systems, in both natural resource contexts and other contexts.

Schemes related to natural resources

As noted earlier, the only jurisdiction in the world that has a formal, ongoing direct distribution scheme is the state of Alaska, which in 1982 began to pay annual "dividends" from the Alaska Permanent Fund to each long-term resident in the state (children included). Today there is only a one-year residency requirement to receive payment. Under the state constitution, 25 percent of extractive revenues are paid into the permanent fund, whose principal may not be drawn down. The dividend amounts roughly correspond to the five-year annual average return on the investment of the fund's assets (calculating the return only after enough has been added to the principal to keep its real value from being eroded by inflation).

Studies of the effects of the Alaska scheme are surprisingly scarce, but three documented facts are relevant to this discussion. First, the system is virtually irreversible, not just because of its constitutional anchoring, but also because it would be politically suicidal for any politician to try to change it (Goldsmith 2002). Second, the distribution of dividends has coincided with, and most likely contributed to, a decrease in income inequality.[15] Third, by and large, recipients seem to save their dividend payments rather than to use them to fund consumption sprees, which suggests that one of the common misgivings about cash payouts is misplaced (Hsieh 2003).

There are a smattering of examples of ad hoc direct distribution—that is, one-time cash payments that were financed by natural resource revenue but that did not continue in any regular or institutionalized way: in 2006, for example, the Canadian province of Alberta paid a C$400 "rebate cheque" to its residents. These ad hoc distributions were derived from windfall public revenues that occurred when commodity prices were unexpectedly high, and probably resulted from electoral or other political calculation. Cash payments have also been made as compensation for environmental damage or expropriation; the Chad-Cameroon pipeline project was reported to have made one-time payments to farmers who lost mango trees during the construction (*Economist* 2003).

Though Alaska's approach has not been replicated in other countries, proposals have not been lacking. A few advocates (including this author) argue that direct distribution should become part of the standard set of policy options considered by resource-rich countries and by the international institutions and nongovernmental organizations that are active in natural resource governance (Shaxson 2007; Shaxson and Sandbu 2009). More commonly, proposals for direct distribution schemes are made for specific countries. Manuel Rosales, the opposition candidate for president in Venezuela's 2006 election, included such a scheme in his platform, but he lost the election (*BBC News* 2006). Scholars, politicians, and policy analysts have proposed direct distribution schemes for Bolivia, Ghana, Iraq, and Nigeria.[16] Libya's leader, Muammar Qaddafi, has ordered—somewhat

---

[15] In the 1990s, income inequality fell considerably in Alaska: the incomes of the poorest quintile increased by 28 percent and those of the richest quintile by only 7 percent. This stood in marked contrast to the United States as a whole, where the corresponding income increases were 12 percent for the poorest and 26 percent for the richest quintiles (Goldsmith 2002). Though other explanations cannot be ruled out, the drop in inequality is most likely attributable to Alaska Permanent Fund dividends.

[16] On Bolivia, see *La Razón* (2009). On Ghana, see Moss and Young (2009). On Nigeria, see Sala-i-Martin and Subramanian (2003). With respect to Iraq, in 2008, U.S. senators Hillary Clinton and John Ensign sponsored a "sense of the Senate" resolution that advocated an oil revenue trust fund with a direct distribution component (S. 3470: Support for Iraq Oil Trust Act of 2008). Policy analysts who have recommended something similar include Palley (2003) and Birdsall and Subramanian (2004).

quixotically—that government ministries be abolished and that direct distribution replace public goods.

Among the most exciting initiatives at the time of writing was the reported interest, on the part of the Nigerian president, to implement direct distribution as part of a scheme to end the debilitating conflict in the Niger Delta. According to news reports, 10 percent stakes in the government's oil ventures could be transferred to delta residents, with the explicit goal of bypassing corruption and waste at all levels of government and giving citizens an incentive to support oil exploration in the region, rather than to view it as the source of their sufferings (Burgis 2009a, 2009b). But the plan is still in its infancy, and it remains unclear whether and how it will be implemented—in particular, whether there will be cash distributions or whether the alternative suggestion, for community trust funds, will be adopted. If authorities choose the trust fund option, there is reason to fear that it will simply recreate, at the local level, the problems of corruption and waste that have ruined Nigerian governance at the federal and state levels. A positive sign, however, is that the Movement for the Emancipation of the Niger Delta, the main armed resistance group in the delta, has given the proposals a cautious welcome. All observers and practitioners interested in the conflict-resolving potential of direct distribution will be closely following developments in Nigeria.

Evidence from other contexts

Two other sets of evidence are relevant to assessing the possible consequences of direct distribution. One, mentioned earlier in the chapter, is evidence on how well the private sector manages windfall revenue in comparison with the government. The studies conducted by David L. Bevan, Paul Collier, and Jan Willem Gunning (1987, 1989, 1992) of a Kenyan coffee boom that produced windfalls for both the private and public sectors show that the private sector had a much higher propensity to save out of windfall income than the public sector.

Some countries use nearly unconditional cash distributions—which are not linked to resource revenue—to alleviate poverty. The most thoroughly studied examples are Mexico's Progresa and Oportunidades programs, through which cash payments have been made to female heads of households, provided that the children go to school and have annual medical exams.[17] Contrary to stereotype, poor recipients of cash transfers spend the money, in part, to buy more nutritional food—essentially an investment in human capital—and the payments do not reduce the likelihood that adults will work (Skoufias and McClafferty 2001). Moreover, a significant share of the money (about 25 percent) is used on investment goods such as animals (Gertler, Martinez, and Rubio 2005).

---

[17] Mexico established Progresa (an acronym for Programa de Educación, Salud y Alimentación—the Education, Health, and Nutrition Program) in 1997; in 2002 the name was changed to Oportunidades.

Despite the seemingly positive effects of the simple conditions associated with Mexico's program, many advocates of direct distribution caution against setting any conditions. The reason is that in resource-rich countries, it is particularly important to close off opportunities for corruption and embezzlement; the more complex the system is—and that includes any conditions attached to the distribution—the easier it is to hide the fact that funds are being diverted. Moreover, in post-conflict settings, conditions can easily become real or perceived ways of excluding certain groups from the benefit, inflaming latent conflict. It is thus best to view previous experiences with cash transfers elsewhere as primarily demonstrating how little evidence there is for the notion that the poor cannot manage regular cash transfers wisely.

CONCLUSION

Direct distribution is gradually being recognized as having the potential to produce highly beneficial effects in resource-dependent countries: by increasing both the motivation and the ability of a population to hold its political leaders to account, it can counteract the nefarious effects of extractive resource rents on the countries that receive them.

This brief analysis of direct distribution suggests that it can be particularly useful in post-conflict environments. In the immediate aftermath of violent conflict, direct distribution can, on the one hand, offer a quick peace dividend to a traumatized population, and on the other hand, create incentives for political leaders to provide for the well-being of the populace, and to be perceived to do so. In the medium term, direct distribution may help kick-start economic growth and increase the likelihood that such growth will become sustainable. This, in turn, may reduce the risk that underdevelopment will spur renewed conflict. Although there are clear dangers, and any direct distribution scheme must be planned with extreme care, the time may well be ripe to give the policy a chance.

REFERENCES

Atkinson, A. B. 1995. On targeting Social Security: Theory and Western experience with family benefits. In *Public spending and the poor: Theory and evidence,* ed. D. van de Walle and K. Nead. Baltimore and London: Johns Hopkins University Press / World Bank.

Auty, R. M., ed. 2001. *Resource abundance and economic development.* New York: Oxford University Press.

BBC News. 2006. New life for Venezuela opposition? October 3. http://news.bbc.co.uk/1/hi/world/americas/5389460.stm.

Bevan, D. L., P. Collier, and J. W. Gunning. 1987. Consequences of a commodity boom in a controlled economy: Accumulation and redistribution in Kenya, 1975–83. *World Bank Economic Review* 1 (3): 489–513.

———. 1989. Fiscal response to a temporary trade shock: The aftermath of the Kenyan coffee boom. *World Bank Economic Review* 3 (3): 359–378.

———. 1992. Anatomy of a temporary trade shock: The Kenyan coffee boom of 1976–9. *Journal of African Economies* 1 (2): 271–305.
Birdsall, N., and A. Subramanian. 2004. Saving Iraq from its oil. *Foreign Affairs* 83 (4): 77–89.
Burgis, T. 2009a. Nigeria offers "revolutionary" oil deal to delta. *Financial Times*. October 19.
———. 2009b. Guarded welcome for Niger Delta oil plan. *Financial Times*. October 21.
Collier, P., and J. W. Gunning, eds. 1999. *Trade shocks in developing countries*. New York: Oxford University Press.
Collier, P., and A. Hoeffler. 1998. On economic causes of civil war. *Oxford Economic Papers* 50 (4): 563–573.
Economist. 2003. Can oil help the poor? December 4.
———. 2009. Iran's presidential election. June 4.
Fearon, J. D., and D. Laitin. 2003. Ethnicity, insurgency, and civil war. *American Political Science Review* 97 (1): 75–90.
Gary, I., and T. L Karl. 2003. *Bottom of the barrel: Africa's oil boom and the poor*. Baltimore: Catholic Relief Services.
Gertler, P., S. Martinez, and M. Rubio. 2005. Investing cash transfers to raise long term living standards. Unpublished manuscript. http://emlab.berkeley.edu/users/webfac/emiguel/e271_s05/investing.pdf.
Global Witness. 2004. *Time for transparency: Coming clean on oil, mining and gas revenues*. London.
Goldsmith, O. S. 2002. The Alaska Permanent Fund dividend: An experiment in wealth distribution. Paper presented at the Ninth Congress of Basic Income European Network, September 12–14, Geneva. www.basicincome.org/bien/pdf/2002Goldsmith.pdf.
Gurr, T. R. 1970. *Why men rebel*. Princeton, NJ: Princeton University Press.
Hayek, F. A. 1945. The use of knowledge in society. *American Economic Review* 35 (4): 519–530.
Herb, M. 2003. Taxation and representation. *Studies in Comparative International Development* 38 (3): 3–31.
Hsieh, C. 2003. Do consumers react to anticipated income changes? Evidence from the Alaska Permanent Fund. *American Economic Review* 93 (1): 397–405.
Humphreys, M., and M. Sandbu. 2007. The political economy of natural resource funds. In *Escaping the resource curse*, ed. M. Humphreys, J. Sachs, and J. Stiglitz. New York: Columbia University Press.
Isham, J., M. Woolcock, L. Pritchett, and G. Busby. 2002. The varieties of rentier experience: How natural resource endowments affect the political economy of economic growth. World Bank. http://info.worldbank.org/etools/docs/voddocs/171/352/rentier.pdf.
Karl, T. L. 1997. *The paradox of plenty: Oil booms and petro-states*. Berkeley: University of California Press.
Krugman, P. 1987. The narrow moving band, the Dutch disease, and the competitive consequences of Mrs. Thatcher: Notes on trade in the presence of dynamic scale economies. *Journal of Development Economics* 27:41–55.
La Razón. 2009. La concesión de bonos. October 28.
Le Billon, P. 2008. *Resources for peace? Managing revenues from extractive industries in post-conflict environments*. Public Finance in Post-Conflict Environments: A Policy Paper Series. Political Economy Research Institute. Center on International Cooperation.

New York University. February. www.cic.nyu.edu/peacebuilding/docs/CIC_paper5_ LeBillon_FINAL.pdf.

Leite, C., and J. Weidmann. 1999. Does Mother Nature corrupt? Natural resources, corruption and economic growth. Working Paper WP/99/85. Washington, D.C.: International Monetary Fund.

Mehlum, H., K. O. Moene, and R. Torvik. 2006. Institutions and the resource curse. *Economic Journal* 116 (508): 1–20.

Miguel, E., S. Satyanath, and E. Sergenti. 2004. Economic shocks and civil conflict: An instrumental variables approach. *Journal of Political Economy* 112 (4): 725–753.

Morales, J. A. 2007. Distribución directa a las personas de la renta hidrocarburífera: Impactos macroeconómicos. Coloquios Económicos no. 8. Fundación Milenio. www.fundacion-milenio.org/publicaciones/coloquios/fmilenio-coloquio.economico.08.pdf.

Moss, T., and L. Young. 2009. Saving Ghana from its oil: The case for direct cash distribution. Working Paper 186. Washington, D.C.: Center for Global Development.

Palley, T. I. 2003. Lifting the natural resource curse. *Foreign Service* 80 (12): 54–61.

Robinson, J. A., and R. Torvik. 2005. White elephants. *Journal of Public Economics* 89 (2–3): 197–210.

Ross, M. L. 2001a. Does oil hinder democracy? *World Politics* 53 (3): 325–361.

———. 2001b. *Timber booms and institutional breakdown in Southeast Asia.* New York: Cambridge University Press.

———. 2004. Does taxation lead to representation? *British Journal of Political Science* 34 (2): 229–249.

Sachs, J. D., and A. M. Warner. 1995. Natural resource abundance and economic growth. Working Paper 5398. Washington, D.C.: National Bureau of Economic Research.

Sala-i-Martin, X., and A. Subramanian. 2003. Addressing the natural resource curse: An illustration from Nigeria. Working Paper 9804. Washington, D.C.: National Bureau of Economic Research.

Sandbu, M. E. 2006. Natural wealth accounts: A proposal for alleviating the natural resource curse. *World Development* 34 (7): 1153–1170.

Shaxson, N. 2007. *Poisoned wells.* London: Palgrave Macmillan.

Shaxson, N., and M. E. Sandbu. 2009. Give the people their resource wealth. *Financial Times.* June 4.

Skoufias, E., and B. McClafferty. 2001. Is PROGRESA working? Summary of the results of an evaluation by IFPRI. FCND Discussion Paper 118. International Food Policy Research Institute. www.ifpri.org/sites/default/files/publications/fcndp118.pdf.

PART 4

Allocation and institution building

Introduction

Institutional quality and capacity largely determine how natural resources and the accompanying revenues are managed, and the long-term effects of resource extraction and revenue spending on development and peace. The challenge, in societies that have been traumatized by conflict, is to create structures that will help to ensure an immediate peace, while simultaneously supporting the creation or restoration of self-sustaining institutions for the long term.

In post-conflict countries blessed by high-value natural resources, revenue allocation may be the determining factor in the creation of a sustainable peace—or a spoiled future. But efficient and equitable allocation is difficult to achieve in post-conflict situations, where corruption is often prevalent and effective institutions are lacking. Several chapters in part 4 highlight the ways in which resources can be a curse, rather than a blessing, if resources and revenues are not managed properly and institutions function poorly.

In "High-Value Natural Resources, Development, and Conflict: Channels of Causation," Paul Collier and Anke Hoeffler identify six mechanisms by which natural resources can lead to conflict and describe remedies for addressing each mechanism. Arguing that no one policy option can work on its own, the authors focus on four related categories of intervention: revenue transparency, expenditure scrutiny, commodity tracking, and reduced exposure to price shocks. Collier and Hoeffler also observe that revenue expenditure is a neglected area, and that it is essential for the international community to pay more attention to the issue.

"Petroleum Blues: The Political Economy of Resources and Conflict in Chad," by John A. Gould and Matthew S. Winters, examines the management of Chad's oil revenues after the construction of the Chad-Cameroon pipeline. With the intent of making Chad a model for the equitable and efficient management of resource revenues—and the successful avoidance of the resource curse—the World Bank imposed a number of conditions on the loan for the pipeline, which were reflected in a petroleum revenue management law; the Bank also required Chad to establish a national oversight body to monitor the government's spending of oil revenues. The Bank's goal—to ensure that the allocation of oil revenues would promote equity, peace, and development—was laudable, but neither law nor institutional capacity was sufficient to rein in the power of established patronage systems or to compensate for lack of transparency and accountability. Gould and Winters argue that the Bank could have built more capacity before the oil revenues started pouring in, and should also have demanded more provisions to protect human rights and prevent conflict.

When it comes to post-conflict natural resource management, it is easy to find examples of failure; two chapters in part 4, however, focus on the Liberia Forest Initiative (LFI), which is widely considered a success story. In "Leveraging High-Value Natural Resources to Restore the Rule of Law: The Role of the

Liberia Forest Initiative in Liberia's Transition to Stability," Stephanie L. Altman, Sandra S. Nichols, and John T. Woods argue that the LFI has achieved four main goals: preventing forest revenues from becoming a source of conflict financing; ensuring sustainable forest management; restoring accountability and transparency to the forest industry; and including civil society in decision making. While implementation is far from complete, transformation has been significant. The LFI has also provided a model for other institutional reforms in Liberia. One of the main differences between Liberia's experience and that of other countries, such as Chad, Iraq, and Nigeria, is political will at the highest level: in Liberia, it was the leadership of President Ellen Johnson Sirleaf that drove the reforms.

In "Forest Resources and Peacebuilding: Preliminary Lessons from Liberia and Sierra Leone," Michael D. Beevers points out that despite the apparent success of the LFI, implementation has been slow and fraught with contention. Beevers also argues that the forest industry has not contributed as much to the economic recovery as was expected, and that the industry still harbors corruption and patronage. Nevertheless, Beevers believes that that the LFI played a valuable role in peacebuilding by making it possible for the state and civil society to engage in a dialogue about natural resource management—something that would not have been possible a few years earlier. Neighboring Sierra Leone, in contrast, may have missed a peacebuilding opportunity by failing to undertake post-conflict forest sector reform.

While Liberia stands out for its effort to build institutions to manage resources and the associated revenues, Nigeria's failed efforts to properly allocate revenues from the oil-rich Niger Delta have left the region in a state of poverty and unrest. In "An Inescapable Curse? Resource Management, Violent Conflict, and Peacebuilding in the Niger Delta," Annegret Mähler explores a number of failed initiatives to allocate resource revenues efficiently and equitably. Mähler attributes the failure to three principal sources: poor design (specifically, measures that fail to target the principal causes of conflict, and a lack of measures to ensure participation, monitoring, and evaluation); weak political institutions; and extensive corruption.

Sometimes, instead of being addressed in a peace agreement, or in the constitution or other laws adopted immediately after peace, the management of high-value natural resources is intentionally deferred until a later time. The absence of a clear legal framework, however, can lead to the emergence of grievances regarding resource extraction and revenue management. "The High Cost of Ambiguity: Conflict, Violence, and the Legal Framework for Managing Oil in Iraq," by Mishkat Al Moumin, highlights the tensions that resulted from vague language in Iraq's post-war constitution. The document's failure to specify, among other things, which entity has the authority to manage oil resources and their associated revenues has led to tensions both within the central government and between the national and subnational governments. As Al Moumin points out, the absence of a clear and effective legal framework is particularly dangerous in a country that is already traumatized by war, and where many have easy access to weapons.

Allocation and institution building 295

When it comes to institution building, scholars and development agencies alike tend to place the greatest emphasis on political institutions. Economic institutions, however, should not be forgotten. In "The Capitalist Civil Peace: Some Theory and Empirical Evidence," Indra de Soysa argues that economic reform is central to institution building and sustainable peace. Because free markets provide economic opportunities to many, instead of to a few, they reduce the need to resort to rent seeking and other unproductive economic activities. Using statistical analyses, de Soysa demonstrates that free markets have a dampening effect on both conflict onset and political repression.

Taken together, the chapters in part 4 highlight one of the principal lessons of this volume: accountability is the key to wise revenue spending. The chapters also emphasize the importance of reforming resource sectors and the institutions that manage them, establishing a clear and strong legal framework, and building healthy economic, as well as political, institutions.

High-value natural resources, development, and conflict: Channels of causation

Paul Collier and Anke Hoeffler

Natural resources are not distributed equally randomly across the globe. Some countries have few or no valuable natural resources, and others have many. Moreover, natural resources are more abundant in some regions within countries than others. Abundance brings opportunities for greater income—and, historically, resources such as coal and iron ore have been critical triggers for development. But at least since the early 1970s, resource abundance has often been associated with unfulfilled potential for economic growth and high risk of large-scale violent conflict.

That good fortune should yield problems is evidently avoidable, and the international community has recently become interested in identifying feasible collective actions that could significantly mitigate what has come to be known as the "resource curse." Such endeavors are of particular concern to post-conflict societies, because the use and distribution of resource revenues can be pivotal to peacebuilding.

In order to identify possible interventions, it is useful to consider the reasons why natural resource dependence might have adverse effects. Of course, addressing the cause of a problem will not necessarily remedy it; nevertheless, without an understanding of causes, one can have little confidence in proposed remedies. Such an understanding is of particular importance in post-conflict settings because many countries struggle to maintain peace; in fact, about 40 percent of peacebuilding

---

Paul Collier is a professor of economics and director of the Centre for the Study of African Economies at the University of Oxford. Anke Hoeffler is a research officer at the Centre for the Study of African Economies and a research fellow at St. Antony's College, University of Oxford. This chapter is an adapted and updated version of Paul Collier, "Natural Resources, Development, and Conflict: Channels of Causation and Policy Interventions," originally published in *Economic Integration and Social Responsibility*, ed. F. Bourguignon, P. Jacquet, and B. Pleskovic, Annual World Bank Conference on Development Economics: Europe 2004 (Washington, D.C.: World Bank, 2007). Copyright 2007 The International Bank for Reconstruction / The World Bank. Adapted by permission of the publisher.

attempts fail within the decade, leading to renewed civil war (Collier, Hoeffler, and Söderbom 2008).

This chapter is divided into four sections: (1) a brief consideration of some statistical studies addressing the relationship between natural resources and conflict; (2) a consideration of six major routes that lead from natural resource dependence to development problems; (3) an analysis of potential policy responses; and (4) a brief conclusion.

NATURAL RESOURCES AND CONFLICT: STATISTICAL STUDIES

The first statistical study to find a relationship between natural resources and the risk of civil war was published in 1998 (Collier and Hoeffler); the latest version of that work (Collier, Hoeffler, and Rohner 2009), which analyzed eighty-four large-scale civil wars that occurred between 1960 and 2004, showed that the risk of conflict is substantially increased when primary commodity exports (that is, commodities in their raw or unprocessed state) make up a higher share of gross domestic product (GDP). The relationship is complex, however: at low levels of primary commodity exports, the risk is low, but it increases with higher levels of primary commodity exports. The risk of civil war is at its highest point when primary commodity exports make up about 25 percent of GDP; at still higher levels, the risk decreases.

The study also found that when primary commodity exports at similarly high levels of dependence are compared, oil stands out: high levels of oil dependence are even more likely to be associated with conflict. It should be stressed that natural resource dependence—or primary commodity dependence—is far from being the only factor that is statistically significant in the risk of conflict. In particular, the level of per capita income strongly influences the risk of conflict. At high levels of per capita income, the risk of civil war is negligible, with or without natural resources. Hence, societies such as Norway and Australia, which are highly dependent upon natural resource exports but are also rich, do not face any significant risk from their natural resource endowments.

Of the studies that have investigated the relationship between natural resources and the duration of conflict (as distinct from the risk of its initiation), two studies found that resource dependence increases the duration of civil war (Fearon 2004; Collier, Hoeffler, and Söderbom 2004). One of these studies distinguished between the effects of initial dependence and the effects of the world price of the commodity exports during the conflict (Collier, Hoeffler, and Söderbom 2004). The world price is a particularly reliable causal variable: it is both easily observed and almost entirely unrelated to an individual conflict. Unsurprisingly, the effect of the price depends on the initial level of resource exports: for example, assuming a fairly high level of primary commodity exports at the start of the conflict—30 percent of GDP—a subsequent and sustained 10 percent increase in the world price of the export would extend the duration of the conflict by 12 percent. The study also found a negative association between natural resource dependence and longer-term growth—a finding that is of particular importance in post-conflict situations because economic growth supports the peacebuilding process (Collier, Hoeffler, and Söderbom 2008).[1]

FROM NATURAL RESOURCE DEPENDENCE TO DEVELOPMENT PROBLEMS

By their nature, statistical studies are rarely well suited to explaining why associations exist. This section, which suggests six causal mechanisms, relies on a mix of theory and evidence from statistical and case studies.

Gaining access to honeypots

One obvious potential explanation of the link between natural resources and conflict is that natural resources constitute a valuable honeypot over which interest groups might fight. Surprisingly, the evidence for this hypothesis is relatively weak. If this were a valid explanation, one would expect it to apply to aid: some governments receive very large amounts of aid, so it should be advantageous to capture the government in order to gain access to the aid. Although one economic theorist, Herschel Grossman (1992), proposed precisely this relationship, tests have found no relationship between aid and the risk of conflict (Collier and Hoeffler 2002). Nevertheless, natural resources may be a more evident source of rent than aid.

Some case studies suggest that in particular instances, a pure rent-seeking motive may be important.[2] In Fiji, for example, a businessman who was the local representative of a private American company that was seeking a logging contract attempted to launch a violent coup shortly after the contract had been awarded to a different company (Van Duesen 2008). In Sierra Leone, as part of the 1999 Lomé Peace Agreement, Foday Sankoh, the leader of the Revolutionary United Front rebel group, was offered a role that was analogous to the vice presidency—but he refused until the offer was changed to include chairmanship of the board

---

[1] A large body of additional research confirms the negative relationship between resource dependence and growth. In the best known of the statistical studies, Sachs and Warner (2000) found that natural resources reduce growth. In subsequent studies, Robinson, Torvik, and Verdier (2006) and Mehlum, Moene, and Torvik (2006) used the Sachs and Warner data to investigate why political processes might be dysfunctional in the context of resource rents, and suggested that the problem may be remedied through appropriate institutions. There are also many good case study collections. Gelb (1989) is a particularly good analysis of oil economies, and Auty (2001) is a useful broader analysis.

[2] For the purposes of this chapter, *rent* is defined as those payments to a factor of production that are in excess of the minimum payment necessary to have that factor supplied. For further discussion of rent, see Varian (2006).

that controlled diamond-mining interests (Bangura 2000; GOSL and RUF 1999, art. 5, sec. 2).

Although the rebel leaders in both Fiji and Sierra Leone offered a different explanation, it is difficult to avoid concluding that the desire to obtain control of natural resource rents played a substantial role in their actions. Nevertheless, it is often difficult to distinguish between purely criminal predation and that which is intended to fund a political objective. And the objective can sometimes change over time. For example, FARC (Revolutionary Armed Forces of Colombia) began as a radical rural political movement but is now predominantly a drug-trafficking operation (DOJ 2006; Peceny and Durnan 2006). Presumably, as drug revenues became increasingly central to what the organization was doing, recruits motivated by ideology became less likely to join, and criminals attracted by wealth and violence became more likely to join. Similarly, in the Niger Delta, a movement that had initially protested against injustice and environmental degradation has relatively rapidly been drawn into gang warfare over control of protection and kidnapping rackets.

Making secessionist movements credible

A variant on the honeypot hypothesis, for which there is much better evidence, is that natural resource abundance promotes violent secession. Just as the worldwide distribution of natural resources is not equal, so within countries some locations are more favored than others. Those who live in the vicinity of the natural resource endowment have an obvious economic interest in claiming the resources for themselves, to the exclusion of their fellow nationals. And since natural resources are typically treated as public rather than as private property, such a claim for local ownership is tantamount to a claim for independence.

Many nations are agglomerations of previously distinct political entities, and the process of consolidation is often contested. Hence, in many situations, natural resources will be located in regions where some political groups—albeit often on the fringe—are already claiming autonomy. The presence of natural resources enables such groups to add a credible economic argument to what might otherwise be a largely romantic appeal. An example of this transformation is the (nonviolent) rise of Scottish nationalism, which can be precisely dated to the period between the 1970 and 1974 elections. During the 1970 election, as in all previous elections, the Scottish National Party won only a tiny share of the vote and gained only a single seat in parliament—but in the 1974 elections, its share of the vote rose to 30 percent. The transforming event that brought about this change was surely the dramatic rise in world oil prices that occurred as a result of the 1973 Arab-Israeli War. During this period, the Organization of the Petroleum Exporting Companies appeared to have the power to raise the price almost without limit, and the Shah of Iran began referring to "the noble fuel," giving oil endowments an aura of unrivaled majesty. In this setting, the oil off the shores of Scotland was suddenly seen as valuable, and the Scottish National

Party campaigned using the slogan "It's Scotland's oil" (McBrewster, Miller, and Vandome 2009).[3]

A similar oil-influenced secessionist movement—this time violent—occurred in the Biafra region of Nigeria. Biafra's attempt at violent secession began in 1967, after the central government decided to treat oil revenue as a national asset. Although ethnic tensions were also at play in Nigeria, virtually all African countries have several ethnic groups; what is striking is that the ethnic groups in Africa that have attempted to secede—such as those in Biafra, where there is oil, and in Katanga, in the Democratic Republic of the Congo, where there are diamonds—have usually been resource-rich.[4]

A 2006 statistical analysis of secession (Collier and Hoeffler) relied on the political science classification of civil wars as either secessionist or ideological. Although this is not an immaculate distinction—because it depends, to an extent, on the ostensible objectives of rebel groups—the goal was to determine whether primary commodity exports have differing effects on the risk of the two types of civil war. The study found that dependence on primary commodities does indeed increase the risk of secessionist war more than it increases the risk of ideological war. Another finding worth noting was that if an oil-exporting country experiences a civil war, it is almost certain to be a secessionist war; this is in contrast to non-oil-exporting countries, which often experience ideological civil wars.

Oil may be distinctive in its ability to evoke romantic notions of affluence. The GAM (Free Aceh Movement), for example, which has been attempting to achieve secession of Aceh from Indonesia, has used the analogy of Brunei in its propaganda, claiming that the population of Aceh could be equally rich if Aceh could retain the revenues from the extraction of natural gas in the province. This is a massive—and presumably deliberate—exaggeration, but it may well appeal to the popular imagination.

Financing rebel groups

Rebellions require resources. Recruits are usually full time, and need to be housed, clothed, and fed; but most would-be rebel groups simply cannot finance their activities on a sufficiently large scale, beyond minor acts of predation. Thus,

---

[3] Indeed, debate at the time may well have inflated the value of the oil in excess of its true value.
[4] Usually, ethnic groups in regions that are poorly endowed do not press for secession, for the obvious reason that they would be worse off. However, in cases where "romantic" secessionists manage to build a politically powerful demand for secession—perhaps because they have an unusually charismatic leader—the other regions of the country may decide to grant secession peacefully, since violent opposition would not be worthwhile. This was the case in Czechoslovakia, where the larger and richer Czech region permitted the poorer region of Slovakia to secede peacefully.

another hypothesis about the relationship between natural resources and civil war is based on the vulnerability of such resources to appropriation by rebel groups that need financing to pursue violence.

Natural resource predation is by no means the only source of financing for a rebel army, but where natural resources abound in rural areas, they are uniquely vulnerable: lucrative, immobile, and difficult to defend. The task of extorting rents from rurally based natural resource industries also requires armaments and organization that are similar to those that rebel groups would need in any case. (In urban-based extortion rackets, in contrast, virtually anything beyond basic handguns would be an encumbrance rather than an asset.)

Diamonds offer the most spectacular examples of rebel groups funded by natural resources. UNITA (the National Union for the Total Independence of Angola) and the Revolutionary United Front both came to be remarkably big organizations: when UNITA was disbanded, over 90,000 excombatants took part in a demobilization and reintegration program (MDRP 2008). Standing armies of this size are expensive and depend upon correspondingly substantial predation businesses. Alluvial diamonds are particularly well suited for predation because the extraction process is sufficiently simple that it does not require large corporations. Thousands of small individual operators are much less able to defend themselves than large companies, so a rebel organization can easily intimidate and "tax" producers. Timber is also technologically suited to rebel predation, as was demonstrated by the Khmer Rouge in Cambodia. Where technology requires large companies, as in the case of oil, rebel groups can still be predatory, but the nature of the predation changes: companies are threatened with sabotage, and their employees are kidnapped and ransomed.[5] Legislation and increased public pressure have made it more difficult, however, for multinational corporations to make such payments to rebel groups.[6]

As Philippe Le Billon (2001) argues, it is likely that point resources (oil, for example) and diffuse resources (coffee, alluvial diamonds) generate different types of rents. Whereas point resources *motivate* rebellion, rents from diffuse resources may be used to *finance* rebellion, because rents from such resources can more easily be appropriated while fighting is ongoing. Point resource extraction and sales, in contrast, typically involve international companies that are unwilling to operate during a war. Once rebels have won a civil war, however, they anticipate international involvement in resource extraction.

---

[5] A related phenomenon is "war-booty futures" (Ross 2005), in which a rebel group actually needs a large company to which it can sell the highly risky prospect of extraction rights, contingent upon subsequent rebel victory.

[6] Nongovernmental organizations such as Global Witness have raised awareness of the links between resource extraction and violence. The USA PATRIOT Act is an example of legislation that regulates financial transactions, particularly those involving foreign individuals and entities.

Detaching the government from the electorate

Historically, representative government arose because states needed to raise large amounts of revenue in order to fight wars, and they found that conceding some degree of representation to taxpayers was the necessary price for compliance with taxation (Tilly 1975; Acemoglu and Robinson 2000). A common political economy argument—encapsulated in the central demand of the American Revolution, "No taxation without representation"—holds that taxation provokes scrutiny from citizens. But when a state receives income through aid, natural resources, or both, the need for taxation is reduced, as is popular scrutiny of government. In their discussion of the problems associated with aid, Deborah A. Brautigam and Stephen Knack, for example, point out that "when revenues do not depend on the taxes raised from citizens and businesses, there is less incentive for government to be accountable to them" (2004, 265).[7] Resource rents are a nontax revenue that is somewhat analogous to aid.

In an empirical investigation of the link between taxation and representation, Michael L. Ross (2004a) found that the larger the share of government expenditures financed through taxation, the more likely the government was to become representative.[8] People are less concerned about the misuse of public money if they have not been taxed in order to generate it. The power of this argument depends, however, on the sophistication of the electorate. In principle, the opportunity cost of misused public money is the same, regardless of its source. But governments that misuse public funds can more easily disguise the amount of revenue from natural resources than they can disguise the amount of revenue from taxation. It may also be easy to co-opt the relatively small groups of informed critics of natural resource misuse.

To the extent that a government is more detached from electoral concerns when it has substantial natural resource revenues, this detachment is both bad in itself and a potential cause of rebellion, including secession. The perception that resources are being embezzled by a corrupt elite is, at the very least, convenient for rebel groups. Although there is seldom a single motivation for rebellion, the perception of government corruption can be a contributing factor even if it is not, by itself, a significant trigger of violence.

Dutch disease

In the late 1970s and early 1980s, economic scholars made much of the problem of Dutch disease—the apparent relationship between an increase in natural resource exploitation and a decline in the manufacturing sector.[9] Economic theory suggests

---

[7] Moore (1998) has also investigated the relationship between state capacity, democracy, and aid and come to similar conclusions.
[8] This is consistent with the state-formation hypothesis developed by Charles Tilly (1975).
[9] The term *Dutch disease* was coined by the *Economist* (1977). The first formal economic model was developed by Corden and Neary (1982).

that an increase in natural resource revenues will deindustrialize a nation's economy by raising the exchange rate, and thereby making the manufacturing sector less competitive (Corden and Neary 1982). As this perspective suggests, the response—deindustrialization—is simply an efficient allocation of resources: resources move into the nontradable sector, where they are used to produce the goods that are demanded by the now-richer society but that cannot be supplied through imports.

For such changes to be categorized as a disease—that is, as a problem that warrants attention—one or the other of two additional characteristics must typically be present. First, the increase in the exchange rate is temporary, but private actors fail to recognize this; as a result, the resources that have been lured into the nontradable sector are marooned once prices revert, leading to excessive adjustment costs. Second, assuming that one of the main engines of economic growth—namely, learning by doing—occurs mostly in the manufacturing sector, rather than in the natural resource extraction industry, as the manufacturing sector contracts (and with it one of the engines of growth), overall growth rates decline. Whether Dutch disease requires intervention is likely to depend on both the scale of the resource revenues and on the policy environment. But there is overwhelming statistical evidence that since the 1960s, countries that are rich in natural resources have experienced lower growth rates,[10] and that low growth rates are robustly correlated with a higher risk of civil war (Miguel, Satyanath, and Sergenti 2004; Collier and Hoeffler 2004; Collier, Hoeffler, and Rohner 2009).

Since aid has the same effect as natural resource extraction in raising the real exchange rate, it has sometimes been criticized for causing changes that are analogous to those associated with Dutch disease. Indeed, the effect of aid on growth has been extensively debated. In a study that controlled for policy—and thus controlled, in principle, for the "detachment" effect that both aid and natural resources are likely to have in common—the findings showed that aid has diminishing returns that depend, in turn, on policy (Collier and Dollar 2002).[11] The study authors used "saturation point" to refer to the point at which the effect of aid on growth becomes negative. When policies are reasonable and aid is no more than 30 percent of GDP, aid contributes to growth. When policies are poor, the saturation point occurs when aid is around 10 to 15 percent of GDP. Since natural resource revenues are closely analogous to aid, at least for a given policy environment, one would expect the same range of absorptive capacity to apply to both. The diminishing returns that drive the economy to the saturation point, beyond which aid—and, by implication, natural resources—actually reduces

---

[10] See, for example, Sachs and Warner (2000), Gylfason (2001), and Gylfason and Zoega (2006) for an analysis of the mechanisms by which a decline in the formation of human and physical capital reduces growth in resource-rich economies.

[11] The "detachment effect" refers to the phenomenon, discussed in the previous section, in which the government is removed from the concerns of the electorate because most of its funding comes from other sources.

growth, might well reflect Dutch disease. In other words, up to a point, resources might have a beneficial effect that is subject to the normal pattern of diminishing returns; beyond that point, an adverse effect—Dutch disease—becomes preponderant.

Many countries that have abundant natural resources are indeed likely to breach the saturation point—partly because revenues are sometimes very high (in excess of 30 or even 40 percent of GDP, as in Nigeria), but also because policies are often very poor, perhaps because of the detachment effect, which may cause the saturation point to set in at relatively low levels of revenue. Indeed, there may be an inherent trap in the dynamics of revenue and policy: when policies are poor and natural resource revenues are high, the non-natural-resource part of the economy is likely to have slow or even negative growth, and so to diminish relative to the natural resource component. It is then in a weak position to lobby for reform. In Nigeria, for example, the non-oil segment of the economy has been virtually stagnant for a long period.[12]

Exposure to shocks

Finally, natural resources and other primary commodities can be problematic for development because they expose the economy to price shocks. Large negative shocks tend to produce episodes of severe economic contraction that compound the direct loss of income. Such episodes directly increase poverty by causing a drop in export income; they also tend to reduce the growth rates of output over the medium term (Collier and Dehn 2001). Over and above the income and output losses, episodes of rapid economic decline substantially increase the risk of civil war (Collier and Hoeffler 2004; Miguel, Satyanath, and Sergenti 2004). Even positive shocks sometimes destabilize economic management, thereby creating missed opportunities.

Distinguishing between competing hypotheses

Although there is plenty of evidence for all six linkages between natural resource abundance and violent conflict, the proxies of natural resource abundance are often too crude to allow one to distinguish the precise transmission mechanisms. The question is, how can one distinguish between competing hypotheses?

A 2004 study used a general measure of primary commodity exports that included agricultural products, oil, and minerals, but not diamonds (Collier and Hoeffler 2004). This measure, which was first used by Jeffrey Sachs and Andrew M. Warner (2000), has been criticized, however, because it aggregates such a variety of resources. Michael Ross (2004b) and James Fearon (2005) have also raised doubt about whether the Sachs and Warner (2000) measure is robustly correlated with civil war.

---

[12] For an overview of the Nigerian economy, see Collier, Pattillo, and Soludo (2008).

A number of studies—for example, James Fearon and David Laitin (2003) and Päivi Lujala (2010)—have found that oil exporters have a higher risk of civil war. There is also some evidence that oil and gas reserves increase the duration of conflict (Lujala 2009), a finding that may be interpreted in different ways. Because oil-producing countries tend to have weaker institutional capacity (Isham et al. 2005), they may be unable or unwilling to distribute their oil wealth evenly, thus causing grievances that lead to civil war, or they may be unable to effectively deter rebellion. Another possibility is that oil is a honeypot that motivates rebellion. Macartan Humphreys (2005) has examined this last hypothesis by analyzing the role of oil reserves rather than current oil production. But his results are not conclusive, perhaps because current oil production and known reserves are highly correlated: "proven" reserves are more likely to be an economic than a geological concept: oil companies explore reserves only if the political and economic situation is conducive to exploitation (Collier and Hoeffler 2005). Thus, it is likely that proven reserves are considerably underestimated in fragile countries (Collier 2010), and that available data therefore do not permit an investigation of the hypothesis that natural resource reserves motivate rebellion.

Indra de Soysa and Eric Neumayer (2007) have used a measure of resource rents to distinguish between two rival hypotheses: (1) that resources provide financing and motive for conflict and (2) that resources weaken state capacity, which in turn fosters conflict. They found that higher rents from the energy sector were positively associated with the risk of civil war (which supports the "state capacity" hypothesis), but they found no evidence that mineral rents increased the risk of civil war. Since energy rents are more likely to accrue to the state, whereas mineral rents can be appropriated either by the state or by rebels, they rejected the finance and motive hypothesis. This stands in contrast to Lujala (2010)—who, using subnational data, found a positive relationship between the location of violent conflict and the location of diamonds, providing some evidence that the diamonds might have been used to finance conflict.

POLICY RESPONSES

Clearly, no single policy intervention will simultaneously address all six of the causal mechanisms that link natural resources to conflict. If all are indeed credible routes to conflict, as seems likely, a package of interventions that collectively addresses all the routes will be required. In the absence of a package, interventions that address only a single route may have limited effect: closing one connection may simply increase opportunities for the other connections to take effect.

This section considers the four components of a feasible package of interventions: revenue transparency, expenditure scrutiny, commodity tracking, and reduced exposure to price shocks. (Although there are six routes, some interventions address more than one of them, so an effective package need have only four components.)

Revenue transparency

Revenue transparency is useful in several respects. Clearly, it is necessary for scrutiny of expenditures: unless revenues are known, it is pointless to ask how they are used. In terms of the six routes discussed earlier in the chapter, transparency is necessary to address the problem of detachment; it can also reduce secessionist pressure.

As the example of the GAM in Aceh illustrated, rebel movements may deliberately exaggerate the value of natural resource revenues. Far from keeping the population quiescent, secrecy is likely to facilitate such exaggeration. Because the populations of many developing countries do not trust their governments to provide accurate information, especially on such contested matters, transparency alone cannot counter such propaganda: a government campaign to demonstrate that revenues from natural resources are lower than the figures cited by a rebel group would simply set off claims, on the part of the rebels, that the government is engaging in embezzlement. Hence, any system of transparency must also be credible to the domestic population.

Post-conflict countries can now participate in programs such as the Extractive Industries Transparency Initiative, which supports improved governance in resource-rich countries through the verification and publication of company payments and government revenues from oil, gas, and mining.[13] The Natural Resource Charter, currently an international convention in the making, is a set of economic principles that governments can use to increase the prospects of sustained economic development from natural resource exploitation.[14] The strategies recommended by the Natural Resource Charter should further improve government accountability—and, thereby, the use of resource incomes for development and security. Developed through a participatory process that was guided by academic research, the charter begins with the premise that the development of natural resources should be for the maximum benefit of the citizens of the source country, then specifies how this can be achieved. The precepts cover issues that range from achieving transparency and informed public oversight to best practices in contracting with and paying natural resource extraction companies.

Expenditure scrutiny

Although scrutiny depends on transparency, transparency is not in itself scrutiny. Citizens and their representatives are the legitimate beneficiaries of public revenues; hence, scrutiny is predominantly a domestic process. The international community may also have a legitimate interest in scrutiny, to the extent that it is putting resources into the country, but this interest is distinctly secondary to the domestic interest. The international community should nevertheless support

---

[13] For additional information on the Extractive Industries Transparency Initiative, see Eddie Rich and T. Negbalee Warner, "Addressing the Roots of Liberia's Conflict through the Extractive Industries Transparency Initiative," in this volume.
[14] See www.naturalresourcecharter.org.

domestic efforts to increase scrutiny; in some countries, institutions that can conduct scrutiny need to be established from scratch. The precise architecture of scrutiny will vary from country to country, depending on what is already in place.

Citizens of post-conflict countries have experienced either state fragility or complete state failure and are thus more likely to feel detached from their governments. Transparency and scrutiny can counterbalance the problem of detachment, at least to some extent. Gradually, the population may come to recognize that natural resource revenues are indeed owned by the nation, and that decisions about their use are a core issue of domestic politics.

Commodity tracking

Commodity tracking directly addresses the fact that natural resources have historically been used to finance rebel movements. The Kimberley Process, a certification scheme designed to ensure that rough diamonds are "conflict free," should reduce financing opportunities for rebel movements and thereby decrease the risk of violent conflict.[15] By improving transparency, commodity tracking also addresses the problems of secession and detachment: the government is seen to be attempting to curtail the illicit use of revenues.

The physical tracking of commodities can also be usefully combined with information on the corresponding financial transactions.[16] Banks' reporting requirements are currently increasing in any case, as a means of curbing corruption and international terrorism, and the reporting requirements for the physical movement of commodities are also being increased—but the two have yet to be combined. The integration of financial reporting systems, for which banks are responsible, and physical consignments, which are reported by customs authorities, would be relatively straightforward with modern information technology, and would greatly augment transparency.

Reduced exposure to price shocks

It is currently difficult for post-conflict countries to guard against price shocks: opportunities to cushion price shocks through private and public insurance are

---

[15] For additional information on the Kimberley Process, see Clive Wright, "The Kimberley Process Certification Scheme: A Model Negotiation?"; J. Andrew Grant, "The Kimberley Process at Ten: Reflections on a Decade of Efforts to End the Trade in Conflict Diamonds"; Harrison Mitchell, "A More Formal Engagement: A Constructive Critique of Certification as a Means of Preventing Conflict and Building Peace"; and Kazumi Kawamoto, "Diamonds in War, Diamonds for Peace: Diamond Sector Management and Kimberlite Mining in Sierra Leone," all in this volume.

[16] One development along these lines is a U.S. law, the Dodd-Frank Wall Street Reform and Consumer Protection Act, which was signed on July 21, 2010. Designed to increase transparency in the trade of minerals financing conflict in the Democratic Republic of the Congo (DRC) and surrounding areas, the act requires companies to trace the source of "conflict minerals" that are used in production of their goods.

limited for governments, and because stabilization funds can be difficult to administer,[17] they are therefore slow to respond and would be in danger of working procyclically (that is, in times of economic growth the fund would release money, while in times of economic downturn the fund would withhold the money). One strategy for protecting against price shocks is to diversify the economy—that is, to make it less vulnerable to price changes in the natural resource sector by increasing activities in other sectors, such as services and manufacturing. But diversification takes time, and the benefits to peacebuilding will be slow to materialize.

In combination with transparency and scrutiny, however, diversification can help to reduce the problem of Dutch disease. Dutch disease is best thought of in terms of absorptive capacity: how much natural resource revenue can the government productively use? Absorptive capacity depends, in turn, on the quality of the policy environment. Reducing economic fluctuations and improving the effectiveness of public expenditures increase absorptive capacity, rendering countries less likely to suffer from the adverse effects of natural resources and more able to use them to rebuild their societies.

CONCLUSION

Development aid typically dominates the public debate when it comes to assisting poor countries, many of which are post-conflict societies. Scholars do not agree on whether aid has a positive impact on development. Sachs (2006) stresses the positive impact of development aid, while Easterly (2006) argues that aid has impeded development. Collier (2007) takes the middle ground, suggesting that aid has had positive but small effects on development. If this view is correct, it is desirable to continue to focus on aid effectiveness and policy coherence in the poorest countries. Aid effectiveness refers to the need to increase the impact of aid on economic growth and poverty reduction; policy coherence refers to efforts to align apparently disparate policy arenas (such as aid and trade), to ensure that they are all supportive of development.

The natural resource revenues that accrue to developing countries are far larger than aid flows, but they are analytically similar. Policy coherence demands that the international community focus on raising the returns from natural resource revenues, just as it has struggled to raise the returns on aid. Indeed, the payoff for raising the returns on natural resource revenues dwarfs the effects of raising the returns on aid. Some of the actions required—such as domestic scrutiny—are similar; others are very different. But the prolonged international debate on the effectiveness of aid contrasts sharply with the neglect that has prevailed, until recently, with respect to international policy toward natural resources.

---

[17] Stabilization funds are designed to reduce the economic impact of volatile revenue from nonrenewable resources.

REFERENCES

Acemoglu, D., and J. Robinson. 2000. Why did the West extend the franchise? Growth, inequality and democracy in historical perspective. *Quarterly Journal of Economics* 115 (4): 1167–1199.

Auty, R., ed. 2001. *Resource abundance and economic development*. Oxford, UK: Oxford University Press.

Bangura, Y. 2000. Strategic policy failure and governance in Sierra Leone. *Journal of Modern African Studies* 38 (4): 565.

Brautigam, D., and S. Knack. 2004. Foreign aid, institutions and governance in sub-Saharan Africa. *Economic Development and Cultural Change* 52 (2): 255–285.

Collier, P. 2007. *The bottom billion: Why the poorest countries are failing and what can be done about it*. Oxford, UK: Oxford University Press.

———. 2010. *The plundered planet*. London: Penguin Books.

Collier, P., and J. Dehn. 2001. Aid, shocks and growth. Policy Research Working Paper 2688. World Bank. www-wds.worldbank.org/external/default/WDSContentServer/IW3P/IB/2001/11/06/000094946_01102304052049/Rendered/PDF/multi0page.pdf.

Collier, P., and D. Dollar. 2002. Aid allocation and poverty reduction. *European Economic Review* 46 (8): 1475–1500.

Collier, P., and A. Hoeffler. 1998. On the economic causes of civil war. *Oxford Economic Papers* 50 (4): 563–573.

———. 2002. Aid, policy and peace: Reducing the risks of civil conflict. *Defence and Peace Economics* 13 (6): 435–450.

———. 2004. Greed and grievance in civil wars. *Oxford Economic Papers* 56 (4): 563–595.

———. 2005. Resource rents, governance, and conflict. *Journal of Conflict Resolution* 49 (4): 625–633.

———. 2006. The political economy of secession. In *Negotiating self-determination*, ed. H. Hannum and E. F. Babbitt. Lanham, MD: Lexington Books.

Collier, P., A. Hoeffler, and D. Rohner. 2009. Beyond greed and grievance: Feasibility and civil war. *Oxford Economic Papers* 61 (1): 1–27.

Collier, P., A. Hoeffler, and M. Söderbom. 2004. On the duration of civil war. *Journal of Peace Research* 41 (3): 253–273.

———. 2008. Post-conflict risks. *Journal of Peace Research* 45 (4): 461–478.

Collier, P., C. Pattillo, and C. Soludo, eds. 2008. *Economic policy options for a prosperous Nigeria*. Basingstoke, UK: Palgrave Macmillan.

Corden, W. M., and J. P. Neary. 1982. Booming sector and de-industrialisation in a small open economy. *Economic Journal* 92 (368): 825–848.

de Soysa, I., and E. Neumayer. 2007. Natural resource wealth and the risk of civil war onset: Results from a new dataset of natural resource rents, 1970–1999. *Conflict Management and Peace Science* 24 (3): 201–218.

DOJ (U.S. Department of Justice). 2006. United States charges 50 leaders of narco-terrorist FARC in Colombia with supplying more than half of the world's cocaine. March 22. www.justice.gov/opa/pr/2006/March/06_crm_163.html.

Easterly, W. 2006. *The white man's burden: Why the West's efforts to aid the rest have done so much ill and so little good*. Oxford, UK: Oxford University Press.

Economist. 1977. The Dutch disease. November 26.

Fearon, J. 2004. Why do some wars last so much longer than others? *Journal of Peace Research* 41 (3): 275–301.

———. 2005. Primary commodities exports and civil war. *Journal of Conflict Resolution* 49 (4): 483–507.
Fearon, J., and D. Laitin. 2003. Ethnicity, insurgency and civil war. *American Political Science Review* 97 (1): 75–90.
Gelb, A. 1989. *Oil windfalls: Blessing or curse?* Oxford, UK: Oxford University Press.
GOSL (Government of Sierra Leone) and RUF (Revolutionary United Front of Sierra Leone). 1999. Peace agreement between the Government of Sierra Leone and the Revolutionary Front of Sierra Leone. July 7, Lomé, Togo.
Grossman, H. 1992. Foreign aid and insurrection. *Defence Economics* 3 (4): 275–288.
Gylfason, T. 2001. Natural resources, education, and economic development. *European Economic Review* 45 (4): 847–859.
Gylfason, T., and G. Zoega. 2006. Natural resources and economic growth: The role of investment. *World Economy* 29 (8): 1091–1115.
Humphreys, M. 2005. Natural resources, conflict, and conflict resolution: Uncovering the mechanisms. *Journal of Conflict Resolution* 49 (4): 508–537.
Isham, J., M. Woolcock, L. Pritchett, and G. Busby. 2005. The varieties of resource experience: Natural resource export structures and the political economy of economic growth. *World Bank Economic Review* 19 (2): 141–174.
Le Billon, P. 2001. The political ecology of war: Natural resources and armed conflicts. *Political Geography* 20:561–584.
Lujala, P. 2009. Deadly combat over natural resources: Gems, petroleum, drugs, and the severity of armed civil conflict. *Journal of Conflict Resolution* 53 (1): 50–71.
———. 2010. The spoils of nature: Armed civil conflict and rebel access to natural resources. *Journal of Peace Research* 47 (1): 15–28.
McBrewster, J., F. P. Miller, and A. F. Vandome, eds. 2009. *Scottish National Party*. Mauritius: Alpha Publishing.
MDRP (Multi-Country Demobilization and Reintegration Program). 2008. MDRP-Supported Activities in Angola. www.mdrp.org/PDFs/MDRP_ANG_FS_1208.pdf.
Mehlum, H., K. Moene, and R. Torvik. 2006. Institutions and the resource curse. *Economic Journal* 116 (508): 1–20.
Miguel, E., S. Satyanath, and E. Sergenti. 2004. Economic shocks and civil conflict: An instrumental variables approach. *Journal of Political Economy* 112 (4): 725–753.
Moore, M., 1998. Death without taxes: Democracy, state capacity and aid dependence in the Fourth World. In *Towards a democratic developmental state*, ed. G. White and M. Robinson. Oxford, UK: Oxford University Press.
Peceny, M., and M. Durnan. 2006. The FARC's best friend: U.S. antidrug policies and the deepening of Colombia's civil war in the 1990s. *Latin American Politics and Society* 48 (2): 95–97.
Robinson, J. A., R. Torvik, and T. Verdier. 2006. Political foundations of the resource curse. *Journal of Development Economics* 79 (2): 447–468.
Ross, M. L. 2004a. Does tax lead to representation? *British Journal of Political Science* 34:229–249.
———. 2004b. What do we know about natural resources and civil war? *Journal of Peace Research* 41 (3): 337–356.
———. 2005. Booty futures. Unpublished manuscript. www.sscnet.ucla.edu/polisci/faculty/ross/bootyfutures.pdf.
Sachs, J. 2006. *The end of poverty: Economic possibilities for our time*. New York: Penguin Press.

Sachs, J., and A. M. Warner. 2000. Natural resource abundance and economic growth. In *Leading issues in economic development,* ed. G. M. Meier and J. E. Rauch. 7th ed. Oxford, UK: Oxford University Press.

Tilly, C. 1975. *The formation of national states in Western Europe.* Princeton, NJ: Princeton University Press.

Van Duesen, C. 2008. Fiji Pine Limited: A case study of long term privatization and stakeholder conflict. *Online Journal of International Case Analysis* 1 (2): 18.

Varian, H. R. 2006. *Intermediate microeconomics: A modern approach.* 7th ed. New York: W.W. Norton.

Petroleum blues: The political economy of resources and conflict in Chad

John A. Gould and Matthew S. Winters

In July 2003, Chad—a poor and landlocked state—joined the league of oil-exporting nations. Reaching this point required several consortiums of international oil companies; extended analysis and consultation with environmentalists, anthropologists, and activists; the passage of a law detailing how the government could spend oil revenues; the creation of oversight bodies at the national and international levels; and the construction of a 1,070-kilometer pipeline terminating off the port of Kribi, Cameroon.

The World Bank was at the center of this effort. As the gatekeeper for international investment, the Bank hoped to make Chad into a model of responsible resource extraction among poor countries beset by conflict and weak governance. Unfortunately, the Bank's efforts to hold the government accountable for its spending failed in the face of Chad's illiberal governance and entrenched patronage politics, allowing President Idriss Déby and his inner circle to benefit disproportionately from the revenues and sparking a renewal of conflict.[1]

This chapter describes the World Bank's attempt to ensure the equitable use of oil revenues through the creation of new laws and institutions, and analyzes why it went astray. The years from 2000 to 2003, when the oil pipeline was

---

John A. Gould is an associate professor of political science at Colorado College. Matthew S. Winters is an assistant professor in the Department of Political Science at the University of Illinois at Urbana-Champaign. The authors would like to thank Amanda Cronkhite, Nicole Gruttadauria, and Edward Moe for research assistance on this project. They would also like to thank Marielle Debos and their dear friend Karen Ballentine (1961–2010) for their helpful suggestions on earlier drafts of this paper.

[1] As used in this chapter, *liberal* and *illiberal* refer to the accountability of a government and to the civil and political rights of its citizens. An illiberal political environment is one in which executive power is unchecked by other authorities; citizens' political choices are not heeded; and civil and political rights are violated. *Patronage politics* occur when those who control resources (patrons) provide favors or preferential treatment to individuals of lower socioeconomic status (clients), with the expectation that the clients will reciprocate by offering general support and assistance (Scott 1972). Patron-client relationships are particularly likely in countries where state officials control access to jobs and basic services and enjoy significant discretion in allocating them (Chandra 2004, 2009).

constructed, were a period of relative calm in Chad's tumultuous history. Historically, government transitions in Chad have occurred only by force—and at any given moment, there have been at least a handful of rebel groups trying to wrest control of the government from the incumbent. Nevertheless, as the oil pipeline project was realized, President Déby seemed to have relatively firm control of the country, an appearance that was reinforced by his victory in a flawed 2001 presidential election. But beginning with a mutiny of the presidential guard in 2004, Chad reverted to its old ways. Rebel attacks in April 2006 and February 2008 both came close to toppling the Déby regime. Déby was able to hang on in no small part because of new military hardware that had been purchased using oil revenue.

Contrary to the Bank's hopes, natural resource revenue seems to have reignited conflict and led to little development outside the bank accounts of the president's inner circle. Patron control over revenues fueled jealousies and resentments among those who had been part of patronage networks in the past and among others who felt consistently excluded. Oil revenues also allowed the president to take a more militaristic stance on the country's eastern border, adjacent to the conflict-torn Darfur region of Sudan. Threatened from abroad and within, Déby secured the Bank's reluctant approval to take oil funds that had been earmarked for development and use them for government and army salaries instead (Massey and May 2005). In 2008, in the face of additional local conflict and the government's wholesale lack of compliance with the original agreement, the Bank withdrew from the project entirely.

The chapter does not contend that the addition of oil revenues to Chad's volatile political mix is at the root of its conflicts. Chad has a history of significant internal and transboundary strife, both before and since it became an oil-producing state (Pegg 2009; Massey and May 2005). Yet oil has proven to be a catalyst for increased conflict. It enriches those who hold power and provides unprecedented incentive to rebels to seize the state apparatus. To protect his power, President Déby has invested heavily in state capacity. Sadly, it is capacity of the wrong sort: what Déby has "purchased" is the ability to maintain power indefinitely and to spend Chad's new resource wealth as he sees fit.

The chapter is divided into four major sections: (1) a summary of the theoretical relationship between oil and conflict that has informed events in Chad; (2) a review of the history of conflict in Chad; (3) a description of the development, and subsequent dissolution, of Chad's oil-revenue management framework; and (4) a brief conclusion.

OIL AND THE POLITICAL ECONOMY OF CONFLICT

Oil has subtly altered the shape of politics in Chad. First, the regime's distributional choices have altered the stakes of the political game. Second, the political geography of Chad's oil resources has shaped the strategies of Chad's diverse competing actors. Finally, oil revenues have allowed Chad to build new state capacity—although

not necessarily of the sort that one would wish. In combination, these three factors have added a deadly new chapter to Chad's history of illiberal politics.

Distributional choice

The means of distributing oil revenues in a low-capacity, illiberal political environment can affect the stakes of conflict and shape opportunities to build more accountability into governance structures.[2] A simple distributional model can be used to clarify this point: at one end of the spectrum of distributional possibilities,

---

[2] In the context of this chapter, *state capacity* refers to the government's ability to provide essential public goods, such as security, to its inhabitants. A low-capacity state, for example, may not have a monopoly on the use of force within its territory, may fail to provide basic infrastructure and services to its citizens, and may maintain a bureaucracy that puts its own interests above those of its citizens.

the state may allow oil revenues to concentrate in the hands of a narrow group of political elites. Where this happens and oil revenues are significant in size, politics are likely to be characterized by a "winners take all" model in which time horizons tend to be short and resentments among losers may provide incentives for armed conflict. With millions of dollars of oil revenues in play, those who benefit from the revenues will strive to maintain power by any means.

This outcome is bad news for those who wish to consolidate the political expectations of the elite around institutions that promote liberal governance.[3] Oil beneficiaries are likely to feel threatened by domestic political institutions that offer rivals access to political power. They will therefore have an incentive to undermine liberal political accountability in all its forms—accountability to the citizenry through regular, free, and fair elections; accountability to other branches of government in the form of checks, balances, and institutional independence; and accountability to a civil society that is capable of monitoring government activities, resisting government encroachment, and demanding policy changes. Where large resource rents are on the line,[4] incumbent elites are more likely to see the rule of law as an encumbrance and civil society as a nuisance. Resources become a "curse" rather than a blessing (Fish 2005; Easterly 2006). Oil does not cause illiberalism, but it does have the potential to reinforce weak and illiberal institutions where they already exist.

At the other end of the spectrum, the state facilitates broad regional or social distribution of the benefits from oil revenues. Such distribution patterns offer an opportunity to build "win-win" politics that can serve as the basis for a wider social peace between formerly hostile factions. Broad and equitable distribution of resource revenues can also lower the cost of losing the political game and reduce the incentive to attempt to win power through extra-institutional means. In other words, distribution based on broad regional or social formulas might encourage social peace and permit the political behavior of the elite to consolidate around an emerging set of liberal political institutions. Thus, under the right conditions, oil revenues might encourage liberal institution building.

There are two caveats to this argument, however. First, while broad distribution is preferable to "winners take all," it may fail to build the sorts of civic structures characteristic of a strong society. In fact, centralized patronage structures may simply be replaced by more dispersed patronage structures, leading citizens to meet their basic political needs by relying on local power brokers rather than on

---

[3] Institutional consolidation occurs when elite political actors confine their political behavior to a given framework of formal and informal rules, norms, and decision-making procedures. Behavior can consolidate around either liberal or illiberal institutions. Liberal democratic consolidation occurs when democratic rules of the game are, to quote Juan Linz and Alfred Stepan, "the only game in town" (1996, 5).

[4] The term *rent* is used to refer to revenue that is not derived from productive activity but instead accrues simply through the fact of ownership (George 1920).

civic organizations and democratic participation. Local and regional patronage risks reinforcing clan or tribal identities—and, in ethnically divided societies, may also reinforce the tendency for democratic elections to serve as referenda on ethnicity (Collins 2004).[5] Second, regardless of how an illiberal government distributes oil benefits, a government that can raise enough revenue to function without taxation is less dependent on societal cooperation to maintain its rule (Ross 1999). Thus, societies can exert little leverage over illiberal governments with access to natural resource revenues: when a government has ready access to oil rents, demands for self-restraint on the part of the state are backed by less social leverage—and, when asked to engage in self-restraint, governments have fewer reasons to do so (Gould and Sickner 2008).

Introducing oil revenues in illiberal, low-capacity states can thus create pernicious incentives that limit opportunities for both conflict resolution and institution building. The more narrowly concentrated the benefits of oil revenues are, the more intense these effects are likely to be. Yet oil revenues also offer an opportunity for a low-capacity state to build its functional competence and to provide important public goods—including education, infrastructure, justice, basic health care, and internal and external security—that it could not provide before. The major difficulty is that most public goods require soldiers, police, and bureaucrats. Unless these three elements are incorporated into a governance system that is accountable and responsive to citizens, capacity-building efforts can go badly wrong. Soldiers and police can prey on citizenry rather than protecting them, or they may focus on guarding the interests of a narrowly constituted ruling clique or clan. Similarly, bureaucrats in a patronage-based political system can make biased decisions in areas where the economy and the state intersect—most notably by ensuring that favored clients get preferential treatment in bidding, contracts, and the application of laws and regulations.

In sum, more state capacity is arguably desirable, but it must be capacity of the right sort. Good governments provide crucial public goods—and, most importantly, protect rather than prey upon their citizens. In the absence of improved government transparency and accountability, efforts to build state capacity can potentially fuel conflict and a broader sense of injustice. The ideal is to build capacity within an accountable state.

---

[5] Regional and social distribution schemes may also be easily disrupted by rapidly changing demographics—an influx of refugees, for example. In addition, fluctuations in oil prices may threaten politically important distributional agreements: payouts established when international market prices are high are difficult to reduce when prices are low. As will become clear later in the chapter, such risks can be overcome, but only through the creation of stabilization funds—something the World Bank tried to do in Chad. Without the stability provided by such funds, governments may be forced to take on costly foreign debt when prices drop, in order to avoid upsetting the delicate and potentially explosive distributional schemes that have been used to purchase social peace. For more on this issue, see Pegg (2006).

Political geography

Oil can also affect the strategies that rival political actors choose in attempting to resolve their conflicts. Philippe Le Billon has noted that oil is a geographically concentrated "point resource" that is accessible only to capital-intensive modes of extraction (2007). Capturing oil rents thus requires capturing the apparatus of the state (or forming a new state or other entity that has a local monopoly on the use of force in the vicinity of the extractive facilities). Efforts to capture oil rents are therefore likely to take one of two forms: a coup d'état or a war of secession. The fact that oil is a point resource certainly does not prevent other forms of conflict from occurring, but Le Billon has predicted that secessionist movements will be the more likely form of rebellion when the oil sector is located far from the center of power ("distant" resources), in areas that can more easily be "carved out" by insurgent groups. Where the state has firm control over point sources ("proximate" resources), as in Chad, Le Billon has argued that the most likely path to riches is through control of the state itself (Le Billon 2007).

CONFLICT IN CHAD

Chad is a highly fractionalized society made up of many relatively small ethnic groups.[6] Nomadic Toubou, Gorane, and Zaghawa—three groups that are generally practitioners of Islam—live in the Saharan north; a mix of sedentary and nomadic people live in the Sahelian central region; and the Sara, a traditionally Christian group—and the largest ethnic group in Chad—live in the tropical south. When the country gained independence, in 1960, the dominant political party was predominantly made up of Sara.

François Tombalbaye, a Sara, led Chad for its first fifteen years—transforming it, in 1962, into a single-party state and dissolving parliament the following year. In the view of Muslims in the north, the government was both unrepresentative and actively discriminatory; the particular points of contention were allegedly unfair—and violently enforced—taxation practices (e.g., head taxes on cattle that disproportionately affected the nomadic people of the north), exclusion from civil service (despite the Sara's lack of bureaucratic training), and cultural restrictions (e.g., the prohibition of turbans, part of the traditional garb in the north) (Azevedo 1998). In 1966, the country descended into civil war, with the regimes in Libya and Sudan sponsoring various northern rebel groups. Although French intervention restored some semblance of order in 1968, rebel groups continued to fight against the government into the 1970s. They never formed a single coalition, however, and were known for fighting against each other as much as against the Tombalbaye government.

In 1969, Chad granted Conoco, a U.S. company, the right to explore for oil. By 1975, oil deposits had been confirmed in the south of the country (see figure 1).

---

[6] This section draws, generally, on Massey and May (2005), Fearon, Laitin, and Kisara (2006), and ICG (2009).

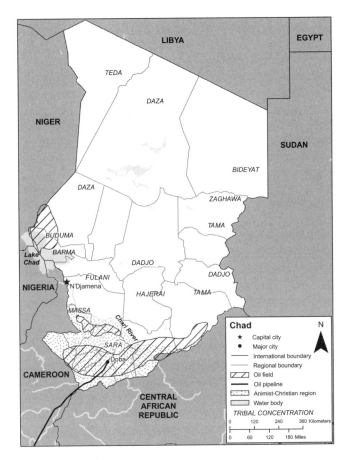

Figure 1. Oil and tribal concentrations in Chad
Source: World Bank (2001).

That same year, General Noël Milarew Odingar, another Sara, led a coup in which Tombalbaye was killed. Although the coup was preceded by growing tensions between Tombalbaye and the military, there were allegations that France provided support for the coup in response to the government's decision to award the oil contract to a U.S. company (ICG 2009). Regardless of its causes, the coup caused enough concern among international investors to delay progress toward oil extraction. Odingar peacefully transferred control to the Supreme Military Council, which elected Félix Malloum, a southern politician and soldier, as president.

In 1978, Malloum brokered a peace with a major rebel group led by Hissen Habré, a northerner living in exile in Sudan. Habré successfully negotiated an equal sharing of government positions between northerners and southerners, but the military government never implemented the agreement. In 1979, ethnic riots pushed the country into anarchy. For the next three years, Chad existed as a patchwork of small, warlord-controlled territories. In 1982, Habré unified the country under his command and gained the support of both France and the United States, which saw him as a counterweight to Libyan influence in the region.

In April 1989, Idriss Déby, the nation's chief military adviser, mounted an unsuccessful coup against Habré, then fled to the Darfur region of Sudan, where he recruited both Chadian and Sudanese members of his Zaghawa ethnic group into a Libyan-funded rebel movement. (Throughout his rule, Habré had been in nearly constant conflict with Libya.) In 1990, Déby's rebels took N'Djamena. The United States was preoccupied with the 1990–1991 Gulf War, and the French refused to assist Habré.[7]

Déby was not afforded much of a honeymoon. He soon faced challenges from two new rebel groups: the National Revival Committee for Peace and Democracy (Comité de Sursaut National pour la Paix et la Démocratie, or CSNPD) and the Armed Forces for a Federal Republic (Forces Armées pour la République Fédérale, or FARF). The CSNPD, which formed in 1992, allegedly wanted to prevent the Déby government from exploiting oil in the Doba Basin (Buijtenhuijs 1998). It also demanded the introduction of federalism in Chad, as a means of keeping oil revenues local. The FARF, which was based in the oil-rich region of Logone, was a breakaway faction of the CSNPD that formed in 1994, when the CSNPD signed a cease-fire with Déby's government. Through violence and negotiation, Déby was able to obtain a settlement with the FARF in 1998; the settlement granted general amnesty for FARF members, the integration of both civilian and military rebels into the Chadian bureaucracy and army, and the legalization of the movement as a political party (Europa Publications 2004; Massey and May 2005).

As Déby moved toward exploitation of the southern oil fields near Doba, he risked alienating his core constituency: the Zaghawa in the northeastern part of the country. The south had long been the more prosperous part of Chad—what the French called *le Tchad utile* (the useful Chad)—and northerners feared that oil exploitation would further consolidate southern economic dominance over the country (Massey and May 2005). As is detailed later in the chapter, once oil extraction began in the early 2000s, this resentment spurred some of the subsequent conflict.

Chad's oil-revenue management framework

In 1988, when Chad was still ruled by Habré, a consortium made up of Exxon, Chevron, and Royal Dutch Shell signed a thirty-year exploration and extraction agreement whose terms have been described as "abusive" because of the limited share of oil profits assigned to Chad (Massey and May 2005, 253). In 1992, the French company Elf Aquitaine replaced Chevron in the consortium.[8] The following

---

[7] Millard Burr and Robert O. Collins (1999) have argued that France was trying to improve its relations with both Libya and Sudan in order to gain access to oil; Mario Joaquim Azevedo (1998) claims that the French were upset because Habré was considering granting oil exploitation rights to an American company.

[8] There have been allegations that French intelligence services supported Déby's 1990 rebellion in exchange for his favoring French commercial interests (ICG 2009); in other words, the involvement of Elf Aquitaine may have been the realization of a quid pro quo.

year, geologists determined that the reserves near Doba were substantial: around 900 million barrels.[9]

The consortium made some progress toward beginning exploitation, but significant capital investments were still required. Because Chad is landlocked, the oil would need to be piped to port by means of a 1,000-kilometer pipeline. In addition to the construction of the pipeline itself, this arrangement would require the construction of an offshore facility and intermediate pumping stations. Moreover, because of the low quality of the oil, the pipeline would need to be heated in order to reduce resistance to flow.

Given these high start-up costs, the consortium—and the Western banks that were underwriting the initial expenditures—sought both protection against government expropriation and promises of noninterference in operations. They also wanted to deflect criticism, from nongovernmental organizations (NGOs), of new natural resource exploitation in Africa (Mallaby 2004). With these goals in mind, the consortium approached the World Bank, requesting that it act as an intermediary. Exxon flatly stated that it would not proceed without World Bank support "to help defray risks and complications" (Runyan 2000, 10).[10]

Consultations between the oil companies, the government, and the World Bank continued under Déby. In line with its core mission, the World Bank was interested in ensuring that the natural resource wealth would be used for poverty alleviation; in fact, the Bank saw the Chadian case as an opportunity to demonstrate that the "resource curse" could be overcome if the appropriate legal framework were in place. The Bank therefore worked to design mechanisms that would require the government to channel oil revenues to antipoverty projects.

As it appeared more likely that the Bank would sign off on the pipeline project, international NGOs—including Amnesty International and the Environmental Defense Fund—became increasingly strident in their opposition. Critics argued that the consortium's community "consultation" did more to market the project among the people affected than to incorporate their needs. Despite Bank measures in 1998 to stiffen environmental safeguards, critics felt they were inadequate. In July of that year, eighty-six NGOs from twenty-eight countries sent an open letter to World Bank president James Wolfensohn, calling on the Bank to suspend its participation. The letter included descriptions of civilian massacres at the hands of Chadian security forces and noted the Chadian government's failure to investigate these incidents. The Bank responded with a nineteen-volume analysis and strategy for managing environmental risks but did not directly respond to the human rights concerns (Hernandez Uriz 2001; Horta and Nguiffo 1998).

During the second half of the 1990s, as the World Bank negotiated with the oil companies, the government of Chad, and international NGOs, Déby won a

---

[9] Note that in terms of global reserves, 900 million barrels is not that much. Worldwide, about a hundred oil fields have estimated reserves of more than 1 billion barrels. Chad's estimated reserves are comparable to those of Australia, Brunei, Colombia, or Equatorial Guinea.
[10] See also Horta and Nguiffo (1998).

1996 presidential vote, and his party dominated a 1997 general election that appeared to have been rigged in its favor (May and Massey 2000). Ngarlejy Yorongar, the Doba-based leader of the Federation, Action for the Republic (Fédération, Action pour la République, or FAR) political party and a critic of the pipeline, spread rumors that the oil consortium had provided Déby with illegal election funding (Massey and May 2005). Summarizing the elections that were held as Chad inched toward beginning oil extraction, one international observer said, "Oil is really what is at stake" (*Africa Research Bulletin* 1997, 12530).

The World Bank formula

In January 1999, after several years of negotiations with the World Bank, the Chadian parliament passed the Petroleum Revenue Management Law 001 (PRML).[11] The new law met the Bank's conditions: (1) it provided a specific spending schedule for direct oil revenues (royalties and dividends), and (2) it created a governance institution, the Petroleum Revenue Oversight and Control Committee (Collège de Contrôle et de Surveillance des Ressources Pétrolières), to oversee this spending.[12] In addition, the International Advisory Group—an entity created and funded by the World Bank, with members appointed by the Bank, in consultation with the governments of Chad and Cameroon—would monitor the project from abroad.

The PRML promised to address many of the aspects of oil extraction that threatened to contribute to conflict in Chad. The law created a broadly distributive framework that was intended to knit together the nation's regions through poverty reduction and equitable distribution of resources. It also included provisions that were designed to reduce vulnerability to the boom-bust cycles that afflict oil-dependent states. Finally, the law was designed to increase state capacity to ensure fairness and transparency. In sum, the PRML was "an unprecedented regulatory arrangement designed to ensure transparency and accountability" (Massey and May 2005, 254). At the same time, however, because the law would dictate overall budget allocations and require the creation of a new governance institution, it could also be viewed as undermining state sovereignty—leading former U.S. ambassador to Chad Donald Norland to grumble about the Bank's "infringement on the independence of a newly independent African country" (*Religion & Ethics Newsweekly* 2002). The pipeline project was thus a test of how far the Bank could push a key clause in its charter, which prohibited interference in the internal affairs of sovereign states.

---

[11] Loi No. 001/PR/99 Portant Gestion des Revenus Pétroliers (Petroleum Revenue Management Law).

[12] Indirect revenues, which were not covered by the agreement, included those from taxation. Ultimately, these were a substantial portion of the overall revenues accruing to the Chadian government.

The distributional framework of the PRML

The World Bank's primary concern was to reduce poverty and to build state capacity to ensure that oil resources were managed wisely and transparently. But the agreement with the Bank, as expressed in the law, also made a lot of sense from the perspective of conflict reduction. The Bank's negotiators sought to ensure that the benefits of oil revenues would be shared socially, regionally, and even across generations; the law also placed precise limitations on how the government could spend direct oil revenues from the project. The Bank requested that by the end of January 2003 the government of Chad develop a mechanism for disbursing the funds.

The distributional framework of the PRML was designed as follows:

- Revenues would gather in a Citibank escrow account in London that the World Bank had the power to freeze.[13] To avoid fostering inflation and to help isolate the national economy from boom-bust cycles in the international price of oil, revenue from this account could be steadily reintroduced into Chad's economy. While this provision was designed to avoid the well-known phenomenon of "Dutch disease" (Pegg 2006),[14] it would also reduce pressure on the government, during a downturn in the oil market, to make the sorts of budget cuts that could lead to distributional conflict.
- After deductions for debt service payments, 10 percent of the revenues would go to the Future Generations Fund, a means of redistributing money from the current generation to later generations that will inherit a Chad drained of oil.
- Of the remaining 90 percent of post-debt-service oil revenues, the PRML allocated 80 percent to priority development sectors—including health, education, rural development, and the environment—to ensure that the revenues would help the population at large rather than Chad's political and economic elite.
- Five percent of the remaining revenues were earmarked to develop the Doba oil-producing region. Doba is a Christian region in a largely Muslim country, and

---

[13] As with escrow accounts in real estate or business transactions, the purpose of such an account is for the commercial bank to hold the money until both parties acknowledge that the terms of the agreement have been met. In this specific case, Citibank was to hold Chad's direct oil revenues until the World Bank certified that Chad was meeting the conditions specified under the PRML, at which point the money would be released to Chad.

[14] *Dutch disease* is a phenomenon in which the discovery of substantial natural resource wealth negatively affects a nation's economy. The discovery often causes sudden appreciation in the value of the nation's currency—which, in turn, decreases the nation's competitiveness in the international commodity markets. This reduces the country's exports of manufactured and agricultural commodities and increases its imports. At the same time, the natural resource sector draws a substantial share of domestic resources such as labor and materials, increasing their cost to other sectors. Moreover, when the initially booming resource sector eventually declines, the non-resource-based sectors may find it difficult to recover. The higher prices also reduce the capacity of nonresource sectors. See Pegg (2006) and Sachs and Warner (1995).

this cinq pour cent fund was implicitly designed to alleviate conflict by reassuring the Christian south that the Muslim north would not expropriate the benefits of the oil revenues.
- The remaining 15 percent could be used completely at the government's discretion.

Efforts to build capacity

In addition to requiring a fair and broad distributional formula, the World Bank sought to help Chad build the capacity to ensure that revenues would be effectively spent. The purpose of the Collège was to oversee governmental spending. Nongovernmental Collège members included one representative each from Chadian NGOs, unions, human rights organizations, and religious groups. State representatives included two parliamentarians, the head of the central bank, the director of the treasury, and a supreme court justice. While state officials technically outnumbered civil society representatives five to four, the institutional diversity of the state appointments appeared to ensure independence from the president.

In January 2000, the World Bank provided a US$17.5 million capacity-building loan that was intended to build budgeting and auditing capacity and to upgrade financial management software. The funds were allotted to both the Collège and to other government ministries. A second capacity-building loan, of US$23.7 million, followed six months later. Two major components of this loan were capacity building for environmental management and the creation of a pilot development fund for the Doba region (World Bank 1999, 2000).

Patronage politics trump institution building

The PRML was an innovative attempt to ensure that oil revenues would help to reverse illiberal trends in Chad and build the state capacity that was needed to govern the country responsibly and fairly. Conflict reduction—through broad distribution of revenues specifically targeted to benefit the poor and the oil-producing region—was an implicit part of this approach. Unfortunately, however, the Bank's efforts failed to overcome Chad's heritage of illiberal politics, patronage, and conflict. Between 2000 and 2006, President Déby reshaped the Bank's broad revenue-distribution scheme to meet his own political needs and systematically undermined the power of the Collège to call him—and his increasingly muscular state apparatus—to account. Instead of creating good governance, social peace, and equitable development, the Bank-sponsored oil pipeline ultimately funded the further consolidation of an authoritarian political system based on centrally controlled patronage.

Patronage was already built firmly into Chad's politics. Déby's government was staffed by a close inner circle of ministers and officials drawn from Déby's kinsmen and allied tribal groups. At the same time, special deals were constructed to maintain the loyalty of groups that might otherwise have felt left out: the prime minister was traditionally a southerner, for example.[15]

Given Chad's illiberal heritage, the Bank had trouble persuading skeptics that its intervention would actually improve things. In 1999, despite the Bank's safeguards, Elf Aquitaine and Royal Dutch Shell withdrew from the consortium— after having been persuaded by international NGOs that the human rights and environmental issues associated with the project made the risk to their reputations too high.[16] After James Wolfensohn, president of the World Bank, personally intervened, Chevron and Petronas, the Malaysian state-owned oil company, stepped in to take the place of Elf Aquitaine and Royal Dutch Shell. Construction of the pipeline from the Doba fields to the port in Cameroon began in 2000.

With a consortium of investors firmly in place, Déby spent one-fifth of a US$25 million investment signing bonus on weaponry, at a time when the country was appealing for international food aid (Massey and May 2005). The purchases were technically legal under the PRML, and Déby was facing a rebellion in the far north, led by the Movement for Democracy and Justice in Chad (Mouvement pour la Démocratie et la Justice au Tchad),[17] but many observers felt that the weapons purchases violated the spirit of the law (Raeburn 2001).

In May 2001, Déby engineered his reelection. During the run-up to the vote, the opposition parties lamented the government's control of the media and of the Independent National Electoral Commission; documented the government's use of intimidation tactics to influence voting; and accused the government of simultaneously excluding eligible voters from the electoral list and adding ghost voters in the pro-Déby north (May and Massey 2003). Déby celebrated his manufactured victory by having all six opposition candidates arrested; Wolfensohn again personally intervened, this time to secure the candidates' release (Massey and May 2005).

A general election held in 2002 was boycotted by many of the opposition parties, allowing pro-Déby forces to take 113 of the 155 seats in the parliament. As a nod to the pipeline region, Déby's government allowed the Doba-based FAR to claim the ten seats that it had won. Déby also appointed a prime minister from the south. These measures helped the pipeline project gain support among former opponents in the south.

The years 2002 and 2003 were a period of relative calm in Chad. Construction proceeded apace on the pipeline, and the government faced fewer armed challenges (ICG 2009). By early 2004, the project seemed to be quite successful: the pipeline, which employed 13,000 people from Chad and Cameroon during construction (IFC n.d.), finished a year ahead of schedule. Oil began flowing to Cameroon in July 2003, and the first tanker filled with Chadian oil left Kribi in October.

---

[15] It is important to note, in this context, that the cinq pour cent fund may not have come into existence without pressure from the FAR.
[16] The withdrawal of Elf Aquitaine led to protests outside of the French embassy in N'Djamena.
[17] Thanks to Marielle Debos for pointing this out.

In 2004, as exports mounted, oil revenues from the London escrow account augmented the budget, and the Collège began to review the government's fiscal performance. Critics, meanwhile, pointed out that the rapid completion of the pipeline had outstripped the Bank's emphasis on capacity building, creating a "two-speed problem" in which oil revenues would accrue to the government before it had developed the institutions to ensure that they would be spent in accordance with the letter and the spirit of the PRML (Pegg 2006; International Advisory Group 2001).

Worse, just as oil revenues began to take on significant proportions, Chad's apparent stability disintegrated. First, Déby further centralized power, undermining the Bank's efforts to build social and institutional checks on Chad's growing state capacity. Déby's particular target was the Bank's formula for broad social and regional distribution of benefits. Second, new patterns of conflict emerged, largely as a result of the Déby regime's growing resource wealth and the resentment it generated.

Déby centralizes power

Part of the two-speed problem may have originated in the reluctance of Déby and his supporters to tolerate an independent monitoring body. Déby began undermining the independence of the Collège even before oil revenues began to return to Chad. As noted earlier, the opposition's 2002 electoral boycott delivered 72 percent of the parliamentary seats to Déby's supporters. In 2003, Déby replaced the southern prime minister with a close relative (a northerner), ensuring firm control over the legislature's choice of two parliamentary appointments to the Collège. Déby also placed his brother-in-law in charge of the central bank, thus securing his influence over the bank's Collège representative. A year later, in violation of the constitution, Déby selected a new head of the supreme court, thereby securing influence over yet another member of the Collège. By 2004, the president had strengthened his sway over the actions of a majority of the members of the Collège. Although the government had already gained apparent majority control, international civil society groups accused it of interfering in the selection of the nongovernmental members of the Collège (Gary and Reisch 2005).

In 2004, the Collège nevertheless delivered a relatively critical summary report, citing "incidents of irregularities in transfers of funds; poor quality of, and long delays in the delivery of goods and services; lack of competitive bidding processes, and cases of overpricing of goods and services" (World Bank 2005b). But the Collège, in addition to being underfunded and understaffed (Gary and Reisch 2005), lacked the legal standing to compel the government to act on its findings.

The erosion of the influence and independence of the Collège was part of the president's larger effort to concentrate and retain power. Déby campaigned for constitutional amendments that would allow him to run for a third term, replace the upper house with a presidentially appointed council, and amend the constitution at will. In 2005, in another flawed process that included the intimidation of journalists and the creation of progovernmental (and hence obedient) NGOs that diluted the voice of legitimate members of civil society, Déby won the referendum (Economist Intelligence Unit 2006; Gary and Reisch 2005).

Meanwhile, a smoothly functioning patronage system was shaping the government's use of the new oil revenue. According to anecdotal evidence collected by various observers, firms with ties to the president received preferential consideration and were engaging in overbilling, contract padding, and other forms of corruption (Gary and Reisch 2005). Such arrangements siphoned resources away from legitimate government activities and made it difficult for the civil service to provide public goods (Economist Intelligence Unit 2006). Déby's political vehicle, the Patriotic Salvation Movement, even created NGOs in order to win lucrative contracts associated with the spending of oil revenue in priority development sectors (Gary and Reisch 2005).

Thus, as the government's fiscal resources grew, state capacity failed to keep pace; this had a devastating effect on the PRML's social and regional distribution scheme because much of the money designated for poverty reduction was instead diverted to politically connected subcontractors. In the south, cinq pour cent funds were slow to disburse because the government had failed to develop a mechanism for their distribution, despite having promised to do so. When the government finally did distribute the funds, through subnational government agencies operating in the Doba area, the money went to a mere seven projects in two cities, and the largest project—a new stadium that absorbed 39 percent of the total fund—had only marginal potential to alleviate poverty. Despite claims of decentralization, Stephen Reyna has reported that the projects undertaken through the cinq pour cent funds originated in the president's office and were awarded to politically connected firms from the north. In the east, meanwhile, development was limited to the construction of an east-west road used primarily for military purposes (Reyna 2007). As part of its Petroleum Sector Management Capacity Building Project, the World Bank had established a pilot social development fund, but it had only a small budget (US$3.5 million) and was ultimately described by the International Advisory Group as "disappointing" (International Advisory Group 2004).

Major conflict returns to chad

Conflict in Chad takes many forms—but, in keeping with Le Billon's prediction, growing oil revenues coincided with an increase in attempted coups and other assaults on the capital. Although the 1999–2003 period was relatively stable by Chad's standards, conflict intensified in May 2004, when Déby's personal guard launched a small-scale military revolt—a prelude to the emergence of a larger rebel movement that would renew pressure on the regime.

The conflict had two origins: first, in discontent about the way in which the Déby regime was spending the oil revenues; second, in Déby's attempt to defuse discontent by becoming newly enmeshed in the conflict in Darfur between rebel groups opposed to the Sudanese government and the government-allied

Janjaweed militia. In 1990, Déby's movement to take power in Chad had originated in Darfur, where his Zaghawa ethnic group has a stronghold.[18] After becoming president, Déby developed an arrangement with Omar al-Bashir, the president of Sudan, in which each refused to support rebel bases in their territories that were arrayed against the other nation.

In 2003, violence intensified in Darfur, and refugees began to spill across the border into Chad. At first, Déby remained uninvolved, even though his Zaghawa kinsmen were the targets of the Sudanese government and the *Janjaweed* militia. Déby even spoke out publicly against his older brother—a strong supporter and a financial backer of two Darfur-based insurgent groups (Marchal 2008).

Members of the Zaghawa group, meanwhile, were allegedly disappointed that Déby's patronage system did not extend beyond his innermost circle of supporters (Marchal 2008). After Zaghawa contingents within Chad's army rebelled in 2005, Déby shifted his stance on Darfur in an attempt to regain the support of his Zaghawa kinsmen (Prunier 2008). In 2005, he concluded a "gentleman's agreement" with the Sudan-based Zaghawa Justice and Equality Movement, allowing the group to attack Sudanese forces in Darfur from bases in Chad. According to some observers, he soon extended this arrangement to the Sudan Liberation Army, another Sudanese insurgent group, and began to use oil revenues to finance military supplies for groups opposed to the Sudanese government. At the same time, the Sudanese government began to actively support Chadian rebels on its territory (Marchal 2008; Sany and Desai 2008).

Meanwhile, Déby intensified his use of patronage in an ultimately failed attempt to consolidate support at home. First, he improved his position in the south by appointing a southern prime minister and thereby restoring the traditional link between southern Chad and that political office (Economist Intelligence Unit 2006). Second, he worked throughout 2005 to integrate rebel soldiers into the national army or otherwise provide them with jobs (Grawert 2008).[19]

Chad's showdown with the World Bank

By the end of 2005, however, Déby's push to resolve the various conflicts—with the Zaghawa, with the south, and with the various armed groups threatening Chad from Sudan—had reached its fiscal limits. Most of Déby's military spending went to improve the capabilities of his intelligence service and his personal guard, leaving little to pay the salaries of the rank-and-file military—which generated resentment and new rounds of defections, like those of May 2004. Significant numbers of former rebels deserted the army and became rebels again, many of them joining the groups that had formed in the wake of the May 2004 coup

---

[18] Zaghawas make up less than 2 percent of the population of Chad—but across the border in Darfur, they make up 10 percent of the population (Grawert 2008; Sany and Desai 2008).

[19] See also Debos (2008).

attempt (Grawert 2008). Déby faced similar pressures from his civil servants, who went on strike to demand that their salaries be paid.

Déby's patronage needs had simply outstripped his growing resources from the oil royalties and dividends (which were covered under the PRML) and from the taxes (which were not). Instead of restructuring government spending to eliminate corruption and waste, the president used the crisis to demand that the Bank release a greater proportion of oil revenues for discretionary use. In late 2005, the Chadian government informed the World Bank of its intention to alter the PRML to gain access to more oil revenue and use it for nondevelopment purposes. Government officials claimed that the PRML had been "a leap into the unknown," creating a budget crisis that had pushed the government's "back to the wall" (White 2006, 7). Given the importance of patronage to Déby's political support, fiscal restraint—that is, reducing the level of patronage transfers—could indeed have threatened his political survival.[20] In an October 2005 meeting with European leaders, Déby called for the immediate release of the resources in the Future Generations Fund.

On December 8, 2005, the World Bank issued a formal response, urging Chad "to take urgent and credible measures to strengthen the safeguards in the management of the country's public finances" and offering to help uncover the sources of the country's fiscal problems and improve its financial management (World Bank 2005a). Undaunted, parliament revised the law unilaterally. In return, the World Bank froze the oil revenues in the escrow account and suspended its other lending to Chad.

As Déby battled the World Bank in negotiations in Paris, he faced an increasingly hostile atmosphere at home. In March 2006, Déby's twin nephews, Timane and Tom Erdimi, took control of a coup that had been undertaken by mutinous army forces led by one of the nephews. Timane was the secretary-general of the presidential administration, and Tom was the former coordinator of the oil project. Both were Bideyet, a Zaghawa subgroup.[21] Allegedly, they resented Déby's efforts to exclude them from decision making and from the benefits of the oil money. After the coup failed, they fled to Darfur and founded the Rally of Democratic Forces (Rassemblement des Forces Democratique). Déby, for his part, accused his nephews of having used their positions to siphon oil revenues for personal use (ICG 2009).

In April 2006, a second coalition of rebel forces, the United Front for Change (Front Uni pour la Changement), marched on N'Djamena from Darfur, demanding a national forum, a transitional government, and new democratic elections. With logistical assistance from the French government, Chadian troops beat back the rebel attack (Mekay 2006). Déby blamed the attack on Sudan and threatened to expel 200,000 Sudanese refugees if the international community did not do more to stop rebel activities (Neuhaus 2006).

---

[20] The International Crisis Group (2009) has argued that growing Sudanese support for rebel groups was an additional factor in Déby's decision to challenge the existing rules.

[21] Thanks to Marielle Debos for pointing out this detail.

Later in April, oil minister Mahmat Hassan Nasser threatened to cut off oil flows in three days unless the World Bank ended the freeze on the escrow account or the oil consortium paid US$125 million directly to the state treasury. Despite four months of tough talk, the World Bank capitulated. At the end of April 2006, Chad and the World Bank reached an agreement that loosened the conditions on the spending of oil revenues; a July 2006 memorandum of understanding institutionalized the changes. Chad agreed to greater oversight of its expenditures and pledged to support the Collège, while the Bank allowed Déby to fundamentally reorient the PRML's revenue distribution framework.

Given the weakness of the Collège, Chad's side of the agreement amounted to little, but the Bank's concessions were devastating to the original spirit of the PRML: Déby fundamentally revised the Bank's social and regional distributional scheme so as to gain the freedom to spend much more of the oil revenues as he saw fit. The first casualty was the cinq pour cent development program for Doba. Remarkably, under the original PRML, the president had already been given the discretion to eliminate this fund. But by explicitly cutting distributions to the Doba region, Déby violated the norm of interregional solidarity that had been established by the Bank. Déby also eliminated the Future Generations Fund. By far the biggest concession, however, was the Bank's agreement to allow oil revenues to be spent in the governance and justice sectors—thereby permitting Déby to strengthen the state security services and increase the number of police and military personnel.

The World Bank appears to have backed down because of pressure from Western donors, most notably France and the United States. Ironically, the threat to the regime's stability ultimately served as a bargaining chip for Chad. Simon Massey and Roy May have noted that American companies had a 65 percent stake in the oil project; they also cite the importance of Chad in the U.S. Global War on Terror, and argue that World Bank president Paul Wolfowitz ultimately "succumbed to U.S. pressure" in reaching a deal with Chad (Massey and May 2005; 2006, 446–447). The International Crisis Group (2009) has also observed that the standoff came at exactly the time when the United States was trying to diversify its energy sources by expanding African oil imports. French pressure on the Bank in favor of its ally was apparently also intense (Massey and May 2006).

Déby followed up on his victory over the Bank by renegotiating Chad's taxation scheme with Chevron and Petronas—charging them a higher rate and pocketing an additional US$450 million in the process. Both companies were acutely aware that the Chinese were willing to take their place should they fail to come to an agreement with the government (*Economist* 2006; *Chad News* 2006).[22]

---

[22] Obsolescing bargain theory, which predicts that outside investors have bargaining leverage before they make their investment and then rapidly lose it afterward, provides insight into how the Bank could have done more to protect against a loss of its leverage over Chad after signing the initial agreement. For additional information on this issue, see Gould and Winters (2007).

In March 2007, giving in to its lack of resources, independence, and capacity, the Collège stopped reporting on budget allocations. The following year, with oil prices on the rise, Chad earned US$1.2 billion on 53 million barrels. Much of this money was devoted to large public works projects, for which members of Déby's inner circle won numerous contracts (ICG 2009).

Winners take all

Earlier in the chapter, it was argued that a winners-take-all model—that is, the concentration of oil benefits in the hands of a narrow group of political elites—would raise the stakes of political competition and weaken opportunities to consolidate elite expectations around more liberal institutions. Chad's record of almost constant conflict since the 2006 memorandum of understanding confirms that greater centralized discretion over oil revenues has done little to build the foundations of a lasting peace. As predicted, the prospects for liberal institutional consolidation are now more remote than ever.

In keeping with Le Billon, Chad's history since oil extraction began demonstrates that attempts to capture state control of point resources are likely to take the form of coups and rebellions. Since the 2006 presidential election, rebellion has served as the primary vehicle for attempted government turnover. In October 2007, Déby attempted a peace deal with several rebel groups during a meeting in Tripoli, but by January of the following year, Chad had launched attacks on rebel bases in Darfur. Later that same month, with Sudanese support, a 4,000-man coalition of forces entered N'Djamena and attacked the presidential palace, and, allegedly, the radio station. Meanwhile, civilians allegedly sacked the oil ministry (ICG 2009; Small Arms Survey 2009). The rebellion came close to succeeding, but a lack of unity, superior firepower in the area of the capital, and some minor support from southern-based government troops and the Sudan-based Justice and Equality Movement (a Zaghawa-dominated group) prevented a government collapse (Prunier 2008; Marchal 2008; ICG 2009). In May 2009, rebels launched yet another major attack from Darfur, but the government, with its increasingly impressive arsenal, was able to easily repel it.

Between 2000 and 2009, Chad's annual military spending rose from about US$14 million to about US$315 million (ICG 2009). The International Crisis Group has described Déby's military as "one of the best-equipped" in sub-Saharan Africa (2009, 13). In February 2010, Chad and Sudan agreed to normalize relations, to stop sheltering rebel groups that were launching attacks against the other nation, and to set up a joint border patrol to improve stability. But in April, Chad had to again repel an insurgency near the Sudanese border. Despite the relative civility of relations between the governments of Chad and Sudan since the February agreement, analysts speculate that the insurgents are unlikely to have attacked without at least tacit Sudanese backing (*BBC News* 2010). Although the agreement may make it more difficult for Darfur-based rebels to attack Chad, whether the détente will last remains to be seen. As new oil fields come on line in Chad, they are likely to serve as continued objects of contention—sources of wealth being fought over by competing factions in Chad's political landscape—rather than as sources of national unity or peacebuilding.

Conclusion

Oil did not cause the conflict in Chad, nor is it the source of the country's illiberal government. Oil did, however, shape both conflict and governance in mutually reinforcing and ultimately destructive ways. In particular, the pattern of armed conflict in Chad demonstrates how oil revenues can build up the military capacity of the state while undermining the consolidation of political institutions. Granted, Chad's competing elites have never fully accepted the legitimacy of either the formal or the informal rules that shape the political game in Chad. Yet oil, for all its promise, appears to have made things worse.

The Bank designed the PRML to ensure that oil revenues would promote equity, peace, and development. The most notable potential beneficiaries of the law were the poor, the oil-producing region, and the future generations that will inherit a Chad without oil. The agreement was to have been policed by the Collège and monitored by the International Advisory Group. But as oil flows provided the government with unprecedented fiscal resources to fight poverty and fund development, Déby's patronage networks asserted increasing control (Pegg 2009). The Bank's broad social and regional distribution scheme deteriorated as wealthy, politically connected clients, mostly from the north, siphoned wealth from public projects and demanded side deals in exchange for political support. With wealth flowing to some but not others, resentment was bound to fuel conflict. As Le Billon (2007) predicts, elites fell out over control of the state apparatus and the associated oil rents, and conflict took the form of elite-led coup attempts and armed marches on the capital.

The Collège proved remarkably courageous at first, but in practice remained ineffectual throughout its short life. While the Bank might have done more to ensure that its capacity-building efforts proceeded at the same pace as the pipeline, the project suffered from a more fundamental flaw: the Bank created the Collège as if Chad already had a semblance of checks and balances on executive power. As Bank negotiators must have known, this was not the case: with the agreement in place, the executive easily leashed, then neutered, his watchdog. A larger budget, more resources, and better training would likely have done little to alter this outcome.

Déby, of course, bears much of the blame for the country's prolonged civil and international conflicts. In particular, in 2005 he disturbed a fragile entente with Sudan by supporting his Zaghawa kinsmen in Sudan in their struggle against Khartoum. One wonders, however, whether he would have had the courage to take this step had he not had access to oil revenues. Déby's state apparatus, which has become increasingly well armed since the fiscal crisis of 2005–2006, may eventually stand a chance of establishing a monopoly of force within its boundaries and defending itself from incursions from the east. Yet it is hard to find solace in a state that has built military capacity without accountability. Not coincidentally, Chad's rise to oil riches has accompanied the consolidation of Déby's personal power and a further erosion of the formal institutions of democracy. Seven years following the first rush of petroleum through the pipeline, power in Chad is more concentrated and exercised more arbitrarily than ever.

From 1999 to 2008, the World Bank made an extensive effort to use oil revenues to reduce conflict, relieve poverty, and establish good governance. In 2008, having accomplished only a fraction of its goals, the Bank ended its efforts to ensure that oil revenues would be funneled toward reducing poverty in Chad, giving up its requirements that Chad adhere to a specific spending schedule, its support for the Collège, and its control over an off-shore escrow account into which Chad's direct oil revenues were flowing. The Bank left the remainder of its Chad portfolio intact: as of August 2010, seven World Bank projects continue to operate in Chad, although only one new project has been approved since 2007 (World Bank n.d.).

The intervention of the World Bank has arguably done Chad's people irreparable harm. In 2000 Chad was an illiberal, conflict-ridden country without oil; today it is an illiberal, conflict-ridden country *with* oil. The main things that have changed are that the benefits of retaining power are vastly higher, and that the government now has the money to buy arms. While revenues may eventually be used to broker peace agreements, the prospects for building democratic institutions have never been lower.

The authors are sympathetic to the argument that Chad needs oil revenues to enhance the capacity of the state; the Bank's original intent, which was to use its leverage to direct oil revenues toward education and development, was compelling. Nor do the authors deny that Chad's people deserve a government that can protect its citizens from the depredations of internal rebellion and foreign attack. But greater capacity is a dual-edged sword. In Chad, the Bank inadvertently helped create capacity without restraint. By facilitating the extraction of oil, the Bank bears some responsibility for providing a brutal dictatorship with the revenue it needs to retain its repressive hold on power. Ultimately, the World Bank placed too much faith in its ability to create capacity for good governance in an illiberal political setting.

Could things have turned out differently? That is doubtful. The Bank might have done more to front-load capacity-building projects into its initial agreement. It might even have demanded provisions in the PRML under which revenues would have been withheld, pending improvement in interregional equity, human rights, progress toward resolving inter- and intraclan conflicts, and the creation of effective checks and balances on executive power. But the Bank's charter prohibits such heavy intervention in the domestic politics of recipient countries, and it is unlikely that any African leader would have accepted such conditions. Sadly, the authors believe that the Bank did just about as well as it is likely ever to do in such a context. For this reason, the Bank would be well-advised to exercise much greater caution in any future efforts to develop oil resources in low-capacity, illiberal countries.

REFERENCES

Africa Research Bulletin: Political, Social and Cultural Series. 1997. Chad: Elections at last. 34 (1): 12530–12531. Quoted in S. Massey and R. May, Dallas to Doba: Oil and Chad, external controls and internal politics, *Journal of Contemporary African Studies* 23 (2): 256.

Azevedo, M. J. 1998. *Roots of violence: A history of the war in Chad.* Amsterdam: Gordon and Breach.

BBC News. 2010. "Hundred killed" in Chad clashes. April 30. http://news.bbc.co.uk/2/hi/8653357.stm.

Buijtenhuijs, R. 1998. Chad in the age of the warlords. In *History of Central Africa: The contemporary years since 1960*, ed. D. Birmingham and P. M. Martin. London: Longman.

Burr, M., and R. O. Collins. 1999. *Africa's Thirty Years War: Libya, Chad, and the Sudan, 1963–1993.* Boulder, CO: Westview Press.

Chad News. 2006. Chad, oil companies resolve tax dispute. October 11. www.africanoiljournal.com/10-11-2006%20chad%20chevron%20and%20petronas%20resolve%20tax%20dispute.htm.

Chandra, K. 2004. *Why ethnic parties succeed: Patronage and ethnic headcounts in India.* Cambridge, UK: Cambridge University Press.

———. 2009. Why voters in patronage democracies split their tickets: Strategic voting for ethnic parties. *Electoral Studies* 28 (1): 21–32.

Collins, K. 2004. The logic of clan politics: Evidence from the Central Asian trajectories. *World Politics* 56 (2): 224–261.

Debos, M. 2008. Fluid loyalties in a regional crisis: Chadian "ex-liberators" in the Central African Republic. *African Affairs* 107 (427): 225–241.

Easterly, W. 2006. *White man's burden: Why the West's efforts to aid the rest have done so much ill and so little good.* New York: Penguin Press.

Economist. 2006. Pump priming. 31 August.

Economist Intelligence Unit. 2006. Country Report Chad. December.

Europa Publications. 2004. Chad. In *The Europa world year book 2004.* Vol. 1. London.

Fearon, J., D. Laitin, and K. Kisara. 2006. Random narratives. Chad. Ethnicity, Insurgency, and Civil War project. Department of Political Science. Stanford University. www.stanford.edu/group/ethnic/Random%20Narratives/ChadRN2.6.pdf.

Fish, M. S. 2005. *Democracy derailed in Russia: The failure of open politics.* Cambridge, UK: Cambridge University Press.

Gary, I., and N. Reisch. 2005. *Chad's oil: Miracle or mirage?* Washington, D.C.: Catholic Relief Services / Bank Information Center.

George, H. 1920. *Progress and poverty.* 25th Anniversary Edition. New York: Doubleday / Page and Company.

Gould, J. A., and C. Sickner. 2008. Making market democracies? The contingent loyalties of post-privatization elites in Azerbaijan, Georgia and Serbia. *Review of International Political Economy* 15 (5): 740–768.

Gould, J. A., and M. Winters. 2007. An obsolescing bargain in Chad: Explaining shifts in leverage between the government and the World Bank. *Business and Politics* 9 (2): 1–34.

Grawert, E. 2008. Cross-border dynamics of violent conflict: The case of Sudan and Chad. *Journal of Asian and African Studies* 43 (6): 595–614.

Hernández Uriz, G. 2001. To lend or not to lend: Oil, human rights, and the World Bank's internal contradictions. *Harvard Human Rights Journal* 14: 197–231.

Horta, K., and S. Nguiffo. 1998. Open letter to Mr. James D. Wolfensohn, president of the World Bank, from 86 NGOs in 28 countries, concerning the Chad/Cameroon oil & pipeline project. Washington, D.C.: Africa Action.

ICG (International Crisis Group). 2009. Chad: Escaping from the oil trap. *Africa Briefing* 65 (26 August). www.crisisgroup.org/en/regions/africa/central-africa/chad/B065-chad-escaping-from-the-oil-trap.aspx.

IFC (International Finance Corporation). n.d. The International Finance Corporation (IFC) played a leading role in facilitating the oil pipeline between Chad and Cameroon. www.ifc.org/ifcext/africa.nsf/AttachmentsByTitle/ChadCamProjectOverview/$FILE/ChadCamProjectOverview.pdf.

International Advisory Group. 2001. Report of mission to Cameroon and Chad, November 14–25, 2001. December 21. www.gic-iag.org/doc/IAGReportofMission14-25Nov.pdf.

———. 2004. Report of mission 8 to Chad, October 10–26, 2004. www.gic-iag.org/doc/IAG_Mission_8_Chad_en.pdf. Quoted in I. Gary and N. Reisch, *Chad's oil: Miracle or mirage?* (Washington, D.C.: Catholic Relief Services / Bank Information Center, 2005), 78.

Le Billon, P. 2007. Geographies of war: Perspectives on "resource wars." *Geography Compass* 1 (2): 163–182.

Linz, J., and A. Stepan. 1996. *Problems of democratic transition and consolidation: Southern Europe, South America, and post-communist Europe.* Baltimore, MD: Johns Hopkins University Press.

Mallaby, S. 2004. *The world's banker: A story of failed states, financial crises, and the wealth and poverty of nations.* New York: Penguin Books.

Marchal, R. 2008. The roots of the Darfur conflict and the Chadian civil war. *Public Culture* 20 (3): 429–436.

Massey, S., and R. May. 2005. Dallas to Doba: Oil and Chad, external controls and internal politics. *Journal of Contemporary African Studies* 23 (2): 253–276.

———. 2006. Commentary: The crisis in Chad. *African Affairs* 105:443–449.

May, R., and S. Massey. 2000. Two steps forward, one step back: Chad's protracted "transition to democracy." *Journal of Contemporary African Studies* 18 (1): 108–132.

———. 2003. Presidential and legislative elections in Chad, 2001–2002. *Electoral Studies* 22 (4): 765–772.

Mekay, E. 2006. Chad gets World Bank over a barrel. Inter Press Service. May 4.

Neuhaus, L. 2006. Chad president backs off threat to expel Darfur refugees, extends deadline on oil. Associated Press. April 18.

Pegg, S. 2006. Can policy intervention beat the resource curse? *African Affairs* 105 (14): 1–25.

———. 2009. Chronicle of a death foretold: The collapse of the Chad-Cameroon pipeline project. *African Affairs* 108 (431): 311–320.

Prunier, G. 2008. Chad: Caught in the Darfur crossfire. *Le Monde diplomatique.* English edition. http://mondediplo.com/2008/03/05chad.

Raeburn, P. 2001. Commentary: This clean oil project is tainted already. *Business Week,* April 9.

Religion & Ethics Newsweekly. 2002. The Chad pipeline. June 28. www.pbs.org/wnet/religionandethics/week543/cover.html. Quoted in S. Massey and R. May, Dallas to

Doba: Oil and Chad, external controls and internal politics, *Journal of Contemporary African Studies* 23 (2): 256.

Reyna, S. P. 2007. The traveling model that would not travel: Oil, empire, and patrimonialism in contemporary Chad. *Social Analysis* 51 (3): 88–89.

Ross, M. L. 1999. The political economy of the resource curse. *World Politics* 51 (2): 297–322.

Runyan, C. 2000. Chad/Cameroon oil pipeline moving forward. *World Watch* 13 (4): 10.

Sachs, J., and A. Warner. 1995. Natural resource abundance and economic growth. Working Paper 5398. Cambridge, MA: National Bureau of Economic Research.

Sany, J., and S. Desai. 2008. Transnational ethnic groups and conflict: The Zaghawa in Chad and Sudan. *Conflict Trends* 10 (2): 25–29.

Scott, J. C. 1972. The erosion of political-client bonds and social change in rural Southeast Asia. *Journal of Asian Studies* 32 (1): 5–37.

Small Arms Survey. 2009. Echo effects: Chadian instability and the Darfur conflict. *Sudan Issue Brief* 9 (February): 1–12.

White, D. 2006. Chad-Cameroon pipeline: A leap into the unknown? *Financial Times*, March 1.

World Bank. 1999. *Project appraisal document for management of the petroleum economy project*. Project Document No. 19427. Washington, D.C.: World Bank Group.

———. 2000. *Project appraisal document for petroleum sector management capacity building project*. Project Document No. 19342. Washington, D.C.: World Bank Group.

———. 2001. Oil and tribal concentrations in Chad. World Bank Map 31455. web.worldbank.org/WBSITE/EXTERNAL/EXTINSPECTIONPANEL/0,,contentMDK:20228587~pagePK:64129751~piPK:64128378~theSitePK:380794,00.html.

———. 2005a. World Bank statement on Chad. Press release No. 2006/194/AFR. http://web.worldbank.org/WBSITE/EXTERNAL/NEWS/0,,contentMDK:20749536~menuPK:34463~pagePK:34370~piPK:34424~theSitePK:4607,00.html.

———. 2005b. World Bank reaction to Chad-Cameroon pipeline oversight committee's report on mission to sites of projects financed by oil revenues. Press release No. 2006/038/AFR. http://web.worldbank.org/WBSITE/EXTERNAL/NEWS/0,,contentMDK:20597333~menuPK:34463~pagePK:34370~piPK:34424~theSitePK:4607,00.html.

———. n.d. Chad. http://web.worldbank.org/WBSITE/EXTERNAL/COUNTRIES/AFRICAEXT/CHADEXTN/0,,menuPK:349881~pagePK:141159~piPK:141110~theSitePK:349862,00.html.

Leveraging high-value natural resources to restore the rule of law: The role of the Liberia Forest Initiative in Liberia's transition to stability

Stephanie L. Altman, Sandra S. Nichols, and John T. Woods

On January 16, 2006, Liberia inaugurated the first democratically elected female president in Africa, Ellen Johnson Sirleaf. The historical significance was immeasurable. After fourteen years of civil war—fueled, in large part, by "conflict timber"—Liberia ushered in a new era, with a new government that recognized the role that natural resources had played in the war.[1] As one of her first orders of business, President Johnson Sirleaf restored lawful government control of the forest sector and made clear her intention to govern it transparently, equitably, and sustainably. To put an end to years of illegal distribution of forest resources, the president issued Executive Order No. 1—which, among other measures, declared all forest concessions null and void and assigned the Forestry Development Authority (FDA), in collaboration with the Liberia Forest Initiative (LFI), the task of overseeing forest sector reform (GOL 2006b).[2] The executive order demonstrated the president's commitment to reining in the manifold abuses of the Taylor regime and creating a new system for managing the forest sector (LFI 2004a).

This chapter focuses on the role of the LFI in the reform of Liberia's forest sector. A partnership made up of U.S. government agencies, international development agencies, and international and Liberian nongovernmental organizations (NGOs), the LFI was created to support the government of Liberia in establishing an approach to forest management that would address international demand for reforms and ensure the appropriate use and management of forest resources; the

---

Stephanie L. Altman is an attorney advisor at the National Oceanic and Atmospheric Administration's Office of General Counsel for International Law. She formerly worked in Liberia as a legal advisor to the Ministry of Agriculture and as an envoy to the European Commission on Forestry Law Enforcement, Governance and Trade. Sandra S. Nichols is a senior attorney at the Environmental Law Institute. John T. Woods is the former managing director of the Forestry Development Authority in Liberia.

[1] For further discussion of timber in Liberia, see Michael D. Beevers, "Forest Resources and Peacebuilding: Preliminary Lessons from Liberia and Sierra Leone," in this volume.

[2] The FDA is a public authority that is responsible, among other things, for managing and conserving forest resources and ensuring that forest resources are devoted to productive use (GOL 1976).

338 High-value natural resources and post-conflict peacebuilding

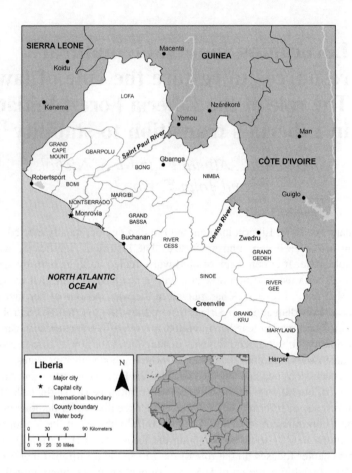

LFI was also tasked with developing, in partnership with the government, a revised legal framework for forest management.

In particular, the chapter explores the LFI's contributions to the redistribution of resources and power and to the restoration of peace and security. The emphasis is on the period after the violent conflict, when Liberia faced a choice: either to continue the lawless and iniquitous abuse of the forest sector or to establish equity, good governance, and the rule of law. Under international pressure and with support from the LFI, Liberia has focused on fundamental reforms that are designed to avert conflict and support broader peacebuilding goals.

The chapter is divided into five parts: (1) a description of the background against which the reforms were undertaken; (2) a history of the National Forestry Reform Law and its accompanying regulations, with particular emphasis on the role of the LFI; (3) a discussion of efforts to strengthen governance and prevent a return to conflict; (4) a review of lessons learned; and (5) a brief conclusion.

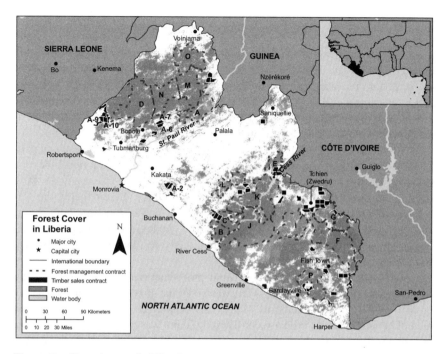

Figure 1. Forest cover in Liberia
Source: Adapted by Sean Griffin from data in Christie et al. (2007).

BACKGROUND

A West African coastal nation, Liberia is blanketed by rich tropical forests that support its economy, ecology, and society (see figure 1) (*FAO Newsroom* 2006). The country contains more than 40 percent of the remaining Upper Guinean Forest, a particularly rich ecosystem (GOL 2004; World Bank 2006). Over centuries, the sixteen different ethnic groups that inhabit Liberia's forests have developed social traditions and religious beliefs founded on interaction with the natural world; an estimated 40 percent of Liberians adhere to traditional, forest-based religions and culture (Olukoju 2006). Forests are also important sources of nontimber products such as meat, fish, medicines, and resins, which are used both for livelihoods and for subsistence (Peal 2000; *VoANews.com* 2009).

In 1821, under the auspices of the American Colonization Society, freed American slaves began to settle along the coast of what would become Liberia, gradually gaining dominance over indigenous communities (U.S. Department of State n.d.). The territory, which was initially a U.S. commonwealth, declared independence in 1847. The freed slaves and their descendants, commonly known as Americo-Liberians, maintained control over the wealth and power of the nation until 1980, when President William R. Tolbert's proposal to raise the price of rice was met with violent opposition. Despite Tolbert's claim that the price increase was meant to encourage consumption of local rice and to reduce dependence on imported rice, riots ensued, leaving the Tolbert administration vulnerable to a coup. In the wake of the riots, Samuel Doe, an ethnic Krahn, took over the country. By the late 1980s, economic collapse and Doe's arbitrary rule had set the stage for civil war. In 1989, the National Patriotic Front of Liberia, a militia under the control of the warlord Charles Taylor, overran much of the countryside. Taylor had two goals: first, to establish himself as Liberia's leader; second, to reestablish Americo-Liberians as the ruling political faction.

While the exploitation of natural resources was not the express cause of Liberia's civil war, it was one of the many ways in which the Americo-Liberians had oppressed the indigenous majority. Most critically, natural resources were instrumental in prolonging the conflict (Fairhead 2001). Taylor fueled the war with conflict resources, including timber, diamonds, and rubber,[3] and both Taylor and Doe used timber concessions to garner power, money, and patronage (Blundell 2008).[4] In some cases, arms were traded directly for logging rights (Woods, Blundell, and Simpson 2008).

As the war continued, timber contracting procedures fell by the wayside. During the six years (1997–2003) that the FDA was under the direction of Charles Taylor's brother, Bob Taylor, the authority largely abandoned accounting procedures and recordkeeping. Without proper recordkeeping, there was no way to calculate fees or to control the use of the fees that were collected.[5] All factions traded timber for arms and financial support (UNEP 2004): from 1990 to 1994, for example, US$53 million in timber was exported from areas that were controlled by armed factions (Greenpeace 2007). Contractors built roads at their convenience, regardless of ecological consequences, and employed armed militias against both civil society groups and local populations. A warlord economy developed that was outside the legal system and beyond the reach of regulatory institutions (UNEP 2004).

The war left 250,000 dead, reduced Liberia's gross domestic product by 50 percent, and decimated critical industries such as manufacturing, iron mining, rice, and rubber (UNEP 2004).[6] Uncontrolled extraction of high-value natural resources—timber, diamonds, and gold—filled this economic void. As the economy

---

[3] Taylor's use of conflict resources led some to suggest that his principal motivation was to consolidate power over the resources themselves (Reno 1998).

[4] For example, Oriental Timber Corporation, an Indonesian-owned company registered in Liberia, deposited millions of dollars into Taylor's personal bank account in exchange for tax credits. Similarly, Doe traded the largest timber concession in West Africa to obtain military training for an antiterrorist unit (Blundell 2008).

[5] From 2000 to 2002, forestry was the biggest industry in Liberia, representing 50 to 60 percent of export earnings and 26 percent of gross domestic product, so recordkeeping failures had significant implications. A 2005 study by the Forest Concession Review Committee showed that by the end of the war, concessionaires owed the FDA US$64 million (FCRC 2005a).

[6] Before the war, iron mining was responsible for more than 50 percent of Liberia's export earnings (UNEP 2004).

contracted sharply, the unregulated and unrestrained use of Liberia's forests transformed timber into a leading economic sector. By the end of Taylor's regime, timber represented over 50 percent of Liberia's income (McAlpine, O'Donohue, and Pierson 2006; *FAO Newsroom* 2006). Taylor used the timber revenues to buy weapons, draining the very lifeblood of the nation to support the protracted and devastating conflict (Price 2003).

As chaos and destruction spread from Liberia to neighboring West African countries, the international community began to intervene. In March 2001, the UN Security Council (UNSC) issued a resolution that (1) prohibited member nations from conducting weapons training in Liberia and from selling arms to Liberia, (2) barred member nations from importing rough diamonds from Liberia, and (3) created a panel of experts to investigate the links between natural resource exploitation and the financing of warfare in the region, particularly in Guinea and Sierra Leone (UNSC 2001b).[7] The reports of the panel of experts revealed the details of President Taylor's control of timber concessions and provided documentation that timber profits were being used to buy arms (UNSC 2001a, 2002).

In August 2001, Taylor responded to international pressure by issuing a plan to use timber revenue to foster development projects in counties that had significant sources of timber (UNSC 2002).[8] But Liberian NGOs were not convinced that Taylor's initiative was credible; nor did they believe that it was sufficient to address the enormity of the problem. They began lobbying other elements of Liberian civil society, as well as the international community, to expose what they knew of Taylor's true intentions—namely, to continue to use timber revenues to support the war (Rochow 2009). On May 6, 2003, in recognition of the role that timber revenue played in the acquisition of arms for Taylor's government, the UNSC issued Resolution 1478, which prohibited member states from importing round logs originating in Liberia (UNSC 2003a).[9] Fighting continued until June 2003; in August 2003, international pressure forced Taylor to step down.

By the end of the war, Liberia's infrastructure had largely been destroyed, and most of the population lacked access to electricity, to running water, and to basic goods and services. Under these conditions, forests were more essential than ever for meeting subsistence needs (UNEP 2004). Between 1990 and 2005, pillaging—for both commercial and subsistence needs—led to the loss of approximately 33,000 hectares of forest per year. Nevertheless, as of 2005, approximately 4.5 million hectares of Liberian forest remained (Bayol 2009).

---

[7] The panel of experts found that the value of round logs exported in the first six months of 2001 was between US$7 million and US$18 million, but only US$4.6 million was officially reported and taxed.

[8] In January 2002, Taylor further agreed to establish a system of protected areas, consisting of 30 percent of Liberia's remaining forest areas, but he did not follow through with this plan.

[9] In 2003, sanctions were imposed for a provisional period of ten months; they were later renewed, and were finally lifted in June 2006.

PLANNING, DESIGNING, AND IMPLEMENTING REFORM

In June 2003, at peace talks in Accra, Ghana, the warring Liberian factions signed the Comprehensive Peace Agreement, which formally ended hostilities and established the two-year National Transitional Government of Liberia (UNMIL n.d).[10] The UN Mission in Liberia (UNMIL) was installed in September 2003; its mandate was to provide humanitarian assistance, to stabilize and improve security, and to prepare the country to hold elections in 2005. Subsequently, as the need for such assistance became clear, the UN assigned UNMIL an additional responsibility: to help establish proper administration of natural resources (UNSC 2003b).

Though peace agreement did not address natural resources, the transitional government, the international community, and Liberian NGOs viewed natural resource reforms as key to the transition to peace. So critical was timber reform that in 2004, while UNMIL was still attempting to establish security, the U.S. Department of State convened a group of representatives from U.S. governmental agencies, international development agencies, and international and Liberian NGOs to develop a forest sector reform process (McAlpine, O'Donohue, and Pierson 2006). This group became known as the LFI.[11]

The LFI partners recognized that to respond to the increasing demands on forest resources, Liberia would need to ensure that those resources were managed sustainably from generation to generation (McAlpine, O'Donohue, and Pierson 2006).

The LFI was designed to facilitate collaboration, information sharing, and support for peacebuilding. The initiative coordinated the contributions of donors and partners to achieve shared aims but retained a flexible structure; this approach averted wasteful overlap of effort while simultaneously allowing donors and partners to focus their work on those aspects of the forestry sector that were most important to them. Finally, the existence of the LFI created a sense of critical mass that spurred stakeholder involvement (Lowe 2009).

Even at the earliest stages of the LFI's development, a tension emerged between the goal of lifting sanctions (which would allow the government to export timber and generate revenue) and the goal of achieving broad, sustainable reform

---

[10] The National Transitional Government was chaired by Gyude Bryant, a Liberian politician, and was in power from October 2003 through January 2006, when President Ellen Johnson Sirleaf took office.

[11] Ultimately, the LFI was made up of fifteen international partners: the Center for International Forestry Research, Conservation International, the Environmental Law Institute, the European Commission, Flora and Fauna International, the UN Food and Agriculture Organization, Forest Partners International, the International Monetary Fund, the International Union for Conservation of Nature, the UN Environment Programme, the U.S. Agency for International Development, the U.S. Department of State, the U.S. Forest Service, the World Agroforestry Centre, and the World Bank. See www.fao.org/forestry/site/lfi.

in the forestry sector (McAlpine, O'Donohue, and Pierson 2006). Nevertheless, the LFI was able to agree on four priorities (commercial, conservation, community—the "three Cs"—and financial management and transparency) and on four framework issues (governance and rule of law, institutional capacity, information management, and security) (LFI 2004a).

The LFI plan of action

In 2004, Conservation International, the Environmental Law Institute (ELI), the European Commission, the Food and Agriculture Organization, the International Union for Conservation of Nature, the U.S. Forest Service (USFS), the U.S. Department of State, and the World Bank carried out two field missions in Liberia to prepare an action plan for coordinating the work of the LFI partners (LFI 2004a, 2004b).[12] The plan laid out actions designed to address the four priorities and the four framework issues; it also identified five essential areas for the LFI to focus on within one year (LFI 2004b):

- Financial and institutional reform of the FDA.
- Transparent, substantive review of all forest concessions.
- Control of forest resources.
- The development of a training plan for FDA staff.
- Enforcement of the rule of law in protected areas.[13]

Assessments: FDA management, legislative structure, and existing concessions

As the first step in the implementation of the action plan, the LFI undertook a series of assessments. To reestablish control of forest resources as soon as possible, the LFI assigned priority to (1) evaluating the institutional and financial management of the FDA and (2) reviewing the pre-2003 forest management system. Two parallel evaluations of the FDA were conducted: one by the European Commission and another by the U.S. Treasury Department, working in collaboration with the USFS and the World Bank. These assessments found critical gaps in the accounting process for invoicing logging, which had prevented the FDA accounting division from verifying the fees charged for exported products. Lack

---

[12] To create a more collaborative environment and to prevent the rivalries among agencies and donor nations that had occurred in other post-conflict settings (IFRC 2005), the partners synchronized their missions to Liberia (Lowe 2009). Open and continuing dialogue—through regular in-person meetings and video conferences—further facilitated coordination (McAlpine, O'Donohue, and Pierson 2006).

[13] During the missions, the LFI partners decided to exclude security from the action plan because they determined that it was largely an external factor and outside of their control (LFI 2004a).

of verification, in turn, had enabled companies to evade both taxes and fees: by misrepresenting their production rates, they were able to export larger quantities of wood than they were reporting to the government. A subsequent audit of the FDA accounting division revealed that the government had grossly mismanaged timber revenues.

The LFI's assessment of the legislative structure for the timber sector, which was designed to determine whether Liberia had the basic legal tools for effective forest management, showed that the previous abuses could not be blamed on an antiquated legal system. During the 1970s and 1980s, the FDA had succeeded, under the existing legislation, in managing timber concessions so as to contribute to government revenues. The assessment also revealed that the existing legislation addressed conservation and community objectives.[14]

The most critical assessment was a comprehensive review of the seventy existing timber concessions. Although the FDA had conducted two previous reviews after UN sanctions had been imposed, neither had been accepted by Liberian NGOs or by the general public (Rochow 2008), and the NGOs had continued to insist that a comprehensive review was essential. In July 2004, the transitional government established the Forest Concession Review Committee to conduct a third review; the committee was made up of Liberian government officials, representatives of civil society groups, UNMIL staff, and LFI partners (Rochow 2009).[15]

The review committee established a three-step process for evaluating the concession claims and the companies that held them. The approach was designed to provide transparency, public notice, and opportunity to comment, as well as evidence that each company had been operating legally (Rochow 2009). For each concession, the review committee determined whether the firm met the minimum legal requirements to operate under a timber license and assessed the history of the company's operations (FCRC 2005b). It then decided which concessions were valid and could be allowed to proceed, and which had to be cancelled. To meet the minimum legal requirements, (1) a firm had to be a bona fide business entity; (2) there could be no prior contract rights to the concession (that is, no overlapping claims to harvest in the same area); (3) the appropriate parties had to have signed a valid contract under Liberian law; and (4) all documents had to have been submitted to the committee under oath.

---

[14] For example, the 1953 Act for the Conservation of the Forests of Liberia had provided for the creation of communal forests and for native authority over forest reserves, and the forest-related provisions of both the 1956 Liberia Code of Law, and of the 1976 law that had established the FDA, provided a basis for conservation, management, and consideration of community benefits and needs (McAlpine, O'Donohue, and Pierson 2006).

[15] The review committee was supported by a technical secretariat that paired Liberian technical and legal experts with international counterparts. The combination of Liberian and international experts on the secretariat was key to the success of the review committee.

After a thorough review, not one company met all four criteria (Blundell 2008), and only one-third of the firms met the first one—operating as a legitimate business entity.[16] When the review committee investigated the companies' histories, they found that overharvesting was rampant and that twelve of the companies had openly participated in the conflict, traded timber for arms, or aided and abetted civil instability (Woods, Blundell, and Simpson 2008).[17] Finally, the review committee discovered that the government, in its eagerness to reap the benefits of granting concessions, had given different companies the right to harvest the same trees: although the total amount of forest in Liberia is less than 4.5 million hectares, approximately 10 million hectares had been allocated to concessionaires (Woods 2007). In May 2005, the review committee concluded that all existing timber concessions should be declared null and void (Blundell 2009). However, to the disappointment of many Liberians and international partners—including those involved with the LFI and those working on related issues outside of the LFI—there was no formal disbarment process or attempt to prosecute companies that were suspected of having purchased guns with revenues from commercial timber.

Design and enactment of the reforms

Following the assessment stage and in light of the findings of the concession review, the Forest Concession Review Committee designed a set of reforms intended to improve transparency in financial management, introduce democratic decision making into contracting procedures, and ensure the traceability of forest resources. In a May 2005 report, the committee recommended that the transitional government take a series of actions: First, the committee recommended that no further concessions be awarded until adequate reforms were implemented.[18] Second, to ensure that reforms were undertaken, the committee recommended the establishment of a monitoring committee. Third, the committee recommended the enactment of legislation that would address the gaps that had been identified in the concession review (FCRC 2005a; McAlpine, O'Donohue, and Pierson 2006). Finally, the committee recommended that the transitional government, through an executive order, endorse the committee's recommendations (FCRC 2005a).

---

[16] To establish that it was a legitimate business entity, a company had to produce articles of incorporation or a business license.

[17] These companies were BIN Liberia Inc., Forestry and Agricultural Products Corporation, Inland Logging Corporation, Jasus Liberian Logging Corporation, Liberia Forest Development Corporation, Lofa Logging Company, Maryland Wood Processing Industry, Mohammed Group of Companies, Oriental Timber Corporation, Royal Timber Corporation, Togba Timber Corporation, and United Logging Corporation.

[18] Specifically, the review committee recommended that the reform of management practices include the following components: land use planning, allocation of future concessions by means of competitive bidding, reform of concession contracts, reform of forest sector revenue collection, and efforts to strengthen public participation and the rule of law.

The transitional government did not take action on any of these recommendations, but the LFI pressed ahead with proposed management reforms by developing the *FDA Reform Manual*, which provides technical guidance on commercial forestry in Liberia (McAlpine, O'Donohue, and Pierson 2006). Subsequently, the LFI legal team, with legal drafting led by the Environmental Law Institute (ELI), began preparing to implement the changes that had been recommended by the review committee by developing legislative reforms that focused on four areas:[19]

- *Incorporating sound forestry and environmental principles.* Liberia's existing laws required concessionaires to manage their concessions according to international principles of forest and environmental management, but the current legislative framework, forest management plans, or concession contracts did not reflect these principles (ELI 2005). The LFI legal team worked closely with foresters from the FDA and the USFS to incorporate updated principles and practices into forestry regulations, forest management plans, and concession contracts.
- *Strengthening financial transparency and improving community access to the benefits of forest resources.* In the realm of financial transparency, there were two principal issues: the government was underreporting the payments it was receiving from timber companies, and timber companies were overreporting their payments to the government; the result was significant leakage of forest fees. To make matters worse, companies were assigning fraudulent classifications to trees in order to avoid paying the appropriate fees. In the realm of benefits, it was unclear whether the taxes and fees collected from timber concessions actually benefited adjacent communities. To deal with these two sets of issues, the LFI legal team (1) provided the FDA with technical assistance to review and enhance revenue management and (2) suggested strategies for strengthening the mechanisms for benefit sharing, primarily by increasing public participation in governance (ELI 2005).
- *Drafting environmental impact regulations.* Although existing statutes required environmental impact assessments (EIAs), they provided little guidance for concessionaires on how to conduct or when to submit EIAs, and few criteria for the Liberian Environmental Protection Agency (EPA) and the FDA to use in evaluating EIAs (ELI 2005). The LFI legal team worked with the EPA and the FDA to draft regulations and guidelines for forest sector EIAs.
- *Revising the concession allocation process.* The concession review had revealed systematic failures within the concession allocation process. The

---

[19] ELI's activities included the following: (1) developing and drafting the legal and regulatory framework, in collaboration with the FDA and other LFI partners; (2) designing and implementing a broad-based public participation program to ensure meaningful public review of, and comment on, laws and regulations; and (3) building the capacity of Liberians to implement and enforce the new law and the accompanying regulations.

process was revised to ensure that it was transparent, fair, competitive, and in keeping with good business practices (ELI 2005). The reforms completely reconceived the system under which the Liberian government would agree to commercial timber harvesting. Under previous contractual arrangements, the timber companies owned the trees. Under the new law, companies had no ownership rights; instead, they would be permitted to sustainably harvest trees on the condition that they met all legal requirements (Myers 2009b).

While the LFI legal team was conducting research and consultations and drafting the new forestry law, the Liberia Media Centre and the Press Union of Liberia, as communications experts and civil society organizations, carried out a public awareness campaign and gathered public comments on the proposed reforms. Liberia Media Centre staff conducted public meetings to promote understanding of the proposed new law and worked to directly engage the public in the development of the law (Myers 2008).

The consultation and drafting paid off when, shortly after coming into office in January 2006, President Johnson Sirleaf made an audacious move to advance forest sector reform (McAlpine, O'Donohue, and Pierson 2006). In Executive Order No. 1, issued in February 2006, Johnson Sirleaf adopted the recommendations of the Forest Concession Review Committee, canceled all existing timber concessions, and placed a moratorium on all timber exports and new timber concessions until new legislation could be promulgated. The order also established the Forestry Reform Monitoring Committee to carry out the recommendations and oversee legal reforms. The monitoring committee was installed within the FDA and led by the LFI.

In June 2006, in response to the president's strong reform stance, the UNSC lifted the ban on Liberian timber exports (UNSC 2006). Johnson Sirleaf's cancellation of logging concessions and the creation of the monitoring committee were specifically cited as key steps in getting sanctions lifted. Although the lifting of sanctions represented international commendation of the reforms that had been undertaken so far, the UNSC warned that sanctions would be reinstated if the government did not adopt the LFI's proposed forest legislation (UNSC 2006).

Promulgation of regulations

In the course of the legal drafting process, the legal team identified ten core regulations that would be necessary to restart commercial logging and fully implement the law. Among other things, the core regulations addressed public participation, conservation of biodiversity, sustainable forest management, reporting requirements, and forestry fees. Once the National Forestry Reform Law (NFRL) of 2006 had been signed into law (GOL 2006a), the LFI legal team, the monitoring committee, and the FDA revised the preliminary drafts of the regulations to send them out for public comment.

In 2007, to ensure broad public involvement in the development of the final regulations, ELI, the USFS, and two Liberian NGOs (Green Advocates and the Sustainable Development Institute) designed and implemented the first notice-and-comment rule-making process ever to take place in Liberia. In the course of this process, the public received notice of release of the draft regulations and was given the opportunity to comment on them. In addition, the FDA, the Liberia Media Centre, and the Press Union of Liberia conducted a public awareness campaign throughout Liberia, collecting feedback at twenty-one public meetings held in twelve of Liberia's fifteen counties. The FDA received hundreds of written and oral comments from forest-dependent communities, representatives of industry and NGOs, legal and forestry experts, Liberian government officials, and other stakeholders. The comments were incorporated into the revised regulations, which were approved by the FDA board on September 11, 2007 (Myers 2008).[20]

Major elements of the NFRL

The NFRL and the accompanying regulations have been called the most progressive forest management legislation in Africa (Pichet 2009). The NFRL establishes a framework for managing the Liberian timber sector based on the three C's (commercial, conservation, and community) agreed upon by the LFI in 2004; it also establishes commercial provisions and gave the FDA a mandate to draft a community rights law and a wildlife conservation law.[21]

The law divides Liberia's forests into three categories: protected areas, areas where communities can engage in logging and wood processing, and commercial logging areas. The law also institutes rigorous contracting requirements, including competitive bidding and prequalification standards for logging contracts, requirements that timber companies disclose their corporate structure and financial and technical capacity, freedom of information requirements, and a chain-of-custody system. Under the new contracting requirements, a permit is required for timber export, and the government must closely manage payments. Finally, the law includes a social agreement requirement, which is designed to redress the past exclusion of forest communities from the benefits of commercial forestry by compensating them directly. Overall, the law supports improved and more transparent forest management and more equitable access to forest resources.

The regulations address key aspects of commercial forestry, as outlined by the NFRL. The chain-of-custody requirements, for example, are designed to trace every log from the forest to the port, to provide transparency, and to ensure that taxes, land rental fees, and other forest-related fees are paid to the government

---

[20] The first ten regulations under the NFRL covered public participation; forest land use planning; bidder qualifications; tender, award, and administration of contracts and permits; major prefelling operations; benefit sharing; forest fees; a chain-of-custody; penalties; and the rights of private landowners.

[21] The Community Rights Law was passed in November 2009; as of September 2011, the wildlife law was still in draft form.

(FDA 2007d). Under the social agreement requirement, timber companies must negotiate directly with affected communities to reach agreement on compensatory benefits for restrictions of access to, or use of, forest resources that arise directly or indirectly from the contract (FDA 2007c).[22] No new contract can be issued until such an agreement has been reached.[23] Land rental fees, unlike the benefits provided through social agreements, are divided among the local community, the county, and the central government, through a formula and process outlined in the law (GOL 2006a, sec. 14.2.e.ii). Finally, the new legal regime features broad rights for the public: for example, communities must be given notice and provided with the opportunity to comment before contractual rights to forest land are granted to private parties; local communities also have greater access to information and enhanced legal standing (GOL 2006a, secs. 3.1, 4.5, 5.8, 8.2, 18.5, 20.10, 20.11; FDA 2007b).

Institutional reform

The development of the NFRL and the accompanying regulations was only one aspect of reform. The reform also sought to restructure the FDA and to ensure that the FDA's fiscal administration was in line with its new institutional objectives. Because the transitional government was unwilling, on its own, to improve financial transparency, leading members of the international donor community pressured the transitional government to institute GEMAP, the Governance and Economic Management Assistance Program.[24] Under GEMAP, (1) each of the six major state-owned enterprises, including the FDA, was overseen by an outside, independent financial and management controller, and (2) international advisors worked with key government agencies to establish financial management systems, train Liberian staff, and report to the public on progress. As part of the program, all Liberian agencies are required to submit monthly financial statements, including accounting records and account reconciliations, to the Ministry of Finance.

In August 2009, the FDA became the first participating government agency to graduate from GEMAP and take complete ownership of its financial systems. Key reforms in the accounting and auditing departments of the FDA are complete. At a press conference in Monrovia in August 2009, the mission director of the U.S. Agency for International Development (USAID) noted that the FDA had instituted modern systems to improve efficiency and deter corruption (Sonpon 2009). The authority now uses a computerized accounting system, and clearly defined procedures and guidelines for public disclosure are now in place.

In addition to improving fiscal administration, the LFI addressed the institutional structure of the FDA. The USFS and USAID took the lead, improving the FDA's personnel policies and procedures, conducting training, and bringing the

---

[22] These benefits are separate from and in addition to other forestry-related fees or taxes.
[23] In an attempt to depart from the dark history associated with timber concessions in Liberia, the term *concession* has been replaced by *contract*.
[24] For more information on GEMAP, see www.gemap-liberia.org/about_gemap/index.html.

size of the staff to the appropriate level. Like other Liberian government agencies, the FDA had been overstaffed,[25] and severe political interference had undermined staff motivation and competence (UNDP 2007). To reduce staffing by almost 40 percent, the FDA offered retirement packages to qualified employees; nearly two hundred staff members accepted. To complete the restructuring, the FDA created four new departments to fill the institutional gaps, including law enforcement, legal support, research and development, and strategic planning.

Training and implementation

Once the law and its accompanying regulations were in place, the LFI and the FDA identified the steps that were necessary to resume commercial logging and build technical expertise within the FDA. As mandated by the new law, the FDA and the LFI developed forest management procedures, including field manuals on contract preparation, harvesting practices, forest management, chain of custody, contract administration, and social agreements between concessionaires and affected communities.

The LFI, aware that international funding would not continue indefinitely, and mindful that the new system would succeed only if Liberians took ownership of it, conducted training for FDA staff on strategically chosen topics, including forest inventory techniques, forest economics research, contract administration, low-impact logging, and the new legal framework. In July 2007, to improve the FDA's institutional capacity, ELI, the FDA, Flora and Fauna International, Green Advocates, the USFS, and other LFI partners conducted two days of introductory training for Monrovia-based FDA staff, which introduced nearly 50 percent of the staff to the history, framework, and implications of the new forestry law and engaged them in a careful study of the language of the law. To carry the process forward, a small group of FDA staff—eventually named the Trainers of Trainees (ToT)—worked with ELI to become the first trained and designated capacity-building team within the agency. The ToT then trained the rest of the Monrovia-based FDA staff (Myers 2008). In April 2008, ELI and the ToT conducted a training course for FDA field staff; in October 2009, the team conducted a course for community forest development committees, which were set up under the NFRL to represent communities affected by commercial logging.

Transparency and accountability have been incorporated into the timber harvesting process through various means, including through LiberFor, Liberia's new chain-of-custody system. As mandated by the NFRL, all logs and wood products will be tracked from point of origin to port of export (or to domestic markets), through LiberFor's computerized information system. Currently based in Monrovia, LiberFor is being managed by the SGS (Société Générale de Surveillance), under a five-year contract with the FDA.

---

[25] When President Johnson Sirleaf came into office, approximately 69,000 people were employed in the Liberian civil service (IRIN 2006).

SGS is working with FDA staff to conduct a systematic forest inventory and develop a corresponding database, to introduce best practices for forest management, and to train government staff to oversee and implement the chain-of-custody system. Once LiberFor is operational and financially self-sustaining (through export fees and stumpage fees, which are based on the type and amount of timber harvested), and FDA staff have been adequately trained to manage the system, SGS will transfer management and operations to the FDA (FDA 2009b).[26]

The resurrection of commercial forestry

On February 29, 2008, after four years of aggressive reform efforts and a three-year moratorium on timber exports, the FDA opened bids for six timber sales contracts (TSCs)—short-term licenses for less than 5,000 hectares and less than three years (FDA 2008). Eight companies were prequalified, but only three offered bids on four contracts. By early 2010, the first four TSCs were operational and proceeding through the chain-of-custody system. The next step was to put up three forest management contracts (FMCs) for bid; FMCs are long-term licenses for the management of 50,000 to 400,000 hectares for twenty-five years. Three agreements were reached, and the companies proceeded with prefelling requirements. Four more FMCs were tendered for bid in February 2009 and ratified in September 2009. Three were held up when timber companies alleged improper conduct in the tendering process, but by November 2009, all seven were engaged in prefelling operations (FDA 2009a). From February 2008 through the end of 2009, the Liberian government allocated 1,037,266 hectares, or approximately one-fourth of Liberia's forests, for commercial timber extraction (SDI 2010).

Unresolved issues

The new legal structure addresses many past problems, but the implementation of the 2006 law and its accompanying regulations has raised some practical and policy challenges. Some matters are simply questions of interpretation, such as whether advertising contracts on the FDA web site meets the standard for international advertising, and under what conditions the FDA can terminate contracts. Broader policy questions have been raised by initial efforts to negotiate social agreements. More detailed requirements are needed to clarify the standards for social agreements and to protect communities in their negotiations with timber companies.

---

[26] LiberFor is particularly important as Liberia continues its negotiations to participate in a Voluntary Partnership Agreement with the European Union's Forest Law Enforcement, Governance and Trade (FLEGT) initiative. The FLEGT initiative is a licensing system that is designed to prevent illegally logged timber from entering the European Union. For more information on Liberia and the FLEGT initiative, see Duncan Brack, "Excluding Illegal Timber and Improving Forest Governance: The European Union's Forest Law Enforcement, Governance and Trade Initiative," in this volume.

The intense pressure to produce timber revenue is causing concern about the time between opening bids and shipping logs. The law requires the legislature to ratify new FMCs, a step that can add significant time to the contracting process. Moreover, the prefelling requirements for FMCs are elaborate and can take up to one year.[27] Some FDA staff have gone so far as to say that the reforms are "overly comprehensive, complicated and detailed," and have suggested that they are an impediment to the government's immediate financial needs (Altman 2009).

Potential investors have raised questions about whether the size and the duration of the TSCs are sufficient to attract meaningful investment. While the intent of this contract category is to allow small-scale Liberian enterprises to participate in commercial forestry, it is not clear whether this will work. Investors have also questioned the fact that there is no contract type for concession areas with between 5,001 and 49,999 hectares. Finally, Liberian timber companies have argued that the contracting requirements (including bid payments, taxes, and forest fees) effectively price out Liberian companies that would otherwise bid on contracts (Altman 2009).

Although the forest law's recognition of community rights is an important step forward, the law has been criticized for failing to precisely define who is included in the community (Unruh 2009).[28] In particular, the law does not specifically mention women and children; these two groups have suffered the most from Liberia's history of oppression and exclusion, and both stand to benefit from changes in the timber sector (GOL 2006a).[29] As noted earlier, under the

---

[27] One of the prefelling requirements, for example, requires the concession holder to develop a forest management plan within twelve months after the ratification of a contract and at least ninety days before the start of the annual logging season. The FDA, in collaboration with the USFS, is reviewing the requirement to determine whether it is realistic to require a company to provide a forest management plan within one year of ratification, when it can take two to four years to conduct a comprehensive field inventory and develop a complete plan. As an interim measure, the FDA has recommended a two-step process in which concessionaires would submit an initial, one-year operations plan two to three months after ratification, then submit a final, five-year operations plan within one to two years (Cohen 2009). The FDA supports this solution, even though the approach could allow logging to begin before the full plan is complete.

[28] The drafters of the law struggled with the terminology and ultimately decided that it was best to use the broad term *affected communities* (GOL 2006a, sec. 1.3; Myers 2009b). In 2008, the meaning of this phrase was narrowed to apply only to communities that live within the forest or within three kilometers of the forest (FDA n.d.). The Community Rights Law (GOL 2009a), adds new definitions for "community" and the associated rights.

[29] If both the formal and the informal economies are included, women make up 54 percent of Liberia's workforce. But 90 percent of these women are employed in the informal sector or in agriculture; in forestry, men outnumber women by a ratio of almost 4:1. Thus, increased opportunities in the timber sector would help Liberian women. Similarly, Liberian youth could benefit from timber sector employment. UNICEF estimates that 15,000 Liberian children fought in the civil war. The timber industry could potentially provide some of these demobilized soldiers with jobs or could provide funding for schools and other institutions that would help former child soldiers adjust to life after war (UNICEF 2003).

social agreement requirement, timber companies must negotiate with communities before a new contract can be issued. While the law provides for a consultative process when a company negotiates a social agreement with "affected communities," the law lacks qualitative details and specifications (e.g., requirements for the length of a road), verifiable targets for the delivery of benefits, and mechanisms to monitor the implementation of social agreements.

As Liberia struggles to implement this paragon of a forest management system, one might wonder whether the LFI and its partners, swept away by the opportunity to start with a clean slate, created a system that was too prescriptive for a country recovering from decades of civil war. One might also wonder, as Liberia's new governance systems continue to be tested, how long the government can sustain its political will for reform in the face of competing short-term economic and investment interests.

STRENGTHENING GOVERNANCE AND PREVENTING A RETURN TO CONFLICT

The reforms designed by the LFI were structured to achieve four goals:

- To redress the conditions that had enabled the Taylor regime to plunder natural resources and use them to fuel conflict.
- To restore sustainable forest harvesting and management.
- To reestablish accountability and transparency in the executive branch of government.
- To increase the participation of civil society in decision making about, and management of, the forest sector.

The legal and institutional reforms that are now in place can largely be attributed to the careful strategic thinking that guided the reform process from the beginning. While the situation in Liberia remains fluid (7,952 UNMIL troops were still in place as of July 2011), and there were reports, in 2009, of conflict over natural resources and land, overall development indicators are improving (UN 2009). Moreover, the reform process itself has offered capacity-building experiences to many in Liberia.

The LFI's achievements can be traced to careful planning and coordination and to factors that are specific to Liberia, including the political will for reform, a history of corruption and inequity, external pressure to conform to international standards for forest management, and the role of Liberian civil society. These and other factors are discussed briefly in the sections that follow.

Political will for reform

The political will of the government of Liberia—in particular, the backing of President Ellen Johnson Sirleaf—was critical to the success of the reform process led by the LFI (Woods 2007). In contrast to the transitional government that preceded her, President Johnson Sirleaf (1) clearly communicated a vision of national priorities to the country and to national and international investors; (2) declared all existing timber concessions null and void; (3) linked reforms within the forest sector to "broader financial, economic, and political reform efforts" (McAlpine, O'Donohue, and Pierson 2006, 91); and (4) empowered the LFI by providing government support for the reform efforts.

Without the president's support, no amount of money or expertise could have yielded the substantial changes that occurred immediately after the president's election (McAlpine, O'Donohue, and Pierson 2006). During her campaign and her initial days in office, the president consistently decried the role of timber in perpetuating conflict in Liberia. Through Executive Order No. 1 and subsequent actions, the president continued to demonstrate her commitment to forest reform—and, more broadly, to good governance, rule of law, and economic stability.

A suite of reforms

While the LFI was undertaking targeted reforms in the forest sector, broader reforms were under way in Liberia, of which GEMAP was an example. The GEMAP model used for the reform of other state-owned enterprises followed the model that the LFI had established for the forest sector (McAlpine, O'Donohue, and Pierson 2006); at the same time, GEMAP reforms reinforced the LFI's efforts.

History of Liberia

Liberia's bloody history, and the pivotal role of timber and land rights in the corruption and social inequities that had led to the conflict, shaped the final form of the NFRL. One of the goals in updating Liberia's forest sector legislation was to eliminate opportunities for corruption. Given the history of the executive branch exerting autocratic control over the timber sector, Liberian civil society groups insisted on requiring legislative ratification of timber contracts (Myers 2009a). But this authority has created opportunities for corruption: the fact that legislators have requested bribes from concessionaires to guarantee ratification of contracts is a topic of open discussion in the media and among the general public.

Land tenure

The unsettled state of Liberian land tenure policy further complicated timber sector reform. Significant questions remain regarding the ownership of land, including forest lands. As of this writing, all forest resources, except those located in communal forests and forest resources that have been developed on private or deeded land through artificial regeneration, "are held in trust by the Republic of Liberia for the benefit of the People" (GOL 2006a, sec. 2.1). Communal forests are defined as areas "set aside by statute or regulation for the sustainable use of Forest Products by local communities or tribes on a non-commercial basis" (GOL 2006a, sec. 1.3).

Liberians have submitted claims to approximately 3.2 million hectares of land, some of which overlap (FDA 2007a). Broader questions about ownership rights and overall land tenure policy are being addressed by the Land Commission, which was established in 2009 to hear claims and to develop a land tenure policy (GOL 2009b).

Sanctions as leverage

UN sanctions on Liberian timber remained in place while assessments were being conducted and reforms were being designed; they were lifted only when President Johnson Sirleaf adopted the Forest Concession Review Committee's recommendations in Executive Order No. 1. In lifting the sanctions, the UNSC recognized the government's "commitment to transparent management of the country's forest resources for the benefit of Liberians and its reforms in the timber sector" (UNSC 2006). While the sanctions were in place, the UNSC and its panel of experts, in consultation with the LFI, used them as leverage to push for reform in Liberia's forest sector. Although it is difficult to prove a direct causal link between the sanctions and Liberia's robust reforms, the government did strategically align its reform efforts with the conditions that the UNSC had set for the lifting of sanctions. It is thus arguable that the Liberian experience demonstrates the utility of sanctions as a means of fostering reform.[30]

The role of civil society

A reform process of such depth and breadth could not have been achieved without the sustained work of knowledgeable and engaged civil society groups. From the start, Liberian civil society rejected Taylor's calculated response to international pressure for an end to the abuse of forest resources. Later, dissatisfied with the results of the first two concession reviews, civil society groups mounted intense pressure for the government to undertake a third concession

---

[30] The timing of the lifting of the sanctions could be interpreted as offering support to the new Johnson Sirleaf administration, rather than to the timber sector. Had the UNSC extended the sanctions, it could perhaps have protected the FDA from pressure to produce economic benefits, which would have given it more time to develop new systems and build the institutional and financial capacity to implement them. Maintaining sanctions would thus have given priority to natural resource objectives, but potentially at the cost of economic redevelopment. On the other hand, if history reveals that sanctions were lifted before the timber sector was ready to function independently, economic redevelopment may have suffered in any case.

review process through the LFI, and thereby established the LFI as central to reform.

During the early days of the reform efforts, Liberian and international NGOs facilitated community involvement in the LFI and assisted in building local communities' capacity to contribute to reform efforts. Liberian NGOs led the effort to present the LFI's objectives to communities, to seek community input and ensure community participation, and to incorporate stronger benefit-sharing mechanisms for communities into the NFRL and its accompanying regulations. These efforts ensured that the public would be included in reform initiatives and placed significant pressure on the transitional government to adopt the recommendations of the Forest Concession Review Committee (McAlpine, O'Donohue, and Pierson 2006).

Partnership with the UN

Initially, 15,000 UN peacekeeping troops were assigned to Liberia; the goal was to provide a level of security that would permit the country to focus on its long-term objectives. Through the UN mission, the LFI gained access not only to resources (such as helicopters and security forces), but also to staff and financial and technical assistance.

The LFI also developed a reciprocal relationship with the UN panel of experts: by collaborating directly with the panel, the LFI was able to focus on strategic actions that could lead to the repeal of sanctions; the two entities also worked together to identify (1) constraints on reform and (2) actions that would help to reestablish the rule of law in the timber sector (McAlpine, O'Donohue, and Pierson 2006). The UN panel and the LFI made a strategic decision not to focus on short-term actions that would result in a hasty lifting of sanctions, but to implement sustainable reforms that would prevent a return to the conditions that had led to the original conflict. This decision was backed by a willingness, on the part of the UNSC, to maintain sanctions until sufficient reforms had been accomplished.

The United States and the LFI

On the basis of assessments conducted in the early post-conflict period, the U.S. government determined that a strong and coordinated international role in forest reform would be necessary to ensure sustainable forest management and prevent a return of violence. In 2004, in recognition of the historical relationship between Liberia and the United States, the U.S. Congress, at the request of President George W. Bush, allocated over US$200 million in aid for Liberia, US$4 million of which was designated for forest sector reform, including the LFI. The LFI leveraged U.S. political and financial support to gain attention and funding from additional partners, including the European Commission and the World Bank.

The value of the resource

The great value of the remaining Liberian forests was critical to reform. Within Liberia, the financial value of timber inspired citizens to work for reform; outside Liberia, the international community was galvanized by the ecological value of the forests, which constitutes the largest remaining portion of the Upper Guinean Forest. Neither the financial nor the ecological aspect was lost on the Johnson Sirleaf administration. Economic pressure, which was exacerbated by the timber sanctions, forced the FDA and the LFI to pursue many aspects of reform at once—including financial management, contract administration, and sustainable commercial harvesting—while simultaneously recreating the FDA as an institution that could effectively manage the forests for the benefit of all Liberians.

In addition to creating revenue for the government, the timber sector is a catalyst for job creation, livelihood opportunities, and infrastructure development. Potential direct employment from logging and related economic activities is estimated to be between 7,000 and 10,000 jobs (Woods 2007). In Liberia's Poverty Reduction Strategy of 2008, commercial forestry is the cornerstone of economic revitalization in rural areas.[31]

LESSONS LEARNED

At the time of writing, the reform of Liberia's forest sector had yet to be finalized or fully implemented. Thus, the lessons presented here apply only to the contained universe in which the comprehensive reforms were developed, not to the larger universe in which they will be put into practice. And although Liberia's particular history—including its historical connection to the United States—does make the story of the LFI unique, it is still worth considering how the successes of this initiative can be distilled into a set of transferable principles that could be applied in similar settings.

Factors critical to success

Addressing the management of natural resources early in the post-conflict period was critical to avoiding a return to conflict. Arguably, the peacebuilding effort could have focused on the human rights and legal conundrums associated with land tenure. But the impatience with which timber revenue is currently anticipated suggests that Liberians would not have tolerated sorting out the tangle of land tenure before taking steps to revive the economic engine of timber.

---

[31] The Poverty Reduction Strategy projected that in 2008–2009 the timber sector would contribute 14.4 percent of gross domestic product and revenues of US$24.3 million, rising to US$46.1 million by 2011 (GOL 2008). But it became clear during the development of the 2009–2010 budget that unrealized revenues from the timber sector would create cash flow problems.

To marshal the substantial resources that were needed to initiate reforms following the cessation of conflict, it was critical for the Liberian public, for international relief and development organizations, and for the environmental community to understand the need to take action. It was through the sanctions that Liberian NGOs and the international community were able to leverage sufficient support to address the reform of the timber sector.

The structure of the LFI presented international NGOs and donor nations with a unique opportunity for efficient collaboration: drawing from experiences in other countries, key members of the LFI focused on carefully coordinating resources to avert both conflict and redundancy. Through a partnership approach, the LFI leveraged funding and technical support; at the same time, it maintained a sufficiently flexible structure so that partners could choose which components of the initiative to pursue.

The LFI's contribution to capacity building was also fundamental to the success of the reform process. For example, the LFI conducted workshops and on-the-job training for stakeholders and FDA staff, and collaborated with the FDA to develop field manuals that complemented the technical knowledge gained in the classroom. Day-to-day interactions with LFI partners also provided FDA staff with informal training. Since its inception, the LFI has maintained its office within the FDA's building, allowing a daily exchange of information and technical support.

In a deliberate effort to break with Liberia's past, the LFI emphasized public participation in all its initiatives. During the concession review process, for example, the review committee, in coordination with local NGOs, conducted regional forums and town hall meetings (Rochow 2006)—an effort that brought out communities' grievances about their historic exclusion from the concession approval process (SDI 2006). The LFI legal team continued to do public outreach, through initiatives that included public vetting of work plans and a formal notice-and-comment period for the ten core regulations that accompanied the new law. Meaningful inclusion in the reform process was cathartic for communities that were being consulted—for the first time—about decisions affecting the forests they called home. Consultation yielded decisions that were appropriate and sustainable because they were based, in part, on the communities' perspectives and desires. And because the reform process called for communities to be informed about their new rights and responsibilities, it built their capacity to participate further.

Obstacles to implementation

Notwithstanding the gains made in reforming the timber sector, significant challenges remain. In 2009, after having spent approximately US$4 million to reform Liberia's commercial sector, the U.S. government, in the wake of allegations of irregularities during the bidding process for the first seven FMCs, elected to discontinue support.[32] This policy decision left the FDA with responsibility for a large suite of reforms that it does not have the capacity to implement. Consequently, the structure and leadership of the LFI have changed, and priorities are being reassessed. The FDA, Liberian civil society, and foreign consultants have identified the following areas, among others, as critical for maintaining momentum (Altman 2009):

- Technical and financial capacity building.
- A review of the current legal framework to determine whether it is too complex to be effectively implemented in a post-conflict climate.
- Additional monetary support.
- Further clarification and refinement of the mechanisms by which benefits will flow to communities that are affected by commercial forestry.

Neither the LFI's effective coordination of the reform efforts nor the inclusion of the public in decision making could prevent expectations from outrunning reality.[33] Companies have complained that the new payment structure has made up-front costs prohibitive. FDA staff and representatives of the small-scale timber industry have argued that the contract allocation procedures detailed in current legislation are too cumbersome, and that certain steps could be curtailed without sacrificing good governance (Altman 2009).

The tension between objectives and reality may reflect the critical lesson of the LFI experience: in planning for reform in a post-conflict country, the leaders of the effort must include support for implementation—specifically, financial and technical capacity building—and create reasonable expectations for when the benefits of the reform will be garnered. As of January 2011, more than five years after reform was initiated and three years after sanctions were lifted, only nine containers of logs had been legally exported under the new system. Many companies seem to be taking a wait-and-see approach, allowing other companies to test the system before they join in. Nor has the global economy been conducive to launching the fledging system.

Limited government resources and the magnitude and complexity of the new legal framework make it imperative for the LFI to focus on continued

---

[32] In September 2009, U.S. government funding for the LFI ended, and a World Bank forest advisor was nominated to coordinate the LFI's work and to serve as a liaison between the LFI and the FDA's strategic planning unit. As of June 2011, the LFI had held coordination meetings only irregularly, although they are supposed to be quarterly.

[33] As of January 2011, eight TSCs and six FMCs were operational, but desperately needed revenues from these contracts were not expected within the time frame predicted by the government, under Liberia's Poverty Reduction Strategy (Deshmukh 2009). As of March 20, 2010, the government had received only US$8 million of the US$12.6 million in land-rental and bid fees owed by contract holders.

capacity building for all affected groups, including judges, FDA staff, local and national NGOs, and community-based organizations (Myers 2008). Under pressure from the central government and other segments of Liberian society to generate revenue from the forestry sector, the FDA is implementing the new legal framework as rapidly as possible, and without sufficient capacity to ensure that effective controls, such as a functioning enforcement division, are in place.[34] Although many foreign experts have worked with the FDA since the reform process started, only three FDA employees have had the opportunity to obtain formal training or to pursue higher education in foreign countries.

In the era of unregulated timber harvesting, companies engaged in commercial forestry became accustomed to a lawless environment. One of the goals of the reforms is to undo this culture. Under the new system, the FDA has successfully completed at least one enforcement action; however, amid the rush to get the forest sector up and running, allegations that the FDA has engaged in corrupt prequalification and contracting practices have surfaced (UNSC 2009; NGO Coalition of Liberia 2008). As of December 2009, however, no such allegations had been proven.

Additional international support will be needed to fully implement the reforms. LiberFor, the chain-of-custody system, is largely in place, but the system is far from being fully implemented. To ensure that the forest sector contributes to good governance, further financial and technical capacity building is essential. More work will also be needed to ensure that social agreements are meaningful and are negotiated according to the required legal procedures (Siakor 2009; Deshmukh 2009).[35] As the NFRL is being implemented, both timber companies and the FDA are finding areas in the law that need further clarification; it will be important to address these concerns in the near term, so that they can be incorporated into the next round of administrative regulations (Wogbeh 2009).

Unresolved policy questions

Beyond the legal and institutional aspects of commercial forestry are several policy issues that may completely change the terrain in the forest sector. First, in this era of intense focus on opportunities for using carbon capture to mitigate climate change, the international market has discovered particular value in Liberia's forests. In response, President Johnson Sirleaf's special advisor on climate change has established a technical working group to focus on carbon (Donovan 2009). While the working group is developing a national strategy to consider carbon options, others in the forestry sector are asking whether the

---

[34] For example, the FDA's enforcement division does not have a single automobile or motorbike with which to monitor the activities of logging companies.

[35] In one case, a community insisted that a company provide a concrete bridge; the company refused—claiming, with the support of the FDA, that the demand was unreasonable.

social and economic benefits of setting aside forests for carbon credits would match the potential benefits of commercial logging.

Second, it is not yet clear how the balance between conservation, community, and commercial—the three C's of Liberian forest management—will play out. Although the reforms of commercial forestry are in the early stages of implementation, conservation and community are at even earlier stages: legislation and regulations that will affect the forest sector are still being drafted and have yet to be implemented. In November 2009, after more than two years of intermittent discussion and consultation, the Community Rights Law (GOL 2009a) was passed by the legislature and signed into law by the president. The law recognizes the right of forest communities to own and manage forest resources in Liberia; however, in its present form, the law represents a derogation of the act that the government of Liberia, through the FDA, originally presented to the legislature in early 2009. It also includes numerous provisions that conflict with the NFRL.[36]

Finally, and perhaps most importantly, the underlying questions of land tenure have not yet been addressed. As of June 2011, the Land Commission was in the early stages of gathering information, but its policy recommendations will certainly have implications not only for the forestry sector, but also for the future of Liberia overall.

CONCLUSION

The government of Liberia, in partnership with the LFI, has taken substantial steps toward restructuring the forestry sector and mitigating threats to peace. To date, the reforms are being implemented haltingly, but they represent formidable steps toward restoration of the rule of law. A number of requirements—including notice-and-comment rule making, social agreements, and benefit sharing—are reversing the history of exclusion and oppression that fed the conflict. Transparency and the application of legal procedures—from planning, to granting concessions, to allocating benefits—will inspire new trust in the government. Open and lawful commercial transactions that occur within a reformed accounting structure; the reporting requirements mandated under the NFRL; and the chain-of-custody system will create the opportunity for genuine economic development—and, most critically, will eliminate timber as a source of funding for future conflict.

Through forest sector reform, the LFI has improved Liberia's economic, social, and political stability and has contributed to the peacebuilding process. Now that reform is in place, long-term success will depend on increasing the technical capacity of the FDA so that it can implement the reforms, and on the stakeholders' stamina, force of will, and commitment to ensuring that the fledging

---

[36] An early draft of the law challenged the government's authority over forest resources and placed communities in control of all commercial forestry—an arrangement that was far beyond what the final version provides.

system is monitored and enforced. Stakeholders will need to exercise patience and determine how best to attract investment during a global economic crisis. The reforms facilitated by the LFI represent an extraordinary opportunity for Liberia to avert conflict and overcome the resource curse.

REFERENCES

Altman, S. 2009. FDA board retreat notes. February. (On file with authors.)

Bayol, N. 2009. Corrections to reference data in forest resources assessment 2005. (On file with authors.)

Blundell, A. 2008. *Scoping study on the benefits of incorporating forestry into the Extractive Industries Transparency Initiative with specific reference to Liberia.* Natural Capital Advisors, LLC. www.afdb.org/fileadmin/uploads/afdb/Documents/Project-and-Operations/LEITI%20forestry%20report.pdf.

———. 2009. Personal communication. November 15.

Christie, T., M. K. Steininger, D. Juhn, and A. Peal. 2007. Fragmentation and clearance of Liberia's forests during 1986–2000. *Oryx* 41 (4): 539–543.

Cohen, B. 2009. Personal communication to the Liberia Forest Initiative (LFI) from an LFI coordinator with the U.S. Forest Service. May 5.

Deshmukh, I. 2009. Comments made by the head of ARD (Associates in Rural Development) Liberia during a Liberia Forest Initiative conference call. May 5.

Donovan, J. 2009. Comments made during a meeting of the Liberia Forest Initiative by the technical director of Conservation International. May.

ELI (Environmental Law Institute). 2005. Strengthening Liberia's forest governance. ELI project document. March 25. (On file with authors.)

Fairhead, J. 2001. International dimensions of conflict over natural and environmental resources. In *Violent environments,* ed. N. L. Peluso and M. Watts. Ithaca, NY: Cornell University Press.

FAO Newsroom. 2006. Liberia forestry sector emerges after fourteen years of conflict and mismanagement. October 5. www.fao.org/newsroom/en/news/2006/1000415/index.html.

FCRC (Forest Concession Review Committee). 2005a. Report of the Concession Review Committee. (On file with authors.)

———. 2005b. Report of the Concession Review Committee: Phase III. www.fao.org/forestry/29659/en/.

FDA (Forestry Development Authority). 2007a. *National forest management strategy.* www.fda.gov.lr/doc/NFMgmtStrategy.pdf.

———. 2007b. Regulation 101-07: Regulation on public participation in promulgation of regulations, codes, and manuals. In *Forestry Development Authority: Ten core regulations.* www.fda.gov.lr/doc/FDATENCOREREGULATIONS.pdf.

———. 2007c. Regulation 104-07: Regulation on tender, award, and administration of forest management contracts, timber sale contracts, and major forest use permits. In *Forestry Development Authority: Ten core regulations.* www.fda.gov.lr/doc/FDATENCOREREGULATIONS.pdf.

———. 2007d. Regulation 108-07: Regulation on establishing a chain of custody system. In *Forestry Development Authority: Ten core regulations.* www.fda.gov.lr/doc/FDATENCOREREGULATIONS.pdf.

———. 2008. Bids officially opened for six timber sale contracts. March 5. www.fda.gov.lr/press.php?news_id=123.
———. 2009a. Forestry Development Authority annual report, 2009. (On file with authors.)
———. 2009b. *Liberian Forestry Brief* 1. March.
———. n.d. Draft of social agreement handbook. (On file with authors.)
GOL (Government of Liberia). 1976. Liberia Forestry Development Authority act of 1976.
———. 2004. *Liberia's national biodiversity strategy and action plan.* www.cbd.int/doc/world/lr/lr-nbsap-01-p1-en.pdf.
———. 2006a. An act adopting the National Forestry Reform Law of 2006. www.fda.gov.lr/doc/finalforestrylawPASSEDBYLEGISLATURE.pdf.
———. 2006b. Executive Order No 1: GOL Forest Sector Reform. www.emansion.gov.lr/doc/EXECUTIVE%20ORDER%20_%201%20-%20Forest%20Sector%20Reform.pdf.
———. 2008. *Poverty reduction strategy.* www.emansion.gov.lr/doc/Final%20PRS.pdf.
———. 2009a. An act to establish the Community Rights law of 2009 with respect to forest lands. www.fda.gov.lr/doc/Liberia%20Forestry%20-%20CRL%20October%202009%20-%20official.pdf.
———. 2009b. An act to establish the Lard Commission.
Greenpeace. 2007. *Logs of war: The relationship between the timber sector, arms trafficking and the destruction of the forests in Liberia.* www.greenpeace.org/raw/content/international/press/reports/logs-of-war.pdf.
IFRC (International Federation of Red Cross and Red Crescent Societies). 2005. Information black hole in Aceh. In *World Disasters Report 2005.* www.ifrc.org/publicat/wdr2005/chapter4.asp.
IRIN (Integrated Regional Information Networks). 2006. Liberia: "Bloated" war-time workforce gets the peace-time axe. *IRIN Humanitarian News and Analysis.* March 23. www.globalsecurity.org/military/library/news/2006/03/mil-060323-irin02.htm.
LFI (Liberia Forest Initiative). 2004a. *Action plan for forest sector rehabilitation and reform.* Washington, D.C.: U.S. State Department.
———. 2004b. Aide memoire: Multidonors Liberia Forest Initiative. Joint USG/World Bank/FAO/EC/IUCN/CI Mission, October 18–27. www.fao.org/forestry/lfi/29663/en/.
Lowe, P. 2009. Personal communication from World Bank technical advisor. May 15.
McAlpine, J. L., P. A. O'Donohue, and O. Pierson. 2006. Liberia: Forests as a challenge and an opportunity. *International Forestry Review* 8 (1): 83–92.
Myers, B. 2008. ELI final report to the USDA. November 26. (On file with authors.)
———. 2009a. Personal communication from senior attorney, Environmental Law Institute. May 6.
———. 2009b. Personal communication from senior attorney, Environmental Law Institute. June 1.
NGO Coalition of Liberia. 2008. Reform in jeopardy: Reflections on the forest sector reform process in Liberia. July 31. www.illegal-logging.info/uploads/NGOs080731BriefingReformsInJeopardy.pdf.
Olukoju, A. 2006. *Culture and customs of Liberia.* Westport, CT: Greenwood Press.
Peal, A. 2000. Green spot in Africa. www.unep.org/ourplanet/imgversn/112/peal.html.

Pichet, T. 2009. Comments made by the manager of the Société Générale de Surveillance Liberia during a meeting on the Liberian concession process sponsored by the United States Forest Service International Program Office.

Price, S. V., ed. 2003. *War and tropical forests: Conservation in areas of armed conflict.* Binghamton, NY: Haworth Press.

Reno, W. 1998. *Warlord politics and African states.* Boulder, CO: Lynne Rienner.

Rochow, J. K. W. 2006. *Lessons learned from the Liberia forest review.* Washington, D.C.: World Bank. August.

———. 2008. Stuck in stages: The evolving role of enforcement in Liberia forest sector reform. In *Eighth International Conference on Environmental Compliance and Enforcement: Conference proceedings*, ed. J. Gerardu, D. Jones, M. Reeves, T. Whitehouse, and D. Zaelke. www.inece.org/conference/8/proceedings/63_Rochow.pdf.

———. 2009. Personal communication. September.

SDI (Sustainable Development Institute). 2006. *Technical report for project ref.: 76479-000.* (On file with authors.)

———. 2010. Liberia—The promise betrayed. January. www.wrm.org.uy/countries/Liberia/Promise_Betrayed.pdf.

Siakor, S. 2009. Comments made during a Liberia Forest Initiative conference call by the director of the Sustainable Development Institute. May 5.

Sonpon, L. M., III. 2009. FDA graduates from USAID-GEMAP financial management dependency. August 5. www.liberianobserver.com/node/372.

UN (United Nations). 2009. Eighteenth progress report of the Secretary-General on the United Nations Mission in Liberia. S/2009/86. February 10. http://unmil.org/documents/sgreports/sg18pr.pdf.

UNDP (United Nations Development Programme). 2007. United Nations Development Programme Vacancy Announcement No. UNDP/ISSA/2007/04. April 10. www.lr.undp.org/hrv55.htm.

UNEP (United Nations Environment Programme). 2004. *Desk study on the environment in Liberia.* http://postconflict.unep.ch/publications/Liberia_DS.pdf.

UNICEF (United Nations Children's Fund). 2003. Liberia's child soldiers dream of return to normal life. September 25. www.unicef.org.uk/press/news_detail_full_story.asp?news_id=182.

UNMIL (United Nations Mission in Liberia). n.d. History. http://unmil.org/1content.asp?ccat=history&zdoc=1.

Unruh, J. D. 2009. Land rights in postwar Liberia: The volatile part of the process. *Land Use Policy* 26 (2): 425–433.

UNSC (United Nations Security Council). 2001a. Report of the panel of experts pursuant to Security Council Resolution 1343 (2001), paragraph 19, concerning Liberia. S/2001/1015. www.un.org/Docs/sc/committees/Liberia2/1015e.pdf.

———. 2001b. Resolution 1343. S/RES/1343 (2001). March 7. www.unhcr.org/refworld/pdfid/3b00f554c.pdf.

———. 2002. Report of the panel of experts pursuant to Security Council Resolution 1395 (2002), paragraph 4, in relation to Liberia. S/2002/470. www.un.org/Docs/sc/committees/Liberia2/470e.pdf.

———. 2003a. Resolution 1478. S/RES/1478 (2003). May 6.

———. 2003b. Resolution 1509. S/RES/1509 (2003). September 19.

———. 2006. Resolution 1689. S/RES/1689 (2006). June 20.

———. 2009. Midterm report of the panel of experts on Liberia submitted pursuant to paragraph 4 of Security Council Resolution 1854 (2008). www.frontpageafrica.com/documents/panelreport.pdf.

U.S. Department of State, Office of the Historian. n.d. Founding of Liberia. www.state.gov/r/pa/ho/time/dwe/16337.htm.

VoANews.com. 2009. Illegal mining threatens Liberian rainforest. February 20. www.voanews.com/english/archive/2009-02/2009-02-20-voa57.cfm?CFID=240807175&CFTOKEN=40223098&jsessionid=88308d1930faad226986435b4f7237185747.

Wogbeh, M. 2009. Comments made during a meeting of the Liberia Forest Initiative by the manager of the Community Forestry Division of the Forestry Development Authority. May.

Woods, J. T. 2007. Liberia forest sector governance and reform. PowerPoint presentation to Liberia Forest Initiative steering committee. Monrovia, March 13.

Woods, J. T., A. G. Blundell, and R. Simpson. 2008. Investment in the Liberian forest sector: A road map to legal forest operations in Liberia. Forest Trends. http://forest-trends.org/~foresttr/documents/files/doc_1320.pdf.

World Bank. 2006. Project appraisal document on a proposed grant from the trust fund for Liberia in the amount of US$2.0 million to the government of Liberia for a development forestry sector management project. Report No. 37389-LR. September 6. www-wds.worldbank.org/external/default/WDSContentServer/WDSP/IB/2006/09/27/000160016_20060927113040/Rendered/PDF/37389.pdf.

Forest resources and peacebuilding: Preliminary lessons from Liberia and Sierra Leone

Michael D. Beevers

The 1990s were characterized by extended violent conflicts that were primarily internal in origin, but that tended to spill over into neighboring countries. These conflicts, most of which erupted in the developing world, came to be known as "new wars" because they seemed to be a novel species of civil war (Kaldor 1999; Duffield 2001). The new wars created a cottage industry of scholars who attempted to understand their causes and consequences; they also led to the evolving concept of peacebuilding: defined broadly, peacebuilding consists of efforts, on the part of international actors, to avoid conflict relapse by consolidating peace. Peacebuilding operations include maintaining security, providing humanitarian relief, fostering social and political reconciliation, and supporting economic development. Because peacebuilding is based on an underlying logic that stresses "building states to build peace," it also includes initiatives that are designed to strengthen state institutions and the relationship between citizens and the state (Call 2008, 5).[1]

A substantial number of new wars appeared to be related to natural resources or the environment, which led to research that explored the links between conflict and resources. Much of the resulting literature has focused on the role of resource scarcity, resource abundance, and specific "conflict resources" in the onset or duration of civil war.[2] There has also been an emerging awareness that natural resources and the environment are potentially critical to avoiding conflict relapse. Although peace depends on a number of factors, competition over natural resources, persistent environmental problems, and the inability to meet livelihood needs may reignite

---

Michael D. Beevers is an assistant professor of environmental and international studies at Dickinson College.

[1] For example, Roland Paris (2004) suggests that peacebuilding rests on a normative logic based on the "elixir of liberalization," which assumes that market-oriented economic systems and democratization can enhance peace. For further exploration of this issue, see Indra de Soysa, "The Capitalist Civil Peace: Some Theory and Empirical Evidence," in this volume.

[2] See, in particular, Homer-Dixon (1991, 1999); Collier and Hoeffler (1998, 1999); Deudney and Matthew (1999); Diehl and Gleditsch (2001); Peluso and Watts (2001); Bannon and Collier (2003); and Ross (2004).

368 High-value natural resources and post-conflict peacebuilding

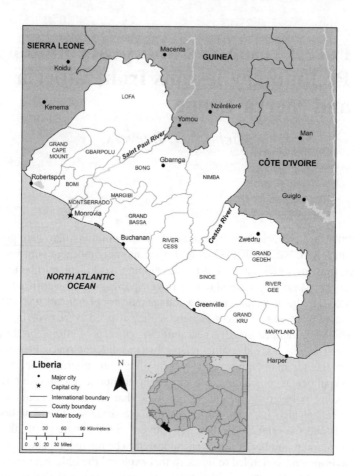

conflict. Indeed, preliminary research confirms that during the first five years after a peace agreement, internal armed conflicts that involve natural resources are twice as likely to recur as those that do not involve natural resources (Binningsbø and Rustad 2008). The proper management of natural resources and the environment may thus help initiate peace and energize post-conflict development (Bijlsma 2005; UNEP 2009).

This chapter compares the management of forest resources in two very different post-conflict contexts: Liberia and Sierra Leone (see figure 1).[3] In Liberia, forests were recognized as an important factor in fueling the conflict; as a result, com-

---

[3] This chapter is based on fieldwork and documentary evidence collected in Liberia and Sierra Leone between October 2008 and May 2009. As part of a doctoral research grant funded by the U.S. Institute for Peace, interviews were conducted with government officials, representatives of international organizations, members of local civil-society organizations, activists, and residents of local communities. The chapter also incorporates information collected in the course of a United Nations Environment Programme mission to Sierra Leone, May 3–15, 2009.

Forest resources and peacebuilding 369

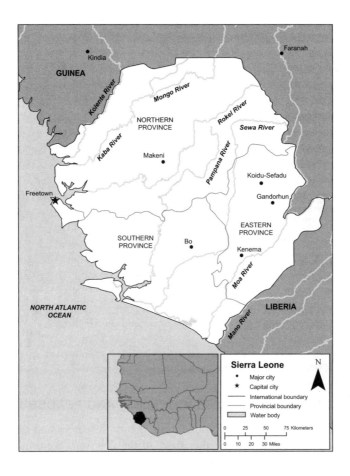

prehensive forest reforms were a central component of the peacebuilding agenda.[4] In Sierra Leone, where forests were of only marginal importance in what was essentially a "diamond war," post-conflict forest reforms were not undertaken. The role of forest reform in these two countries reveals preliminary lessons about three mechanisms that can contribute to peacebuilding: fostering dialogue, promoting economic recovery, and supporting sustainable livelihoods.

The chapter is divided into five major sections: (1) a discussion of scholarly perspectives on the relationship between forests, conflict, and peacebuilding; (2) a review of post-conflict management reforms in Liberia; (3) a review of forest management in post-conflict Sierra Leone; (4) a summary of lessons learned; and (5) a brief conclusion.

---

[4] This chapter defines *forest reform* as formal efforts that (1) are undertaken by national and international actors to alter how individuals and groups behave in relation to forests and forest resources and (2) are embodied in new laws, institutions, policies, and practices.

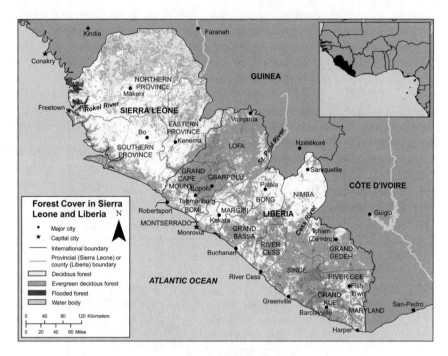

Figure 1. Forest cover in Sierra Leone and Liberia
Source: FAO (2009).

PERSPECTIVES ON FORESTS, CONFLICT, AND PEACEBUILDING

In the course of exploring the links between natural resources and conflict, one question scholars asked was whether some of the new wars were being fought over forests.[5] Wil de Jong, Deanna Donovan, and Ken-Ichi Abe, for example, have suggested that forests and conflict are strongly correlated, noting that at least half the conflicts of the twentieth century occurred in forested areas, and that "countries affected by violent conflict are home to more than 40 percent of the world's tropical forests" (2007, 1–2). Nevertheless, there is considerable ambiguity about the precise linkages between forests and violent conflict (Rustad et al. 2008).

According to one perspective, forest degradation or scarcity, combined with population pressure and poor or inequitable management, can foster violent competition over dwindling livelihood assets (Homer-Dixon 1991; Kaplan 1994). Although this forest-scarcity hypothesis has come under criticism (Hauge and Ellingsen 1998; Peluso and Watts 2001), it continues to have a widespread effect on policy (UNEP 2009). Another perspective suggests that rough terrain can provide insurgents with safe havens from which to launch wars and destabilize governments (Kaimowitz 2003). The notion that forests are a terrain that offers opportunities for initiating or prolonging conflict finds little support in the empirical record, however (Rustad et al. 2008).

---

[5] Examples of this work include Austin and Bruch (2000); Price (2003); USAID (2005); and de Jong, Donovan, and Abe (2007).

Other research argues that countries whose economies depend on valuable natural resources are more susceptible to conflict because resource abundance can lead to slow growth; increased poverty; and weak, corrupt, and less accountable governments (Ross 2003). Such explanations also emphasize the economic motives of combatants and the entrepreneurial, "self-financing" character of new wars that leverage natural resource revenues to fuel conflict (Ballentine and Sherman 2003, 1). In cases where a country relies excessively on timber revenues, dependence can make the government weak, corrupt, and less accountable. For example, timber revenues can bypass government procedures, and concessions can be arranged outside the structures of public accountability. Timber wealth can further weaken governments and foster violence if shadow states emerge that compete with the state for revenues and authority (Reno 1998, 2000).[6] Finally, looting, the sale of concessions by combatants, and competing ownership claims—all of which are associated with conflict timber—can trigger, perpetuate, and fuel conflict (Collier and Hoeffler 1999; Reno 2000). While few studies support the notion that abundant forest resources cause conflict, a combination of factors—including stalled economic growth, endemic poverty, weak government, and the availability of substantial timber revenues—can, under certain conditions, prolong and exacerbate violence (Thomson and Kanaan 2003; Global Witness 2004; Ross 2004).

The perception that new wars appeared to be linked to natural resources led to international efforts to manage those resources, with the goal of ending conflict and promoting peace.[7] Despite a historical reluctance among consuming countries and international organizations to attempt global control of the trade in valuable commodities (Crossin, Hayman, and Taylor 2003), the United Nations, international financial institutions, various Western governments, and international nongovernmental organizations (NGOs) established a number of mechanisms—including legal instruments, voluntary initiatives, and normative standards—designed to curtail the trade in conflict resources, starve combatants of the revenues that were fueling and prolonging conflict, and thereby force combatants to the negotiating table (Le Billon 2003).[8]

---

[6] William Reno (1995, 1) defines a shadow state as a "parallel political authority" that exercises control over informal markets and natural resources in order to build political and economic power outside the realm of state institutions.

[7] See Ballentine and Nitzschke (2005) and Rustad, Binningsbø, and Le Billon (2009).

[8] With respect to Liberia, for example, the UN imposed an arms embargo and prohibited trade in round logs and other timber products; for Sierra Leone, the UN imposed sanctions on the import of rough diamonds. And in both countries, the UN used expert panels to gather information and report back to the Security Council. Meanwhile, a group of Western governments, international NGOs, and businesses established the Kimberley Process Certification Scheme to prevent the international sale or shipment of conflict diamonds. Of course, restricting revenues is no guarantee that a conflict will be shorter or less violent. For example, combatants may respond to a drop in revenue by attacking a neighboring country, by inflicting revenge on the civilian population, or by breaking up into different factions, which can make negotiations more difficult. Efforts to curtail revenues may also make it harder for one side to attain victory—thereby prolonging rather than shortening the conflict (Le Billon 2003).

Once a peace agreement is in place, peacebuilding generally focuses on immediate needs, and natural resource management is rarely a priority.[9] But as the national government begins to reestablish authority and rebuild institutions, natural resource management receives increasing attention, predominantly at the insistence of international actors; such initiatives often involve consultation with local civil-society organizations. Specifically, natural resources form the core of export strategies that can contribute to economic growth, provide employment, and create the national revenues that are vital to peacebuilding. Natural resource management can also address environmental problems and ensure the accessibility of the natural resources on which sustainable livelihoods depend (UNEP 2009).[10] Finally, natural resource management can help transcend political and societal cleavages and establish the trust that is necessary for long-term peace (Conca and Dabelko 2002; UNEP 2009).

In sum, proper management of natural resources can help consolidate peace. In practical terms, the management interventions occur through reforms—laws, institutions, policies, and practices—that are designed to strengthen state institutional control over natural resources. Although it is still unclear how much reforms matter for peace, there are ongoing efforts to understand how and to what extent these management interventions shape peacebuilding trajectories.

LIBERIA

Liberia has an estimated population of 4 million and suffers from the endemic poverty common in other parts of sub-Saharan Africa.[11] While estimates vary, approximately 80 percent of the country is forested, of which 35 percent is characterized as "undisturbed forest" (UNEP 2004, 44–45). The rest of the country is made up of regenerating wooded areas or land used for shifting cultivation.[12] Most Liberians live in rural areas and depend on agricultural and forest products for their livelihoods. Approximately 55 percent of the population lives in forest areas, and nearly all the population uses either charcoal or firewood for energy (UNEP 2004); the forests are also central to cultural practices.

---

[9] Peacebuilding efforts are typically focused on establishing security; meeting humanitarian needs; demobilizing, disarming, and reintegrating combatants; supporting elections; repairing infrastructure; reestablishing the rule of law; and opening up the economy to foreign investors.
[10] Sustainable livelihoods depend on the availability of resources (natural, economic, social, and human) and are shaped by formal and informal institutions.
[11] In 2008, Liberia was ranked 176 out of 179 countries on the UN Human Development Index (UNDP 2008).
[12] *Shifting cultivation* is a farming system in which land is cultivated on a rotational basis to maintain productivity. In Liberia, patches of forest are cleared for rice, cassava, or other crops every few years, after which the land is left fallow, to be reclaimed by natural vegetation.

Perspectives on the roots of the conflict in Liberia

Throughout the Liberian conflict (1989–2003), scholars and the media tried to comprehend the causes of a brutal civil war while the international community tried to engineer an end to it. The origins and character of the conflict remain subject to debate,[13] but considerable attention has centered on the economic imperatives of Charles Taylor—first as a rebel leader and warlord, and later as president (1997–2003)—who used his control over conflict resources (such as diamonds, iron ore, rubber, and especially timber) to amass power and personal wealth (Reno 1998; Smillie, Gberie, and Hazleton 2000; UNSC 2001). William Reno (1998), for example, has argued that Taylor wanted to win the war not because of political ambitions but in order to consolidate authority over natural resource markets. The conflict has also been blamed on Liberia's natural resource wealth—most notably, its vast supplies of timber and other forest resources—of which both the government and rebel elements attempted to gain control in order to finance military operations (Reno 1998; Global Witness 2002, 2004; Baker et al. 2003; UNSC 2001, 2004).

Substantial evidence links Taylor and other combatants to natural resources. Liberia's timber exports drastically increased in the 1990s (Baker et al. 2003; World Bank 2005) and became Taylor's most lucrative conflict commodity.[14] While he was president of Liberia, Taylor financed weapons purchases by selling the largest timber concession in the country to the Oriental Timber Company (UNSC 2001; Global Witness 2004). Reports also alleged that Taylor gained control of Sierra Leone's extensive diamond-mining areas in order to finance violence (Smillie, Gberie, and Hazleton 2000). Even Taylor's enemies reportedly used timber and diamonds to finance their operations (Global Witness 2004; World Bank 2005).

Reports of the connections between natural resources and the Liberian conflict mobilized the UN, which had tried—but thus far failed—to alter the trajectory of the conflict.[15] The result was a variety of mechanisms designed to stop the flow of resource revenues that was fueling and perpetuating the conflict. In July 2000, for example, UN Security Council Resolution 1306 banned the import of all diamonds from Sierra Leone (UNSC 2000); and in May 2003, Resolution 1478 banned the import of "all round logs and timber products" originating in Liberia (UNSC 2003, 4). It is uncertain whether these interventions directly brought about an end to the war, but one thing is clear: by throwing a spotlight on conflict resources and Charles Taylor's economic agenda, international media

---

[13] See Sawyer (1992); Richards (1996); Reno (1998); Ellis (1999); and Levitt (2005).
[14] When Taylor became president, timber production surged. From 2000 to 2002, forestry was the country's most important economic activity, representing 50 to 60 percent of exports and 26 percent of gross domestic product (UNEP 2004).
[15] The UN and the Economic Community of West African States were involved in at least thirteen peace agreements (including the Abuja Accords, which led to the election of Taylor), all of which collapsed.

reports helped to frame the way in which the UN and other peacebuilders understood the Liberian war.

Framing the conflict in terms of purely economic motives, or as an example of competition over valuable natural resources, overlooks its more complex and overlapping sociopolitical and economic roots and their connection to natural resources. Jeremy Levitt (2005) suggests that the conflict originated in resentment against a long line of oligarchic, dysfunctional, and oppressive governments, of which Taylor's was just the latest. While Liberia's abundant natural resources may have been a source of tension, Levitt argues that the tension did not result from the resources themselves, but from unfair land ownership and tenure rights that had been devised in the 1800s. Under these rules, certain groups (mostly Americo-Liberians) had the right to individual land ownership, but indigenous populations were forced to remain under systems of collective land ownership that were dominated by customary authorities (Richards et al. 2005).[16] These patterns were still in place in the 1950s and 1960s, as Liberia was opening its forests and minerals to international markets. During that period, the government moved to take control of the most valuable lands, assigning benefits to a small group of landowners, political leaders, and foreign-owned businesses. These arrangements left most of the country underdeveloped and a large segment of the population disenfranchised, with few opportunities for sustainable livelihoods and little access to land.

In keeping with Levitt's focus on the history of oppression and exclusion in Liberia, the conflict can also be viewed in the context of patronage, a system in which political leaders divert state revenues to shore up their own power. Ultimately, patronage systems can lead to the formation of shadow states, which undermine the state by (1) diverting to political supporters revenues that would otherwise be used to provide basic services, (2) marginalizing rural populations and urban elites,[17] and (3) empowering local strongmen who can eventually become warlords (Reno 2000). Patronage networks are essential for political power: leaders must purchase support and are thus financially dependent on natural resource revenues. Patronage tends to thrive in places like Liberia, where most revenues come from natural resources and where concessions have historically been arranged with little transparency or accountability (Reno 2000; Richards 1996).

In sum, a fuller account of the conflict and its links to natural resources would emphasize, in addition to economic motives, both historical grievances and the patronage system. Economic and political motives are deeply intertwined

---

[16] *Americo-Liberians* is the term used to refer to the descendants of free African Americans and freed American slaves who, in 1822, under the auspices of the American Colonization Society, settled in what would eventually become Liberia—where, for much of the nation's history, they politically dominated the region's indigenous populations.

[17] Urban elites can became marginalized when political leaders' access to formal or informal revenues diminishes, making it increasingly difficult to dispense patronage in exchange for support.

in Liberia, and Taylor's wholesale looting of the country's natural resources can be viewed as an effort to buy loyalty and to dispense the patronage that was needed to acquire political power.

Forests and peacebuilding in Liberia

Despite the importance of Liberia's forests to livelihoods, the main purpose of forest reforms was to persuade the UN to lift timber sanctions, which would allow the national government to harness the financial potential of its forest resources for peacebuilding. The sanctions demanded that Liberia gain "full authority and control of timber producing areas" and take "all necessary steps to ensure that government revenues . . . are not used to fuel conflict." The sanctions also mandated systems of transparency and accountability to ensure that timber revenues would "benefit the Liberian people, including development." Finally, the sanctions mandated environmentally sustainable business practices, legal reforms, and a review of concessionary agreements (UNSC 2003, 4).

In early 2006, in a first step toward reform, President Ellen Johnson Sirleaf issued Executive Order No. 1, which canceled all forest concessions, placed a moratorium on commercial timber harvests, and established the Forest Reform Monitoring Committee to oversee forest reforms.[18] In June 2006, the UN acknowledged Liberia's progress and conditionally lifted the sanctions (UNSC 2006): however, a permanent withdrawal of sanctions would occur only if comprehensive forest reforms were passed within ninety days and were approved by the Security Council. After three months of consultations by the Forest Reform Monitoring Committee—with input from the Liberia Forest Initiative, Liberian NGOs, and government agencies—the government of Liberia enacted the National Forestry Reform Law (NFRL), which emphasized the government's authority over forests and was oriented around the "three Cs" of forest management: commercial, community, and conservation (GOL 2006a).[19] By acknowledging that Liberia's forests have multiple uses and values, and by highlighting the importance of sustainability and community benefits, the three Cs provided

---

[18] The UN panel of experts recommended canceling all forest concessions as a first step toward forest reform (UNSC 2004).

[19] The Liberia Forest Initiative (LFI), which was founded in 2004, was pivotal in undertaking forest reforms. Led by the U.S. Department of State and the U.S. Agency for International Development, the LFI was a partnership created to provide support for the Liberian forestry sector. Its members include, among other organizations, the Center for International Forestry Research, Conservation International, the European Commission, Flora and Fauna International, the UN Food and Agriculture Organization, the International Monetary Fund, the International Union for Conservation and Nature, the National Transitional Government of Liberia, and the World Bank. For additional information on the LFI, see Stephanie L. Altman, Sandra S. Nichols, and John T. Woods, "Leveraging High-Value Natural Resources to Restore the Rule of Law: The Role of the Liberia Forest Initiative in Liberia's Transition to Stability," in this volume.

something for all stakeholders (GOL 2006a). The NFRL also recognized that "past instances by both Liberian and non-Liberians of political patronage, corruption, tax evasion, violations of the rights of local communities, and lack of transparency have resulted in the unsustainable management of forests, and even fueling conflict" (GOL 2006a, 6).

Given the significance of rebuilding the economy and the central role of raw materials in jump-starting economic growth, it is not surprising that commercial forestry received the lion's share of attention in the reform process (IMF 2008).[20] Liberia's conflict-to-development strategy is based on fast-tracking productive economic sectors in order to revive the economy, create employment opportunities, rebuild infrastructure, and supply basic services (GOL 2006b).[21] By "reviving the traditional engines of growth" and restructuring the economy, with the assistance of foreign investment and exports, the government hopes to alleviate poverty and support a peaceful post-conflict trajectory (IMF 2008, 21).

Indeed, Liberia's forests represented an enormous opportunity for a cash-strapped country ravaged by years of conflict and institutional decay. But because of Liberia's history of corruption and patronage, the grievances associated with forests, and the role of timber in fuelling the conflict, the recommercialization of forests would require oversight to ensure transparency, accountability, and the rule of law; safeguards incorporated into the NFRL included monitoring of new concession agreements, chain-of-custody contracts, and tracking of timber revenues. To ensure transparency and accountability and improve fiscal administration, partial oversight for the forest sector was handed over to a foreign comptroller, who works under the Governance and Economic Management Assistance Program (GEMAP). The comptroller interacts with the government of Liberia; the Forestry Development Authority (FDA), the government agency that is responsible for managing Liberia's forests; the UN; the World Bank; and donor countries.

Acknowledging communities' historical lack of rights and benefits, the NFRL set out to effect "empowerment" by ensuring that communities were "fully engaged in the sustainable management of forests" and could "equitably participate in and . . . benefit from . . . forests" (GOL 2006a, 34–35). The NFRL also (1) mandated that concessionaires pay fees to affected communities and surrounding counties and (2) required, through regulations, that firms conduct environmental assessments and negotiate social agreements with communities; these agreements detail community benefits and access rights and must be approved by the FDA before commercial activities can begin. Recognizing that forests are essential to

---

[20] Interviews with Forestry Development Authority staff, national government officials, activists, and members of local civil-society organizations, Liberia 2008.
[21] A commercial focus is also the result of Liberia's long history with forestry—including narratives, rooted in the once-booming timber export industry, that remain deeply embedded among residents in particular parts of the country and in the government, specifically the FDA. In interviews in 2008, FDA staff and government officials described a longing for the "better days" of timber exports—before Taylor's era and the stigma of conflict timber (Beevers 2008).

livelihoods, the NFRL assigned broad rights allowing community use of forests. The NFRL also acknowledged the importance of Liberia's forests to national, regional, and international conservation; as a consequence, the reforms address wildlife management and establish new regulations for forest networks and other protected areas.[22]

On paper, the NFRL is comprehensive and perhaps even "cutting edge."[23] But implementation has been slow and fraught with contention. For example, the FDA, which is in charge of implementing the NFRL, has been criticized by Liberian government officials and international financial institutions for the lack of progress in realizing financial returns from commercial timber production. Optimistic scenarios developed by the International Monetary Fund, for example, estimated that the sector would generate US$25 million and create employment opportunities in 2008 (IMF 2008). Although several commercial contracts were awarded, no timber was legally harvested, and no revenue was collected. Part of the problem stems from the FDA's failure to award concessions to reputable companies. Although the FDA was required by law to advertise globally, it did not do so; as a result, when large forest concessions were put out to bid, there were few responses—and none of the companies that did respond had significant experience in forestry or discernable capital with which to carry out timber operations.[24] This suggests not only that companies granted concessions may fail to meet their contractual obligations, but also that they may be shell companies—which, if they are allowed to do business, will increase the risk of corruption.[25] Risks may be associated even with known companies. For example, Global Witness (2009), an international NGO, reported in mid-2009 that the FDA had granted a contract to a timber company that is known for illegal logging in other parts of the world—and thereby failed to follow the law. A mounting number of alleged improprieties in the awarding of concessions have also raised questions about the FDA's commitment to transparency and accountability. According to the UN Panel of Experts on Liberia, in 2008, the FDA altered three forest management contracts on over 235,000 hectares of forest, which would have led to over US$50 million in lost revenue over twenty-five years, while benefiting the companies (UNSC 2008). There have also been persistent reports of forest contracts being altered by the FDA and of a bidding process that is fixed in favor of certain companies.[26] Some government officials and FDA administrators blame international consultants and "agitators" for the fact that commercial forestry has yet

---

[22] Liberia's forests, which include a large swath of the Upper Guinean Forest, are significant for biodiversity and have been identified by international conservation groups as important for the mitigation of climate change.
[23] Interview notes, Liberia 2008.
[24] Interview notes, Liberia 2008.
[25] Shell companies have no active business transactions or assets; they can be used for legitimate business purposes, but they are also used as fronts for illegal business operations.
[26] Interview notes, Liberia 2008.

to produce revenues, claiming that they are getting in the way of post-conflict development by questioning Liberia's commitment to accountability and transparency, and thereby subverting the national interest.[27]

Problems in the commercial timber sector have been compounded by a backlash against what is perceived by some as a "commerce-centric" development agenda, in which community objectives are subordinate to timber production and historical grievances concerning land ownership and tenure remain unaddressed.[28] According to a member of Liberian civil society, "fast-tracking timber has eroded the trust between the government and communities. . . . A more deliberate set of rules of how communities would be integrated into commercial activities needs to be discussed."[29] Some observers feel that in order to mitigate potential conflicts before commercial forestry begins, legitimate conflict resolution structures should be established and certain issues (including land ownership and tenure rules, and the definition of "community") should be resolved.[30]

Contention has also emerged over the Community Rights Law, which was mandated by the NFRL. The controversy began in 2008, when a nine-page community rights bill submitted to the legislature was mysteriously replaced by a thirty-two-page version (Beevers 2008). This sleight of hand was significant because the two versions were very different: the nine-page bill, for example, described the government's obligation to community forestry and recognized tenure rights, but still reserved to the government the authority to manage forest resources. The thirty-two-page version, in contrast, had communal forests as its central organizing principle, and placed forest management directly into the hands of community residents. Whereas the nine-page version would have endowed the state with the power to oversee the commercial timber sector and conservation areas, the thirty-two-page version granted such rights to communities—ostensibly to guarantee that the benefits would go directly to the people, rather than being siphoned off by businesses and the central government.

In the wake of the switching of the documents, which has never been explained, further negotiations were undertaken that resulted in a seventeen-page law that was passed in October 2009: the Community Rights with Respect to Forest Lands Act. Confusion remains, however, about how commercial forestry will be carried out on communal lands; there is also considerable anger in some communities about the fact that the earlier law was watered down, preventing communities from developing "in accordance with their own needs and interests" (Binda 2010). The FDA, for its part, maintains that giving communities full control of the

---

[27] Interview notes, Liberia 2008.
[28] Interview notes, Liberia 2008.
[29] Interview notes, Liberia 2008.
[30] Interview notes, Liberia 2008. Disputes over land are commonplace, and violent conflict related to land claims is on the rise. A report by the Truth and Reconciliation Commission has also stated that land disputes threaten Liberia's national stability (Truth and Reconciliation Commission of Liberia 2009).

forests would exacerbate tensions over competing claims to forests, put more power into the hands of companies, undermine the government's ability to manage the forests for a variety of uses, and deprive the country of the revenues needed for post-conflict recovery.

SIERRA LEONE

Sierra Leone has an estimated population of 6 million and remains one of the poorest countries in the world.[31] While estimates vary, approximately 18 percent of the country is forested, and two-thirds of the remaining land area is "wooded," consisting of secondary and regenerating forests. About 5 percent of Sierra Leone's forests consist of either rainforest, which is located in forest reserves, or mangrove swamps, which are located in coastal areas (Baker et al. 2003). Historically, about 60 percent of Sierra Leone's total land area was rainforest (Baker et al. 2003), but by the early twentieth century, timber extraction by colonial authorities and shifting cultivation had reduced the forest cover to its current level (Richards 1996; Squire 2001). As Paul Richards (1996) has noted, if Liberia was the last country in West Africa to have its forests exported, Sierra Leone was the first.

In Sierra Leone, forests did not contribute significantly to conflict or to the outbreak of violence, and timber was not implicated in funding or sustaining the hostilities (Baker et al. 2003)[32]—probably because Sierra Leone has only a limited amount of commercial timber and neither the rebels nor the government could readily access forest areas.[33] Nevertheless, Sierra Leone's forests were not without a role in the conflict: they served as enclaves for rebel combatants, allowing them to launch attacks and to hide from government forces; they also provided a setting in which the rebels were able to build a sense of community (Richards 1996).

Perspectives on the roots of the conflict in Sierra Leone

The causes of the brutal and protracted conflict in Sierra Leone (1991–2002) have been subject to much debate, but the struggle is often characterized as a spillover from the Liberian war.[34] As is the case with Liberia, explanations have focused on the economic motives of Charles Taylor—who, in order to gain control of Sierra Leonean diamond-mining areas to sustain the Liberian war, helped give rise to and supported the Revolutionary United Front (RUF) in its uprising against the

---

[31] In 2008, Sierra Leone ranked 179 out of 179 countries on the UN Human Development Index (UNDP 2008).
[32] Interviews conducted by the author suggest that considerable illicit timber harvesting was carried out during the conflict, although there is little evidence to back up this claim.
[33] Robert Kaplan (1994), in a largely discredited but stubbornly persistent account, assigned the causes of the Sierra Leonean war to environmental collapse triggered by a history of deforestation and poor agricultural practices.
[34] For discussions of the origins of the Liberian conflict, see Kaplan (1994); Richards (1995, 1996, 2001); Reno (1998); Bangura (2004); Gberie (2005); and Keen (2005).

government of Sierra Leone (Global Witness 2000; UNSC 2001).[35] The war in Sierra Leone is also portrayed as having been fuelled and prolonged by diamonds, if not directly triggered by these valuable global commodities.[36] David Keen, for example (2005), has observed that collusion over the spoils of war—between rebels and soldiers as well as between diamond companies, brokers, and government officials—provided substantial incentive to continue the conflict and undermine any overtures toward peace.

A consistent flow of reports from international NGOs (such as Global Witness and Partnership Africa Canada) documenting Taylor's greed and the trade in conflict diamonds helped to mobilize the UN and various Western governments and led to a set of interventions aimed at managing diamond exports and the resulting revenues. In July 2000, the UNSC passed Resolution 1306, which prohibited the direct or indirect import of rough diamonds from Sierra Leone and required the Sierra Leonean government to establish a certificate-of-origin system before the diamond trade could resume (UNSC 2000).[37] After a succession of coups, elections, and failed peace agreements, hostilities finally ceased. Although many factors contributed to ending the war, it was ultimately the international attention to conflict resources and to Taylor's economic agenda that provided sufficient leverage for the international actors that were trying to end the conflict (Keen 2005).

The focus on Taylor's greed and on conflict diamonds, however, tends to overlook the roots of the conflict that were particular to Sierra Leone and that made the rebellion possible. Specifically, a long history of patronage and undemocratic government, widespread underdevelopment, and grievances associated with natural resources generated resentment (Richards 1996; Bangura 2004; Keen 2005). This resentment was deepened by a number of factors. First, Sierra Leone's population was aware of the country's abundance—and also aware that it had not benefited from it. Second, land was a source of conflict, largely because agriculture had to compete with other uses, such as diamond mining. Finally, the chiefs—the customary custodians of land outside Freetown (the capital)—had the power to distribute land and to arbitrate land-based disputes, and these customary arrangements for land ownership and tenure often conflicted with people's aspirations

---

[35] For discussions of Charles Taylor's role in the Sierra Leonean conflict, see Zack-Williams and Riley (1993) and Le Billon (2006).

[36] For discussions of the role of diamonds in the Sierra Leonean conflict, see Smillie, Gberie, and Hazleton (2000); Farah (2001); and Keen (2005).

[37] The system eventually put into place, the KPCS, was designed to ensure that diamonds can be traced from the point of extraction to the place of export, to ensure that they do not originate in conflict areas. For additional perspectives on the KPCS, see J. Andrew Grant, "The Kimberley Process at Ten: Reflections on a Decade of Efforts to End the Trade in Conflict Diamonds"; Clive Wright, "The Kimberley Process Certification Scheme: A Model Negotiation?"; and Harrison Mitchell, "A More Formal Engagement: A Constructive Critique of Certification as a Means of Preventing Conflict and Building Peace," all in this volume.

and livelihood needs (Keen 2005). In particular, young rural men had little access to productive land and few employment opportunities outside of diamond mining.

Sierra Leone's historically unjust and corrupt political system, which began with British colonialism and continues today, is based on patronage networks that have exploited the country's resource base (first forests, and now minerals) to gain personal enrichment and consolidate political power. In addition to looting the country's natural resources, these networks marginalized segments of the population and undermined government authority by creating shadow states (Reno 1995).

Siaka Stevens, who was president of Sierra Leone from 1968 to 1985, helped set the stage for conflict and for the failure of the state. In the 1970s, in order to strengthen his political power, Stevens centralized state control of diamond mining, exacerbating already inequitable land relationships and rendering small-scale diamond mining, on which many Sierra Leoneans relied for their livelihoods, illegal. Under Stevens' autocratic rule, diamond revenue was also diverted from state institutions to patronage networks, which led to declines in state spending on education and health. In the early 1980s, the global economic decline led to a national fiscal crisis in Sierra Leone—and caused Stevens to further consolidate power in urban areas and to withdraw support for rural communities altogether (Keen 2005). These actions produced a disaffected urban elite that was outside of Stevens' patrimonial system and that had political (rather than simply economic) motives for war, as well as a disenfranchised group of young men who could easily be absorbed into the RUF (Richards 1996; Abdullah 2004). While the role of Taylor and diamonds in explaining the war should not be underestimated, a more nuanced account would also highlight two other factors: the importance of diamond revenues in maintaining patronage systems, and the ways in which underdevelopment and grievances about access to land laid the foundations for violence.

Forests and peacebuilding in Sierra Leone

An estimated 70 percent of Sierra Leone's population lives in rural areas, relying on agricultural production and forest resources for their livelihoods; the forests are also a cultural asset. In addition to their importance to the shifting cultivation of rice and other sustenance crops, forests provide most construction materials and are used by 95 percent of the population to obtain firewood and charcoal (Baker et al. 2003). Despite the significance of the forests to Sierra Leone's rural population, forest management is not a peacebuilding priority, either for the national government or for the international actors—the UN, the World Bank, donor governments, and international NGOs—that are assisting with peacebuilding efforts.

Sierra Leone's peacebuilding strategy emphasizes economic growth, youth employment, and revenues from mining and agriculture. The World Bank and the government of Sierra Leone regard these sectors as the primary drivers of long-term economic recovery and poverty reduction—and, ultimately, of peace (World Bank 2005). According to the peacebuilding priorities articulated in *The Agenda for Change*, the government's planning document for post-conflict development, only a "transformation of the economy" can set the country on a path to peace (GOSL 2008a, 1). Peacebuilding objectives, as expressed in the *Agenda*, therefore focus on foreign investment in agribusiness and mineral extraction (of diamonds, rutile, and bauxite, for example), in order to provide the necessary revenues and employment needed to spur economic recovery and provide basic services (World Bank 2005; GOSL 2008a).

Because patronage, corruption, and grievances have been associated with the use of natural resources, the *Agenda* stresses transparency and accountability. As described in the *Agenda*, natural resource management will be largely focused on harnessing Sierra Leone's comparative advantages (large mineral deposits, abundant fertile land, and a deep harbor) for the betterment of the country, although "ensuring clear land ownership" is mentioned in the document (GOSL 2008a, 5). Forests are mentioned in World Bank documents not as a critical component of sustainable livelihoods but only in relation to deforestation, poor land use, and loss of biodiversity, all of which are presumed to deepen poverty (World Bank 2005).

Current wildlife and forestry regulations—the Wildlife Act and the Forestry Act—were passed in 1972 and in 1988, respectively, although the Forestry Act was revised in 1990, before the war began. New wildlife regulations and forest policies were drafted in 1997 and 2003 but were not passed, and no comprehensive attempt to address forests has occurred since. Since 2008 however, growing concerns about Sierra Leone's forests have mobilized a small group of UN agencies, donor governments, national civil-society organizations, and Sierra Leonean government officials to discuss comprehensive forest and trade reforms (GOSL 2008b; Howard 2009).[38] The concerns stem, in part, from a perception among stakeholders that the government lacks control over its remaining forest areas, and from reports of illicit timber harvesting in parks and reserves (Ford 2008). There is also a desire among stakeholders to conserve Sierra Leone's remaining forests, which are under pressure from agriculture, mining, hunting, urban development, and timber harvesting (Howard 2009). In 2008, to regain control of the forests, the government placed a temporary ban on all timber exports until forest reforms can be introduced (Ford 2008).

There are conflicting views on where the threats to Sierra Leone's forests come from and on whether such threats can undermine peace. For example, Sierra Leonean activists and civil-society groups claim that illicit timber harvesting is sanctioned by local chiefs and government officials, both of whom profit from the revenue. The worry is that even small-scale trade in forest products may sustain shadow states, which may deprive local communities of needed resources,

---

[38] In early 2009, the Ministry of Agriculture restructured forest management to mirror the approach used in Liberia; it is now organized according to conservation, commercial, and community goals.

exacerbate forest- and land-based grievances, and foster conflict. Other observers, however, mostly from government and international organizations, claim that hunting and "slash and burn" agricultural practices—which are expected to rise in tandem with future population growth and diminished opportunities to "get rich" in diamond mines—will lead to deforestation and the loss of biodiversity.[39] This view suggests that forest scarcity may threaten peace by fostering competition over remaining stands of forest, and by limiting the opportunities for youth who are looking for livelihoods that are tied to forest resources rather than to diamonds. Still other observers have suggested that conservation organizations have "overplayed" deforestation in Sierra Leone, and that both the sustainable use of forest products and the conversion of forests to agricultural land are necessary to meet the livelihood needs of forest communities.[40] Adherents of this view are concerned that government attempts to control forests may diminish livelihood opportunities for local communities and thereby increase tension between communities and customary chiefs and between communities and the government.

LESSONS LEARNED

Contrasting the experiences of Liberia and Sierra Leone makes it possible to draw preliminary lessons about how forest reforms—or a lack thereof—can affect peacebuilding. The focus in this section is on three mechanisms that can help strengthen peacebuilding: fostering dialogue, promoting economic recovery, and supporting sustainable livelihoods.

Fostering dialogue

As noted at the outset of the chapter, efforts to manage natural resources may help transcend political and societal cleavages and establish the trust that is necessary for long-term peace. In Liberia, forest reform has created opportunities for substantive dialogue between a broad array of stakeholders, including the government, international actors, community activists, and Liberian civil-society groups. Communication, however, is only part of the process, and whether it will succeed in building trust, confidence, and cooperation is uncertain.

By providing a public forum to discuss historical grievances and expose the corruption and patronage that have historically been associated with Liberia's forests, reform has sparked contentious debates about the ownership and control of forests—topics that have historically been off-limits in public discourse. The debates illustrate the central role that forests play in community livelihoods. The contention does not originate with the reforms, which are comprehensive, but from suspicions about the government's ability to manage forests and timber revenue for the good of the country—in particular, for the good of local communities.

---

[39] Interview notes, Sierra Leone 2009.
[40] Interview notes, Sierra Leone 2009.

Indeed, the reform process is increasingly characterized by distrust between key actors.[41] The FDA, for example, has accused international actors, including NGOs and consultants that have an interest in the success of the reform process, as well as Liberian civil society, of openly thwarting development by publicly questioning the FDA's motives. The FDA asserts that holding the forest sector to such strict standards and holding up genuine errors on the part of FDA staff as examples of corruption has slowed down the process of awarding contracts: each time a new allegation arises, the activities of the commercial sector are put on hold because of public pressure.[42] At the same time, Liberian civil-society groups blame the government for circumventing the law and undermining the country's fragile peace by fast-tracking commercial forestry and resorting to the "old ways" of doing business.[43] The rhetoric has heated up to the point where stakeholders are accusing each other of pitting the "state against society," "communities against the government," and "communities against communities."[44] In short, while fostering dialogue that would have seemed impossible only a few years ago, the reform process may also be fostering cycles of suspicion that can only slow economic development and create deep divisions between stakeholders.

In Sierra Leone, the absence of forest reforms may be a missed opportunity. Although most of the international attention has focused on conflict diamonds, which are viewed as the primary natural resource and therefore a principal means of supporting peacebuilding, forests can help consolidate peace in rural areas. Forests may have played only a marginal role in the conflict, but grievances over land ownership and tenure rights, and the availability of livelihoods, are connected to forest management. Without a forest reform process in Sierra Leone, there is no opportunity to discuss the uses and value of forests, the opportunities they provide for alternative livelihoods (particularly for youth), or potential changes in customary land arrangements. Without reforms, the patronage systems and the resulting grievances long associated with forests will persist, leaving the root causes of tension and conflict to fester. Given the several decades of government neglect of rural areas that began under Stevens, forest reforms would allow communities to participate in decision making and feel that they are a part of the country's future. Although recent discussions of forest reform are a step in the right direction, they need to be expanded to incorporate a larger group of stakeholders.

Promoting economic recovery

Because they foster growth, provide employment, and generate revenue, valuable natural resources are often key to peacebuilding. In Liberia, commercial forestry is a crucial component of economic recovery—but, contrary to expectations, only

---

[41] Interview notes, Liberia 2008.
[42] Interview notes, Liberia 2008.
[43] Interview notes, Liberia 2008.
[44] Interview notes, Liberia 2008.

a small fraction of the projected US$24 million in revenue for 2008–2009 was collected (UNSC 2008). Moreover, the shortage of reputable timber companies, coupled with reports of alleged improprieties in handling bidding and contracts, has raised questions about transparency and accountability. While the improprieties may have resulted from poor judgment or lack of capacity, they may also represent parallel systems of doing business. Reform can change the law, but it is more difficult to change the underlying culture, in which patronage and corruption have historically functioned alongside state institutions. If, because of lack of oversight, forest reforms simply recreate patronage systems, the reforms may ultimately legitimize and strengthen those systems, weaken the government, and siphon revenues away from peacebuilding priorities (Chabal and Daloz 1999).

To genuinely promote economic recovery, forest reforms must alter prewar social, economic, and political dynamics; given the tremendous stakes involved in the control and use of forests, however, this will not be easy. The increasingly public forum in which Liberia's forest issues are discussed suggests that an emphasis on accountability and transparency is challenging the old ways of doing things, but robust state institutions cannot survive unless international actors make a long-term commitment to support Liberian civil society, actively seek the participation of forest communities in decision making, and ensure continued oversight from GEMAP and other international entities.

The example of Liberia also demonstrates that when forests are central to economic recovery, they may spur contention. The contention is not about whether forest reforms were needed, but about whether the particular reforms that were instituted will effectively address prewar grievances associated with forests and land. Given the connections between politics and the exploitation of Liberia's forests and forest peoples, and between timber and the war, it should not be surprising that international actors, activists, Liberian civil-society organizations, and local communities have little trust in the FDA's ability to manage the forest sector, direct timber revenues to development, or focus on priorities that are in line with those of communities.

Tension and mistrust will continue to sow discontent and slow down the reform process. The government and the FDA must continue to work with communities and local civil-society groups—and these groups must, in turn, acknowledge the efforts of the government and the FDA. Building trust and confidence will take years, if not decades—and it may take an equally long time to determine how, and to what extent, forest resources contribute to economic recovery and peace.

Supporting sustainable livelihoods

There is little question that ensuring access to the natural resources on which livelihoods depend is important for consolidating peace. Nevertheless, peacebuilding tends to focus on the high-stakes resources that are thought to fuel conflict—the result, in part, of a built-in bias that assigns priority to the formal economy as the center of economic growth. In both Liberia and Sierra Leone, forests are vital to livelihoods and remain at the center of rural life. While economic recovery is a prerequisite for peace, so, too, is access to sustainable livelihoods.

But sustainable livelihoods—in this case, agricultural production and the use of forest products—are generally considered low-stakes elements of the informal economy; hence, livelihoods receive little attention in peacebuilding efforts. Indeed, interviews conducted in both Liberia and Sierra Leone revealed a widely held perception that communities, and their livelihoods, are being left behind in the peacebuilding process.[45]

Liberia's focus on commercial forestry needs to be matched with comparable efforts to rebuild communities and ensure food security, with input from the communities themselves. As dialogue (and contention) about community rights and benefits increases, slow progress is being made. In Sierra Leone, a first step would be to push forward with forest reforms that place priority on livelihoods in rural areas, especially those that offer opportunities for youth. While reforms in the diamond sector have sought to address community and livelihood concerns, attention remains focused on jump-starting commercial mining, rather than on creating new livelihood opportunities. A second step for both countries would be to increase efforts to resolve land ownership and tenure rights, since these issues affect access to forests, and therefore to sustainable livelihoods.[46] When patronage systems or perverse rules associated with land ownership and tenure rights prevent communities from meeting their livelihood needs, grievances develop. Dialogue about land ownership and tenure rights would not only bring these long-held grievances to the surface, but would also set an example demonstrating that sustainable livelihoods and rural communities matter to both national governments and international actors.

CONCLUSION

The observations offered in this chapter are preliminary but can provide insights into the connection between natural resource management and peacebuilding. First, since reforms alter people's relationship to natural resources, they inherently bring people together or divide them over time. Reform is thus not an end in itself but a slow and contentious process that can establish trust, although this is by no means easy or assured. Second, natural resource management tends to focus on specific resources that fit particular economic narratives (for example, they are related to the conflict, or they have the power to spur post-conflict recovery). As a result, forests are a peacebuilding priority in Liberia, but not in Sierra Leone.

---

[45] Interview notes, Liberia 2008 and Sierra Leone 2009.
[46] In both Liberia and Sierra Leone, efforts to address land ownership and tenure rights have begun, albeit slowly. In Liberia, the Governance Reform Commission has been tasked with addressing land and property rights issues. In Sierra Leone, land reforms are addressed in the Land Policy and in the Land Commission Act, which established the Land Commission to review policy and interpret law.

But assigning priority to economic dimensions has two disadvantages: it underemphasizes the role of historical grievances, patronage networks, and the quest for political power in explaining conflict, and it overemphasizes the impact of economic recovery as a peacebuilding tool.

Peacebuilders tend to frame natural resource management in economic terms because they are ill equipped to see political grievances or to understand how political and economic motives are linked. For reform to be effective, natural resource management needs to consider the livelihood needs of the population *and* the combined political and economic agendas of those who are in power. More specifically, for natural resource management to contribute to peace, it must engage with local communities, address their everyday needs, and work to bring to the surface the systems of power and patronage that fuel grievances and sow discontent in the first place.

REFERENCES

Abdullah, I. A., ed. 2004. *Between democracy and terror: The Sierra Leone civil war.* Dakar, Senegal: CODESRIA.

Austin, J. E., and C. E. Bruch, eds. 2000. *The environmental consequences of war: Legal, economic and scientific perspectives.* Cambridge, UK: Cambridge University Press.

Baker, M., R. Clausen, R. Kanaan, M. N'Goma, T. Roule, and J. Thomson. 2003. *African cases.* Vol. 3 of *Conflict timber: Dimensions of the problem in Asia and Africa.* Washington, D.C.: U.S. Agency for International Development.

Ballentine, K., and H. Nitzschke. 2005. *Profiting from peace: Managing the resource dimensions of civil war.* Boulder, CO: Lynne Rienner.

Ballentine, K., and J. Sherman, eds. 2003. *The political economy of armed conflict: Beyond greed and grievance.* Boulder, CO: Lynne Rienner.

Bangura, Y. 2004. The political and cultural dynamics of the Sierra Leone war. In *Between democracy and terror: The Sierra Leone civil war*, ed. I. A. Abdullah. Dakar, Senegal: CODESRIA.

Bannon, I., and P. Collier, eds. 2003. *Natural resources and violent conflict.* Washington, D.C.: World Bank.

Beevers, M. 2008. Understanding environmental and natural resources governance in war-torn societies: Initial observations from forest politics in Liberia. Paper presented at the annual convention for the International Studies Association, February 15–18, New York.

Bijlsma, M. 2005. Protecting the environment. In *Postconflict development*, ed. G. Junne and W. Verkoren. Boulder, CO: Lynne Rienner.

Binda, S. 2010. Community rights law "secretly" altered. (Liberia) *Daily Observer.* May 24.

Binningsbø, H., and S. A. Rustad. 2008. Resource conflicts, resource management and post-conflict peace. Working Paper. Oslo: Centre for the Study of Civil War, Peace Research Institute Oslo.

Call, C. 2008. Ending wars, building states. In *Building states to build peace*, ed. C. Call and V. Wyeth. Boulder, CO: Lynne Rienner.

Chabal, P., and J. P. Daloz. 1999. *Africa works: Disorder as a political instrument.* Oxford, UK: James Currey Ltd.

Collier, P., and A. Hoeffler. 1998. On economic causes of civil war. *Oxford Economic Papers* 50:563–573.

———. 1999. *Justice-seeking and loot-seeking in civil war*. Washington, D.C.: World Bank.

Conca, K., and G. Dabelko, eds. 2002. *Environmental peacemaking*. Washington, D.C.: Woodrow Wilson Center Press / Johns Hopkins University Press.

Crossin, C., G. Hayman, and S. Taylor. 2003. Where did it come from? Commodity tracking systems. In *Natural resources and violent conflict*, ed. I. Bannon and P. Collier. Washington, D.C.: World Bank.

de Jong, W., D. Donovan, and K. Abe, eds. 2007. *Extreme conflict and tropical forests*. Dordrecht, Netherlands: Springer.

Deudney, D., and R. Matthew, eds. 1999. *Contested grounds: Security and conflict in the new environmental politics*. Albany: SUNY Press.

Diehl, P. F., and N. P. Gleditsch, eds. 2001. *Environmental conflict*. Boulder, CO: Westview Press.

Duffield, M. 2001. *Global governance and the new wars*. London: Zed Books.

Ellis, S. 1999. *The mask of anarchy: The destruction of Liberia and the religious dimension of an African civil war*. New York: New York University Press.

Farah, D. 2001. Al Qaida cash tied to diamond trade. *Washington Post*. November 2.

FAO (UN Food and Agriculture Organization). 2009. Land cover in Liberia–Globcover regional. www.fao.org/geonetwork/srv/en/metadata.show?id=37192&currTab=simple.

Ford, N. 2008. Timber exports banned to save forests. *African Business*. March 1.

Gberie, L. 2005. *The dirty war in West Africa: The RUF and the destruction of Sierra Leone*. Bloomington: Indiana University Press.

Global Witness. 2000. *Conflict diamonds: Possibilities for the identification, certification and control of diamonds*. London.

———. 2002. *The logs of war: The timber trade and armed conflict*. Oslo: Fafo Institute for Applied Social Sciences.

———. 2004. *Dangerous liaisons: The continued relationship between Liberia's natural resource industries, arms trafficking and regional insecurity*. London: Global Witness.

———. 2009. Credibility of Liberia's forest reform programme at point of collapse. Press release. August 28.

GOL (Government of Liberia). 2006a. An act adopting the National Forestry Reform Law of 2006. www.unep.org/dec/docs/Liberian%20forestry%20law.pdf.

———. 2006b. *Breaking with the past: From conflict to development*. Interim poverty reduction strategy summary, Republic of Liberia. Monrovia: Government of Liberia.

GOSL (Government of Sierra Leone). 2008a. *The agenda for change: My government's policies for Sierra Leone's poverty reduction strategy*. www.fao.org/docs/up/easypol/forum/31//31_President%27s_Agenda_for_Change.doc%201%20.pdf.

———. 2008b. Forestry development, exploitation and trade reforms. Internal document. Forestry Division. Ministry of Agriculture, Forestry, and Food Security.

Hauge, W., and T. Ellingsen. 1998. Beyond environmental scarcity: Causal pathways to conflict. *Journal of Peace Research* 35:298–317.

Homer-Dixon, T. 1991. On the threshold: Environmental changes as causes of acute conflict. *International Security* 16:76–116.

———. 1999. *Environment, scarcity and violence*. Princeton, NJ: Princeton University Press.

Howard, P. C. 2009. Towards a revision of forestry and wildlife legislation in Sierra Leone. Internal document. Forestry Division. Ministry of Agriculture, Forestry, and Food Security. Government of Sierra Leone.

IMF (International Monetary Fund). 2008. *Liberia: Poverty reduction strategy.* IMF Country Report 08/219. Washington, D.C.

Kaimowitz, D. 2003. *Forests and war, forests and peace.* Bogor, Indonesia: CIFOR.

Kaldor, M. 1999. *New and old wars: Organized violence in a global era.* Stanford: Stanford University Press.

Kaplan, R. 1994. The coming anarchy: How scarcity, crime, overpopulation and diseases are rapidly destroying our planet. *Atlantic Monthly.* February.

Keen, D. 2005. *Conflict and collusion in Sierra Leone.* Oxford, UK: James Currey Ltd.

Le Billon, P. 2003. Getting it done: Instruments of enforcement. In *Natural resources and violent conflict*, ed. I. Bannon and P. Collier. Washington, D.C.: World Bank.

———. 2006. Fatal transactions: Conflict diamonds and the (anti) terrorist consumer. *Antipode* 38:778–801.

Levitt, J. I. 2005. *The evolution of deadly conflict in Liberia: From paternaltarianism to state collapse.* Durham, NC: Carolina Academic Press.

Paris, R. 2004. *At war's end: Building peace after civil conflict.* Cambridge, UK: Cambridge University Press.

Peluso, N. L., and M. Watts. 2001. *Violent environments.* Ithaca, NY: Cornell University Press.

Price, S. V., ed. 2003. *War and tropical forests: Conservation in areas of armed conflict.* Binghamton, NY: Food Products Press.

Reno, W. 1995. *Corruption and state politics in Sierra Leone.* Cambridge, UK: Cambridge University Press.

———. 1998. *Warlord politics and African states.* Boulder, CO: Lynne Rienner.

———. 2000. Shadow states and the political economy of civil wars. In *Greed and grievance: Economic agendas in civil war,* ed. M. Bergdal and D. M. Malone. Boulder, CO: Lynne Rienner.

Richards, P. 1995. Rebellion in Liberia and Sierra Leone: A crisis of youth? In *Conflict in Africa,* ed. O. W. Furley. London: Tauris.

———. 1996. *Fighting in the rainforest: War, youth and resources in Sierra Leone.* Oxford, UK: Heinemann Educational Books.

———. 2001. Are forest wars in Africa resource conflicts? The case of Sierra Leone. In *Violent environments*, ed. N. L. Peluso and M. Watts. Ithaca, NY: Cornell University Press.

Richards, P., B. S. Archibald, B. Bruce, W. Modad, E. Mulbah, T. Varpilah, and J. Vincent. 2005. Community cohesion in Liberia: A post-war rapid social assessment. World Bank Social Development Paper 21. Washington, D.C.: World Bank.

Ross, M. 2003. The natural resources curse: How wealth can make you poor. In *Natural resources and violent conflict,* ed. I. Bannon and P. Collier. Washington, D.C.: World Bank.

———. 2004. How do natural resources influence civil war? Evidence from thirteen cases. *International Organization* 58:35–67.

Rustad, S. A., H. Binningsbø, and P. Le Billon. 2009. Do resource-related peacebuilding initiatives build peace? Paper presented at the annual convention for the International Studies Association, February 15–18, New York.

Rustad, S. A., K. J. Rød, W. Larsen, and P. N. Gleditsch. 2008. Foliage and fighting: Forest resources and the onset, duration, and location of civil war. *Political Geography* 27:761–782.

Sawyer, A. 1992. *The emergence of autocracy in Liberia: Tragedy and challenge.* San Francisco: Institute for Contemporary Studies.

Smillie, I., L. Gberie, and R. Hazleton. 2000. *The heart of the matter: Sierra Leone, diamonds and human security.* Ottawa: Partnership Africa Canada.

Squire, C. 2001. *Sierra Leone's biodiversity and the civil war.* Washington, D.C.: Biodiversity Support Program.

Thomson, J., and R. Kanaan. 2003. *Conflict timber: Dimensions of the problem in Asia and Africa.* Washington, D.C.: U.S. Agency for International Development.

Truth and Reconciliation Commission of Liberia. 2009. Final report. http://trcofliberia.org.

UNDP (United Nations Development Programme). 2008. Human development indices: A statistical update 2008. http://hdr.undp.org/en/statistics/.

UNEP (United Nations Environment Programme). 2004. *Desk study on the environment in Liberia.* Nairobi.

———. 2009. *From conflict to peacebuilding: The role of natural resources and the environment.* Nairobi.

UNSC (United Nations Security Council). 2000. Resolution 1306. S/RES/1306 (2000). July 5.

———. 2001. Report of the panel of experts pursuant to Security Council Resolution 1343 (2001), paragraph 19, concerning Liberia. S/2001/1015. www.un.org/Docs/sc/committees/Liberia2/1015e.pdf.

———. 2003. Resolution 1478. S/RES/1478 (2003). May 6.

———. 2004. Report of the panel of experts, concerning Liberia.

———. 2006. Resolution 1689. S/RES/1689 (2004). June 20

———. 2008. Report of the panel of experts submitted pursuant to paragraph 1 of Security Council resolution 1819 (2008) concerning Liberia. S/2008/785. www.securitycouncilreport.org/atf/cf/%7B65BFCF9B-6D27-4E9C-8CD3-CF6E4FF96FF9%7D/Liberia%20S%20 2008%20785.pdf.

USAID (U.S. Agency for International Development). 2005. *Forests and conflict: A toolkit for intervention.* Washington, D.C.

World Bank. 2005. *Republic of Sierra Leone joint IDA–IMF advisory note on the poverty reduction strategy paper.* Report number 31775-SL. Washington, D.C.: World Bank.

Zack-Williams, A., and S. Riley. 1993. Sierra Leone: The coup and its consequences. *Review of African Political Economy* 56 (March): 91–98.

An inescapable curse? Resource management, violent conflict, and peacebuilding in the Niger Delta

Annegret Mähler

The Niger Delta is home to nearly thirty million people and to the greatest concentration of oil production in the country. Since 1999, when Nigeria transitioned to democracy, the central government has undertaken three major resource management initiatives for the conflict-ridden region:

- The reform of the derivation formula, which regulates the distribution of oil revenue.
- The establishment of the Niger Delta Development Commission and the Niger Delta Regional Development Master Plan.
- The creation of the Ministry of the Niger Delta and the launching of the Niger Delta Technical Committee.[1]

The intent of the initiatives was to reduce violence and to improve socioeconomic conditions in the delta.[2] While studies by Philippe Le Billon (2008) and the United Nations Environment Programme (2009) have demonstrated that natural resource management may contribute to peacebuilding, in the case of the Niger Delta, such policies have so far had little success.[3] Indeed, violence and forced displacements have increased significantly since the end of the 1990s, causing tremendous social and economic damage. In 2008, more than 1,000 people were

---

Annegret Mähler is a research fellow at the German Institute of Global and Area Studies in Hamburg, Germany.

[1] Although there were a few initiatives before 1999, they were not substantial, and the military government's response to increasing unrest in the Niger Delta was dominated by harsh military repression. The democratization that occurred in 1999 therefore seems to be a sound starting point for assessing resource management initiatives.

[2] The Niger Delta is located in southern Nigeria. As defined in this chapter, the region includes nine states: Abia, Akwa Ibom, Bayelsa, Cross River, Delta, Edo, Imo, Ondo, and Rivers.

[3] For more information on the causal relationship between natural resources and violence, see Päivi Lujala and Siri Aas Rustad, "High-Value Natural Resources: A Blessing or Curse for Peace," the introductory chapter of this book.

392 High-value natural resources and post-conflict peacebuilding

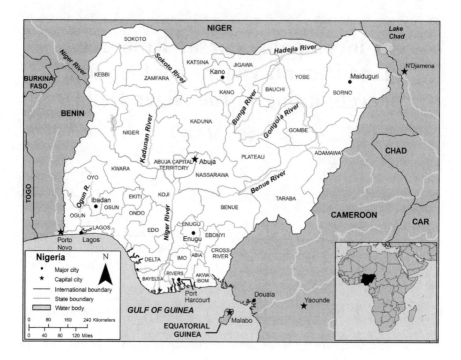

killed—a historical peak (IRIN 2009b). With a view to providing insights for improving future resource management in the Niger Delta and beyond, this chapter explores the reasons for the limited success of the initiatives.

The failure to reduce violence and improve socioeconomic conditions in the delta—and thereby establish a durable peace—can be attributed to four main causes:

- Conceptual weaknesses in the initiatives themselves, which failed to adequately address the complex political, social, and economic causes of the conflicts—in particular, the socioeconomic distortions caused by the oil industry's effects on employment.
- The weakness of political institutions, which undermines the effectiveness of all government initiatives.
- The presence of an oil-based "economy of violence" that is fostered by a number of parties—including politicians, security forces, local authorities, and international actors—that have a vested interest in continued conflict.
- The government's military intervention in the delta, which has been marked by the disproportionate use of violence and is drawing segments of the Niger Delta population into active or passive support for militant groups.

The chapter is divided into six major sections: (1) a brief history of the conflict; (2) a discussion of the central resource management initiatives; (3) an evaluation of the initiatives' effects on socioeconomic development and violent conflict;

(4) an examination of general constraints on the outcomes of the initiatives; (5) a list of lessons learned; and (6) recommendations for next steps.

CONFLICT IN THE NIGER DELTA: A BRIEF HISTORY

Commercial oil production began in Nigeria in 1956, four years before the country became independent. By 1970, oil production already accounted for more than 50 percent of the country's export revenues; by the end of the 1970s, it accounted for about 95 percent (UN Comtrade n.d.). Since then, the high dependence on oil has changed little; in 2005, for example, oil revenues accounted for 88 percent of government income (Lubeck, Watts, and Lipschutz 2007).

Ever since oil production in the Niger Delta began, the area has suffered from violent, oil-related conflicts. The attempted secession of Biafra, which is situated within the Niger Delta, led to a bloody civil war (1967–1970) that was motivated—

not exclusively, but strongly—by disputes between the federal government and the regional political and military elites over the sharing of oil revenues (Harneit-Sievers 1992; Oyefusi 2007).[4]

Between the mid-1970s and the end of military rule, in 1999, the central government gradually reduced the share of oil revenues allotted to producing states. The struggle between the federal government and regional activists over what constitutes fair distribution remains one of the central causes of conflict in the Niger Delta.

In addition to fueling violence, oil exploitation in the Niger Delta has had disastrous ecological consequences: massive contamination of water resources, destruction of farmland, and dispersion of toxic substances (Obi 2001). Between 1986 and the end of the 1990s, distress associated with environmental damage was exacerbated by a deep economic crisis that led to a rise in unemployment and poverty. Between 1985 and 1995, the portion of the Niger Delta population living in poverty rose from 44 to 59 percent (UNDP 2006). The government responded to the economic crisis by introducing, in 1986, a structural adjustment program that involved deep cuts in public expenditures for health and education.

By the beginning of the 1990s, the combination of environmental damage and harsh economic circumstances had led to increasing grassroots mobilization (Ukeje 2003). The struggle first gained international attention when Ken Saro-Wiwa founded the Movement for the Survival of the Ogoni People (MOSOP). In 1990, MOSOP presented its manifesto, the Ogoni Bill of Rights,[5] to the government and the people of Nigeria. The document demanded fair compensation for oil pollution, a more equitable distribution of oil revenues, and more political autonomy for the Ogoni people. Although MOSOP was a nonviolent movement, it encountered severe governmental repression; Saro-Wiwa and eight of his fellow activists were executed, several hundred other activists were detained, whole villages were devastated, and numerous people were killed (Ibeanu and Mohammed 2001).[6] By 1995, the government had succeeded in crushing the protest movement, and the level of conflict in the Niger Delta dropped temporarily—but the root causes of the conflicts remained.

In March 1997, a decade-long dispute between the Itsekiri, the Urhobo, and the Ijaw peoples over the ownership of Warri, a town located in Delta State, was reignited by the creation of a new jurisdiction known as Warri South West, and

---

[4] On May 30, 1967, after the central government put in place a territorial realignment that implied that the Igbo majority would lose control over the oil-producing areas of the Niger Delta, the Biafran region, under the command of the Igbo military governor Odumegwu Ojukwu, declared its independence.

[5] The Ogoni Bill of Rights can be viewed at www.waado.org/nigerdelta/RightsDeclaration/Ogoni.html.

[6] In addition, it has been reported that the military regime, under General Sani Abacha, triggered violent boundary conflicts between the Ogoni people and other ethnic groups (Ibeanu and Mohammed 2001; Human Rights Watch 1995). According to Human Rights Watch (1995), for example, Nigerian soldiers participated in secret military raids that were designed to look like violent intercommunal conflicts, and government soldiers joined with Andoni fighters in attacking Ogoni villages.

the location of its headquarters in an Itsekiri area rather than in an Ijaw area (Human Rights Watch 2003). The ethnic violence was indirectly linked to oil, however: private oil companies had assigned disproportionately high financial benefits to the Itsekiri people, intensifying interethnic resentment (Human Rights Watch 1999).[7] In addition, in order to attract public attention to the demands for local control of oil revenues, some local activists—mainly Ijaw youths—seized oil installations and took staff hostage. The conflict over Warri cost hundreds of lives (Bergstresser 1998; Human Rights Watch 2003).

Since the Warri crisis, a complex interplay of interethnic and intercommunal conflicts has continued to feed periodic violent eruptions throughout the Niger Delta. This violence has been marked, since the late 1990s, by an increase in hostage taking (ICG 2006a) and in the sabotage of oil pipelines (Zinn 2005). Clashes with government security forces—notorious for human rights violations and for their immoderate use of force (Human Rights Watch 1999, 2002, 2006)— have also increased, destroying the credibility of the government in the delta and fostering increasingly violent responses from militant youth groups.

Although there is no question that oil has played a major role in violent conflict in the Niger Delta, oil fails to provide an exhaustive explanation of the violence.[8] There are essentially three roots of the conflict, all of which predate the oil era: cultural and political cleavages, weak political institutions, and an as-yet unconsolidated statehood (World Bank 2003). Nevertheless, oil continues to serve as an additional trigger for conflict:

- The massive environmental damage that has resulted from oil production has created a tremendous sense of grievance.
- Struggles over the distribution of oil revenues have exacerbated interethnic and intercommunal conflict.
- By causing distortions in the national economy, oil has indirectly increased the risk of violent conflict.[9]

---

[7] In the absence of a responsible state, some oil companies had began to provide—partly unofficially—financial assistance to their host communities to pacify them.

[8] The following findings are based on a research project of the German Institute of Global and Area Studies; the research was funded by the DFG (German Research Foundation) and supervised by Dr. Matthias Basedau.

[9] Since the 1970s, because of its almost total dependence on oil exports, Nigeria has increasingly suffered from "Dutch disease"; at the same time, financial mismanagement has been rampant. As noted in the text, the deep economic crisis that began in 1986 led to rising unemployment and poverty in the 1990s; see Mähler (2010) for details. (*Dutch disease* is a phenomenon in which the discovery of substantial natural resource wealth negatively affects a nation's economy. The discovery often causes sudden appreciation in the value of the nation's currency—which, in turn, decreases the nation's competitiveness in the international commodity markets. This reduces the country's exports of manufactured and agricultural commodities and increases its imports. At the same time, the natural resource sector draws a substantial share of domestic resources such as labor and materials, increasing their cost to other sectors. Moreover, when the initially booming resource sector eventually declines, the non-resource-based sectors may find it difficult to recover.)

- By funding patronage networks, oil has further corrupted Nigeria's weak political institutions.
- By indirectly funding militant groups, oil serves as a catalyst for violence.

RESOURCE MANAGEMENT INITIATIVES

Although the government's initial (and continuing) response to conflict in the Niger Delta was military suppression, this strategy has been accompanied by peacebuilding and conflict-prevention initiatives, especially since democratization in 1999. For example, the government has launched various law enforcement initiatives, including the seizure of weapons and machinery and the prosecution of arms smugglers, and has agreed to periodic (and usually short) cease-fires.

The government has also intensified efforts to build peace by reforming resource management. As noted earlier, the three principal initiatives in this area are the reform of the derivation formula; the establishment of the Niger Delta Development Commission and the development of the Niger Delta Regional Development Master Plan; and the creation of the Ministry of Niger Delta Affairs and the Technical Committee on the Niger Delta.[10]

Reform of the derivation formula

The derivation formula determines the share of oil revenues distributed to the regions where the oil was extracted. Until the end of the 1960s, the producing states received a share of 50 percent. In the wake of Nigeria's political and fiscal centralization,[11] this percentage was steadily reduced: from 45 percent (1969–1975), to 20 percent (1975–1979), to between 0 and 3 percent (1979–1999) (UNDP 2006). With the transition to democracy, in 1999, the share was increased to 13 percent.

Although per capita oil revenue is relatively small in Nigeria, even a 13 percent stake is by no means marginal, especially in view of the strong increase in the price of oil in recent years. The derivation formula is set forth in the Nigerian constitution, but there are no regulations dictating how the revenues should be spent (ANEEJ 2004), and there are hardly any local or regional mechanisms of fiscal control (Human Rights Watch 2007).

Because of the southern states' persistent discontent with the derivation formula, reform of the formula became the topic of debate in 2005, at the National

---

[10] Although further initiatives were undertaken by civil society groups, oil companies, and international organizations, evaluation of these efforts is beyond the scope of this chapter. For comprehensive studies of nongovernmental initiatives, see Ibeanu (2006), Ogonor (2003), and Ngomba-Roth (2007).

[11] Beginning in 1975, the (almost exclusively) military governments transferred more and more responsibility from the local and regional levels to the federal level, in order to strengthen Nigeria's internal stability—but also to extend their personal power.

Political Reform Conference.[12] While the delegates from the northern states were willing to accept an increase to 17 percent, the Niger Delta delegates insisted on at least 25 percent, with an eventual increase to 50 percent over the long term. This contentious issue was left unresolved, however, and was not addressed in the closing statement of the conference. The end result was further polarization of oil-producing and non-oil-producing states (UNDP 2006).

The legislative representatives of the Niger Delta—and the vast majority of the Niger Delta population—view the existing regulation as unjustifiably depriving them of revenues that are theirs by right. And for most of the militant groups, a higher share of oil revenues is one of the central official justifications for armed struggle (Olukoya 2009).

The Niger Delta Development Commission

In 2000, faced with growing violence in the delta, the administration of President Olusegun Obasanjo made a second effort to address violent conflict by creating the Niger Delta Development Commission (NDDC). The NDDC replaced the Oil Mineral Producing Areas Development Commission (OMPADEC), which had been established by the military regime in 1992. As stipulated in the Niger Delta Development Commission Act No. 2, 1999, the NDDC's mandate was to "conceive, plan and implement, in accordance with set rules and regulations, projects and programmes for the sustainable development of the Niger-Delta area" (Nigerian National Assembly 1999 part II, title 7, 1.b). Specifically, the NDDC was to focus on the "development of social and physical infrastructures; technology; economic/environmental remediation and stability; human development; pursuit of a peaceful environment that allows tourism to thrive and supports a buoyant culture" (UNDP 2006). The NDDC was also charged with developing a long-term master plan for the delta, which would integrate strategies proposed by a variety of stakeholders, including the central and regional governments, oil companies, and nongovernmental organizations (NGOs).

Guide to Abbreviations

MEND:	Movement for the Emancipation of the Niger Delta
MNDA:	Ministry of Niger Delta Affairs
MOSOP:	Movement for the Survival of the Ogoni People
NDDC:	Niger Delta Development Commission
NDPVF:	Niger Delta People's Volunteer Force
NDRDMP:	Niger Delta Regional Development Master Plan
OMPADEC:	Oil Mineral Producing Areas Development Commission
TCND:	Technical Committee on the Niger Delta

---

[12] The broader objective of the conference, which was convened by then-president Olusegun Obasanjo, was to discuss future political and constitutional reforms and socioeconomic development in Nigeria, with the ultimate goal of strengthening security, sustainable development, and internal stability. The conference was held between February and July 2005, and was attended by about four hundred participants: six delegates from each state, plus representatives from government-approved social interest groups such as labor unions, business and professional associations, nongovernmental organizations, and ethnic organizations.

By law, the NDDC is an agency of the central government and is directly under the control of the presidency; all commission members are federal political appointees (UNDP 2006). The governing board is made up of nineteen members: the chairman, nine representatives from the oil-producing states, three from the north, and six from the oil and gas industry, federal ministries, and the commission itself (Omeje 2006).[13] Unlike OMPADEC, the new commission draws on various sources—not just on oil revenues—for funding. Most of the funding (between 2001 and 2004, about 78 percent) comes from the federal government (UNDP 2006). Commission members from the oil and gas industry pay 3 percent of their annual budgets toward the support of the NDDC, and member states pay 50 percent of their Ecological Fund allocations (Omeje 2006).[14]

The Niger Delta Regional Development Master Plan (NDRDMP) was developed by GTZ International Services, a German cooperative enterprise for sustainable development that now operates worldwide as GIZ; a Nigerian consulting company; and the NDDC. In March 2007, after an initial delay, President Obasanjo launched the plan. But his successor, President Umaru Musa Yar'Adua, failed to implement the plan when he became president in May 2007.[15]

The NDRDMP identifies the main social, economic, and environmental problems in the Niger Delta,[16] and provides corresponding policy recommendations designed to achieve sustainable development in the region. The recommendations cover twenty-five sectors, the central ones being infrastructure, health, education, agriculture, and conflict resolution (TCND 2008). The plan is designed to be implemented over a fifteen-year period and assumes a financial investment of US$50 billion (ICG 2007).

The Ministry of Niger Delta Affairs and the Technical Committee on the Niger Delta

In September 2008, after repeatedly delaying the implementation of the NDRDMP, President Yar'Adua launched two new initiatives: the Ministry of Niger Delta Affairs (MNDA) and the Technical Committee on the Niger Delta (TCND). The MNDA's mandate is focused on infrastructure development, environmental protection, and youth empowerment—especially the provision of employment (Roll 2008).

---

[13] The commission consists of the governing board, eleven directorates, the Managing Committee, and the Niger Delta Development Advisory Committee (for further details, see Nigerian National Assembly (1999).

[14] The Ecological Fund was established in 1981 to ameliorate ecological problems; it also finances environmental research.

[15] In February 2010, Vice President Jonathan Goodluck, a former governor of the Niger Delta state Bayelsa, became interim president. In May 2010, President Yar'Adua died, and Goodluck assumed the office of president.

[16] The collection of new demographic and socioeconomic data on the Niger Delta was part of the NDRDMP's mandate.

The MNDA was put in charge of all development efforts in the region (*Africa Research Bulletin* 2009); thus, the NDDC became answerable to the new federal ministry. Initially, the central government announced that the MNDA would be located in the delta—to facilitate coordination with the NDDC and as a signal of the federal government's responsiveness to the wishes of the Niger Delta population. However, the MNDA was ultimately based in Abuja, the national capital. Obong Ufot Ekaette, the new minister of Niger Delta affairs, was born in the delta, but by the time of his appointment, he had already served the federal bureaucracy for many years; hence, his appointment was not very popular in the delta (ICG 2009).

The TCND's mandate was to review all previous reports and initiatives on the Niger Delta—starting with the 1958 Willinks' Report, issued during colonial rule, and including the NDRDMP. On the basis of this review, the TCND was to make recommendations on how "to achieve sustainable development, peace, human and environmental security in the Niger Delta region" (TCND 2008, vi). The forty-four-member committee, chaired by Ledum Mitee, the president of MOSOP, submitted its report to the president at the end of 2008. The TCND urged the federal government to initiate a compact with multiple stakeholders confirming its commitment "to support critical short-term changes" (TCND 2008, 59); it also stated that this compact should include, among other things, an immediate increase in the derivation formula to 25 percent (TCND 2008).

In comparison to past efforts to resolve violent conflict and improve socioeconomic conditions in the Niger Delta, the recommendations place greater emphasis on "good governance, transparency and accountability" (TCND 2008, 65) and on "the sustainable utilisation of the resources of the Niger Delta," which "holds the key to the successful reintegration of the Region into a productive national economy" (TCND 2008, 82). In addition, the TCND recommendations focus on economic development and human-capital development, through the improvement of health care and education and the empowerment of women and young people.

OUTCOMES OF THE INITIATIVES

The following evaluation of the peacebuilding initiatives is divided into two complementary parts: the first assesses specific achievements and limitations of the initiatives; the second is a more general analysis of the government's success in achieving its main objectives—namely, reducing violent conflict and improving socioeconomic conditions in the delta. While it is too early for a conclusive evaluation of the latest initiatives (the MNDA and the TCND), a somewhat more definitive assessment of the NDDC—and, with some reservations, of the NDRDMP—is possible.

Achievements and limitations of the initiatives

The mere creation of the NDDC can be considered a breakthrough in the federal government's commitment to the Niger Delta. Both in concept and in terms of financial support, the NDDC is an improvement over OMPADEC—which, according to several sources, was underfunded, plagued by internal corruption, and failed to achieve any improvement in the development of the region (ANEEJ 2004; Omotola 2007).

According to the NDDC's own reports, by the beginning of 2006 it had initiated over 2,000 development projects and 300 electrification projects (ICG 2006b).[17] However, as Kenneth Omeje (2006) reports, a study published in September 2003 revealed that of 358 projects that had been conceived by the NDDC, only 100 were operational. A 2004 study by the African Network for Environment and Economic Justice (ANEEJ) supported Omeje's report, finding widespread abandonment of projects in Akwa Ibom State, for example. Although the NDDC has unquestionably made *some* progress in local infrastructure development (ANEEJ 2004; ICG 2006b), the initiative has not had substantial or wide-ranging impact. In short, the NDDC has yet to meet the development needs of the region or the expectations of the populace; as a consequence, delta residents have less and less confidence in the capacity and reliability of the commission.

Explanations of the NDDC's poor performance focus on the lack of funding; numerous sources have reported that neither the federal government, the state government, or the oil companies have met their financial obligations.[18] For instance, a December 2007 report by the International Crisis Group notes that since 2000 the NDDC should have received US$4 billion; instead, it had received US$1.9 billion (ICG 2007). And a November 2008 TCND report "recommends that ALL OUTSTANDING FUNDS due to NDDC be paid IMMEDIATELY as these are legitimate amounts due to the Region"—clearly underlining the serious and persistent financial constraints under which the NDDC operates (TCND 2008, 73).

Another major shortcoming of the NDDC's efforts is the lack of mechanisms for monitoring and evaluating the allocation and implementation of projects (Omeje 2006). Without monitoring and evaluation, it is impossible to compare project conceptions, the effectiveness of contractors, or empirical outcomes. Moreover, the lack of transparency opens the way for widespread corruption—which, indeed, has been reported to be pervasive in the NDDC (Omotola 2007).

Both in conception and implementation, the NDDC is burdened by a top-down approach: as noted earlier, all the members of the governing board are federal appointees; moreover, there is no mechanism to ensure that members of the local population are included on the commission (Higgins 2008). Programs and projects are thus conceived and designed without the involvement of those who will be most directly affected (Omeje 2006). Understandably, many inhabitants of the delta regard the NDDC as an imposition by the federal government (UNDP 2006); as Ben Aigbokhan (2007, 195) notes, delta residents, "particularly the youth," have a "hostile attitude . . . towards the NDDC."

---

[17] Projects included the construction of roads, schools, health centers, and electrical facilities.

[18] See, for example, ANEEJ (2004); Omeje (2006); and UNDP (2006).

Although the NDRDMP was developed under the aegis of the NDDC, it has several advantages over its parent initiative: first, it is inherently more participatory than both the NDDC itself and the NDDC's earlier projects. For example, the NDRDMP was developed on the basis of broad consultation with Niger Delta residents (Rühl 2004).[19] Second, because of the recognized flaws in the NDDC, the master plan places much more emphasis on monitoring and evaluation (TCND 2008).

Despite being "considered comprehensive by many development experts" (ICG 2009, 11), the NDRDMP has a central flaw, however: it remains essentially unimplemented. The beginnings of the plan date back to late 2001, when GTZ, in collaboration with a Nigerian consulting company and the NDDC, helped to create a broad development plan for the region. The government officially launched the plan in March 2007. Implementation was repeatedly delayed, however, until—as noted earlier—President Yar'Adua launched two new initiatives, the MNDA and the TCND, then gave them mandates that at least partly duplicated the work that had been carried out during the development of the master plan.

Given the history of the NDDC and the NDRDMP, the future of the TCND should also be regarded somewhat skeptically. What speaks in its favor are three factors: (1) its relatively broad membership (as the president of MOSOP, Ledum Mitee, the chair of the TCND, has a great deal of legitimacy in the delta); (2) its participatory character; and (3) its coherent and comprehensive recommendations, which were based on an extensive critical review of former initiatives and development plans (ICG 2009).

Nevertheless, the TCND's report has so far evoked little government response. Instead, in February 2009, several months after receiving the TCND's report, President Yar'Adua announced that he wanted to create yet another government committee to study the TCND's recommendations and propose some strategies for carrying them out (IRIN 2009a). His actions exacerbated the frustration of Niger Delta residents and reinforced their view that the government is unwilling to provide any concrete solutions to the region's problems.

On the one hand, delta residents—many of whom have lost confidence in the NDDC—may view the creation of a completely new agency, the MNDA, as a symbol of a resurgence of the government's commitment to change in the region. On the other hand, the ministry's credibility has been undermined by the decision to locate it in Abuja rather than in the delta, and by the MNDA's "unclear guiding principles" (ICG 2009, 1): unless the ministry's mandate is clarified, its responsibilities and those of the NDDC are likely to overlap (ICG 2009), leading to inefficiency, coordination problems, and the waste of financial resources. Moreover, the ministry's effectiveness may be constrained by low funding. Under the 2009 budget, it was set to receive less funding than the NDDC has received in recent years, making it unlikely that the MNDA will succeed in meeting the

---

[19] Bettina Rühl (2004) reports that consultants undertook extensive qualitative surveys on the current situation, needs, and expectations of Niger Delta residents.

ambitious aims set by the federal government.[20] Among delta residents, views of the new ministry's ability to foster change are mixed; some are doubtful (Walker 2008a), whereas others—including Chief Edwin Clark, a prominent Ijaw leader—are more positive (ICG 2009).

Socioeconomic development and violence in the Niger Delta since 1999

Has the Niger Delta experienced any significant improvement in the principal socioeconomic indicators since 1999? Predominant opinion, both in the literature and among delta residents, is that the government's resource-based initiatives have had little, if any, success (Aigbokhan 2007; Higgins 2009; Omotola 2007). Although current and accurate data are hard to come by, available information appears to support this assessment.[21] For example, according to data from the UN Development Programme, between 1996 and 2004, the incidence of poverty in the Niger Delta decreased somewhat, from 59.0 percent of the population to 50.5 percent—but the poverty level is still above 1980s levels (UNDP 2006).[22] Thus, although there may be a causal relationship between the decline in poverty and the implementation of NDDC programs, the reform of the derivation formula, or both, the decline has not been substantial.

The incidence of poverty is not the sole indicator, however, that socioeconomic conditions have improved little if at all. The Niger Delta is still characterized by poor infrastructure and limited access to health care; in fact, as of 2006, delta residents' access to health care was worse than that of any other region (Aigbokhan 2007). Housing, too, continues to be of poor quality (UNDP 2006). Although there are no reliable data that would allow a comparison between the 1990s and the first decade of the twenty-first century, as of 2006, unemployment was extremely high in the Niger Delta, and was higher there than in the rest of the country (Aigbokhan 2007; UNDP 2006).

Finally, oil production in the Niger Delta continues to cause severe environmental damage. So far, despite directives from the central government ordering oil companies to end gas flaring, no substantial reduction has occurred (UNDP 2006; Amnesty International 2009).[23] Oil spills continue to contaminate water resources, destroy farmland, and disperse toxic materials. Indeed, the absolute

---

[20] In fact, as noted earlier, the NDDC did not receive the designated budget at all; it is conceivable that the MNDA might suffer the same fate.

[21] For example, even the TCND's report, which was published in November 2008, relies on a survey published in 2000 for its data on health care access in the delta.

[22] According to the UNDP report, poverty rates in 1980 ranged from a low of 7.2 percent (in Rivers State and Bayelsa State) to a high of 24.9 percent (in Ondo State).

[23] Oil drilling is usually accompanied by escaping gas. In Nigeria, most of the gas is burned as waste; "gas flaring," as it is called, causes air pollution, acid rain, noise, and elevated ambient temperature, grievously harming wildlife, farmland, and human populations.

number of oil spills seems to have increased between 2004 and 2009 (TCND 2008).[24] Referring to general socioeconomic conditions in the Niger Delta, Nnamdi Obasi, head of the ICG's Nigeria bureau, stated in 2009 that "although no recent comprehensive studies have been done on living conditions in the region, residents in several states say the development situation 'has deteriorated' since the 2006 UN Development Programme . . . report on development indicators" (IRIN 2009b).

With respect to the second major objective—ending violent conflict in the delta—empirical results are even more disturbing. Violence (defined as death and displacement) has increased overall since 1999, and at an even more rapid rate since 2003 (Hazen and Horner 2007; HIIK n.d.). One cause of the uptick in violence that began in 1999 was the transition to democracy: politicians began recruiting young men, most of whom were unemployed, and providing them with weapons to intimidate voters and combat political opponents. Since most of the weapons have not been returned (Hazen and Horner 2007; Human Rights Watch 2004), a considerable number of well-armed, disillusioned young men—many of whom were dismissed after the elections, as the politicians no longer had any use for them—are at large, and have become the main actors in the violent uproar raging in the delta (Obi 2006).[25]

In addition to engaging in armed clashes with security forces, militant groups—including the Movement for the Emancipation of the Niger Delta (MEND), the Niger Delta Vigilante, and the now-weakened Niger Delta People's Volunteer Force (NDPVF)—have sabotaged oil pipelines, attacked oil installations, and kidnapped staff members. Although the exact number of sabotage attacks is contested, data indicate that the incidence of sabotage has increased considerably since the late 1990s (TCND 2008).[26] Hostage taking is on the rise

---

[24] Not all of the oil spills result from poorly maintained pipelines; some are caused by sabotage, either as an act of protest or for the purpose of theft (Amnesty International 2009).

[25] As of 2011, the most visible armed group is the Movement for the Emancipation of the Niger Delta (MEND), which has played a prominent role in the region since 2006. Although MEND is largely made up of young Ijaw, it does not make exclusively ethnic demands. MEND's three major demands are the withdrawal of government troops from the Niger Delta; the release from prison of Dokubu Asari, the former leader of an armed group, the Niger Delta People's Volunteer Force (NDPVF); and local control over oil revenues (Hanson 2007). Some MEND members appear to be former members of the NDPVF, an Ijaw militant group, founded in 2003 by Dokubo Asari, that fractured after Asari was arrested in 2005. In contrast to most of the other militant groups, MEND is said to be a loose coalition of armed groups, lacking a stable internal structure (Hazen and Horner 2007). Also unlike other militant groups, MEND has not specifically called for the delta to secede from the rest of Nigeria (*BBC News* 2006).

[26] Oil companies claim a high incidence of sabotage, for which they blame both militant groups and local communities. Community leaders and representatives of national and international NGOs, however, claim that some of the damage to oil installations results not from sabotage, but from erosion caused by poor maintenance (ICG 2006a).

as well (ICG 2006a), with 167 kidnappings in 2007 alone (ICG 2009). While the victims are mainly foreign oil workers, a growing number of wealthy Nigerians have also been taken hostage. In addition to drawing public attention to militant demands, hostage taking is used to finance militant activities.[27]

According to IRIN (2009b), the UN news agency, 2008 was "the Delta's most dangerous year on record"; in the first nine months of the year, 1,000 people were killed and 300 were taken hostage. Because of intensified military operations under way since May 2009, clashes between government forces and militant groups have increased; the resulting waves of displacement have affected thousands of people.

In August 2009, the government offered amnesty to all militants who hand over their arms; those who renounce violence will receive financial compensation and be given access to rehabilitation programs. Although some militant groups, including MEND, initially resisted participation, many relented shortly before the deadline: ultimately, at least 8,000 militants are reported to have joined the amnesty program, and thousands of guns were collected (Vanguard 2009). Although the amnesty is only a first step, there are signs that, at least in the short term, federal funds will be used for rehabilitation programs for former militants. Nevertheless, given the unsolved socioeconomic crisis in the delta, the remaining weapons arsenals, and the failure of similar amnesty programs in the past, some observers remain skeptical about the long-term success of the amnesty (*BBC News* 2009; Duffield 2009).

CONSTRAINTS ON OUTCOMES

The Nigerian government's efforts to support peacebuilding in the Niger Delta through resource management suffer from three major constraints, two of which are conceptual and the third of which is structural:

- Especially during the first years after the transition to democracy, program planning occurred without sufficient public participation.
- Implemented projects are not subject to adequate external monitoring or self-evaluation.
- The oil industry is capital intensive, but it is not labor intensive (Karl 2007). This structural problem is particularly pronounced in Nigeria, where virtually no oil is processed within the country; instead, it is generally exported immediately. As a result, the oil industry provides very few jobs in Nigeria; it thereby contributes directly to the extremely high unemployment in the delta, and indirectly to conflict in the region. This issue has not been addressed sufficiently

---

[27] In addition, criminal copycats engage in hostage taking simply to make money (Hazen and Horner 2007).

within the conception of the initiatives so far, at least not in a sustainable and structural manner.[28]

These conceptual and structural problems are not the only constraints on the government initiatives, however. Broader contextual constraints—both political and social—also impede the effectiveness of the initiatives. First and foremost is the persistent weakness of Nigeria's political institutions (Lewis 2007), which are characterized by lack of transparency, corruption, patronage, and the absence of democratic leadership (especially, but not exclusively, at the state and local levels) (Ologbenla 2007; Higgins 2009). The authors of a 2009 report published by Control Risks, found, for example, that despite "limited progress, . . . coping with corruption remained a major challenge" (Gosztonyi, Taylor, and Bray 2009, 5). Thus, money allocated for socioeconomic development is often used by state and local politicians for private gain (Omeje 2006)—which helps to explain why, despite significant increases in revenues resulting from the reform of the derivation formula, many of the funds are not reaching the local population.

More broadly, the weakness of political institutions generally undermines the effectiveness of *all* government initiatives—including efforts to improve socioeconomic conditions and resolve conflict (Bergstresser 2007). The NDDC's lack of funding and the postponed implementation of the NDRDMP and of the recommendations of the TCND cannot be traced solely to the weakness of political institutions, however: the more immediate causes are lack of government commitment and insufficient opportunities for members of the political opposition, or for civil society groups, to pressure both the government and the oil companies to increase their financial accountability.

Another contextual constraint is the relative weakness and fragmentation of civil society (Bertelsmann Stiftung 2007)—the legacy of extreme ethnic diversity and decades of repressive military rule. Civil society groups are central to peacebuilding; where they are weak and fragmented, development is inevitably hampered.

A number of geographic and demographic characteristics also complicate peacebuilding efforts. The Niger Delta is rough territory, composed largely of marshland and forest and crossed by an extensive network of creeks. As a consequence, it is extremely difficult to provide sustainable infrastructure to the region, and the area provides an excellent hiding place for militant groups. The population density in the habitable parts of the Niger Delta is very high (UNDP 2006) and constantly on the rise; population pressure has rendered land scarce and complicated local development efforts, especially job-creation programs. Moreover, because of Nigeria's large population, per capita oil revenues are low in comparison to those of other oil-producing countries. In 2008, for example, when oil prices were high, per capita oil revenue in Nigeria was only US$409

---

[28] Nigeria engages in almost no oil processing; in fact, almost all of Nigeria's refined oil products are imported (EIA 2009). Although there are four existing state-owned refineries, their capacity is very low, and Nigeria has no private petroleum refineries.

(about US$1.10 per day), versus US$8,291 in Saudi Arabia (EIA 2009). Thus, even if oil wealth were distributed equally, the extent to which peace could be "bought" (or sustainable economic development promoted) would still be limited (Basedau and Lay 2009).[29]

Finally, there is one more crucial contextual factor, which is an indirect consequence of the enduring weakness of political institutions: powerful actors profit, directly or indirectly, from the violent conflict and are fostering its continuation. Since 2000, Nigeria has been home to a thriving trade in weapons and stolen oil that is supported by numerous entities: militant groups; members of the national security forces (Amnesty International 2005; ICG 2006a);[30] politicians (especially at the local and federal levels); the so-called godfathers (wealthy and powerful individuals);[31] and international businesses (both legitimate and less so) (Hanson 2007; Hazen and Horner 2007; Marquardt 2007). Illegal oil trading has increased since 2000 (UNODC 2009). According to the ICG (2006a, i), various industry experts have estimated that "Nigeria loses anywhere from 70,000 to 300,000 barrels per day to illegal bunkering," which is equivalent to between 3 and 12 percent of the country's total oil production. By providing militant groups with weapons and financial resources, the illegal oil trade has fueled an autonomous economy of violence.

LESSONS LEARNED

Since 1999, Nigeria's democratic governments have launched a number of efforts to reduce violence and improve socioeconomic conditions in the Niger Delta; as this chapter has demonstrated, these initiatives have had little success so far. The failure of the initiatives derives, in part, from conceptual problems inherent in their design—namely, a lack of participation and a lack of monitoring and evaluation. However, the Nigerian government seems to have learned some lessons from past experience: more recent initiatives—the NDRDMP and the TCND—are, at least theoretically, more participatory, and have included civil society groups in their planning efforts. Although the NDRDMP also stresses the importance of monitoring projects, self-evaluation is still lagging in practice, and will remain an important future challenge.

---

[29] For a further exploration of this point, see Basedau and Lay (2009), which argues that per capita resource wealth, despite having been largely neglected by previous studies, is pivotal: petrostates with low per capita resource wealth tend to be prone to violence, whereas those with high per capita resource wealth tend to have little violence. Oil-wealthy countries manage to maintain stability through large-scale distribution of wealth, high spending on the security apparatus, and the assurance of protection from external allies (for instance, oil-importing countries that have an interest in protecting cooperative governments).

[30] There are allegations of particular involvement by the Nigerian navy (ICG 2006a).

[31] Godfathers exert crucial political influence in Nigeria: in return for their support for political candidates (which often involves violence), they demand personal benefits, control of political decisions, and shielding from the consequences of their illegal activities, including oil theft (Walker 2008b).

Moreover, the government has so far failed to develop a comprehensive strategy for addressing the economic distortions caused by the oil industry, especially with respect to creating sustainable employment opportunities. Any long-term solution must entail both capacity-building programs and an effort to strengthen the processing industry (and related industries) throughout the country.[32]

As discussed in the previous section, the federal initiatives have also been constrained by broad contextual issues—principally, the weakness of Nigeria's political institutions. Although the federal government appears to have become increasingly aware of the consequence of this weakness—and has, for example, intensified anticorruption initiatives—both political capacity and political will, especially at the state and local levels, are still lacking.[33] More comprehensive approaches are also needed to address oil theft and weapons trading, both of which perpetuate violent struggle. Finally, because local infrastructure has been repeatedly and seriously damaged during military raids, the excessive violence associated with military action in the Niger Delta (Amnesty International 2005; ICG 2006c) has constrained and counteracted the few development efforts that have been achieved so far. Perhaps even more important, military suppression is gradually destroying the government's credibility and indirectly creating support (either active or passive) for militant groups.

CONCLUSION AND NEXT STEPS

It is impossible, within this brief chapter, to provide a complete set of recommendations for successful peacebuilding through resource management in the Niger Delta, but some further insights that may be of help are offered here.

First, in the short term, the vicious cycle of violence—and the associated reinforcement of socioeconomic grievances—was broken, in August 2009, by an amnesty program for all militants who hand over their weapons. As of this writing, 8,000 militants had reportedly accepted the amnesty offer, many more than were initially expected. This is a window of opportunity that should be seized to immediately satisfy some of the basic needs of the local population. Such a step could prevent further frustration among the residents of the Niger Delta—frustration that would otherwise foster active or passive support for armed struggle and facilitate continued recruitment of young militants. Oil revenues could be used to create special funds to finance rehabilitation programs for former militants, as well as basic improvements in physical and social infrastructure.

In the medium term, comprehensive reforms that take into consideration the "lessons learned" are absolutely indispensable. Thus, the federal government should

---

[32] Capacity-building efforts should include infrastructure development, the improvement of both general and specialized education, and enhancement of local and regional administrative expertise.

[33] This is evident in the conception of the NDRDMP, for example, and in the creation of the Economic and Financial Crimes Commission in 2002.

give much greater priority to the weaknesses of Nigeria's political institutions and should strive to eliminate support for corruption and patronage. Although Nigeria's participation, since 2004, in the international Extractive Industries Transparency Initiative (EITI)—which calls for action not only on the part of the Nigerian government, but also on the part of the oil companies—is a move in the right direction, it must be accompanied by comprehensive reforms of the political system and the political culture.[34] An important first step would be the creation of internal control mechanisms to ensure transparency and accountability for state governments, with respect to both revenues and expenditures.

Furthermore, the excessive violence associated with the government's military action in the Niger Delta must be contained. This does not necessarily mean that security forces should be completely withdrawn (which would be unrealistic), but military action and the excessive use of force must be restricted. Efforts should also be made to eliminate the sometimes rapacious culture that is associated with the security forces and the police. Here, the first step should be fundamental reform focused on improving education and ensuring adequate compensation.

Efforts to combat oil theft and weapons trading must not only strengthen internal transparency and control mechanisms, but must also accord greater emphasis to the international aspects of the problem, which have been largely neglected. At the regional level, the Economic Community of West African States could play a much more important role, by helping to eradicate cross-border trafficking in weapons and oil. As the problem also has global dimensions, which cannot be solved solely by the governments of West Africa, international efforts have to be strengthened as well. For instance, oil-importing countries must be held more responsible for even passive involvement in trafficking, and international oil-trade channels must be made more transparent.

The Nigerian government's resource-based peacebuilding initiatives have failed to address the complex issues underlying the violent conflicts. To succeed, the initiatives must be integrated into comprehensive policies that speak to those underlying issues. In the long term, the only sustainable approach to resource management will be to reduce Nigeria's excessive dependence on oil exports and to aggressively develop alternative economic engines throughout the country.

REFERENCES

Africa Research Bulletin. 2009. Nigeria: Oil facilities targeted. *Africa Research Bulletin* 46 (6): 18010B–18012B.

---

[34] Under the EITI, the Nigerian government committed to providing detailed, publicly accessible information about oil- and gas-company revenues; the oil and gas companies must also disclose payments made to the Nigerian government. Thus, not only is the Nigerian government under pressure to make transparent and accountable use of the revenues, but the oil companies are also under greater scrutiny, and therefore less able to engage in corruption or bribery.

Aigbokhan, B. E. 2007. Reconstruction of economic governance in the Niger Delta region in Nigeria: The case of the Niger Delta Development Commission. In *Reconstructing economic governance after conflict in resource-rich African countries*, ed. K. Wohlmuth and T. Urban. Berlin: LIT Verlag.

Amnesty International. 2005. *Ten years on: Injustice and violence haunt the oil delta.* www.amnesty.org/en/library/asset/AFR44/022/2005/en/63b716d6-d49d-11dd-8a23-d58a49c0d652/afr440222005en.pdf.

———. 2009. *2009: Nigeria, petroleum, pollution and poverty in the Niger Delta.* www.amnesty.org/en/library/asset/AFR44/017/2009/en/e2415061-da5c-44f8-a73c-a7a4766ee21d/afr440172009en.pdf.

ANEEJ (African Network for Environment and Economic Justice). 2004. Oil of poverty in Niger Delta. www.aneej.org/Documents/OIL%20OF%20POVERTY%201.pdf.

Basedau, M., and J. Lay. 2009. Resource curse or rentier peace? The ambiguous effects of oil wealth and oil dependence on violent conflict. *Journal of Peace Research* 46: 757–776.

BBC News. 2006. Nigeria's shadowy oil rebels. April 20. http://news.bbc.co.uk/2/hi/africa/4732210.stm.

———. 2009. Nigerian militant amnesty starts. August 6. http://news.bbc.co.uk/2/hi/africa/8186816.stm.

Bergstresser, H. 1998. Nigeria 1997. In *Afrika-Jahrbuch 1997: Politik, Wirtschaft und Gesellschaft in Afrika südlich der Sahara*, ed. R. Hofmeier. Opladen, Germany: Leske und Budrich.

———. 2007. Polit-ökonomische Kurzanalyse Nigeria. Unpublished report. Hamburg: German Institute of Global and Area Studies.

Bertelsmann Stiftung. 2007. *BTI 2008—Nigeria country report.* Gütersloh, Germany.

Duffield, C. 2009. Will amnesty bring peace to the Niger Delta? *BBC News*, October 5. http://news.bbc.co.uk/2/hi/africa/8291336.stm.

EIA (U.S. Energy Information Administration). 2009. Country analysis briefs: Nigeria. www.eia.doe.gov/cabs/Nigeria/Oil.html.

Gosztonyi, K., A. Taylor, and J. Bray. 2009. Facing up to corruption in Nigeria. www.crg.com/PDF/nigeria_corruption_2009_final.pdf.

Hanson, S. 2007. MEND: The Niger Delta's umbrella militant group. March 22. www.cfr.org/publication/12920/.

Harneit-Sievers, A. 1992. Kriegsfolgen und kriegsbewältigung in Afrika: Der nigerianische bürgerkrieg, 1967–70. Unpublished report.

Hazen, J. M., and J. Horner. 2007. Small arms, armed violence, and insecurity in Nigeria: The Niger Delta in perspective. Small Arms Survey Occasional Paper 20. www.smallarmssurvey.org/files/sas/publications/o_papers_pdf/2007-op20-Nigeria.pdf.

Higgins, K. 2009. Regional inequality and the Niger Delta. Policy Brief No. 5. Overseas Development Institute. www.odi.org.uk/resources/download/2507.pdf.

HIIK (Heidelberger Institut für Internationale Konfliktforschung). n.d. Conflict barometer. http://hiik.de/de/konfliktbarometer/index.html.

Human Rights Watch. 1995. The Ogoni crisis: A case-study of military repression in southeastern Nigeria. www.hrw.org/en/reports/1995/07/01/ogoni-crisis.

———. 1999. The price of oil: Corporate responsibility and human rights violations in Nigeria's oil producing communities. www.hrw.org/en/reports/1999/02/23/price-oil.

———. 2002. The Niger Delta: No democratic dividend. www.hrw.org/en/reports/2002/10/22/niger-delta.
———. 2003. The Warri crisis: Fueling violence. www.hrw.org/en/reports/2003/12/17/warri-crisis.
———. 2004. Nigeria's 2003 elections: The unacknowledged violence. www.hrw.org/en/reports/2004/06/01/nigeria-s-2003-elections-0.
———. 2007. Chop fine: The human rights impact of local government corruption and mismanagement in Rivers State, Nigeria. www.hrw.org/en/reports/2007/01/30/chop-fine.
Ibeanu, O. 2006. *Civil society and conflict management in the Niger Delta*. Monograph series 2. Lagos, Nigeria: Cleen Foundation.
Ibeanu, O., and F. K. Mohammed, eds. 2001. *Oiling violence: The proliferation of small arms and light weapons in the Niger Delta*. Lagos, Nigeria: Friedrich Ebert Stiftung.
ICG (International Crisis Group). 2006a. Fuelling the Niger Delta crisis. *Africa Report* 118 (September 28). www.crisisgroup.org/home/index.cfm?action=login&ref_id=4394.
———. 2006b. Nigeria's faltering federal experiment. *Africa Report* 119 (October 25). www.crisisgroup.org/home/index.cfm?action=login&ref_id=4464.
———. 2006c. Want in the midst of plenty. *Africa Report* 113 (July 19). www.crisisgroup.org/home/index.cfm?id=4274.
———. 2007. Nigeria: Ending unrest in the Niger Delta. *Africa Report* 135 (December 5). www.crisisgroup.org/home/index.cfm?id=5186&l=1.
———. 2009. Seizing the moment in the Niger Delta. *Africa Briefing* 60 (April 30). www.crisisgroup.org/home/index.cfm?action=login&ref_id=6080.
IRIN (Integrated Regional Information Networks). 2009a. Nigeria: Timeline of recent events in Niger Delta. *IRIN Humanitarian News and Analysis,* May 28. www.irinnews.org/PrintReport.aspx?ReportId=84606.
———. 2009b. Nigeria: Violence creates "human security" crisis in Delta. *IRIN Humanitarian News and Analysis,* May 13. www.irinnews.org/PrintReport.aspx?ReportId=84371.
Karl, T. L. 2007. Oil-led development: Social, political and economic consequences. CDDRL Working Papers 80: 1–34. http://iis-b.stanford.edu/pubs/21537/No_80_Terry_Karl_Effects_of_Oil_Development.pdf.
Le Billon, P. 2008. Resources for peace? Managing revenues from extractive industries in post-conflict environments. Public finance in post-conflict environments: A policy paper series. February. New York: New York University Center on International Cooperation. www.cic.nyu.edu/peacebuilding/docs/CIC_paper5_LeBillon_FINAL.pdf.
Lewis, P. M. 2007. *Growing apart: Oil, politics, and economic change in Indonesia and Nigeria*. Ann Arbor: University of Michigan Press.
Lubeck, P., M. Watts, and R. Lipschutz. 2007. *Convergent interests: U.S. energy security and the "securing" of Nigerian democracy*. CIP International Policy Reports. February. Washington, D.C.: Center for International Policy. http://ciponline.org/NIGERIA_FINAL.pdf.
Mähler, A. 2010. Nigeria: A prime example of the resource curse? Revisiting the oil-violence link in the Niger Delta. German Institute of Global and Area Studies Working Papers 120.
Marquardt, E. 2007. Mujahid Dokubo-Asari: The Niger Delta's Ijaw leader. *Terrorism Monitor* 5 (15): 1–4.

Ngomba-Roth, R. 2007. *Multinational companies and conflicts in Africa: The case of the Niger Delta—Nigeria.* Münster, Germany: LIT Verlag.

Nigerian National Assembly. 1999. Niger Delta Development Commission Act No. 2, 1999. Abuja.

Obi, C. 2001. Oil minority rights versus the Nigerian state: Conflict and transcendence. University of Leipzig Papers on Africa. Politics and Economics Series 53.

———. 2006. Youth and the generational dimensions to struggles for resource control in the Niger Delta. CODESRIA Monograph Series. Council for the Development of Social Science Research in Africa. www.codesria.org/IMG/pdf/Cyril_Obi.pdf.

Ogonor, B. O. 2003. The impact of training on the conflict resolution ability of rural women in the Niger Delta, Nigeria. *International Journal of Lifelong Education* 22 (2): 172–181.

Ologbenla, D. K. 2007. Leadership, governance and corruption in Nigeria. *Journal of Sustainable Development in Africa* 9 (3): 97–118.

Olukoya, S. 2009. The Niger Delta and violence. Unpublished study.

Omeje, K. 2006. *High stakes and stakeholders: Oil conflict and security in Nigeria.* Aldershot, UK: Ashgate Publishing Limited.

Omotola, J. S. 2007. From the OMPADEC to the NDDC: An assessment of state responses to environmental insecurity in the Niger Delta, Nigeria. *Africa Today* 54 (1): 73–89.

Oyefusi, A. 2007. Oil and the propensity to armed struggle in the Niger Delta region of Nigeria. World Bank Policy Research Working Paper No. 4194. http://ssrn.com/abstract=979666.

Roll, M. 2008. "Baba Go-slow." Hintergrundinformationen aus der internationalen Entwicklungszusammenarbeit Afrika, September 30. http://library.fes.de/pdf-files/iez/05766.pdf.

Rühl, B. 2004. Masterplan im Niger Delta. Akzente 1. www2.gtz.de/dokumente/akz/deu/AKZ_2004_1/Nigeria_Nigerdelta.pdf.

Sala-i-Martin, X., and A. Subramanian. 2003. Addressing the natural resource curse: An illustration from Nigeria. IMF Working Paper 03/139. http://ssrn.com/abstract=420318.

TCND (Technical Committee on the Niger Delta). 2008. Report of the technical committee on the Niger Delta. www.stakeholderdemocracy.org/uploads/Other%20publications/Nigeriareport.pdf.

Ukeje, C., ed. 2003. *Oil and violent conflicts in the Niger Delta.* Ile-Ife, Nigeria: Centre for Development and Conflict Management Studies.

UN Comtrade (United Nations Commodity Trade Statistics Database). n.d. UN Statistics Division. http://comtrade.un.org/db.

UNDP (United Nations Development Programme). 2006. *Niger Delta human development report.* Abuja, Nigeria.

UNEP (United Nations Environment Programme). 2009. *From conflict to peacebuilding. The role of natural resources and the environment.* Policy Paper 1. Nairobi.

UDODC (United Nations Office on Drugs and Crime). 2009. Transnational trafficking and the rule of law in West Africa: a threat assessment. Vienna.

Vanguard. 2009. Amnesty: FG to destroy recovered weapons. October 11. www.vanguardngr.com/2009/10/11/amnesty-fg-to-destroy-recovered-weapons/.

Walker, A. 2008a. Doubts over Niger Delta ministry. *BBC News*, September 11. http://news.bbc.co.uk/2/hi/africa/7609904.stm.

———. 2008b. "Blood oil" dripping from Nigeria. *BBC News*, July 27. http://news.bbc.co.uk/2/hi/africa/7519302.stm.

World Bank. 2003. Nigeria strategic conflict assessment. *Social Development Notes* 11 (May 2003). http://siteresources.worldbank.org/INTCPR/214578-1111751313696/20480272/SDN83CPR11.pdf.

Zinn, A. 2005. Theory versus reality: Civil war onset and avoidance in Nigeria since 1960. In *Understanding civil war: Evidence and analysis, Volume 1—Africa,* ed. P. Collier and N. Sambanis. Washington, D.C.: World Bank.

The legal framework for managing oil in post-conflict Iraq: A pattern of abuse and violence over natural resources

Mishkat Al Moumin

In 2005, observers were optimistic about the prospects for the new Iraqi constitution, which was intended to strengthen democracy, create oil revenues and distribute them fairly to the Iraqi people, and achieve sustainable peace.[1] Instead, the oil provisions of the constitution have created a vague and conflicting legal system that has pitted government agencies, levels of government, and religious and ethnic groups against one another, threatening the entire peacebuilding process. Specifically, the constitution failed to clearly and explicitly address three key issues:

- Who owns the oil.
- How the oil reserves are to be managed.
- How the oil revenues are to be distributed.

Transparent and equitable oil management and revenue sharing are crucial for peacebuilding in resource-rich states.[2] Oil exports generate more than 90 percent of Iraq's government revenue (Blanchard 2009), but the national budgetary process lacks a detailed legal framework for revenue sharing and distribution. In the current system, "sovereign expenditures" (supporting expenses for a range of government functions, including the production of oil exports and the administration

---

Mishkat Al Moumin is the chief executive officer of Women & the Environment Organization and is the former minister of the environment for the interim Iraqi government. The chapter is current as of March 2011; it does not address subsequent developments. The author is grateful for research assistance provided by Andrew Beckington, Daniel Brindis, Mona Funiciello, Gabriel Elias, and Heather Croshaw.

[1] Although natural gas is also important in Middle Eastern economies, this chapter deals solely with oil resources.

[2] Under the constitutions of Kuwait and the United Arab Emirates, for example, the state and the emirates, respectively, serve as trustees, with both the legal authority and responsibility to preserve and exploit the resources for the good of their national economies and national security (Bunter 2004). Thus, the state's "ownership" of the oil resources is limited, not absolute, and the state is required to ensure that the oil revenues are used for the benefit of all (Maitland 1905).

of the National Cabinet, the Ministry of Foreign Affairs, and the Ministry of National Defense) are allocated first. From the remaining funds, 17 percent are allocated to the Kurdistan Regional Government (KRG), and the rest are distributed to the other governorates. The allocation among the governorates is based on population, need, and political negotiation (Blanchard 2009; Kane 2010; *Revenue Watch* 2005). In the absence of a specific legal framework, this default arrangement has fostered a sense of inequity among various groups—and, ultimately, fierce disputes over oil resources.

This chapter is divided into seven parts: (1) a brief review of Iraq's oil endowment, population, and governance structure; (2) a description of oil management under the 1970 Iraqi constitution; (3) a description of the oil provisions of the 2005 constitution; (4) a discussion of conflict over the authority to manage oil; (5) a discussion of disputes over the distribution of oil revenues; (6) a consideration of recent developments in oil management; and (7) a brief conclusion.

BACKGROUND: IRAQ'S OIL, POPULATION, AND GOVERNANCE STRUCTURE

Including both proven crude reserves of 115 billion barrels and the potential for an additional 45 to 100 billion barrels of recoverable oil, Iraq has the fourth-largest endowment of oil in the world (EIA 2009). The most significant oil fields are in the north, in Kirkuk Governorate near the Kurdish semi-autonomous region, and in the south, in Shiite areas (see figures 1 and 2). As of 2006, only seventeen of Iraq's eighty oil fields had been developed; the most significant are in Kirkuk Governorate, in the north, and in the Rumaila field near the Basra Governorate (Kumins 2006).

Iraq is dominated by two ethnic groups: Arabs make up 75 percent of the population and Kurds 20 percent. (Turkmen and other groups make up the remaining 5 percent). Approximately 97 percent of Iraqis are Muslim. The two main Muslim groups are the Shiites, who make up two-thirds of Iraqi Muslims, and the Sunnis, who make up one-third; the majority of Kurds are Sunni Muslim (O'Leary 2002). A small portion of the population consists of Christians and other religious minorities (World Almanac Books 2009).[3] As can be seen in figure 1, Shiite Arabs live to the south and east of Baghdad, Sunni Arabs live in the northwestern part of the country, and the Kurds live the north.

Iraq is a federal state that consists of the central government, the parliament, and the supreme court. At the subnational level, Iraq has one autonomous region (the KRG) and eighteen governorates.[4]

---

[3] Because the Iraqi government has never conducted a survey to determine the precise percentages of ethnic or religious groups, these numbers are estimates. See Kassim (2010) and Mahdi (2010).

[4] Under article 119 of the constitution, one or more governorates can combine to form a region. After the 1990–1991 Gulf War, the Arbil, Sulaimaniyah, and Dahuk governorates combined to create the Kurdistan Regional Government.

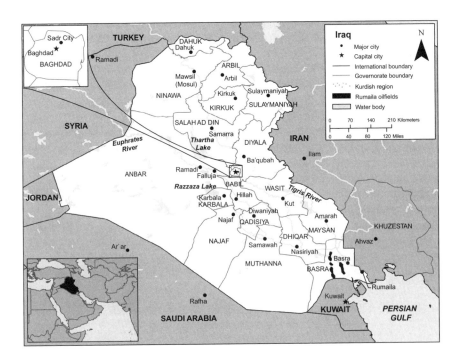

OIL MANAGEMENT UNDER THE 1970 IRAQI CONSTITUTION

The 1970 Iraqi constitution reflected an effort on the part of the Ba'ath Party to formally concentrate its control over oil resources. According to article 13 of the 1970 constitution, "natural resources and basic means of productions are owned by the people. The central government will manage these resources directly according to the national plan" (ROI 1970). Despite granting ownership of oil to all Iraqis, this provision failed to detail the means by which "the people" would participate in managing the resource; thus, the grant of ownership was essentially meaningless.

In 1979, Saddam Hussein became president of Iraq; using a narrow interpretation of article 13, the Ba'ath Party claimed legal authority to centralize and manage oil resources on behalf of the Iraqi people, instead of relying on a participatory process that would have (1) given all Iraqis a role in decision making about oil and (2) held leaders accountable for their actions. Having centralized power over oil resources, Hussein's regime ultimately used its control over oil revenues to wage war against Iran (1980–1988) and Kuwait (1990–1991) (Revenue Watch 2005). The intent of these wars was to gain further oil reserves, but they caused considerable damage to Iraq's oil sector, infrastructure, and overall economy.

With the invasion of Iran, Hussein hoped to regain control over Iran's oil-rich Khuzestan region, which is along the southeastern border of Iraq and the southwestern border of Iran. But the resulting damage to oil facilities limited Iraq's ability to produce oil: production fell from three million to less than one million

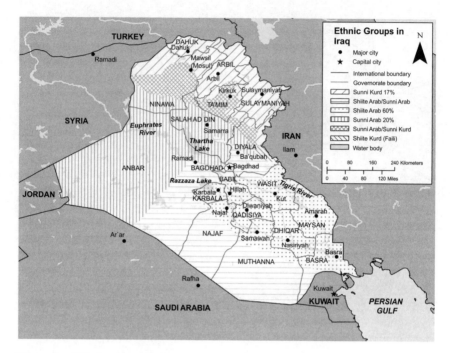

Figure 1. Ethnic groups in Iraq
Source: University of Texas libraries (1978).

barrels per day (Alnasrawi 2001a). Although production rebounded to 2.5 million barrels per day toward the end of the war, oil prices remained low when compared with the historic highs of 1980 and 1981. The result was a significant drop in revenues, from US$26 billion in 1980 to US$11 billion in 1988 (Alnasrawi 2001b).[5]

One source of the drop in oil prices was overproduction on the part of Kuwait and Saudi Arabia (Krupa 1997), both of which had been producing more oil than was allowed by the quotas set by the Organization of the Petroleum Exporting Countries (OPEC) (Alnasrawi 2001a). But because both nations had supported Iraq in its war against Iran, Iraq initially ignored the overproduction. Among the sources of Kuwait's overproduction was the Rumaila field, which is located under both Kuwait and southern Iraq (Hayes 1990). In May 1990, at an emergency meeting of the Arab League, Saddam Hussein's regime claimed that the Kuwaiti violations of the OPEC quota had cost Iraq US$14 billion per year since 1988 (Hayes 1990). Iraq also accused Kuwait of "slant drilling" across the Iraqi border to extract more oil from the Iraqi side of the field (Alnasrawi 2001a; Hayes 1990).

---

[5] The high oil prices of 1980–1981 were attributable, in large part, to global anxiety about the oil supply, which had been triggered by a series of events: the 1979 Iranian Revolution, the Iran hostage crisis, arbitrary price increases imposed by the Organization of the Petroleum Exporting Countries, and the start of the Iran-Iraq war.

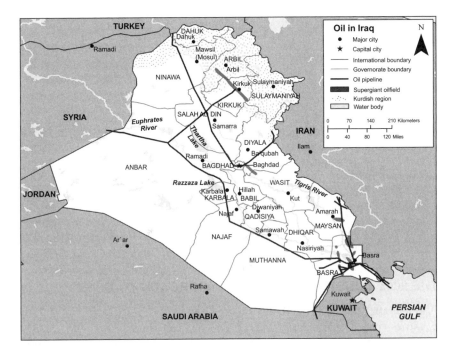

Figure 2. Oil in Iraq
Source: EIA (2003).

When it invaded Kuwait, in August 1990, the Hussein regime cited the slant drilling as the reason; in other words, Hussein was once again prepared to go to war to obtain oil-rich territory (Terrill 2007). Hussein hoped that the Kuwait war would help end Iraq's economic crisis, assist with paying back Iraq's foreign debt, and restore the regime's credibility with the Iraqi people. Instead, the invasion—which ended with the 1990–1991 Gulf War—resulted in restrictive sanctions and brought about a humanitarian crisis (Alnasrawi 2001a).[6] Under the sanctions, Iraq was forced to shut down 97 percent of its oil exports. Moreover, it was unable to buy the spare parts to maintain oil exploration and production, further hindering oil development (Alnasrawi 2001a; UNSC 2000). In 2000, a group of UN experts reported that

> the decline of conditions of all sectors of the oil industry continues, and is accelerating in some cases. This trend will continue, and the ability of the Iraqi oil industry to sustain the current reduced production levels will be seriously compromised, until effective action is taken to reverse the situation (UNSC 2000, 11).

---

[6] Under United Nations Security Council (UNSC) Resolution 661, passed in August of 1990, Iraq was placed under an oil embargo, and its financial assets were frozen (UNSC 1990). Because Iraq imports between 70 and 80 percent of its food, these sanctions caused a food shortage, and food prices increased from 200 to 1,800 percent (Provost 1992).

In April 1995, to address the dire humanitarian situation, the UNSC adopted Resolution 986, which established the legal basis for the Oil-for-Food Programme (UN 2010). Under this program, which operated from December 1996 through March 2003, Iraq was permitted, under UN supervision, to sell oil in exchange for food and medicine.[7]

After the fall of Hussein's regime, Iraq was engulfed by a civil war that some analysts attribute solely to religious conflict. Other observers, however, have called attention to conflict between ethnic groups and various levels of government over how power is to be shared, how Iraq's "massive energy reserves" are to be managed (Holland and Jarrar 2007), and how oil revenues are to be distributed (Cockburn 2006).[8] In theory, the constitution should have resolved such conflicts, but the vague and ambiguous language with which it addresses the key and contentious issue of oil prevents it from playing the role that was envisioned for it—as a legal document that describes how wealth and power will be shared, and thereby contributes to peacebuilding.

THE 2005 CONSTITUTION AND ITS APPROACH TO OIL

A month after the March 2003 invasion of Iraq by a U.S.-led coalition of thirty countries (U.S. Department of State 2003), Saddam Hussein's regime fell. The U.S.-appointed Coalition Provisional Authority oversaw Iraq until June 2004, when the Transitional Administrative Law (TAL) came into force (CPA 2004;

---

[7] During the seven years of its implementation, the Oil-for-Food Programme helped deliver food rations to Iraqi residents, resulting in a large reduction in the malnutrition rate among Iraqi children (UN Office of the Iraq Programme Oil-for-Food 2003). However, as the result of two problems—the UN Security Council's failure to clearly define the parameters of the program and the Hussein regime's ability to shape the program's design and implementation—the regime was able to collect an estimated US$10 billion from the program through illegal surcharges and commissions (UN Office of the Iraq Programme Oil-for-Food 2003; Hsieh and Moretti 2006; IIC 2005; Botterill and McNaughton 2008). Ultimately, corruption led to the disbandment of the program in 2003, at which point control was transferred to the Coalition Provisional Authority. Between March 20, 1996, and November 21, 2003, the Iraqi government spent US$31 billion on humanitarian operations and US$1.6 billion on spare parts and equipment for oil operations. Although the Oil-for-Food Programme formally ended in March 2003, over US$6.9 billion in additional oil sales occurred before 2005. During the life of the program, approximately 3.4 billion barrels of oil, worth about US$65 billion, were exported. After December 2000, about 72 percent of the funds were allocated to humanitarian needs: 25 percent to pay for damages caused by the Iraqi invasion of Kuwait, 2.2 percent to UN operations, and 0.8 percent to weapons inspections in Iraq (UN 2010).

[8] According to the Iraq Body Count project, civilian deaths increased from 10,751 in 2004 to 14,849 in 2005, and violence continued to increase during 2006 and 2007. Beginning in 2008, however, violence began to decrease (Iraq Body Count 2008, 2010).

U.S. Institute of Peace 2005).[9] The TAL provided for the creation of a transitional national assembly and the establishment of a timeline for the development of a new constitution (CPA 2004, arts. 30–34, 60, 61). In 2005, countrywide elections were held to create the National Assembly, and a thirteen-member constitutional committee, drawn from the newly elected representatives, began to draft a new constitution. Among the committee's charges was to bring together rival ethnic groups to form a united government (CPA 2004; U.S. Institute of Peace 2005).[10]

Most of the drafters of the constitution believed that any system with strong central power would lead to the kind of authoritarian rule that had existed under Hussein. The Kurds, in particular, felt that the new government should vest more power in the governorates. Other groups, including members of Sunni and Shiite Arab Communities, suggested granting authorities to the governorates under the umbrella of the federal government (Blanchard 2009; CPA 2004, art. 52).[11] The new political system that was ultimately created—a federal-style, decentralized system that favors regional governments—represents a dramatic shift for Iraq, and particularly for its state agencies, which had no experience with decentralization and are still adjusting to the change.

Although the constitutional committee had the opportunity to create a legal framework for the equitable and transparent management of oil reserves and revenues, political feasibility dictated the use of vague language. In the short term, this language made it possible to sidestep thorny problems, such as how to define "fair compensation" for damage from past wars.[12] But it also led to new problems, and ultimately created opportunities for disenfranchised ethnic and religious groups to incite violence.

AUTHORITY TO MANAGE OIL: CONSTITUTIONAL ORIGINS OF CONFLICT

Under the 2005 Iraqi constitution, oil ownership and management are governed primarily by articles 111 and 112 (the annex to this chapter includes selected

---

[9] The purposes of the TAL (officially, the Law of the Administration for the State of Iraq for the Transitional Period) were (1) to establish state structure and protect human rights in the period before "the formation of an elected Iraqi government pursuant to a permanent constitution" and (2) to define the parameters of a future, permanent constitution (CPA 2004).

[10] To protect minorities during the development of the constitution, article 61(c) of the TAL stated that no permanent constitution could be ratified if it were rejected by two-thirds of the voters in three or more of Iraq's eighteen governorates (CPA 2004).

[11] The Iraqi parliament is a mix of Shiites, Sunnis, Kurds, Christians, and Turkmen; its members have a range of political orientations and differing views on the role of the state.

[12] Compensation for damage from past wars is to be paid from oil revenues. The controversy surrounding the allocation of compensation is discussed in more detail in "Conflict over the Distribution of Oil Revenues," a later section of this chapter.

articles from the 2005 constitution). Under article 111, "oil and gas are owned by all the people of Iraq in all the regions and governorates." This language is somewhat similar to that of article 13 of the 1970 constitution, which stated that "natural resources and basic means of production are owned by the people," but the 2005 constitution specifically mentions "regions and governorates." It is unclear why article 111 includes this phrase—perhaps to leave open the possibility of regional and governorate ownership? In any case, the vague language has led to tension—and, in some cases, to violence.

Article 112 of the 2005 constitution describes how decisions will be made about oil management and revenue sharing:

> First: The federal government, with the producing governorates and regional governments, shall undertake the management of oil and gas extracted from present fields, provided that it distributes its revenue in a fair manner in proportion to the population distribution in all parts of the country, specifying an allotment for a specified period for the damaged regions which were unjustly deprived of them by the former regime, and the regions that were damaged afterwards in a way that ensures balanced development in different areas of the country, and this shall be regulated by a law.
> Second: The federal government, with the producing regional and governorate governments, shall together formulate the necessary strategic policies to develop the oil and gas wealth in a way that achieves the highest benefit to the Iraqi people using the most advanced techniques of the market principles and encouraging investment.

Thus, article 112 vests authority for the management of oil in both the federal government and the regional and governorate governments, but it fails to specify how the various levels of government are to work together to achieve (or even to establish) their chosen aims. To further complicate matters, other articles in the constitution can be interpreted as granting significant authority to the regions and governorates. Article 115, for example, which addresses the distribution of authority between the regional, governorate, and federal governments, notes that "all powers not stipulated in the exclusive powers of the federal government belong to the authorities of the regions and governorates that are not organized in a region. With regard to other powers shared between federal government and the regional government, priority shall be given to the law of the regions and governorates not organized in a region in case of dispute." Similarly, the first paragraph of article 121, which also addresses the distribution of authority, grants the regional governments "the right to exercise executive, legislative, and judicial powers in accordance with this Constitution, except for those authorities stipulated in the exclusive authorities of the federal government." Furthermore, the second paragraph of article 121 states that when there is "a contradiction between regional and national legislation in respect to a matter outside the exclusive authorities of the federal government, the regional power shall have the right to amend the application of the national legislation within that region."

There are two key controversies regarding oil management: (1) how the federal and the subnational governments will determine oil investment procedures and (2) who has the authority to award oil contracts.

It is not difficult to see how the wording of the constitution has created conflict over the role of various levels of governments in the management of oil resources. Because articles 115 and 121 grant considerable authority to regions and governorates, these levels of government would appear to have a legitimate and genuine argument for asserting control over oil reserves found within their boundaries. A number of other arguments have been marshaled in support of this view:

- Article 110, which lists the exclusive powers of the federal government, does not include oil development or management (Deeks and Burton 2007).[13]
- The third and sixth paragraphs of article 114 list the areas of "shared" competency between federal and regional governments, including environmental policy making and public educational policy.
- Finally, although article 112 does not use the word *shared*, as articles 114 and 115 do, it does appear to contemplate shared power over oil resources.

In sum, articles 115 and 121 do appear to grant significant authority to regions and governorates, which is further bolstered by articles 110, 112, and 114. A number of observers, however, have raised counterarguments—claiming, for example, (1) that the provisions for the management of oil in article 112 were set off separately from article 114, which specifically addresses areas of concurrent authority, and (2) that article 112 represents a "careful compromise on oil"— which, according to Ashley Deeks and Matthew Burton, is not to be disrupted by articles 115 or 121 (Al-Adhadh 2008; Deeks and Burton 2007, 65–66).

Disputes over oil management at the federal level

Under Hussein's regime, the Iraqi oil ministry administered oil exploration and production. Although the new constitution does not specify which governmental institution is responsible for managing oil on behalf of the Iraqi people, article 111 does state that all Iraqi people own the nation's oil resources. Since article 49 designates parliament as the entity that represents the Iraqi people, these provisions can be interpreted as favoring a parliamentary role in oil management—if not absolute control, then at least oversight.

The silence of the 2005 constitution on the question of which federal institution—parliament or the oil ministry—has authority over oil contracts has

---

[13] Ashley Deeks and Matthew Burton note, however, that article 115 could be interpreted to mean that the federal government has the power to legislate outside the areas listed, in article 110, as exclusive to the federal government. One of their arguments is that a number of other articles in the constitution "contemplate that the federal legislature will enact laws" (Deeks and Burton 2007, 67).

led to conflict between the executive and legislative branches (Jiyad 2010). On June 30, 2009, without consulting parliament, the Iraqi Ministry of Oil awarded an oil development contract for the Rumaila oil field to an oil consortium led by BP (British Petroleum) (Al-Zubaidi 2009; Blanchard 2009). After the contract was issued, 140 members of parliament (out of 275 at the time) submitted a petition requesting the oil minister to come to parliament to answer questions about oil contracts (Carlisle 2009).[14] Although the minister did not face a vote of no confidence, the formal questioning was indicative of the seriousness of the concern (Blanchard 2009).

Parliament based its objection on Law No. 97 of 1967, which had been issued by President Abed Alrahman Araf before the Ba'ath Party took power (Al-Zubaidi 2009; Donovan 2010). Under Law No. 97, the parliament must adopt all oil contracts with foreign companies by passing a law. Thus, the oil ministry would not have had the authority to sign the 2009 BP contract without parliamentary action (Guardian 2009; Macalister 2009). In defense of his action, the Minister of Oil stated that, as an elected figure, he represents the Iraqi people as a whole and can therefore sign the contract on their behalf (Baxter 2009). Nonetheless, some members of parliament continue to question the award of the contract, as well as the minister's authority to award oil contracts in general. In the absence of a clear allocation of responsibilities in the legal framework governing oil management, this dispute is likely to arise again, creating confusion and uncertainty for the federal government and oil investors.

Disputes between the federal government and the governorates

The Rumaila contract has also led to disputes between the federal government and the governorates. Arguing that article 111 of the constitution—"oil and gas are owned by all the people of Iraq in all the regions and governorates"—means that oil and gas are owned by the residents of the regions and governorates from which the oil is being extracted (Ahmed 2009), the Governorate Council of Basra, where the Rumaila field is located, has taken the position that the oil ministry cannot award oil contacts without consulting with the elected bodies of the producing governorates, and that the BP contract should therefore be void. To further support its assertion, the council has cited the second paragraph of article 112, which states that "the federal government, *with* the producing regional and governorate governments *shall together* formulate the *necessary strategic policies* to develop the oil and gas wealth in a way that achieves the *highest benefit* to the Iraqi people" (emphasis added) (Ahmed 2009; Aswat Al Iraq 2009).

Indeed, article 111 could arguably be interpreted to favor local over federal ownership of oil. Specifically, the phrase "in all the regions and governorates," which modifies "people of Iraq," suggests an emphasis on the inhabitants of

---

[14] As of 2010, the parliament had 325 members, having increased in size with the Iraqi population.

particular regions and governorates. At the same time, however, article 111 refers to ownership "by *all the people of Iraq*" (emphasis added), not necessarily by any governmental authority. Moreover, in article 112, the federal government is described as making decisions in consultation with the regions and governorates and not vice-versa, which may argue in favor of federal management, if not ownership. And yet, article 115 favors the laws of the regional governments and governorates in the case of a dispute.

In failing to consult with the Governorate Council of Basra, the oil ministry awarded a contract that may have violated article 112 and may therefore be unconstitutional. In July 2009, the Basra council submitted an unsuccessful plea to Prime Minister Nouri al-Maliki, requesting that he acknowledge the council's right to award contracts in accordance with the constitution. The council has also asked the federal government to pay the governorate 3 percent of the price the federal government receives for each barrel exported from Basra (Ahmed 2009).

Disputes between the federal and regional governments

In August 2007, relying on articles 111 and 112 of the 2005 Iraqi constitution, the KRG amended Iraqi oil laws by passing the Petroleum Act of the Kurdistan Region of Iraq, then awarded over twenty contracts to a variety of small companies to explore for oil in the Kurdish region (Khalil 2009; KRG 2010).[15] Iraq's oil ministry evaluated these contracts and ruled them illegal. The federal government backed the ministry's actions and blacklisted the companies in question, prohibiting them from competing for future Iraqi oil contracts—a move that sent a strong message to other oil companies hoping to operate in Iraq (Khalaf, Mahtani, and Negus 2008). Later that same month, the dispute led to clashes between the Iraqi National Guard and the *peshmerga*, the defense forces of the Kurdistan region. The clashes occurred near the Green Line, which separates the Kurdish region from the rest of Iraq (Shadid 2009). The dispute quieted briefly in August 2008. One year later, the federal government agreed to approve the contracts, provided that the KRG would agree not to seek an increase in Kurdistan's share of government-provided oil revenues (Chorev 2007).

Although the Kurdish Petroleum Act attempts to clarify the ambiguity over whether the central or subnational governments have the authority to award oil contracts, it has created a parallel approval process for oil contracts (KRG 2006). Oil companies seeking to do business in Kurdistan now need to sign two separate contracts and adhere to the laws of two governments: the Kurdish government in Arbil and the central government in Baghdad (Khalaf, Mahtani, and Negus

---

[15] The text of the Petroleum Act cites articles 111 and 112 of the 2005 Iraqi constitution as authorization: "Petroleum in the Kurdistan Region is owned in a manner consistent with article 111 of the Constitution of Iraq. The Regional Government shall share Revenue derived from Petroleum with all the people of Iraq, pursuant to Article 112 of the Constitution of Iraq and this Act."

2008). Nor does signing a contract with one government necessarily grant or facilitate the approval of the other government (Peters 2010). The existence of two separate approval processes adds to the cost of doing business in Iraq and may deter international oil companies from bidding on contracts. Moreover, it is unclear which government should be approached first, the KRG or the federal government. Moreover, procedural missteps can lead to harsh consequences, such as blacklisting (Khalaf, Mahtani, and Negus 2008).

CONFLICT OVER THE DISTRIBUTION OF OIL REVENUES

Iraqi political parties are founded on ethnic and religious identities, with specific parties representing Shiites, Sunnis, Kurds, and other religious and ethnic groups. Thus, in the January 2005 transitional elections, the representatives to the National Assembly were elected on the basis of religion or ethnicity: Sunnis elected Sunnis, Shiites elected Shiites, and Kurds elected Kurds, regardless of political platform.

Because religious and ethnic distinctions have a profound effect on the Iraqi political system, they have equally profound implications for the distribution of oil revenues. Since the removal of the Ba'ath Party, which had monopolized oil revenues for thirty-five years, Iraq's ethnic and religious groups have been fighting for as large a share of the revenues as possible. And because relations between Shiites and Sunnis and between Kurds and Arabs are largely hostile, each group fears that the other will dominate oil revenues.

Like the disputes discussed earlier in the chapter, disagreements over revenue distribution stem from ambiguity in article 112 of the Iraqi constitution, which fails to clarify (1) which institution will determine which group or region should receive how much revenue from oil and (2) which criteria should be applied in making these decisions. The use of the phrase "present fields"—which could be interpreted to mean only currently operating fields, not future fields—creates further room for conflict (Baker et al. 2006).

Although the first paragraph of article 112 states that oil and gas revenues shall be distributed "in a fair manner" with special consideration to "damaged regions which were unjustly deprived" of revenues by the former regime, it does not clarify how this is to be achieved. The subjective criterion of fairness has created room for various political parties to mobilize their constituencies in the quest for their fair share of oil revenues.[16]

Kurds and Shiites, for example, who were systematically deprived of oil revenues under Saddam Hussein's regime, should be compensated for their losses. But how much, and for how long? Until Iraq can agree, as a whole, on what

---

[16] Because of the wording of the first paragraph of article 112, both the Shiites and the Kurds, which are historically neglected groups, are eager to lay claim to the status of "damaged regions." The Sunnis, too, refer to their region as underdeveloped, neglected, ignored, and without oil reserves (Al-Fadhal 2010).

amount of oil revenue is just compensation, ethnic and religious groups, with their corresponding political parties, will continue to compete for the biggest share, denouncing other parties' claims and hindering the reconciliation process. By provoking a debate on fairness and by failing to provide a methodology, guidelines, or criteria that would allow the reconciliation of divergent views, the constitution leaves the issue of distribution vulnerable to political rhetoric and offers no means of progress toward peace.

In the absence of constitutional guidance, the governorates or distribution of oil revenues has been relegated to the political arena, where the regions that believe they are being treated unfairly feel that they have only one option: standing against the government. In a post-conflict environment, where there is widespread access to weapons, such opposition can quickly become violent: both the Sunni and the Shiite insurgencies came from cities such as Fallujah and Sadr City that had been given less priority in the federal government's distribution of oil revenues (Chiarelli and Michaelis 2005; Al-Hashimi 2009). Furthermore, the regions and governorates where the oil is located have an incentive to expand their boundaries.

Kirkuk Governorate offers an example of the connections between religion, ethnicity, the management of oil reserves, and the distribution of oil revenue. The conflict over Kirkuk, an oil-rich governorate located 150 miles north of Baghdad, is one of the main threats to peace in Iraq (Borger 2008; ICG 2008). Kirkuk's inhabitants belong to a number of different ethnic groups (Kurds, Arabs, Turkmen, and Shabaks, among others) and adhere to a variety of different religions, including Christianity, Islam—both Sunni and Shiite—and Mandaeism (Thaler 2007). On the surface, the Kirkuk dispute concerns whether Kirkuk is part of the Kurdish region. But the real issues are the ownership and management of Kirkuk's large oil reserves and the distribution of the associated revenues.[17]

As noted earlier, article 111 of the Iraqi constitution grants ownership of oil and gas to "all the people of Iraq in all the regions and governorates"; and under article 112, "the federal government, with the producing governorates and regional governments," has a say in the management of oil. But neither article provides a framework for ensuring that the various religious and ethnic groups within a region or governorate receive their fair share of oil revenues; nor do the articles specify how much influence governorates have in relation to the federal government.

If the constitution is interpreted to mean that oil and its associated revenues are owned by the region or governorate in which the oil is found, then controlling Kirkuk Governorate is equivalent to controlling all of Kirkuk's oil. Control of Kirkuk and its oil by one ethnic or religious group is likely to provoke internal disputes over the control of the governorate. But if the constitution is interpreted to mean that both oil management and revenue distribution will be shared by the

---

[17] According to the U.S Energy Information Administration, as of 2009 Kirkuk Governorate had 8.6 billion barrels of oil reserves (EIA 2009).

federal government and the regions and governorates, then Kirkuk Governorate will likely attempt to strengthen its position in relation to the federal government—which may, in turn, create more unity within the governorate. One option for Kirkuk is to advocate for de facto control of the resource (e.g., by controlling the contracting process); another is to seek an extra share of the revenues, on the grounds that the governorate of origin should receive preferential treatment. A third option is to join the KRG, which already receives preferential treatment with respect to the distribution of oil revenues. For its part, the KRG would probably welcome the addition of Kirkuk to the region, because obtaining control over Kirkuk's oil would increase the KRG's direct revenues from oil.

The stakes are high, and the absence of a clear legal framework has created fierce competition—and violent conflict—between the city's two largest communities: the Kurds and the Arabs (Shadid 2009). It is not clear which group makes up the majority. The Kurds claim that they make up the majority of the population, and that Kirkuk should therefore be part of Kurdistan. The Arabs claim that they make up the majority of the population, and that Kirkuk is an Iraqi governorate subject to the control of the central government. Both sides believe that whichever ethnic group is larger will receive a larger share of oil revenues (Anderson and Stansfield 2009), and each has accused the other of attempting to change the demographics of Kirkuk to gain an advantage (Mackey 2005; Varner 2008; Williams 2009). The Kurds claim that under an "Arabization" policy implemented by Saddam Hussein's regime, thousands of Kurds and Turkmen were expelled from Kirkuk, while Arabs from central and southern Iraq were encouraged to migrate to the region. Similarly, the Arabs claim that the Kurds took advantage of the period following the fall of Hussein's regime to relocate more Kurds in Kirkuk (Khalil 2009).[18]

RECENT DEVELOPMENTS IN OIL MANAGEMENT

Despite the obvious need to do so, the Iraqi parliament has yet to pass an oil and gas law to address the ambiguities in the constitution. In February 2007, members of the Iraqi cabinet drafted a hydrocarbon legislative package that included provisions for oil and gas management and revenue sharing. But because of disagreements over key parts of the law, the legislation was still pending at the time of

---

[18] At the end of the 1990–1991 Gulf War, Hussein's regime focused on "Arabizing" Kirkuk. For example, Kurds, Turkmen, and Assyrians were pressured to sign "ethnic correction forms" renouncing their ethnicity and registering as Arabs. Those who refused received formal expulsion letters and were forced to leave government-controlled areas of northern Iraq (see Human Rights Watch 2004). In 2003, after the fall of Hussein's regime, the *peshmerga* crossed the Green Line and entered Kirkuk, in order to strengthen Kurdish claims that Kirkuk is part of Kurdistan. Arabs and Turkmen sought protection from the federal government, and in August 2008, Prime Minister Maliki deployed Iraqi army troops to Kirkuk, in an effort to push back against the Kurdish influence (ICG 2009).

writing. Three areas of particular contention are (1) authority to award oil contracts, (2) division of authority between the national and subnational governments, and (3) the extent of foreign participation in Iraq's oil and gas production (Blanchard 2009; Kane 2010). Although all ethnic and religious groups in Iraq would seem to have a common interest in the development of specific formulas and mechanisms for revenue sharing, that is not the primary focus of the law.

In an attempt to reduce tensions over revenue distribution, the Iraqi parliament has approved an annex to the 2010 national budget under which all governorates (but not the KRG) will receive US$1 for each barrel of oil produced by oil fields within their territory (*Al-Mada* 2010; *Shab Al Yomia* 2009). But the policy fails to specify a methodology for collecting and distributing the funds (*Freedom Space* 2010).[19] For example, it is unclear how the additional funds will be distributed in governorates whose populations are a mix of ethnicities and religious groups.[20] Despite its progressive intentions, the ambiguity of the policy could undermine efforts to achieve equity.

CONCLUSION

Oil exports account for more than 75 percent of Iraq's gross domestic product (EIA 2009). This level of dependence makes it imperative to create a positive business environment—one that will encourage foreign companies to invest in Iraq's future and help support the reconstruction process. However, the confusion generated by the constitutional framework for oil management has the potential to reduce the funds available for reconstruction, and ultimately undermine peacebuilding.

For the long term, Iraq needs to determine the practical implications of articles 111 and 112 and find answers to the following questions:

1. Under article 111, do all Iraqis own oil, or do the regions and governorates from which the oil is extracted have a special ownership status?
2. Under article 112, how should the federal and subnational governments work together to formulate policies for oil management and distribution of its revenues?
3. Which authority, national or subnational, supercedes the other?

Efforts to interpret articles 111 and 112 must be undertaken against the backdrop of other articles in the constitution. For example, article 115 which vests

---

[19] At the time of writing, the Ministry of Finance was attempting to develop such a methodology.
[20] For example, the Kurds who returned to Kirkuk after the fall of Hussein's regime are suffering from lack of basic services. Since they all live in one part of the governorate, it is easy to deprive them of such services, while providing services to other ethnic groups (Hassan 2010).

regions and governorates with all powers not vested exclusively in the federal government, heavily favors local autonomy. Since oil management is not an exclusively federal domain, the implication could be that regions and governorates have broad powers over oil management. Furthermore, with respect to "other powers shared" between the national and subnational governments, article 115 states that in case of dispute, "priority shall be given to the law of the regions and governorates not organized in a region." Similarly, in areas outside exclusive federal authority, the second paragraph of article 121 explicitly allows regional governments to amend federal laws that contradict regional laws. Taken together, articles 115 and 121 allow regional and governorate governments to override federal laws that are not constitutionally mandated.

By failing to address key questions, articles 111 and 112 foster inevitable conflicts between the oil laws of the national and subnational governments. These conflicts need to be resolved soon, if the constitution is to fulfill its aim of serving as the foundation for a peaceful, cohesive country.

Some senior members of the Iraqi oil industry have suggested that establishing a national oil company could reduce political tension. Under such an arrangement, management authority would be vested in an independent technical body instead of being under the control of a political body. Regional leaders are suspicious of this proposal, arguing that local communities should have direct access to the flow of oil revenues (Baker et al. 2006).

Ultimately, no matter who is granted oil management authority, all sides must recognize that the constitution grants *all* Iraqis ownership of the nation's oil. However, that is not enough. Iraq urgently needs a legal and regulatory framework that incorporates detailed mechanisms for exercising and enjoying the ownership of oil and its associated revenues. Until such a framework is adopted, Iraq is likely to experience continued conflict over oil.

REFERENCES

Ahmed, R. 2009. Provincial council held session because of the oil contracts. *Iraqi National News Agency*, July 1. www.wna-news.com/inanews/news.php?item.24606.5. (In Arabic.)

Al-Adhadh, K. 2008. Optimization policies for the management of the Iraqi oil extraction industry. Gulf Organization for Industrial Consulting. www.iraqistudies.org/English/conferences/2008/papers/alAdhadh.pdf.

Al-Fadhal, M. 2010. Compensating Iraqis who suffered damage under Saddam's regime. *Al Hewar Al Her*, June 25. www.ahewar.org/debat/show.art.asp?aid=216859. (In Arabic.)

Al-Hashimi, T. 2009. Author's interview with the vice-president of Iraq, Washington, D.C., December 12.

Al-Mada. 2010. Parliament approves the allocation of one dollar per barrel of oil to support investment projects. January 27. http://almadapaper.net/news.php?action=view&id=10235. (In Arabic.)

Alnasrawi, A. 2001a. Iraq: Economic sanctions and consequences: 1990–2000. *Third World Quarterly* 22 (2): 205–218.

———. 2001b. Oil, sanctions, debt and the future. *Arab Studies Quarterly* 23 (4): 1–14.

Al-Zubaidi, W. 2009. Controversy over the Iraq oil contracts. *Al Jazeera*, December 13. (In Arabic.)
Anderson, L., and G. Stansfield. 2009. *Crisis in Kirkuk: The ethnopolitics of conflict and compromise*. Philadelphia: University of Pennsylvania Press.
Aswat Al-Iraq. 2009. Basra City Council decides to send a commission of parliament to allocate 3% of oil revenues. December 16. http://ar.aswataliraq.info/?p=189000. (In Arabic.)
Baker, J. A., L. H. Hamilton, L. Eagleburger, V. Jordan Jr., E. Meese III, S. Day O'Connor, L. E. Panetta, W. J. Perry, C. S. Robb, and A. K. Simpson. 2006. *The Iraq Study Group report*. Washington, D.C.: United States Institute of Peace. http://media.usip.org/reports/iraq_study_group_report.pdf.
Baxter, K. 2009. Iraq's oil minister survives parliamentary mauling. Arabian Oil and Gas.com. June 23. www.arabianoilandgas.com/article-5740-iraq_oil_minister_faces_questions_in_parliament/.
Blanchard, C. M. 2009. Iraq: Oil and gas legislation, revenue sharing, and U.S. policy. Congressional Research Service. www.fas.org/sgp/crs/mideast/RL34064.pdf.
Borger, J. 2008. Conflict in Kirkuk is "main threat" to peace. *Guardian*, October 28. www.guardian.co.uk/world/2008/oct/28/kurds-iraq-kirkuk-conflict.
Botterill, L. C., and A. McNaughton. 2008. Laying the foundations for the wheat scandal: UN sanctions, private actors, and the Cole inquiry. *Australian Journal of Political Science* 43 (4): 583–598.
Bunter, M. 2004. The Islamic (Sharia) law and petroleum developments in countries of North Africa and the Arab world. *Transnational Dispute Management* 1 (2): 1–25.
Carlisle, T. 2009. Iraqi oil minister called to explain deals. *National*, June 16. www.thenational.ae/apps/pbcs.dll/article?AID=/20090616/BUSINESS/706169900/0/SPORT.
Chiarelli, P. W., and P. R. Michaelis. 2005. Winning the peace: The requirements for full-spectrum operations. *Military Review* (July/August): 4–17. www.au.af.mil/au/awc/awcgate/milreview/chiarelli.pdf.
Chorev, M. 2007. Iraqi Kurdistan: The internal dynamics and statecraft of a semistate. *Al Nakhlah: The Fletcher School Online Journal for Issues Related to Southwest Asia and Islamic Civilization*. (Fall):1–11. http://fletcher.tufts.edu/al_nakhlah/archives/Fall2007/Matan_Chorev_AN.pdf.
Cockburn, P. 2006. Iraq is disintegrating as ethnic cleansing takes hold. *Independent*, May 20. www.independent.co.uk/news/world/middle-east/iraq-is-disintegrating-as-ethnic-cleansing-takes-hold-478937.html.
CPA (Coalition Provisional Authority). 2004. Law of administration for the state of Iraq for the transitional period. March 8. www.iraqcoalition.org/government/TAL.html.
Deeks, A. H., and M. D. Burton. 2007. Iraq's constitution: A drafting history. *Cornell International Law Journal* 40 (1): 1–87. http://organizations.lawschool.cornell.edu/ilj/issues/40.1/burtondeeks.pdf.
Donovan, T. W. 2010. Ratification of federal oil tenders: The debate continues. *International Law Office*, February 1. www.internationallawoffice.com/newsletters/detail.aspx?g=695e6436-3165-4646-8304-94095a09ab29&redir=1.
EIA (U.S. Energy Information Administration). 2003. Iraq oil map. www.eia.gov/emeu/security/esar/esar_bigpic.htm.
———. 2009. Iraq energy statistics, information, and analysis. www.eia.doe.gov/cabs/Iraq/Oil.html.

Freedom Space. 2010. Al Fayhaa TV. One dollar per barrel for all producing governorates: Mechanism and methods of spending on infrastructure or political projects. February 4. www.alfayhaa.tv/alfayhaa-programs/daily-programs/freedome-space/24339.html. (In Arabic.)

Guardian. 2009. Iraq parliament promises to push Shell out of gas deal. April 18.

Hassan, S. The returned Kurdish refugees to Kirkuk explain their suffering, including lacking services in their areas. Misalliances. *Kurdish News Agency*, October 18.

Hayes, T. 1990. The oilfield lying below the Iraq-Kuwait dispute. *New York Times*, September 3.

Holland, J., and R. Jarrar. 2007. The battle for Iraq is about oil and democracy, not religion! *AlterNet*, September 10. www.alternet.org/world/62042.

Hsieh, C.-T., and E. Moretti. 2006. Did Iraq cheat the United Nations? Underpricing, bribes, and the oil for food program. *Quarterly Journal of Economics* 121 (4): 1211–1248.

Human Rights Watch. 2004. Claims in conflict: Reversing ethnic cleansing in northern Iraq. August 2. www.hrw.org/en/node/11985/section/1.

ICG (International Crisis Group). 2008. Oil for soil: Toward a grand bargain on Iraq and the Kurds. *Middle East Report* 80:1–42.

———. 2009. Iraq and the Kurds: Trouble along the triggering line. *Middle East Report* 88:1–37.

IIC (Independent Inquiry Committee). 2005. Independent Inquiry Committee finds mismanagement and failure of oversight: UN members states and secretariat share responsibility. Press release. September 7. www.iic-offp.org/story07Sept05.htm.

Iraq Body Count. 2008. Post-surge violence: Its extent and nature. December 28. www.iraqbodycount.org/analysis/numbers/surge-2008/.

———. 2010. Documented civilian deaths from violence. www.iraqbodycount.org/database/.

Jiyad, A. M. 2010. The legality of Iraqi oil contracts remains questionable. *Middle East Economic Survey* 52 (2).

Kane, S. 2010. Iraq's oil politics: Where agreement might be found. United States Institute of Peace. www.usip.org/files/resources/iraq_oil_pw64.pdf.

Kassim, R. 2010. Political disagreements delay the Iraqi census. *Dar Al Hayat*, November 28. www.daralhayat.com/portalarticlendah/206766.

Khalaf, R., D. Mahtani, and S. Negus. 2008. Forbidden fields: Oil groups circle the prize of Iraq's vast reserves. *Financial Times*, March 20.

Khalil, L. 2009. Stability in Iraqi Kurdistan: Reality or mirage? Working Paper Number 2. Saban Center for Middle East Policy at the Brookings Institution. www.brookings.edu/~/media/Files/rc/papers/2009/06_kurdistan_khalil/06_kurdistan_khalil.pdf.

KRG (Kurdistan Regional Government). 2006. Petroleum act of the Kurdistan Region of Iraq: Final draft for submission to the parliament of Kurdistan. September 9. http://web.krg.org/pdf/Kurdistan_Petroleum_Act_Final_Draft.pdf.

———. 2010. The Kurdistan Region in brief. April 23. www.krg.org/articles/detail.asp?lngnr=12&smap=03010300&rnr=140&anr=23911.

Krupa, M. 1997. Environmental and economic repercussions of the Persian Gulf War on Kuwait. Case Number 9. ICE Case Studies. www1.american.edu/ted/ice/kuwait.htm.

Kumins, L. 2006. Iraq oil: Reserves, production, and potential revenues. CRS Report for Congress. www.usembassy.it/pdf/other/RS21626.pdf.

Macalister, T. 2009. West's access to Iraqi oil in doubt. *Sun Herald*, April 19.

Mackey, S. 2005. The coming clash over Kirkuk. *New York Times*, February 9. www.nytimes.com/2005/02/09/opinion/09mackey.htm.
Mahdi, O. 2010. Political disagreements destroyed the last chance to hold the Iraqi census. *ELAPH*, December 5. http://elaph.com/Web/news/2010/12/615966.html?entry=article TaggedArticles. (In Arabic.)
Maitland, F. W. 1905. Moral personality and legal personality. *Journal of the Society of Comparative Legislation* 6 (2): 192–200.
O'Leary, C. A. 2002. The Kurds of Iraq: Recent history, future prospects. *Middle East Review of International Affairs Journal* 6 (4). http://meria.idc.ac.il/journal/2002/issue4/jv6n4a5.html.
Peters, P. 2010. Iraq: Political and legal risk in Kurdistan; Business as usual? *Mondaq*, June 9. www.mondaq.com/article.asp?articleid=102478.
Provost, R. 1992. Starvation as a weapon: Legal implications of the United Nations food blockade against Iraq and Kuwait. *Columbia Journal of Transnational Law* 30 (3): 577–639.
Revenue Watch. 2005. Protecting the future: Constitutional safeguards for Iraq's oil revenues. Report No. 8. May. www.iraqrevenuewatch.org/reports/052605.pdf.
ROI (Republic of Iraq). 1970. Constitution of the Republic of Iraq. July 16.
———. 2005. Iraqi constitution. October 15. www.uniraq.org/documents/iraqi_constitution.pdf.
Shab Al Yomia. 2009. Analytical report: Maliki's government faces challenges in the absence of political consent. April 17 http://arabic.people.com.cn/31662/6639085.html.
Shadid, A. 2009. Worries about a Kurdish-Arab conflict move to the fore in Iraq. *Washington Post*, July 27.
SOK (State of Kuwait). 1963. Constitution. January 29. www.kuwait-info.com/a_state_system/state_system_articles1.asp.
Thaler, K. 2007. Iraqi minority group needs U.S. attention. *Yale Daily News*, March 9. www.yaledailynews.com/opinion/guest-columns/2007/03/09/iraqi-minority-group-needs-us-attention/.
Terrill, W. A. 2007. Kuwaiti national security and the U.S.–Kuwaiti strategic relationship after Saddam. Strategic Studies Institute. www.strategicstudiesinstitute.army.mil/pdffiles/pub788.pdf.
University of Texas Libraries. 1978. Iraq: distribution of religious groups and ethnic groups. Perry Castañeda Library Map Collection. Map No. 503930. www.lib.utexas.edu/maps/middle_east_and_asia/iraq_ethnic_1978.jpg.
UN (United Nations). 2010. Office of the Iraq programme: Oil-for-food. June 15. www.un.org/Depts/oip/.
UN Office of the Iraq Programme Oil-for-Food. 2003. Statement to the Security Council by the Secretary-General on the closure of the Oil-for-Food Programme. November 20. www.un.org/Depts/oip/background/latest/sgstatement031119.html.
UNSC (United Nations Security Council). 1990. Resolution 661. S/RES/661 (1990). August 6.
———. 2000. Report of the group of United Nations experts established pursuant to paragraph 30 of the Security Council resolution 1284. www.un.org/Depts/oip/background/reports/oilexpertsreport.pdf.
U.S. Department of State. 2003. Press briefing: Boucher announces coalition for immediate disarmament of Iraq. March 18. www.america.gov/st/washfile-english/2003/March/20030318202511nosmohtp0.3604242.html.

U.S. Institute of Peace. 2005. Iraq's constitutional process: Shaping a vision for the country's future. *Special Report* 132 (February 2005): 1–14. www.usip.org/files/resources/sr132.pdf.

Varner, B. 2008. Kurd-Arab Kirkuk clash is "ticking time bomb," UN mediator says. *Bloomberg*, February 28. www.bloomberg.com/apps/news?pid=20601087&sid=aQOVnZuH7k4U&refer=home.

Williams, T. 2009. U.N. report lays out options for an oil-rich Iraqi region. *New York Times*, April 23. www.nytimes.com/2009/04/23/world/middleeast/23iraq.html?_r=1.

World Almanac Books. 2009. Nations of the world: Iraq. In *World Almanac and Book of Facts*, ed. C. A. Joyce. New York: Simon and Schuster.

ANNEX

Excerpts from the 2005 Iraqi Constitution

Section One: Fundamental Principles

Article 1:
The Republic of Iraq is a single federal, independent and fully sovereign state in which the system of government is republican, representative, parliamentary, and democratic, and this Constitution is a guarantor of the unity of Iraq.

Section Three: Federal Powers

Article 49:
First: The Council of Representatives shall consist of a number of members, at a ratio of one seat per 100,000 Iraqi persons representing the entire Iraqi people. They shall be elected through a direct secret general ballot. The representation of all components of the people shall be upheld in it.

Section Four: Powers of the Federal Government

Article 110:
The federal government shall have exclusive authorities in the following matters:
First: Formulating foreign policy and diplomatic representation; negotiating, signing, and ratifying international treaties and agreements; negotiating, signing, and ratifying debt policies and formulating foreign sovereign economic and trade policy.
Second: Formulating and executing national security policy, including establishing and managing armed forces to secure the protection and guarantee the security of Iraq's borders and to defend Iraq.
Third: Formulating fiscal and customs policy; issuing currency; regulating commercial policy across regional and governorate boundaries in Iraq; drawing up the national budget of the State; formulating monetary policy; and establishing and administering a central bank.
Fourth: Regulating standards, weights, and measures.

Fifth: Regulating issues of citizenship, naturalization, residency, and the right to apply for political asylum.
Sixth: Regulating the policies of broadcast frequencies and mail.
Seventh: Drawing up the general and investment budget bill.
Eighth: Planning policies relating to water sources from outside Iraq and guaranteeing the rate of water flow to Iraq and its distribution inside Iraq in accordance with international laws and conventions.
Ninth: General population statistics and census.

Article 111:
Oil and gas are owned by all the people of Iraq in all the regions and governorates.

Article 112:
First: The federal government, with the producing governorates and regional governments, shall undertake the management of oil and gas extracted from present fields, provided that it distributes its revenue in a fair manner in proportion to the population distribution in all parts of the country, specifying an allotment for a specified period for the damaged regions which were unjustly deprived of them by the former regime, and the regions that were damaged afterwards in a way that ensures balanced development in different areas of the country, and this shall be regulated by a law.
Second: The federal government, with the producing regional and governorate governments, shall together formulate the necessary strategic policies to develop the oil and gas wealth in a way that achieves the highest benefit to the Iraqi people using the most advanced techniques of the market principles and encouraging investment.

Article 114:
The following competencies shall be shared between the federal authorities and regional authorities:
First: To manage customs, in coordination with the governments of the regions and governorates that are not organized in a region, and this shall be regulated by a law.
Second: To regulate the main sources of electric energy and its distribution.
Third: To formulate environmental policy to ensure the protection of the environment from pollution and to preserve its cleanliness, in cooperation with the regions and governorates that are not organized in a region.
Fourth: To formulate development and general planning policies.
Fifth: To formulate public health policy, in cooperation with the regions and governorates that are not organized in a region.
Sixth: To formulate the public educational and instructional policy, in consultation with the regions and governorates that are not organized in a region.
Seventh: To formulate and regulate the internal water resources policy in a way that guarantees their just distribution, and this shall be regulated by a law.

Article 115:
All powers not stipulated in the exclusive powers of the federal government belong to the authorities of the regions and governorates that are not organized in a region. With regard to other powers shared between the federal government and the regional government, priority shall be given to the law of the regions and governorates not organized in a region in case of dispute.

Section Five: Powers of the Regions

Chapter One: Regions

Article 116:
The federal system in the Republic of Iraq is made up of a decentralized capital, regions, and governorates, as well as local administrations.

Article 117:
First: This Constitution, upon coming into force, shall recognize the region of Kurdistan, along with its existing authorities, as a federal region.
Second: This Constitution shall affirm new regions established in accordance with its provisions.

Article 119:
One or more governorates shall have the right to organize into a region based on a request to be voted on in a referendum submitted in one of the following two methods:
First: A request by one-third of the council members of each governorate intending to form a region.
Second: A request by one-tenth of the voters in each of the governorates intending to form a region.

Article 121:
First: The regional powers shall have the right to exercise executive, legislative, and judicial powers in accordance with this Constitution, except for those authorities stipulated in the exclusive authorities of the federal government.
Second: In case of a contradiction between regional and national legislation in respect to a matter outside the exclusive authorities of the federal government, the regional power shall have the right to amend the application of the national legislation within that region.
Third: Regions and governorates shall be allocated an equitable share of the national revenues sufficient to discharge their responsibilities and duties, but having regard to their resources, needs, and the percentage of their population.
Fourth: Offices for the regions and governorates shall be established in embassies and diplomatic missions, in order to follow cultural, social, and developmental affairs.

Fifth: The regional government shall be responsible for all the administrative requirements of the region, particularly the establishment and organization of the internal security forces for the region such as police, security forces, and guards of the region.

Article 140:
First: The executive authority shall undertake the necessary steps to complete the implementation of the requirements of all subparagraphs of Article 58 of the Transitional Administrative Law.
Second: The responsibility placed upon the executive branch of the Iraqi Transitional Government stipulated in Article 58 of the Transitional Administrative Law shall extend and continue to the executive authority elected in accordance with this Constitution, provided that it accomplishes completely (normalization and census and concludes with a referendum in Kirkuk and other disputed territories to determine the will of their citizens), by a date not to exceed the 31st of December 2007.

Source: ROI (2005).

The capitalist civil peace: Some theory and empirical evidence

Indra de Soysa

Post-conflict societies are often characterized by weak economic and political institutions and domination by entrenched interests. The end of violence creates an opportunity to put a stop to the "institutional sclerosis" that results when rent seeking holds back socioeconomic progress (Olson 1982).[1] But the question of how best to take advantage of this opportunity remains controversial. In a 2008 publication on post-conflict economic recovery, the United Nations Development Programme (UNDP) described recovery as "building back differently and better" (UNDP 2008, 1). But what, exactly, should be done "differently" and "better"?

The reality is that aid has generally failed to deliver development; instead, as many have argued, development is driven by entrepreneurial activity. And the extent of such activity is largely determined by the structure of incentives that motivate investment endogenously (Easterly 2006). While multilateral organizations (such as the UN) and many nongovernmental organizations (NGOs) pay homage to building markets and encouraging private economic activity, there is generally a visible bias in favor of "getting the politics right," as opposed to encouraging free markets (Collier 2009; Paris 2004). And most of the post-conflict peacebuilding literature emphasizes improving coordination among donor countries and making the delivery of aid more effective; there is generally little focus on identifying and nurturing endogenous sources of domestic peace and recovery (Call and Cousens 2008).

One consequence of the emphasis on state building and on undertaking reconstruction from the "outside" is a failure to examine the role of free markets in establishing social peace. This chapter argues that free markets matter, and

---

Indra de Soysa is a professor of political science and the director of globalization research at the Norwegian University of Science and Technology in Trondheim, Norway, and an associate scholar at the Centre for the Study of Civil War, Peace Research Institute Oslo.

[1] *Rent seeking* refers to attempts to capture economic benefits without contributing to overall economic production. For example, producers seek rents when they lobby governments for higher tariffs, and monopolists seek rents when they try to prevent competition.

that they can both spur and support endogenous efforts to build functional states and institutions. The approach is both theoretical and empirical: what are the arguments and evidence for a relationship between free markets and social harmony?

Many liberals believe that systems that discourage the formation of monopolies and entrenched interests escape perverse political and economic outcomes; correspondingly, they believe that systems that encourage individual liberties and free market transactions improve welfare and increase social harmony.[2] But the efforts of the international community to promote more open economic systems have recently come under question (Cramer 2009; Paris 2004); the argument is that fragile societies cannot handle the competitive, conflictual situations bred by democracy and free markets.[3] Nevertheless, post-conflict recovery has to start somewhere. It is precisely this issue of where to start—and why—that is the focus of this chapter.

The chapter is divided into four major sections: (1) a discussion of the theoretical basis for establishing economic freedom in post-conflict settings; (2) an explanation of why peace fails under autarkic economic environments; (3) analyses of data that illustrate a strong connection between economic freedom and social harmony; and (4) a brief conclusion.

WHY ECONOMIC FREEDOM? SOME THEORETICAL EXPLANATIONS

How might market institutions, the more neglected aspect of the liberal peace, matter? In the eighteenth century, classical liberals such as Adam Smith, David Ricardo, and Bernard Mandeville argued that when individuals pursue self-interest, they serve a higher social purpose "as if by a hidden hand" (Stilwell 2006). Free markets thus provide the basis for prosperity—while other desired outcomes, such as peace, arise from cooperation among people who are acting out of self-interest. In this view, cooperation stems from the expectation of gain, rather than from religious (or other) ethics or from inherent feelings of sympathy for others.

---

[2] For the purposes of this chapter, *liberalism* refers to the classical liberal position on free markets, political liberty, and individual freedoms. Classical liberals such as John Milton, Montesquieu, David Hume, John Locke, Adam Smith, Immanuel Kant, and adherents of the Manchester School believed that individual freedoms, particularly in the economic realm, would lead to vibrant markets that were free of interference from politics—and that such freedoms would therefore be good for prosperity and peace (Hirschman 1977; Holmes 1995). (For further discussion of classical liberalism, see Hall [1987]). The mountain of empirical evidence that links democracy and trade dependence to peace at the international level has rekindled the idea of promoting open trade and democracy in order to promote civil peace (Russett 1993; Russett and Oneal 2001).

[3] In this chapter, liberal economic systems, free markets, capitalism, and economic freedom are regarded as similar both conceptually and operationally and are used interchangeably. See Berger (1993) for an extended discussion of these terms.

Such arguments were expanded by political philosophers—including John Locke, Immanuel Kant, John Stuart Mill, and Norman Angell—who saw the expansion of trade, or the "spirit of commerce," as the triumph of exchange and civility over plunder and predation (Kant 1991). Commercial liberalism advocated free markets; republican liberalism called for the creation of representative states, to ensure that the rules of the free market would generally be impartially enforced and could not be subverted by the powerful. Economic and political freedom were thus inextricably linked, because people who were free to engage in mutually beneficial economic activity would form associations to check the power of states and vested interests.

Classical liberalism also held that self-interested economic activity produces wealth more efficiently than autarkic systems, which are designed to increase the welfare of rulers and states. The goal of mercantilism, the dominant economic system at the time that classical liberalism emerged, was to increase the wealth of kings. Arguments that capitalism was superior to mercantilism were based on the premise that markets could create and distribute goods and services (i.e., wealth) more efficiently, increasing the welfare of *all*—including the king. Consider the following observation, made in the 1830s by Alexis de Tocqueville, a keen observer of how democracy, rather than chaos, was taking root in the newly formed United States of America:

> You have some difficulty in understanding how men so independent do not constantly fall into the abuse of freedom. If on the other hand, you survey the infinite number of trading companies in operation in the United States . . . you will comprehend why people so well employed are by no means tempted to perturb the state, nor to destroy the public tranquility by which they all profit (de Tocqueville 1956, 118–119).

Those who invest money wish to avoid war because violence would disrupt profits. Thus, the growth of commerce apparently made war—which would damage the interests of everyone—unnecessary.

In keeping with classical liberal theory, several contemporary studies report a positive relationship between economic freedom, properly functioning markets, and civil peace, and describe a number of different channels through which good market institutions, such as respect for property rights, can temper social conflict (de Soysa and Fjelde 2010; de Soysa and Binningsbø 2009; Eriksen and de Soysa 2009; Mousseau and Mousseau 2008; Steinberg and Saideman 2008). David A. Steinberg and Stephen M. Saideman (2008), for example, found that the less the state is able to manipulate economic policies in favor of ethnic majorities, the less fear and mistrust will be generated among minorities. In other words, economic freedom matters: more open markets dampen the fear and mistrust associated with ethnic nepotism. This suggests, in turn, that the primary concern of ethnic groups might be economic, rather than political, well-being.

Other researchers, including Michael Mousseau and Demet Yalcin Mousseau (2008), argue that people who are free to engage in contracts respect the rights of others and promote the welfare of others. Using the density of life insurance contracts as a measure of market norms, Mousseau and Mousseau found that high levels of contracting lead to respect for individual rights, regardless of caste, creed, ethnicity, or other characteristics.

The explanation of the link between free markets and social peace offered in this chapter complements the broadly social explanations of Steinberg and Saideman (2008) and Mousseau and Mousseau (2008). The theory presented in the following section seeks to explain why economic autarky sets the stage for rebellion rather than for peace—and, by implication, why peace may be more likely under conditions of economic freedom.

WHY ECONOMIC AUTARKY ENCOURAGES REBELLION-SPECIFIC CAPITAL

The theory that free markets encourage social peace is founded on a single observation: *violent armed conflict has to be feasible to occur*. The question is, what renders armed conflict feasible? First of all, war is a costly endeavor; it will not occur if those who invest in it do not expect the returns from war to be higher than the returns from peace. Thus, grievances alone are unlikely to bring about armed conflict: challenging the state requires significant financing and relatively large numbers of volunteers. But if people are capable of sufficiently organizing human and financial resources to launch a rebellion, why wouldn't they channel that energy to obtain relief from grievances *without* engaging in violence?

Theoretical and empirical analyses conducted by two sets of researchers—Paul Collier and Anke Hoeffler (2004) and James D. Fearon and David D. Laitin (2003)—show that *opportunity*, rather than grievance, explains the onset of civil war: that is, conflict will occur where organizing for violent purposes is viable (Collier, Hoeffler, and Rohner 2009). Viability, in turn, is shaped by many factors, including the size and nature of the payoffs for investing in violence rather than in other potentially "profitable" enterprises. In the "loot-seeking" model of rebellion, for example, in which high-value resources render rebellion both attractive and viable, loot is the expected payoff for the "investment" in rebellion.

But the argument that rebellion is opportunistic behavior fails to take into account the opportunity costs associated with organized violence: in a globalized world with ample opportunity for profitable investment, any potential rebel could just as easily be a "corporation"—exporting natural resources and paying taxes to the state—instead of a warlord who has to invest much of the loot in continued conflict (not to mention the discomfort of living in the bush). In an environment that provides incentives for investment and enforces rules that safeguard profits, investing in production will be more attractive than investing in war. In fact, in a number of advanced market economies, the high costs of remaining illegal have led many "loot-seeking" groups, like the Mafia, to move into the quasi-legitimate business world.

On the other hand, if the state monopolizes all economic activity and expropriates the surpluses that are created in an economy—serving, in Mancur Olson's terms, as a "roving" rather than as a "stationary" bandit—there will be few incentives to invest in taxable enterprise and "go legit" (Olson 1993).[4] Where property rights are insecure and capricious political processes govern economic life, productive enterprises are at risk, and there is motivation to organize in the shadows, by capturing rents and defending them (Skaperdas 2003).

Although shadow economies are often thought to emerge during war and its aftermath, in all likelihood they exist before war even begins. Consider the Mexican drug cartels, for example, which are engaged in a lucrative trade that lacks a legal infrastructure for handling transactions. The groups organize and fight in Mexico because violence is more viable there, but the impetus for the killing is the high demand for drugs across the border. Globally, such shadowy groups are now responsible for a large part of violent conflict (Mueller 2004).[5] These groups survive and thrive because they have "rebellion-specific capital": that is, organizational advantages over states, from armaments and tunnels to sophisticated command and communications networks.

Stergios Skaperdas (2003) holds that because the incentives that govern markets shape the behavior of *homo economicus* (economic man), the economy cannot be divorced from its governance—a perspective that is in keeping with the thesis of this chapter. The conflict that plagues northern Mexico, for example, cannot be solved without governance-based efforts to alter the payoffs that accrue to those who invest in conflict-specific capital. In practical terms, there are two ways to address this issue—either militarily (that is, by suppressing the violence), or legislatively (that is, by legalizing drugs in the United States and thereby eliminating the payoff for smuggling).

Ultimately, bad—that is, incompetent—governments are the primary source of violent conflict, not the ethnic and cultural clashes that are often held responsible (Mueller 2004). Thus, the peacebuilding initiatives currently in fad might have to focus more intently on how to build economic and political institutions that support economic competition and ensure low barriers to entry for legitimate business. All too often, however, post-conflict peacebuilding efforts are designed to remove broad societal grievances, rather than to promote markets by removing the risks of investing.

A vast literature addressing the "resource curse" demonstrates that rulers of resource-rich states fail to build good institutions (Jensen and Wantchekon 2004;

---

[4] In the view of Mancur Olson (1982), capricious governance is analogous to roving banditry, where the arbitrary nature of theft (i.e., high tax rates) gives producers an incentive to hide their goods and to underproduce. A stationary bandit, in contrast, will avoid stealing because if producers believe that their goods are safe, they will produce a surplus that will increase the absolute value of the bandit's takings (i.e., the tax base). Thus, a stationary bandit provides a predictable tax rate that elicits optimal production—a win-win situation.

[5] For a comparative view of warlordism, see Marten (2006).

Olsson and Congdon Fors 2004; Ross 2001).[6] But this raises a question: if resources provide lootable income, and resource-rich nations tend to have weak governments, why haven't rulers used the resource wealth to increase state capacity? The most convincing argument is that rulers fear being replaced, and therefore will resist building institutions that would create alternative bases of power (Acemoglu and Robinson 2006). If capitalism, which is one such institution, builds alternative sources of economic power, then the rulers of resource-rich countries have little incentive to create the kind of open economy that would eventually lead to reform—and, ultimately, to the loss of rents (Congdon Fors and Olsson 2007). A large body of literature on the "rentier state" is based on similar arguments (Beblawi 1990; Bellin 2004; Ross 2001).[7]

Countries with high-value resources—oil and diamonds, in particular—are at very high risk of conflict (Fearon and Laitin 2003; Lujala 2010). How might greater economic freedom moderate this risk? Knowing that there is a resource curse does not break the spell. Poor countries that are blessed by nature cannot ignore their largesse and "keep it in the ground." Over the past several decades, a number of schemes to manage the resource curse—such as state ownership, development funds, and various revenue-sharing schemes—have been tried, with mixed results (Weinthal and Luong 2006). After reviewing the evidence, Erika Weinthal and Pauline Jones Luong (2006) offer one solution that they believe may be the best: allowing competitive private ownership of resources. With illustrative evidence from Russia, Weinthal and Luong show that what prevents rulers from mismanaging wealth is ownership structure; therefore, assigning private ownership to extractive activities leads to the demand for better—that is, impartial—institutions to manage the transactions between private actors.

Although most of the internal wars being fought today are devoid of political content (Collier, Hoeffler, and Rohner 2009; Mueller 2004), the notion persists, particularly among global governance agencies, that war is "politics by other means." As this section has made clear, however, where countries are rich in natural resources and booty makes it possible to organize and maintain violence, war is more likely to be "economics by other means." In other words, when state institutions are weak or unwilling to adjudicate fairly, warlords are essentially businessmen for whom engaging in organized violence is an occupational hazard; mafias, after all, have historically begun as private protection rackets (Gambetta 1993).

---

[6] The term *resource curse* refers to economic, political, and social maladies that stem from the perverse incentives that resources provide for anyone who wishes to capture them. For a more detailed explanation of the resource curse, see Paul Collier and Anke Hoeffler, "High-Value Natural Resources, Development, and Conflict: Channels of Causation," in this volume.

[7] The term *rentier state* refers to states that are dependent on rents rather than taxes.

ECONOMIC FREEDOM AND CIVIL PEACE: EMPIRICAL EVIDENCE

Capitalistic—that is, production-friendly—environments may be capable of breaking the link between natural resources, weak states, and civil war (Fearon 2005), but there is a dearth of evidence that effectively ties free markets to peace and demonstrates how the two can work symbiotically. In fact, because of the risk that the state will be captured by private interests, free markets are typically viewed as weakening, rather than strengthening, the state (Cramer 2009; Paris 2004; Stiglitz 2007).[8] The few studies that have addressed free markets in post-conflict settings have found that economic freedom does have short-term destabilizing effects (Paris 2004): privatization of the economy, for example, can be dangerous without good institutions. But what remains unclear is how one gets to long-term stability without starting somewhere, particularly if it is unclear whether capitalist institutions are worth building in the first place.

This chapter argues that free markets produce viable civil societies, which act as a counterweight to the capture of democracy by vested interests that have access to state power (Bermeo and Nord 2000). Economic institutions that ensure economic competition and low barriers to entry for legitimate business increase the motivation to organize openly and legally, rather than in the shadows. The next task is to present evidence for the connection between free markets and civil peace.

The broad trend: A bivariate analysis

Since the end of the Cold War, the world has become much safer in terms of armed conflict (Gleditsch 2008; Hewitt, Wilkenfeld, and Gurr 2008; Human Security Report Project 2005). The question is, can the growth in free-market capitalism account for the change?

Figure 1 compares global trends in civil armed conflict with scores on the 2010 Index of Economic Freedom. (The index assigns scores to ten categories of economic freedom—including labor freedom, business freedom, trade freedom, investment freedom, property rights, and freedom from corruption—which are then averaged to create an overall score.)[9] The contrast is quite stark. In countries with below-average levels of economic freedom (not shown in the figure), the risk of civil war is over twice that of countries with above-average levels of economic freedom. In fact, low performers on economic freedom accounted for much of the spike in civil wars that occurred during the early 1990s (Economic Freedom Network n.d.).

---

[8] This is an old debate that goes back to Adam Smith and Marxist critiques of capitalism.
[9] For detailed explanations of the Index of Economic Freedom, see Gwartney and Lawson (2005). The data are available at Economic Freedom Network (n.d.).

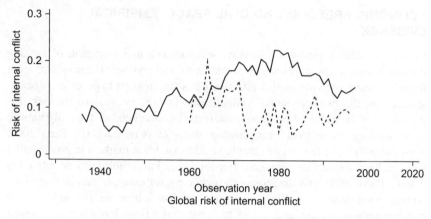

Figure 1. Economic freedom and the risk of internal armed conflict (>25 battle deaths), 1970–2008
Sources: UCDP (n.d.); Economic Freedom Network (n.d.).
Notes:
1. To compute the risk of internal conflict, the number of ongoing civil wars was divided by the total number of countries.
2. Above-average economic freedom was defined as anything above the mean value of economic freedom, which for the global sample was 5.88 points.

This simple, bivariate reckoning clearly demonstrates that peace and greater economic freedom have gone together. It also contradicts the claim—made by many who see the imposition of free-market policies through structural adjustment programs as destabilizing to social harmony—that it was the imposition of neoliberal policies by the International Monetary Fund and the World Bank that led to conflicts in the 1980s and 1990s (Abouharb and Cingranelli 2007).[10] The drop in civil war that has occurred since the end of the Cold War is also interesting: if the risk of civil war is largely driven by the resource curse, can it be that the shift toward neoliberal policies that has occurred since the early 1990s renders peace possible, even in resource-wealthy countries with weak governance?

The comparison of bivariate averages provides preliminary evidence that peace and free markets are positively linked, but this inference may be too broad and is perhaps unreliable. For example, the measure of economic freedom may actually reflect income or some other factor, such as European heritage. To determine whether the broad trends in liberalization and the end of civil war are connected, the bivariate correlations need to be tested more carefully and precisely, using multivariate models that can account for other possible explanatory factors. The

---

[10] Structural adjustment programs were policies imposed by multilateral donors in an effort to open up closed economies.

next section will show that the positive correlation between peace and free markets holds even when several relevant factors are controlled for.

Free markets, organized violence, and human rights: Multivariate analyses

Figure 1 suggests that countries with higher levels of economic freedom are less likely to suffer from internal conflict. But this result could have been driven by a number of factors: richer countries, for example, may be less subject to civil war. To determine the net effect of economic freedom on civil war—that is, the effect of one variable considered independently of other (potentially explanatory) variables—one must use multivariate regression models, which make it possible to gauge the size and direction of the impact of any one variable while other variables are held constant. In the analyses described in this section, standard data sets, independently collected by other researchers, were used to measure the phenomena under study; this approach minimizes any biases the author may have introduced to the coding of data.

The two subsections that follow describe two types of assessments:

- The impact of economic freedom on organized violence.
- The combined impact of natural resource wealth and economic freedom on human rights.

The goal is to demonstrate, through more sophisticated means, that the results shown in figure 1 are not spurious—in other words, that economic freedom has a direct effect on civil peace and human rights, even when considered apart from "good institutions." The models employ several control variables, which were gleaned from the findings of Collier and Hoeffler (2004); Collier, Hoeffler, and Rohner (2009); and Fearon and Laitin (2003), all standard-bearers in the field.[11]

Economic freedom and civil war

For the main variable of interest, economic freedom, the analysis relies on data from the Fraser Institute that measure the extent to which an economy is (1) free from state interference and (2) allows private economic activity that is supported by impartial institutions (Gwartney and Lawson 2005). Economic freedom is judged according to twenty-two criteria, both objective (e.g., the government's share of the economy, trade openness, restrictions on capital) and subjective (e.g., the level of independence of the judiciary).[12] The index ranges from 0 (total

---

[11] See the chapter annex for a detailed explanation.
[12] These data, which were obtained from the Fraser Institute, are available for five-year intervals until 2000 and at one-year intervals thereafter. For the period between 1970 and 2000, interpolations were made for the time between the five-year intervals. For full details on the data, see the Fraser Institute's web site, www.freetheworld.com.

autarky) to 10 (total freedom). In 2010, for example, the highest and lowest scores, respectively, were assigned to the free-trade port of Hong Kong (9.05) and Zimbabwe (3.57).

The main dependent variable (i.e., the outcome to be explained) in this analysis is the onset of civil war; the onset of conflict is relevant because one purpose of the analysis is to determine whether countries with high levels of economic freedom can maintain peace. The data used to measure armed conflict were obtained from the UCDP/PRIO Armed Conflict Dataset v4-2008 (Gleditsch et al. 2002; Harbom and Wallensteen 2009).[13] In the context of that data set, an intrastate armed conflict is defined as a contested incompatibility between a government and one or more opposition groups that results in at least twenty-five battle deaths in a year.

As shown in table 1, countries with higher levels of economic freedom have a lower risk of civil war (as is indicated by the negative sign of the coefficient); moreover, this result is highly statistically significant (indicated by the three asterisks after the coefficient).[14] Interestingly, per capita income, which is often touted as one of the most robust explanations for the onset of civil war (Hegre and Sambanis 2006), is not statistically significant, so the result is not explained by the fact that richer countries have higher levels of economic freedom. In robustness checks, which are designed to determine whether results are sensitive to changes in the models, the inclusion of measures of good institutions (such as lack of corruption), made no difference to the effects of economic freedom on the risk of civil war.[15]

But in real-world terms, how might economic freedom affect the risk of civil war? One way to explore this question is to ask to what extent economic freedom dampens the risk of civil war in a post-conflict setting. For a poor country (where the income is in the lowest 25th percentile) emerging from civil conflict, an improvement in the level of economic freedom from the 25th to the 75th percentile reduces the annual risk of civil war from 4.7 to 2.7 percent, a reduction of almost 60 percent.[16] The following three comparisons will help put this shift in perspective:

- Moving the level of economic freedom from the 25th to the 75th percentile is analogous to instituting Botswana's level of economic freedom in Sierra

---

[13] The UCDP/PRIO Armed Conflict Dataset is a collaborative project between the Department of Peace and Conflict Research at Uppsala University and the Centre for the Study of Civil War at the Peace Research Institute Oslo. For additional information, see the web site of the Uppsala Conflict Data Program, www.ucdp.uu.se.

[14] A statistically significant result is one that is extremely unlikely to have occurred by chance; the smaller the standard errors (shown in parentheses in the table) relative to the size of the coefficient, the greater the statistical significance.

[15] A number of methods were used to check for robustness when the parameters of the models were changed, but the fundamental negative (and statistically significant) effect of economic freedom on the risk of conflict held up (see the annex for a discussion of this point).

[16] All variables apart from economic freedom, income, and conflict history were held at their mean. All substantive effects were estimated using Clarify software (King, Tomz, and Wittenbeng 2000).

Table 1. The effect of economic freedom on the onset of civil war, 1946–2005

Variable	Effect on the onset of intrastate armed conflict[b]
Economic freedom$_{t-1}$	−0.33***
	(0.11)
Per capita income$_{log, t-1}$	−0.27
	(0.20)
Growth in per capita income$_{t-1}$	0.02
	(0.02)
Population size$_{log}$	0.48***
	(0.08)
Oil exporter	0.14
	(0.28)
Ethnic fractionalization	8.98***
	(2.12)
Ethnic fractionalization squared[a]	−7.99***
	(2.29)
Democracy	−0.12
	(0.24)
Autocracy	−0.18
	(0.25)
Incidence of conflict$_{t-1}$	−0.31
	(0.29)
Brevity of peace	0.90**
	(0.41)
	(1.67)
Number of observations	3,028
Number of countries	117

Sources: Data were drawn from CSCW (2008); Gleditsch et al. (2002); and Harbom, and Wallensteen (2009).
Notes:
1. Robust standard errors are in parentheses. These standard errors are robust to statistical problems arising from heteroscedasticity (nonnormality of error terms) and serial correlation, or the correlation of the error term across panels.
2. The "log" subscripts indicate that the data were log transformed to reduce the effects of extreme values.
3. The "t−1" subscripts indicate that the independent variable was measured one year before the year of civil war onset.
4. Economic freedom data are available only from 1970.
*** $p < .01$; ** $p < .05$;
a. Ethnic fractionalization squared models the quadratic effect of fractionalization. (This is useful for testing whether conflict is dependent on ethnic fractionalization in a linear or nonlinear way. In a linear relationship, if one variable changes, the other changes by a corresponding amount.)
b. An intrastate armed conflict is defined as a contested incompatibility between a government and one or more opposition groups that results in at least twenty-five battle deaths in a year.

Leone: had Sierra Leone adopted Botswana's level of economic freedom at the end of its civil war, in 2002, it would have roughly halved its risk of reverting to conflict.
- In the absence of improvements in economic freedom, a similar reduction in risk would take a full eight years of post-conflict peace.
- In terms of the effect on the risk of civil war, moving the level of economic freedom from the 25th to the 75th percentile has the same impact as moving from the 25th to the 75th percentile in per capita income distribution.

Although the war-averting effect of greater economic freedom is comparable to that of higher per capita income, it is presumably much easier for a country to reduce the risk of war by improving policies and building institutions than by becoming wealthier.

Economic freedom and political repression

This segment of the analysis addresses the following question: Can economic freedom calm social dissent, as measured by state repression of people's rights? It also tests natural resource wealth in relation to economic freedom to see whether economic freedom can moderate the effects of resource extraction on the political repression of dissent.[17] In other words, given that resource extraction is supposedly associated with the risk of political repression, can economic freedom reduce that risk?

Although it is true that a state may successfully suppress conflict through repressive means, the very existence of such repression signals a high level of social dissent, short of all-out civil war (Poe 2004); this level of social and political upheaval can be captured by data on state repression. The analysis focuses on the most odious forms of repression: violations of "physical integrity rights" (disappearances, imprisonment, political murder, and torture). Scores on the Cingranelli-Richards (CIRI) index of physical integrity rights range from 0 to 8, where 0 represents total repression of rights and 8 represents perfect respect for all rights.[18]

As can be seen in table 2, economic freedom has a statistically significant dampening effect on political repression—a result that is unaffected by per capita income or other relevant controls. And, as in the previous analysis, the presence of good institutions had no effect on the interaction between economic freedom and political repression.[19]

---

[17] "Testing interactive terms" means determining the effect that occurs when two variables are in play concurrently. In practical terms, it involves multiplying two variables to create a new variable.

[18] The CIRI human rights data and documentation are available at http://ciri.binghamton.edu/. The CIRI Human Rights Dataset, which is generated from the country reports created by Amnesty International and the U.S. State Department, is designed to capture the patterns and sequence of the severity of repression, freeing the researcher from making assumptions about various questions (e.g., whether torture matters more than death and disappearances) (Cingranelli and Richards 1999).

[19] Most of the results confirmed previous findings. Per capita income has a strong negative effect on repression, as do democracy, ethnic fractionalization, and the time since the last civil war. Population size and ongoing civil war, on the other hand, show positive effects on repression. These findings are highly consistent with those reported previously by others (see Landman 2005). While the British and socialist legal systems show negative effects on repression, which is consistent with the results reported previously, the effects are highly fragile.

Table 2. The effect of economic freedom on political repression, 1981–2006

Variable	Effect on political repression
Economic freedom	−0.286
	(3.71)***
Oil exporter	0.310
	(1.54)
Per capita income	−0.158
	(2.00)**
Growth in per capita income	−0.010
	(1.54)
Democracy	−0.628
	(4.84)***
Population size	0.293
	(6.79)***
British legal system	−0.015
	(0.10)
Socialist legal system	−0.246
	(1.09)
Civil war	1.132
	(7.27)***
Years of civil peace	−0.017
	(4.54)***
Ethnic fractionalization	−0.520
	(1.86)*
Number of observations	2,586
Number of countries	111

Sources: Data were drawn from World Bank (2007), Fearon and Laitin (2003), and Gurr and Jaggers (1995).
Notes: Panel-corrected z-statistics are in parentheses. Year dummies (not shown) were computed with all tests.
*** $p < .01$; ** $p < .05$; * $p < .10$

The direct substantive effects of economic freedom are large. For comparison's sake, if all the nations in the world were frozen at the mean level of economic freedom (holding all other variables equal), and if economic freedom alone were changed to its maximum value, one could expect a 60 percent reduction in the risk of political repression.[20] Remarkably, this is twice the impact associated with a shift from the average level of civil war to a world free of civil wars.

The next part of the analysis was designed to address the following question: in resource-wealthy countries where the goal of peacebuilding policy

---

[20] Marginal effects were computed as follows: (1) starting with a predicted probability for the model (at the value of 5 on the CIRI scale, which is roughly the mean of the sample); (2) holding all the control variables at their mean values; (3) recomputing the original prediction, using the maximum value of economic freedom while holding all other variables at their means; then (4) examining the differences between the two predictions. Alternatively, one could pick the values of economic freedom for two countries, such as Sierra Leone and Botswana. (Incidentally, if the world had Sierra Leone's level of economic freedom in 2000 and then changed to the level of Botswana in 2000, a 60 percent reduction in political repression could be expected.)

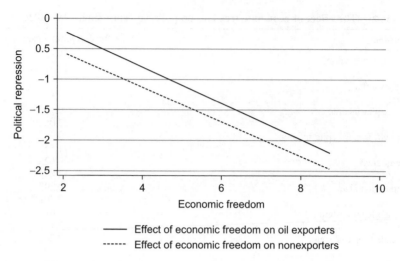

Figure 2. Effects of economic freedom on political repression in oil-exporting states and non-oil-exporting states
Source: Data were drawn from World Bank (2007), Fearon and Laitin (2003), and Gurr and Jaggers (1995).

is to improve governance and decrease dissent, should policy favor economic or political freedoms? To get at this issue, the analysis compared the effects of oil wealth and economic freedom on political repression with those of oil wealth and democracy on political repression, in order to determine whether economic freedom or democracy was the better moderating factor.[21]

As shown in figure 2, economic freedom dampens political repression among both oil-exporting and non-oil-exporting countries. Although oil exporters clearly experience greater repression, the risk of repression among oil exporters and non-oil-exporters converges slightly as economic freedom increases.

The results of this analysis clearly suggest that resource-wealthy states can avert dissent and repression through institutional reforms that support markets and economic entrepreneurship. Although democracy alone has strong negative effects on political repression—as reported by many researchers (Davenport and Armstrong 2004; de Soysa and Nordås 2007) and as shown by the negative sign of the coefficient in table 2, in the presence of oil wealth, repression increases as democracy moves from 0 to 1 (figure 3).[22] In non-oil-exporting countries, however, democracy has no effect on repression. Even if these results suggest only tentatively that it is economic freedom, rather than democracy, that tempers the effects of

---

[21] Of course, peacebuilders could also use both, so the analysis also included a test of the combined effects of democracy and economic freedom, which may in fact be complementary. The results of this test are not shown.

[22] Democracy is a discreet variable that takes the value 1 if the Polity scale is above 6, and the value 0 if the Polity scale is below 6.

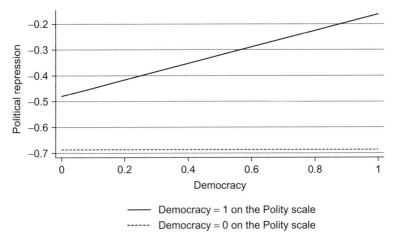

Figure 3. Effects of democracy on political repression in oil-exporting states
Source: Data were drawn from World Bank (2007), Fearon and Laitin (2003), and Gurr and Jaggers (1995).
Note: The Polity scale works as follows: if Polity is greater than 6, democracy takes the value 1; if Polity is less than 6, democracy takes the value 0. If Polity is greater than −6 but less than 7, semidemocracy takes the value 1; if not, semidemocracy takes the value 0. If Polity is less than −6, autocracy takes the value 1; if not, autocracy takes the value 0.

oil on repression, they do provide further confirmation of the power of economic freedom, as opposed to political freedom alone, to moderate capricious rule.

As shown in figure 4, as economic freedom increases, autocracies seem to lower their levels of repression (dotted line) as do democracies (solid line), although the decline in democracies is faster (shown by the steeper slope of the line). Interestingly, up to a threshold of roughly 4, economic freedom in autocracies is associated with a lower risk of repression than in democracies. In other words, at low levels of economic freedom, even democracies have higher levels of political repression, suggesting that democratic countries may have higher levels of social dissent when economic freedom is low, but as economic freedom increases, the level of political repression rapidly decreases. Thus, the figure clearly confirms that economic freedom and democracy are working in tandem.

Taken together, the analyses provide empirical evidence that resource wealth distorts relations between the state and society in violently repressive ways that do not reach the level of organized armed conflict. The results also suggest that resource-wealthy states are more likely to take repressive measures independently of macro political factors such as regime type—as is illustrated by the positive sign of the coefficient of the "oil exporter" variable in table 2. In other words, even when stability is defined as the absence of organized violence, the stability of oil-wealthy states may come at a rather high price. Nor does it seem that rulers of oil-wealthy states are "buying" stability without engaging in political repression—which suggests that many of the maladies faced by such states may be related to the repression of those who are calling for good governance (Jensen

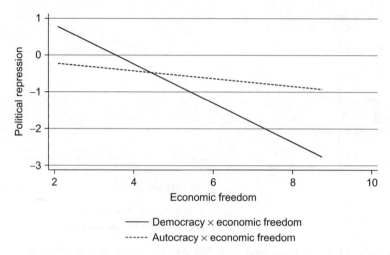

Figure 4. Effects of democracy and economic freedom on political repression
Source: Data were drawn from World Bank (2007), Fearon and Laitin (2003), and Gurr and Jaggers (1995).
Note: The Polity scale works as follows: if Polity is greater than 6, democracy takes the value 1; if Polity is less than 6, democracy takes the value 0. If Polity is greater than −6 but less than 7, semidemocracy takes the value 1; if not, semidemocracy takes the value 0. If Polity is less than −6, autocracy takes the value 1; if not, autocracy takes the value 0.

and Wantchekon 2004; Ross 2001). These findings concur with those of Collier and Hoeffler (2005), who have argued that democracy might not be the answer for managing natural resource-related problems. In sum, it is economic freedom, not political liberalization, that seems to moderate political repression in oil-exporting countries. Given this finding, peacebuilders interested in obtaining social peace should pay closer attention to building institutions that encourage markets.

CONCLUSION

Serious scholarly treatment of what it means to build back "differently and better" is just beginning (Collier 2009; Paris 2004; Paris and Sisk 2009; UNDP 2008). As noted earlier, a number of observers have rejected the idea of using economic liberalization as a blueprint for building better states, principally because such freedoms may be temporarily destabilizing, even if they are desirable in the long run (Cramer 2009; Paris 2004). The (quite legitimate) argument is that nascent state institutions should be allowed to become "institutionalized" before rapid economic liberalization occurs. The dilemma is that such institutionalization can occur only *after* institutions that would serve particular functions—such as ensuring the enforcement of the proper "rules of the game" within the polity and economy—are put in place. Privatization, for example, should *begin* at some point *before* it becomes institutionalized: it is the very success of nascent institutions that allows them to develop legitimacy—and, eventually, to become institutionalized.

Germany and Japan, for example, still cleave to many of the institutions that were imported (and even imposed) during the post-war years for one simple reason: they worked.

To determine whether capitalism weakens or strengthens states, this chapter measured two forms of social breakdown: the onset of civil war and the repression of human rights, particularly under conditions of resource wealth. The goal was to determine whether market institutions can help secure peace, or whether such institutions should simply be abandoned if short-term destabilization occurs. The results are clear: economic freedom—the proxy used for a market-friendly economic environment—promotes peace and decent governance. One possible explanation is that economic freedom is associated with strong states that are capable of protecting property: the more fair and equitable economic rules are, the more likely market actors are to invest in institutions and processes that cauterize both war and economic loss.

It might very well be that impartial, market-supporting institutions are hard to establish under the lawless conditions that characterize post-conflict societies, but to assume that market-supporting institutions should therefore not be established would be to confuse the symptoms of the disease with its cause. Where rent seeking is the norm, powerful actors will naturally resist the creation of impartial institutions that support markets, but the end of conflict certainly offers a great opportunity to impose such institutions from outside, as was the case with Germany and Japan.

It is precisely when the international community has the leverage to constrain powerful actors that such institutions should be created, with an eye to long-term gains. Markets seem to pacify, so they need to be built, and when it comes to reducing bad governance (defined as governance that elicits social dissent), markets and free political institutions seem to be complementary rather than at odds. The empirical evidence offered in this chapter shows that free economies promote peace and decent governance, particularly under the risky conditions of natural resource extraction. Future work might focus on the promises and pitfalls of the practical side: how to build markets in post-conflict societies where existing political forces have massive incentives to secure their positions and power, and those of their allies.

ANNEX

Data and Methods

Data and robustness checks for the civil war analyses

To estimate the effect of economic freedom on civil war and human rights, several confounding factors must be simultaneously accounted for in the models. Per capita income has proved to be one of the strongest predictors of civil war; thus, the effects of economic freedom were estimated net of the modernity and productivity of an economy, as measured by per capita income. Data on per capita income were obtained from the World Bank's World Development Indicators CD-ROM and log transformed to reduce the effect of extreme values (World Bank 2007). Because growth in per capita income is also thought to decrease the risk of an onset of civil war, it was included in the model, but the effect of the main variable of interest remained unchanged.

Countries with large populations also seem to have a greater risk of civil war, and size is an important control variable because the extent of a country's desire to be economically open and free might be a function of the size of its domestic market. To control for country size, total population was included in the model; like per capita income, it was log transformed to reduce the impact of extreme values (World Bank 2007).

Country size and the extent of social fractionalization are generally linked. Tests of the effect of social fractionalization on the risk of civil war have yielded mixed results and are subject to theoretical controversy (Collier, Hoeffler, and Rohner 2009; Esteban and Ray 2008; Fearon and Laitin 2003). The model included a measure of ethnic fractionalization obtained from Fearon and Laitin (2003) in linear and quadratic form (the quadratic term was added to model the nonlinear shape of the effect). The reasoning behind this approach is that moderate fractionalization, which corresponds relatively closely to polarization (two large groups), might matter more than low fractionalization or very high fractionalization.

Since politics can be vital to whether and how conflict develops, the model also controlled for regime type, relying on the Polity IV scale, a widely used measure of democracy that ranges from −10 to 10 and features a set of discrete variables (Gurr and Jaggers 1995).[23] Semidemocracies were left out as the reference category in the models, making it possible to estimate how perfect democracy and perfect autocracy explain the risk of civil war when compared with countries whose regimes fall between these two categories. Controlling for regime type is particularly useful when trying to estimate the effect of economic freedom on conflict, because democracies might be judged favorably by those who are coding measures of economic freedom. The models also include a variable measuring resource wealth by using a dummy variable coded 1 if the country exports more than one-third of its gross domestic product as petroleum and 0 if it does not. This measure was taken from Fearon and Laitin (2003).

To address the possibility that conflict may affect economic freedom, the models lagged the independent variables by one year and recorded the brevity of peace—that is, the time since the last conflict onset. Since the legacy of a previous armed conflict is likely to be nonstationary, this variable was specified

---

[23] The Polity scale works as follows: if Polity is greater than 6, democracy takes the value 1; if Polity is less than 6, democracy takes the value 0. If Polity is greater than −6 but less than 7, semidemocracy takes the value 1; if not, semidemocracy takes the value 0. If Polity is less than −6, autocracy takes the value 1; if not, autocracy takes the value 0.

as a decay function.[24] Accounting for the proximity of conflict addresses potential biases that may have been created if coders of economic freedom had coded down the level of economic freedom when observing political tensions and violence, or if violence had in some way tended to constrain policies that were supportive of economic freedom. The model also controlled for conflict in the country within the previous year.

A number of robustness checks were conducted to determine the sensitivity to the testing method and to changes in the parameters of the model used to create table 1. First, because civil war will surely bias the coding of economic freedom, the variable measuring the brevity of peace was dropped, and the Fearon and Laitin (2003) method (testing onset with a lagged civil-war variable to indicate whether a conflict was ongoing the previous year) was used instead. This alternative specification produced almost identical results.

The rate of income growth was not statistically significant. Various insignificant variables were also dropped, but none of these specification changes influenced the effect of economic freedom on the risk of civil war. Even lagging the index of economic freedom by two, three, four, or five years made no difference to the results.

Data and methods for the political repression analyses

The control variables for the repression models were quite similar to those used in the civil war models and are from the same sources. Per capita income and political democracy are strong predictors of lower repression (Davenport and Armstrong 2004; de Soysa and Nordås 2007; Landman 2005; Poe, Tate, and Keith 1999), while population size (Landman 2005), oil wealth (de Soysa and Binningsbø 2009; Kisangani and Nafziger 2007), and the incidence of civil war (measured as conflict between a government and an organized rebel group resulting in at least twenty-five deaths in a single year) increase political repression (Poe, Tate, and Keith 1999). Surprisingly, in contrast to the civil war literature, most empirical studies find that ethnic fractionalization reduces political repression (de Soysa 2009; Lee et al. 2004). Given arguments about the detrimental effects of fractionalization on good economic policies, this term was included in the model (Easterly and Levine 1997).

Because there have been some findings that socialist legal systems and British legal systems reduce repression (Poe, Tate, and Keith 1999), the inclusion of these variables was important, since any effect of capitalism might in fact be an effect of a British legal heritage or of the absence of a socialist legal heritage.

---

[24] The function of time that has passed without conflict is given by 2 to the power of − (time since last onset of conflict/α), where α is the half-life parameter (Raknerud and Hegre 1997). After the log-likelihood of different models had been compared, a functional form was chosen in which the influence of the last conflict decays over time, with a half-life of two years.

Because these variables were included in the model, it was possible to estimate the effect of economic freedom without the influence of either legal heritage. Since it is also important to estimate the effects of economic structure, as measured by the rate of income growth, annual per capita economic growth was included in the model (World Bank 2007). A term for the history of peace, or a count variable representing the years of peace since 1946, was also included in the model; and, in order to account for any trending in the measures over time, year dummies were entered. (In other words, if human rights and capitalism both trend upward over time, each was separately accounted for.)

Because pooled time-series, cross-section data are characterized by complicated correlation structures between and within units (Beck and Katz 1995), they raise several thorny estimating issues. For the ordered probit estimations, the cluster option in the statistical software program STATA 11 was used, which computes Huber-White corrected robust standard errors with the assumption that observations are independent across units but nonindependent within (Wiggins 1999). These robust standard errors are robust to heteroscedasticity and serial correlation (Wiggins 1999). As an alternative, the repression models were also tested with and without lagged dependent variables, and by means of ordinary least squares with panel-corrected standard errors.

REFERENCES

Abouharb, R. M., and D. L. Cingranelli. 2007. *Human rights and structural adjustment.* Cambridge, UK: Cambridge University Press.

Acemoglu, D., and J. A. Robinson. 2006. Economic backwardness in political perspective. *American Political Science Review* 100 (1): 115–131.

Beblawi, H. 1990. The rentier state in the Arab world. In *The Arab state,* ed. G. Luciani. Berkeley: University of California Press.

Beck, N., and J. N. Katz. 1995. What to do (and not to do) with time-series cross-section data. *American Political Science Review* 89 (3): 634–647.

Bellin, E. 2004. The political-economic conundrum: The affinity of economic and political reform in the Middle East and North Africa. Carnegie Paper No. 53. Washington, D.C.: Carnegie Endowment for International Peace.

Berger, P. L. 1993. The uncertain triumph of democratic capitalism. In *Capitalism, socialism, and democracy revisited,* ed. L. Diamond and M. F. Plattner. Baltimore, MD: Johns Hopkins University Press.

Bermeo, N., and P. Nord, eds. 2000. *Civil society before democracy: Lessons from nineteenth-century Europe.* Lanham, MD: Rowman and Littlefield.

Call, C. T., and E. M. Cousens. 2008. Ending wars and building peace: International responses to war-torn societies. *International Studies Perspectives* 9 (1): 1–21.

Cingranelli, D. L., and D. L. Richards. 1999. Measuring the level, pattern, and sequence of government respect for physical integrity rights. *International Studies Quarterly* 43 (2): 407–417.

Collier, P. 2009. *Wars, guns, and votes: Democracy in dangerous places.* New York: HarperCollins.

Collier, P., and A. Hoeffler. 2004. Greed and grievance in civil war. *Oxford Economic Papers* 56 (4): 563–595.
———. 2005. Democracy and resource rents. Unpublished paper. Centre for the Study of African Economies, Oxford University.
Collier, P., A. Hoeffler, and D. Rohner. 2009. Beyond greed and grievance: Feasibility and civil war. *Oxford Economic Papers* 61 (1): 1–27.
Congdon Fors, H., and O. Olsson. 2007. Endogenous institutional change after independence. *European Economic Review* 51 (8): 1896–1921.
Cramer, C. 2009. Trajectories of accumulation through war and peace. In *The dilemmas of statebuilding: Confronting the contradictions of postwar peace operations*, ed. R. Paris and T. D. Sisk. London: Routledge.
CSCW (Centre for the Study of Civil War at Peace Research Institute Oslo). 2008. UCDP/PRIO armed conflict dataset: Armed conflicts version 4-2008. www.prio.no/CSCW/Datasets/Armed-conflict/UCDP-PRIO/Old-Versions/4-2007/.
Davenport, C., and D. A. Armstrong II. 2004. Democracy and the violation of human rights: A statistical analysis from 1976 to 1996. *American Journal of Political Science* 48 (3): 538–554.
de Soysa, I. 2009. Hell is other people? Social fractionalization and state repression, 1980–2004. *Politische Vierteljahresschrift* 43:100–127.
de Soysa, I., and H. M. Binningsbø. 2009. Devil's excrement or social cement? Oil wealth and repression, 1980–2004. *International Social Science Journal* 57 (1): 21–32.
de Soysa, I., and H. Fjelde. 2010. Is the hidden hand an iron fist? Capitalism and the onset of civil war, 1970–2005. *Journal of Peace Research* 47 (3): 287–298.
de Soysa, I., and R. Nordås. 2007. Islam's bloody innards? Religion and political terror, 1980–2000. *International Studies Quarterly* 51:927–943. www.svt.ntnu.no/iss/Indra.de.Soysa/published/Islams%20bloody%20Innards.pdf.
de Tocqueville, A. 1956. *Democracy in America*. London: Penguin.
Easterly, W. 2006. *The white man's burden: Why the West's efforts to aid the rest have done so much ill and so little good*. Oxford, UK: Oxford University Press.
Easterly, W., and R. Levine. 1997. Africa's growth tragedy: Policies and ethnic divisions. *Quarterly Journal of Economics* 112:1203–1250.
Economic Freedom Network. n.d. Annual reports: Economic freedom of the world. www.freetheworld.com/release.html.
Eriksen, S., and I. de Soysa. 2009. A fate worse than debt? International financial institutions and human rights, 1981–2003. *Journal of Peace Research* 46 (4): 485–503.
Esteban, J., and D. Ray. 2008. Polarization, fractionalization and conflict. *Journal of Peace Research* 45 (2): 163–182.
Fearon, J. D. 2005. Primary commodities exports and civil war. *Journal of Conflict Resolution* 49 (4): 483–507.
Fearon, J. D., and D. D. Laitin. 2003. Ethnicity, insurgency, and civil war. *American Political Science Review* 97 (1): 1–16.
Gambetta, D. 1993. *The Sicilian Mafia: The business of private protection*. Cambridge, MA: Harvard University Press.
Gleditsch, N. P. 2008. The liberal moment fifteen years on. *International Studies Quarterly* 52 (4): 691–712.
Gleditsch, N. P., P. Wallensteen, M. Eriksson, M. Sollenberg, and H. Strand. 2002. Armed conflicts 1946–2001: A new dataset. *Journal of Peace Research* 39 (5): 615–637.

Gurr, T. R., and K. Jaggers. 1995. Tracking democracy's third wave with the Polity III data. *Journal of Peace Research* 32 (4): 469–482.
Gwartney, J., and R. Lawson. 2005. *Economic freedom in the world 2003: The annual report*. Vancouver, B.C., Canada: Fraser Institute.
Hall, J. A. 1987. *Liberalism*. London: Paladin.
Harbom, L., and P. Wallensteen. 2009. Armed conflicts, 1946–2008. *Journal of Peace Research* 46 (4): 577–587.
Hegre, H., and N. Sambanis. 2006. Sensitivity analysis of empirical results on civil war onset. *Journal of Conflict Resolution* 50 (4): 508–535.
Hewitt, J., J. Wilkenfeld, and T. R. Gurr. 2008. *Peace and conflict 2008*. Boulder, CO: Paradigm.
Hirschman, A. O. 1977. *The passions and the interests: Political arguments for capitalism before its triumph*. Princeton, NJ: Princeton University Press.
Holmes, S. 1995. *Passions and constraints: On the theory of liberal democracy*. Chicago: University of Chicago Press.
Human Security Report Project. 2005. *Human security report 2005: War and peace in the 21st century*. Oxford, UK: Oxford University Press.
Jensen, N., and L. Wantchekon. 2004. Resource wealth and political regimes in Africa. *Comparative Political Studies* 37 (7): 816–841.
Kant, I. 1991. Perpetual peace: A philosophical sketch. In *Kant's Political Writings*, 2nd ed., edited and with an introduction by Hans Reiss; translated by H. B. Nisbet. Cambridge, UK: Cambridge University Press.
King, G., M. Tomz, and J. Wittenberg. 2000. Making the most of statistical analyses: Improving interpretation and presentation. *American Journal of Political Science* 44 (2): 341–355.
Kisangani, E., and W. E. Nafziger. 2007. The political economy of state terror. *Defence and Peace Economics* 18 (5): 405–414.
Landman, T. 2005. *Protecting human rights: A comparative study*. Washington, D.C.: Georgetown University Press.
Lee, C., R. Lindström, W. H. Moore, and K. Turan. 2004. Ethnicity and repression: The ethnic composition of countries and human rights violations. In *Understanding human rights violations: New systematic studies*, ed. S. Carey and S. C. Poe. Aldershot, UK: Ashgate.
Lujala, P. 2010. The spoils of nature: Armed civil conflict and rebel access to natural resources. *Journal of Peace Research* 47 (1): 15–28.
Marten, K. 2006. Warlordism in comparative perspective. *International Security* 31 (3): 41–73.
Mousseau, M., and D. Y. Mousseau. 2008. The contracting roots of human rights. *Journal of Peace Research* 45 (3): 327–344.
Mueller, J. 2004. *The remnants of war*. Ithaca, NY: Cornell University Press.
Olson, M. 1982. *The rise and decline of nations: Economic growth, stagflation, and social rigidities*. New Haven, CT: Yale University Press.
———. 1993. Dictatorship, democracy, and development. *American Political Science Review* 87 (3): 567–575.
Olsson, O., and H. Congdon Fors. 2004. Congo: The prize of predation. *Journal of Peace Research* 41 (3): 321–336.
Paris, R. 2004. *At war's end: Building peace after civil conflict*. Cambridge, UK: Cambridge University Press.

Paris, R., and T. D. Sisk. 2009. *The dilemmas of statebuilding: Confronting the contradictions of postwar peace operations*. London: Routledge.

Poe, S. C. 2004. The decision to repress: An integrative theoretical approach to the research on human rights and repression. In *Understanding human rights violations: New systematic studies*, ed. S. Carey and S. C. Poe. Aldershot, UK: Ashgate.

Poe, S. C., C. N. Tate, and L. C. Keith. 1999. Repression of the human right to personal integrity revisited: A global cross-national study covering the years 1976–1993. *International Studies Quarterly* 43 (2): 291–313.

Raknerud, A., and H. Hegre. 1997. The hazard of war: Reassessing the evidence for the democratic peace. *Journal of Peace Research* 34 (4): 385–404.

Ross, M. L. 2001. Does oil hinder democracy? *World Politics* 53 (3): 325–361.

Russett, B. 1993. *Grasping the democratic peace*. Princeton, NJ: Princeton University Press.

Russett, B., and J. Oneal. 2001. *Triangulating peace: Democracy, interdependence, and international organizations*. London: W.W. Norton and Company.

Skaperdas, S. 2003. Restraining the genuine *homo economicus*: Why the economy cannot be divorced from its governance. *Economics and Politics* 15 (2): 135–162.

Steinberg, D. A., and S. M. Saideman. 2008. Laissez fear: Assessing the impact of government involvement in the economy and ethnic violence. *International Studies Quarterly* 52 (2): 235–259.

Stiglitz, J. E. 2007. What is the role of the state? In *Escaping the resource curse*, ed. M. Humphreys, J. D. Sachs, and J. E. Stiglitz. New York: Columbia University Press.

Stilwell, F. 2006. *Political economy: The contest of economic ideas*. Oxford, UK: Oxford University Press.

UCDP (Uppsala Conflict Data Program). n.d. UCDP database. www.ucdp.uu.se/gpdatabase/search.php.

UNDP (United Nations Development Programme). 2008. *Crisis prevention and recovery report 2008: Post-conflict economic recovery—Enabling local ingenuity*. www.undp.org/cpr/content/economic_recovery/PCERreport.pdf.

Weinthal, E., and P. J. Luong. 2006. Combating the resource curse: An alternative solution to managing mineral wealth. *Perspectives on Politics* 4 (1): 35–53.

Wiggins, V. 1999. *Comparing XTGLS with regress cluster*. College Station, TX: Stata Corporation.

World Bank. 2007. *World development indicators*. CD-ROM. Washington, D.C.: World Bank.

PART 5

Livelihoods

Introduction

It is essential for national and subnational governments, international organizations, and civil society to acknowledge the importance of resource exploitation for local livelihoods, and to take account of the tensions that can result from overlapping claims to the same resources, or to different resources in the same area. In many resource-rich countries, the small-scale exploitation of high-value natural resources, such as diamonds or forest products, may be well established before conflict, or may develop as a coping strategy during conflict. Such exploitation, which is often unofficial and even illegal, may be the economic backbone of war-torn communities. Local populations may accordingly view any disruption of their livelihoods—through large-scale exploitation or through attempts to curb peace spoilers' access to valuable resources, for example—as a negative side effect of peace. Economic development must therefore be approached on two fronts: by fostering resource projects that will maximize fiscal returns, and by formalizing and supporting the resource economies on which conflict-affected populations depend.

Tensions over access to resources have the potential to ignite old conflicts and create new ones. In a given area, those seeking livelihood opportunities in the wake of conflict—and therefore competing for access to resources—may include established residents, returning refugees, displaced persons, excombatants, and migrants. Meanwhile, national and subnational governments may be attempting to reestablish their authority over resources, and companies may be looking for opportunities to begin commercial exploitation. Under these circumstances, tensions may emerge about overlapping claims, unclear rights to resources, and differing views on which entities have the authority to grant resource rights and access; such tensions may be further aggravated by environmental damage related to resource exploitation. The resulting disputes between communities, various levels of government, and extractive firms can undermine, destabilize, or even derail the peacebuilding process.

Such issues are at the core of the fifth part of the volume. The first two chapters in part 5 focus on Afghanistan, where local livelihoods often depend on opium poppy cultivation. In "Counternarcotics Efforts and Afghan Poppy Farmers: Finding the Right Approach," David M. Catarious Jr. and Alison Russell examine the evolution of national and international policy regarding opium poppy in Afghanistan. Because of their view that opium poppy was primarily a source of criminality and conflict financing, both the Afghan and the U.S. governments initially focused on eradication and the development of alternative livelihoods. Noting that such policies have had transitory success at best—and have undermined rural livelihoods—Catarious and Russell conclude that farmers are the key to successfully reducing poppy cultivation. To develop solutions that will make it possible for farmers to quit poppy cultivation, policy makers need to understand the complex context in which the farmers operate—that is, the economic, security, political, and environmental challenges that farmers face, and the needs that poppy cultivation meets.

In "The Janus Nature of Opium Poppy: A View from the Field," Adam Pain argues that opium poppy cultivation provides a means of coping in a country where both the national government and the international community have failed the population on many counts. Poppy cultivation provides jobs, reduces poverty, serves as hedge against the failure of other crops, and may even contribute to local conflict resolution. Thus, for many poppy farmers—whom Pain describes as the most vulnerable and victimized actors in the opium trade—the opium economy has yielded greater positive effects than reconstruction efforts and counternarcotics projects. Pain argues that a deeper understanding of the opium economy, the welfare benefits it provides, and the informal institutions of which it is a part would have led to a more appropriate response to the challenges of opium poppy cultivation and trade.

In "Peace through Sustainable Forest Management in Asia: The USAID Forest Conflict Initiative," Jennifer Wallace and Ken Conca illustrate how the U.S. Agency for International Development (USAID), a major player in the field of development assistance, identified and sought to address the problem of forest conflict. The goal of the USAID Forest Conflict Initiative was to increase understanding and awareness, both within and outside USAID, of the role that forests played in conflict, and to develop more conflict-sensitive approaches to management of the forest sector. The chapter describes the key obstacles that USAID encountered in its efforts to communicate the new approaches, and stresses the importance of such approaches—not only to USAID but to governments, the private sector, the donor community, and local stakeholders.

As essential as it is to recognize the significance and value of resource-based livelihoods, it is equally important to address problems that may be associated with them. "Women in the Artisanal and Small-Scale Mining Sector of the Democratic Republic of the Congo," by Karen Hayes and Rachel Perks, describes the efforts of Pact, a nongovernmental organization based in Washington, D.C., to address gender-related issues among women living and working in artisanal mining communities in the Democratic Republic of the Congo. Women artisanal miners, many of whom are driven to mining by economic need, face discrimination, unequal participation in decision making, and the risk of violence and abuse. Hayes and Perks point out that by sidelining women, both mining communities and the country as a whole miss out on opportunities to develop the mining sector and strengthen peacebuilding.

In "Forest User Groups and Peacebuilding in Nepal," Tina Sanio and Binod Chapagain describe community forest user groups (CFUGs), a national approach to securing livelihoods that depend on forest products. In addition to managing community forests, which are an integral part of rural livelihoods, CFUGs have made a positive contribution to peace by assisting in reconciliation, reintegration, and reconstruction; mediating negotiations over property; providing returnees with access to community forests and building materials; granting low-interest loans; and supporting small-scale enterprises. The peacebuilding potential of such groups is rarely acknowledged by governments or international agencies, however; instead, local communities tend to be viewed as passive recipients of third-party interventions. In Nepal, for example, the central government has not included CFUGs in national peacebuilding initiatives.

The final chapter in part 5 illustrates how resource exploitation can lead to wide-ranging environmental damage, put local livelihoods in danger, and create tension in a country already riddled with conflict. In "Lurking Beneath the Surface: Oil, Environmental Degradation, and Armed Conflict in Sudan," Luke A. Patey argues that if environmental destruction continues to damage livelihoods, the expectation that oil will foster development may be undermined, which would lead to an increase in oil-related conflicts. So far, violence has been sporadic and primarily directed against oil companies, but simmering conflicts have the potential to pit local groups against each other or against the government. To avoid further conflict, Patey argues for assigning priority to environmental protection and to compensation for environmental damage.

Because of their role in conflict financing, local resource economies can pose challenges to peacebuilding; at the same time, however, they can provide economic opportunities. Artisanal mining and the harvesting of forest products, for example, are labor intensive, have relatively low start-up costs, can be started quickly, and have the potential for quick economic returns for local communities. Acknowledging the importance and peacebuilding potential of local resource economies, involving the local population in resource management, and securing local livelihoods are keys to gaining the support of local populations for the peacebuilding process.

Counternarcotics efforts and Afghan poppy farmers: Finding the right approach

David M. Catarious Jr. and Alison Russell

Afghanistan's opium trade provides funding for insurgents, corrupt government officials, regional warlords, and criminal elements; it also undermines political stability. Despite efforts to stem the trade, poppy cultivation has not only persisted but expanded: in 2009, Afghanistan's poppies produced approximately 95 percent of the world's opium, and the total export value of opium and its refined products— that is, morphine and heroin—was estimated to be US$2.8 billion (UNODC and GOA 2009).[1]

This chapter, which focuses largely on U.S. and Afghan counternarcotics efforts,[2] argues that these initiatives have failed because they have ignored the motivations and needs of farmers, who are the most vulnerable and victimized link in the opium trade: of all of the links in the opium value chain, farmers make the least amount of money; domestic and international traffickers, drug processors, and criminal organizations make far more (Martin and Symansky 2006). In 2009, over 6 percent of Afghanistan's population cultivated poppy (UNODC and GOA 2009), and in many regions of the country, poppy cultivation is critical to supporting farmers and their families. But because poppy cultivation is simultaneously a source of economic security and political instability, policies to stem cultivation must be designed and implemented with care: the goal must be to support Afghan farmers rather than to punish them, and to protect the stability and viability of the central government and the rural population. It is

---

David M. Catarious Jr. was an analyst and project director at CNA, a nonprofit think tank based in Washington, D.C. Alison Russell is an analyst and project director at CNA. The authors would like to thank the following people for sharing their experiences: Eric Bone, Michael Kleinman, Matt Korade, Carter Malkasian, Gerald Meyerle, and Major Piet Wit. The authors would also like to thank other interviewees who were kind enough to share their thoughts and experiences off the record.

This chapter was developed with support from the Center for Global Partnership of the Japan Foundation.

[1] Opium has been used for thousands of years, both for medicinal purposes and for its psychological effects. Since the 1800s, opium has been processed to create more powerful derivatives, including morphine, codeine, and heroin (DEA 2001).

[2] The chapter focuses on the actions of the U.S. and Afghan governments because they have been the most engaged in the country since the Afghan conflict began in 2001.

also important to recognize that counternarcotics programs cannot be judged in a vacuum; they are just one element among the many that must fall into place if farmers are to move away from poppy.

This chapter is divided into seven major sections: (1) a brief overview of the relationship between conflict and narcotics in Afghanistan; (2) an analysis of factors that affect poppy cultivation; (3) a description of the principal Afghan and U.S. counternarcotics policies and programs; (4) a discussion of factors that undermine counternarcotics efforts; (5) a description of counternarcotics efforts in Uruzgan Province; (6) a list of lessons learned; and (7) a brief conclusion.

CONFLICT AND NARCOTICS IN AFGHANISTAN

Once traversed by the ancient Silk Road, Afghanistan has historically been a key location along the trade route between East and West. It is a geographically, ethnically, linguistically, and religiously diverse country: Pashtuns make up the largest ethnic group (about 40 percent of the population), followed by Tajiks (27 percent); other ethnic groups include Hazaras, Uzbeks, Aimaks, Turkmens, and Balochs. Dari and Pashto are the predominant languages (CIA 2010). Since 1979, Afghanistan has been witness to extraordinary upheaval and political unrest—and, amid the chaos, the country's opium trade has rapidly expanded.

From Soviet invasion to civil war: 1979–1994

In 1979, the Soviet Union invaded Afghanistan, provoking a ten-year war between Soviet forces and armed factions—known as mujahideen—who opposed the Communist government and were supported largely by the United States, China, Iran, Pakistan, and Saudi Arabia (Goodhand 2005). The late 1970s saw a marked increase in poppy cultivation—and, during the conflict, opium producers and drug traffickers strengthened their position in Afghanistan. Opium production continued to increase throughout the decade: by the end of the 1980s, opium producers—including mujaheddin groups—were producing about 1,570 metric tons of opium each year, more than six times the rate of annual production during the previous decade (Goodhand 2005; Martin and Symansky 2006).

The defeated Soviets withdrew in 1989, but conflict subsequently erupted among major ethnic groups. The resulting disorder and burgeoning illegal economy provided room for the opium trade to grow: from 1992 to 1995, annual production ranged from 2,200 to 2,400 metric tons (Goodhand 2005; Shaw 2006).

The emergence and rule of the Taliban: 1994–2001

The Taliban, an Islamic fundamentalist group, arose amid the disorder, conquering the southern city of Kandahar in 1994 and Kabul, the capital, in 1996. By 1998, the Taliban controlled 90 percent of Afghanistan; the only military opposition came from a group of former mujaheddin in the northern regions, who were known as the United Front or Northern Alliance (Rashid 2000).

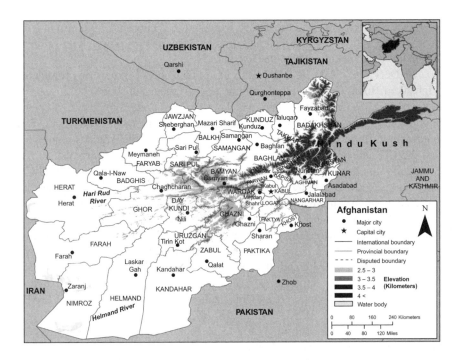

Over 96 percent of the land used for poppy cultivation was governed by the Taliban, who allowed cultivation to continue. In 1999, the peak year for production, 4,500 metric tons of opium were produced: three-quarters of the world's supply (Goodhand 2005; Shaw 2006). But in 1999, Taliban leader Mullah Omar ordered poppy cultivation to be cut by one-third (Goodhand 2005). The following year, the Taliban issued an unconditional ban on poppy cultivation (Davis and Chouvy 2002); the resulting drop in opium production (to 185 metric tons, a decrease of more than 90 percent) wiped out 70 percent of the world's supply (Goodhand 2005; Martin and Symansky 2006; Davis 2001).[3]

The overthrow of the Taliban and the post-conflict insurgency

In September 2001, al Qaeda operatives attacked the United States. In October of that year, in a mission dubbed Operation Enduring Freedom (OEF), a coalition

---

[3] The exact reason for the poppy ban is unknown. Some experts have speculated that the ban was not intended to stop opium production but to increase the value of the Taliban's own opium stockpile. (Between 1994 and 2000, opium prices ranged from US$23 to US$40 per kilogram. After the Taliban's poppy ban, prices spiked tremendously, reaching $380 per kilo by April 2001 and US$700 by September 2001.) Others believe that the ban was an effort to win approval and development aid from the international community (Goodhand 2005, 2008; IMF 2003).

led by the United States and the United Kingdom (UK) invaded Afghanistan and removed the Taliban—which had harbored al Qaeda—from power. The Taliban leadership fled, seeking refuge in Pakistan.

In December 2001, the United Nations convened a group of prominent Afghans in Bonn, Germany, to determine how Afghanistan should be governed in the post-Taliban era. What came to be known as the Bonn Agreement set up an interim government—the Afghan Interim Authority—and established a process for determining future governance. As part of the agreement, the Afghans requested that the UN and other international bodies assist the interim government in its efforts to "combat international terrorism, cultivation and trafficking of illicit drugs and provide Afghan farmers with financial, material and technical resources for alternative crop production" (Bonn Agreement 2001, annex III, sec. 6).

The Bonn Agreement also established the International Security Assistance Force (ISAF) in Afghanistan, a UN-mandated peacekeeping force that was commanded on a rotational basis by individual governments (including Germany, Turkey, and the UK). Although the initial focus of ISAF was on Kabul and the surrounding areas, its activities expanded beyond Kabul over time. In August 2003, NATO (North Atlantic Treaty Organization) forces took command of ISAF, and in October 2003, the UN expanded ISAF's mission to include all of Afghanistan. Over the ensuring years, ISAF took command of military forces throughout the country—culminating in October 2006, when the final American-led coalition forces were transferred to the command of ISAF (NATO n.d.). Currently, ISAF's mission is to assist the Afghan government with security, stability, and reconstruction.

Meanwhile, within a year of having been routed, the Taliban launched an insurgency campaign; by 2005, they had regained control of many districts in the southern provinces, which had traditionally been their stronghold (Malkasian and Meyerle 2009a). As of this writing, the Taliban continue to have a destabilizing effect on the new, internationally supported Afghan government.

Until 2004, the resources and energy of the U.S. military were focused on locating and destroying Taliban and al Qaeda forces in Afghanistan; in that year, however, OEF's mission was expanded to include counternarcotics operations. The international community, particularly under the auspices of the UN, has also been engaged in stemming the flow of illegal narcotics in Afghanistan. One of the most notable entities involved in this work is the United Nations Office on Drugs and Crime (UNODC)—which, since 1994, has used survey teams and satellite imagery to monitor poppy production and verify eradication efforts in Afghanistan (UNDCP 2000).

Since 2001, the drug trade in Afghanistan has undergone a number of changes. Probably because of increasing prices, more people have become involved in the trade. In addition, the loose networks that benefited from the opium trade in the 1990s have been replaced by more professional traffickers, who have streamlined smuggling operations. The changes to the narco-trade have increased the complexity of Afghanistan's security situation—which has, in turn made the

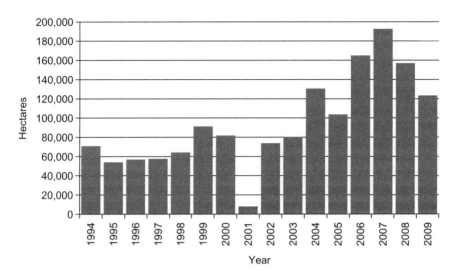

Figure 1. Poppy cultivation in Afghanistan, 1994–2009
Source: Data from UNODC and GOA (2005, 2009).

fight against the Taliban more difficult (UNODC and GOA 2009; Peters 2009b; Wright 2006).

Despite the counternarcotics efforts undertaken by the Afghan government, the United States, and the international community, poppy cultivation has proliferated since 2001 (figure 1). After the defeat of the Taliban, a number of factors, including insecurity and high opium prices, contributed to this growth, particularly in the south and east. Since 2004, cultivation has become increasingly concentrated in the southern and western provinces that are both Taliban and criminal strongholds: in 2009, the seven provinces in the south and west that were controlled by the Taliban produced 99 percent of the country's poppy. As of 2009, overall opium production remained high (6,900 metric tons), but had decreased from its 2008 level (7,700 metric tons) (UNODC and GOA 2009).

FACTORS AFFECTING POPPY CULTIVATION

National and international counternarcotics efforts in Afghanistan must be understood in a broad context that includes the most fundamental figures in the poppy trade: the poppy farmers themselves. In 2008 surveys conducted by UNODC, farmers who had never cultivated poppy cited a number of reasons, the most widespread being that the Koran prohibits the use of narcotics and that the production of narcotics is widely believed to be un-Islamic (UNODC and GOA 2008). Other reasons also cited were (1) the illegality of poppy cultivation, (2) respect for the instructions of elders and local councils, and (3) respect for the government's ban on poppy production. But farmers who *do* choose to cultivate poppy do not, by and large, lack respect for Islam or for their local leaders; nor do they cultivate poppy in order to support the insurgency or to assist corrupt politicians, drug traffickers, or other criminal elements.[4] In fact, the presence of these groups in the poppy trade has prevented some farmers from engaging in poppy cultivation (Crawley 2007).[5]

Instead, Afghan farmers who cultivate poppy base their decisions on a complex mix of agricultural, economic, and security considerations (Mansfield and Pain 2008). The pattern of cultivation in Nangarhar Province between 2004 and 2007 exemplifies the range and complexity of the influences on farmers' decisions. In 2004 and 2005, the number of hectares being used for poppy cultivation dropped by 96 percent—from 28,213 hectares to 1,093. The change resulted from a combination of factors—primarily, leadership on the part of the governor and local officials, development support for alternative agricultural crops, and cooperation from farmers (UNODC and GOA 2009). But by 2007, the area under cultivation had rebounded to 18,739 hectares. Researchers have attributed this increase to several factors (Mansfield and Pain 2007). First, although crops such as wheat were initially substituted for poppy, they could not provide sufficient income to support the farmers' basic needs. Second, because poppy cultivation is more labor intensive than wheat cultivation, the decrease in income associated with the transition to wheat was exacerbated by a decrease in income from labor. Third, because development aid was not sufficient to account for income shortfalls, farmers were forced to sell their production equipment and seek loans to provide for their families. With mounting pressures from income loss, lack of equipment, and debt, farmers turned back to poppy to generate income.

Agricultural factors

In many parts of Afghanistan, poppies are an ideal agricultural crop (IRIN 2004). Although they thrive in the well-irrigated regions of the south, poppies are also more drought resistant than other crops, which makes them attractive during water shortages (DEA 2001). Afghanistan's history of producing poppies means that a trained workforce is available to harvest them. Because transportation infrastructure is inadequate in much of Afghanistan, particularly in rural areas

---

[4] In the southern provinces, where there is an increasing concentration of Taliban, there have been many reports of farmers being pressured to grow poppy through threats and intimidation—not only from the Taliban, but from other sources as well, including warlords, tribal leaders, traffickers, drug barons, local militias, and landowners. Despite the prevalence of such reports in the literature (Crawley 2007; GAO 2006; NATO n.d.; UNODC and GOA 2004), survey results indicate that only 1.9 percent of farmers regarded external pressure as the primary cause of their decision to cultivate poppy (UNODC 2005).

[5] In interviews undertaken between 2006 and 2008, several former officials who had worked on counternarcotics programs in Uruzgan Province noted that many farmers and local officials are eager to be free of their ties to regional warlords and the Taliban, even if that means losing some income by turning away from poppy.

far from population centers, the journey from farm to market can be hot and time-consuming. The dried latex that is scraped from poppy pods can withstand long trips and heat, is easy to transport, and can be stored for months at a time.[6] The portion of the poppies remaining after the latex is harvested can also provide cooking oil, winter fuel, and animal fodder (Pain 2008). Finally, their relative hardiness and ability to generate income make poppies work well as a hedge against the failure of other crops. Even if poppy is not their primary crop, many Afghan farmers are willing to include poppy in their fields.

Economic factors

For many of the growing seasons since 2001, poppy provided farmers with the level of income they needed to support themselves and their families.[7] In late 2001, for example, poppy was planted heavily because the Taliban's 2000 ban on cultivation had created a tenfold increase in prices, making it the most lucrative crop available (IMF 2003; Goodhand 2008). Only in late 2008 did prices drop to the levels characteristic of the late 1990s (UNODC and GOA 2009).

Because poppy is a labor-intensive crop, it provides employment for many workers who do not own land themselves (Mansfield 2002; Mansfield and Pain 2007). In fact, poppy is the only means for landless farmers in many areas to gain access to land, which they do through sharecropping arrangements (sharecroppers lease plots, then grow crops on them in order to pay for the use of the land). Once sharecroppers have access to land, they can also grow food crops to support themselves and their families.

Poppy cultivation is also a means of obtaining loans. Many farmers do not have access to official lending institutions (or to the collateral that is required in order to receive a legal loan), so they turn to other individuals and organizations (including insurgent groups and drug traffickers) for informal loans (Pain 2008; GAO 2006). Although poppy-related loans are commonly viewed as driving farmers into debt,[8] field research has found that loans obtained in exchange for poppy cultivation have a net positive result for Afghan farmers—and have brought more Afghans out of debt than into it. Particularly in rural areas, debt is a critical means for farmers, especially the poorest ones, to support their families when crops are not in season (Pain 2008). It also provides access to the capital that farmers need to buy seeds, fertilizer, and food; to pay workers; and to make (illicit) payments to local officials (Pain 2008; UNODC and GOA 2004).

---

[6] Farmers harvest opium (latex) directly from the pods, without removing them from the plants, then sell the raw opium to traders. Morphine is extracted from the raw opium at small laboratories (DEA 2001).
[7] In a 2008 UNODC survey, 92 percent of farmers cited "poverty alleviation" as their motivation for growing poppy; 66 percent also cited the high price of opium. The survey also showed that the incomes of farmers who grew poppy were 53 percent higher than the incomes of those who did not (UNODC and GOA 2008).
[8] See, for example, Martin and Symansky (2006).

This is not to say that all debt has been good for poppy farmers; whether debt benefits farmers often depends on other variables, such as opium prices, agricultural conditions, and government actions. For example, after the Taliban's poppy ban in 2000, some lenders in Kandahar and Nangarhar monetized debt that had previously been denominated in opium. But because of the price increase that had occurred in response to the ban, farmers whose debt was converted from opium to dollars owed far more than they had when they first took out the loans; many defaulted or lost their property. Farmers whose poppy fields have been eradicated have also been forced deeper into debt by the resulting loss of income (Pain 2008).

Security factors

Particularly in Taliban-occupied regions, Taliban forces and affiliated insurgent groups, corrupt officials, and criminal elements recognize the lack of security as an opportunity and use it to their advantage with the rural and farming population. The Taliban, for example, have gained popular support by protecting farmers' fields against the government's eradication efforts (*Jane's Islamic Affairs Analyst* 2008). Taliban propaganda emphasizes the value of such protection, portraying the group as caring more about the livelihoods of the local population than the national government does (*Jane's Terrorism and Security Monitor* 2007). Protection is provided through bribery, by means of political arrangements with allied or sympathetic officials, or through a show of force. In exchange for protection, the Taliban and other drug trafficking and criminal groups charge farmers a tax (known as *zakat* or *ushr*) of at least 10 percent on the value of the poppy they produce (Pain 2006).[9]

The Afghan government's inability to enforce the rule of law affects farmers in other ways as well. Because the lack of infrastructure and the presence of the Taliban and drug traffickers can make trips dangerous, farmers are reluctant to incur the risk and expense of traveling to markets. But opium traders are willing to purchase the crop at the farm gate—an important advantage in an insecure environment (Mansfield and Pain 2007). Farmers in Helmand and Kandahar provinces, for example, continued to cultivate poppy even in 2008, when opium prices dipped below those of wheat, because checkpoints and harassment had

---

[9] By protecting the drug traffickers' convoys and heroin laboratories, the Taliban is able to extract further funds from the trade. Various organizations estimate that the Taliban, al Qaeda, drug traffickers, and other nonstate armed groups (such as warlords and transnational criminal organizations) collect between US$200 million and US$500 million annually from the opium trade (Kraeutler 2008; Peters 2009; Orszag-Land 2004; Makarenko 2002; Wright 2008). These groups also make money by smuggling the chemical precursors for heroin production into Afghanistan from Central Asia and Pakistan (Wright 2008).

made it dangerous and prohibitively expensive to transport crops to market (Mansfield and Pain 2008).[10]

COUNTERNARCOTICS POLICIES

Since early 2002, when the Afghan Interim Authority first assumed power, the Afghan government and the international community have continuously refined their counternarcotics efforts. The Afghan government has combated poppy cultivation by creating national strategies; forming government-sponsored teams to implement those strategies; and assigning provincial governors with the task of eliminating poppy cultivation.

As noted earlier, U.S. involvement in Afghanistan was initially focused on military operations targeting al Qaeda and Taliban forces. As operations evolved, the U.S. military and other U.S. agencies (e.g., the Department of State and the Department of Justice) have become more engaged in counternarcotics activities.

While American counternarcotics initiatives have included a variety of activities, including judicial reform and drug interdiction, the focus here is on the policies that directly affect poppy farmers: eradication, alternative livelihood development, and public information. Eradication involves physically halting cultivation: crops may be dug up by tractors or by hand, or destroyed by herbicides. Alternative livelihood development, which may involve skills training and support for alternative crop production, focuses on providing farmers with economically viable income sources. Public information campaigns are designed to educate farmers about the government's ban on poppy cultivation, to ensure that they are aware of alternatives, and to persuade them to switch from cultivating poppy to other sources of livelihood.

Afghan counternarcotics initiatives

The counternarcotics efforts of the Afghan Interim Authority initially focused on bans and eradication. Although the Afghan government subsequently expanded its approach, eradication and alternative livelihood development are central to its strategy.

The Ministry of Interior (MOI), the lead ministry in charge of counternarcotics, released the country's first cohesive national strategy in October 2002 (Blanchard 2008). This strategy was replaced in 2003 by the Afghan National Drug Control Strategy (NDCS), which established two goals: reducing poppy cultivation by 70 percent by 2008 and eliminating it entirely by 2013. Also in

---

[10] In some instances, dependence on opium traders has led to a decline in poppy production. In 2007, for example, in Ghor Province, which is far from the main trafficking routes, a decrease in both production and prices led to a drop in the number of opium traders operating in the province. As a result, farmers who could generate income from alternative sources did so (Mansfield and Pain 2007).

2003, Hamid Karzai (who had become interim president in 2002) assigned provincial governors responsibility for eradicating poppy from their provinces. This approach, known as governor-led eradication (GLE), produced some positive results in certain areas, particularly where local populations respected the governors and viewed them as legitimate representatives of the central government. In 2004, a large majority of the eradication that occurred was undertaken through GLE programs (UNODC and GOA 2005).

In December 2004, two days after having been elected president, Karzai launched a major effort against poppy cultivation, opium production, and drug trafficking (Mikhos 2006). As part of this initiative, he redistributed responsibility for drug interdiction by elevating the Counternarcotics Division of the MOI to the cabinet level; giving it a new name, the Ministry of Counternarcotics (MCN); and assigning it responsibility for developing overall policy and ensuring that counternarcotics efforts were aligned with the goals of the NDCS. Meanwhile, the MOI and its special deputy for counternarcotics retained responsibility for the implementation of counternarcotics strategy; thus, most of the domestic units responsible for eradication fell under the MOI. In 2006, the Afghan government updated the NDCS; the most notable change was the elimination of the deadlines for meeting the poppy eradication goals (Islamic Republic of Afghanistan 2006).

The MOI and the MCN have separate chains of command and have created implementing entities that are responsible for specific types of missions. The Poppy Elimination Program (PEP), for example, which is under the MCN, supports eradication at the provincial level. PEP teams—which generally have six to eight members, including Afghan officials and international experts—are responsible for assessing cultivation levels and monitoring eradication efforts; PEP teams also conduct public information campaigns to discourage poppy cultivation and support alternative livelihoods. Because PEP operates at the provincial level, the teams often work with governors, who are charged with leading local eradication efforts (Blanchard 2008).

The MOI administers several entities that are focused at least partially on eradication:

- The Counternarcotics Police of Afghanistan, the lead drug enforcement agency in the country, has intelligence, investigation, and interdiction capabilities and receives training from the United States and the UK (Mikhos 2006).
- The Central Eradication Planning Cell, a UK–led organization, relies on information gleaned from surveys and sophisticated technology to target poppy fields and monitor eradication efforts (Blanchard 2008).
- The U.S.-backed Afghan Eradication Force, formerly known as the Central Poppy Eradication Force, enforces the poppy ban in areas where local initiatives have been unsuccessful (Blanchard 2008). The eight-hundred-member force, which is broken into several smaller teams, has mobile units and air support.

U.S. and international counternarcotics initiatives

Like those of the Afghan government, the counternarcotics initiatives of the U.S. government and the international community have expanded since 2002. At an April 2002 meeting in Geneva, donor countries—including Germany, Italy, Japan, the UK, and the United States—developed a plan to support reconstruction and the establishment of security in Afghanistan; one result was the assignment of various missions to particular nations and organizations (Holt 2002). Counternarcotics operations were assigned to the UK, where 90 percent of the heroin is Afghan in origin (Orszag-Land 2004), and the United States agreed to train a 70,000-member Afghan National Army (Rohde 2006).

In January 2003, to support reconstruction, the United States and ISAF introduced provincial reconstruction teams (PRTs), joint civilian-military teams that are usually commanded by a military officer and consist of a military member (e.g., a civil affairs officer), a civilian police officer, and experts from civilian U.S. government agencies (e.g., the U.S. Agency for International Development, the Department of State, the Department of Agriculture, and the Department of Justice); for security, each PRT is accompanied by a platoon of military personnel. The PRTs' reconstruction and development efforts focus on agriculture, including alternative livelihood development; the teams are also involved in governance programs and in promoting the rule of law. Because PRTs were initially located in hot spots, they did not interact with nongovernmental organizations (NGOs) or international agencies. They have since spread throughout the country and have been taken over by countries other than the United States. As of late 2009, nearly thirty PRTs were operating in Afghanistan (Malkasian and Meyerle 2009b).

As noted earlier, U.S. military forces initially focused on military activities, not on reconstruction or counternarcotics. In fact, the United States relied on the UK and the Afghan government to handle counternarcotics, because the U.S. military depended on opium traffickers, including warlords, for information on the Taliban and al Qaeda. But as the country continued to destabilize—and as it became increasingly clear that poppy cultivation was contributing to the destabilization—the United States changed strategy. Between 2003 and 2004, U.S. aid increased from US$982 million to US$2.4 billion; the U.S. Agency for International Development (USAID) doubled its staff in Afghanistan; the U.S. military increased its deployment of PRTs in the south and east, where poppy was strong and security was weak (Rohde 2006); and Zalmay Khalilzad, the U.S. ambassador to Afghanistan, shifted policy and requested NATO assistance with counternarcotics efforts (Tarnoff 2009; Brownfield 2004). Of the US$2.4 billion, US$532 million was for USAID and U.S. Department of State counternarcotics efforts, including US$258 million for eradication, US$180 million for alternative livelihood development, and US$5 million for public information; the balance was for drug interdiction and law enforcement (GAO 2006). The U.S. counternarcotics plan closely matches that of the Afghan government, in that it focuses primarily on eradication and alternative livelihood development.

Responsibility for supporting U.S. counternarcotics efforts is distributed among several U.S. agencies:

- The Bureau of International Narcotics and Law Enforcement Affairs (INL), which is under the authority of the U.S. State Department, is responsible for helping the Afghan government with both eradication and public information (Inspectors General 2007). The INL collaborates with the GLE programs; provides guidance to the PEP teams; and cooperates closely with the UK counternarcotics efforts (through the Joint Narcotics Analysis Center, in London, and the International Operations Coordinating Center, in Kabul).
- The Office of National Drug Control Policy coordinates with INL in providing guidance for counternarcotics policy (Kerlikowske 2009).
- USAID has assumed most of the responsibility for reconstruction efforts, which includes administering the U.S.'s alternative livelihood programs. In Afghanistan, these programs include crop substitution, diversification (e.g., crop rotation and animal husbandry), distribution of cash in exchange for labor, and training courses to allow Afghans to obtain new jobs in a different sector.[11]
- The U.S. Department of Defense, through the PRTs, provides intelligence, logistics, and protection for eradication operations.

FACTORS THAT UNDERMINE POPPY ELIMINATION EFFORTS

Both the government of Afghanistan and the international community have set goals for reducing poppy cultivation, but the statistics show that these goals are far from being attained: since 1994, when UNODC began measuring cultivation, production was highest from 2004 through 2009; and of the ten years that production was highest, eight were from 2002 through 2009 (UNDCP 2000; UNODC and GOA 2009).

It would be misleading, however, to hold counternarcotics programs fully responsible for changing patterns of poppy cultivation: as field researchers David Mansfield and Adam Pain have argued, the larger context must be taken into account (Mansfield and Pain 2008). The price of poppy ebbs and flows, as do those of other crops. Agricultural conditions change from year to year. Provincial and regional leaders shift, and with them the level of corruption and the focus on counternarcotics efforts. Finally, the influence of insurgents and criminal elements varies with the level of security. When a farmer makes a decision about planting poppy, all of these factors are considered—not simply the government's counternarcotics actions.

Nevertheless, counternarcotics programs can be evaluated according to their impact on farmers and their ability to address farmers' reasons for choosing to cultivate poppy. Counternarcotics efforts that address farmers' motivations may

---

[11] A number of other organizations, including NGOs, international agencies, and the PRTs, are also engaged in alternative livelihood programs.

prove helpful, assuming that other factors beyond the immediate control of counternarcotics programs—such as weather, or the global opium market—are aligned. On the other hand, counternarcotics efforts that are designed and implemented improperly can undermine their intended objectives.

The authors' observations of the impacts of counternarcotics efforts on Afghan farmers reveal three themes:

- Eradication, alternative livelihood development, and public information campaigns are extremely difficult to implement in areas where insecurity is high or where public officials are complicit with or directly involved in the narco-trade.
- Eradication efforts undermine the financial well-being of farmers and may cause the population to turn against the government.
- Alternative livelihood programs can help move farmers away from poppy in the short term but are difficult to sustain under long-term pressure from other factors.

These themes will be explored in more detail in the three subsections that follow.

Insecurity and complicity

From the perspective of their impact on farmers, eradication, alternative livelihood development, and public information programs have had mixed results. In some cases, the programs have been undermined by lack of security or by the complicity or direct participation of public officials in the narco-trade. Where both of these characteristics are present, such as in the southern, Taliban-controlled provinces, counternarcotics efforts have been severely curtailed.

Corruption—which runs from the highest levels of government down through provinces and districts—has undermined efforts to combat the Taliban and the drug trade. Early in the post-Taliban era, many former leaders of the United Front who had been heavily involved in the narco-trade were installed at the Ministry of Interior, the agency that leads counternarcotics operations, and many opium-trading warlords were elevated to parliament or to key positions in provincial and district governments and various police forces (*Jane's Islamic Affairs Analyst* 2007); in fact, it has been estimated that 25 percent of the Afghan parliament is involved in the narco-trade. In one of the more notorious examples, the then-governor of Helmand Province was discovered to have nine tons of opium in his basement; he went onto become a senator (Inspectors General 2007). Of Afghanistan's thirty-four provinces, the former governors of fourteen (including Helmand) have been implicated in the drug trade; one of the most prominent Afghans in the trade is Ahmed Wali Karzai, the brother of President Hamid Karzai and a high-level political figure in Kandahar Province (*New York Times* 2010).

In the least secure regions, farmers and insurgent groups have opposed eradication by force or other measures. In many cases, insurgent groups have fired on eradication teams; farmers have also flooded fields to prevent tractors from destroying the crops. Even in relatively secure areas, the complicity of local officials in the narco-trade can significantly undermine counternarcotics efforts. In some cases, for example, when fields are being selected for eradication, GLE teams or local police commanders have targeted only the fields of their competitors or of small and powerless farmers, while protecting their own and those of their allies (Byrd and Buddenberg 2006); in other cases, farmers have been targeted on the basis of tribal affiliations, exacerbating tensions among rival ethnic groups (*Jane's Islamic Affairs Analyst* 2008).

In some of the early efforts at eradication, farmers were paid to eradicate their fields—which some did—but the money was never distributed by the governors or the local police commanders. In other cases, numbers were manipulated so that provincial officials could profit both from the sale of the opium and from its supposed eradication. In still other instances, farmers have succeeded in bribing eradication teams to leave the crops—and the farmer's livelihoods—unmolested (Peters 2009a; Morarjee 2006).

Eradication, economics, and the central government

The principal problem with eradication programs is that they target farmers, instead of alleviating the pressures that drive farmers to growing poppy. In fact, field research indicates that farmers, more than any other actors in the opium trade, have been victimized by eradication programs—and that as a consequence, the programs have helped turn the rural population against the government (Mansfield and Pain 2008; Pain 2008). The primary effect of eradication is economic: by destroying a farmer's income source, eradication can lead to poverty and drive farmers deeper into debt to landholders and lenders. The timing of eradication can exacerbate the problem: if poppy crops are eradicated after planting season, farmers may be left with no other income source (Davis and Chouvy 2002). Moreover, if farmers' financial security is undermined during one season, they may be forced to grow more poppies during the following harvest to make up for lost revenue, assuming that poppy prices are high enough.

In the international community, aerial eradication—that is, spraying pesticides from aircraft in order to destroy the crops—has been one of the most contentious areas of debate. The United States has advocated aerial eradication on the basis of speed, efficacy, and safety for eradication personnel, but the Afghan and other governments have objected because the pesticides damage all crops that are sprayed, not just poppy; there is also concern is that aerial eradication will further encourage farmers to turn toward insurgent groups for protection (*PakTribune* 2005).

Alternative livelihood programs

Unlike eradication programs, which can harm poppy farmers, alternative livelihood programs are designed to move farmers away from poppy by providing them with other sources of sustainable income. In much of the country, except in the least secure areas, USAID, among other agencies, has undertaken programs that are specifically intended to alleviate some of the pressures that push farmers toward poppy cultivation; the forms of support include providing irrigation for crops, providing seeds for alternative crops at no cost, providing loans, and building roads to create easier access to markets (USAID n.d.).

Alternative livelihood programs have shown promise in some areas but have succumbed, in the long term, to the other pressures that spur poppy cultivation. Development projects, for example, have been cited as a key reason (along with the cooperation of the provincial governor) for the 96 percent reduction in poppy cultivation in Nangarhar Province between 2004 and 2005 (Mansfield 2008b). Unfortunately, such projects have proven unsustainable: eventually, local goodwill and short-term support from donor nations and agencies are overcome by agricultural, economic, and security pressures.

It is important to note, however, that farmers do not necessarily require alternative livelihood programs to decide to try crops other than poppy. Farmers have demonstrated a willingness to switch to other crops when, on account of economic, agricultural, or security considerations, those crops offer higher returns. In 2007 and 2008, for example, when a notable shift to wheat production occurred in a number of provinces, researchers attributed the change to four factors: high wheat prices, falling opium prices, pressure from authorities, and farmers' concerns about low levels of food crop cultivation (Mansfield 2008a). But such shifts may be short-lived, depending on how conditions evolve. If alternative crops cannot sustain higher levels of profit, poppies are often the best choice from an economic perspective.

COUNTERNARCOTICS EFFORTS IN URUZGAN PROVINCE

Uruzgan Province encapsulates many of the issues associated with counternarcotics efforts in Afghanistan as a whole.[12] A Taliban stronghold, Uruzgan is in southern Afghanistan—and, like many provinces in that region, is home to a variety of players in the poppy trade, including criminal elements and Taliban insurgents and their allies. The province is the fourth-largest producer of poppy in the country and borders Helmand and Kandahar, the two largest producers. As shown in figure 2, after peaking in 2004 and dropping dramatically in 2005, poppy cultivation in Uruzgan remained fairly constant from 2006 through 2009.

In May 2004, when the U.S. military established a base of operations in Tirin Kot, the provincial capital, Uruzgan was one of the last Taliban strongholds. As of this writing, ISAF controls the southern region of Afghanistan; a PRT deployed by the Netherlands in February 2006 is under the direction of ISAF; and USAID and a PEP team (based in Tirin Kot) are also active in the province,

---

[12] This section is based on interviews with USAID officials and members of PRTs who were operating in Uruzgan Province between 2006 and 2008.

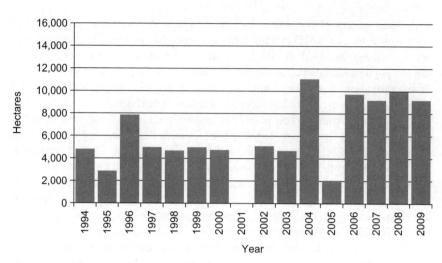

Figure 2. Poppy cultivation in Uruzgan Province, 1994–2009
Source: Data from UNODC and GOA (2005, 2009).

as are ISAF-directed Australian forces. Both on their own and in collaboration with other entities, all these organizations have undertaken counternarcotics efforts in the region, including eradication, alternative livelihood development, and public information programs.

Alternative livelihood and public information programs

Conditions in Uruzgan Province made it difficult to implement alternative livelihood and public information programs. Although the province used to have productive orchards (which yielded nuts and pomegranates, and were also used to produce dried fruits), the trees have vanished, most having been cut down for firewood. The violence of the past several decades has contributed to loss of agricultural production and led to a decline in the experience base of the local population. The alternative livelihood campaigns undertaken by USAID and the PRT were delayed by lack of transportation and lack of local capacity. According to the agricultural expert on the PRT, there is "nothing like a working agricultural extension service; there are no functioning demonstration farms or agricultural colleges."

In 2006, to support development in Uruzgan, USAID focused on labor-intensive projects that would provide non-poppy-related work for the local population. Among the successful projects were the installation of irrigation systems and the construction of small roads and bridges. USAID also funded the distribution of seeds and agricultural products and undertook "train-the-trainers" programs.[13]

---

[13] In a "train-the-trainers" program, agencies train local individuals, who then conduct subsequent training; such programs can be a cost-effective means of building capacity.

Although these operations were somewhat successful, it takes time to get agricultural operations up and running and to rebuild the marketplace. As a consequence, turning the population away from poppy was a difficult undertaking.

Both the PEP teams and the PRT found it difficult to conduct public information campaigns and to win the trust of the local population. With small groups of farmers spread out across a wide area of land and no central communication network, communication was difficult and time-consuming. And because the Taliban had eliminated many local leaders, what would otherwise have been a conduit to the local population was lost. In addition, local Afghans who worked on PEP teams became targets for those in the poppy trade;[14] the work was so dangerous that the team collecting information about poppy cultivation levels had to pretend that it was performing other, unrelated activities.

Yet another problem was that the PEP teams' public information campaigns were not necessarily well received by the farmers. Even though the campaigns emphasized the fact that poppy growing was counter to Islamic principles, they were unable to discourage farmers from growing poppy. Nor was it effective to warn that the government would eradicate the poppy fields: because of the weakness of the central government, the farmers did not regard the threats as credible.

Insecurity and complicity

Alternative livelihood programs faced a number of challenges, but the most serious were lack of security and the complicity of local officials in the narco-trade. Because security was available mainly through association with the PRT, most development actions were undertaken by or in coordination with the PRT. For example, USAID first undertook alternative livelihood development programs in the province in 2004, after the arrival of military forces that could provide the necessary security.[15]

Although the Taliban and affiliated groups had a large presence in Uruzgan between 2006 and 2008, there were not many combat operations in the area. The Taliban and their allies focused their military operations in Helmand and would retreat to Uruzgan between operations. Despite the relatively low level of violence, overall insecurity limited counternarcotics efforts. For example, lack of security prevented the Afghan MCN from operating freely in Uruzgan. In order to compensate governors who were undertaking eradication as part of the GLE program, the MCN and UNODC were in the practice of sending verification teams throughout the country; but in Uruzgan (as well as other areas), pervasive insecurity made

---

[14] According to a former PEP team member, PEP teams were threatened on many occasions.
[15] Because being associated with the military or the government may jeopardize their security or undermine their effectiveness as independent organizations, NGOs often eschew cooperation with military forces. Hence, most NGOs chose not to operate in Uruzgan Province.

it too dangerous for the teams to verify eradication reports. As a consequence, according to an interviewee, provincial officials were able to make unverified, and likely inflated, claims about how much poppy had actually been eradicated.

Another consequence of insecurity was the difficulty of bringing legal crops to market. The one road leading from Tirin Kot to Kandahar was commonly obstructed by roadblocks that the Taliban and other forces (including the Afghan National Police) had set up for the purpose of extracting taxes or bribes; these high "transportation" expenses could exceed what farmers could earn from their sale (Mansfield 2008a).

Public officials' support of the narco-trade further undermined counter-narcotics efforts: the director of transport was suspected of growing poppy, as was then-governor Abdul Hakim Munib (Anderson 2007). As one expert interviewed by the authors noted, "in Uruzgan, the poppy trade was connected to everything." Another interviewee also reported that the governor of Uruzgan was corrupt and supported the poppy trade. According to this source, the governor allowed the PEP team to operate from within his compound but did not support eradication; in fact, poppy was reportedly being grown on his compound. The governor also held talks with community leaders, but instead of instructing them to not grow poppy, he would tell the leaders that the PEP team had come to take away their livelihoods. Finally, the source noted that although the governor received funds to participate in GLE programs, his eradication efforts targeted only small, poor farms owned by people who had no political influence, not the larger and more productive holdings that belonged to powerful individuals.

LESSONS LEARNED

Stemming the cultivation of poppies in Afghanistan is a critical step in stabilizing the country, but it must be done with care, so as to retain the support of the population. Afghan, U.S., and international efforts to stem the poppy trade reveal several lessons:

- Counternarcotics efforts should not punish the poppy farmers, who represent the most vulnerable and victimized link in the opium trade.
- Large-scale eradication should not be undertaken until viable livelihood alternatives to poppy have been established.
- Because of the complexity of the various factors that influence poppy cultivation, the success of particular policies and programs should be judged only over the long term.

Provide support for poppy farmers

Evidence from the field has made it clear that, by and large, the farmers who cultivate poppy do so not because they support criminal or antigovernment elements but because of a complex mix of agricultural, economic, and security considerations. In fact, in numerous instances, farmers in various regions of the country have been willing to move away from poppy, at least in the short term, when a sufficient level of support has been provided—or even promised—to mitigate these other factors. When it comes to the poppy trade, the farmers are not the enemy and should not be punished; counternarcotics efforts should focus instead on supporting farmers and undermining the traffickers and others who profit the most from the trade.

Establish viable alternatives to poppy

In many regions of the country, particularly in Taliban-controlled areas where infrastructure is limited and insecurity is widespread, poppy remains the only crop that can enable farming families to meet their basic needs. Thus, before eradication begins, it is essential to establish alternative means for Afghan farmers to earn an income. Specifically, counternarcotics efforts should provide farmers with economic security to protect them against the failure of alternative crops, subsidize the income from less profitable crops, provide access to loans, provide the necessary farming equipment, and establish safe access to markets. Building a lawful rural economy and establishing security in Afghanistan are necessary preconditions to achieving a sustainable reduction in poppy cultivation; eradication efforts, which have undermined both these goals, should be pursued only sparingly. The Afghan government, the U.S. government, and the international community must develop goals and priorities that reflect this perspective.

Judge success over the long term

Many observers have declared that several localized decreases in poppy cultivation are successes: the example that is perhaps cited most often is the 96 percent decrease in poppy cultivation between 2004 and 2005 in Nangarhar Province.[16] During that period, Nangarhar's governor focused on reducing poppy cultivation and, through USAID, obtained large investments in alternative livelihood programs. Although the governor's commitment and USAID support may indeed have contributed to the decrease, they were not enough to overcome the other forces that eventually pushed the province back into poppy cultivation. To achieve long-term success, counternarcotics strategies must be resilient enough to withstand pressures that are beyond the control of local officials and international actors, including price fluctuations, weather, and insecurity.

Evaluations of farm-level counternarcotics efforts must focus on the long term and must take into account the larger context, including economic, agricultural, security, and location-specific influences (Mansfield and Pain 2008). Counternarcotics efforts must not only recognize the influence of factors such as price changes,

---

[16] See, for example, Martin and Symansky (2006).

droughts or floods, insurgent attacks, the commitment of local leaders, and the availability of development assistance, but must also ensure that operations designed to improve the lives of Afghan farmers address these factors over the long term, as they continue to evolve. Attributing success—or failure—to specific and narrow counternarcotics policies may lead to misguided strategies.

CONCLUSION: THE WAY AHEAD

At the time of writing, Afghanistan was the world's largest producer of opium. The country is in the throes of an evolving conflict, and its future is highly uncertain. In the fall of 2009, in a national election that was marred by corruption, President Karzai was reelected for a second five-year term. Meanwhile, U.S. policy toward Afghanistan has shifted under the administration of President Barack Obama.

On the military side, President Obama announced in December 2009 that 30,000 additional American troops would be deployed to Afghanistan; if conditions permit, they will begin returning to the United States in mid-2011 (Obama 2009). U.S. counternarcotics policy in Afghanistan has also undergone a major shift: holding that eradication is counterproductive and harmful to poor farmers, the United States will discontinue poppy eradication efforts and will focus instead on agricultural development and reform, and drug interdiction (Kaufman 2009; Bruno 2009). This is a sharp departure from the policies of the Bush administration, which had advocated the use of herbicides to stem poppy cultivation (Barry 2009).[17]

In December 2009, as part of its regional strategy to improve stability in Afghanistan and Pakistan, the Obama administration noted that its "top reconstruction priority is implementing a civilian-military agriculture redevelopment strategy to restore Afghanistan's once vibrant agriculture sector" (USDA 2010, 1). The Afghan government has indicated—through the Ministry of Agriculture, Irrigation, and Livestock—that it regards agricultural reform as critical (Bruno 2009).

From 2002 to 2007, roughly 14 percent of the US$6 billion spent by USAID in Afghanistan was allocated to agriculture and alternative livelihood development (USAID n.d.); it is unclear how much this allocation will change under the new strategy. USAID's counternarcotics efforts have focused on substituting other high-value crops for poppy; those programs are expected to continue (Bruno 2009). The U.S. Army has also begun to shift its agricultural development efforts. In eastern Afghanistan, instead of having PRTs run agricultural programs, the army has turned those programs over to agribusiness development teams led by National Guard members (Bruno 2009). The U.S. Department of Agriculture has also provided a great deal of assistance—US$256 million from 2003 through 2009—mainly in the form of food and economic development (USDA 2010).

---

[17] The Afghan government, the UK, and the European Union opposed the eradication policies of the Bush administration. Nevertheless, other nations, including Russia, continue to pressure the United States to pursue eradication.

All of these shifts in counternarcotics policies that affect Afghan farmers are promising developments. But regardless of the strategies adopted for ongoing operations, it is clear that poppy cultivation in the fields of Afghanistan is a problem that will not be resolved in the short term.

REFERENCES

Anderson, J. L. 2007. The Taliban's opium war: The difficulties and dangers of the eradication program. *New Yorker,* July 9.

Barry, E. 2009. Russia, plagued by heroin use, to press U.S. on destroying Afghan poppy crops. *New York Times,* September 23.

Blanchard, C. M. 2008. Afghanistan: Narcotics and U.S. policy. RL32686. Congressional Research Service. January 24.

Bonn Agreement (Agreement on Provisional Arrangements in Afghanistan Pending the Re-Establishment of Permanent Government Institutions). 2001. www.un.org/News/dh/latest/afghan/afghan-agree.html.

Brownfield, A. 2004. The threat from within Afghanistan. *Jane's Islamic Affairs Analyst,* September 1.

Bruno, G. 2009. Nourishing Afghanistan's agricultural sector. May 26. www.cfr.org/publication/19478/nourishing_afghanistans_agricultural_sector.html.

Byrd, W. A., and D. Buddenberg. 2006. Introduction and overview. In *Afghanistan's drug industry: Structure, functioning, dynamics, and implications for counter-narcotics policy,* ed. D. Buddenburg and W. A. Byrd. www.unodc.org/pdf/Afgh_drugindustry_Nov06.pdf.

CIA (U.S. Central Intelligence Agency). 2010. Afghanistan. *The World Factbook.* https://www.cia.gov/library/publications/the-world-factbook/geos/af.html.

Crawley, V. 2007. Afghan drug trade closely linked to Taliban insurgency. *America.gov,* June 26. www.america.gov/st/peacesec-english/2007/June/20070626170626MVyelwarC0.4788324.html?CP.rss=true.

Davis, A. 2001. Afghan drug output wanes—but only under Taliban. *Jane's Intelligence Review,* October 1.

Davis, A., and P.-A. Chouvy. 2002. Afghanistan's opium production rises post-Taliban. *Jane's Intelligence Review,* December 1.

DEA (U.S. Drug Enforcement Administration). 2001. Opium poppy cultivation and heroin processing in Southeast Asia. DEA-20026. http://permanent.access.gpo.gov/websites/usdojgov/www.usdoj.gov/dea/pubs/intel/20026/20026.html.

GAO (U.S. Government Accountability Office). 2006. Afghanistan drug control: Despite improved efforts, deteriorating security threatens success of U.S. goals. GAO-07-78. November. www.gao.gov/new.items/d0778.pdf.

Goodhand, J. 2005. Frontiers and wars: The opium economy in Afghanistan. *Journal of Agrarian Change* 5 (2): 191–216.

———. 2008. Corrupting or consolidating the peace? The drugs economy and post-conflict peacebuilding in Afghanistan. *International Peacekeeping* 15 (3): 405–423. www.informaworld.com/smpp/ftinterface~content=a793322435~fulltext=713240930~frm=content.

Holt, V. 2002. Peace and stability in Afghanistan: U.S. goals challenged by security gap. Peace Operations Factsheet Series. Henry L. Stimson Center. www.stimson.org/fopo/pdf/AfghanSecurityGapfactsheet_063102.pdf.

IMF (International Monetary Fund). 2003. *Islamic state of Afghanistan: Rebuilding a macroeconomic framework for reconstruction and growth.* IMF Country Report No. 03/299. September. www.imf.org/external/pubs/ft/scr/2003/cr03299.pdf.

Inspectors General, U.S. Department of State and U.S. Department of Defense. 2007. Interagency assessment of the counternarcotics program in Afghanistan. U.S. Department of State Report No. ISP-I-07-34. U.S. Department of Defense Report No. IE-2007-005. July.

IRIN (Integrated Regional Information Networks). 2004. Afghanistan: Opium and alternative livelihoods. August 24.

Islamic Republic of Afghanistan, Ministry of Counter Narcotics. 2006. National Drug Control Strategy. January. www.afghanconflictmonitor.org/AFGHANISTAN_NationalDrug ControlStrategy_January2006.pdf.

Jane's Islamic Affairs Analyst. 2007. Afghanistan: The organized narco-state. February 1.

———. 2008. Divisions emerge in Afghan drug strategy. August 28.

Jane's Terrorism and Security Monitor. 2007. Opium and the Afghan insurgency. September 12.

Kaufman, S. 2009. U.S. scraps Afghan crop eradication in favor of interdiction. *America.gov*, July 29. www.america.gov/st/sca-english/2009/July/20090729184555esnamfuak0.4385187.html.

Kerlikowske, G. 2009. Testimony of Gil Kerlikowske, director, Office of National Drug Control Policy. U.S. House Oversight and Government Reform Committee. Domestic Policy Subcommittee. May 19.

Kraeutler, K. 2008. UN reports that Taliban are stockpiling Afghan opium to ensure income source. *New York Times*, November 27.

Makarenko, T. 2002. Bumper Afghan narcotics crop indicates resilience of networks. *Jane's Intelligence Review,* April 22.

Malkasian, C., and G. Meyerle. 2009a. A brief history of the war in southern Afghanistan. CRM D0019791.A1/SR1. Washington, D.C.: CNA.

———. 2009b. Provincial reconstruction teams: How do we know they work? Strategic Studies Institute. U.S. Army War College. www.strategicstudiesinstitute.army.mil/pdffiles/PUB911.pdf.

Mansfield, D. 2002. The economic superiority of illicit drug production: Myth and reality. Paper presented at the International Conference on Alternative Development in Drug Control and Cooperation. January 7–12, Feldafing, Germany.

———. 2008a. Responding to risk and uncertainty: Understanding the nature of change in the rural livelihoods of opium poppy growing households in the 2007/08 growing season. A report for the Afghan Drugs Inter Departmental Unit of the UK Government. www.davidmansfield.org/data/Field_Work/UK/FINAL_UK_DRIVERS_REPORT_08.pdf.

———. 2008b. *Resurgence and reductions: Explanations for changing levels of opium poppy cultivation in Nangarhar and Ghor in 2006–07.* Case Study Series. Water Management, Livestock and the Opium Economy. Afghanistan Research and Evaluation Unit. www.davidmansfield.org/data/Field_Work/AREU/OpiuminNangarharandGhor ResurgenceandReductionCS.pdf.

Mansfield, D., and A. Pain. 2007. Evidence from the field: Understanding changing levels of opium poppy cultivation in Afghanistan. Briefing Paper Series. Afghanistan Research and Evaluation Unit. November. www.davidmansfield.org/data/Policy_Advice/AREU/EvidenceFromtheFieldOpiumBriefingPaper.pdf.

———. 2008. Counter-narcotics in Afghanistan: The failure of success? Briefing Paper Series. Afghanistan Research and Evaluation Unit. December. www.areu.org.af/index .php?option=com_docman&task=doc_details&gid=617&Itemid=99999999.

Martin, E., and S. Symansky. 2006. Macroeconomic impact of the drug economy and counter-narcotics efforts. In *Afghanistan's drug industry: Structure, functioning, dynamics, and implications for counter-narcotics policy*, ed. D. Buddenburg and W. A. Byrd. www.unodc.org/pdf/Afgh_drugindustry_Nov06.pdf.

Mikhos, A. 2006. Analysis: Afghanistan's drugs challenge. *NATO Review*. Spring. www.nato.int/docu/review/2006/issue1/english/analysis.html.

Morarjee, R. 2006. Afghan peasants bear the brunt of curbs on opium. *Financial Times*. May 10. www.ft.com/cms/s/0/f27cffa0-dfc0-11da-afe4-0000779e2340.html#ixzz19bs5aDSs.

NATO (North Atlantic Treaty Organization). n.d. History. International Security Assistance Force: Afghanistan. www.isaf.nato.int/history.html.

New York Times. 2010. Ahmed Wali Karzai. Times Topics. March 31. http://topics.nytimes.com/topics/reference/timestopics/people/k/ahmed_wali_karzai/index.html.

Obama, B. 2009. Obama's address to the nation on the way forward in Afghanistan and Pakistan, December 2009. Essential Documents. Council on Foreign Relations. December 1. www.cfr.org/publication/20871/obamas_address_to_the_nation_on_the_way_forward_in_afghanistan_and_pakistan_december_2009.html?breadcrumb=%2Fregion%2Fpublication_list%3Fid%3D280.

Orszag-Land, T. 2004. Afghanistan's deadly harvest. *Jane's Islamic Affairs Analyst*, March 26.

Pain, A. 2006. Opium trading systems in Helmand and Ghor. Issues Paper Series. Afghanistan Research and Evaluation Unit. www.areu.org.af/index.php?option=com_docman&task=doc_details&gid=353&Itemid=99999999.

———. 2008. Opium poppy and informal credit. Issues Paper Series. Afghanistan Research and Evaluation Unit. October. www.areu.org.af/index.php?option=com_docman&task=doc_details&gid=602&Itemid=26.

PakTribune. 2005. U.S. backs away from Afghan aerial spraying. January 23. www.paktribune.com/news/index.shtml?91300.

Peters, G. 2009a. Holbrooke's drug war. *Foreign Policy*, August 10. http://afpak.foreignpolicy.com/posts/2009/08/03/holbrookes_drug_war.

———. 2009b. *Seeds of terror: How heroin is bankrolling the Taliban and al Qaeda*. New York: Thomas Dunne Books.

Rashid, A. 2000. *Taliban: Militant Islam, oil, and fundamentalism in Central Asia*. New Haven, CT: Yale University Press.

Rohde, D. 2006. An Afghan symbol for change, then failure. *New York Times*, September 5.

Shaw, M. 2006. Drug trafficking and the development of organized crime in post-Taliban Afghanistan. In *Afghanistan's drug industry: Structure, functioning, dynamics, and implications for counter-narcotics policy*, ed. D. Buddenburg and W. A. Byrd. www.unodc.org/pdf/Afgh_drugindustry_Nov06.pdf.

Tarnoff, C. 2009. Afghanistan: U.S. foreign assistance. R40699. CRS Report for Congress. Congressional Research Service. www.fas.org/sgp/crs/row/R40699.pdf.

UNDCP (United Nations International Drug Control Programme). 2000. Afghanistan annual opium poppy survey 2000. www.unodc.org/pdf/publications/report_2000-12-31_1.pdf.

UNODC (United Nations Office on Drugs and Crime) and GOA (Government of Afghanistan), Counter Narcotics Directorate. 2004. *Afghanistan: Opium survey 2004*. www.unodc.org/pdf/afg/afghanistan_opium_survey_2004.pdf.

UNODC (United Nations Office on Drugs and Crime) and GOA (Government of Afghanistan), Ministry of Counter Narcotics. 2005. *Afghanistan: Opium survey 2005*. www.unodc.org/pdf/afg/afg_survey_2005.pdf.

———. 2007. *Afghanistan: Opium survey 2007.* October. www.unodc.org/documents/crop-monitoring/Afghanistan-opium-Survey-2007.pdf.

———. 2008. *Afghanistan: Opium survey 2008.* November. www.unodc.org/documents/crop-monitoring/Afghanistan_Opium_Survey_2008.pdf.

———. 2009. Afghanistan opium survey 2009: Summary findings. September. www.unodc.org/documents/crop-monitoring/Afghanistan/Afghanistan_opium_survey_2009_summary.pdf.

USAID (U.S. Agency for International Development). n.d. Budget and obligations. Afghanistan. http://afghanistan.usaid.gov//en/Page.Budget.aspx.

USDA (U.S. Department of Agriculture), Foreign Agricultural Service. 2010. USDA at work for agriculture in Afghanistan. March. www.fas.usda.gov/country/Afghanistan/FAS%20Afghanistan%20Fact%20Sheet_3.10.10.pdf.

Wright, J. 2006. The changing structure of the Afghan opium trade. *Jane's Intelligence Review*, September 9.

———. 2008. Applying pressure: Tackling Afghanistan's insurgents. *Jane's Intelligence Review*, May 13.

The Janus nature of opium poppy: A view from the field

Adam Pain

Opium, with its dream-inducing effects, is linked to Greek mythology: one of its derivatives, morphine, is named after Morpheus, the Greek god of sleep and dreams. But this chapter draws its inspiration from Roman mythology—specifically from Janus, the god of gates, doorways, and beginnings and endings. The figure of Janus, which is characteristically depicted with two heads facing in opposite directions, is used here to suggest that despite pervasive views of opium's damaging effects, it also offers transformative potential for peacebuilding in Afghanistan. This potential can be realized in three areas: the crop can (1) directly improve household welfare; (2) help smooth the way for the resolution of local conflicts; and (3) serve as a strategic resource, both to build governance and to provide the basis for building a social contract at the local level. The purpose of the chapter is not to advocate the cultivation of opium poppy but to argue that as long as opium poppy exists, a more strategic response—one that takes into consideration the opportunities it creates—may be in order.

To many observers, opium poppy is associated with greed, criminality, and the Taliban insurgency that arose after the U.S.-led invasion in 2001—and is, by definition, destructive to efforts to build a state and create a durable peace. But this view fails to recognize that opium poppy cultivation is not so much a *cause* as a *symptom*: opium reflects the failure of the state prior to 2001—and, since then, the failure of the orthodox state-building model, which has yet to provide Afghanistan with a transition to security, a political settlement, or strong socioeconomic development (Goodhand and Sedra 2007).

That opium contributes to the financing of the insurgency is undeniable, although its magnitude as a funding source is open to debate (Guistozzi 2007). Nevertheless, its significance in Afghanistan's informal economy is well documented (Ward and Byrd 2004), and there can be no doubt of its contribution to the rise of a shadow

---

Adam Pain is a visiting professor in rural development at the Swedish University of Agricultural Sciences and co-principal investigator of a research program on livelihood trajectories in Afghanistan funded by the Economic and Social Research Council, United Kingdom.

state.[1] But the focus on opium's role in the war and in the black economy—which has driven counternarcotics policy since 2001—largely ignores the more complex role that opium poppy plays in the rural economy, where 90 percent of the participants in the opium value chain are found (Pain 2010a).[2] Evidence from the field suggests that from a rural economy perspective, opium has done more to offer social protection;[3] generate economic growth; and, more controversially, contribute to local conflict resolution, than anything else on offer. Even more important, it has set the standards by which efforts to mitigate the wider costs of the opium economy can be judged.

Afghanistan's conflicts are deep-rooted and multilayered, and local conflicts are intertwined with regional or national conflicts. The focus in this chapter is on the local dimension, on the grounds that the Afghan family and village are the only durable institutions in the country's fractured landscape (Dupree 2004) and that they provide, however imperfectly, the fundamental public good of security that the state has historically failed to deliver. The chapter is divided into four sections: (1) a description of the context of opium poppy cultivation since 2001; (2) an examination of the factors that have driven the spread of cultivation; (3) a discussion of the effects of this spread; and (4) a consideration of opium's transformative potential in the peacebuilding process.

THE CONTEXT OF OPIUM POPPY CULTIVATION SINCE 2001

The globalization of opium as a commodity owes much to the presence of the British in India, during the nineteenth century, and to the presence of the United States in Southeast Asia, during the twentieth. The irrepressible market for opium has been driven primarily by demand from the West, although usage elsewhere is growing. But the West has remained largely unaccountable for the effects of that demand.

Afghanistan has a long history of opium poppy cultivation and was legally exporting opium until cultivation was officially banned in the late 1940s. Cultivation continued at low levels into the 1960s and 1970s. The political instability that began in the late 1970s fuelled an increase in cultivation, but the greatest expansion has taken place since 2001; the timing alone makes it clear that opium production has been incidental to the deeper history of conflict in Afghanistan.[4]

---

[1] In a shadow state, government officials use their positions to pursue their own or others' interests, and provide services in return for payments.

[2] *Value chain* refers to the activities—from production to processing to final product—that add value to a product.

[3] *Social protection* refers to actions on the part of the state or communities that provide a safety net in times of shock (e.g., famine) or that address the effects of long-term poverty.

[4] The banning of cultivation in Iran (1955), Turkey (1972), and Pakistan (in the 1980s) undoubtedly encouraged the persistence and spread of opium poppy cultivation within Afghanistan.

The Janus nature of opium poppy   493

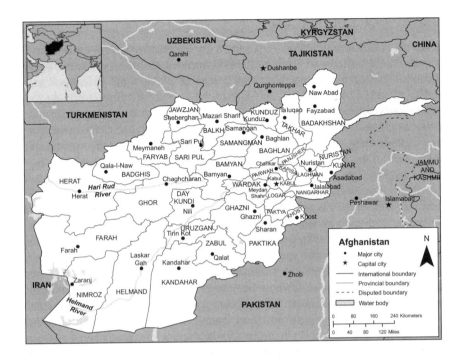

The response to the expansion of cultivation has evidenced an awkward tension between politics and governance. From one perspective, unprecedented expansion (between 2002 and 2007, a near tripling of the area devoted to the crop) can be regarded as a crisis that requires an immediate response; from another perspective, the expansion can be regarded as a development issue, which requires a longer-term response that is focused on causes, rather than a short-term response that is focused on symptoms. In other words, there is a tension between the "public good" of the West and decentralized, participatory approaches, which are fundamental to good governance and recognize individual rights, including the right to secure the means to a living. So far, the public good of the West—in practical terms, criminalization and eradication of cultivation—has had the advantage.[5]

---

[5] It is important to note here that the notion of legality is not absolute but is contingent on circumstances. Because the use of opium as a narcotic is widely defined as illegal, the production of opium for this market is criminalized in the West. But there is a second, legal market for opium—as a source of morphine and other pharmaceutical agents (such as codeine and thebaine); for such uses, opium can be legally cultivated, as it is in the United Kingdom.

DRIVERS OF CULTIVATION

If the cultivated area devoted to any other crop had nearly tripled—from an estimated 74,000 hectares in 2002 to 193,000 hectares in 2007—while remaining localized and occupying no more than 5 percent of the total agricultural land (UNODC and GOA 2004, 2006, 2007), an exploration of the processes driving such cultivation would have been a likely response. Those concerned with counternarcotics policy might also have been concerned about the geographical spread of cultivation: as of 2000, three provinces—Nangarhar, Helmand, and Kandahar—contained 80 percent of the area devoted to opium poppy; by 2003, cultivation had spread across twenty-eight provinces, and the area devoted to the crop in the three core provinces represented only 47 percent of the total (UNODC and GOA 2007). By 2007, however, cultivation was again concentrated in the three core provinces, which held 71 percent of the area in cultivation. Instead, however, the definition of policy success has largely focused on aggregate area—a statistic that is of questionable precision and reveals little about the sources of the change (Mansfield and Pain 2008).

First, why these three core provinces? In Helmand, the reasons can be traced to the 1990s, when a breakdown in the management of the province's centralized irrigation system caused water scarcity, and the loss of subsidized inputs (credit and fertilizer) led farmers to shift from cotton to an alternative cash crop that had a functioning market (Pain 2006); similar factors may have played a role in Kandahar. In the case of Nangarhar, cultivation has been centered in small farms in resource-poor areas where there have been acute concerns about food security (Mansfield 2004). In all three cases, strong links to opium trading systems have been fundamental to cultivation.

After 2001, the expansion of cultivation was largely driven by price: before 2001, the price was US$50 to US$100 per kilogram, but it rose to a peak of US$600 to US$700 per kilogram between 2001 and 2003. Although the price declined to between US$100 and US$200 per kilogram in 2004–2005, the total area devoted to opium poppy cultivation continued to rise, reflecting the price advantage of opium over other crops, and the fact that its market functioned well. Although price fluctuations have contributed to shifts in and out of cultivation in many areas (Mansfield and Pain 2008), prices have, overall, been an important "pull" factor in the dynamics of cultivation.

The influence of social structures that regulate markets also has to be considered. Until 2001, the informal social regulation of the opium market—that is, the effect of class, ethnicity, and gender on regulating access to markets—was probably influential in keeping cultivation centered in the three core provinces;[6] in Balkh, for example, control of the market by Pashtuns from Kandahar prevented other ethnic groups from accessing the opium market.[7] After 2001, social regulation appears to

---

[6] On the role of class, ethnicity, and gender in regulating access and returns in commodity markets in India, see Harriss-White (2003).
[7] See Pain (2007a).

have relaxed, despite continued evidence that ethnic identity—and, therefore, access to the main traders—determines price (Pain 2006). Yet another aspect of the opium market is that it continues to function under conditions of insecurity, providing both credit and purchase at the farm gate (Mansfield and Pain 2008).

But general explanations are not sufficient to explain the dynamics of cultivation at the province and local level. Longitudinal fieldwork in four provinces (Badakhshan, Balkh, Ghor, and Nangarhar) has shown that resource availability, as well as market access and terms of trade, is a crucial driver in the dynamics of cultivation (Mansfield and Pain 2007).[8] (So, for example, more remote, resource-poor areas have led the return to cultivation, while more central areas—with better access to land, water, and markets—have made more durable shifts away from the cultivation of opium.) Under the effects of these three drivers, opium poppy cultivation takes on the characteristic features of a "footloose crop"—that is, one that rapidly shifts location according to pressure gradients.[9] For example, in Nangarhar—which, unlike Balkh, is a relatively ethnically homogeneous province (Mansfield 2004)—cultivation has had a particularly dynamic pattern, collapsing in 2005 because of threats and promises from the provincial governor, but rising again in 2006 and 2007 when promises were not delivered on, particularly in remote, resource-poor areas.

In Balkh, where the history of cultivation is tied to complex historical settlement patterns (resulting from Pashtun immigrants' deliberate settlement of upstream areas) and to water availability, there have been four phases of cultivation (Pain 2006). First, before 1994, there was limited cultivation for local use. Second, between 1994 and 2001, cultivation was intensive but highly concentrated in upstream locations—in particular, in Pashtun communities. During the third phase, after 2001, there was more general cultivation, but it was affected by water availability. It is this period that offers evidence that deep, ethnically based tensions—generated by conflicts that began before 2001—were markedly tempered by the growth of the opium economy (Pain 2010b). This tempering effect occurred for two reasons: first, labor was mobilized across community divides; second, communities that had formerly been at odds were aware that they had a shared interest in the opium market and its benefits (Pain 2010b). This phase lasted until 2006, when informal coercive power exerted by provincial authorities in support of their own interests created an effective ban on opium cultivation (Pain 2008b). The transitions between the phases "have been driven largely by structures of informal power—socially determined, ethnically based . . . and associated with powerful individuals

---

[8] Counternarcotics measures have had both direct and indirect effects on these drivers, intensifying their effects at times and mitigating them at others. The interaction of these factors is complex and is context- and time-specific. For example, depending on the level of the perceived threat of eradication, opium prices can either increase (to respond to the increased risk) or decrease (if the risks are seen to be very high), thus pushing cultivation elsewhere.

[9] This phenomenon is also sometimes known as *ballooning*.

and groups" (Mansfield and Pain 2007, 8); specifically, the more powerful groups were located upstream, and were therefore in control of water distribution.

Both pull and push factors (formal and informal counternarcotics actions that drive opium out of an area) explain the specific patterns of opium poppy cultivation. Price and market structures—that is, the ways in which informal market regulation affects price and availability—have been key promoters of expansion, which has occurred in response to deeply entrenched rural poverty. Such poverty was, in many areas, exacerbated by the 1998–2001 drought, which led many rural households to deplete their assets and go into debt. Poverty, however, is both socially and spatially differentiated. Specific patterns of cultivation—as in Balkh, for example—can be related to social and spatial characteristics: for example, poorer villages and households are more likely to be found downstream, and richer villages upstream; Pashtun villages are more likely to be upstream, and other ethnic groups to be downstream.

From this perspective, conflict is not a key driver of the dynamics of opium poppy cultivation, but it is not without a role. For example, despite indications that increased cultivation may temper conflict, conflicting evidence can be drawn from the contrary situation, when opium cultivation declines. In the case of both Nangarhar and Balkh, insecurity and violence increased (Mansfield and Pain 2008). There is certainly a correlation between insecurity and opium poppy cultivation: cultivation is a symptom of underlying livelihood and physical insecurity, and opium poppy is a low-risk crop in a high-risk environment. But field evidence is not kind to generalized explanations, including those derived from multiple regression models, which hold that opium poppy production is conflict induced.[10]

OPIUM, DEBT, AND ECONOMIC SECURITY

Early accounts of the spread of opium poppy after 2001 emphasized the role of debt,[11] often denominated in opium, as a key reason for the continued cultivation of the crop. It was argued, moreover, that cultivation was leading farmers further into debt—and that, given the high interest rates being charged on loans against future crops, opium traders were, in effect, "narco-usurers" (UNODC 2003a). But advance loans against future crops are not unique to opium; moreover, although interest rates in 2002–2004 may have been higher for opium than for other crops, the higher rates could well have reflected the riskiness associated with the crop (because of the potential for crop failure, price fluctuations, and eradication) (Pain 2008b). Nevertheless, a perspective that linked opium to debt creation persisted. Thus, for example, the United Nations Office of Drugs and Crime concluded that "financing costs banking on informal credit, without a proper banking system

---

[10] For an example of studies that rely on multiple regression models, see Lind, Moene, and Willumsen (2010).
[11] See Pain (2008b).

in place, have been extremely high in Afghanistan and have clearly contributed to the spread of opium poppy cultivation in country" (2003b, 122).

In the core provinces, cultivators who took opium-based loans before the price increase of 2001 subsequently experienced a dramatic increase, in dollar terms, of their overall debt.[12] It is far from clear, however, that the expansion of opium beyond the core provinces was linked to opium-denominated debt, although it may have been linked to the general decapitalization of the rural economy (that is, the outflow of capital) that resulted from the 1998–2001 drought. But the policy leap—from assumptions about a link between opium and debt, and the fact that credit is available only at high interest rates (Goeldner 2004)—to claims that opium cultivation evidenced a general lack of rural credit is simply not justified by the evidence. In fact, informal credit practices are widespread (Klijn and Pain 2007); most rural households have access to them—and, more to the point, much of the credit is interest free. More broadly, there is a tendency to regard "the informal" as problematic and to see it through the lens of opium poppy—as occurs, for example, with respect to the *hawala* system of money transfer. This tendency raises wider issues about approaches to peacebuilding and state building that emphasize the formal and neglect the positive attributes of the informal; these issues are returned to in the final section.

A 2008 examination of the linkages between opium and credit, based on fieldwork in Badakhshan and Balkh (both of which had seen significant expansion of cultivation after 2001), found opium poppy cultivation more likely to relieve than to create debt (Pain 2008b). According to detailed household histories, beginning in the 1990s, political instability, drought, and a growing need for credit had led to a general increase in the cost of informal credit; this increase predated the rise of opium cultivation. These histories also showed that in both Balkh and Badakshan during the key opium cultivation years, cultivation was primarily a means of securing food and relieving debt (Pain 2008b). Household members looked back on those years as a time of prosperity and viewed the decline of the opium economy as having had a primarily negative effect on their food security.

The benefits of opium poppy cultivation have been widespread; however, because of underlying social inequities, they have not necessarily been equally distributed (Pain 2007a). Landowners in areas with abundant resources have enjoyed the highest returns. But because of the higher labor demands associated with opium poppy, more land has been sharecropped out for opium cultivation than for wheat. This has led to increased demand for farm labor—which has led, in turn, to a substantial increase in labor wages.[13] Opium poppy cultivation has

---

[12] Because the debt remained opium denominated, as the price increased so did the dollar debt. For a review of the evidence, see Pain (2008b).

[13] When landowners do not have the labor resources to cultivate opium themselves, they use sharecroppers. Sharecropping is a tenancy arrangement in which rent is paid through a share of the crop harvest; the proportion of the share depends on what portion of the inputs of production (land preparation, seed, fertilizer, etc.) were provided by the tenant.

also had significant multiplier effects on the rural economy.[14] John Mellor (2005), for example, estimates that for each farm job that is directly related to opium, an additional 5.6 nonfarm jobs have been created.

In summary, the growth in opium cultivation since 2001 has had largely beneficial effects on the rural population: reducing poverty, relieving debt, and providing employment and food security. This supports the view that opium has transformed household welfare. Moreover, these benefits have dwarfed any that have been gained from the reconstruction effort.[15] In July 2008, during a visit to Balkh, the minister for counternarcotics openly admitted that the government had failed to develop the region and apologized for the government's disregard for the area.[16]

And what of the linkages between opium and conflict? Here one must be careful to distinguish between localized conflict between villages over resources and the more specific interconnection between the opium economy and the insurgency in the south.[17] The focus here is on the former—on a history of localized conflict that has often been linked to the control of natural resources and land. The limited evidence that exists, from Jan Koehler and Christoph Zuercher (2007), indicates that because of its poverty-reducing effects, opium has in some cases subdued or mitigated conflict. Koehler and Zuercher also note that opium has played an indirect role in ongoing conflicts, by rekindling land disputes and destabilizing the local power balance. Similar observations can be drawn from Balkh—both at the local level and, more interestingly, at the provincial level, where the rise and consolidation of the governor's political power, which was built on the opium economy, has contributed to a regime of relative security; a similar level of security has not been achieved in the neighboring province of Kunduz, where opium has not been grown (Pain 2010b).

THE TRANFORMATIVE POTENTIAL OF THE OPIUM ECONOMY

Much of the policy response to opium poppy emphasizes its negative dimensions—and, despite the policy rhetoric, much of the practical effort has focused on opium eradication, an approach that has triggered resentment, protest, and resistance (Mansfield and Pain 2008; Pain 2010a). Moreover, there is little evidence to support claims, for example, of the beneficial effects of alternative livelihood programs that have been designed to replace opium.[18] Thus, it is difficult to disagree with the judgment of Richard Holbrooke, who, as U.S. Special Representative to Afghanistan and Pakistan, described the U.S. counternarcotics effort in

---

[14] The dynamic effects of the opium economy on the immediate rural economy have been widely noted. See, for example, Mansfield (2004) and Pain (2006, 2007b).
[15] See Pain (2008a).
[16] See "Minister Apologises for Lack of Progress in Balkh," cited in Pain (2008a, 2).
[17] Much of the literature on conflict in Afghanistan focuses on the connection between opium and the insurgency.
[18] See Pain (2008a), specifically on Balkh.

Afghanistan as "the most wasteful and ineffective program I have seen in 40 years in and out of the government" (*BBC News* 2009).

Opium poppy cultivation has to be viewed in relation to the wider peace-building and state-building efforts in Afghanistan, which suffer from a number of problems (Suhrke 2006; Goodhand and Sedra 2007):

- The limitations of the original Bonn agreement.[19]
- The conflation of a war on terror with a counternarcotics response and a state-building project.
- The creation, through excessive aid, of a rentier state.[20]
- The application of an inappropriate model of state building.

With respect to state building, Lant Pritchett and Michael Woolcock (2004) have pointed out that in many development programs, the solution is the problem: the assumption that one can "skip straight to Weber" imposes a universal model of what a state should be and ignores historical processes of state building (Pritchett and Woodcock 2004,193).[21] The state-building model being applied in Afghanistan has also failed to attend to, and build on, the only durable institutions in the landscape: the family and the village.

Opium poppy offers opportunities that could have been integrated into the state-building process. First, for producers, opium poppy has directly reduced poverty and provided livelihood security at a time when little else was on offer. Opium poppy cultivation has thus played a transformative role in the welfare of rural populations, but it could also have provided breathing space, during which resources could have been put in place that would have fostered a continuing shift out of poverty. There is also evidence, albeit tentative, that the opium economy has, in some circumstances, reduced tensions between communities and households, and thereby reduced potential for conflict. A more sensitive and strategic counternarcotics effort, to respond to Holbrooke's judgment, would have taken both of these aspects into account and used the opium economy to gain time and to sustain support for wider state-building initiatives. Instead of defaulting to the eradication impulse, such an approach would have involved participatory and governance-building measures, at the local level, that were focused on the reduction of opium poppy cultivation.

A more sophisticated counternarcotics response would also have sought to understand opium-diffusion processes—and would have thereby discovered that social inequalities are the root issue underlying most conflicts in Afghanistan. In

---

[19] The Bonn Agreement (Agreement on Provisional Arrangements in Afghanistan Pending the Re-Establishment of Permanent Government Institutions) was signed on December 22, 2001, and resulted from a meeting, held under the auspices of the United Nations, between leading Afghan figures. The goal was to establish an interim authority in the country.

[20] A rentier state derives a substantial part of its revenue from external sources.

[21] Max Weber's views on the role and functions of the state include a monopoly on the legitimate use of violence and an impartial and rule-bound bureaucracy.

this view, opium cultivation is largely a symptom of fundamental failures in state building—that is, a homegrown response to what the state had failed to deliver. Instead of attempting to destroy one of the few sources of welfare provision available to the rural poor, a more calibrated response would have taken notice of the standards and achievements, however imperfect, set by the opium economy. Such a response would have assigned greater value to informal and customary institutions and structures, including those that are central to dispute resolution. It would also have required a fairly substantial rethinking of the state-building model that is currently being applied in Afghanistan.

REFERENCES

BBC News. 2009. Envoy damns U.S. Afghan drug effort. March 21. http://news.bbc.co.uk/2/hi/south_asia/7957237.stm. Quoted in Christopher Blanchard, Afghanistan: Narcotics and US Policy, Congressional Research Service 7-5700. (Washington, D.C.: CRS, 2009).

Dupree, N. 2004. The family during crisis in Afghanistan. *Journal of Comparative Family Studies* 35 (2): 311–329.

Goeldner, K. 2004. Roles and opportunities for rural credit initiatives in Afghanistan's opium economy. Workshop Paper #2. Rural finance in Afghanistan: The challenge of the opium economy. http://siteresources.worldbank.org/INTAFGHANISTAN/Resources/AFRFW_2_Rural_Credit_Initiatives.htm.

Goodhand, J., and M. Sedra. 2007. Bribes or bargains? Peace conditionalities and "post conflict" reconstruction in Afghanistan. *International Peacekeeping* 14 (1): 41–61.

Guistozzi, A. 2007. *Koran, Kalashnikov and laptop: The neo-Taliban insurgency in Afghanistan.* London: Hurst.

Harriss-White, B. 2003. *India working: Essays on society and economy.* Cambridge, UK: Cambridge University Press.

Klijn, F., and A. Pain. 2007. *Finding the money: Informal credit practices in rural Afghanistan.* Synthesis Paper. Kabul: Afghanistan Research and Evaluation Unit. www.areu.org.af/index.php?option=com_content&task=view&id=41&Itemid=86 .

Koehler, J., and C. Zuercher. 2007. Statebuilding, conflict and narcotics in Afghanistan: The view from below. *International Peacekeeping* 14 (1): 62–74.

Lind, J. T., K. O. Moene, and F. Willumsen. 2010. Opium for the masses? Conflict-induced narcotics production in Afghanistan. Working Paper, Department of Economics, University of Oslo. www.esop.uio.no/research/working-papers/OpiumfortheMasses.pdf.

Mansfield, D. 2004. *Diversity and dilemma: Understanding rural livelihoods and addressing the causes of opium poppy cultivation in Nangarhar and Laghman, Eastern Afghanistan.* Internal Document No. 2, Project for Alternative Livelihoods in Eastern Afghanistan. http://palinfo.org/index.php?option=com_docman&task=cat_view&gid=13&limit=5&limitstart=30&order=name&dir=DESC&Itemid=43.

Mansfield, D., and A. Pain. 2007. *Evidence from the field: Understanding changing levels of opium poppy cultivation in Afghanistan.* Briefing Paper. Kabul: Afghanistan Research and Evaluation Unit.

———. 2008. *Counter-narcotics in Afghanistan: The failure of success?* Briefing Paper. Kabul: Afghanistan Research and Evaluation Unit.

Mellor, J. 2005. Poppies and agricultural development in Afghanistan. Presentation to the Ministry of Agriculture, January 18, Kabul.

Pain, A. 2006. Opium trading systems in Helmand and Ghor provinces. In *Afghanistan's drug industry: Structure, functioning, dynamics and implications for counternarcotics policy*, ed. D. Buddenberg and W. A. Byrd. Kabul: United Nations Office on Drugs and Crime / World Bank.

———. 2007a. *The spread of opium poppy cultivation in Balkh*. Case Study Series. Kabul: Afghanistan Research and Evaluation Unit.

———. 2007b. *Water management, livestock and the opium economy: The spread of opium poppy cultivation in Balkh*. Kabul: Afghanistan Research and Evaluation Unit.

———. 2008a. *"Let them eat promises": The closing of the opium poppy fields in Balkh and its consequences*. Case Study Series. Kabul: Afghanistan Research and Evaluation Unit.

———. 2008b. *Opium poppy and informal credit*. Issues Paper. Kabul: Afghanistan Research and Evaluation Unit.

———. 2010a. Narcotics and counternarcotics: Responding to an irrepressible market? Forthcoming. In *Deconstructing the Afghan security sector*, ed. E. Cole, A. Dowling, and C. Karp. Security Governance Series. Geneva: Geneva Centre for the Democratic Control of Armed Forces / LIT Verlag.

———. 2010b. The opium revolution: Continuity or change in rural Afghanistan? In *The comparative political economy of development: Africa and South Asia*, ed. B. Harriss-White and J. Heyer. London: Routledge.

Pritchett, L., and M. Woolcock. 2004. Solutions when the solution is the problem: Arraying the disarray in development. *World Development* 32 (2): 191–212.

Suhrke, A. 2006. When more is less: Aiding state-building in Afghanistan. Working Paper 26. Madrid: FRIDE.

UNODC (United Nations Office on Drugs and Crime). 2003a. Opium poppy cultivation in a changing policy environment: Farmers' intentions for the 2002–2003 growing season. Strategic Study No. 9. Kabul.

———. 2003b. The opium economy in Afghanistan. Vienna.

UNODC (United Nations Office on Drugs and Crime) and GOA (Government of Afghanistan), Ministry of Counter Narcotics. 2004. *Afghanistan: Opium survey*. Vienna: UNODC; Kabul: GOA.

———. 2006. *Afghanistan: Opium survey*. Vienna: UNODC; Kabul: GOA.

———. 2007. Afghanistan: Opium winter rapid assessment survey. February. www.unodc.org/documents/crop-monitoring/Afghan-winter-survey-Feb08-short.pdf.

Ward, C., and W. A. Byrd. 2004. *Afghanistan's opium drug economy*. Report No. SASPR-5, South Asia Region PREM Working Paper Series. Washington, D.C.: World Bank.

Peace through sustainable forest management in Asia: The USAID Forest Conflict Initiative

Jennifer Wallace and Ken Conca

This chapter examines a multiyear initiative within the U.S. Agency for International Development (USAID) that was designed to promote greater awareness of forest-related conflict and encourage a more conflict-sensitive approach to natural resource management (NRM). The initiative consisted of two separate projects: the Conflict Timber Project (CTP), which was undertaken in 2002–2003 and was designed to obtain a clearer picture of timber-related conflict and its drivers in Asia and Africa; and Managing Conflict in Asian Forest Communities (MCAFC), which was undertaken between 2003 and 2007 and sought "to analyze the types and causes of forest conflict; identify approaches to reducing conflict; and communicate the seriousness of this problem to governments, the private sector, the donor community, and the US public" (USAID 2007, 1).

Guide to Abbreviations

ANE:	USAID Bureau for Asia and the Near East
ARD:	Associates in Rural Development
CTP:	Conflict Timber Project
DCHA:	USAID Bureau for Democracy, Conflict and Humanitarian Assistance
MCAFC:	Managing Conflict in Asian Forest Communities
NRM:	natural resource management
OTI:	USAID Office of Transition Initiatives
RAFT:	Responsible Asia Forestry and Trade program
TFD:	The Forests Dialogue
USAID:	U.S. Agency for International Development

The chapter focuses on the characterization of forest conflict in the CTP and on the practical efforts to address it that were carried out through the MCAFC project. This two-part initiative on "conflict timber" provides a unique opportunity to explore how a bilateral development assistance agency conceptualized the problem of forest conflict; attempted to raise awareness of the issue and promote more conflict-sensitive practice; and identified and engaged with the audiences it had selected to receive its message. The initiative also provides an opportunity to evaluate the effects of greater awareness

---

Jennifer Wallace is a Ph.D. candidate in the Department of Government and Politics at the University of Maryland and an affiliate of the Harrison Program on the Future Global Agenda. Ken Conca is a professor of international relations in the School of International Service at American University, where he directs the Global Environmental Politics Program. The authors wish to express their thanks to the individuals who made various published and unpublished documents and data available to them. This chapter was developed with support from the Center for Global Partnership of the Japan Foundation.

on practice. Finally, a conflict-sensitive approach to NRM has great salience for peacebuilding: many of the sites involved were post-conflict settings, and the more diffuse conflicts associated with forest access and resources are among the quickest ways to undermine a fragile peace.

The chapter has four goals:

- To identify the assumptions that were reflected in the way the CTP conceptualized forest conflict. The focus here is on identifying aspects of the conceptual framework that are new or innovative when compared with past practice, and on the particular linkages between that framework and NRM in post-conflict settings.
- To trace the linkages between the conceptual and analytic, awareness-raising, and policy-advisory aspects of the initiative. The objective here is to explore how the combination of three factors—the project's conceptual framework, the characteristics of the agency, and the characteristics of the wider stakeholder community—led to a particular pattern of ideational diffusion and policy adoption.
- To ask what lessons can be learned from the difficulties observed in (1) turning the analytical concepts and framework into actionable recommendations at the programmatic level within USAID and (2) spreading the message to stakeholder groups within and outside the agency.
- To draw lessons from this case that can be applied to post-conflict NRM. The focus here is on both the initiative's substantive findings about forest conflict and on institutional lessons that can be gleaned from an effort to raise the profile of a new and cross-cutting issue in the programmatic operations of a bilateral development assistance agency.

The chapter is divided into five major sections: (1) a review of the literature on the relationship between forests, conflict, and peacebuilding; (2) an overview of the origins and goals of the USAID Forest Conflict Initiative; (3) a description of the agenda, goals, and achievements of the CTP; (4) a description of the agenda, goals, and achievements of the MCAFC project; and (5) concluding commentary on the effectiveness and implications of the Forest Conflict Initiative, with particular attention to the future integration of conflict-sensitive NRM into peacebuilding initiatives.[1]

BACKGROUND: CONFLICT, FORESTS, AND PEACEBUILDING

The early literature linking the environment to violent conflict focused on a thread that led from environmental degradation to material scarcity to the exacerbation of social tensions; later work highlighted resource abundance as a potential catalyst for

---

[1] Some information for this chapter was drawn from interviews with (1) participants in the USAID initiative (USAID staff, consultants, and implementing partners) and (2) individuals who had extensive experience in forestry projects in Southeast Asia. Because of the potential sensitivity of the subject matter, interview subjects were promised anonymity.

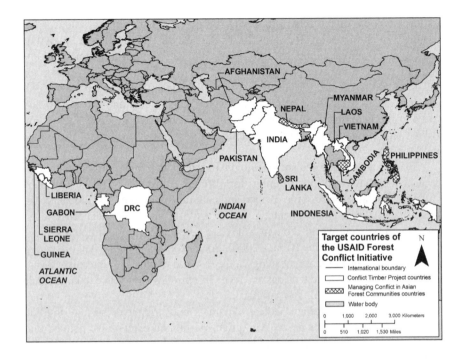

conflict.[2] Forests illustrate many of the conflict dynamics posited in the ecoconflict literature, ranging from violent clashes in the wake of accelerated deforestation rates to conflict timber episodes in which forest resources are used to sustain and fund belligerents. But a narrow focus on social responses to perceived scarcity or abundance misses the wide array of conflict dynamics that occur in and around forests—specifically, conflicting claims to the land and its resources; conflict between the different levels of governance that regulate access, use rights, and concessions; and tensions between local practices and the rules, regulatory modes, and development aims of the state.

Philippe Le Billon, for example, traces the transition in Cambodia from a classic case of conflict timber, during the civil war, to post-war social conflict rooted in forest exploitation and commodification: in Le Billon's account, elite control of Cambodia's most valuable resource contributed to corruption, political factionalization, and unsustainable economic development (Le Billion 2000). Paul Richards argues that the rebellion staged by Sierra Leone's Revolutionary United Front, rather than being grounded in mere economic rapaciousness, was a violent social project intended to address both the social exclusion experienced

---

[2] On the role of resource abundance in conflict, see Paul Collier and Anke Hoeffler, "High-Value Natural Resources, Development, and Conflict: Channels of Causation," in this volume.

by the members of the rebel group and the perceived misappropriation of the country's mineral wealth (Richards 2001). And Yayoi Fujita, Khamla Phanvilay, and Deanna Donovan argue that forests were the target of military attack in Laos during the Indochina War precisely because they provided the cover, resources, and livelihoods critical for survival. Migration during the war led to discord, which persists to this day, between customary landholders and those who laid claim to the land during or after the conflict, and between lowland agricultural villages and migrant villages that depend on forest resources (Fujita, Phanvilay, and Donovan 2007).

Forests are among the socioecological systems that generate social conflict because they have multiple meanings for different stakeholders: for nearby communities, they are sources of livelihood and cultural significance; for global actors, such as international environmental groups or activists, they are critical ecosystems; and in a globalizing world economy, they are potentially commodified resources with growing market value (Conca 2006). Social conflict occurs when one group seeks to impose one of these meanings at the expense of others. The result can vary in intensity, from localized tensions and sporadic episodes of violence to larger-scale and more continuous forms of conflict.

But just as forest-related social dynamics may trigger or sustain conflict, they may do the same for peace. As Adrian Martin and others have pointed out, social interaction involving natural resources inevitably offers opportunities for both conflict and cooperation (Martin 2005). In societies emerging from war or other forms of civil violence, effective forest governance can thus be essential to establishing peace.

Forests are most vulnerable in the early stages of peacebuilding, when other economic activities have yet to recover from the disruption of violent conflict, and government institutions have yet to establish authority. For example, Judy Oglethorpe and colleagues have noted that weakened governing institutions may attempt to jump-start devastated economies by granting concessions for unsustainable exploitation of forest resources, while the private sector simultaneously takes advantage of peace—and of institutional weakness—by moving in and extracting resources illegally. In addition, demands on forests increase during and immediately after war, when agricultural systems have been destroyed or disrupted and local populations, refugees, and internally displaced persons are more dependent on wild plant and animal products (Oglethorpe et al. 2002). Several factors—the increase in demand for forest resources during and after violent conflict, the conflict between the survival and livelihood needs of local actors and the efforts of governing regimes to establish authority, and unclear or contested rights of access—may threaten a fragile peace. The effective management of forests in post-conflict contexts is thus an essential element of peacebuilding strategies.

In sum, simple measures of material abundance or scarcity are likely to be poor predictors of conflict; social interactions involving forests may be a source of both conflict and peaceful cooperation; and forest-related dynamics play out in a variety of social contexts and at different spatial scales.[3] Although the causes of forest conflict are complex and multidimensional, the extent of the problem is clear. USAID has identified twelve countries in Asia alone that are affected by forest conflict. In Indonesia, for example, between 6.6 and 19.6 million people—as much as 10 percent of the total population—are affected. And in Cambodia, 1.7 million people, or about 12 percent of the population, are affected (USAID 2006b).

THE CONFLICT TIMBER PROJECT

The CTP was undertaken jointly by the USAID Office of Transition Initiatives (OTI) and its Bureau for Asia and the Near East (ANE). OTI is part of the Bureau for Democracy, Conflict and Humanitarian Assistance (DCHA), one of the functional bureaus at USAID; ANE is one of the agency's geographic bureaus.[4]

Setting the agenda

The idea for the CTP began to take shape in 2001; the first contract in support of the project was agreed to in 2002. Two key developments led to the creation of the CTP. The first was a meeting in which Patrick Alley, a founding director of the advocacy organization Global Witness, briefed USAID administrator Andrew Natsios on a report that Global Witness had just released: *Taylor-Made: The Pivotal Role of Liberia's Forests and Flag of Convenience in Regional Conflict*, which documented links between logging, the arms trade, and regional conflict (Global Witness 2001). This meeting and the report's wider reception among policy makers and activists put conflict timber on the agenda of the USAID administrator. After the meeting, Natsios asked OTI to lead the development of an action plan to address the relationship between logging and conflict; ANE was to provide technical assistance.

In attempting to respond to this directive, OTI and ANE found that there was insufficient information to generate a complete understanding of the problem. As noted in the final report of the CTP:

---

[3] For example, Siri Aas Rustad and colleagues (2008) found little statistical support linking forest cover to conflict onset or duration; however, the complexity of the interactions in and around forests might have confounded statistical analysis, producing inconsistent or insignificant results.

[4] In addition to administrative offices, the USAID Washington, D.C., headquarters consists of functional and regional bureaus. The functional bureaus include Legislative and Public Affairs; Global Health; Economic Growth, Agriculture and Trade; Foreign Assistance; Democracy, Conflict and Humanitarian Assistance; and Management. USAID has both regional and local field missions outside of Washington. In 2008, the Bureau for Asia and the Near East was divided into two separate regional bureaus: the Asia Bureau and the Middle East Bureau. The Central Asian republics, which were previously grouped in USAID's Europe and Eurasia Bureau, were relocated to the Asia Bureau.

While the Action Plan identified illustrative steps the Agency could take to monitor and reduce conflicts over timber, it also noted a general lack of information, and moreover a lack of careful analysis of the nexus between the economic, financial, political, ecological, social and security aspects of conflict timber. In an effort to address these informational and analytical gaps, and as a first step toward developing the foundation for well-targeted and effective programming, the Action Plan called for further analysis of the problem of conflict timber (USAID 2003a, 2).

Thus, the action plan delivered to Natsios in January 2002 called for further research on the issue of conflict timber.

The second development that raised the visibility of forest conflict was the arrival, in 2001, of the ANE senior advisor for NRM, whose role was to support the region's missions in their efforts to address NRM. En route to her post, the advisor heard a number of accounts of violence that was linked to access to forests and other resources, prompting her to ask program officers in the country-level field missions what could be done about forest-conflict linkages. Thus, at the same time that the USAID administrator was raising the profile of conflict timber within the agency, ANE had an internal champion who supported a more active role for the bureau in addressing forest conflict. The interest generated within ANE by the senior advisor for NRM and the administrator's directive to OTI to investigate conflict timber were the key developments that led to ANE's participation, with OTI, in the development of the action plan.

After the release of the action plan, ANE and OTI designed the first phase of the USAID Forest Conflict Initiative, the CTP. To implement the CTP, ANE and OTI contracted with Associates in Rural Development (ARD), a consulting firm, which was to carry out a nine-month comprehensive study of conflict timber in Asia and Africa. The project, which was undertaken in two phases, had three stated goals (USAID, 2003a, 3):

- To provide, through preliminary country surveys and follow-up case studies, a descriptive account of conflict over forests.
- "To assess the role of forests in peace processes."
- To identify suitable programmatic responses, both at the field-office level and from Washington, D.C.

During the first phase of the CTP, ARD developed an analytical framework for identifying, understanding, and assessing forest-related conflicts and developed conflict-timber profiles for fifteen countries in Asia and Africa; the profiles were based on information obtained from interviews, the media, nongovernmental organizations (NGOs), and international agencies. The framework, which emphasized the commodity, market, and governance characteristics of forest conflict, was presented to USAID for internal review. The second phase of the CTP involved in-depth case studies in the Democratic Republic of the Congo and Indonesia. The final output of the project, which combined the lessons learned from both phases, was a diagnostic analysis, *Conflict Timber: Dimensions of the Problem in Asia and Africa* (USAID 2003a, 2003b, 2003c).

Conceptualizing forest conflict

The framework developed by ARD had three elements: a two-part definition of forest conflict, an emphasis on the commercial chain of timber production, and country-level case studies. In the two-part definition of forest conflict, Type I conflicts were defined as "conflict financed or sustained through the harvest and sale of timber"; Type II conflicts were defined as "emerging as a result of competition over timber or other forest resources" (USAID 2003a, iii). Examples of Type II conflicts included competition between forest inhabitants and illegal land-grabbers, and between commercial operators and rural populations. Since such competition may be either violent or nonviolent, USAID used an expansive definition that "extends ... beyond violent confrontation to include situations where people who are dependent on forest resources are restricted from using them to the point of seriously affecting their livelihoods or social structure" (USAID 2006b, 1). In other words, the perspective of forest conflict that emerged from the framework was both differentiated and expansive—differentiated in the sense that it drew a sharp distinction between the two forms of conflict, yet expansive in the sense that it bundled together the two forms for the purpose of raising awareness and promoting conflict-sensitive programming. Both forms of conflict were identified as central to conflict management, and both were in play during the empirical, awareness-raising, and policy-advisory phases of the initiative.

A second key aspect of the framework was an emphasis on the commercial chain of timber production—often referred to in scholarly circles as a "commodity chain" or "supply chain" approach.[5] In contrast to analytical frameworks that stress spatially defined units of analysis (such as countries), the commodity chain approach frames production and trade as a sequential chain consisting of linked nodes. Key nodes in the timber commodity chain include logging, the processing of round logs, the fabrication and assembly of timber products, and the marketing and retail sales of the completed products. Figure 1 illustrates a typical supply chain for wood-based products.

One advantage of the commodity chain approach is that it reveals the connections between local forest-related activities and the larger economic forces that drive at least some of the extractive activity—particularly export-oriented activity. A second advantage is that it sheds light on power relations up and down the chain, highlighting potential points of regulatory intervention. For example, it may be more effective to focus regulatory efforts on the nodes in the supply chain where power is more concentrated (e.g., end users) than on diffuse and geographically

---

[5] On commodity chains, see Gereffi and Korzeniewicz (1994). In 1998, S. Tjip Walker (1998), who was employed by OTI at the time, wrote a doctoral dissertation that emphasized this approach.

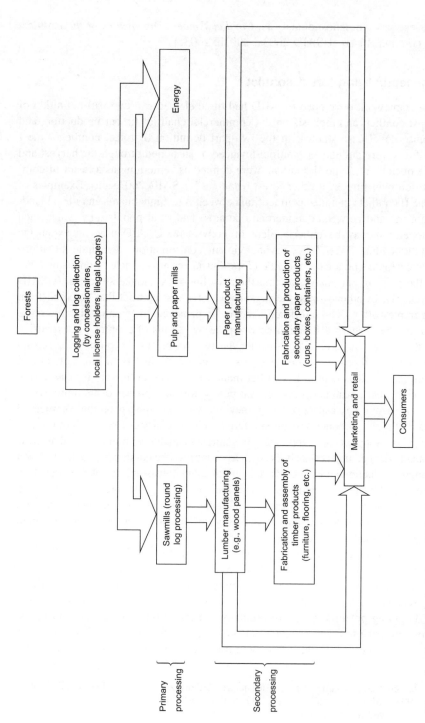

Figure 1. Supply chain for wood-based products

dispersed activities (e.g., illegal logging) that are easily shifted from one location to another. In a global economy, the most powerful nodes of commodity chains may be on the financial side of an industry or in marketing and retailing; they are not necessarily the nodes around which violent conflict coalesces—in this case, logging activities that are undertaken at specific sites.[6] A third and related advantage is that by focusing on material flows and power relations among economic agents, the commodity chain approach can be applied, at least in principle, to both legal and illegal resource extraction.

The commodity chain approach is not without limitations, however.[7] By stressing market relations among profit-driven actors, it may underemphasize political, social, or cultural influences, actors, and relationships. An exclusive focus on the material dimensions of actors' interests may be appropriate for profit-driven actors, but will fail to capture the symbolic or normative significance that a commodity holds for other actors, such as local communities and international activist groups. For example, under the commodity chain approach, an indigenous community or an ethnic minority may simply be viewed as a local group of extractors—a view that potentially oversimplifies conflict dynamics.

As noted earlier, ARD's conceptual framework was based on three analytic categories—commodity characteristics, market characteristics, and governance characteristics—each of which was associated with critical variables that were assumed to shape the propensity for, and the characteristics of, forest-related conflict (see table 1). For example, among commodity characteristics, lootable and more easily concealable products, such as diamonds, are more attractive as a means of financing armed conflict. Similarly, among market characteristics, the larger the number of buyers and sellers, the easier it is to hide individual transactions—which may be useful for actors who extract timber illegally or who wish to hide the source of timber from chain-of-custody monitoring. In addition to suggesting propensity for forest conflict, commodity, market, and governance characteristics suggest points of policy intervention for the prevention or management of forest conflict.

The third element of the analytic framework was a set of country-level case studies. As noted earlier, ARD developed fifteen profiles of countries in Africa and Asia; the goal was to collect data on the commodity chain characteristics and variables shown in table 1 (USAID 2003b, 2003c). Table 2 lists the countries for which profiles were assembled and shows how each country was characterized with regard to the presence of Type I and Type II forest conflict. Notably, all but one of the Africa cases yielded evidence of Type I forest conflict, but little in the way of Type II conflict.[8] The Asia profiles, in contrast, revealed

---

[6] See Conca (2001).
[7] For a useful review of the commodity chain literature, see Uddhammar (2006). See also Clancy (1998); Collins (2000); and Raikes, Jensen, and Ponte (2000).
[8] The relative lack of Type II conflict in Africa can perhaps be attributed to the lack of infrastructure for large-scale commercial timber operations, the presence of which drives much of the Type II conflict in Asia.

Table 1. Variables that influence forest conflict

Analytic category	Key variables
Commodity characteristics	Importance to livelihoods Accessibility Lootability Weight-to-value ratio Concealability Fungibility
Market characteristics	Level of assured demand Number of buyers and sellers Capital intensity of the production process
Governance characteristics	Accountability Ability to make and enforce the rule of law Level of, and trends in, social welfare Degree of social heterogeneity Presence and strength of civil society groups Presence and scope of tenure issues associated with land or other resources

Source: Adapted from USAID (2003a).

widespread Type II conflict, along with Type I conflict in half of the countries profiled. As discussed later in the chapter, these regional differences led to very different patterns of ideational diffusion, policy adoption, emphasis, and follow-up at the programmatic level.

Table 2 also shows the status of each profiled country with respect to armed conflict between 1989 and 2007. As the table indicates, the fifteen profiled countries are a heterogeneous set when it comes to violent conflict. Several are emerging from conflict and may plausibly be characterized as post-conflict (Cambodia, Indonesia, and Nepal in Asia; Liberia and Sierra Leone in Africa). Others have one or more ongoing armed conflicts of varying degrees of intensity (Afghanistan, Myanmar, India, and Pakistan in Asia; Guinea in Africa). A few fit both categories, in that they are emerging from one armed conflict while other armed conflicts endure (the Philippines in Asia; the Democratic Republic of the Congo in Africa). Finally, a few are classified as conflict-free (Laos and Vietnam in Asia; Gabon in Africa).

In the countries listed in table 2, the variations in the level of forest conflict highlight the complexity of the dynamics surrounding forest conflicts. While in some cases forest conflict does not escalate sufficiently to result in a high number of fatalities, in other cases forests are inextricably linked to violent conflict. As noted earlier, violent conflict can also intensify the extraction of forest resources and undermine the rule of law, indirectly contributing to forest conflict.

The target audience: Field missions

The CTP, the first phase of the forest conflict initiative, was not simply intended to address an information gap that had been identified by OTI and ANE; it was

Table 2. Forest conflict and armed conflict in the countries profiled during the Conflict Timber Project

	Forest conflict (as of 2003)		Armed conflict since 1989 (as of 2008)		Forest conflict (as of 2003)		Armed conflict since 1989 (as of 2008)
Asia	Type I	Type II		Africa	Type I	Type II	
Afghanistan	•		War 1989–2001; minor conflict 2003–2004; war since 2005	Democratic Republic of the Congo	•		War 1996–2000; minor conflict 2001 and 2006–2008
Cambodia	•		Minor conflict 1990–1998	Gabon	•		No armed conflict
India	•		Minor conflict on multiple fronts since 1989; intermittent war and minor conflict in Punjab and Kashmir	Guinea		•	Intermittent minor conflict and one-sided violence since 2000
Indonesia	•		Minor conflict 1999–2005 (Aceh); intermittent minor conflict 1989–1998 (Timor-Leste); no conflict since 2005	Liberia	•		Minor conflict 2000–2002; war 2003; no conflict since 2003
Laos	•		Minor conflict 1989–1990; no conflict since 1991	Sierra Leone	•		Minor conflict 1991–1997; war 1998–1999; minor conflict 2000; no conflict since 2001
Myanmar	•		Minor conflicts on multiple fronts and occasional war since 1989				
Nepal	•		Minor conflict 1996–2001; war 2002–2005; minor conflict 2006				
Pakistan	•		Intermittent minor conflict and war on three fronts since 1989				
Philippines	•		War late 1980s, early 1990s; minor conflict since 1993; war 2000; minor conflict since 2001 (Mindanao)				
Vietnam		•	No armed conflict				

Sources: USAID (2003a); Gleditsch et al. (2002); Harbom and Wallensteen (2009).
Notes: The Uppsala Conflict Data Program (UCDP 2008) defines *armed conflict* as "a contested incompatibility that concerns government and/or territory where the use of armed force between two parties, of which at least one is the government of a state, results in at least 25 battle-related deaths." *Minor armed conflict* (which appears in the table as "minor conflict") is defined as 25 to 999 battle-related deaths in one year; *war* is defined as 1,000 or more battle-related deaths in one year. *One-sided violence* is "the use of armed force by the government of a state or by a formally organised group against civilians which results in at least 25 deaths in a year."

also intended to raise consciousness, in USAID country-level field missions, about forest conflict and to promote conflict-sensitive programming. USAID has local missions in twenty-two Asian countries, and the regional field office for ANE is located in Bangkok. While the bureaus in the Washington headquarters are tasked with providing support to the local and regional field missions and making programmatic recommendations, they do not have the authority to allocate resources. As a project initiated at the headquarters offices of OTI and ANE, the CTP therefore had to generate interest and "buy-in" from the country-level field missions; in order for the issues that had been identified in the final CTP report to be addressed, the country-level field missions would first have to be willing to embrace and support the necessary activities.

THE MCAFC PROJECT

Following the publication of the final report, in 2003, which brought the CTP to an end, DCHA and ANE continued to cooperate, to a limited extent, on the forest conflict issue.[9] But ANE also launched (and solely supported) the more comprehensive Managing Conflict in Asian Forest Communities project. The impetus for this project came primarily from the ANE senior advisor for NRM; there was no similar spin-off in the Africa bureau. The MCAFC project was designed to achieve four primary objectives:

- Identifying categories, causes, and patterns of community-level conflict over forests and water.[10]
- Developing approaches to monitoring and managing these conflicts.
- Recommending mechanisms for building these approaches into USAID country-level programming or into the work of partner organizations.
- Communicating the nature and magnitude of natural resource conflict to host-country governments, other donor organizations, NGOs, and the U.S. public and private sectors, particularly wood-based industries (ARD 2006).

The MCAFC project was carried out from August 2003 to February 2007. Working directly with USAID missions in Cambodia, Nepal, the Philippines, and Sri Lanka, project staff sought to obtain more detailed information about forest conflict than had been possible under the CTP, and also to raise the visibility of the forest conflict issue among a broader audience. The original objectives of the CTP—raising awareness, within the Washington headquarters and at the

---

[9] In 2005, the DCHA Office of Conflict Management and Mitigation; the USAID Bureau for Economic Growth, Agriculture and Trade; and ANE jointly produced a tool kit on forests and conflict; it was one in a series of tool kits designed to assist development agencies in addressing the risk factors that contribute to violent conflict (USAID 2005).

[10] Because of the potential for deforestation to cause absolute decline in water supplies and exacerbate conflict, the MCAFC project adopted a holistic approach to NRM that included land, water, and forest resources.

field-mission level, of forest conflict and encouraging the missions to engage in conflict-sensitive programming—gave way to the goal of reaching actors outside the agency, who were viewed as having greater potential to influence activities on the ground. This wider audience included the international donor community, national and international NGOs and civil society groups, and the defense and private sectors. In practice, the MCAFC project consisted of three components— community stakeholder workshops, forums designed to engage international actors, and communications outreach. Over the life of the project, the emphasis shifted in the direction of widening and internationalizing the audience, in order to bring additional actors into efforts to address forest conflict; this shift required greater focus on the forums and communications outreach.

Early MCAFC efforts focused on generating localized information on forest conflict and establishing partnerships at the community level. In 2004, two country assessments were conducted: a comprehensive assessment of forest conflict in Cambodia and a focused assessment of conflicts over natural resources in Sri Lanka, at the watershed level (this assessment was more limited because of ongoing conflict). The Cambodia assessment was followed by a local stakeholder workshop, "Community-Level Impacts of Forest and Land Conflicts in Mondulkiri," which was held in the provincial capital of Sen Monorom and hosted by the USAID Cambodia field office. The workshop included seventy-seven people from indigenous communities, local government, and national and local NGOs. For USAID, one of the most important achievements of the workshop was the presence of thirty-nine members of indigenous communities, who traveled from remote areas to participate in the dialogue and to learn about their rights to land and forest resources under Cambodian law (USAID 2007). After the workshop, the MCAFC project financially supported the work of two Cambodian NGOs that helped forest communities defend their forest use rights —and manage conflicts with encroachers and those with competing claims to the land—by raising awareness of laws, collaborating with local authorities, and engaging in participatory land use planning that included all stakeholders.

In the same month as the Cambodia workshop, a similar workshop was held in the Philippines, in collaboration with the USAID Philippines field office and with strong support from the Philippine Department of Environment and Natural Resources. The workshop included seventy-five participants from the national and local government, NGOs, donors, the private sector, and other experts. Participants identified areas that were under threat from natural resource conflicts and came up with a list of priority actions, such as resolving discrepancies in policies and developing dispute resolution mechanisms. With respect to the workshop, the MCAFC final report noted that

> a leader of an upland farmer federation said this was the first time they were able to discuss and share their experiences with such a diverse audience. He believed that previous development projects failed because they did not identify conflict over natural resources as a critical issue (USAID 2007, 50).

USAID sources have credited the success of both workshops as much to the participatory nature of the project planning phase, which engaged multiple stakeholders, as to the workshops themselves.

In the wake of the in-country workshops, USAID and its implementing partners undertook initiatives designed to bring forest conflict to the attention of a wider international audience. In November 2005, the World Wildlife Fund, in coordination with USAID, hosted a meeting in Washington, D.C., on forest conflict in Asia that was attended by participants from some fifteen environmental, conflict-resolution, and humanitarian-relief NGOs, along with USAID staff (Pendzich 2005). The goals of the meeting were (1) to assess "the impacts related to forest conflict that are of concern to the three major NGO sectors"; (2) to identify "some broad, preferably synchronized actions that can be taken by government, donors, NGOs and industry to reduce and manage forest conflict"; and (3) to help frame the agenda for a subsequent USAID stakeholder workshop with a wider array of participants (Pendzich 2005, 1–2). The attendees discussed the impact of conflict on the environment and key issues that contribute to environmental conflict; they also analyzed current approaches to generate a list of lessons learned. One of the most important observations made at the meeting was that NGOs, which are active primarily at the community level, have the potential to raise awareness among policy makers and thereby facilitate integrated programming that recognizes the interface between conflict and the environment (Pendzich 2005).[11]

In December 2005, USAID and The Forests Dialogue (TFD) jointly sponsored a multi-stakeholder meeting in Washington, D.C. TFD is a forum that brings together owners of private forests and representatives from forest product businesses and environmental- and social-advocacy NGOs. This meeting brought together U.S. government officials and leaders from intergovernmental organizations, NGOs, and the timber industry; the goal was to build partnerships through which each set of actors, in their own spheres of activity, could reduce forest conflict.

Another key outreach event, held in Brussels in February 2006, was a meeting entitled "Security, Development and Forest Conflict: A Forum for Action." Supported by the Center for International Forestry Research, the European Tropical Forest Research Network, the Netherlands Ministry for Foreign Affairs, the UK Department for International Development, and USAID, the meeting was designed to extend the dialogue about forest conflict into Europe and to reach out more directly to the defense and security community.

The Brussels meeting was unique among MCAFC activities in that its primary focus was to bring together various members of the donor community; the sixty participants included national security officials from the United States and several European countries, as well as representatives from the diplomatic corps, foreign-aid agencies, and environment- and security-oriented NGOs. Like other awareness-raising events, the meeting highlighted the governance and commodity

---

[11] See also USAID (2007).

chain aspects of forest conflict, but it also focused on two key objectives: (1) integrating NRM into the broader security agenda (specifically by incorporating natural resource conflict into the work of UN security and peacebuilding institutions) and (2) promoting better coordination between diplomatic, development, and defense organizations' efforts to address forest conflict.

At the same time that the MCAFC project was reaching out more broadly to the donor community and generating awareness among security and development officials in Washington, the project was expanding its activities in Asia. A third detailed assessment, carried out in Nepal in 2005 in conjunction with the USAID field mission, led to programmatic recommendations focused on forest conflict in that country.

Finally, throughout the project, substantial emphasis was placed on developing and implementing a communications strategy. The three major elements of the strategy were the following:

- Reports and brochures to disseminate the information that had been collected during the assessments and to highlight the issue of forest conflict.
- Presentations at meetings of key partners, such as international NGOs and donor agencies.
- A web site that made project output available to policy makers, academics, and the general public.[12]

As a follow-on to the meeting sponsored by TFD and USAID, the Environmental Change and Security Program at the Woodrow Wilson International Center for Scholars, in Washington, D.C., hosted a public panel discussion in December 2005. USAID also produced a film on forest conflict in Cambodia that was shown to a number of audiences; in 2007, it was among the films selected for the Washington, D.C., Environmental Film Festival. In 2007, the final year of the project, three additional outreach activities were undertaken: a second special event was held at the Wilson Center, to present the project's key findings; a video was produced in the Khmer language to foster discussion among Cambodian audiences about reducing conflict and improving livelihoods; and ARD produced the final report on the MCAFC project, which highlighted the many dimensions of forest conflict and the project's major accomplishments.[13]

The forest conflict framework

The framework developed for the CTP, the first phase of the USAID Forest Conflict Initiative, included important conceptual innovations that shaped adoption by key actors in the subsequent MCAFC project. First was the identification, under

---

[12] See www.forestconflict.com.
[13] The data are available on the project web site (www.ardinc.com/us/projects/asia-managing-conflict-in-asian-forest-communities.html).

the broader rubric of forest conflict, of two very different types of conflict (Type I and Type II). In addition to helping to raise the profile of Type II conflict at a time when Type I was the principal focus of media attention, the two-part definition of forest conflict had implications for conflict management. In the realm of post-conflict NRM, the international community had been much more successful at creating frameworks to address Type I conflict than at helping war-torn societies manage Type II conflict.

A second innovative aspect of the framework was the way in which it linked different levels of analysis. Previous work undertaken by bilateral or multilateral aid agencies tended to apply what one interview subject referred to as either top-down or bottom-up frameworks for understanding forest conflict. In a top-down framework, the links between timber commodity extraction and violent conflict are analyzed from a global perspective. A bottom-up approach, in contrast, stresses local land-tenure disputes and other clashes between competing user groups, but not necessarily the transnational markets within which some parties' interests are embedded.

As an example of the top-down approach, one interview subject referred to a 2005 report that was undertaken by Adelphi Research for the USAID Office of Conflict Management and Mitigation (USAID 2005). The report, billed as a tool kit for managing forest conflict, identifies key issues, including the role of timber sales in financing conflict, the use of forests as safe havens by parties in conflict, and low-level violent conflict over logging. But because the tool kit recommendations are applicable only to the global scale rather than to local conditions, they are limited to general policy measures stressing democratic participation, sustainable management, land rights, and effective governance. The top-down approach is useful in framing a problem, raising awareness, and helping to identify strategic priorities. But it has limited utility as a programmatic guide. During interviews with the authors, consultants to USAID on the Forest Conflict Initiative indicated that they understood that their task was to move beyond a general, top-down framework and connect local conditions to broader systemic forces, particularly in international timber markets.

Third, despite the limitations of the commodity chain perspective, the USAID framework allowed a more nuanced approach to the problem because it linked the global trade in forest products to conflicts that had previously been regarded as purely local. One interview subject contrasted the USAID approach with that of the World Bank—which, he said, viewed forest conflict solely as a governance issue. The same interviewee noted that the private sector, as well, tended to focus narrowly on the illegal logging aspect of forest conflict. Because the USAID framework both deepens and enlarges the definition of forest conflict, and thereby expands potential approaches to conflict management, it is an improvement on previous models used by key players.

By highlighting certain social relations and causal mechanisms at the expense of others, analytical frameworks influence what researchers "see"—and therefore what they recommend. The three sections that follow consider the effects of the USAID framework on the Forest Conflict Initiative.

field-mission level, of forest conflict and encouraging the missions to engage in conflict-sensitive programming—gave way to the goal of reaching actors outside the agency, who were viewed as having greater potential to influence activities on the ground. This wider audience included the international donor community, national and international NGOs and civil society groups, and the defense and private sectors. In practice, the MCAFC project consisted of three components—community stakeholder workshops, forums designed to engage international actors, and communications outreach. Over the life of the project, the emphasis shifted in the direction of widening and internationalizing the audience, in order to bring additional actors into efforts to address forest conflict; this shift required greater focus on the forums and communications outreach.

Early MCAFC efforts focused on generating localized information on forest conflict and establishing partnerships at the community level. In 2004, two country assessments were conducted: a comprehensive assessment of forest conflict in Cambodia and a focused assessment of conflicts over natural resources in Sri Lanka, at the watershed level (this assessment was more limited because of ongoing conflict). The Cambodia assessment was followed by a local stakeholder workshop, "Community-Level Impacts of Forest and Land Conflicts in Mondulkiri," which was held in the provincial capital of Sen Monorom and hosted by the USAID Cambodia field office. The workshop included seventy-seven people from indigenous communities, local government, and national and local NGOs. For USAID, one of the most important achievements of the workshop was the presence of thirty-nine members of indigenous communities, who traveled from remote areas to participate in the dialogue and to learn about their rights to land and forest resources under Cambodian law (USAID 2007). After the workshop, the MCAFC project financially supported the work of two Cambodian NGOs that helped forest communities defend their forest use rights —and manage conflicts with encroachers and those with competing claims to the land—by raising awareness of laws, collaborating with local authorities, and engaging in participatory land use planning that included all stakeholders.

In the same month as the Cambodia workshop, a similar workshop was held in the Philippines, in collaboration with the USAID Philippines field office and with strong support from the Philippine Department of Environment and Natural Resources. The workshop included seventy-five participants from the national and local government, NGOs, donors, the private sector, and other experts. Participants identified areas that were under threat from natural resource conflicts and came up with a list of priority actions, such as resolving discrepancies in policies and developing dispute resolution mechanisms. With respect to the workshop, the MCAFC final report noted that

> a leader of an upland farmer federation said this was the first time they were able to discuss and share their experiences with such a diverse audience. He believed that previous development projects failed because they did not identify conflict over natural resources as a critical issue (USAID 2007, 50).

USAID sources have credited the success of both workshops as much to the participatory nature of the project planning phase, which engaged multiple stakeholders, as to the workshops themselves.

In the wake of the in-country workshops, USAID and its implementing partners undertook initiatives designed to bring forest conflict to the attention of a wider international audience. In November 2005, the World Wildlife Fund, in coordination with USAID, hosted a meeting in Washington, D.C., on forest conflict in Asia that was attended by participants from some fifteen environmental, conflict-resolution, and humanitarian-relief NGOs, along with USAID staff (Pendzich 2005). The goals of the meeting were (1) to assess "the impacts related to forest conflict that are of concern to the three major NGO sectors"; (2) to identify "some broad, preferably synchronized actions that can be taken by government, donors, NGOs and industry to reduce and manage forest conflict"; and (3) to help frame the agenda for a subsequent USAID stakeholder workshop with a wider array of participants (Pendzich 2005, 1–2). The attendees discussed the impact of conflict on the environment and key issues that contribute to environmental conflict; they also analyzed current approaches to generate a list of lessons learned. One of the most important observations made at the meeting was that NGOs, which are active primarily at the community level, have the potential to raise awareness among policy makers and thereby facilitate integrated programming that recognizes the interface between conflict and the environment (Pendzich 2005).[11]

In December 2005, USAID and The Forests Dialogue (TFD) jointly sponsored a multi-stakeholder meeting in Washington, D.C. TFD is a forum that brings together owners of private forests and representatives from forest product businesses and environmental- and social-advocacy NGOs. This meeting brought together U.S. government officials and leaders from intergovernmental organizations, NGOs, and the timber industry; the goal was to build partnerships through which each set of actors, in their own spheres of activity, could reduce forest conflict.

Another key outreach event, held in Brussels in February 2006, was a meeting entitled "Security, Development and Forest Conflict: A Forum for Action." Supported by the Center for International Forestry Research, the European Tropical Forest Research Network, the Netherlands Ministry for Foreign Affairs, the UK Department for International Development, and USAID, the meeting was designed to extend the dialogue about forest conflict into Europe and to reach out more directly to the defense and security community.

The Brussels meeting was unique among MCAFC activities in that its primary focus was to bring together various members of the donor community; the sixty participants included national security officials from the United States and several European countries, as well as representatives from the diplomatic corps, foreign-aid agencies, and environment- and security-oriented NGOs. Like other awareness-raising events, the meeting highlighted the governance and commodity

---

[11] See also USAID (2007).

The definition of forest conflict

The definition of forest conflict adopted as part of the project framework reflected the need to draw attention to localized, endemic Type II conflict. "Hitching a ride" with the higher-profile Type I conflict did garner significant attention for Type II conflict. But given the lack of documented connections between Type I and Type II, the quest for more conflict-sensitive USAID initiatives could go only so far. Without strong evidence that Type II conflict, when left unaddressed, created conditions for Type I conflict, the project findings gave field missions no incentive to manage Type II situations in order to forestall Type I problems. As one USAID staffer noted, the empirical evidence is simply lacking: longitudinal studies would be needed to document how Type II evolves into Type I, but no one has undertaken this type of study. Another USAID staffer not connected to the initiative suggested that from a conflict management perspective, the distinction between Type I and Type II was not particularly relevant; the key question was whether *any* form of conflict attained such scope or intensity that the agency felt obliged to respond programmatically.

The commodity chain approach

As noted earlier, the commodity chain approach, by emphasizing production, consumption, and governance relations up and down the supply chain, focuses attention on certain actors and interests at the expense of others. For example, one interview subject with extensive experience in community forestry noted that community-based NRM tends to be organized at the hamlet level—a level of social aggregation substantially below even the most localized state-based governance. NRM activities at this level—or conflicts that occur when such systems clash with wider-scale state actions—may not be captured in a commodity chain framework.

A second disadvantage of the commodity chain approach is its limited ability to situate conflicts that are specific to a given node in the supply chain, or that occur between different nodes, within a larger context of violent conflict. Thus, the evidence generated by the USAID framework revealed few or no explicit linkages between Type I and Type II conflict—implying that, from a management perspective, they are largely separable problems. In the absence of an analysis that takes into account both the local aspects of the conflict and the larger international context, it is difficult to establish the relationship, in a particular instance of forest conflict, between conflict that is caused by opportunism and conflict that is caused by grievances or deprivation.

The analytic categories

Of the three sets of characteristics used to assess the propensity for forest conflict—commodity characteristics, market characteristics, and governance characteristics—the first two function not as variables but as constants, because they are difficult to manipulate within the short time horizons available to key stakeholders. Commodity characteristics are largely determined by the nature of forest resources, and market characteristics are not easily influenced at the level of USAID programming, particularly during projects with short life cycles. As a result, the third set—governance characteristics—moved to center stage, as is evident in the 2003 CTP final report, which lists four "key interrelated characteristics" as common to episodes of timber conflict. All four relate to governance:

- "There is a direct and strong link between conflict timber and poor, inequitable systems of governance."
- "Governments are almost always complicit in conflict timber activities."
- "Loose financial oversight generates incentives for powerful individual actors (military, police, politicians) to engage in conflict timber activities."
- "Ambiguous land/resource tenure promotes struggles over timber" (USAID 2003a, iii–iv).

Essentially, the framework construes forest conflict management as a matter of regulating market activity—which translates, in turn, into a focus on the legality of extractive activities and the legal framework governing property rights and forest access.

Laws, rule-making processes, property rights regimes, and oversight mechanisms thus emerge as the key levers for forest conflict management. This approach is somewhat limited, however, because it is not always simple to separate what is legal from what is illegal. The same activities may be legal in one national context and illegal in a neighboring country. For example, encroachment by settlers or extractive industries may cause conflicts with local populations, regardless of whether access is authorized under national law. Similarly, changes in the law can render previously illegal activities legal, or vice versa. Nor does the law have universally legitimate authority: many communities with long-standing ties to forests question the legitimacy of the state's forestry laws (USAID 2003a).

The emphasis on governance—and hence, on legality—has reinforced the view, among some of the USAID-targeted stakeholders, that forest conflict is essentially a problem of illegality. But this approach may fail to adequately address conflicts that arise when legal practice does not reflect the interests of those with traditional or cultural claims, or those who must access forest resources to meet subsistence needs. New standards developed by the Indonesian Ministry of Forestry, with the assistance of USAID, recognize the limits of a narrow legal perspective: under these standards, which were adopted in 2009, the legality of timber concessions is determined, in part, by local community and stakeholder participation and consistency with customary law (Ministry of Forestry 2009).

Adoption by key actors

Although the initial objective of the Forest Conflict Initiative was to raise awareness, among individual USAID missions, of the importance of integrating conflict-sensitive NRM into agency programming, the first phase of the project made it clear that the issue was on a far greater scale than any one mission could address. Given the complex ways that forest conflict was embedded in timber markets, national development plans, and conservation initiatives, and the many levels on which rule making and institution building occurred, it was imperative for the project to raise awareness among a larger and heterogeneous audience.

This realization led to a conscious expansion of the target audience to include four key constituencies:

- Governmental actors in Asia, who were responsible for national forest management policies.
- NGOs that served as the implementing partners for an array of USAID programs in forestry and biodiversity.
- The international donor community, which was in a position to determine whether the issue would receive higher priority in foreign assistance.
- Private-sector actors, who occupied positions of power in international commodity chains for forest products.

The in-country workshops and stakeholder meetings in Washington, D.C., and Brussels were key forums in which the project findings were disseminated among a broader set of actors at the international level.

In particular, the framework developed during the CTP and the subsequent country assessments highlighted the need to engage the private sector. This effort was made easier by recent data demonstrating that illegally harvested timber, much of it tied to violent conflict, was undercutting the market share of major players in international timber markets to a much greater extent than had previously been realized.[14]

A new target: The private sector

Attempting to engage and influence private-sector actors in the region's timber and wood-processing sectors created particular challenges for a bilateral donor agency such as USAID. As noted earlier in the chapter, regulating market activity is challenging because of the short time horizons of the projects. Moreover, some interview subjects regarded such efforts as being outside USAID's mandate,

---

[14] At the USAID's December 2005 workshop, in Washington, in which one of the authors of this chapter participated, several participants stressed the influence of new analyses of the market impacts of illegal timber.

although this was a contested position. One way the agency sought to reach out to the private sector was by providing financial support to the Responsible Asia Forestry and Trade program (RAFT), which had been developed by the Nature Conservancy. RAFT was an outgrowth of the Global Development Alliance to Promote Forest Certification and Combat Illegal Logging in Indonesia (which had also been sponsored by USAID), through which NGOs such as The Nature Conservancy and the World Wildlife Fund partnered with private-sector timber firms in Indonesia to promote sustainable forest management.

RAFT's goal is to build on the initial success of the alliance in Indonesia by expanding it to a regional scale. RAFT engages NGOs, governments, and the private sector in an effort to do the following:

> Increase regional timber trade from legal sources.... Improve sustainability of forest management on the ground.... Strengthen regional cooperation on forest management and trade ... [and] Contribute towards climate change abatement by reducing CO_2 emissions from forest loss and degradation and enhancing regional capacity for sustainable forest management through the emerging international REDD framework (USAID 2006a, 2).

RAFT works with private-sector timber firms to help facilitate compliance with the standards of sustainable and legal logging practice. How RAFT addresses each country in the region depends on its place in the global supply chain—which suggests that the CTP's commodity chain emphasis could translate into policy implementation. In source countries, such as Indonesia, RAFT provides assistance with forest management, whereas in wood-processing countries, such as Vietnam and China, RAFT focuses on establishing and implementing policies to reduce imports from uncertified timber sources. In smaller countries, such as Laos and Cambodia, which have less developed timber industries, RAFT focuses on improving community management through technical assistance and training, rather than on an industrial regulatory model that requires the development and implementation of import policy. By focusing on "pressure points," RAFT has succeeded in changing the behavior of land managers who are influenced by the commercial and regulatory environment.

The military: A missed target?

Although there was no consensus on this point, some interview subjects (both inside and outside USAID) felt that the military may have been underemphasized as a target audience. Apart from the Brussels meeting, there is little evidence that attempts were made to actively bring the defense sector into the process.

Engaging the national military in efforts to address forest conflict is a complex and context-specific undertaking. Some interview subjects suggested that because of its direct contact with local military organizations, the U.S. military could, through cooperative activities, contribute to peacebuilding. Interview subjects stressed the importance of context, however. When a country is using timber to finance conflict—as was the case, for example, in Indonesia under Suharto—engaging the military in that country may be essential in order to break the timber-conflict link, and military-to-military contacts could conceivably play a role in doing so. But where the sale of timber is an illegal, renegade activity, the interests of military forces may be at odds with the peacebuilding effort because the military itself is engaged in logging for self-financing, or is providing access and protection to private loggers. One interview subject with many years of experience in the region dismissed the importance of the military-to-military channel, arguing that it was not central in cases where local military forces were not involved, and unworkable in cases where they were.

The original target: Country-level missions

The original intent of the USAID Forest Conflict Initiative—to persuade country-level USAID missions to address forest conflict in their programming—appears to have had mixed results. Conversations with USAID staff and observers of the agency's forest-related activities yielded a set of variables that seemed to influence policy adoption at the mission level and that are worthy of more targeted field research:

- *Relevance to the mission's current programming.* Mission staff were more likely to be receptive if the implementing partners of the Forest Conflict Initiative could contribute to the mission's existing program objectives or provide evidence and attention that would support current post-conflict programming. In Cambodia, for example, mission staff reportedly did not view the objectives of the Forest Conflict Initiative as fitting closely with the mission's priorities, whereas mission staff in Nepal viewed the project as providing further corroboration of their perspective on conflict dynamics in the country, and as a means of generating visibility in Washington.
- *Availability of resources.* Where mission activities related to forest conflict were supported by funds from Washington, the project was not viewed as competing with the mission's own activities, funding, or goals; this helped to generate support.
- *The perspectives of staff on the connections between forests and conflict, and on the tractability of forest conflict.* In some instances, where forest conflict stemmed from competing pressures generated by economic development, poor governance, and local subsistence needs, mission staff viewed the problems as complex and endemic processes that they could not directly address. Moreover, the direct connections between these conflicts and violent conflict were not always readily apparent, which increased the mission staff's perception that the project's objectives were outside of the scope of post-conflict programming. In some instances, the implementing partners had to actively sell the Forest Conflict Initiative as a strategic opportunity for the missions.

- *Ties and tensions between USAID headquarters in Washington and the mission.* In a few cases, mission staff experienced a disconnect between mission-level programming and the programming priorities generated by the Washington headquarters; when mission staff felt that they were being told what to do by people who were not engaged in the day-to-day realities of the situation, they were sometimes resistant. Although the USAID organizational structure makes such tensions inevitable, several factors here—including the complexity of forest-conflict linkages, the variability of conditions within and across the forests of the region, and a similar variability in the dynamics of violent conflicts and peace processes—combined to make the tensions between headquarters and the field missions a particular challenge.
- *Timing.* In some cases, the extent of policy adoption or the nature of the response at the mission level was simply a matter of personalities and timing. Changes in mission staff affected the level of interest in programming that integrated a more conflict-sensitive approach to NRM, as did internal personnel constraints and opportunities presented by a change in the local political situation, which could bring new actors or interests to the fore. For example, one interview subject with project experience in many countries in the region suggested that political transitions provide leverage for efforts to enact change, citing Indonesia as an example of a place where the USAID initiative may have had an easier time gaining traction when the political situation was in flux.

CONCLUSIONS: EFFECTIVENESS AND IMPLICATIONS

The expansion, transformation, and implementation of the USAID Forest Conflict Initiative lead to some observations about the effectiveness of the project. These observations, in turn, suggest some broader lessons on the integration of conflict-sensitive NRM into peacebuilding.

The effectiveness of the Forest Conflict Initiative in Asia

Overall, the effectiveness of the USAID Forest Conflict Initiative was mixed. Several important achievements emerged from the CTP and the MCAFC project:

- USAID developed a heightened awareness of forest conflict.
- An analytic framework was developed that combined local factors with wider systemic influences—which increased awareness of the more pervasive, but less attention-grabbing, Type II forest conflicts.
- In a few countries in the region, national workshops brought together representatives from government, NGOs, and local communities.
- Links were forged between a variety of international stakeholder groups.

These achievements led, in turn, to a more explicit recognition of forest conflict in mission-level programming in Asia, and to the integration of local-level conflict resolution into environmental agendas in the region.

The initiative also shed light on key variables that seem to shape the integration of issues such as forest conflict into field-level USAID operations (and perhaps bilateral donor agency operations more generally): relevance, resources, staff perspectives, tensions between missions and headquarters, and timing. In this particular case, these variables often interacted in ways that limited full understanding and appreciation of the message about the need for a conflict-sensitive approach to NRM. As a result, at least with regard to forests, conflict-sensitive NRM has yet to be fully integrated into USAID peacebuilding strategies (whether they are labeled explicitly as such or not).

Another limitation on the impact of the initiative came from the tendency of key international constituencies to "hear what they want to hear" when confronted with a complex problem such as forest conflict. For some private sector actors, the issue quickly became a matter of certifying that timber extraction was legal and "sustainable" (variously defined). For others, such as local NGOs, dealing with forest conflict was a matter of empowering communities to more effectively report information about abuses, as a means of catalyzing supportive advocacy. Still others emphasized empowering local communities through the reform of property rights and rules of access. While each of these approaches may play a key role in the challenge of managing forest conflict, the centrality of conflict management can be lost in the application of narrower strategies that reflect the familiar objectives of industry, or environmentalists, or aid agencies.

The initiative's analytic framework also influenced its effectiveness. On the one hand, two characteristics of the framework—the links between localized conflicts and global commodity chains, and the inclusion of both Type I and Type II conflicts—made it possible to consider the problem more comprehensively and to bring together constituencies that had not previously engaged in dialogue on forest conflict. For example, it was through the initiative that NGOs dealing with forest conservation; humanitarian aid to war-torn societies; and conflict resolution, peacebuilding, and reconciliation were brought together to discuss forest conflict. Similarly, by highlighting the market implications of illicit timber extraction, the commodity chain approach helped to mobilize legitimate commercial actors to engage in broader discussions of the problem.

On the other hand, the commodity chain approach and the key variables on which it focused (commodity, market, and governance characteristics) clearly pushed the effects of the initiative in specific directions. Because both commodity and market characteristics were essentially constants, policy conversations converged on the common ground of governance—which, although it is a crucial element of conflict-sensitive forest management, fails to address a number of issues. What happens, for example, when Type II conflict is played out at the hamlet or village level, outside the state's reach? What happens when unsustainable and unjust timber extraction are, within the prevailing governance patterns, entirely legal? How do governance strategies for Type I conflict, which stress legalization, regulation, and certification, affect Type II conflicts, which often exist not because of the absence of governance but because some stakeholders resist or reject the legitimacy of state-based rules?

Finally, the number and variety of actors that USAID was trying to engage forced the initiative to balance two objectives: generating mission-level programming guidelines within USAID and catalyzing action among key actors in the larger environment within which the agency operates. Essentially, the initiative reached the water's edge of two important, but very different, accomplishments: creating the sort of detailed operational tool kit that would be useful at the mission level, and creating a sustained stakeholder network that could keep attention focused on forest conflict within the wider political context of agency activities.

Implications for post-conflict peacebuilding

The USAID Forest Conflict Initiative was not framed explicitly as post-conflict peacebuilding. Nevertheless, the agency's experience yields some important lessons for this volume. Many of the countries on which the initiative focused are emerging from protracted violent conflict. The data generated by the initiative provide the closest look, to date, at the dynamics of forest conflict in those settings and have yielded a number of insights, a few of which stand out.[15]

First, Type II conflicts—which involve competing uses of forests; contested understandings of what rules, claims, and practices are legitimate; and differing capacities, among actors, to press their claims under existing governance mechanisms—are pervasive in Asia. Nevertheless, among some actors that the initiative tried to (or could have tried to) engage, the absence or indirectness of connections between Type II and Type I conflict reduced the salience of forest conflict in general. In the post-conflict setting, however, it is precisely through the more diffuse Type II conflicts that poor forest governance is most likely to derail peacebuilding.

Second, the data generated by the initiative revealed the pervasive presence of state-based actors in both Type I and Type II conflicts, the often ambiguous character of tenure systems and rules of access, and the varying degrees of legitimacy that local actors ascribe to state-based rule systems. This combination of conditions raises some profound questions about the meaning of such staple concepts of peacebuilding as "the rule of law" and "good governance," particularly in the context of forest management. As the analysis has shown, better governance may not be a sufficient solution when the state is complicit in the exploitation of forests and national legal codes conflict with traditional local practices. Effective solutions must therefore take into account the various stakeholders and levels of government involved in the conflict.

---

[15] Available in the final reports and on the forest conflict web site (www.forestconflict.com).

Another set of lessons derives from the empirical picture of an initiative, conducted inside a bilateral aid agency, which sought to raise the salience of forest conflict for a range of actors both inside and outside the agency. To improve conditions on the ground, it is essential to understand the obstacles to adoption of integrated post-conflict programming. If attention to NRM is central to peacebuilding, then the capacity of bilateral donors to promote greater conflict sensitivity in NRM, as well as greater NRM sensitivity in post-conflict settings, is certainly one key to establishing a sustainable peace.

Finally, a wider theme stands out. Although the framework used by the initiative succeeded in bringing key stakeholders to the table, it became clear that the more nuanced framework that would be needed to move beyond awareness to sustained action at any particular node in the commodity chain was lacking. Hence, a dilemma: without a unifying narrative, it is impossible to assemble the requisite cast of players to address a problem as complex and multilayered as forest conflict. But that same unifying narrative risks narrowing the focus to core concepts—timber, commodity chains, governance—that are of limited value for understanding and managing forest resources, and the conflicts that surround them, in a post-conflict setting.

REFERENCES

ARD (Associates for Rural Development). 2006. Asia: Managing conflict in Asian forest communities. www.ardinc.com/projects/detail_sector.php?id=84.

Clancy, M. 1998. Commodity chains, services and development. *Review of International Political Economy* 5 (1): 122–148.

Collins, J. L. 2000. Tracing social relations in commodity chains: The case of grapes in Brazil. In *Commodities and globalization: Anthropological perspectives,* ed. A. Haugerud, M. P. Stone, and P. D. Little. Oxford, UK: Rowman & Littlefield.

Conca, K. 2001. Consumption and environment in a global economy. *Global Environmental Politics* 1 (3): 53–71.

———. 2006. *Governing water: Contentious transnational politics and global institution building.* Cambridge, MA: MIT Press.

Fujita, Y., K. Phanvilay, and D. Donovan. 2007. Past conflicts and resource use in postwar Lao PDR. In *Extreme conflict and tropical forests,* ed. W. De Jong, D. Donovan, and K. Abe. Dordrecht, Netherlands: Springer.

Gereffi, G., and M. Korzeniewicz, eds. 1994. *Commodity chains and global capitalism.* Westport, CT: Praeger.

Gleditsch, N. P., P. Wallensteen, M. Eriksson, M. Sollenberg, and H. Strand. 2002. Armed conflict 1946–2001: A new dataset. *Journal of Peace Research* 39 (5): 615–637.

Global Witness. 2001. *Taylor-made: The pivotal role of Liberia's forests and flag of convenience in regional conflict.* London.

Harbom, L., and P. Wallensteen. 2009. Armed conflict 1946–2008. *Journal of Peace Research* 46:577–587.

Le Billon, P. 2000. The political ecology of transition in Cambodia 1989–1999: War, peace and forest exploitation. *Development and Change* 31 (4): 785–805.

Martin, A. 2005. Environmental conflict between refugee and host communities. *Journal of Peace Research* 42 (3): 329–346.

Ministry of Forestry (Indonesia). 2009. Director general of forestry production development's regulation number: P.6/Vi-Set/2009 concerning standards and guidelines on assessment of performance in sustainable production forest management and timber legality verification. Jakarta.

Oglethorpe, J., R. Ham, J. Shambaugh, and H. van der Linde. 2002. Overview C: Conservation in times of war. In *Conserving the peace: Resources, livelihoods and security,* ed. R. Matthew, M. Halle, and J. Switzer. Winnipeg: International Institute for Sustainable Development / International Union for Conservation of Nature.

Pendzich, C. 2005. A conservation and development perspective on forest conflict. Paper presented at the USAID workshop "Building Partnerships to Reduce Forest Conflict in Asia," November, Washington, D.C.

Raikes, P., M. F. Jensen, and S. Ponte. 2000. Global commodity chain analysis and the French *filière* approach: Comparison and critique. *Economy and Society* 29 (3): 390–417.

Richards, P. 2001. Are "forest wars" in Africa resource conflicts? The case of Sierra Leone. In *Violent environments,* ed. N. L. Peluso and M. Watts. Ithaca, NY: Cornell University Press.

Rustad, S. A., J. K. Rød, W. Larsen, and N. P. Gleditsch. 2008. Foliage and fighting: Forest resources and the onset, duration and location of civil war. *Political Geography* 27 (7): 761–782.

UCDP (Uppsala Conflict Data Program). 2008. UCDP database. www.ucdp.uu.se/database.

———. n.d. UCDP definitions. www2.pcr.uu.se/research/UCDP/data_and_publications/definitions_all.htm.

Uddhammar, E. 2006. Development, conservation and tourism: Conflict or symbiosis? *Review of International Political Economy* 13 (4): 656–678.

USAID (U.S. Agency for International Development). 2003a. *Conflict timber: Dimensions of the problem in Asia and Africa. Volume I: Synthesis report.* Washington, D.C.

———. 2003b. *Conflict timber: Dimensions of the problem in Asia and Africa. Volume II: Asia cases.* Washington, D.C.

———. 2003c. *Conflict timber: Dimensions of the problem in Asia and Africa. Volume III: Africa cases.* Washington, D.C.

———. 2005. *Forests and conflict: A toolkit for intervention.* Washington, D.C.

———. 2006a. Environmental cooperation—Asia (ECO-Asia): Responsible Asia forestry and trade. www.usaid.eco-asia.org/files/fact_sheets/RAFT.pdf.

———. 2006b. *Forest conflict in Asia: How big is the problem?* Washington, D.C.

———. 2007. *Forest conflict in Asia: Causes, impacts and management.* Final report of the Managing Conflict in Asian Forest Communities Project. Washington, D.C.

Walker, S. T. 1998. Both pretense and promise: The political economy of privatization in Africa. Ph.D. diss., University of Indiana.

Women in the artisanal and small-scale mining sector of the Democratic Republic of the Congo

Karen Hayes and Rachel Perks

This chapter focuses on women who work and live in the diverse, complex, and often-neglected artisanal and small-scale mining (ASM) communities of the Democratic Republic of the Congo (DRC). ASM encompasses both the manual extraction and processing of minerals and their subsequent trade. Much of ASM is informal, and it is often characterized by dangerous practices and harmful social and environmental impacts.[1] Although many ASM communities have existed for years or even centuries, other communities have begun to engage in mining relatively recently, mostly as a result of poverty.

Although women throughout the DRC continue to be affected by protracted conflict and the aftermath of war, there are several reasons to focus on women in ASM. First, ASM supports 16 to 20 percent of the population of the DRC and is a critical economic driver in the country's move out of war (World Bank 2008). Because women make up as much as 50 percent of the ASM labor force and are often their families' principal providers (Hinton, Veiga, and Beinhoff 2003), what happens in the ASM sector has tremendous economic implications for the country as a whole. As ASM transitions from an informal and unregulated sector—historically associated with war and corruption—into a more efficient and formal labor economy, it will face massive challenges. To the extent that women can play an equal role in that transition, they have the opportunity not only to achieve greater empowerment and participation in social and political life, but to help

---

Karen Hayes is the Africa director for corporate community engagement at Pact. Rachel Perks, currently a Ph.D. candidate at the School for Agriculture, Policy and Development at the University of Reading, is the former country director for Pact in the Democratic Republic of the Congo.

[1] In the DRC, ASM is legal under the conditions defined in the 2002 Mining Code and in the ASM Code of Conduct, which is included in the 2003 Mining Regulations. For ASM to be legal, a miner must operate only within officially designated artisanal mining zones; hold a valid artisanal miner's license; be over eighteen years of age; respect environmental standards; and not use mercury or explosives. Since there is only one legal artisanal mining zone in the entire country, virtually all ASM occurs outside the law.

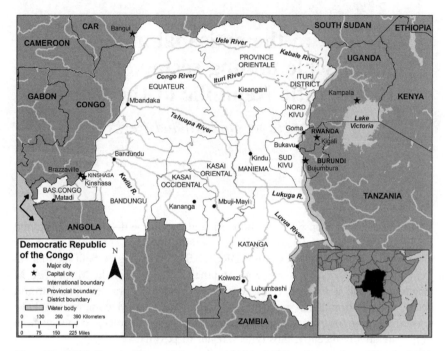

Note: The DRC Constitution, which was ratified in 2005 and came into effect in 2006, mandates that within three years the eleven provinces be redivided into twenty-six. As of June 2011, the redivision had not yet taken place.

move the country forward. Second, because of complex historical and cultural factors, the DRC is currently suffering from an epidemic of sexual and gender-based violence (SGBV), which includes not only rape, but also precocious marriage and forced prostitution. During the war, rape was used as a weapon, but the practice did not end with the war. The legacy of SGBV is being perpetuated in ASM communities; it therefore makes sense, from a practical perspective, to emphasize the prevention and reduction of SGBV in those communities.

Women in ASM communities are doubly at risk—as residents of rural or peri-urban areas that are emerging from war or suffering from reduced livelihood opportunities, and as informal workers subject to precarious social, economic, and environmental conditions. Nevertheless, ASM represents a tangible—and, in the short term, valuable—economic opportunity for both men and women in the DRC. ASM needs little advance investment or lead time, and therefore has significant potential to provide quick economic returns. If the sector's association with conflict and abuse could be removed, its potential to generate peace dividends could be great. But for such a transition to occur, a deliberate and comprehensive recognition of the current and potential role of women who work in ASM is required.

Although the DRC has technically been at peace since 2002, when the transitional government was put in place, security remains fragile, particularly in the east. DDR (demilitarization, demobilization, and reintegration) has been fraught with problems, and the pillars of local governance, economic opportunity, and social cohesion are being rebuilt at an alarmingly slow pace. Moreover, as is often the case in a society emerging from conflict, the structures and norms that once guided social practice have lost some of their potency. In ASM communities in particular, the traditional leadership has often been replaced, corrupted, or coerced by the new hierarchy of mine control;[2] in this void, certain behaviors flourish, particularly among men: survivalism, a sense of impunity, and a tendency to escape through drug and alcohol abuse. Women, meanwhile, remain extremely vulnerable, which curtails their impact on the peacebuilding process.

People who have suffered through protracted conflicts tend to gauge the value of peace by the social, economic, and political benefits they derive from it. Though such benefits are often judged on the basis of essential social services (e.g., education, health care, clean water), the "peace dividend" must also include the ability to go about daily activities without experiencing serious physical or psychological threats, and to actively participate in economic and political decision making.

Though many Congolese women would argue that prewar social practice did not promote respect or equal opportunity for women, they would nevertheless agree that before the conflict, traditional structures provided some positive influence and some degree of security. In the DRC, peacebuilding at the local level requires reestablishing the security of communities where men and women play equally important, though perhaps different, roles. Security is not limited to physical protection but includes all aspects of life—most notably economic opportunity, health and well-being, and participation in community governance.

In the spirit of UN Security Council Resolutions 1325 and 1820,[3] which reaffirm the central role of women in peacebuilding, this chapter focuses on the intersection of high-value resources and gender roles in the post-conflict setting. Specifically, it draws on efforts to address the needs of women working in the

---

[2] This hierarchy may include the mine owners, the investors who finance the activity, the traders who purchase the material, official and unofficial security forces, the police, the army, rebel soldiers, and predatory officials who take advantage of lack of knowledge of the law to assign themselves self-designed roles.

[3] Security Council Resolution 1325, adopted unanimously on October 31, 2000, created a political framework that makes women—and a gender-based perspective—relevant to negotiating peace agreements, planning refugee camps and peacekeeping operations, and reconstructing war-torn societies (UNSC 2000). Security Council Resolution 1820, adopted June 19, 2008, demands that parties to armed conflict adopt concrete measures to end sexual violence, including training troops, enforcing military discipline, and upholding responsibility along the chain of command. It also asserts the importance of women's participation in all processes, including peace talks, that are related to ending sexual violence in the context of conflict (UNSC 2008c).

copper and cobalt mines of Katanga Province and in the gold mines of Ituri District, in Orientale Province.

The chapter is divided into five major sections: (1) background on the relationship between ASM and conflict; (2) a discussion of gender roles in the post-conflict environment of the DRC; (3) a description of two programs that have been used to empower women in ASM communities; (4) a list of recommendations for the future; and (5) a brief conclusion.

BACKGROUND: ASM AND CONFLICT

The DRC has one of the greatest mineral resource endowments of any country in the world, including gold, diamonds, copper, cobalt, tin, tantalum, tungsten, uranium, and semiprecious gemstones. From the 1880s to 1960, when the country was under colonial rule, industrial mining flourished; even when production deteriorated, under Mobutu's rule (1965–1997), mining still accounted for 70 to 80 percent of export earnings and about 8 percent of gross domestic product. Since the early 1990s, however, industrial mining has declined substantially; extraction is now dominated by ASM, which accounts for 90 percent of all mineral production and provides full-time, seasonal, or supplementary livelihoods for roughly two million people (World Bank 2008). ASM occurs in every province of the country, but it is most concentrated in the diamond fields of the Kasai provinces and in the provinces along the eastern frontier (Orientale, Nord Kivu, Sud Kivu, Maniema, and Katanga).

ASM is characterized by basic, manual mining techniques. It is largely unregulated, and miners are exposed to a wide range of physical hazards. It is also associated with a number of social and economic problems, including diversion of livelihoods from more sustainable activities; squalid camp conditions, where substance abuse and sexual promiscuity create health risks; child labor; environmental damage and localized inflation. Nevertheless, ASM makes possible the exploitation of ore bodies that are too small or too remote to justify the investment required for large-scale, commercial mining—and thus has an important role to play in the mining sector. As currently practiced in the DRC, however, ASM is inefficient because the technical skills required to identify, plan, develop, and exploit mines to their full potential are lacking. As a consequence, ASM ends up degrading the overall value of the ore body while simultaneously consuming or contaminating other resources—such as wood, land, and water—which could be essential to livelihoods once the ore is exhausted. As currently conducted, ASM may deliver short-term financial gains to the miners and traders who are directly involved, but it may also exacerbate local poverty in the long term.

In the DRC, ASM has been associated with, and at times directly linked to, conflict. In what became known as Africa's World War (1996–2002), foreign armies, local militias, and foreign, nonstate armed groups sought control of mining sites throughout the country, both for their long-term value and as a means of financing the war effort (Hartung and Moix 2000). Minerals extracted by artisanal workers were used, in part, to purchase arms and fund other costs associated with the conflict.[4]

The broader conflicts surrounding resource extraction are complicated, and ASM does play a role in those conflicts. But it should not be assumed that all ASM communities are rife with armed groups and are directly involved in violent conflict. Outside of the mines that are controlled by the Congolese army and by Congolese and foreign militias in the eastern provinces, conflicts are often localized, and tend to be linked to pricing at the point of sale, competition over access to mineral deposits, and corrupt government entities that are benefiting at the expense of artisanal miners. But whatever conflicts are occurring at either the macro or the micro level, one form of conflict is pervasive in the DRC: the exploitation and abuse of women.

WOMEN IN ASM

During and after conflict, societies adapt, and the roles of men and women may change to buffer socioeconomic shocks and stresses. For example, when men are away at war, women most often remain at home to provide for their families. Although such shifts in gender roles may be temporary or permanent, they are likely to continue if DDR and post-conflict reconstruction are largely unsuccessful. Even when families are not directly affected by conflict, the economic impacts of war reverberate throughout society, typically producing unemployment in the formal economy. The result, in many African countries, is that both men and women seek informal livelihood sources. The effects of such livelihood adaptations are visible in ASM communities across the DRC.

A lack of documentation and research makes it difficult to determine how women's involvement in ASM has evolved over the years. In several mineral-rich countries, shifts toward artisanal mining (and away from other rural livelihoods, such as farming) are known to have occurred since the 1980s (Hilson 2010); however, a fuller understanding of the drivers of women's involvement in ASM in the DRC, in particular, warrants further research. Field research undertaken in Kolwezi, a town hosting thirty thousand artisanal miners in the copper belt of southern Katanga Province, shows that during the years after the conflict, women's involvement in ASM increased as a consequence of two factors: a general economic downturn and decreased livelihood opportunities in traditional sectors, such as agriculture. The research also found that women's involvement in ASM was primarily poverty driven: 75 percent of the women interviewed in 2007 had been mining for less than two years, and 70 percent were their families' sole earners (Pact 2007).

---

[4] See UNSC (2003, 2004, 2005a, 2005b, 2006, 2007a, 2007b, 2008a, 2008b, 2009a, 2009b, 2010).

Artisanal mining has become an important source of livelihood for women in the DRC because of its relative ease of entry in comparison to other sectors: it requires virtually no formal education or skills, and little or no capital. Thus, ASM provides women with economic opportunities that would otherwise be unavailable. Nevertheless, ASM is not without serious impacts on individual and family well-being.

Women assume a variety of roles in ASM; they may be directly involved in mining and trading or may work in the subsidiary businesses (such as bars, hotels, and restaurants) that support mining communities. Women and young girls may also be part of the sex trade.[5] Because of the transient nature of ASM communities, the presence of many young men who are without their families, the daily flow of cash, and the high rates of alcohol and substance abuse, prostitution is part and parcel of mining life. Women in the sex trade often migrate alongside artisanal workers who are in search of new prospects in other parts of the country; they may enter the trade when a mine is set up near their home; or they may travel to a mine to engage in prostitution temporarily, before returning to school or to home. But once a woman is known to have been involved in the sex trade, the shame attached to prostitution may make it difficult for her to reintegrate into her family or community, or to attract or retain a husband.

Among the women who work in the mines, gender discrimination is common—a pattern that is consistent with the findings of several studies on women in ASM in other parts of Africa, and in Asia and the Americas.[6] Despite similar working hours and levels of effort, women are often paid only a fraction of what men receive. Moreover, women tend to work at the lower ends of the production chain, performing tasks such as washing, sorting, or transporting; because they have only limited presence in the higher levels of production and trade, they are often excluded from the decisions that determine the level of payment for various services and the organization of the mining teams. Being excluded from key aspects of economic governance profoundly undermines women's well-being and economic standing, and is particularly damaging in light of their increasing role as principal breadwinners.

Gender-based discrimination is usually cultural in origin, reflecting long-standing traditions and taboos. In the diamond mines of Kasai Oriental Province, for instance, women are required to surrender any high-value stones to the male mine owners or diggers and are permitted to keep only low-grade stones. In the copper mines of southern Katanga Province and the gold mines of northern

---

[5] The destructive effect of this vicious cycle on traditional Congolese society is vividly illustrated by the fact that women and young girls from as far away as Kasai Oriental Province or northern Katanga Province can be found working as prostitutes in artisanal areas along the DRC's southern border with Zambia.

[6] For more information on women in ASM in Asia, see Lahiri-Dutt (2008). On Suriname, see Heemskerk (2003). For an overview of the situation in Africa, see Hinton, Veiga, and Beinhoff (2003).

Orientale Province, women are not even permitted to enter the mines, for fear that their presence will make the minerals "disappear"; thus, they are excluded from the tasks performed in mines, which often reap the highest wages. (Though a woman's presence may be blamed if a mine "goes bust," taking a girl's virginity is believed to increase a male miner's chances of striking it rich. Taboo and myth are thus finely manipulated to support both discrimination against and violation of women in artisanal communities.)[7]

In the DRC, because of the lack of other child care options, women are often compelled to bring their children to the mines. This affects the children's well-being in several ways: (1) they are exposed to contamination from minerals, unsafe water, and poor sanitary conditions; (2) they may be forced to forgo education in order to work in the mines; (3) because it is difficult for such children to resume their education in later years, they may lack the requisite skills to enter other labor markets and may be forced to remain in mining permanently.

Young children begin by performing whatever tasks they are capable of doing around the mine, and may eventually begin mining when they are physically able to do so. In Kolwezi, it is estimated that around 24 percent of child miners work alongside their mothers (the rest work independently or on teams); it also appears that having been brought to the mines by their mothers led the children to work in the mines (Pact 2007).

Despite the disadvantages noted, it would be inaccurate to imply that women are always in subordinate positions in ASM in the DRC. The authors have witnessed cases in which the women managers of artisanal mines have prohibited child labor; women traders who are more successful than their male counterparts because they are believed to be more fair; and diamond-sorting sites where only women are allowed to handle the stones because the site managers regard them as more honest. Although such examples are rare, they provide potential models for improving the circumstances of women in ASM.

PACT'S APPROACHES

Pact, a nonprofit organization based in Washington, D.C., has been in the DRC since 2003. Pact's DRC country program focuses solely on the responsible management of natural resources, which Pact regards as a fundamental requirement for sustaining peace and preventing further conflict. Pact works with private

---

[7] A related and particularly serious problem is the belief, prevalent in the mining areas of Katanga, that having sex with a virgin or a very young child will prevent or cure HIV/AIDS. This belief allegedly originated with truck drivers from Southern Africa, where the rates of HIV infection are much higher than in the DRC, and where both the belief and the practice have been documented (Shell 2000). Because artisanal miners are highly mobile and because such beliefs are an important part of everyday life in the DRC, there is a grave risk that such stories will increase the incidence of SGBV in the ASM community.

mining companies, local communities, and the national government, and is funded by a variety of partners.[8]

The next two sections describe Pact's efforts to address gender issues in ASM communities in the DRC. Economic development, through responsible and regulated natural resource extraction, is an important pillar of post-conflict recovery in the DRC; if one adds the staggering scale of employment in ASM, it is clear that recasting the roles of men and women in ASM is essential to peacebuilding.

Economic empowerment

In 2006, 150 women enrolled in a Pact program designed to support and empower women as they moved out of the most precarious forms of mine labor and into more permanent work in other small-scale economic activities. The program focused on helping participants to achieve literacy, establish village savings banks, obtain vocational training, and start small businesses. Although the initiative was based on WORTH, a Pact program designed for rural settings, it was modified to reflect the circumstances of artisanal women in a peri-urban mining town in southern Katanga Province.[9]

The women, who wished to leave the ASM sector and seek alternative livelihoods, were organized into literacy and support groups, each with about twenty members. Each group selected two "literacy days" each week; on those days, they learned to read and write under the guidance of a literacy volunteer—typically, an educated person from the community, such as a teacher or a member of the clergy—who was chosen by the group but was not a member. (The women were free to meet more than twice a week, but this was often difficult because of their household responsibilities.) One day a week, often on one of the literacy days, the women put a certain amount into a village savings bank; the women themselves determined the amount, and individual contributions could vary from one woman to the next. When the savings reached a certain level, the group could begin lending money to members who wished to undertake small business projects.

Village savings schemes are not unique to Pact or to the DRC. What made this model unique was the way in which literacy, numeracy, and group education functioned interdependently, building social capital among the members: for example, even the books used in the literacy component specifically addressed

---

[8] Between 2006 and 2009, Pact entered into a three-year agreement that created the Extractive Industries Network, a partnership that also included four mining companies listed on international stock exchanges and the U.S. Agency for International Development (USAID). Working in Katanga and Orientale provinces, the network addressed a range of challenges in the ASM sector, including social development and security around mines.

[9] WORTH was first developed and implemented by Pact in Nepal and has since been replicated in Cambodia, the DRC, Ethiopia, Kenya, Tanzania, and Zambia.

business and entrepreneurship, and were designed to focus on the savings-and-loan aspect of the program. Participants who had been involved in previous microsavings and credit schemes agreed that the emphasis on literacy—and the opportunity to meet regularly for purposes beyond evaluating the status of loans that had been made to members—strengthened solidarity and reduced the chance of default.[10]

In addition to increased literacy and access to economic opportunities, the women who participated in the program noted other benefits: social empowerment (because they are running their own small businesses); an increase in economic standing, both within their families and within the community; and the ability to participate more fully in community governance and decision making (because of increased literacy). Such outcomes—which are examples of peace dividends, broadly defined—help support the kinds of social and economic changes that are necessary for women to both benefit from, and participate in, post-conflict recovery and peacebuilding. For instance, the more long-standing WORTH groups have used their solidarity to strengthen security for women, addressing issues such as precocious marriage and the promotion of respect for the security of women and girls. In one village, a local WORTH group brought to the attention of Pact a spate of rapes in which artisanal miners (and young men influenced by the artisanal mining lifestyle) had victimized girls as young as three years of age. With Pact's assistance, the women reported these incidents to UNICEF and were able to access medical treatment, reporting services, and some initial counseling.

Preventing SGBV

Although miners in and around ASM communities are not the sole perpetrators of SGBV—the presence of armed public security agents, militia members, and self-appointed security guards, many of whom are unpaid and uncontrolled, can also increase insecurity and the risk of SGBV—the incidence of SGBV in ASM communities should not be surprising; mining areas are characterized by a confluence of key factors:

- Traditional village authority that is weak or nonexistent.
- The limited presence of police and judicial authorities.
- A workforce that consists largely of men who are single or far from their families and wives.
- Cultural patterns that assign a socially inferior role to women, especially young women and girls (which, in turn, fosters a sense of impunity with regard to abuse).

---

[10] An internal evaluation and the final program report, which were submitted to USAID in October 2009, include participants' testimonies (Pact 2009a, 2009b).

- The perpetuation, by local witch doctors (*fétisheurs*), of beliefs and practices that encourage SGBV.
- The prevalence and acceptance of the sex trade, which places women at particular risk of abuse.

There are two key approaches to restoring reciprocity between men and women, in order to reestablish norms of mutual respect—and, hence, community security. One is to address ideas about what constitutes a man, and the other is to address the powerlessness of women. In the first approach, attributes of maleness other than raw power, such as those related to protection, fatherhood, responsibility, and support, need to be brought to the fore. In the second approach, women need first to be empowered, and second to be recognized (by men, by themselves, and by each other) for their familial, social, and economic roles; their leadership potential; and their capacity to contribute to community harmony. Both approaches need to be grounded in the everyday lives of community members—which, in the case of ASM, depend on natural resources.

As is the case with any effort to address inequality in gender roles, initiatives that are focused solely on women can alienate them from the broader society and make men even more resistant to change; such initiatives can even produce violent backlashes, which would only intensify women's insecurity. Thus, efforts to address gender issues in the ASM sector need to be undertaken within a broader framework for social change—and to address men, women, and the relationships between them.

The prevention of SGBV requires a broad-based approach that incorporates the following elements: strengthening the judicial system; promoting social (and judicial) recognition of rape as a serious crime; and redefining gender roles. In addition, victims of SGBV need physical and psychological treatment, as well as support for economic and social reintegration.

Working with mining companies, local women's groups, civil society organizations, and several UN partners, Pact piloted SGBV prevention models in artisanal mining areas of both Katanga Province and Ituri District, in Orientale Province. From an initial focus on educating communities about UN mechanisms for reporting and addressing SGBV, the pilots expanded to include literacy and savings programs, to build social and economic capital; public education campaigns, to familiarize communities with SGBV law and with the resources available for victims; and support for economic transition out of ASM. By encouraging the pursuit of economic opportunities that do not require migration or the prolonged absence of men from their homes, the pilots fostered opportunities for family reunification and eventual stabilization.

Sexual and gender-based violence in the Democratic Republic of the Congo: A brief overview

For peacebuilding to be inclusive and effective, all actors, both men and women, must have the opportunity to participate freely, without fear of reprisal or prejudice, and with the expectation of respect, understanding, and appreciation of their concerns, perspectives, and priorities. In the Democratic Republic of the Congo (DRC), one factor that prevents such engagement is the prevalence of sexual violence and the impunity commonly granted to its perpetrators.

The effects of sexual violence include permanent bodily damage, infection with sexually transmitted diseases, mental trauma, family rejection, marital breakup, and loss of future opportunities. In the DRC, where torture during rape is commonplace, sexual violence is particularly damaging. In 2008, United Nations Under-Secretary-General John Holmes described the DRC as "the worst place in the world to be a woman or girl" and noted that "the levels and brutality of violence against women are almost unimaginable." Writing in the *Los Angeles Times*, Holmes said that "despite many warnings, nothing quite prepared me for what I heard from survivors of a sexual violence so brutal it staggers the imagination and mocked my notions of human decency" (Holmes 2007).

Sexual and gender-based violence (SGBV) has become endemic in parts of the DRC, especially in Sud Kivu and Nord Kivu provinces. This has occurred in the wake of intense conflict, during which armed groups—both Congolese public security forces and foreign armed militias—used rape as a weapon of war. In Sud Kivu, for example, even after the 2006 peace agreement, estimates indicate that forty women were raped every day (Rodriguez 2007). Nevertheless, SGBV is not limited to the provinces traditionally regarded as conflict zones. In Katanga—a province that is often considered to be peaceful and lawful, and that has attracted significant foreign investment in recent years—2008 statistics indicate that as many as twenty women and girls may be raped each day (UNFPA 2008). Although most reports and estimates have focused on female victims, a March 2010 study conducted in Nord and Sud Kivu and Ituri District revealed that of all reported incidents of sexual violence, women were the victims in 39.7 percent of cases and men in 23.6 percent of cases (children were the victims in the remainder of the cases). The survey also revealed that women are increasingly reported as perpetrators—a pattern that indicates a need for more inclusive policies in efforts to address SGBV in the DRC (Johnson et al. 2010).

Although it is difficult to obtain an accurate picture of the prevalence of SGBV across the DRC, one thing is clear: SGBV cannot be reduced unless obstacles to reporting are overcome.* Historically, SGBV has been chronically underreported because (1) health and medical centers lack the capacity to provide data to national databases; (2) victims and their families are afraid of reprisal and are unfamiliar with reporting mechanisms; and (3) victims' geographic isolation makes it difficult for them to reach the support services through which SGBV would be reported.

In addition to problems associated with reporting, a complex mix of interwoven—and mutually reinforcing—cultural, institutional, and political factors contribute to the problem of SGBV:

- A traditional failure to recognize women as equal citizens, which undermines their standing and legal rights in Congolese society.
- Repeated exposure to violence and abuse, which appears to have habituated both men and women to such behavior.
- Physical displacement, which has led to the breakdown of traditional authority and the deterioration of social cohesion.
- Failure to recognize rape as a serious crime.**
- Lack of capacity in the rural legal system (stemming from failure to pay the judiciary, lack of expertise with such cases, and the sheer volume of cases that would have to be addressed).
- A culture of impunity, which is fostered by the fact that those cases that are reported are rarely prosecuted or punished.
- A lack of political will and capacity on the part of the state, which prevents it from establishing a culture of "zero tolerance."

---

* Some provinces report high rates, but in those that do not, the rates may reflect a paucity of information rather than a lower incidence of SGBV.

** In many cases, a family will settle a rape case for as little as a goat, which has an average market price of US$50–60.

INTEGRATING ASM INTO THE PEACEBUILDING AGENDA: RECOMMENDATIONS FOR THE FUTURE

Although the approaches described are certainly not unique to Pact, what sets the Pact model apart is its focus on ASM communities. Pact regards ASM areas as crucial to the overall peacebuilding agenda for DRC for the following reasons:

- ASM offers the potential for substantial economic dividends for both individuals and families—dividends that could be even more significant if ASM were properly organized and responsibly managed.
- Women working in ASM face significant social and health consequences whose long-term impact remains unknown. Increasing security for women and ensuring that ASM meets basic health and safety standards would help mitigate negative impacts and potentially increase women's productivity in the sector.
- The ASM sector remains subject to resource governance conflicts that are pertinent to the DRC's larger peacebuilding agenda. For example, several reports published by Pact and International Alert address the importance of improving governance to ensure more equitable remuneration for artisanal miners (Pact 2010; Spittaels 2010). Women's concerns are intricately linked to this overall reform agenda.

Artisanal miners are among the most economically and socially vulnerable laborers in the country, and mining camps are precarious and dangerous environments, especially for women and young girls. ASM communities confront a range of sustainable livelihoods challenges, including those relating to gender discrimination and sexual exploitation, and it is therefore essential that they be integrated into the development agenda. If viable ways can be found to strengthen the role of women in these communities, the positive contribution to peacebuilding could be extremely significant. Unfortunately, artisanal mining is often beyond the vision or reach of nongovernmental organizations (NGOs) and aid agencies (Hayes 2008; Perks 2011).

The following recommendations, based on Pact's experience with women in ASM communities, could improve the overall peacebuilding agenda for natural resource management in the DRC:

- A coordinated policy framework that takes advantage of the skills and resources of all interested actors would maximize the impact of limited resources and increase the efficacy of initiatives. Gender mainstreaming—in which the opinions, needs, status, and role of women are viewed as equal to those of men—is integral to such a framework.[11] As things stand now, interventions in the ASM

---

[11] In July 1997, the UN Economic and Social Council defined *gender mainstreaming* as follows: "Mainstreaming a gender perspective is the process of assessing the implications for women and men of any planned action, including legislation, policies or

sector are ad hoc and are driven by the agendas, needs, or opportunities of individual organizations or sectors.
- Donor governments, NGOs, investors, and Congolese civil society should continue to lobby the DRC government and UN agencies to respond to the specific challenges faced by women in ASM communities and rural areas. For example, when broader development programming in the areas of HIV/AIDS and SGBV is being undertaken, outreach aimed specifically at women artisanal miners would help them access much-needed support and services.
- Public-private partnerships should be established with mining companies and their supply chains that (1) reflect global development objectives and standards,[12] and (2) are in line with the DRC government's national development plans. Even if companies do not wish to fund ASM reform (given the fact that most ASM is carried out illegally, and the risk of criticism if a company is perceived to be connected to conflict, child labor, the sex trade, etc.), companies can still find limited ways to participate, while remaining within their comfort zone.[13] For media-wary companies, gender issues may be one of the less controversial points of entry.
- It is important to recognize that women may want to stay in ASM. Thus, livelihood initiatives should view regulated ASM as a viable economic opportunity for women as well as men, and should focus attention on supporting women to achieve greater equity and security in the sector.
- Small pilot opportunities for collaboration with UN agencies and other development organizations should be created. A strong component of such efforts could be to improve access to health and reproductive services for women artisanal miners; for example, local clinics could provide testing services and health education.
- The current resurgence of international interest in "conflict minerals" in eastern DRC should be used as an opportunity to emphasize UN Security Council Resolutions 1325 and 1820, which reaffirm the pivotal role of women in peacebuilding. The resolutions should be essential elements in any new initiatives that are proposed, funded, or implemented.

---

programmes, in any area and at all levels. It is a strategy for making the concerns and experiences of women as well as of men an integral part of the design, implementation, monitoring and evaluation of policies and programmes in all political, economic and societal spheres, so that women and men benefit equally, and inequality is not perpetuated. The ultimate goal of mainstreaming is to achieve gender equality." (ECOSOC 1997).

[12] One example of such standards is the due diligence guidelines developed by the Organisation for Economic Co-operation and Development for mineral extraction in high-risk, conflict-affected areas; see OECD (2010).

[13] Such efforts do work, as is clear from the accomplishments of the Extractive Industries Network. In this effort, which was carried out in Katanga and Orientale provinces, the companies focused primarily on social development, which was clearly within their purview. Through a partnership with USAID, however, they were also able to work on more challenging and contentious issues related to ASM and women's security.

CONCLUSION

One of the many questions facing the DRC is how to most efficiently transform the country's mineral resources into a driver of sustainable long-term development. Some ore bodies are deep and vast, and cannot be effectively exploited without industrial-scale mining (and foreign capital); others are more accessible and can be exploited through small-scale, semi-industrial mining; and still others cannot justify major investment and are suitable only for manual extraction through ASM, assuming that ASM could be undertaken safely and legally. Finding the right mix of approaches is crucial not only to economic recovery but also to securing safe and sustainable livelihoods for those who work in extractive industries.

The scale of change needed to build lasting peace in the DRC is enormous and will require many different approaches and actors working in myriad settings. Artisanal mines can be one such setting. In these mines, the risks women face are severe and their position is precarious—but, given the right mix of external factors and internal empowerment, the dynamics can change. Given its large scale and economic potential, and the mobility of its workers, ASM should be regarded as a social phenomenon and an opportunity rather than as a localized problem. Women acting as leaders, agents of social change, and peacebuilders in artisanal mining communities could act as catalysts for wider peace and stabilization initiatives in the DRC.

REFERENCES

ECOSOC (United Nations Economic and Social Council). 1997. Coordination of the policies and activities of the specialized agencies and other bodies of the United Nations system: Mainstreaming the gender perspective into all policies and programmes in the United Nations system; Report of the Secretary-General. E/1997/66. www.un.org/documents/ecosoc/docs/1997/e1997-66.htm.

Hartung, W. D., and B. Moix. 2000. Deadly legacy: U.S. arms to Africa and the Congo war. World Policy Institute Arms Control Reports. February 3. http://repositories.lib.utexas.edu/bitstream/handle/2152/5829/2290.pdf?sequence=1.

Hayes, K. 2008. Artisanal & small-scale mining and livelihoods in Africa. Common Fund for Commodities. www.pactworld.org/galleries/default-file/CFC_Paper_ASM_Livelihoods_in_Africa-FINAL.pdf.

Heemskerk, M. 2003. Self-employment and poverty alleviation: Women's work in artisanal gold mines. *Human Organisation* 62 (1): 62–73.

Hilson, G. 2010. "Once a miner, always a miner": Poverty and livelihood diversification in Akwatia, Ghana. *Journal of Rural Studies* 26:296–307.

Hinton, J. J., M. M. Veiga, and C. Beinhoff. 2003. Women and artisanal mining: Gender roles and the road ahead. In *The socio-economic impacts of artisanal and small-scale mining in developing countries*, ed. G. Hilson. Lisse, Netherlands: A. A. Balkema.

Holmes, J. 2007. Congo's rape war. *Los Angeles Times*, October 11. www.latimes.com/news/opinion/la-oe-holmes11oct11,0,6685881.story?coll=la-opinion-center.

Johnson, K., J. Scott, B. Rughita, M. Kisielewski, J. Asher, R. Ong, and L. Lawry. 2010. Association of sexual violence and human rights violations with physical and mental health in territories of the eastern Democratic Republic of the Congo. *Journal of the American Medical Association* 304 (5): 553–562.

Lahiri-Dutt, K. 2008. Digging to survive: Women's livelihoods in South Asia's small mines and quarries. *South Asian Survey* 15 (2): 217–244.

OECD (Organisation for Economic Co-operation and Development). 2010. Draft due diligence guidance for responsible supply chains of minerals from conflict-affected and high-risk areas. www.oecd.org/dataoecd/13/18/46068574.pdf.

Pact, Inc. 2007. Kolwezi economic development and governance transition strategy: Final report. www.pactworld.org/galleries/default-file/Kolwezi_Economic_Development_and _Gov...Final.pdf.

———. 2009a. The Extractive Industries Global Development Alliance Network (EIN) for the Democratic Republic of the Congo, September 2006–September 2009: Final technical report. (On file with authors.)

———. 2009b. Evaluation of WORTH and agriculture components in Kolwezi and Fungurume, GDA Program. (On file with authors.)

———. 2010. PROMINES study: Artisanal mining in the Democratic Republic of Congo. http://pactworld.org/cs/pact_promines.

Perks, R. 2011. How can public-private partnerships contribute to security and human rights policy and practice in the extractive industries? A case study of the Democratic Republic of Congo (DRC). *Resources Policy*.

Rodriguez, C. 2007. Sexual violence in South Kivu. *Forced Migration Review* 27:45.

Shell, R. C. H., and R. Zeitlin. 2000. Positive outcomes: The chances of acquiring HIV/AIDS during the school-going years in the Eastern Cape, 1990–2000. *Social Work Practitioner-Researcher* 12 (3): 139–154.

Spittaels, S., ed. 2010. *The complexity of resource governance in a context of state fragility: An analysis of the mining sector in the Kivu hinterlands*. International Alert. www.international-alert.org/pdf/1210KIVUGL.pdf.

UNFPA (United Nations Population Fund). 2008. Rapport des nouveaux cas des violences sexuelles survenus au Katanga au cours du premier trimestre. Initiative Conjoint de Lutte contre les Violences Sexuelles Faites aux Femmes, aux Jeunes, aus Enfants et aux Hommes en RDC. March. (Internal report; on file with authors.)

UNSC (United Nations Security Council). 2000. Resolution 1325. S/RES/1325 (2000). October 31. www.un.org/events/res_1325e.pdf.

———. 2003. Final report of the panel of experts on the illegal exploitation of natural resources and other forms of wealth of the Democratic Republic of the Congo. S/2003/1027. October.

———. 2004. Report of the group of experts on the Democratic Republic of the Congo. S/2004/551. July. www.un.org/ga/search/view_doc.asp?symbol=S/2004/551.

———. 2005a. Report of the group of experts on the Democratic Republic of the Congo. S/2005/30. January. www.un.org/ga/search/view_doc.asp?symbol=S/2005/30.

———. 2005b. Report of the group of experts on the Democratic Republic of the Congo. S/2005/436. July. www.un.org/ga/search/view_doc.asp?symbol=S/2005/436.

———. 2006. Report of the group of experts on the Democratic Republic of the Congo. S/2006/53. January. www.un.org/ga/search/view_doc.asp?symbol=S/2006/53.

———. 2007a. Final report of the group of experts on the Democratic Republic of the Congo. S/2007/423. July. www.un.org/ga/search/view_doc.asp?symbol=S/2007/ 423.

———. 2007b. Interim report of the group of experts on the Democratic Republic of the Congo, pursuant to Security Council resolution 1698 (2006). S/2007/40. January. www.un.org/ga/search/view_doc.asp?symbol=S/2007/40.

———. 2008a. Final report of the group of experts on the Democratic Republic of the Congo. S/2008/773. December. www.un.org/ga/search/view_doc.asp?symbol=S/2008/773.

———. 2008b. Report of the group of experts on the Democratic Republic of the Congo. S/2008/43. February. www.un.org/ga/search/view_doc.asp?symbol=S/2008/43.

———. 2008c. Resolution 1820. S/RES/1820 (2008). June 19.

———. 2009a. Final report of the group of experts on the Democratic Republic of the Congo. S/2009/603. November. www.un.org/ga/search/view_doc.asp?symbol=S/2009/603.

———. 2009b. Interim report of the group of experts on the Democratic Republic of the Congo. S/2009/253. May. www.un.org/ga/search/view_doc.asp?symbol=S/2009/253.

———. 2010. Interim report of the group of experts on the Democratic Republic of the Congo. S/2010/252. May. www.un.org/ga/search/view_doc.asp?symbol=S/2010/252.

World Bank. 2008. Democratic Republic of Congo: Growth with governance in the mining sector. Report No. 43402-ZR. May. http://siteresources.worldbank.org/INTOGMC/Resources/336099-1156955107170/drcgrowthgovernanceenglish.pdf.

Forest user groups and peacebuilding in Nepal

Binod Chapagain and Tina Sanio

In Nepal, community forest user groups (CFUGs) are emerging as important institutional assets, capable of supporting peacebuilding by assisting with reintegration and reconstruction and providing livelihood assistance. CFUGs are democratic, local institutions that engage in the sustainable management of forest resources. Nepal has more than 14,500 such groups, which manage over 1.2 million hectares of forest. More than 1.65 million households (40 percent of the national population) belong to CFUGs—the highest membership of any civil society organization in Nepal.

This chapter is based on a study that was designed to identify the role of CFUGs in local peacebuilding in Nepal—specifically in the areas of conflict transformation and reconstruction efforts. The study compared three districts: Sankhuwasabha, in the eastern hills; Rolpa, in the mountains of the midwest; and Nawalparasi, in the plains.[1]

The principal focus of the chapter is the link between peacebuilding and natural resource management in post-conflict settings. The chapter is divided into six major sections: (1) a description of community forestry in Nepal, (2) the presentation of a theoretical framework that is useful in understanding the role of CFUGs in peacebuilding, (3) the case studies, (4) a list of factors affecting outcomes, (5) a list of lessons learned, and (6) a brief conclusion.

COMMUNITY FORESTRY IN NEPAL

The livelihoods of most rural Nepalis depend on livestock and agriculture, of which forests have always been an integral part. Farmers rely on wood for fuel,

---

Binod Chapagain previously worked for the Livelihoods and Forestry Programme in Nepal, and is currently a Ph.D. candidate at the Research School of Humanities and Arts, Australian National University. Tina Sanio is a social anthropologist with extensive experience in Mongolia, Nepal, and Thailand; she is a freelance consultant currently working in Germany for GIZ.

[1] The authors conducted individual interviews and group discussions with employees of international organizations, Nepalese government agencies, and national and local Nepalese nongovernmental organizations (NGOs); they also spoke with approximately three hundred CFUG members, land rights activists, and informal community leaders. The interviews took place as part of ongoing research conducted between February 2007 and November 2009. Secondary information was obtained from previous studies, national and international NGOs, and Nepalese government agencies.

timber for buildings and agricultural implements, and leaves for animal bedding and fodder. Nevertheless, community forestry was not introduced until 1978; until then, the government had control over forests.

In 1978, under amendments to the Forest Act of 1961, some government forests were turned over to village-level political units known as *panchayats*, an arrangement that lasted until 1993, when passage of the Forest Act turned over the management of most national forests to CFUGs.[2] CFUGs are legally recognized, democratic entities. The household is the legal unit of membership, and all households that are in proximity to a community forest are eligible for membership. According to data from the Livelihoods and Forestry Program (LFP) of the United Kingdom's Department for International Development, of the 255,000 households in LFP districts that are identified as marginalized based on participatory well-being ranking, about 244,000 poor and very poor households are members of CFUGs (LFP 2008).[3]

Each CFUG must elect an executive committee and develop a constitution and operational plans to guide the management of the resources; a CFUG is recognized as legitimate only after an authorized government forest officer approves its constitution and operational plans. CFUGs obtain funds from membership fees and from the sale of forest products, including fodder, timber, firewood, and herbs; they also accept grants from governmental and nongovernmental agencies working in the same geographical area. Because they generate their own resources, CFUGs serve as vehicles for local development in rural Nepal. In 2008, CFUGs spent about 53 percent of their revenue on community development initiatives, including income-generating efforts, safe drinking water, improvements to rural roads and trails, scholarships for poor children, health emergencies, and the creation of revolving loan funds that are used for emergencies and for the support of microbusinesses (LFP 2008). Thus, sustainable forestry practices allow communities to survive and to be financially independent—that is, to meet many of their own basic needs.

Community-led forest management is an exceptional development in Nepal: CFUGs are fully responsible for managing forests, collecting revenues, and deciding on the use of available funds. Community-based management has improved the condition of the forests and generated resources for local development. CFUGs are also active in conservation—and, particularly in the hills and mountains, they serve as a counterbalance to looters and poachers, whom they actively pursue.[4]

All CFUG members meet at least once a year. Decisions are made by consensus, but if consensus cannot be reached, votes are taken. The forest is divided into blocks, and the members agree on management plans for each block.[5] Expenditure

---

[2] Passage of the Forest Act was spurred by Nepal's transition to democracy in 1990.
[3] The LFP works in fifteen administrative districts that are defined by the government of Nepal.
[4] Some CFUGs, however, have reportedly engaged in smuggling timber from Terai.
[5] Forest maintenance (cleaning, thinning, and pruning) is undertaken by group as a whole.

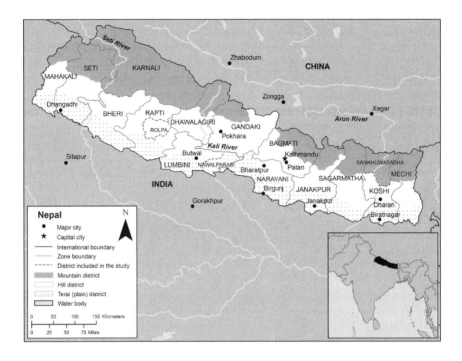

reports and budget plans for the coming year are also presented to the group for approval. The workings of the CFUGs are thus participatory and transparent, and the members trust each other to manage the forest and use revenues wisely.

Both men and women have an equal right to membership, and each CFUG's executive committee is required to have at least 33 percent women. Thus, CFUGs offer women an opportunity to take an active part in decision making—an opportunity that hardly exists in any other sphere in their lives.[6] Moreover, at least in the case of women, the CFUGs may provide broader platforms for leadership development. A study of the Koshi Hills, for example, found that about 80 percent of the women who were elected to local governing bodies in 1998 were members of CFUGs.

It is important to note that CFUGs are not without conflict. When conflict does occur, it is managed through traditional, informal practices. Issues that arise are discussed in general meetings of the group, where a variety of conflict-resolution strategies are employed (Upreti 2006). As a result, CFUG members have experience with collaborative, interest-based approaches to conflict management, including mediation and negotiation. Despite the CFUGs' strengths as

---

[6] CFUGs also foster the development of interest-based subgroups in which women can play active roles; for example, a CFUG might have a women's group, an entrepreneurs' group, and a nontimber forest products group.

democratically based institutions, however, they have by no means escaped the influence of traditional hierarchies and power relationships; inequalities continue to affect the user groups' internal dynamics and their relationship to the community at large, creating potential for conflict.

CFUGs and village development committees

In order to understand the role of community-based natural resource management in local peacebuilding efforts, it is important to grasp the larger environment in which the CFUGs operate. CFUGs exist alongside village development committees (VDCs), which are the lowest administrative element in the government of Nepal and serve as the official means of access to higher levels of government. Although the VDCs are part of the Ministry of Local Development, they have the authority to collect certain taxes and to develop annual plans and budgets independently; they also receive annual funding from the central government to implement their plans. VDCs are responsible for ensuring that rural residents have an element of control over development; they also monitor the use and distribution of state funds and facilitate cooperation between higher-level government officials, nongovernmental organizations (NGOs), and funding agencies. Finally, VDCs oversee education, water supplies, sanitation, basic health, and the collection of some government revenues.

Each district has several VDCs, and there are, in theory, 3,913 throughout the country. In practice, however, VDCs are often nonfunctional or nonexistent—creating a vacuum that, in many cases, CFUGs have filled.[7] Because CFUGs often serve as the primary engines of local development, they are frequently in conflict with VDCs.

In comparison to VDCs, CFUGs are flexible, responsive, inclusive, and nonbureaucratic: community residents have easy access to CFUGs and their resources, regardless of whether they are members, and joining a CFUG is a simple process. Obtaining access to VDC resources, in contrast, is a lengthy process: applicants may need to wait a year for budget-related decisions. Finally, VDC staff are appointed by the central government, whereas CFUGs employ their own local staff as required. Thus, community members—including internally displaced persons (IDPs)—would be more likely to approach CFUGs than local government (where it exists).

The war years

The Maoist insurgency that began in February 1996 was rooted in a 250-year history of economic stratification, ethnic tension, and regional economic imbalance

---

[7] Some VDCs are simply understaffed; others were entirely put out of commission during the conflict that began in 1996; and still others have not had any elected representatives since the conflict, because no elections have been held since the dissolution of all VDCs in 1998.

(Banjade and Timsina 2005).[8] Although almost 80 percent of Nepalis live in rural areas, repressive social structures had denied most rural residents the opportunity to own land, which is the sole means of obtaining a secure livelihood.[9] Discrimination on the basis of sex, ethnicity, and caste was common, and poor and marginalized populations were denied access to natural resources—particularly forests, land, and water (Basnet 2008).[10]

When the insurgency began, poverty was rampant: at some point during 1996, 60 percent of landholding households were unable to meet their daily food needs—and of these, 78 percent could not meet their needs for four to six months (DFID n.d.). In rural Nepal, land ownership is a symbol of security; thus, not owning land is a mark of poverty and vulnerability. During the war, the poor were targeted by both rebels and government security forces: the rebels tried to persuade them to join their army by holding out promises of a better life, and the security forces viewed them with suspicion, as informers and rebel supporters.

The ten-year war left more than 13,000 dead, and severely affected seventy-three of Nepal's seventy-five districts: because government employees—including employees of the forest department—were not allowed to enter villages during the conflict, service quality declined in rural areas (Upreti 2006).[11] Moreover, if the Royal Nepal Army thought that Maoist insurgents were hiding in the forest, they prohibited CFUGs from entering those areas, thus preventing the CFUGs from doing their work. Both Maoist rebels and government security forces used the forests for shelter and as training grounds, and both groups—but particularly rebels—extracted forest products, especially timber, from some areas without the consent of user groups and without consideration for sustainability (Roka 2007; Upreti 2006).

Although reports of the effect of the war on the CFUGs are mixed, there is no question that the CFUGs were in a difficult position during the conflict. CFUG leaders were under pressure from both sides, and those who refused to follow orders were either kidnapped or tortured (Upreti 2006). Some CFUG leaders were forcibly removed from office because of their political affiliations; others left as the result of threats from either the government or the rebels. Although in some areas forests were protected and the supply of forest products was

---

[8] The Maoists' principal demands were for "revolutionary" land reforms (essentially, seizing land from the landlords and distributing it to the poor); the institution of a people's democracy; rural development; and equality for men and women (including land ownership for women), for all ethnic groups, and for people from different castes. Although forests as such were not a cause of the conflict, they were an element in land tenure issues and therefore linked to the overall conflict.
[9] Approximately 5.5 million Nepalis are landless, out of a total population of 26 million (CSRC 2009; CBS n.d.).
[10] Until the Forest Act was passed in 1993, forest land was either state property or the property of the king and his family.
[11] Although the forests are managed by the CFUGs, employees of the forest department provide technical services, such as conducting inventory and managing nontimber forest products.

maintained, several studies have shown that the conflict undermined the leadership of the CFUGs and prevented the groups from properly managing the forests (Rechlin et al. 2007; Roka 2007). In particular, the conflict interfered with the formation of new CFUGs—and when new groups did form, the war prevented established CFUGs from meeting and planning with them (Roka 2007). In some cases, the rebels also challenged the authority of existing groups and prohibited CFUG members from leaving their villages in order to work in the forests.

Nevertheless, one study claims that the insurgents accepted the CFUGs because they were democratic institutions that had been formed at the village level; had local support; and functioned independently of the central government (Rechlin et al. 2007). The VDCs, in contrast, were often targeted by Maoist rebels for their perceived failure to support the people. In this view, the CFUGs played a neutral role during the war, generally accommodating multiple development interests and providing a forum for the discussion of village concerns (Rechlin et al. 2007; Roka 2007).

THEORETICAL BACKGROUND

The work of the CFUGs can be viewed as an example of conflict transformation: a process-oriented peacebuilding effort that focuses on structure and outcomes, and that is designed to bring an end to structural, cultural, and direct violence.[12] According to John Burton (1990, 1993), Ronald J. Fisher (1983), and Marieke Kleiboer (1996), other approaches to conflict management, such as conflict resolution and conflict settlement, focus primarily on horizontal relationships—that is, on the actions of parties that are of relatively equal status—whereas conflict transformation involves vertical relationships among parties of unequal status.[13] Moreover, conflict resolution and conflict settlement tend to view grassroots leaders and civilian populations as passive recipients of third-party interventions—but, as will be clear later in the chapter, community-based organizations such as CFUGs are not passive: they are center stage, and when it comes to peacebuilding, they are setting their own agenda (Reimann 2004). John Paul Lederach explains that conflict transformation must actively envision, include, respect, and promote the human and cultural resources from a given setting and not see the people in it as the problem and the outsider as the answer (Lederach 1995).

The actors and strategies associated with conflict transformation are reflected in Track III of table 1. Putting the table into the context of Nepal, Track I actors would include representatives of the government, the Maoists, the former king, the People's Liberation Army, and the Royal Nepal Army. Track II actors would include representatives of United Nations agencies, international NGOs, political

---

[12] As Johan Galtung (1998) has observed, social injustice can be described as structural or institutional violence.

[13] For further discussion of conflict settlement, see Bercovitch (1984, 1996) and Fisher and Ury (1981).

Table 1. Actors and strategies involved in conflict management

	Track I	Track II	Track III
Actors	Political or military leaders act as mediators for and/or as representatives of the parties who are in conflict.	A variety of third parties may be involved in conflict resolution, including private individuals; academics; professional mediators; and local, national, or international nongovernmental organizations; civil mediation (i.e., mediation led by "insiders") and "citizen diplomats" may also be used.	A variety of actors may be involved in conflict resolution, including local leaders (both formal and informal); community members; grassroots organizations; local, national, and international development agencies; human rights organizations; community organizations; and humanitarian assistance organizations.
Strategies	Outcome-oriented: Tools range from official and coercive measures such as sanctions, binding arbitration, and mediation by major powers, to noncoercive measures such as facilitation, direct negotiation, mediation, fact-finding missions, and "good offices."[a]	Process-oriented: Tools are mostly nonofficial and noncoercive; primarily facilitation (problem-solving workshops and roundtables, for example).	Process-, structure-, and outcome-oriented; tools include capacity building, trauma work,[b] grassroots training, and development and human rights work.

Source: Adapted from Reimann (2004).
a. Good offices are beneficial services undertaken by a third party, particularly for the purpose of mediating a dispute.
b. Trauma work includes a range of psychotherapeutic, cognitive behavioral, and medical interventions designed to help trauma victims regain a sense of control over their lives.

foundations, and local NGOs whose work focuses on conflict. The CFUGs exemplify the types of actors represented in Track III.

Historically, both the actors and strategies associated with Track III have been ignored, but Tracks I and II fail to capture the richness and complexity of Track III peacebuilding activities. Cordula Reimann (2004) argues that Track III is essential to conflict transformation because it is the Track III actors who deal directly with those who have been most affected by the conflict.[14] In Nepal, for

---

[14] The notion of involving communities at the earliest stages of peacebuilding has been highlighted several times in evaluations of UN-sponsored disarmament, demobilization, and reintegration projects, but practitioners seem to be at a loss as to how to implement such an approach. (See Lederach 1995, 1997).

example, it is the CFUGs that deal directly with IDPs—assisting with reconciliation, reintegration, reconstruction, and livelihood support. An emphasis on Track III recognizes that the potential for peacebuilding already exists and is rooted in the traditional culture of a community or region.[15] Moreover, the inclusion of bottom-up strategies, which are characteristic of Track III, tends to support local efforts to obtain social justice—and, potentially, bring about structural change.

CASE STUDIES

Ten years of conflict between the government and the Maoist rebels left Nepal with thousands of IDPs and a large number of "disappeared." Even in 2009, three years after the signing of the comprehensive peace agreement (CPA), thousands of IDPs did not feel safe enough to return to their homes; they struggled to secure a livelihood, and they lacked dependable access to food, health care, and education (IDMC n.d.).[16]

During the post-conflict period in Nepal, CFUGs contributed to peacebuilding by assisting IDPs to return to their homes, acting as mediators in reconciliation efforts and in negotiations over property, helping to rebuild housing and infrastructure, providing CFUG membership to returnees, and supporting small-scale enterprise development. Thus, the case studies focus on *internal* conflict transformation—that is, on interventions that were not dominated by outside third parties, but by community-based organizations—in this case, the CFUGs.

To assess the effect of community-based natural resource management on peacebuilding, the authors collected qualitative and quantitative data on the CFUGs' work in three districts, between February 2006 and August 2009: Sankhuwasabha (in the eastern hills), Rolpa (in the mountains of the midwest), and Nawalparasi (in the plains). Although all three districts had significant numbers of IDPs,[17] they had differing geographical characteristics and differing histories with respect to CFUGs. In the eastern hills and in the mountains of the midwest, community forestry is well established, whereas it is relatively new in the plains. Because Rolpa was the birthplace of the Maoist insurgency—and therefore of the conflict—it had a particularly high number of IDPs. Of the three,

---

[15] In other words, traditional conflict-management systems should neither be ignored, nor replaced by "invented traditions" that cannot deliver what they should. See, for example, Oomen (n.d.), which discusses the Rwandan juridical system of *gacaca*.

[16] Although Nepal created a national policy for IDPs in February 2007, the policy lacks adequate mechanisms for ensuring safety and security. Moreover, because of a sharply limited definition of the displaced, only displaced persons who have personal or family connections to police, army, or government officials, or to leaders of political parties, are officially designated as IDPs; thus, the majority of IDPs have been excluded from assistance, making it difficult to assess the scope of displacement.

[17] The principal reasons for displacement were as follows: targeting by security forces who believed that the victims were Maoists, murder or abduction of family members by one side or the other, arrest and torture by one side or the other, and arrest without evidence.

Sankhuwasabha had the second-highest number of IDPs.[18] (For statistics on CFUG membership, displaced households, assistance to displaced persons, and infrastructure development, see the accompanying tables.)

Case studies: Summary data tables

District	Number of community forest user groups (CFUGs)	Number of member households	Number of households in the district	Percentage of households that are CFUG members
Sankhuwasabha	267	25,944	30,766	84
Nawalparasi	54	21,465	98,340	22
Rolpa	318	30,385	38,512	79

Community Forest User Groups, by district
Sources: LFP (2007, 2008); Department of Forestry (n.d.).

District	Number of residents who disappeared	Number of residents who were killed	Number of households that were displaced	Number of households that returned
Sankhuwasabha	2	132	118	71
Nawalparasi	0	189	24	18
Rolpa	61	748	2,194	1,099

Displaced households, by district
Sources: INSEC Online (n.d.a, n.d.b, n.d.c).

District	Number of returning households that were granted free CFUG memberships	Number of household enterprises supported by a CFUG	Number of houses whose construction was supported by a CFUG
Sankhuwasabha	25	5	11
Rolpa	856	9	587

Assistance to internally displaced persons, by district
Sources: SODEC (2008, n.d.); INSEC Online (n.d.a, n.d.b, n.d.c).
Note: No data were available for Nawalparasi.

District	Spending (US$)	Number of households directly benefited
Sankhuwasabha	16,333	1,357
Nawalparasi	41,453	364
Rolpa	29,280	2,938

Infrastructure development, by district
Source: LFP (2007).

---

[18] So far, there are no data available on the socioeconomic circumstances, caste, or ethnic affiliation of the IDPs.

Sankhuwasabha

After the signing of the 2006 peace accord, most of the IDPs from Sankhuwasabha wanted to return to their villages but were reluctant to do so. They still feared revenge, either from one side or the other; their houses had been destroyed; and their farmland had been captured or rendered barren by war-related damage. The IDPs knew that they would need assistance in reintegrating. Working in collaboration with the Society Development Centre (SODEC), a local NGO, two CFUGs in Sankhuwasabha started working as mediators, facilitating the reintegration of IDPs.[19] The CFUGs conducted informal meetings with local residents and with representatives of political parties. The aim was to create an environment in which the displaced could return safely, find housing and livelihood support, and resume their lives. SODEC cooperated with—and obtained the backing of— district-level political parties and human rights organizations; SODEC also assured the IDPs that the CFUGs would help them reintegrate safely.

With these assurances, the displaced families began to return; within two months of initiating the process, twenty families were resettled. The CFUGs immediately provided the following assistance:

- Ten households received free timber to rebuild their homes.
- Ten households received a 50 percent subsidy to purchase timber.
- Fifteen households received low-interest loans of NPR78,000 (about US$1,000) for income-generating activities (such as vegetable farming, goat farming, pig farming, or furniture building).
- All returning families received free membership in a CFUG (there is normally a fee of NPR3,000 to NPR5,000).[20]

In addition, the CFUGs facilitated dialogue between returning families and local political leaders, in order to protect returnees from further threats and insecurity.

During the war, 132 residents of Sankhuwasabha were killed, 2 disappeared, and 118 families were displaced. Between 2007 and mid-2009, 71 families—over 60 percent of the displaced households—were resettled. The CFUGs spent over US$16,000 on the reconstruction of the infrastructure in the district, which directly benefited more than 1,357 households.[21]

---

[19] The CFUGs started by working with families that had been displaced from their villages and were residing in district headquarters. After some IDPs had been successfully returned from district headquarters, SODEC reached out to other IDPs. Although many CFUGs were involved in these efforts, this case study is based on information collected from two CFUGs in particular.

[20] Because some of the households received more than one type of benefit, there is some overlap in these descriptions. Poor households, for example, may have received both timber for housing construction and a low-interest loan to start an income-generating activity.

[21] The infrastructure improvements made by Sankhuwasabha (and by the other districts as well) would have been made in any case, and were not made specifically for the IDPs. Nevertheless, the IDPs benefited from them.

The example of Sankhuwasabha demonstrates that as actors in Track III conflict-transformation processes, CFUGs are capable of contributing to successful local peacebuilding through reintegration, reconstruction, and livelihood support. The CFUGs were able to contribute for two reasons: first, because they were experienced in conflict resolution; second, because management of the forest resources provided revenues that could then be used to provide practical assistance to IDPs.

Nawalparasi

Although there were no reports of disappearances from Nawalparasi during the war, 189 people were killed and 24 families were displaced. After the peace accord, eighteen families (75 percent) returned to their villages through the assistance of CFUGs (LFP n.d.). During 2007 and 2008, CFUGs in Nawalparasi spent US$41,453 to rebuild infrastructure, which directly benefited 364 households.[22]

Like many rural residents, Prem Prasad Sharma, of Nawalparasi, owned no land and was forced to work as an unskilled laborer. During the war, he was repeatedly victimized by both rebels and government security forces. In 2006, however, the CFUGs allocated some land to poor families, provided that they agreed to protect the forest resources. Prem said,

> My life . . . changed after CFUG formed a group of poor families . . . and gave us some Community Forests land. . . . Our CFUG called a meeting to talk about setting aside some land for the poor people and conflict victims to grow broom grass to make and sell brooms. The group members were chosen from a participatory well-being ranking, which was based on the food sufficiency. We divided the plot of land among our subgroup members. The CFUG paid us to buy seedlings of broom grass from the forest and also bought seedlings for us. Then, we planted the seedlings ourselves. The first year, I took nine brooms and three loads of grass from my plot: the second year, eighteen brooms and nine loads, and the third year, thirty-eight brooms and twenty-eight loads. We earned NRP25 for each broom if they were of good quality. It made a difference in our situation. There was a dispute when other group members said that there was not enough fodder grass for them. We resolved it by allowing them to cut grass from the allocated plot. They pay for the grass depending on their financial status. It is free for those in the "very poor" rank, but "poor" has to pay some. It is fine that other people cut fodder grass here, but sometimes they cut the

---

[22] The money used to rebuild the infrastructure was drawn from a fund maintained by Nawalparasi CFUGs and the LFP (LFP 2006). Nawalparasi has a limited number of CFUGs because the government of Nepal has been reluctant to hand over productive Terai forests to community-led groups. Of the 114,900 hectares of forests in Nawalparasi, only 3,000 (2.6 percent of the total) are in the hands of community groups (Department of Forestry n.d.). Although the government is under pressure from CFUGs to hand over more forest resources to CFUGs, it is doing so at a very slow pace.

broom grass. Had the group not supported me, I would have been displaced from my village and my children may have been victims (Sharma 2009).

Thus, in addition to assisting 75 percent of the Nawalparasi IDPs to return home and investing more than US$40,000 on infrastructure, the CFUGs used their access to forest resources to enable the very poor to obtain a livelihood: in Prem's case, a piece of forest land that he manages by himself, enabling him to earn money and care for his family through a sustainable enterprise.

Rolpa

As noted earlier, Rolpa is the birthplace of the Maoist revolution, a circumstance that is reflected in the figures associated with the conflict: 61 people disappeared, 748 were killed, and 2,194 families were displaced. After the war, 1,099 families (50 percent) returned to their villages through the assistance of CFUGs. Of these families, 856 were granted free CFUG membership, 9 started small-scale enterprises with the assistance of CFUGs, and 587 received material support from the CFUGs for housing construction. From July 2006 through June 2007, Rolpa CFUGs spent US$29,280 on infrastructure development, directly benefiting 2,938 families (LFP 2007).

Interviews with displaced persons from Rolpa revealed that most of those who fled did so because of threats from security forces or rebels, or because their family members were killed and they were afraid that they, too, would be killed if they remained. Nevertheless, nearly half of these people returned to their villages because of specific actions taken by the CFUGs: the groups actively sought to discover what had happened to the families; encouraged them to move back; mediated in order to bring about reconciliations; and protected those who were threatened upon their return.

During the war, Ram Bahadur Roka was kidnapped by the rebels four times, beaten, and left for dead. The fifth time he was abducted he was kept in custody but managed to escape. Instead of returning to his village, he went to the plains to hide. After the peace accord, CFUG members from his old village persuaded Ram to return; they also met with the rebels to help him get his property back. The CFUG's successful efforts on his behalf made Ram interested in their other activities. He first became an active member in 2007; in early 2009, he was elected chair of the group that he had joined. Ram said that he would never have returned to his home village if the group had not encouraged him to do so (Roka 2009).

FACTORS AND CONSTRAINTS AFFECTING OUTCOMES

As is illustrated by the case studies, CFUGs have engaged in a long and impressive list of initiatives that strengthen and guide local peacebuilding efforts. By actively encouraging IDPs to return to their villages, defending them from threats, assisting them to achieve sustainable livelihoods, and offering them membership

Forest user groups and peacebuilding in Nepal 557

in community-led resource management groups, the CFUGs have demonstrated their capacity for conflict transformation. CFUGs offer new—and substantial—potential for peacebuilding in rural communities.

A number of factors have made it possible for CFUGs to successfully support peacebuilding in post-conflict Nepal:

- Because the CFUGs were firmly established before the war began, they were able to continue to function during the conflict, although at a somewhat lower level, and to survive (and thrive) after the war.
- The CFUGs were established, democratic, grassroots organizations that had the active support of their communities. During the war, the CFUGs delivered key community services, maintained a neutral position, and developed a history of successfully accommodating multiple interests.[23] Because the CFUGs survived the war largely intact, they were in a position to play a strong peacebuilding role during the post-conflict period.
- The CFUGs manage conflict within their groups through traditional practices; the same approaches were effective in addressing other conflicts. For example, traditional practices were used to resolve conflicts between IDPs and either rebel or security forces in the IDPs' home villages; between CFUGs and VDCs, and between CFUGs and other CFUGs (Upreti 2006).

Other factors, however, may constrain the ability of CFUGs to continue (or expand) their work.

- In August 2008, Nepal's Constituent Assembly began drafting a new constitution, which is scheduled to be completed by the end of August 2011.[24] Major issues (such as property rights, ethnicity, and caste) have yet to be addressed; promises to civil society groups and to victims of the conflict have yet to be kept; and the political parties are still fighting over the meaning of "scientific land reform," which was written into the CPA. With the country in transition, the future of community forestry in Nepal is unclear.
- Even if the CFUGs continue as legitimate legal entities, young people are generally migrating away from rural areas, which will make it difficult to find members (and leaders) for CFUGs.
- Most members of CFUG executive committees are drawn from the local elite (that is, higher-caste men from relatively wealthy families).[25] Although women,

---

[23] This may explain, to some extent, why the VDCs were targeted by the rebels during the war, whereas the CFUGs were largely left alone: unlike the VDCs, the CFUGs were perceived as legitimate representatives of the populace.

[24] The adoption of the constitution can be postponed for another six months if the president calls a state of emergency.

[25] Because of domination by members of the rural elite, participation on the executive committee is sometimes referred to by development practitioners as *participulation*—that is, the manipulation of participation.

lower castes, and ethnic groups are represented on the committees, they are largely token presences. For example, women are required to make up 33 percent of the membership of executive committees, but fewer than 20 percent of key decision-making positions (chair, secretary, and treasurer) are held by women. And although ethnic households make up about 35 percent of CFUG members (a figure that is proportionate to the percentage of ethnic citizens in the national population), ethnic households are significantly underrepresented in executive positions (LFP n.d.).[26] Continued domination by elites has created power struggles within CFUGs; at the same time, awareness of discrimination has led some CFUGs to take steps to respond to these inequities.

- Discrepancies between the Forest Act of 1993 and the Local Self-Governance Act of 1999 have created ongoing conflicts between CFUGs and VDCs.
- Some leaders of CFUGs have been subject to the influence of particular political parties, and some CFUG members have served as leaders of political parties. As a consequence, CFUG leaders have sometimes made decisions that served the interests of a particular political party, rather than those of the community.
- Despite the CFUGs' demonstrated success in sustainably managing resources, the government of Nepal does not fully trust community-based natural resource management—and is therefore unlikely to assign CFUGs a role in peacebuilding. For example, although CFUGs have already made effective peacebuilding contributions, they have received no official recognition for their work; nor were they assigned a role in the CPA signed in 2006.[27] Moreover, neither the government nor the other agencies and organizations in tracks I and II have invited the CFUGs to assist with the official reconstruction and reintegration process. There appears to be a general reluctance—mostly on the part of the

---

[26] Historically, Nepal's ruling classes have been made up of Brahmins and Chhetris, who originally migrated from other areas. The phrase *ethnic groups* refers to the traditional tribes of Nepal (including Rai, Gurung, Tamang, Limbu, Magar, and Newar), which have experienced discrimination and marginalization.

[27] During negotiations about the CPA, forest rights activists tried to persuade the leaders of democratic political parties to address community rights as part of the agreement, but they were unsuccessful because the largest network of CFUGs is affiliated with one political party—the Communist Party of Nepal–Unified Marxist-Leninist (CPN–UML)—and the Maoists and the CPN–UML disagree on forest resource management. Although there were rumors, during the negotiations about the CPA, that there were plans to link the forest user groups very closely to local government at the village and district levels, this did not occur. Such an arrangement would have been desirable from the perspective of some political parties and civil society groups, but not from the perspective of the traditional parties and the landlords, both of which have a vested interest in maintaining control over natural resources, especially land. After the CPA was signed, thousands of CFUG members (under the aegis of an umbrella organization, the Federation of Community Forestry Users in Nepal), held a pro-democratic demonstration in Kathmandu, submitted a memorandum to the government requesting that the people be given authority over the forest, and met with leaders of various political parties to advocate for their position.

government of Nepal—to "think outside the box" and try new approaches to resource management and peacebuilding.[28]

LESSONS LEARNED

The principal lesson learned is that CFUGs are major contributors to reconstruction and reintegration in Nepal. Specifically, the CFUGs are shoring up peacebuilding by

- Managing conflict over land, housing, and past events.
- Preventing returning IDPs from being revictimized.
- Providing assistance with livelihoods.
- Providing labor and materials to construct homes, schools, health centers, and other essential infrastructure.
- Turning over land to previously landless residents.

With the exception of conflict management, all other CFUG activities are made possible through the successful management of the forests.

Reintegration is the key to security in a post-conflict environment, and responsibility for reintegration ultimately lies with local communities (UNDP n.d.).[29] In the words of the UN Disarmament, Demobilization, and Reintegration Resource Centre,

> The success of reintegration programmes depends on the combined efforts of individuals, families and communities. Reintegration programs shall be designed through a participatory process that involves ex-combatants and communities, local and national authorities, and other non-government actors in planning and decision-making from the earliest stages (UN DDR n.d.).

Nevertheless, the governments and organizations that oversee peacebuilding rarely undertake participatory needs assessments or participatory planning processes that would ensure involvement at the community level.[30]

The history of the CFUGs in Nepal demonstrates their capacity and their potential to foster constructive dialogue at the district and eventually the national level (through the Federation of Community Forest User Groups of Nepal, a national network). The CFUGs have no formal connection to national post-conflict policy; their members have not been invited to serve as resources or advisors for various commissions (such as land reform, truth and reconciliation, or the subcommittees of the Constituent

---

[28] Speaking on condition of anonymity, a UN official working on peacebuilding in Nepal said in a 2007 interview that there are no plans to develop community-based reintegration strategies in Nepal.

[29] See also UNGA (2005).

[30] Cases compared here were Afghanistan, Burundi, the Democratic Republic of the Congo, Haiti, Côte d'Ivoire, Liberia, Sierra Leone, the Solomon Islands, Sudan, and Uganda (UN DDR n.d.).

Assembly); nor do any of the international organizations that are involved in security sector reform, reintegration, or reconstruction work with CFUG members. The research demonstrates, however, that peacebuilding efforts can benefit from the structures, strategies, experiences, and knowledge of the forest user groups.

CONCLUSION

Rebuilding security and social capital in the wake of a conflict poses a number of challenges, and what the CFUGs have to offer is only part of what is needed. But while the rest of the country languishes in a state of transition, CFUGs are demonstrating both the ability and the will to move forward, and to support peace and security through reconciliation, reconstruction, and livelihood support.

One might ask whether the CFUGs would have been as successful in the post-conflict period if they had not existed before and during the war. It is hard to say; nevertheless, the authors believe that such groups, as long as they are legally sanctioned, can be effective even if they did not exist before a conflict. The value of such groups lies in their ability to effectively manage natural resources, to assist with reintegration, and to oversee reconstruction.

Reimann argues that any conflict-transformation strategy must include Track III actors, as they are the parties who deal most directly with those who have been affected by war. Nevertheless, Track I and Track II actors do not actively seek out community-based groups for participation in peacebuilding. But what would an alternative process look like? From the perspective of disadvantaged groups that have suffered centuries of social injustice, one of the possible results of including Track III actors and strategies in peacebuilding efforts is to generate and support structural change. This possibility raises a further question: have Track III actors been excluded from peacebuilding strategies because structural change is not really what Track I (and sometimes even Track II) actors want?[31] In Nepal, CFUGs are watching the political process carefully and are ready to intervene, to demonstrate, and to fight—peacefully—for their rights, if the future of community forestry appears to be at risk. Because of the country's unstable political situation, community-based groups are vital to creating pressure on the government to ensure access to secure livelihoods.

CFUGs have the potential to play a key role in Nepal's continuing recovery from conflict. But the groups themselves are still far from perfect. CFUG leaders need to make sincere efforts to ensure meaningful participation on the part of women, and on the part of people from different castes, classes, and ethnic backgrounds; in short, those who have traditionally been excluded from community decision making must be brought into the fold.

---

[31] There is also the question of perspective: should the CFUGs' efforts and achievements be viewed as "real" peacebuilding strategies, or as aspects of traditional community empowerment? This very question, however, assumes that Track I and Track II actors are the only parties engaged in genuine peacebuilding.

CFUGs are not only assisting their own country, but are also setting an example that can be used as a standard of best practice. Disseminating information on the work of the CFUGs in Nepal could serve two ends: first, to encourage others who are working to develop community-based natural resource management groups; second, to help persuade national leaders to put more trust in their communities, and to share responsibility with those who rely on the benefits of natural resources.

REFERENCES

Banjade, M. R., and N. P. Timsina. 2005. Impact of armed conflict in community forestry of Nepal. *ETFRN News* 43–44/05. www.etfrn.org/etfrn/newsletter/news4344/articles/4_1_Banjade.pdf.

Basnet, J. 2008. How land reform can promote inclusive growth in Nepal. *Land First: Occasional Journal of Land Rights* 7 (July 20).

Bercovitch, J. 1984. *Social conflicts and third parties: Strategies of conflict resolution.* Boulder, CO: Westview.

———. 1996. *Resolving international conflicts: The theory and practice of mediation.* Boulder, CO: Lynne Rienner.

Burton, J. 1990. *Conflict: Human needs theory.* London: Macmillan.

———. 1993. Conflict resolution as a political philosophy. In *Conflict resolution theory and practice: Integration and application*, ed. D. J. D. Sandole and H. van der Merwe. Manchester, UK: Manchester University Press.

CBS (Central Bureau of Statistics), Government of Nepal. n.d. Population. www.cbs.gov.np/#.

CSRC (Community Self Reliance Centre). 2009. *Land and land tenure security in Nepal.* Kathmandu.

Department of Forestry. n.d. CFUG database. (Internal database; last accessed July 2008).

DFID (Department for International Development). n.d. Key facts. www.dfid.gov.uk/Where-we-work/Asia-South/Nepal/Key-facts/.

Fisher, R., and W. Ury. 1981. *Getting to yes: How to negotiate without giving in.* London: Arrow Books.

Fisher, R. J. 1983. Third party consultation as a method of conflict resolution: A review of studies. *Journal of Conflict Resolution* 27 (2): 301–334.

Galtung, J. 1998. *Friede mit friedlichen mitteln.* Opladen, Germany: Leske und Budrich.

IDMC (Internal Displacement Monitoring Centre). n.d. Nepal: Failed implementation of IDP policy leaves many unassisted. www.internal-displacement.org/8025708F004CE90B/%28httpCountries%29/CC2C3C0FBDAD8F03C125746D002F61D9?opendocument&count=10000.

INSEC Online. n.d.a. Conflict-induced displacement in Nepal up to end 2004. (On file with authors.)

———. n.d.b. No. of victims disappeared by state and Maoist, 13 Feb 1996–31 Dec 2006. (On file with authors.)

———. n.d.c. No. of victims killed by state and Maoist in connection with the "People's War." (On file with authors.)

Kleiboer, M. 1996. Understanding the success and failure of international mediation. *Journal of Conflict Resolution* 40 (2): 360–389.

Lederach, J. P. 1995. *Preparing for peace: Conflict transformation across cultures.* Syracuse, NY: Syracuse University Press.

———. 1997. *Building peace: Sustainable reconciliation in divided societies.* Washington, D.C.: U.S. Institute of Peace.

LFP (Livelihoods and Forest Programme). 2006. Financial report for 2005–2006. Kathmandu. (Internal document; on file with authors.)

———. 2007. LFP progress report 2006–2007. Kathmandu. (Internal document; on file with authors.)

———. 2008. Livelihoods and Forestry Programme, annual report: July 2007–July 2008. Kathmandu.

———. n.d. Context database. (Internal database; last accessed July 2008.)

Oomen, B. n.d. Rwanda's *Gacaca*: Objectives, merits and their relation to supranational criminal law. www.roac.nl/roac/_files/publications%20oomen/Oomen%20Rwanda.pdf.

Rechlin, M. A., W. R. Burch, A. L. Hammett, B. Subedi, S. Binayee, and I. Sapkota. 2007. *Lal salam* and *hario ban*: The effects of the Maoist insurgency on community forestry in Nepal. *Forest, Trees and Livelihoods* 17:1–9.

Reimann, C. 2004. Assessing the state-of-the-art in conflict transformation. Berghof Research Center for Constructive Conflict Management. www.berghof-handbook.net/documents/publications/reimann_handbook.pdf.

Roka, K. B. 2007. Armed conflict and its impact on community forestry in Nepal. *Tropical Resource Bulletin* 26:55–62.

Sharma, P. P. 2009. Interview with Tina Sanio.

SODEC (*Société de développement des enterprises culturelles*). 2008. E-mail from SODEC staff to B. Chapagain. June.

———. n.d. Progress report. (Internal document.)

UNDP (United Nations Development Programme). n.d. Practice note: Disarmament, demobilization and reintegration of ex-combatants. www.undp.org/cpr/whats_new/ddr_practice_note.pdf.

UN DDR (United Nations Disarmament, Demobilization, and Reintegration) Resource Centre. n.d. Social and economic reintegration. www.unddr.org/iddrs/04/30.php.

UNGA (United Nations General Assembly). 2005. Administrative and budgetary aspects of the financing of the United Nations peacekeeping operations: Note by the Secretary-General. A/C.5/59/31. May 24. http://documents-dds-ny.un.org/doc/UNDOC/GEN/N05/357/15/pdf/N0535715.pdf?OpenElement.

Upreti, B. R. 2006. Conflicts in natural resource management: Examples from community forestry. *Jahrbuch der Oesterreichischen Gesellschaft fuer Agraroekonomie* 15:143–155.

Lurking beneath the surface: Oil, environmental degradation, and armed conflict in Sudan

Luke A. Patey

Sudan has a long history of armed conflict. The first North-South civil war (1955–1972) was followed by a decade of relative peace, but by 1983 a second conflict had begun that left over 2 million dead and 4 million internally displaced (ICG 2002). The signing of the comprehensive peace agreement (CPA), in 2005, brought an end to the second North-South civil war, but peace remains elusive in Sudan. As the planned 2011 referendum for the secession of Southern Sudan approaches, environmental degradation linked to oil development—which is among the many causes of armed conflict in the region—continues to inflame violence at the local level.

Oil played a role in fueling violence during the second civil war. The Sudan Armed Forces and progovernment militias orchestrated the killing and displacement of thousands of civilians to make room for the oil sector's undisturbed development. In the years since the signing of the CPA, oil has continued to weigh heavily in recurrent bouts of armed conflict. Nonetheless, civil war between the North and South has been held at bay by a number of factors, one of which is that the Government of National Unity, in Khartoum, and the Government of Southern Sudan, in Juba, have a mutual interest in sharing oil revenues. The resulting political accommodation may well continue in the years beyond 2011, when the peace agreement ends. But the partners in the CPA—the ruling National Congress Party and the Sudan People's Liberation Movement (the dominant southern rebel group)—have largely neglected the social and environmental damage caused by oil development in Southern Sudan.[1]

Luke A. Patey is a project researcher at the Danish Institute for International Studies. Because of the sensitive nature of the subject matter, the author has relied on confidential interviews and materials. This chapter also draws from material originally published in Luke A. Patey, "Crude Days Ahead? Oil and the Resource Curse in Sudan," *African Affairs* 109 (437): 617–636.

[1] In 2010, oil-producing states in Sudan included Unity, Southern Kordofan, and Upper Nile.

Although the violent displacement that was common during the second North-South civil war has subsided, the expansion of the oil sector nonetheless continues to exacerbate grievances in oil-bearing regions. Forced relocations and the contamination of water by oil development at Thar Jath—south of Bentiu, in Unity State—led one local to warn, "If the government ignores us, we will go Nigeria style" (AFP 2008a). In fact, protracted armed resistance that is reminiscent of events in the Niger Delta has already begun to materialize in Southern Sudan. In late 2007, the Darfur rebel group JEM (Justice and Equality Movement), with the assistance of a local armed group made up of ethnic Misseriya from the area, attacked an installation of China National Petroleum Corporation (CNPC) near the Defra oil field, in Southern Kordofan, seizing five Sudanese, an Egyptian, and an Iraqi (Reuters 2007). In May 2008, four Indian oil technicians were kidnapped near the oil town of Heglig; in October of that year, nine Chinese oil workers were taken, and five died in what was apparently a botched rescue attempt by Sudanese authorities (AFP 2008b; *Sudan Tribune* 2008). Local armed groups argue that such attacks are justified by the absence of any peacetime benefit from oil, and by oil-related damage to the environment. Unless the concerns of communities in and around oil-bearing regions are addressed, these violent altercations will likely continue.

Regardless of the outcome of the referendum, assigning priority to—and acting on—the often-neglected environmental consequences of oil development will be fundamental to dampening oil-linked violence in the years to come. Once obfuscated by civil war, the problems of environmental degradation have become more apparent in the post-conflict period. Environmental damage has largely destroyed hope, in oil-bearing regions of Southern Sudan, that oil development will lead to better living standards. And, as environmental degradation continues to damage livelihoods in the region, what has so far been mainly sporadic violence may blossom into organized rebellion. Post-conflict resource management must therefore assign priority to environmental protection and remediation, in order to ensure that fresh grievances do not spark new conflicts.

ENVIRONMENTAL DEGRADATION

The oil sector in Sudan expanded significantly in the years following the signing of the CPA (see figure 1). As the security situation improved, exploratory wells, permanent roads, pipelines, pumping stations, and electrical facilities spread across the region. The Chinese, Malaysian, and Indian state-owned companies that dominate the sector expanded their activities. But as civil war came to a formal end, a variety of environmental concerns associated with oil development began to emerge more clearly. The environmental impact of oil development in Sudan is complex, ranging from oil spills to the ecological imprint of road construction (Cooper and Catterson 2007; El Moghraby 2009). The most worrisome issue, however, is "produced water," which comes to ground along with extracted crude oil and holds toxic concentrations of chemicals and minerals; if it is discharged

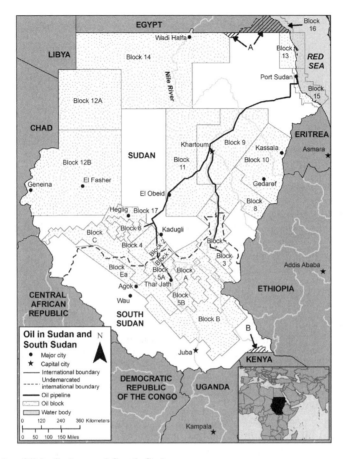

Figure 1. Oil in Sudan and South Sudan
Source: Oil block and oil pipeline data adapted from ECOS (2007).
Notes:
A – The Hala'ib Triangle, claimed by Sudan and de facto administered by Egypt.
B – The Ilemi Triangle, claimed by Ethiopia, Sudan, and Kenya and de facto controlled by Kenya.
For information on ownership of specific concession blocks, see the annex to this chapter.

into the surrounding area without proper treatment, it becomes a severe hazard. The Heglig oil facility alone, for example, generates 10 million cubic meters of produced water a year. Water levels have risen as the Heglig oil field has matured, and the facility's reed bed technology is no longer able to handle the increasing quantity of produced water (UNEP 2007). Contaminated water—as well as hazardous-waste dumping—threatens not only the vast marshland of the Sudd, but also the region's inhabitants: after consuming contaminated water, livestock have died and civilians have fallen violently ill, building further resentment against the oil sector.

Failure to address the issue of produced water stems from a number of factors. First, oil companies tend to underestimate the amount of produced water generated by an oil field. Second, financial constraints and Sudan's lax environmental policies all push companies to cut corners: when it comes to protecting the environment, oil companies have essentially been left on their own. Third, oil companies that operate in Sudan come from countries with poor environmental practices; hence, there has been little regard for international standards and norms. Finally, in a place like Southern Sudan, where there are few roads and only limited infrastructure for waste storage, companies that are keen to slash costs are reluctant to take on the added expense of proper environmental management.

The construction of access roads (for oil exploration) and permanent roads (for production sites) has hampered livelihoods in Southern Sudan by altering local hydrology. Because the oil-bearing regions are predominantly flat, even the slightest depressions can alter the drainage and flood patterns that are critical for irrigation and wildlife. During exploration, which is undertaken in the dry season, oil companies build temporary roads; but to cut costs, they rarely bother to construct the expensive culverts that are required for drainage once the rainy season arrives. And even when drainage is constructed for the permanent roads used to access oil discoveries, the culverts are designed to protect the road, not to ensure the proper flow of water. Thus, during the wet season, the culverts obstruct the flow of water. On the road from Abyei to Agok, for example, the lack of drainage culverts has caused flooding on one side and drought on the other, disrupting irrigation in the area.[2]

Oil-related environmental degradation not only leads to resentment against oil companies—as well as against political leaders, in both the North and South—but can also pit communities against one another. Tainted water (or water that is perceived to be tainted) and alterations to natural hydrology intensify water shortages and force locals to travel longer distances to find fresh sources. Thus, by exacerbating environmental scarcity, oil development in Southern Sudan threatens to intensify local conflict.

THE MISSING PEACE DIVIDEND

The absence of a visible peace dividend is one of the principal grievances of communities in the oil-bearing regions of Sudan. Although the expansion of oil-related infrastructure has yielded wider mobile-network coverage and improved roads, public transportation, and access to markets, it has also threatened livelihoods and uprooted settlements (ECOS 2008).

Oil development has provided local communities with few economic benefits or compensation—and where compensation has been granted, it has occurred

---

[2] Confidential telephone interview with an official from an international organization, January 2009.

through ad hoc agreements, with little governmental or legal oversight. There has been little transparency in how oil funds transferred to producing states are spent. Furthermore, instead of spurring economic development in Southern Sudan, oil production has resulted in calls for economic compensation to cover oil-related environmental damage. For example, when Taban Deng Gai, the governor of Unity State, demanded that his state begin to receive a 15 percent share of oil revenues produced from his state when the CPA ends in 2011, he cited the state's vulnerability to environmental hazards resulting from oil production (Dak 2009).

Finally, employment opportunities in Sudan's oil sector are poor. The oil business does not produce many jobs, particularly for low-skilled workers. Moreover, employment decisions—even for temporary, low-level positions—are often made in Khartoum; as a result, northern Sudanese and foreigners fill most positions.[3] In fact, oil firms often view southerners with suspicion and deny them even casual work. In Abyei, for example, oil companies have employed few Dinka or Misseriya. Those southerners who do find employment are often treated poorly, receive no benefits, and are given lower salaries than their northern counterparts.

POST-CONFLICT ENVIRONMENTAL MANAGEMENT

There is an utter lack of environmental regulation in Sudan's oil sector. Although the CPA states (1) that oil companies should follow "best known practices in the sustainable utilization and control of natural resources," and (2) that communities in oil-bearing regions have the right to participation and compensation, the agreement does not specify any standards for or modes of compensation, and enforcement mechanisms are nonexistent (ECOS 2008).

Not only is the peace agreement vague, but the environmental management procedures that *do* exist in national law are largely ignored. More often than not, the energy and investment sectors take precedence over environmental matters. The law is also hampered by poor enforcement mechanisms, largely because of the variety of government institutions and ministries that are connected to the environment (ECOS 2008). The absence of scrutiny has encouraged poor environmental practices (UNEP 2007); for instance, although it is not uncommon for oil companies to commission environmental impact assessments, the assessments are often conducted after operations have already begun, and are typically shelved after completion.[4] In short, when it comes to the environment, the oil industry is largely self-regulating.

The lack of environmental regulation is fundamentally a failure of the Ministry of Petroleum, in Khartoum, which has neither the will nor the capacity to manage the social and environmental impacts of oil development. And although southern authorities have used strong rhetoric when it comes to the environment, in practice they have been similarly lax. The major foreign oil

---

[3] Unpublished report from an international organization.
[4] Confidential interview with an oil consultant, Khartoum, September 2006.

companies have also failed to take the lead through corporate responsibility. Although some companies provide community development programs, the meager benefits that result are essentially negated by the environmental damage associated with the companies' everyday operations. The oil companies' failure to adhere to international environmental standards, coupled with the lack of peacetime dividends connected to oil, ensures that the sector will continue to be threatened by vandalism, theft, kidnapping, and violence.[5]

The risk of future armed conflict in Sudan can be diminished only if Sudanese political leaders begin to take the condition of the environment seriously. First, for post-conflict resource management to be successful, the domestic institutions responsible for environmental regulation and enforcement require the necessary resources, expertise, and political autonomy. Second, environmental measures must be fully set out in peace agreements, and must reflect international standards—including independent oversight. Although environmental aims may clash with other priorities of political groups, international nongovernmental organizations can assist domestic environmental groups to push environmental issues to the forefront of the government's agenda. A review of the extent to which oil companies' environmental practices meet or violate national law and contractual obligations is essential in any post-conflict setting. In Sudan, the post-conflict environmental assessment conducted by the United Nations Environment Programme offers a valuable starting point for improving environmental management. For specific recommendations, oil companies can turn to the business principles developed by the European Coalition on Oil in Sudan (UNEP 2007; ECOS 2008). Counteracting the environmental degradation caused by oil development is a vital part of building peace in Sudan.

REFERENCES

AFP (Agence France-Presse). 2008a. South Sudan villagers, environment suffer from oil boom. March 5.

———. 2008b. Four Indian oil workers kidnapped in Sudan's Abyei. May 15.

Cooper, J. C., and T. Catterson. 2007. Sudan transitional environment program: Scoping statement for a programmatic environmental assessment of oil exploration and production activities in Southern Sudan. Washington, D.C.: International Resources Group.

Dak, J. G. 2009. Sudan Unity State governor says more oil share post-2011. *Sudan Tribune*, August 19.

ECOS (European Coalition on Oil in Sudan). 2007. Oil: Fuel for a better Sudan? www.ecosonline.org/oilmap/resources/Soedan%20A5%20kleur.pdf.

———. 2008. *Sudan, whose oil? Sudan's oil industry: Facts and analysis*. Utrecht, Netherlands: European Coalition on Oil in Sudan.

---

[5] For a review of the leading international environmental and social standards, see Jill Shankleman, "Mitigating Risks and Realizing Opportunities: Environmental and Social Standards for Foreign Direct Investment in High-Value Natural Resources," in this volume.

El Moghraby, A. I. 2009. Oil development in Sudan. In *Africa and energy security: Global issues, local responses*, ed. R. Beri and U. K. Sinha. New Delhi: Academic Foundation.

ICG (International Crisis Group). 2002. *God, oil, and country: Changing the logic of war in Sudan.* Brussels.

Reuters. 2007. China tells Sudan to ensure safety after attack claim. October 26.

Sudan Tribune. 2008. Conflicting reports on the fate of Chinese hostages in Sudan. October 28.

UNEP (United Nations Environment Programme). 2007. *Synthesis report, Sudan: Post-conflict environmental assessment.* Nairobi.

ANNEX
Ownership of oil concessions in Sudan

Block 1,2,4. Greater Nile Petroleum Operating Company
40% China National Petroleum Corporation
30% Petronas
25% ONGC Videsh
5% Sudapet

Block 3,7. Petrodar Operating Company PDOC Oil production Sudan
41% China National Petroleum Corporation
40% Petronas
8% Sudapet
6% Sinopec
5% Al Thani

Block 5A. White Nile Petroleum Operating Company 1
68.875% Petronas
24.125% ONGC Videsh
7% Sudapet

Block 5B. White Nile Petroleum Operating Company 2
10% awarded to government of South Sudan; composition to be renegotiated
39% Petronas
24.5% Lundin
23.5% ONGC Videsh
13% Sudapet

Block 6. China National Petroleum Corporation International (Sudan)
95% China National Petroleum Corporation
5% Sudapet

Block 8. White Nile Petroleum Operating Company 3
77% Petronas
15% Sudapet
8% Hi Tech

Block 9,11. Sudapak I
85% Zafir
15% Sudapet

Block 10. Free

Block 12A. Qahtani and Others
33% Qahtani
20% Ansan
20% Sudapet
15% Dindir Petroleum
7% Hi Tech
5% A.A. In.

Block 12B. Free

Block 13. China National Petroleum Corporation, Pertamina, and Sudapet
40% China National Petroleum Corporation
15% Pertamina
15% Sudapet
10% Dindir Petroleum
10% Express Petroleum & Gas
10% Africa Energy

Block 14. Petro SA
80% Petro SA
20% Sudapet

Block 15. Red Sea Petroleum Operating Company
35% Petronas
35% China National Petroleum Corporation
15% Sudapet
10% Express Petroleum and Gas
5% Hi Tech

Block 16. Lundin

Block 17. Ansan
66% Ansan
34% Sudapet

Block A. Sudapak II
83% Zafir
17% Sudapet

Block B. Total
32.5% Total
27.5% Kufpec
10% Sudapet
10% Government of South Sudan
20% Open

Block C. APCO
65% Hi Tech
17% Sudapet
10% Khartoum State
8% Hegleig

Block Ea. Free

Building or spoiling peace? Lessons from the management of high-value natural resources

Siri Aas Rustad, Päivi Lujala, and Philippe Le Billon

In June 2010, a team of officials from the U.S. Department of Defense, the U.S. Geological Survey, and the U.S. Agency for International Development announced that Afghanistan has considerable reserves of iron, cobalt, gold, copper, and lithium, with an estimated value of US$900 billion, buried in its soil (*BBC News* 2010). Remarkably, this news was greeted as yet another challenge in the country's painful transition to peace, rather than as an opportunity to diversify the economy, create jobs, bring in foreign currency, and ensure long-term development. Experts have stated, in resounding concert, that the mineral wealth may not be good for Afghanistan and may lead to more conflict in the future.[1]

In Afghanistan and other post-conflict and conflict-affected countries, high-value natural resources present both challenges and opportunities. Although such resources can contribute to renewed conflict, they can also—if properly managed—help to consolidate peace. But what constitutes proper management? Each chapter in this volume sets out, in its own way, to answer that question. The purpose of this concluding chapter is to distill the lessons of the volume as a whole, as well as other literature, in order to point the way forward for future efforts.

Although attempts have been made to improve the management of high-value resources in post-conflict situations, they have met with limited success. As is clear from many of the case studies in this volume, it is extraordinarily difficult to design and implement successful interventions. The point, however, is not that the challenges cannot or should not be addressed, but that program officers, decision makers, and the public need to be realistic about the complexity of the challenges and the commitment that will be required.

Siri Aas Rustad is a researcher at the Centre for the Study of Civil War (CSCW) of the Peace Research Institute Oslo (PRIO) and a Ph.D. candidate in political science at the Department of Sociology and Political Science, Norwegian University of Science and Technology (NTNU). Päivi Lujala is an associate professor in the Department of Geography, NTNU, and a senior researcher in the Department of Economics, NTNU, and CSCW. Philippe Le Billon is an associate professor at the University of British Columbia, where he is affiliated with both the Department of Geography and the Liu Institute for Global Issues.

[1] See, for example, McNeil (2010) and Collier (2010a).

The management of high-value natural resources in post-conflict situations depends, among other things, on the context, including the causes and trajectory of the conflict; the characteristics of the natural resources in question and their role in conflict; the quality of domestic institutions; regional dynamics and international markets; and current and previous approaches to the management of natural resources and the associated revenues. Thus, no one set of policies or programs can ensure success. Instead of attempting to provide a single recipe for the management of high-value natural resources, this chapter highlights a range of policy options and management tools. Some overlap; some work only in combination with other approaches; most are complementary.

This chapter consists of six sections that cover the following topics: (1) assessing the resource base and local resource economies; (2) managing resource extraction and revenue generation; (3) allocating and distributing natural resource revenues; (4) enhancing institutional quality; (5) addressing cross-cutting issues (context, external actors, public engagement, and peace spoilers); and (6) coordinating and sequencing interventions. A brief conclusion highlights central issues in the management of high-value natural resources.

ASSESSING THE RESOURCE BASE AND LOCAL RESOURCE ECONOMIES

In order to engage in realistic peace negotiations, develop judicious and comprehensive recovery policies, and ensure genuine peace dividends for a war-torn populace, two things are required: (1) reliable estimates of the resource base and (2) a thorough understanding of the role of resources in local livelihoods. A number of factors—including the death or flight of staff, illegal or undocumented exploitation, and a lapse in surveys—may make such information hard to come by. Nevertheless, knowledge of the resource base—and of the ways in which local livelihoods depend on it—is essential. People may have high hopes of revenues from resource exploitation, and are likely to be disappointed and aggrieved if their expectations do not materialize. Moreover, those whose incomes depend on the resource economy may be put at risk if their needs are not accounted for in the peace process.

The resource base

An accurate understanding of the extent of the resource base should guide policy decisions and inform public opinion. In the case of peace agreements and revenue-sharing agreements, for example, a common understanding of the scope and value of resources can help all parties to see clearly what is at stake. One option is to use experts to provide impartial information on the resource base. In 2004, for example, to facilitate the Agreement on Wealth Sharing between Sudan and Southern Sudan, experts on oil reserves and oil field development were called in to develop a common understanding, among participants in the negotiations, of the extent of the oil reserves (Wennmann 2012*).[2]

An accurate assessment of the resource base may also render a central government more willing to grant autonomy, a larger share of resource revenues, or both to a region whose resources are relatively small in comparison to those of the nation as a whole, or whose resources are already seriously depleted. During the 2005 peace negotiations between Aceh and the Indonesian government, for example, the depletion of Aceh's reserves made wealth sharing between the government of Indonesia and Aceh less relevant—which probably contributed to the Indonesian government's willingness to grant Aceh better terms, with respect to revenue sharing from oil and gas exploitation in Aceh (Wennmann 2012*).

In some cases, realistic assessments of resource reserves may help a region seeking autonomy realize that resource extraction alone is not a viable basis for the entire regional economy. As Annegret Mähler has observed, even the central government may have inaccurate perceptions of resource reserves and of what can be achieved with them, and may therefore fail to develop other sectors of the economy (Mähler 2012*). The government budget of Southern Sudan (now South Sudan), for example, has been financed almost entirely by oil revenues; unless the country is able to develop the nonoil sectors of its economy, a decline in oil revenues would jeopardize its economic viability as an independent state (Wennmann 2010).

Publicizing information on the size of the resource base also helps to create more realistic expectations. Unrealized expectations may provoke accusations of corruption or failure to adhere to promises made during peace negotiations; even if such accusations are unjust, they can fuel historic grievances and may destabilize the entire peace process. Finally, reliable estimates of reserves are a prerequisite for negotiations with (often) better-informed extraction companies.

Local resource economies

The success of any peacebuilding effort will be measured, in part, against the past and current benefits derived from the local resource economy. In many countries, resource exploitation for the purpose of livelihood support, such as the artisanal mining of minerals, has existed before conflict or develops as a coping strategy during conflict.[3] By serving as the basis for livelihoods, natural resources in the post-conflict period offer employment opportunities; reduce poverty; and provide access to hard currency and construction material (e.g., from forests). In the Democratic Republic of the Congo (DRC), for example, the

---

[2] Citations marked with an asterisk refer to chapters within this volume.
[3] Coping economies, which are also known as *survival economies*, develop when families or population groups survive by engaging in activities such as subsistence agriculture, artisanal mining, and petty trade.

livelihoods of about 15 percent of the population are estimated to depend on artisanal mining (World Bank 2008). Similarly, in the Central African Republic, the artisanal diamond sector provides work for between 50,000 and 80,000 people, and almost 15 percent of the population depends on the sector for survival (Spittaels and Hilgert 2009).

Nevertheless, because exploitation of high-value natural resources for livelihood support is often perceived as a source of financing for conflict, livelihood needs are likely to be forgotten in the rush to curtail rebels' or peace spoilers' access to resources.[4] In separate articles in this volume, Adam Pain and David M. Catarious Jr. and Alison Russell argue, for example, that opium poppy cultivation has been wrongly viewed as providing revenue solely for Afghanistan's conflict economy, and that most counternarcotics efforts in Afghanistan appear to have failed because they ignored farmers' motivations and needs and how the cultivation has contributed to their livelihoods (Pain 2012*; Catarious and Russell 2012*).

Failing to understand the role of resources in the conflict economy may also cause the peace potential of informal (and even illegal) resource extraction to be overlooked. In a chapter focused on Nepal's community forest user groups (CFUGs), Tina Sanio and Binod Chapagain offer a successful example of the peace potential embedded in the local resource economy. CFUGs have facilitated the transition to peace by supporting both livelihoods and civil rights—most particularly by helping to reintegrate internally displaced persons, assisting with the reconstruction of homes, negotiating property rights disputes, and supporting small-scale enterprises (Sanio and Chapagain 2012*). CFUGs were able to accomplish what they did because their sustainable, communal management of forest resources gave them a solid economic and social base from which to operate.

Where exploitation and trade to support livelihoods are the backbone of the local economy, attempts to regulate unofficial or illegal exploitation may severely disturb that economy, causing local populations to view such interference as destructive. It is thus critical, as early in the post-conflict period as possible, to determine how to protect local livelihood opportunities while maximizing fiscal revenues and broad development benefits in the medium and long term. In the case of mineral resources, one possible approach is to set up a mineral rights cadastre—a public registry that grants and administers mineral rights for all types of mining concessions and oversees mining activities from the reconnaissance and exploration phases through extraction (Girones, Pugachevsky, and Walser 2009).[5] In a post-conflict setting, a cadastre can be a source of valuable information about the size of the resource reserves and the expected revenues from both industrial and artisanal exploitation.

---

[4] Peace spoilers are those who have something to lose, either politically or economically, from peace—and who therefore act to undermine it. (Peace spoilers are discussed in later sections of the chapter.)

[5] Some countries that have mineral rights cadastres have also introduced special licenses for artisanal mining.

MANAGING RESOURCE EXTRACTION AND REVENUE GENERATION

Managing resource extraction is challenging even under ordinary circumstances but is particularly so in post-conflict situations. First, regulatory institutions are generally ill prepared to face the massive "resource rush" that often occurs in the wake of conflict. Competent management staff are typically in short supply, governance structures are in flux, and the presence of multiple sources of authority—including transitional administrations, donor projects, and the remnants of past management regimes—may blur the definitions of legality and good practice. Second, because of the vast economic stakes, high-value resource sectors are particularly vulnerable to mismanagement: a single poorly negotiated contract for a major mining venture, for example, can undermine state revenues for decades. At the same time, unofficial or illegal production and smuggling—by civilians, government officials, soldiers, and excombatants—may deprive the state of substantial revenues.[6] Third, warring factions—even those that are technically at peace—have an interest in controlling resource revenues, in order to retain maximum influence over the transition process, preserve the option of rearming in case of a conflict relapse, or cash in as their prospects of maintaining power dwindle. Resource sectors are thus likely to become the focus of politicized, high-stakes contests during the post-conflict transition.

This section discusses three broad lessons related to the management of resource extraction and revenue generation: First, the efforts of the United Nations to restrict peace spoilers' access to revenues have been increasingly effective. Second, the legacy of "odious contracts" signed by previous governments, belligerents, or transitional governments can be addressed through contractual review and renegotiation.[7] Third, commodity-tracking systems can effectively curtail peace spoilers' access to resources and increase state revenues from extractive industries.

United Nations initiatives to regulate access to resources

Since the late 1990s, the UN Security Council (UNSC) has used sanctions, expert panels, and peacekeeping forces to address the role of high-value resources during and after conflict. The increase in the number and diversity of interventions has

---

[6] There are a number of reasons that the end of hostilities is likely to bring about a resource rush, including the following: (1) opportunities may suddenly open up for both foreign investors and local entrepreneurs; (2) domestic authorities and international donors may view resource exploitation as a means of rapidly increasing foreign direct investment and tax revenues, and thereby reducing dependence on foreign aid; and (3) war-affected populations are seeking reconstruction materials and employment to rebuild their lives.

[7] The term *odious contracts* refers to contracts that grant extractive companies unduly high profit margins, generous tax exemptions, or other benefits.

strengthened the influence of the UNSC and UN missions over resource sectors, although the ultimate impacts remain in dispute.

Economic sanctions were rarely deployed until the end of the Cold War; since the mid-1990s, however, seven sanction regimes have included high-value natural resources (Minter and Schmidt 1988). Sanctions have become increasingly effective, for two reasons: more careful targeting and greater diligence on the part of importing companies and countries. The investigative and "naming and shaming" efforts of UN expert panels and nongovernmental organizations (NGOs), such as Global Witness, have also enhanced the effectiveness of sanctions. Expert panels, which were originally created to investigate sanction busting, focused on high-value resource issues for eight conflicts between 1999 and 2007.[8] In some cases, the panels' work has included assessments of resource management—for example, determining compliance with international certification regimes or domestic requirements for resource exploitation, and evaluating the transparency of contracts or revenues.

Although UN peacekeeping forces have rarely been explicitly mandated to regulate access to resources, in 2003, peacekeeping forces from the UN Mission in Liberia were mandated "to assist the transitional government in restoring proper administration of natural resources" (UNSC 2003, 4). And in 2004, the UN Assistance Mission in Sierra Leone (UNAMSIL) was mandated to "support the Sierra Leone armed forces . . . in patrolling the border and diamond mining areas, including through joint planning and joint operations where appropriate" (UNSC 2004, 2). Finally, in 2008, UN peacekeepers in the DRC were directed to prevent "the provision of support to illegal armed groups, including support derived from illicit economic activities"—such as resource extraction and trade (UNSC 2008, 4). Apart from these three mandates, however, UN peacekeepers have played a limited role in the management of high-value resources for various reasons, including the following: given the limited resources and expertise of UN missions, other priorities are more pressing; actions that might involve confrontation with criminal elements increase risks for peacekeepers and civilians alike; political stakeholders are sometimes involved in both the peace process and in questionable or illegal activities—a circumstance that may have to be taken into consideration; and both UN member states and their subnational governments (which may be benefiting economically from the status quo) may be reluctant to have the UNSC meddling in economic affairs.[9]

By deterring peace spoilers' access to conflict commodities, peacekeeping missions could strengthen legitimate, peace-enhancing resource extraction and trade, and curtail peace spoilers' access to resource revenues. In practical terms, this might mean that multidimensional peacekeeping missions would be deployed

---

[8] Expert panels have addressed natural resources in conflicts in Afghanistan (where they also addressed the international activities of al Qaeda), Angola, Côte d'Ivoire, the DRC, Liberia, Sierra Leone, Somalia, and Sudan.

[9] See Le Billon (2012a*), and Taylor and Davis (2012).

in resource production areas (to recover those that are under rebel control), as well as in the vicinity of key transportation hubs or border crossings.[10] However, mandates allowing UN troops to conduct military operations should be carefully considered. Between 2008 and 2010, for example, UN peacekeepers and the Congolese army conducted joint military operations against rebel troops who were controlling mines in the DRC. Although the operations succeeded in reducing the number of mines under rebel control, they were also associated with human rights abuses, population displacement, and extortion by government troops (Global Witness 2010). Nor did the operations succeed in demilitarizing the resource areas (Vircoulon 2011).

Peacekeeping forces can also be used to prevent the escalation of resource-related conflicts, and thereby short-circuit cycles of violence. In January 2002, in Sierra Leone, UNAMSIL peacekeepers had not yet been given an explicit mandate to intervene in resource sectors; nevertheless, as part of their general mandate to maintain peace, they stopped clashes between local youths and demobilized soldiers over access to diamond mines (USAID 2006). This experience shows that a peacekeeping force may intervene in resource-related issues even if it lacks an explicit mandate to do so, if conflicts over resources escalate to the point of physical violence that threatens peace.

By assisting domestic authorities and international agencies overseeing resource sectors, UN mission staff can help to address broader linkages between conflict, resources, and resource revenues. Such assistance might include monitoring activities such as illegal mining, logistical and managerial support, capacity building, and the good offices of UN representatives.[11] In 2010, for example, the Joint Mission Analysis Cell of the UN Organization Stabilization Mission in the DRC, in collaboration with the DRC Ministry of Mines, established five mineral-trading centers in Nord Kivu and Sud Kivu. Because these centers will accept only traceable and certified minerals for trade, they are strengthening both legal trade and the commercialization of minerals.[12]

Review of resource contracts

Before, during, and in the immediate aftermath of conflict, hard-pressed, incompetent, or corrupt government officials may sign contracts that are not in the best interests of the post-transition government or the populace. Sometimes governments under duress may even award concessions to firms providing security services. In 1995,

---

[10] In recent decades, an increasing number of UN peacekeeping missions have been categorized as "multidimensional," which means that they are "composed of a range of components, including military, civilian police, political affairs, rule of law, human rights, humanitarian, reconstruction, public information and gender" (UN DPKO 2003, 5).
[11] For a discussion of good offices, see Conflict Research Consortium (1998).
[12] Personal correspondence from A. Stork, advisor, UN Development Programme, 2011.

for example, the military junta that had seized control of Sierra Leone in 1992 granted business associates of Executive Outcomes, a South African mercenary force, a twenty-five-year mining lease in return for security services (Davies 2000).

Even post-transition governments (occasionally with the assistance of foreign donors) may grant new contracts with very favorable terms, simply to attract major investments. This was the case, for example, with rutile mining in Sierra Leone, which had been the country's main source of export earnings before the war (IMF 2004). According to an internal government review, the agreements that the government of Sierra Leone signed with a foreign titanium extraction firm in 2001 could lead to the loss of about US$8 million per year in tax revenues between 2004 and 2016 (Lambrechts 2009).

In addition to depriving the state of significant revenues poor contracts may also undermine the state's legitimacy in the eyes of the population, if the contracts create the impression that the state is corrupt or incapable of looking after the interests of the country as a whole. Poor contract terms may also foster corruption, give extractive firms too much power in the country's internal affairs, and enable extractive firms to engage in unsustainable resource use. Better contracts may also stipulate improved conditions for workers; establish stricter environmental and social safeguards; and include provisions for local development projects, such as the construction of schools, wells, and roads—all of which provide tangible peace dividends for local populations. For example, the renegotiated contract for Firestone's rubber plantation concession, in Liberia, included better housing for workers (Le Billon 2012b*).

Many post-conflict governments have reviewed, reassessed, and renegotiated resource contracts that were signed during hostilities or during the transitional period. The most complex set of reassessments—which addressed both mining and logging contracts, and involved parliamentarian and interministerial commissions as well as a number of donors and NGOs—took place in the DRC in 2004 and 2007. Although the 2004 Transitional Parliament Commission, which was chaired by opposition leader Christophe Lutundula, made specific recommendations, President Joseph Kabila, who controlled the final renegotiation, took limited (and controversial) action, including the imposition of windfall taxes and the reallocation of some concessions to Chinese companies (Vircoulon 2009).[13]

In Liberia, a review of timber-harvesting contracts (undertaken partly in response to international pressure) revealed that none of the firms under contract could demonstrate the legality of their operations; as a result, Ellen Johnson

---

[13] The commission's recommendations included, among other things: the renegotiation or cancellation of sixteen contracts (which amounted to about half of all the DRC's logging concessions); the imposition of a moratorium on new logging concessions; judicial investigation of twenty-eight Congolese or international companies; and the prosecution of seventeen people for fraud.

Sirleaf, the newly elected president, cancelled all timber concessions (Altman, Nichols, and Woods 2012*). Johnson Sirleaf was also able to renegotiate—and significantly improve—a mining contract that had been signed by Mittal Steel and the transition government (Le Billon 2012b*).

Unfortunately, contract reviews and reappraisals have proved to be slow and contentious processes, as in the case of the DRC. In Liberia, which may be considered a model case, timber sector reform, including the revocation of timber concessions, has been deemed successful; nevertheless, the broader reforms that followed contract reappraisals effectively stalled large-scale timber harvesting for three years, frustrating timber companies and those who were eager to see more revenues flowing to Liberia's strained budget (Beevers 2012*).

Governments that do little (e.g., by failing to follow up on recommendations from contract review commissions), as well as those that undertake substantial measures (e.g., by instituting sweeping reforms that temporarily waylay investments), are both open to criticism. Yet another criticism that has been raised regarding the implementation of contract reviews is the risk of opening new opportunities for corruption or assigning privileged status to particular companies. In the DRC, for example, there was a suspicion, among Western donors and companies, that contracts were being renegotiated in order to facilitate the reallocation of copper and cobalt projects to Chinese companies (Marysse and Geenen 2009).

The meager outcomes of contract reviews can be partly explained by limited expertise and capacity. Other constraints on contract review include inadequate funding, asymmetric information, political fragility, and outright corruption. Finally, the policy recommendations of domestic authorities and international donors may clash with the objectives of ruling elites. Ultimately, as is illustrated by the outcomes in DRC and the Liberia, the successful review of concession contracts depends on political will. In the DRC, recommendations from the concession review foundered because of the president's lack of commitment; in Liberia, in contrast, the president was the driving force in the review process.

To encourage contractual reassessments donors should provide contract review committees with technical assistance and budgetary support. In Liberia, for example, the key to the success of the review was the support of a secretariat that included both Liberian and international technical and legal experts (Altman, Nichols, and Woods 2012*). Donors should also support domestic NGOs. In addition to advancing reform, NGOs often play a direct role in monitoring contract negotiation processes; once contracts have been granted, they may also monitor company operations.

In yet another strategy for supporting contract review, donors could make up for potential revenue losses during review and reform periods. Although budget assistance to the central government and other forms of aid partly address this problem, donors have so far failed to provide funding that is specifically intended to replace revenue losses that may be attributable to reform.

Commodity-tracking systems

Commodity-tracking systems, which trace the path of commodities from production to consumption, reduce the market value of noncertified commodities by making them more difficult to sell. More generally, such systems formalize exploitation and trade, and thereby curtail illegal resource exploitation and direct more revenues to state coffers. The diamond certification scheme created in Sierra Leone in September 2000, for example, targeted illegal production by rebels and soldiers, and also informed official investigations of a prominent government official who was ultimately tried and convicted for engaging in illegal mining.[14]

The Kimberley Process Certification Scheme (KPCS), which was created to prevent rebel groups from profiting from diamond mining and trade, is the best known and most fully developed tracking system to date (Grant 2012*). One of the keys to the success of the Kimberley Process (KP) was that it brought together representatives of governments, civil society, and the diamond industry as equal partners (Wright 2012*; Bone 2012*).[15] The industry's presence, for example, was crucial to the development of a scheme that diamond producers and traders would both endorse and comply with.

Despite the KPCS's success, the value of the system has been subject to debate. The early stages of implementation (before the KPCS was officially established, in 2003) helped rein in the sale of conflict diamonds in both Sierra Leone and Angola. By 2010, less than 1 percent of world's total diamond production consisted of conflict diamonds,[16] and some experts estimate that the proportion of illicit rough diamonds being traded had decreased from 25 to 10 percent.[17] Finally, with the increase in officially registered mining sites and diamond exports, many diamond-exporting countries have experienced an increase in governmental revenues (Mitchell 2012*).

Nevertheless, Philippe Le Billon and Harrison Mitchell are circumspect about the KP's impact (Le Billon 2008b; Mitchell 2012*). As Mitchell points out, although the KPCS has increased state revenues—and thereby indirectly contributed to peacebuilding—its value as a means of preventing or ending conflict is harder to prove. Moreover, especially in countries where certification capacity is low and corruption is high, the scheme has had less than resounding success in preventing illicit mining and accurately documenting the origin of rough diamonds. For example, tax authorities in the Central African Republic

---

[14] The official, who was minister of transport and communications at the time of his arrest, was sentenced to two years of imprisonment (*BBC News* 2001).
[15] As of 2011, the KP had forty-nine members representing seventy-five countries (KP n.d.).
[16] The conflict diamonds that are still being mined and traded come from Côte d'Ivoire, where the Forces Nouvelles rebel group taxes the rough diamond trade (UNSC 2011).
[17] Personal communication, Ian Smillie, chairman of the board of directors, Diamond Development Initiative International, 2010. The figures are rough estimates.

(CAR)—a member state of the KP—estimate that between 25 and 70 percent of CAR diamonds are exported illegally (Jensen, Halle, and Lehtonen 2009); and in the DRC, a considerable proportion of diamonds that were actually mined in the conflict-affected eastern DRC are certified as having originated from Kinshasa, the capital (PAC 2009).

Another commodity-tracking scheme is the Forest Law Enforcement Governance and Trade (FLEGT) initiative of the European Union (EU), which encourages timber-producing countries that export to EU markets to adopt a voluntary timber-licensing system (Brack 2012*). In exchange, the EU funds capacity building and institutional development in the forest sector. FLEGT was not specifically designed for peacebuilding, but given its potential to improve forest governance, it may lend itself to peacebuilding purposes in places such as Liberia and the CAR. As of August 2011, six countries (Cameroon, the CAR, Ghana, Indonesia, Liberia, and the Republic of the Congo) had concluded negotiations with the EU, and the DRC, Gabon, Malaysia, and Vietnam had begun negotiations. Among the fifteen other countries that have expressed interest in the FLEGT initiative are Bolivia, Burma, Colombia, Côte d'Ivoire, and Sierra Leone (FLEGT VPAs n.d.).

In 2010, the Organisation for Economic Co-operation and Development (OECD) created the OECD Due Diligence Guidance for Responsible Supply Chains of Minerals from Conflict-Affected and High-Risk Areas. The guidance is intended for firms that are involved in mineral exploitation and trade, and is designed to assist such firms to protect human rights and avoid contributing to conflict (OECD 2010). The guidance, which applies to all phases of the supply chain that occur in conflict-affected or high-risk areas,[18] specifies a number of actions that firms should undertake to achieve compliance with the OECD due diligence standards, including the following:

- Suspending or ceasing trade operations with dubious suppliers.
- Taking steps to increase leverage over suppliers to bring them into conformance with the standards.
- Developing relationships with local governing authorities, who may be involved in implementing the standards.
- Publicly reporting the findings of due diligence investigations and the measures that have been taken to ensure compliance with the guidelines.

Although the OECD guidance was not developed for any geographic region in particular, they were first endorsed, in 2010, by the International Conference on the Great Lakes Region (ICGLR 2010), an intergovernmental organization that promotes sustainable peace and development in the Great Lakes Region of Africa.

---

[18] The phases of the supply chain include extraction, transport, handling, processing, trading, manufacturing, and selling.

An example of commodity tracking imposed by an economically powerful country is the Dodd-Frank Wall Street Reform and Consumer Protection Act, which is intended to curtail the use of conflict minerals, such as coltan, from the DRC. Signed by President Barack Obama in July 2010, the act requires U.S. companies that purchase certain minerals from the DRC or bordering countries to engage in due diligence and to provide details on the chain of custody to both the public and the U.S. Securities and Exchange Commission (Kersch 2010). Finally, the Tin Supply Chain Initiative (iTSCi) of the International Tin Research Institute, an industry-based scheme, is designed to track the supply chain for tin in the DRC, from the mining site to the export point (Pistilli 2010; ITRI 2011).

All these initiatives—FLEGT, the OECD Due Diligence Guidance, the Dodd-Frank Act, and iTSCi—are emerging and promising means of extending the chain-of-custody approach to timber, and to tin and other minerals that may finance conflict. It is too early to identify lessons from these initiatives, but they do merit careful evaluation and monitoring to assess and improve their effectiveness.

ALLOCATING AND DISTRIBUTING RESOURCE REVENUES

Because most high-value resources are nonrenewable, they are irretrievably lost once exploited; thus, the distribution and allocation of the resulting revenues is of paramount importance. In fact, revenue allocation—specifically, ensuring that revenues are expended in such a way as to support medium- and long-term development—is potentially the most decisive factor in determining whether the future will bring sustainable peace (Collier and Hoeffler 2012*). Unfortunately, the expenditure side of resource management is often overlooked.

Revenue distribution—that is, revenue sharing between the central government and subnational entities (producing regions in particular) is a source of tension in many resource-rich countries. Grievances related to distribution may stem from a number of sources: for example, producing regions may believe that they are not receiving their fair share of resource-related revenues or being adequately compensated for the side effects of resource extraction, such as environmental degradation. Sometimes, such grievances rise to the level of violent conflict—as occurred in Bougainville, Papua New Guinea, in 1988—and need to be addressed as part of peace negotiations.

This section considers four lessons related to revenue allocation and distribution. First, the principal objective of revenue allocation is to foster peace and development; this objective cannot be accomplished in the absence of transparency and accountability. Second, natural resource funds are a valuable means of regulating allocation and mitigating the shocks associated with volatile commodity prices. Third, revenue-sharing arrangements must balance the rights and needs of producing and nonproducing regions. Finally, the grievances caused by resource extraction must be addressed.

Revenue allocation

Nigeria is an illustrative example of inefficient revenue allocation. By the early 2000s, despite nearly forty years of oil exploitation, Nigeria's per capita income was about the same as it had been in the 1960s. During the same period, the percentage of Nigerians living in absolute poverty increased from 36 to 70 percent (Sala-i-Martin and Subramanian 2003).[19]

Since the discovery of oil in the 1950s, Nigeria's resource wealth has been managed under chaotic political conditions. Oil revenues have fuelled widespread corruption, both in the oil-producing Niger Delta and in the central government, and efforts to stabilize the country through political and economic reforms have been unsuccessful. The Niger Delta suffers from chronic unrest, and past attempts to pacify and develop the region have failed dramatically (Mähler 2012*). In short, Nigeria—and the Niger Delta in particular—has little to show for the nearly 29 billion barrels of oil pumped from its reserves between 1960 and 2009.[20]

From a peacebuilding perspective, an optimal allocation arrangement harmonizes the political objective of reconciliation and the economic objective of broad development. In practice, this often means balancing revenue allocation between producing regions and the country as a whole, while simultaneously (1) fostering productive long-term investments such as education, infrastructure, and economic diversification, and (2) responding to immediate needs such as health care, sanitation, and nutrition. If revenues are used to increase military power or to repress the population, rather than to benefit society as a whole, even large revenues will fail to strengthen development.

The vast literature on the "resource curse," including the chapters in this volume, suggests that transparency and accountability in revenue flows and expenditures are the keys to successful revenue allocation.[21] Transparency and accountability go hand in hand: without credible data tracking revenue flows from extractive industries to the state, from state agencies to subnational entities or development projects, and through to the final expenditure of revenues, the government cannot be held accountable for expenditures. The primary safeguard

---

[19] In Sala-i-Martin and Subramanian (2003), the meaning of *absolute poverty* is based on the World Bank's definition of the poverty line, under which an individual who subsists on less than one U.S. dollar a day (in 1985 dollars, adjusted for purchasing power parity) is considered to be in a state of absolute poverty.

[20] Calculated on the basis of statistics from EIA (2010).

[21] The term *resource curse*, which was first coined by Richard M. Auty (1993), refers to the fact that when it comes to economic development many resource-rich countries do not perform as well as their resource-poor counterparts. More broadly, the term *resource curse* is used to refer to other negative outcomes, both political and social, that have been associated with abundant natural resources, including the government's detachment from the electorate and an increased risk of armed conflict (Collier and Hoeffler 2012*; Lujala and Rustad 2012*). The resource curse is also known as *the paradox of plenty* (Karl 1997).

against both corruption and inefficiency is to ensure that revenues accruing to the state cannot be concealed, and that money the state claims to have used for development (e.g., to build health clinics and pay teachers' salaries) has in fact been used for that purpose.

The Extractive Industries Transparency Initiative (EITI), perhaps the best-known initiative of its kind, is designed to monitor the transparency of revenue flows from oil, gas, and mining. In Liberia, for example, the EITI has successfully increased public awareness of revenue flows and encouraged broad participation, on the part of both civil society and the public (Rich and Warner 2012*). The EITI is based on voluntary participation—the hope being that if enough countries implement the EITI standards, they will become a widely applied set of transnational rules.[22] By August 2011, eleven countries (Azerbaijan, the CAR, Ghana, Kyrgyzstan, Liberia, Mongolia, Niger, Nigeria, Norway, Timor-Leste, and Yemen) had fully implemented the EITI standards, and twenty-four were in the process of doing so (EITI n.d.a.).

Several initiatives seek to extend EITI-like transparency requirements to the realm of governmental expenditures and to make exploration and exploitation contracts, as well as the prices agreed to by companies and governments, available to the public. The Natural Resource Charter, for example, includes transparency as one of its twelve core principles (Natural Resource Charter n.d.). Similarly, the EU's FLEGT initiative, discussed earlier in this chapter, is designed to increase the transparency of forest management by publishing information on audits and the allocation of rights, among other things (Brack 2012*).

Natural resource funds

One way to improve revenue allocation in post-conflict countries is to set up one or more types of natural resource funds. Savings and stabilization funds are relatively common in resource-rich countries; the largest are found in oil-rich countries such as Kuwait, Norway, Russia, Saudi Arabia, and the United Arab Emirates. Savings funds smooth revenue distribution across generations by creating a revenue base for the future, when the natural resources are used up. The principal aims of stabilization funds are (1) to absorb excess revenues that might overheat or otherwise disturb the economy and (2) to create a protective buffer against bust periods.[23] Stabilization funds work by setting revenues aside when they exceed forecasts or the government's absorption capacity, and releasing reserve funds when revenues decrease.

---

[22] Another transparency initiative, the Publish What You Pay campaign, seeks to establish legal instruments (notably stock exchange rules) to achieve mandatory transparency. See PWYP (n.d.).

[23] An economy overheats when it grows at an unsustainably rapid rate, causing high inflation and creating excess production capacity, which will eventually hinder economic growth and may cause an economic downturn.

In addition to using savings and stabilization funds to save for future generations and cope with revenue fluctuations, most countries draw on their funds to finance current government expenditures. Withdrawals for this purpose often have annual ceilings, and fund regulations may specify the purposes for which fund disbursements can be used. Ideally, such regulations would be designed to move expenditure decisions beyond the realm of everyday politics and to ensure that revenues are used to address long-term development objectives.

Pure savings funds (such as Chad's Future Generations Fund), which are specifically intended to be released only in the future, may not be feasible or appropriate when current needs are overwhelming, as is often the case in post-conflict countries.[24] Stabilization funds, in contrast, may be more appropriate in post-conflict settings because they are designed to mitigate the revenue volatility associated with changes in commodity prices, which can wreak havoc in fragile economies.

Among the technical decisions that must be addressed in the design of savings and stabilization funds are the following: (1) the share of natural resource revenues to be directed to the fund; (2) how the funds will be invested; and (3) how the inflows and disbursements will be regulated. The laws and regulations governing the administration of the funds should be designed to protect against government misuse. One example of regulatory guidelines are the Santiago Principles, which were developed for the twenty-six members of the International Monetary Fund that have sovereign wealth funds.[25] They provide guidance on best practices (including governance and accountability arrangements) for savings and stabilization funds. Notably, the principles identify transparency as a cornerstone of fund structure, objectives, funding, and withdrawals.

Revenue sharing

Revenue sharing is often a prerequisite for a peace agreement and is frequently proposed as a solution for secessionist conflicts (Ross, Lujala, and Rustad 2012*). Tensions over resources tend to be particularly acute in low-income states characterized by substantial inequality between groups with distinct identities, as was the case in Aceh, Bougainville, and Southern Sudan (Stewart 2000).[26]

In their chapter on the decentralization of resource revenues, Michael L. Ross, Päivi Lujala, and Siri Aas Rustad list three avenues for revenue sharing (Ross, Lujala, and Rustad 2012*). First, local governments may be granted the right to levy taxes directly on extractive industries—as, for example, in Canada and

---

[24] President Idriss Déby dissolved the Future Generations Fund in 2006, after the World Bank loosened its control over the expenditure of oil revenues (Gould and Winters 2012*).
[25] See IWG (2008).
[26] Such tensions are likely to be exacerbated where a particular minority group makes up the majority of the population in a resource-rich region.

Russia, where provinces are permitted to levy some types of taxes themselves, or in Sudan, where the peace agreement of 2005 gave states the right to levy property taxes, royalties, and excise taxes (Haysom and Kane 2009).

Second, revenue collection from resource exploitation may be centralized, and subnational entities in a producing region may then receive a set percentage of the revenues originating from that region. This approach is used in Nigeria, where the oil-producing regions receive 13 percent of the revenues that are generated in their region; in Angola, where Cabinda Province receives 10 percent; and in Indonesia, where Aceh receives 70 percent. In the third revenue distribution option, producing regions receive indirect transfers from the central government, through the national budget, with preferential treatment for producing regions.

The first two approaches are decentralized, in that they give subnational entities more power over revenue flows; the third is a more centralized approach. In a completely centralized system, revenues are allocated strictly on the basis of population and needs. In Iraq, for example, after allocating 17 percent of oil and gas revenues to the Kurdistan Regional Government, the central government distributes the remainder according to the population of each governorate, regardless of whether it produces oil and gas.

Acknowledging that it may be impossible to achieve peace without some decentralization of revenue sharing, Ross, Lujala, and Rustad point out that the first two approaches can pose severe challenges in post-conflict countries, which often suffer from corruption and institutional weakness, rendering them unable to levy taxes and handle highly volatile revenue flows (Ross, Lujala, and Rustad 2012). In Chad, for example, most of the 4.5 percent development fund for the Doba region wound up being used for a few high-profile projects, and many of the associated subcontracts were granted to firms with connections to political elites (Gould and Winters 2012*). Similarly, the oil-rich Niger Delta is riddled with corruption and patronage, and the resulting inequalities have led to deep grievances among Delta inhabitants, many of whom feel that they have been deprived of the resource benefits to which they are entitled. Tensions about revenue distribution have led to a vicious cycle of violence and criminal activity, including oil theft (Mähler 2012*).

Three factors are central to the success of revenue-sharing arrangements.[27] First, all parties must have a clear and realistic understanding of what is being shared: for example, does sharing apply to revenues from all natural resources, or only to those from specific natural resources? Will revenues be calculated only on the basis of production, or will those from sources such as exploration rights and signing bonuses be included as well? Does revenue sharing apply only to current exploitation, or to reserves that have not yet been exploited or even discovered?

Second, management and ownership rights (e.g., how decisions will be made about granting exploration and exploitation rights, and by whom) need to be

---

[27] For a more general discussion of natural resource and peace agreements, see Mason, Sguaitamatti, and Gröbli (2012).

addressed. When such issues arise during peace negotiations, however, it may be best to leave them for subsequent discussions. In Sudan, for example, the decision to discuss only revenue sharing during the peace negotiations, and to defer the discussion of management and ownership to a later stage, prevented the early collapse of negotiations (Wennmann 2012*).

Third, issues that are left open in revenue-sharing agreements, or that are negotiated separately from such agreements, need to be considered from a political perspective to ensure that they do not create new tensions. In Iraq, constitutional provisions addressing revenue distribution and the ownership and management of oil resources appear to have been left deliberately vague, in the interests of fostering a sense of collective ownership. Unfortunately, the vague language has provoked fierce disputes about who owns the oil fields, who has the authority to grant exploration and extraction rights, and how revenues will be shared (Al Moumin 2012*).

Ross, Lujala, and Rustad suggest that distributing revenues through the national budget may be the avenue most suited to post-conflict situations. Under this approach, local governments need not create local taxation institutions and are assured stable revenue flows that are not subject to short-term swings in commodity prices or extraction activity. Notwithstanding the potential benefits of distributing benefits through the national budget, stakeholders from the producing region (who may include former rebels) are unlikely to support this distribution method because it confirms the central government's ownership of and authority over the reserves, as well as its control over revenue distribution. It may therefore be difficult to strike a peace deal on the basis of this arrangement.

Revenue distribution typically involves sharing between a central government and a producing region; under this arrangement, the entire region—including nonproducing areas—receives a designated share of revenues. In an approach coming into increasing use in Africa, revenues are distributed more locally, to producing areas and communities. One example of this model is Sierra Leone's Diamond Area Community Development Fund, which was launched in 2001 as part of a post-conflict reform of the diamond sector. The fund receives 0.75 percent of the total value of diamond exports, then disburses the revenues to diamondiferous regions. Payments are earmarked for small-scale development projects such as education, health services, and community infrastructure (Maconachie 2012*). The CAR has a similar model, in which revenues from timber taxes are distributed to community funds that finance employment-generating projects (Jensen, Halle, and Lehtonen 2009).[28]

Under similar arrangements, local councils in Cameroon receive a share of the fees and taxes collected from logging companies operating in the vicinity. The DRC and Gabon have also decided to establish similar benefit-sharing systems

---

[28] Both Sierra Leone and the CAR have experienced challenges, however, in implementing these funds. In the CAR, when revenue shortfalls resulted in unpaid salaries, for example, the government raided the funds (Jensen, Halle, and Lehtonen 2009).

for forestry, but the arrangements have yet to be implemented (Waugh 2010; Morrison et al. 2009). In Liberia, the government has created a trust fund to share benefits from some types of timber concessions with communities that are affected by logging (Waugh 2010, 2011). This approach is based on similar arrangements already in effect in the mining sector: the County Social Development Fund, for example, which was established by the mining firm ArcelorMittal and the government of Liberia, distributes revenues to the three counties where the company operates.

An alternative to the schemes discussed so far involves distributing revenues directly to the population. Because direct payments bypass governmental bureaucracy, they are less subject to corruption; they also provide a tangible peace dividend and can help alleviate tensions arising from historic grievances over resource distribution. Finally, by guaranteeing that everyone will get an equal share of resource revenues without having to compete for it, direct distribution can provide an incentive to keep the peace (Sandbu 2012*).

Compensation for harm related to resource extraction

Although few peace processes or peace agreements take the social and environmental damage associated with extraction into account, failing to compensate the victims of such damage can reignite tensions or fuel new conflict. Nor are the consequences of resource extraction the only source of compensation demands; in many countries, those who have suffered from wartime destruction—including the depletion of natural resources and the loss of livelihoods, shelter, and infrastructure—may demand redress. In Iraq, to compensate ethnic and religious groups that had suffered systematically under Saddam Hussein's regime, the 2005 Iraqi constitution awarded such groups a larger share of oil and gas revenues on a transitional basis, for an unspecified amount of time (Al Moumin 2012*).

In the Niger Delta, the environmental situation is critical, largely as a consequence of oil spills from pipelines and extraction sites. Although most of the spills have been caused by poor extraction practices and badly maintained pipelines, some have resulted from sabotage on the part of militias or from illegal tapping (illegally tapped oil is sold in both local markets and on the international black market) (Asuni 2009). Although Nigerian law holds oil companies liable for environmental damage (DPR 2002), the companies have argued that most of the spills are caused by sabotage and illegal tapping (Amnesty International 2009). If a landowner is lucky enough to be awarded compensation by an oil company, the compensation is typically small in relation to the damage—the equivalent of one year's loss of crop, even though the land has been ruined for years to come (FRN 2008).

The environmental harm that has sparked years of unrest in the Niger Delta is not unique. As Luke A. Patey shows, similar events may be unfolding in South Sudan, as it recovers from over two decades of war (Patey 2012*). Since the late 1990s, the rapid development of Sudan's oil sector has led to widespread soil contamination, hazardous-waste dumping, and the release of tainted water.

As Patey points out, unless the environmental damage is dealt with, there is a danger of persistent, localized conflicts, similar to those in the Niger Delta; such an outcome would be extremely harmful to the region's long-term development.

Governments and private firms share responsibility for developing a framework to address the damage caused by resource extraction. In Sierra Leone, one model under consideration recognizes that extractive industries will cause environmental damage, and therefore would require them to finance environmental cleanup through a remediation bond, which would be paid before extraction begins.[29]

IMPROVING INSTITUTIONAL QUALITY

Institutional quality is key to the sound governance of natural resources; in fact, research suggests that institutional quality is decisive in the transformation of natural riches into economic development. A study by Halvor Mehlum, Karl Moene, and Ragnar Torvik, for example, shows that in countries with higher institutional quality, the adverse effect of natural resources on economic growth is weaker; moreover, in countries with the healthiest institutions, the adverse effect does not occur at all (Mehlum, Moene, and Torvik 2006).[30] In post-conflict situations, the ability to establish commodity-tracking systems, assess and renegotiate contracts, agree on revenue-sharing formulas, and efficiently and effectively invest resource revenues depends, to a large extent, on the quality and capacity of governance. Thus, many of the approaches described in this chapter depend on a post-conflict institutional framework that is at least partly functional. And because robust local and national institutions are crucial to the management of resources and revenues, institutional reform should be a peacebuilding priority.

Approaches to institutional reform

Although wholesale institutional reform is often unrealistic (and potentially destabilizing), various incremental strategies can be used to strengthen institutions in post-conflict settings. A strategic approach to institutional reform that focuses on a few select institutions—for example, those that are crucial for specific resource management tasks or responsible for particular resources—may be more effective than attempting to build capacity in all institutions at once. Liberia's post-conflict forest sector reform, for example, which was undertaken as one of the conditions for the lifting of UN sanctions, focused specifically on improving institutional capacity and financial management in the Forestry Development Authority (FDA),

---

[29] Personal communication, Oli Brown, environmental affairs officer, UN Integrated Peacebuilding Mission in Sierra Leone, July 2011.
[30] To assess institutional quality, Mehlum, Moene, and Torvik use an index, developed by Political Risk Services, that includes measures for rule of law, bureaucratic quality, government corruption, risk of expropriation, and government repudiation of contracts. For more details on the data on institutional quality, see Knack and Keefer (1995).

the public authority that manages the nation's forests. Evaluations conducted as part of the reform process uncovered clear evidence of corruption and large-scale financial mismanagement; it was also determined that the FDA was overstaffed, and that many FDA employees lacked the required qualifications. Through training, restructuring, resizing, and the implementation of new financial management systems, which were put in place under the auspices of the Governance and Economic Management Assistance Program (GEMAP),[31] the FDA has improved efficiency and constrained fraud and corruption (Altman, Nichols, and Woods 2012*).

Within a post-conflict country, some institutions may function more effectively than others; even if those institutions are not related to natural resources, they can sometimes be used to create a foundation for further reform. Another option is to build goodwill and experience by beginning reform in resource sectors where there is less tension. Michael D. Beevers argues, for example, that Sierra Leone may have missed a peacebuilding opportunity by failing to undertake forest reform, which would have created a platform for local communities and the state to discuss resource management. While forestry was not a source of conflict financing in Sierra Leone, as it had been in Liberia, forests and forest products are an important part of rural livelihoods, and could have provided opportunities to debate issues that were associated with less tension than, for example, diamond mining (Beevers 2012*).

Yet another approach is to build experience in awarding concessions and managing resource projects by bidding out smaller concessions and licenses. In Liberia, for example, the first timber contracts put out to bid were for three-year licenses covering less than 5,000 hectares. The next step was to award larger and longer-term contracts (Altman, Nichols, and Woods 2012*).

In some cases, it may make sense to decentralize some aspects of natural resource governance to the state, provincial, or district level. If resources have strategic importance or are the foundation of a country's assets and economy, such an approach may not be feasible nationwide; nevertheless, it may still be possible to grant subnational entities responsibility for governing specific sites or types of resources. For example, the central government may give local governments management rights over diamond deposits that can be mined through artisanal methods, while retaining authority over larger and more valuable sites, such as kimberlite deposits.[32] Such an arrangement could, for example, give subnational governments both authority and responsibility for executive, legislative,

---

[31] GEMAP, a joint effort of the government of Liberia and the international community, is designed to promote good governance through accountability and transparency. Among the key Liberian institutions targeted for GEMAP reform are the Ministry of Finance, the Central Bank, and the National Port Authority. The FDA was the first governmental agency to graduate from GEMAP. For further information, see www.gemap-liberia.org.

[32] Kimberlite mining, industrial-scale mining that requires extensive infrastructure and investment, is used to extract diamonds from naturally occurring underground structures known as kimberlite pipes.

and judicial decisions regarding specific aspects of resource management. Particularly where a resource is the principal source of livelihoods in an area, local management entities may be better able to respond to constraints on resource use and to manage the long-term impacts of resource use than higher-level officials living outside the area (Ratner 2012). Decentralized authority can also increase cooperation (e.g., between various levels of government and between subnational governments and communities) and strengthen both the legitimacy of, and compliance with, the rules governing resource exploitation. The forest user groups that manage and collect revenues from state-owned forests in Nepal offer an example of successful decentralized resource management (Sanio and Chapagain 2012*).

One option is to partially postpone extraction—for example, by developing extraction capacity in the most peaceful regions first, to build capacity and avoid reviving and fuelling past conflicts. In a variant of this approach, larger projects may be postponed until institutional and economic capacity are sufficient to cope with the revenues. Naturally, postponing or suspending extraction is often impossible—and, in the case of resources that can be exploited artisanally, may be both difficult and undesirable. First, it is harder to control the many participants in small-scale (and often unofficial) mining operations than to control the few companies that are engaged in large-scale mining. Second, banning small-scale mining is likely to have severe adverse effects on local livelihoods. For example, in September 2010, when President Kabila banned artisanal mining in three provinces in eastern DRC (Sud Kivu, Nord Kivu, and Maniema) to curtail illegal mining and trade in the region, the ban severely disturbed local livelihoods and the local economy, affecting as many as 50,000 people, according to one local estimate (Seay 2010).[33]

When it comes to institution building, scholars and development agencies alike tend to place the greatest emphasis on political institutions; Indra de Soysa argues, however, that economic reform is also central to institution building (de Soysa 2012*). Economic freedom—which de Soysa defines as encouraging individual liberties and free-market transaction—seems to promote peace, partly by providing entrepreneurial opportunities. Where economic opportunity is available only to the few or to members of specific groups (typically, those with ties to the state), violent rent seeking is more likely to occur.[34] In light of de

---

[33] Personal communication, Hassan Partow, DRC program manager, Post-Conflict and Disaster Management Branch, Department of Environmental Policy Implementation, UN Environment Programme, 2011. The ban was lifted on March 10, 2011.

[34] *Rent seeking* refers to attempts to capture economic benefits without contributing to overall economic production. In the case of high-value natural resources, where revenues are extraordinarily high in relation to the costs of extraction, rent seekers may attempt to capture rents through various means, including corrupt practices and patronage. In addition to the fact that rent seeking does not contribute to overall economic activity, it can directly undermine economic outcomes—by, for example, weakening economic institutions or diverting revenues from activities that are crucial for economic growth, such as education.

Soysa's perspective, it is important for both donors and domestic authorities to acknowledge the value of economic reform as a means of strengthening institutions and promoting peace.

Approval and support from domestic authorities are important to the success of externally supported reform. In post-conflict situations, however, it may be difficult to determine who the legitimate domestic authorities are. This raises two questions: First, should sovereignty over natural resources be suspended during the early phases of post-conflict transition (for example, through a trusteeship, in which a foreign authority takes charge)? Second, will externally designed institutions achieve legitimacy and be effective in the long term? These questions are particularly pressing in post-conflict settings, where foreign actors have major stakes in resource sectors and could thus be perceived as establishing self-serving institutions, as was the case with the Coalition Provisional Authority in Iraq.[35] Because many high-value resource projects have life spans of several decades, external influences on institutions and on the legislation that governs resource contracts can have long-term effects.

Another important issue concerns the role of transitional authorities in reforming resource sectors and allocating resource contracts—a role that should depend on the nature, legitimacy, and capacity of the authority. For example, if the interim administration is a national unity government made up of the members of former armed groups, resource management reforms and exploitation contracts should be postponed until a democratically elected government is in place; otherwise, there is a risk that decisions will be guided by short-term interests (such as the desire to amass campaign funds). But if there is strong sense among the domestic population and the international community that a democratically elected administration may not be able to deliver, within a reasonable time, the types of reforms that will consolidate a just, equitable, and prosperous peace, then an alternative interim administration should step in at an early phase to set the stage for resource reforms. A case for an interim administration can be made, for example, by the UNSC, when it determines the scope of a UN mission's mandate to address natural resource governance failures; by donors, who (in collaboration with domestic leaders) often shape post-conflict institutional configurations; or even by broad social movements, if they have enough power to overcome the influence of established elites. Overall, the qualifications, intent, and incentives of all interim administrations need careful attention, notably on the part of domestic and international NGOs, who are often in a good position to gauge the long-term interests of the country as a whole.

Democracy can help to improve the quality and capacity of governance, but it would be wrong to assume that a general election will automatically improve resource management. Although elections provide political systems with crucial

---

[35] Allegations related to the countries' oil interests in the region called into question the U.S. and UK governments' motives for invading Iraq; both governments denied the allegations (Le Billon and El Khatib 2004).

elements of accountability and legitimacy, they do not guarantee long-term development, sustainable peace, or the emergence of robust institutions.[36] In fact, the first effect of democratization may be a fire sale on resources—first, to generate a visible peace dividend that will attract the notice of the populace; and second, to raise campaign funds for political parties (as occurred in Cambodia, before the July 1998 elections) (Le Billon 2000). Furthermore, although democracy tends to reduce corruption over the long term, the post-conflict transition to democracy may temporarily exacerbate more diffuse and competitive forms of corruption and thereby undermine the prospects for peace. In Cambodia in the mid-1990s, for example, botched elections left the government with two prime ministers and a plethora of provincial vice-governors vying for control of the resources in their provinces (Le Billon 2003, 2008a; Sung 2004).

Domestic institution building can be further supported by a number of external means: (1) international pressure, which may include the use of sanctions to be lifted only when regulations and management authorities meet minimal standards; (2) measures that relieve international pressure;[37] (3) the implementation of programs that grant privileged access to large export markets in return for compliance with set standards, such as the EU's FLEGT initiative; and (4) the passage of home-country legislation, of which the Dodd-Frank Act, passed in 2010 in the United States, is an example.

In some cases, to advance peace, it may be necessary to compromise—by, for example, integrating rebel factions into transitional governing institutions—but the costs of slowing down institution building need to be carefully considered, as does the risk of jeopardizing the long-term goals of justice and development. Awarding authority over resource management to potential peace spoilers for the sake of appeasement, for example, has a poor record of success.[38]

Laws and regulations

When it comes to managing natural resources and their revenues, the establishment of sound institutions goes hand in hand with legal reform. Domestic laws addressing high-value resources define the objectives, standards, procedures, and institutions that govern the management of the resource base, revenue flows, and expenditures. Such laws may incorporate international voluntary standards: Liberia, for example, passed the Liberia Extractive Industries Transparency Initiative Act

---

[36] In fact, according to Paul Collier and Anke Hoeffler, between 1970 and 2001, in developing countries, the combination of high natural resource rents and open, democratic systems reduced growth (Collier and Hoeffler 2009).

[37] For example, by cancelling all or part of the national debt, donors can ameliorate external pressures that may be driving domestic authorities to focus on projects such as industrial mining, which offer the potential for high fiscal returns but create little direct employment and may undermine livelihood opportunities.

[38] Sierra Leone's experience with this strategy is discussed later in the chapter, in the section on peace spoilers.

to implement the core requirements of the EITI. Liberia also added its own set of requirements concerning the publication of extractive companies' licenses and operating contracts, and included the forestry sector on the list of sectors covered by the requirements (Rich and Warner 2012*).

To prevent narrow interest groups from capturing revenues and to reduce the risk of renewed conflict, laws governing resources should safeguard transparency, accountability, representation, and equity. They should also be designed to ensure that natural resource revenues are geared toward activities and investments that will foster sustainable, long-term development while preventing major social and environmental impacts. In practical terms, this may mean that the laws will require specific allocations of expenditures to various sectors, such as infrastructure, health, and education, or the use of environmental impact assessments (EIAs).

Chad offers an example of how difficult it is to establish institutions and implement and enforce laws regarding natural resources and revenues—even when laws are in place, and there is substantial external pressure to abide by them. A landlocked country, Chad was unable to benefit from its oil without a pipeline that would connect its oil fields to the coast. Because international investment in the 1,070-kilometer Chad-Cameroon pipeline could not proceed without World Bank approval, the Bank was able to impose stringent conditions—reflected in the Petroleum Revenue Management Law (PRML)—on Chad's government (Gould and Winters 2012*).[39]

The PRML, passed in 1999, was designed to reduce poverty; secure equitable distribution of revenues (among social groups, regions, and generations); and smooth volatile revenue flows. Among other provisions, the law allocated 10 percent of oil revenues to the Future Generations Fund; over 70 percent of oil revenues to priority sectors, including health, education, rural development, and the environment; and 4.5 percent of oil revenues to the development of Doba, the oil-producing region. The law also established both national and international committees to oversee revenue distribution and expenditures (Gould and Winters 2012*).

To ensure that the Chadian government complied with the PRML, oil revenues flowed directly into an escrow account that the World Bank had the power to freeze. Despite the unusually stringent conditions and careful oversight, the program did not achieve its objectives: the national and international oversight bodies were unable to hold the government accountable for expenditures. Instead, large portions of the oil revenues were spent on the military and channeled into patronage networks, which contributed to a renewal of Chad's internal conflict. The collapse of the program created through the PRML underscores the difficulty and complexity of managing high-value resources in conflict-affected countries, even when the international community—in this case, the World Bank—has

---

[39] Loi No. 001/PR/99 Portant Gestion des Revenus Pétroliers (Petroleum Revenue Management Law).

substantial leverage over government policies.[40] Chad's recent history also highlights the crucial role of the political elite, which must be committed to fair and effective revenue allocation (Gould and Winters 2012*).

Introducing or consolidating resource management legislation and establishing the necessary administrative and oversight bodies to implement it should be priorities for post-conflict state building. Liberia's forest sector legislation and accompanying regulations, which are probably the most progressive in Africa, exemplify best practices with respect to both legislation and institution building. The reform process, which was designed to achieve transparency at every phase of production and trade, yielded the National Forestry Reform Law of 2006 and a set of regulations to guide the management of the timber sector. The regulations address, among other topics, environmental impact assessment, contracts, preharvesting standards, logging, export permits, invoicing, and monitoring of payments (Altman, Nichols, and Woods 2012*).

Legislation governing resource management must be as specific as possible. In Iraq, for example, vague and potentially conflicting constitutional provisions have led to conflict within the central government and between different levels of government, exacerbating post-conflict instability (Al Moumin 2012*). The laws should clearly state, for example, what entities are in charge of granting exploration and exploitation rights, and how revenues are to be shared (Haysom and Kane 2009). In the case of resources such as oil and gas fields, it is important to specify whether legislation refers only to fields that are currently producing, to all known reserves, or to all current and future reserves. The 2001 Indonesian Law on Special Autonomy for the Province Nanggroe Aceh Darussalam (Aceh), for example, failed to specify the basis on which oil and gas revenues were to be shared between the province and the central government, and lacked a baseline assessment of the resource reserves. As a result, the Free Aceh Movement rejected the legitimacy of the law—which was replaced, in 2003, by a purely military strategy on the part of the central government (Wennmann 2012*). Similarly, in Iraq, it is unclear whether only those oil fields that are currently producing, or future fields as well, are subject to the provisions of the 2005 constitution (Al Moumin 2012*).

Corruption and inefficiency

In post-conflict and conflict-affected countries, resource sector reforms often occur in the context of a corrupt or inefficient regulatory environment. Decentralizing some or all aspects of resource management, revenue collection, and expenditures is one means of circumventing corruption or inefficiency at the national level, but the local level is not necessarily without problems: in Nigeria, for example, corruption is in some cases even higher at the subnational level than at the

---

[40] Because of the mismanagement of the oil funds, the World Bank formally withdrew its support of the project in September 2008.

national level. In 2008, the governor of Bayelsa, one of the most oil-rich states in the Niger Delta, began to explicitly address corruption in the state apparatus; among other initiatives, he invited external accountants and other advisers to audit the state finances. In the first year, the audit led to a reduction of more than 20 percent in the procurement budget and revealed that as many as 15 percent of state workers were fictive, allowing substantial reductions in salary costs. The governor is also promoting transparency in revenue flows from the state to local government authorities. In principle, these funds are to be spent for the benefit of local communities, but they are often eaten away by corruption (*Economist* 2009).

Sierra Leone's Diamond Area Community Development Fund, which distributes diamond revenues to local authorities to fund community development projects, offers another example of an effort to tackle revenue mismanagement. In 2006, the Ministry of Mineral Resources stopped disbursements to local governments because of widespread mismanagement of the funds at the local level. The disbursements were resumed in 2009, after more stringent conditions for proposals, contract bids, and monitoring had been put in place. In addition to improving the management of the funds, the new procedures are intended to increase transparency, public participation, and accountability (Maconachie 2012*).

Transparency is the single most important means of curtailing corruption and should be required throughout the natural resource chain, from the signing of contracts for exploration to the point of export. Public auctions of contracts, an effective way to increase transparency, should probably be used more often at both the local and national levels. By compelling companies to compete openly on the basis of price and contract conditions, public auctions limit the ability of extractive firms to hide the true value of extraction rights and subcontracts. In Nigeria, for example, the cost of some public procurement projects decreased by 40 percent after they were opened up for public bidding (Collier 2007).

ADDRESSING CROSS-CUTTING ISSUES

So far, the chapter has considered policy approaches to specific issues associated with the management of high-value resources in post-conflict situations. This section takes a broader view, examining issues that need to be taken into consideration in all settings, regardless of the policy approach (or combination of approaches) being used. The four subsections that follow address context, the role of external actors, public engagement and multi-stakeholder initiatives, and peace spoilers.

Context

Post-conflict natural resource management does not happen in a vacuum; it occurs in a specific context shaped by political, cultural, and historical factors at the local, subnational, national, and regional levels. Efforts to manage high-value natural resources and achieve a durable peace must therefore take account of context—in particular, the types of resources and their particular characteristics; pre-conflict resource management strategies; and domestic and international conditions affecting exploitation.

The specific characteristics of resources, such as their mode of exploitation and livelihood impacts, present different challenges and opportunities for peacebuilding. For example, if the central government can readily access revenues, as in the case of offshore oil, then the main challenges are to maximize and allocate revenues. If, in contrast, the government cannot easily gather revenues, as with alluvial diamonds,[41] the main challenges are to improve livelihoods, curtail peace spoilers' access to revenues, and formalize exploitation. In the case of alluvial diamonds, for example, governments may have to choose between awarding contracts to international companies that will engage in mechanized extraction, in the hope of raising more taxes and curtailing peace spoilers' potential access to revenues, or leaving the sector largely open to artisanal mining, in the hope of providing employment for local populations.

Some resources, such as timber and narcotics, present specific challenges. Because timber is required for reconstruction, it raises issues related to environmental protection and local livelihoods (Le Billon 2000; Le Billon and Waizenegger 2007). And because forests are often the last refuge for rebel groups, forest management must include military considerations. When it comes to narcotics, legalizing production is rarely an official option for governments, and even less so for intervening countries. Nevertheless, some governments tolerate cultivation to secure a conflict settlement, gain the support of local allies, reduce violence, and sustain local livelihoods—not to mention the benefit of narcotics revenues. In Afghanistan, foreign military forces have faced similar dilemmas and have had to make choices (e.g., eradicating poppy fields, and thereby undermining local livelihoods) that affected their relations with local populations (Le Billon 2009; Catarious and Russell 2012*; Pain 2012*).

Prewar resource management is another important contextual consideration. On the one hand, elements of the pre-conflict resource management framework may be sound enough to build on; it is not always necessary to start from scratch. On the other hand, pre-conflict conditions, such as patronage systems and discriminatory customary rules, may have adverse effects that need to be addressed.[42] In Sierra Leone, the Diamond Area Community Development Fund was established to address unequal development in diamond-mining areas and to increase local participation in decisions about community development, but these efforts have so far faced substantial challenges that have undermined their effectiveness.

---

[41] Alluvial deposits are found in sand, clay, and gravel discharged by rivers. Existing or ancient riverbeds can often be mined using simple tools such as shovels, buckets, and pans.

[42] Customary rules are those that govern traditional social structures and behaviors.

One of the main sources of the DACDF's problems was the failure to take account of the power relations and patronage systems that predated the civil war, and that continue to shape local decision making (Maconachie 2012*). In Chad, the new revenue flows from oil exploitation have reinforced existing patronage systems and enabled the political elite to further concentrate its power and undermine the consolidation of political institutions (Gould and Winters 2012*). Thus, in many cases, instead of ignoring existing informal power relationships, it may be more useful to take advantage of them, and to find ways to motivate political and economic elites to support reform. It is therefore important to determine what incentives elites may have to participate in and help implement post-conflict resource management strategies.

In the case of large-scale production, extractive concessions and contracts need to reflect the operating context. Post-conflict states often suffer from low capacity and lack of legitimacy, and war-torn communities may be vulnerable and ill equipped to cope with the additional stresses associated with extractive projects. Companies, meanwhile, may face hostility from local communities, continued insecurity, limited infrastructure, and incompetent and unreliable governmental institutions. To build the trust and knowledge that are required for extractive activities to contribute to peace, a full understanding of context is essential. As Volker Boege and Daniel Franks note, referring to mining in particular, "Every mine that is reopened or developed in a fragile post-conflict setting becomes a part of that setting"—and thus has the potential to contribute to both peacebuilding and conflict relapse (Boege and Franks 2012*, 87).

External actors

As advisers on policy reform and sources of investment and advocacy, external actors are often central to post-conflict resource management. This section focuses on the roles of international agencies and donor governments, extractive companies, and NGOs. Although these different types of external actors are discussed separately, they often work together, and should perhaps do so more frequently (Nichols, Muffett, and Bruch 2012). Among the examples of successful collaboration is the Liberia Forest Initiative, which was established by the U.S. government and included U.S. and Liberian governmental agencies, international development agencies, and Liberian and international NGOs (Altman, Nichols, and Woods 2012*).[43]

---

[43] In another example, the U.S. Agency for International Development (USAID) has provided financial support to the Responsible Asia Forestry and Trade program, which brings together NGOs, governments, and the private sector for the purpose of improving forest management, resolving conflicts among stakeholders, and increasing the trade in legally sourced timber (Wallace and Conca 2012*). In the DRC, PACT, an international NGO, uses a public-private approach that brings together extractive companies, local communities, and the government (Hayes and Perks 2012*).

International agencies and donor governments

Since the early 1990s, international agencies and donor governments have become increasingly involved in post-conflict natural resource management. For example, the UNSC has issued resolutions with major implications for resource sectors, imposing sanctions and external supervision regimes. UN peacekeeping missions have occasionally administered transitional resource management authorities, as in Timor-Leste and Kosovo. Specialized UN agencies—including the UN Food and Agriculture Organization, the UN Development Programme, and the UN Environment Programme—have been active in institutional reforms and capacity building in many post-conflict countries, including Afghanistan, Cambodia, the DRC, Sudan, and Sierra Leone. Both the World Bank and the International Finance Corporation (IFC), the private sector arm of the World Bank Group, have provided extensive support for resource management reform—assisting, for example with the drafting of the mining code in the DRC. The World Bank Group, including IFC, is also involved in lending and in the coordination of foreign assistance.

Many donor agencies have been directly engaged in fostering reform; USAID, for example, has created programs to promote awareness of conflict commodities, such as timber,[44] and the United Kingdom (UK) Department for International Development actively promotes the EITI. The International Monetary Fund was among the early champions of transparency of revenue flows—most notably in Cambodia, with respect to logging, and in Angola, with respect to the oil sector. Regional organizations, such as the EU, have sought to better regulate access to markets; the most prominent example of such efforts is the EU's FLEGT initiative, for timber (Brack 2012*). The EU also participates in the KP, which regulates the diamond trade (Wright 2012*).

Foreign assistance, and the conditions that donors impose on domestic authorities in return for such aid (often referred to as "donor conditionality"), are important and time-sensitive instruments of governance in post-conflict settings.[45] In the immediate post-conflict period, when countries are most dependent on aid, donors can exert a great deal of influence over the pace and nature of reform, in some cases providing direct support for, or supervision of, domestic authorities. For example, donors might pressure local authorities to conduct contract reviews; undertake initiatives designed to increase transparency, accountability, and public participation in resource development; and establish safeguards for the collection and expenditure of revenues. In resource-rich countries, however, the leverage provided by aid dependence may eventually be undermined by increasing resource revenues; it is therefore important for donors to take advantage of the early window of opportunity and to lay the foundation for a successful withdrawal.

---

[44] See, for example, Wallace and Conca (2012*).
[45] See Boyce (2002).

In many instances, donors will urge post-conflict domestic authorities to seek a rapid increase in public revenues. But once revenues begin to flow, domestic authorities may be tempted to bypass long-term reform and capacity-building initiatives, in the hope that fast-rising resource revenues will solve the country's problems. This is a serious error, as the combination of weak institutions and a resource boom has been shown to aggravate the resource curse.[46] To avoid such an outcome, donor conditionality should be sensitive to, and focused on, resource sectors. In addition, donors should provide the central government with the capacity to carry out reform. Although bilateral agencies have large budgets, little of that money is directed toward strengthening government: in Sierra Leone, for example, less than 10 percent of the US$13 million spent by U.S. and UK aid agencies on diamond reform was used to directly improve government capacity (Le Billon and Levin 2009).

One factor that can complicate the donor-recipient relationship is the effort, on the part of donor nations, to further the interests of their own extractive firms. This raises two common issues: first, competition among donors that have distinct commercial interests (e.g., to participate in a major multilateral reconstruction contract); and second, collusion among donors that have shared vested interests (e.g., a desire to see the oil sector opened to foreign companies). These issues have gained particular importance and prominence as a result of two factors: (1) the increasing competition between resource companies from the West and those from the "BRIC" countries (China in particular, but also Brazil, Russia, and India) and (2) the official Chinese policy of noninterference in domestic affairs.

On the one hand, increased competition can have positive implications: host governments should be able to benefit from the fact that various countries are vying for access to their resources, and contracts with Chinese firms do appear to offer a number of potential advantages. On the other hand, despite its name, the noninterference policy has political impact: under the noninterference policy, Chinese extractive firms are willing to accept poor governance standards in host countries, and may have less incentive to engage in socially and environmentally responsible practices. Chinese assistance tends to reduce the leverage of donor countries and international agencies—which can, in turn, undermine the potentially positive effects of Western resource companies. The requirements associated with being publicly traded on a stock exchange, having official commitments to corporate social responsibility, or simply being a well-known commercial brand tend to make Western firms sensitive to reputational risks; such firms may also be subject to specific legislation (such as the U.S. Foreign Corrupt Practices Act); thus, such firms are generally more supportive of social and environmental standards.[47]

---

[46] See Ross (2001) and Mehlum, Moene, and Torvik (2006).
[47] According to Scott Pegg (forthcoming), however, the differences between Western and Chinese companies, when it comes to corporate social responsibility, are not necessarily that large; nor do they matter that much.

Because Chinese labor costs are so low, resource and infrastructure projects import Chinese workers and make little use of local labor, which can create resentment among the local population. On the positive side, in the view of host-country governments, Chinese companies "get things done"; in addition, they often provide infrastructure deals that, under the right conditions, can reduce the risk of corruption and waste in state expenditures, thereby maximizing the public benefits of resource exploitation. In Afghanistan, for example, the contract for China's copper concession called for the construction of major infrastructure, including the first national railway; a coal plant that would not only supply the project, but would also provide energy for portions of Kabul; groundwater systems; and schools, homes, and hospitals for local workers (Landay 2009). Moreover, the fast pace of Chinese infrastructure construction and resource exploitation can rapidly create tangible peace dividends that can consolidate the transition to peace. Finally, mid-level Chinese managers and technicians sometimes provide (cheap) hands-on training for local workers.

Limited exploitation opportunities can indirectly weaken financial, diplomatic, and even military support from Western donors, who are less inclined to provide assistance to post-conflict countries that are benefiting from a resource boom but that are not offering major trade opportunities. Thus, Western companies, possibly in association with major donor agencies, may need to compete by offering to build infrastructure in return for access to resources. At the same time, BRIC governments and firms—especially Chinese ones—need to more broadly support good governance through international agreements, bilateral relations, and corporate social responsibility initiatives.

Extractive industries

When hostilities end, post-conflict countries begin to seek revenues, and donors begin to promote foreign investment. As resource sectors open up, foreign extractive companies often become active players in post-conflict economies.[48] Given the high demand for certain commodities in international markets, foreign direct investment in high-value resource sectors often precedes investment in other sectors. But post-conflict states are typically weak, which puts them at a disadvantage when negotiating with extractive companies. The resulting agreements may prevent the host country from obtaining a fair share of revenues, from gaining access to the best extractive technology, or from including social and environmental safeguards.

Measures are needed to ensure that extraction projects are transparent and conflict sensitive, consult and involve local communities, and are operated responsibly. Voluntary standards that take into account the social and environmental context of resource exploitation can assist extractive firms—and the commercial

---

[48] For a more detailed view of the peacebuilding potential of private sector operations in conflict-affected countries, see Klein and Joras (2012).

banks and international financial institutions that finance them—to play a more constructive role in post-conflict settings. The principal standards are IFC's Performance Standards on Social and Environmental Sustainability, the Equator Principles, and the Voluntary Principles on Security and Human Rights.[49] EIAs are another approach used by donors and post-conflict governments to mitigate or prevent the environmental (and often social) impacts of large projects, including those that extract and process high-value natural resources (Brown et al. 2012; Kelly 2012). EIAs are designed to inform development decisions by identifying the likely impacts of a proposed project, as well as the likely impacts of alternatives. Where impacts cannot be avoided, EIAs usually identify potential mitigation measures.

Two factors have triggered considerable movement, within extractive industries, to develop and apply best practices and to promote efforts such as the EITI: (1) requirements originating with financing institutions or home-country legislation and (2) the desire to secure long-term profitability by establishing a reputation as a "reputable" company. The International Council on Mining and Metals, for example, an umbrella association of eighteen large mining companies, promotes sustainable development,[50] and the Tin Supply Chain Initiative of the International Tin Research Institute tracks the tin supply chain in the DRC.[51]

Unfortunately, multinational petroleum companies operating in countries with weak institutions may be an exception to the general trend toward greater corporate responsibility; Angola is a case in point. According to Arne Wiig and Ivar Kolstad, oil corporations perpetuate Angola's patronage system by helping to finance it, meanwhile reaping benefits from the dysfunctionality of the country's institutions. Wiig and Kolstad argue that although the oil companies have both an opportunity and a moral responsibility to improve governance in the country, they have so far been reluctant to do so (Wiig and Kolstad 2012*).

In Angola and many other post-conflict countries, weak institutional capacity may require private companies to step into the breach. For example, where local populations have been excluded from formal contract negotiations, firms bear the burden of seeking a "social license to operate" from local communities or risk long-term challenges to their operations (Boege and Franks 2012*); company-community relations may thus become central to preventing and alleviating local grievances.

Although extractive firms have primary responsibility for company-community relations, governments are also responsible for providing firms with an opportunity

---

[49] For more information on voluntary standards, see Shankleman (2012*). See also www.ifc.org/ifcext/sustainability.nsf/Content/PerformanceStandards; www.equator-principles.com/documents/Equator_Principles.pdf; and www.voluntaryprinciples.org.

[50] For more information on the International Council on Mining and Metals, see www.icmm.org.

[51] Precept 12 of the Natural Resource Charter also reflects the trend toward greater corporate responsibility; see Natural Resource Charter (n.d.).

to act responsibly and develop good relations with local communities. For example, companies should be granted sufficient time to assess the context they will be operating in and to undertake the necessary consultations before they begin the physical development of a resource extraction project. In many instances, however, the amount of time that a company requests to conduct a participatory social impact assessment is considerably longer than that the government actually allows.[52] Donors should also include capacity building and financial support in their support for mining sector reform. The quality and effectiveness of EIAs are often hampered by the lack of in-country capacity to conduct and review them (Brown et al. 2012; Bouma 2012; Kelly 2012). Thus, donors often separate technical assistance and reform, and fail to see the connections between mining and the environment—and to acknowledge the potentially negative effects of extractive industries.

Dialogue, understanding, and efforts to resolve local concerns are key elements of successful company-community relations. It is also important for companies to take responsibility for past wrongs and damages, particularly when operating in an area where extraction played a role in past conflict. Where extractive firms neglect to engage positively with communities, tensions may arise—as in Sierra Leone, where the failure of a large-scale mining project to deliver the promised amenities led to violent unrest (Kawamoto 2012*), and in Guatemala, where the environmental consequences of a gold and silver mine strained relations between the state, the mining firm, and local communities (Boege and Franks 2012*).

Nongovernmental organizations

International NGOs often cooperate closely with domestic NGOs. Broadly speaking, NGOs serve as checks and balances on the power of both the government and private firms. With respect to natural resources, such organizations generally focus on advocacy and monitoring—that is, efforts to protect local communities from the negative impacts of extractive activities on the environment, local livelihoods, and human rights. A few domestic and international NGOs have taken on a more operational role that includes advocacy campaigns, policy reforms, and partnering with extractive firms to help companies gain a social license to operate and strengthen local development.

International and domestic NGOs have greatly increased their effectiveness by working together. International NGOs, for example, back up domestic NGOs when they call domestic authorities to account, while domestic NGOs provide international NGOs with much-needed information and legitimacy. *Civilian Capacity in the Aftermath of Conflict*, a report by the Senior Advisory Group to

---

[52] Personal communication, Diana Klein, project manager, Peacebuilding Issues Programme, International Alert, 2010.

the UN Secretary-General, sets forth recommendations for how the UN can mobilize support from civil society, in the country and internationally, to support post-conflict peacebuilding in the areas of coordination, finance, and capacity building (UNSG 2011). The ability of domestic NGOs to advance democratic governance has both benefited from, and contributed to, the development of a governance model that is much more sensitive to local demands for accountability and participatory decision making; in fact, many governance and foreign assistance projects now rely on domestic NGOs to advance democratic governance. The EITI, for example, requires EITI-compliant countries to meet the following criterion: "Civil society is actively engaged as a participant in the design, monitoring and evaluation of this process and contributes towards public debate" (EITI n.d.b).

Public engagement and multi-stakeholder initiatives

Public engagement is critical to building support for extractive projects and establishing the legitimacy of more general resource sector reform. Although resource sector interventions often identify transparency and inclusion as goals, the record is mixed when it comes to implementation. Failing to engage the public in resource-related decisions can lead to significant problems, however, especially where communities depend on resources for their livelihoods. Engaging the public in post-conflict decision making, in contrast, appears to improve the long-term legitimacy of institutions and the sustained implementation of laws and regulations governing natural resources (Bruch et al. 2012). Stakeholder consultation is important not only to develop a better understanding of stakeholders' concerns and needs, but also to build trust and a sense of ownership (Carius and Maas 2012).

Effective public engagement means consulting with local stakeholders during the earliest phases of project development (e.g., in the course of conducting social and environmental impact assessments); it also requires continuing dialogue about the negative side effects of extraction projects; benefit-sharing arrangements; and the expenditure of the new revenues accruing to local communities. Various foreign aid agencies, industry associations, and international financing institutions, including the World Bank, have developed environmental and social standards for large-scale projects. Under these standards, extractive firms must, for example, compensate local communities for loss of land, ensure that homes and livelihoods are at least as good as they were before extraction started, and spend at least one year conducting preparatory work before beginning extraction (Shankleman 2012*).

One approach that has been proposed to foster both constructive engagement among stakeholders and improved regulatory capacity (legislation, implementation, and monitoring) is known as a *resource compact* (Le Billon 2008c). A compact is a forum that has two purposes: (1) to build consensus through participatory decision making and (2) to inform the public by establishing a public platform for discussion of the extractive sector. An example of such an initiative at the international level is the UN Global Compact, which fosters corporate social responsibility in the context of post-conflict recovery by promoting practices that improve security, economic development, and local relations while seeking to prevent corruption, grievances, and human rights abuses (UNGC and PRI 2010). Principles for Responsible Investment (PRI), a partner in the UN Global Compact, outlines environmental, social, and corporate governance commitments for the over nine hundred PRI signatories; among the commitments agreed to by the signatories are accountability, transparency, and engagement (PRI n.d.). At the national level, the multi-stakeholders groups that were established as part of the EITI are designed to ensure that civil society organizations and companies are openly involved in the design and validation of the EITI process.

Public forums, which bring together citizens, government officials, and extractive firms, lie at the heart of the resource compact model. The forums have two purposes: (1) to identify and articulate the principles and objectives that are guiding the extractive sector in general and (2) to serve as a platform for the discussion of specific issues related to particular industries or companies. Ideally, the forums would foster accountability by keeping the general population informed about the resource sector, including the potential value of reserves, forecasted revenue streams, and the social and environmental impacts of alternative modes of exploitation. This is similar to the EITI, where community meetings have been held to present reports and to foster transparency (Rich and Warner 2012*). The resource compact would be supported by a secretariat that would be responsible for acquiring, analyzing, and disseminating information.

Another function of the forums would be to improve participation in the development of resource sector policy by providing a national-level platform for stakeholders and for local communities affected by extraction. Such a platform could also help fill the regulatory vacuum that is characteristic of the post-conflict transition period. The 2008 report of the Technical Committee on the Niger Delta urged the immediate establishment of a multi-stakeholder compact for the purpose of tackling a number of critical issues, including environmental concerns, power supply, and the situation of youth (Mähler 2012*). As of July 2011, however, the compact had yet to be established, and the issues addressed in the report remained unresolved, largely because of lack of political will.

Peace spoilers

Stakeholders who have an interest in seeing a peace agreement fail—whether in the short or long term—are called *peace spoilers* (Stedman 1997). Spoilers seek to derail the peace process because they have something to lose from peace, either politically or economically. When high-value resources are involved, the stakes are high, and the temptation to spoil the peace may be intensified; peace processes must therefore ensure that, over the long term, peace is more beneficial than war for most groups, if not all.

A number of different circumstances can foster peace spoiling. Excombatants, for example, may return to illegal exploitation and violence because reintegration programs are inadequate or because of unrealistic expectations regarding the size of peace dividends and the speed at which they can be delivered. Certain groups may wish to spoil the peace out of resentment at having been excluded from the peace process. Others may refuse to participate in the peace process at all, either because they stand to benefit either politically or economically from continued hostilities, or because they view peace as a threat to the revenue opportunities afforded by lootable resources.

Factionalism is a common problem: during or immediately after peace negotiations, splinter groups may persist in seeking more beneficial arrangements for their members or constituencies. The "copycat effect" can also undermine peace agreements: since peace agreements tend to grant benefits to different factions, other groups (some of which come into being specifically for this purpose) may attempt to obtain the same benefits. In Liberia, for example, between 1990 and 1995, twelve peace agreements failed. Abuja II, the thirteenth agreement, signed in 1996, was somewhat more successful, but the conflict did not end until 2003, with the signing of the Comprehensive Peace Agreement (Dupuy and Detzel, forthcoming). Among the various reasons that contributed to the failure of successive peace agreements were two in particular: (1) the copycat effect and (2) a pattern in which groups would sign an agreement (under severe international pressure), then continue business as usual under new names (or by means of splinter groups)—and thereby avoid officially breaking the agreement (Reno 1999).

Gaining a commitment to peace from potential peace spoilers sometimes requires political concessions; for example, rebel groups might be allocated key ministerial posts, other political positions, or authority over certain segments of the natural resource sector.[53] Often, the goal of political appointments is to encourage rebel groups to transform themselves from violent movements into political movements, and to provide rebel groups with other outlets to promote their cause. In Sierra Leone, as part of the 1999 Lomé Peace Agreement, the peace was "bought" by appointing Foday Sankoh, the leader of the Revolutionary United Front (RUF), as the head of the Commission for the Management of Strategic Resources, National Reconstruction and Development, and giving him the status of vice president (Kawamoto 2012*; Binningsbø and Dupuy 2009). In Angola, the 1994 Lusaka Protocol provided the National Union for the Total Independence of Angola (União Nacional para a Independência Total de Angola, or UNITA) with ministerial appointments, including the ministry responsible for mining.

Anna Jarstad and Desiree Nilsson have found, however, that such arrangements have a poor record in sustaining peace: first, they entail limited concessions

---

[53] Other power-sharing options that may be implemented in the wake of conflict include granting party status to former rebel groups; requiring proportional representation for various ethnic groups in parliament and other institutions; and establishing or enlarging the autonomy of subnational entities.

on the part of rebels; second, they can be exploited for the enrichment of rebel groups and private individuals; and third, they are as easily broken as they are established, without either side incurring significant costs (Jarstad and Nilsson 2008). Rebels may also use such appointments as an opportunity to regroup and rearm. In Sierra Leone, Sankoh cancelled all diamond-mining licenses in 2000, but let the RUF continue mining in secrecy (Binningsbø and Dupuy 2009)—an arrangement that benefited both Sankoh and the RUF and enabled the rebels to resume fighting one year after the Lomé Agreement.

Despite its poor track record, granting economic and political concessions to rebel groups may sometimes be the only way to achieve peace, even if only temporarily. In the case of economic concessions, it is important to avoid diverting revenues away from investments that could help alleviate poverty, build health care and education systems, and spur economic growth. In the case of political concessions, it is important to prevent former rebels from mismanaging the posts they are allotted. In Sierra Leone, for example, in an effort to check Sankoh's actions as head of the Commission for the Management of Strategic Resources, National Reconstruction and Development, President Kabbah ensured that the Ministry of Mineral Resources maintained political power and governmental authority over mineral resources (Binningsbø and Dupuy 2009).[54] Checks and balances must also be established for revenue-sharing initiatives, to curb corruption and to create incentives for potential peace spoilers to refrain from conflict; without adequate safeguards, the revenues may disappear before they reach regional authorities or inhabitants, as has been the case in Nigeria (Mähler 2012*). Checks and balances can be strengthened by initiatives that raise the costs of war for potential peace spoilers; in Angola, the DRC, and Sierra Leone, for example, sanctions and commodity-tracking systems have served such purposes.

When revenue-sharing provisions are integrated into peace agreements, it is important that such arrangements not be viewed as rewards for belligerents, which would create incentives for other groups to exert pressure for the same benefits. Although copycat demands are of concern primarily within countries seeking to end conflict, there is an international dimension as well: copycats may turn up in a neighboring country or even on another continent. If violent efforts to obtain greater autonomy (or to secede entirely) are perceived as a successful means of obtaining a higher share of revenues through peace agreements backed by the international community, groups in other countries may try the same approach.

COORDINATING AND SEQUENCING INTERVENTIONS

Because high-value natural resource management engages so many actors, often with differing agendas, priorities, and definitions of best practice, coordination is essential to avoiding unintended outcomes. As noted earlier, in September

---

[54] Apparently, Sankoh assumed that his powers were more extensive than they actually were —which led to his decision, in the spring of 2000, to cancel all diamond mining licenses.

2010, President Kabila banned artisanal mining in eastern DRC; this took the Ministry of Mines by surprise, and disrupted a minerals traceability pilot project that was being conducted by the International Tin Research Institute (Economist Intelligence Unit 2010). Coordination is required not only among domestic authorities, NGOs, peacekeeping missions, and foreign aid agencies, but must also include domestic and international private sector entities. (The sheer number of actors involved in high-value resource management may explain, in part, why there has been so little coordination in the past.)

When coordination fails, the best-intentioned projects may undermine each other. For example, sanctions and drastic regulations can help prevent peace spoilers from gaining access to resource revenues, but they can also undermine economic recovery and local livelihoods. Similarly, foreign direct investment may help boost the economy, but its positive effects may be blunted in the absence of effective management institutions, support from local communities, and fairly negotiated contracts.

In addition to coordinating the activities of various actors, it is also necessary to properly time and sequence management strategies so that they support and build on each other. For example, resource sector management can draw on general governmental capacity building. Alternatively, as in Liberia, resource sector reform may provide a model for the reform of other sectors and non-resource-related governmental institutions (Altman, Nichols, and Woods 2012*).

Robust institutions are the backbone of resource management and peacebuilding. Institution building is difficult under any circumstances, but in post-conflict countries it can seem like an impossible task. Some scholars have observed that there are inherent difficulties involved in implementing peacebuilding tasks: specifically, what must be done in the short term, to create peace, may become a hindrance, in the long term, to economic development and institution building (Jarstad 2008; Sisk 2010). When it comes to implementing institution-building initiatives, the failure to take a long-term view may be accompanied by the notion that institution building cannot, or should not, be undertaken in the short term, but should instead be addressed once peace is more firmly established. It is important to realize, however, that institution building is a long-term goal because it requires a great deal of time, not because it can be postponed to meet the more immediate goal of consolidating peace. Postponing institution building in the short term risks destabilizing a country when donor fatigue sets in, and political elites and rent-seeking groups attempt to regain power over the resource sector.

Perhaps even more worrisome, failure to take immediate action on long-term goals risks missing the window of opportunity that opens immediately after the end of conflict, when the regime is weak and outside leverage is greatest. This is a particular concern in resource-rich countries, in which governments may be able to rely on resource revenues relatively quickly, once conflict ends, and where the goal of consolidating power, in order to acquire control over natural resources and the associated revenues, is often high on the agenda. In sum, the existence of long-term objectives does not justify inaction in the short term; unless immediate action is taken on long-term goals, they may never be achieved.

Paul Collier has argued that, ideally, institution building should precede resource exploitation (Collier 2010b). Unfortunately, donor nations and international agencies often fail to perceive the need to consolidate institutions until contracts have already been signed. Even when preventive interventions take place, they may be too slow in relation to the rapid pace of resource project development, as was the case in Chad: the pipeline and the oil fields were developed ahead of schedule, but institutional capacity building was delayed (Gould and Winters 2012*; Pegg 2009).

Table 1 lists various approaches to post-conflict natural resource management and links them to the two principal stages of the peace process (immediate aftermath and peace consolidation).[55] As noted earlier in the chapter, there is no one recipe for resource management: approaches must be selected and timed to meet the needs of a specific context. Depending on context, some approaches may not be appropriate at all, or may be used in peacebuilding phases other than those suggested in the table.

Ideally, many of the assessments listed in the table would be undertaken before conflict ends. In most cases, a strong regulatory framework should be set up as early as possible, when transparency, participation by civil society, and donor leverage are at their height, and the political field is open. The speed and extent of reforms will vary, however, depending on whether an interim authority or an elected government is in place. The final validation and implementation of reforms should be left to a democratically elected government. It is also important to avoid an abrupt or safeguard-free changeover from a transitional to an elected government: capacity building must continue during the changeover, and a certain level of supervision (on the part of civil society and international agencies) and accountability (through formal mechanisms, such as GEMAP) must be maintained.

Finally, given the limited resources of domestic authorities and peacekeeping missions, it is important to consider whether and how improving high-value natural resource management can support and reinforce other peacebuilding priorities, such as strengthening security; reviving local economies; reintegrating former combatants; and ensuring access to water, food, and basic services. In many cases, synergies can be found to link apparently unrelated objectives. Identifying and taking advantage of such synergies, however, requires information sharing and cooperation, which are not always easy to achieve in an environment where some actors engage in zero-sum competition for reconstruction funding, and cling to narrow, mandate-specific perspectives. Nevertheless, there is a great deal of potential to mobilize extraction firms and local communities to create synergies on the ground. A thriving and supportive local community is often the best guarantee of successful business ventures, and progressive extraction firms can provide, or at least advocate for, improved socioeconomic development.

---

[55] According to the UN Secretary-General, the immediate aftermath of conflict includes the first two years after a peace agreement or military victory (UNSG 2009); the subsequent post-conflict period is referred to as *peace consolidation.*

Table 1. Approaches to managing high-value natural resources in post-conflict situations

	Immediate aftermath	Peace consolidation
Extraction	Assess the natural resource base and identify extraction sites.	Renegotiate unfair contracts.
	Assess the contribution of high-value natural resources to the conflict economy.	Sign new contracts once appropriate processes for negotiation, award, and follow-up are in place.
	Deploy peacekeepers to sensitive extraction sites.	Include and enforce environmental and social standards and safeguards for extractive industries.
	Impose and monitor sanctions on conflict resources.	Formalize small-scale, including artisanal, resource extraction.
	Impose a moratorium on new extraction contracts.	
	Review natural resource concessions and contracts.	If extraction is a source of instability, assist in the development of alternative livelihoods.
	Cancel noncompliant contracts.	Establish systems (e.g., cadastres) to register claims to land and other resources.[a]
	Assess overlapping demands on and claims to land (e.g., on the part of industrial and artisanal mining and agricultural interests).	
	Assess how and to what extent local livelihoods depend on resource exploitation.	Establish secure regional trading centers.[b]
	Support local livelihoods by granting access to extraction areas and providing security.	Repatriate stolen revenues.
	Assess and understand the local land tenure system.	
	Freeze stolen assets.	
Commodity and revenue tracking	Identify and assess existing commodity-trading networks.	Fulfill revenue- and commodity-tracking requirements.
	Place monitors at trading and export hubs.	Establish new commodity-tracking systems.
	Implement existing commodity- and revenue-tracking systems, such as the Kimberley Process Certification Scheme.	Monitor the commodity chain, including production sites, to assess compliance with standards on the part of extractive firms.
	Relocate revenue management from the ministry in charge of resource management to the ministry in charge of finance.	Introduce transparent revenue-tracking systems.

Lessons from the management of high-value natural resources 611

Table 1. Approaches to managing high-value natural resources in post-conflict situations (continued)

	Immediate aftermath	Peace consolidation
Revenue distribution and allocation	Determine whether revenue distribution contributed to the conflict.	Establish transparent revenue sharing and revenue allocation.
	Assess local communities' immediate needs (e.g., food, water, sanitation, energy, and reconstruction of homes).	Set up development and stabilization funds.[c]
	Identify constraints to long-term development (e.g., low general educational attainment, poor health services).	Consider benefit-sharing schemes for local communities.[d]
	Determine how to best distribute and expend natural resource revenues to meet both short- and long-term needs, and address the causes of conflict.	
Institution building	Review institutions, laws, and regulations governing the management of high-value natural resources and their revenues.	Continue support for institutional reform.
	Begin restructuring, reforming, and building capacity in governmental institutions.	Consolidate checks and balances through transparency and accountability mechanisms.
	Establish appropriate accounting procedures, including the auditing of resource revenues, in all government agencies and at all levels of government that deal with the resource sector.[e]	Consolidate and monitor accounting procedures.
	Begin developing or amending the legal framework for resource management.	Enforce laws, regulations, and policies governing the resource sector.
	Identify incentives and power relationships, including patronage networks, that influence resource and revenue management.	Provide training to civil society groups, members of legislative bodies, and journalists to help build awareness of natural resource legislation and reinforce accountability in resource and revenue management.
	Establish schemes to reduce incentives and curtail opportunities for corruption.	
	Institute anticorruption mechanisms.	
	Build up incentives for elites to support and follow up resource strategies.	
	Consider investigating past and ongoing corrupt practices.	
	Use external expertise for technical and managerial support and supervision.	

Table 1. Approaches to managing high-value natural resources in post-conflict situations (continued)

	Immediate aftermath	Peace consolidation
Stakeholder participation	Identify and analyze the interests of stakeholders.	Create awareness of potential sources of new conflicts over resources.
	Through effective participation (including public meetings and broad dissemination of information), build trust and foster dialogue between local communities, extractive companies, local authorities, and the central government.	Create a compact with multiple stakeholders to serve as a platform for oversight and the dissemination of information.
	Include civil society groups in all assessments and policy discussions (e.g., assessments of the causes of past conflicts, and of the environmental impacts of extraction).	Engage civil society in drafting plans for local and national natural resource management.
	Conduct community meetings to present options for local resource development.	
	Assess local grievances and concerns related to extraction, benefit sharing, and resource distribution.	
	Encourage extractive firms to obtain the free, prior, and informed consent of local communities before undertaking extraction.	

Note: Approaches are not listed in any particular order; context will determine when a given approach is implemented. Indentation of entries indicates a potential sequence for related approaches or activities.

a. A cadastre is a public registry that grants and administers rights to land and other resources.
b. Five such centers were established in Nord Kivu and Sud Kivu, in the Democratic Republic of the Congo, to strengthen the legal and commercial trade of minerals.
c. Development funds channel revenues from natural resource extraction to development projects. Stabilization funds create a protective buffer against bust periods by setting revenues aside when they exceed forecasts or the government's absorption capacity, and releasing reserve funds when revenues decrease.
d. For the purposes of this table, *benefit sharing* refers to an approach to sharing revenues that targets producing communities rather than larger regions.
e. Such procedures should be put in place throughout the natural resource extraction chain, from granting exploration rights to awarding concessions and contracts, sharing benefits and revenues, tracking commodities and revenues, and spending revenues.

CONCLUSION

Since the establishment of the UN Peacebuilding Commission in 2005, the UN, the UN Secretary-General, and the World Bank have begun to formulate a conceptual and operational framework for post-conflict peacebuilding. They have noted the importance of natural resources to peacebuilding, and have called on the international community to more effectively address natural resources in the aftermath of conflict (UNSG 2009, 2010; World Bank 2011; UNEP 2009; UN 2011). This book responds to that call, and is intended to catalyze further research and best practice in the realm of peacebuilding and natural resources.

High-value natural resources offer a considerable advantage for countries emerging from armed conflict. If extracted and managed in a careful way, such resources can yield both an economic boost and an incentive for keeping the peace. Resource revenues offer a potential means of alleviating poverty, compensating victims, creating jobs, and rebuilding the country and the economy. Moreover, addressing the management of high-value natural resources can directly and indirectly reinforce other peacebuilding objectives—by, for example, improving livelihoods; fostering democratization; strengthening civil society; and supporting disarmament, demobilization, and reintegration. Natural resource revenues can also help to reduce dependence on international assistance, particularly over the long term. However, as the chapters in this volume show, the opportunities associated with high-value resources are accompanied by considerable challenges. In fact, when it comes to sustaining peace and long-term development, resource-rich countries tend to fare worse than others.

There is no single way to manage high-value resources in post-conflict countries, and many of the approaches that have been used have not yielded the desired results. This does not necessarily mean that the approaches were ill conceived; planning, implementation, and follow-up may have been inadequate, or there may have been unforeseen complications. Sometimes well-intentioned approaches may have unintended consequences. In the worst case, they may create new grievances that reignite conflict or cause new, low-level conflicts. Such results can sometimes be avoided through careful planning; in other cases, additional action may be needed to mitigate the consequences.

The variety of approaches to resource governance considered in this and other chapters in this book does not imply that all approaches are equally important or appropriate to every setting. The goal of this book is to provide a basis for developing an effective, context-appropriate set of strategies and policies. These strategies and policies should, among other things, address the role that natural resources played in the conflict; curtail attempts to spoil the peace; and take account of how resources were managed before the conflict. Other key aspects of natural resource management include transparency, accountability, participatory decision making, and revenue distribution and allocation, all of which are fundamental to securing equitable development and a sustainable peace.

614   High-value natural resources and post-conflict peacebuilding

Many aspects of resource management are not specific to post-conflict settings, but they are of grave importance in such settings: in countries that have high-value natural resources, sound resource management is crucial to peacebuilding. Depending on the context, some or all of the approaches to resource management covered in this book may be relevant to efforts to address resource-related causes of conflict. Even where resources were not related to conflict, they can offer conflict-weary populations tangible peace dividends in the form of improved security and living standards, livelihood opportunities, and compensation for conflict-related damages. They can also help get the economy back on track and help rebuild pre-conflict institutions in ways that are not just different, but better. This, then, is the essence of the post-conflict challenge: to design the best possible interventions and support programs in settings where the policy framework is weak and state capacity is low. The goal of this chapter, and this book, is to provide sound guidance for such efforts.

REFERENCES

Al Moumin, M. 2012. The high cost of ambiguity: Conflict, violence, and the legal framework for managing oil in Iraq. In *High-value natural resources and post-conflict peacebuilding*, ed. P. Lujala and S. A. Rustad. London: Earthscan.

Altman, S. L., S. S. Nichols, and J. T. Woods. 2012. Leveraging high-value natural resources to restore the rule of law: The role of the Liberia Forest Initiative in Liberia's transition to stability. In *High-value natural resources and post-conflict peacebuilding*, ed. P. Lujala and S. A. Rustad. London: Earthscan.

Amnesty International. 2009. *Nigeria: Petroleum, pollution and poverty in the Niger Delta*. London.

Asuni, J. B. 2009. *Blood oil in the Niger Delta*. Special Report 229. United States Institute of Peace. www.usip.org/files/resources/blood_oil_nigerdelta.pdf.

Auty, R. M. 1993. *Sustaining development in mineral economies: The resource curse thesis*. London: Routledge.

BBC News. 2001. Sierra Leone minister arrested. November 1. http://news.bbc.co.uk/2/hi/africa/1632958.stm.

———. 2010. Afghans say US team found huge potential mineral wealth. June 14. www.bbc.co.uk/news/10311752.

Beevers, M. D. 2012. Forest resources and peacebuilding: Preliminary lessons from Liberia and Sierra Leone. In *High-value natural resources and post-conflict peacebuilding*, ed. P. Lujala and S. A. Rustad. London: Earthscan.

Binningsbø, H. M., and K. Dupuy. 2009. Using power-sharing to win a war: The implementation of the Lomé Agreement in Sierra Leone. *Africa Spectrum* 44 (3): 87–107.

Boege, V., and D. M. Franks. 2012. Reopening and developing mines in post-conflict situations: The challenge of company-community relations. In *High-value natural resources and post-conflict peacebuilding*, ed. P. Lujala and S. A. Rustad. London: Earthscan.

Bone, A. 2012. The Kimberley Process Certification Scheme: The primary safeguard for the diamond industry. In *High-value natural resources and post-conflict peacebuilding*, ed. P. Lujala and S. A. Rustad. London: Earthscan.

Bouma, G. 2012. Challenges and opportunities for mainstreaming environmental assessment tools in the post-conflict setting. In *Assessing and restoring natural resources in post-conflict peacebuilding*, ed. D. Jensen and S. Lonergan. London: Earthscan.

Boyce, J. 2002. Investing in peace: Aid and conditionality after civil wars. Adelphi Paper No. 351. Oxford, UK: Oxford University Press for the International Institute for Strategic Studies.

Brack, D. 2012. Excluding illegal timber and improving forest governance: The European Union's Forest Law Enforcement, Governance and Trade initiative. In *High-value natural resources and post-conflict peacebuilding*, ed. P. Lujala and S. A. Rustad. London: Earthscan.

Brown, O., M. Hauptfleisch, H. Jallow, and P. Tarr. 2012. Environmental assessment as a tool for peacebuilding and development: Initial lessons from capacity building in Sierra Leone. In *Assessing and restoring natural resources in post-conflict peacebuilding*, ed. D. Jensen and S. Lonergan. London: Earthscan.

Bruch, C., D. Jensen, M. Nakayama, and J. Unruh. 2012. *Post-conflict peacebuilding and natural resources: The promise and the peril.* New York: Cambridge University Press.

Carius, A., and A. Maas. 2012. Thinking back-end: Improving post-conflict analysis through consulting, adapting to change, and scenario building. In *Assessing and restoring natural resources in post-conflict peacebuilding*, ed. D. Jensen and S. Lonergan. London: Earthscan.

Catarious, D. M., Jr., and A. Russell. 2012. Counternarcotics efforts and Afghan poppy farmers: Finding the right approach. In *High-value natural resources and post-conflict peacebuilding*, ed. P. Lujala and S. A. Rustad. London: Earthscan.

Collier, P. 2007. *The bottom billion.* Oxford, UK: Oxford University Press.

———. 2010a. In Afghanistan, a threat of plunder. *New York Times*, July 19. www.nytimes.com/2010/07/20/opinion/20collier.html?scp=6&sq=sierra%20leone%20diamonds%20&st=cse.

———. 2010b. *The plundered planet.* Oxford, UK: Oxford University Press.

Collier, P., and A. Hoeffler. 2009. Testing the neocon agenda: Democracy in resource-rich societies. *European Economic Review* 53 (3): 293–308.

———. 2012. High-value natural resources, development, and conflict: Channels of causation. In *High-value natural resources and post-conflict peacebuilding*, ed. P. Lujala and S. A. Rustad. London: Earthscan.

Conflict Research Consortium. 1998. UN good offices. www.colorado.edu/conflict/peace/treatment/ungoodof.htm.

Davies, V. A. B. 2000. Sierra Leone: Ironic tragedy. *Journal of African Economies* 9 (3): 349–369.

de Soysa, I. 2012. The capitalist civil peace: Some theory and empirical evidence. In *High-value natural resources and post-conflict peacebuilding*, ed. P. Lujala and S. A. Rustad. London: Earthscan.

DPR (Department of Petroleum Resources). 2002. *Environmental guidelines and standards for the petroleum industry in Nigeria (EGASPIN).* Revised edition. Lagos: DPR. Cited in Amnesty International, *Nigeria: Petroleum, pollution and poverty in the Niger Delta* (London: Amnesty International, 2009).

Dupuy, K., and J. Detzel. Appeasing the warlords: Power sharing and peacebuilding in Liberia. In *Fragile bargains: Civil conflict and power sharing in Africa*, ed. S. Gates and K. Strøm. Unpublished manuscript; on file with authors.

Economist. 2009. Nigeria: Hints of a new chapter. November 12. www.economist.com/ node/14843563?story_id=14843563.
Economist Intelligence Unit. 2010. *Report on the Democratic Republic of Congo.* London.
EIA (U.S. Energy Information Administration). 2010. *Annual energy review 2009.* August. www.eia.gov/totalenergy/data/annual/pdf/aer.pdf.
EITI (Extractive Industries Transparency Initiative). n.d.a. EITI countries. http://eiti.org/ implementingcountries.
———. n.d.b. The EITI criteria. http://eiti.org/eiti/principles.
FLEGT VPAs (Forest Law Enforcement, Governance and Trade Voluntary Partnership Agreements). n.d. VPA partner countries. www.euflegt.efi.int/portal/home/ vpa_countries/.
FRN (Federal Republic of Nigeria). 2008. Interviews with a government advisor to the House Committee on the Niger Delta conducted by S. A. Rustad, Abuja.
Girones, E. O., A. Pugachevsky, and G. Walser. 2009. Mineral rights cadastre: Promoting transparent access to mineral resources. Extractive Industries for Development Series 4. World Bank. June. http://siteresources.worldbank.org/EXTOGMC/Resources/ei_for _development_4.pdf.
Global Witness. 2010. *The hill belongs to them: The need for international action on Congo's conflict minerals trade.* December 14. www.globalwitness.org/sites/default/ files/library/The%20hill%20belongs%20to%20them141210.pdf.
Gould, J. A., and M. S. Winters. 2012. Petroleum blues: The political economy of resources and conflict in Chad. In *High-value natural resources and post-conflict peacebuilding*, ed. P. Lujala and S. A. Rustad. London: Earthscan.
Grant, J. A. 2012. The Kimberley Process at ten: Reflections on a decade of efforts to end the trade in conflict diamonds. In *High-value natural resources and post-conflict peacebuilding*, ed. P. Lujala and S. A. Rustad. London: Earthscan.
Hayes, K., and R. Perks. 2012. Women in the artisanal and small-scale mining sector of the Democratic Republic of the Congo. In *High-value natural resources and post-conflict peacebuilding*, ed. P. Lujala and S. A. Rustad. London: Earthscan.
Haysom, N., and S. Kane. 2009. Negotiating natural resources for peace: Ownership, control and wealth-sharing. Briefing Paper. Centre for Humanitarian Dialogue. October. www.hdcentre.org/files/Negotiating%20natural%20resources%20for%20peace.pdf.
ICGLR (International Conference on the Great Lakes Region). 2010. Lusaka declaration of the ICGLR special summit to fight illegal exploitation of natural resources in the Great Lakes region. www.oecd.org/dataoecd/33/18/47143500.pdf.
IMF (International Monetary Fund). 2004. *Sierra Leone: Selected issues and statistical appendix.* IMF Country Report No. 04/420. December. www.imf.org/external/pubs/ft/ scr/2004/cr04420.pdf.
ITRI. 2011. Tin supply from the Democratic Republic of Congo. www.itri.co.uk/POOLED/ ARTICLES/BF_PARTART/VIEW.ASP?Q=BF_PARTART_310250.
IWG (International Working Group of Sovereign Wealth Funds). 2008. Sovereign wealth funds: Generally accepted principles and practices; "Santiago principles." October. www.iwg-swf.org/pubs/eng/santiagoprinciples.pdf.
Jarstad, A. K. 2008. Dilemmas of war-to-democracy transitions: Theories and concepts. In *War to democracy: Dilemmas of peacebuilding*, ed. A. K. Jarstad and T. Sisk. Cambridge, UK: Cambridge University Press.
Jarstad, A. K., and D. Nilsson. 2008. From words to deeds: The implementation of power-sharing pacts in peace accords. *Conflict Management and Peace Science* 25 (3): 206–223.

Jensen, D., M. Halle, and M. Lehtonen. 2009. Risks and opportunities from natural resources and the environment for peacebuilding in the Central African Republic. Draft mission report. Geneva: United Nations Environment Programme.

Karl, T. L. 1997. *The paradox of plenty: Oil booms and petro-states.* Berkeley: University of California Press.

Kawamoto, K. 2012. Diamonds in war, diamonds for peace: Diamond sector management and kimberlite mining in Sierra Leone. In *High-value natural resources and post-conflict peacebuilding,* ed. P. Lujala and S. A. Rustad. London: Earthscan.

Kelly, C. 2012. Mitigating the environmental impacts of post-conflict assistance: Assessing USAID's approach. In *Assessing and restoring natural resources in post-conflict peacebuilding,* ed. D. Jensen and S. Lonergan. London: Earthscan.

Kersch, A. 2010. Surprising disclosures in the Dodd-Frank Act may burden many companies. Mayer-Brown. November. www.mayerbrown.com/mining/article.asp?id=10066&nid=11926.

Klein, D., and U. Joras. 2012. Natural resources and peacebuilding: What role for the private sector? In *Governance, natural resources, and post-conflict peacebuilding,* ed. C. Bruch, C. Muffett, and S. S. Nichols. London: Earthscan.

Knack, S., and P. Keefer. 1995. Institutions and economic performance: Cross-country tests using alternative institutional measures. *Economics and Politics* 7 (3): 207–227.

KP (Kimberley Process). n.d. What is the Kimberley Process? www.kimberleyprocess.com/home/index_en.html.

Lambrechts, K. 2009. *Breaking the curse: How transparent taxation and fair taxes can turn Africa's mineral wealth into development.* Open Society Institute of Southern Africa, Third World Network Africa, Tax Justice Network, Action Aid International, and Christian Aid. http://news.bbc.co.uk/2/shared/bsp/hi/pdfs/25_03_09_breaking_the_curse.pdf.

Landay, J. S. 2009. China's thirst for copper could hold key to Afghanistan's future. *McClatchy,* March 8. www.mcclatchydc.com/2009/03/08/63452/chinas-thirst-for-copper-could.html.

Le Billon, P. 2000. The political ecology of transition in Cambodia 1989–1999: War, peace and forest exploitation. *Development and Change* 31 (4): 785–805.

———. 2003. Buying peace or fuelling war: The role of corruption in armed conflicts. *Journal of International Development* 15 (4): 413–426.

———. 2008a. Corrupting peace? Peacebuilding and post-conflict corruption. *International Peacekeeping* 15 (3): 344–361.

———. 2008b. Diamond wars? Conflict diamonds and geographies of resource wars. *Annals of the Association of American Geographers* 98 (2): 345–372.

———. 2008c. Resources for peace? Managing revenues from extractive industries in post-conflict environments. Public Finance in Post-Conflict Environments: A Policy Paper Series. www.cic.nyu.edu/peacebuilding/docs/PDF/CIC_paper5_LeBillon_FINAL.pdf.

———. 2009. Natural resource types and conflict termination initiatives. *Colombia Internacional* 70:9–34.

———. 2012a. Bankrupting peace spoilers: Can peacekeepers curtail belligerents' access to resource revenues? In *High-value natural resources and post-conflict peacebuilding,* ed. P. Lujala and S. A. Rustad. London: Earthscan.

———. 2012b. Contract renegotiation and asset recovery in post-conflict settings. In *High-value natural resources and post-conflict peacebuilding,* ed. P. Lujala and S. A. Rustad. London: Earthscan.

Le Billon, P., and F. El Khatib. 2004. From free oil to freedom oil: Terrorism, war and US geopolitics in the Persian Gulf. *Geopolitics* 9 (1): 109–137.

Le Billon, P., and E. Levin. 2009. Building peace with conflict diamonds? Merging security and development in Sierra Leone's diamond sector. *Development and Change* 40 (4): 693–715.

Le Billon, P., and A. Waizenegger. 2007. Peace in the wake of disaster? Secessionist conflicts and the 2004 Indian Ocean tsunami. *Transactions of the Institute of British Geographers* 32 (3): 411–427.

Lujala, P., and S. A. Rustad. 2012. High-value natural resources: A blessing or a curse for peace? In *High-value natural resources and post-conflict peacebuilding*, ed. P. Lujala and S. A. Rustad. London: Earthscan.

Maconachie, R. 2012. The Diamond Area Community Development Fund: Micropolitics and community-led development in post-war Sierra Leone. In *High-value natural resources and post-conflict peacebuilding*, ed. P. Lujala and S. A. Rustad. London: Earthscan.

Mähler, A. 2012. An inescapable curse? Resource management, violent conflict, and peacebuilding in the Niger Delta. In *High-value natural resources and post-conflict peacebuilding*, ed. P. Lujala and S. A. Rustad. London: Earthscan.

Marysse, S., and S. Geenen. 2009. Win-win or unequal exchange? The case of the Sino-Congolese cooperation agreements. *Journal of Modern African Studies* 47 (3): 371–396.

Mason, S. J. A., D. A. Sguaitamatti, and P. R. Gröbli. 2012. Stepping stones to peace? Natural resource provisions in peace agreements. In *Governance, natural resources, and post-conflict peacebuilding*, ed. C. Bruch, C. Muffett, and S. S. Nichols. London: Earthscan.

McNeil, D. G. 2010. Next for Afghanistan, the curse of plenty? *New York Times*, June 19. www.nytimes.com/2010/06/20/weekinreview/20mcneil.html?emc=eta1.

Mehlum, H., K. Moene, and R. Torvik. 2006. Institutions and the resource curse. *Economic Journal* 116 (508): 1–20.

Minter, W., and E. Schmidt. 1988. When sanctions worked: The case of Rhodesia re-examined. *African Affairs* 87 (347): 207–237.

Mitchell, H. 2012. A more formal engagement: A constructive critique of certification as a means of preventing conflict and building peace. In *High-value natural resources and post-conflict peacebuilding*, ed. P. Lujala and S. A. Rustad. London: Earthscan.

Morrison, K., P. O. Cerutti, P. R. Oyono, and M. Steil. 2009. Broken promises: Forest revenue sharing in Cameroon. WRI Forest Note. November. http://pdf.wri.org/broken_promises_forest_revenue_sharing_in_cameroon.pdf.

Natural Resource Charter. n.d. The Natural Resource Charter. www.naturalresourcecharter.org/index.php/en/the-precepts/precept-12.

Nichols, S. S., C. Muffett, and C. Bruch. 2012. Fueling conflict or facilitating peace: Lessons in post-conflict governance and natural resource management. *In Governance, natural resources, and post-conflict peacebuilding*, ed. C. Bruch, C. Muffett, and S. S. Nichols. London: Earthscan.

OECD (Organisation for Economic Co-operation and Development). 2010. OECD due diligence guidance for responsible supply chains of minerals from conflict-affected and high-risk areas. www.oecd.org/dataoecd/62/30/46740847.pdf.

PAC (Partnership Africa Canada). 2009. *Diamonds and human security: Annual review 2009*. www.humansecuritygateway.com/documents/PAC_DiamondsHumanSecurity_AnuualReview2009.pdf.

Pain, A. 2012. The Janus nature of opium poppy: A view from the field. In *High-value natural resources and post-conflict peacebuilding*, ed. P. Lujala and S. A. Rustad. London: Earthscan.

Patey, L. A. 2012. Lurking beneath the surface: Oil, environmental degradation, and armed conflict in Sudan. In *High-value natural resources and post-conflict peacebuilding*, ed. P. Lujala and S. A. Rustad. London: Earthscan.

Pegg, S. 2009. Chronicle of a death foretold: The collapse of the Chad-Cameroon pipeline project. *African Affairs* 108 (431): 311–320.

———. Forthcoming. Social responsibility and resource extraction: Are Chinese oil companies different? *Resources Policy*.

Pistilli, M. 2010. Conflict minerals: ITRI supply chain initiative fails to address major issues. *Street*, April 1. www.thestreet.com/print/story/10716904.html.

PRI (Principles for Responsible Investment). n.d. The principles for responsible investment. www.unpri.org/principles/.

PWYP (Publish What You Pay). n.d. About us. www.publishwhatyoupay.org/en/about.

Ratner, B. D. 2012. Building resilience in rural livelihood systems as an investment in conflict prevention. In *Livelihoods, natural resources, and post-conflict peacebuilding*, ed. H. Young and L. Goldman. London: Earthscan.

Reno, W. 1999. *Warlord politics and African states*. Boulder, CO: Lynne Rienner.

Rich, E., and T. N. Warner. 2012. Addressing the roots of Liberia's conflict through the Extractive Industries Transparency Initiative. In *High-value natural resources and post-conflict peacebuilding*, ed. P. Lujala and S. A. Rustad. London: Earthscan.

Ross, M. 2001. *Timber booms and institutional breakdown in Southeast Asia*. Cambridge, UK: Cambridge University Press.

Ross, M. L., P. Lujala, and S. A. Rustad. 2012. Horizontal inequality, decentralizing the distribution of natural resource revenues, and peace. In *High-value natural resources and post-conflict peacebuilding*, ed. P. Lujala and S. A. Rustad. London: Earthscan.

Sala-i-Martin, X., and A. Subramanian. 2003. Addressing the natural resource curse: An illustration from Nigeria. NBER (National Bureau of Economic Research) Working Paper No. W9804. www.nber.org/papers/w9804.

Sandbu, M. E. 2012. Direct distribution of natural resource revenues as a policy for peacebuilding. In *High-value natural resources and post-conflict peacebuilding*, ed. P. Lujala and S. A. Rustad. London: Earthscan.

Sanio, T., and B. Chapagain. 2012. Forest user groups and peacebuilding in Nepal. In *High-value natural resources and post-conflict peacebuilding*, ed. P. Lujala and S. A. Rustad. London: Earthscan.

Seay, L. 2010. Congo mining ban hurt more than it helped. *Christian Science Monitor*, October 5. www.csmonitor.com/World/Africa/Africa-Monitor/2010/1005/Congo-mining-ban-hurt-more-than-it-helped.

Shankleman, J. 2012. Mitigating risks and realizing opportunities: Environmental and social standards for foreign direct investment in high-value natural resources. In *High-value natural resources and post-conflict peacebuilding*, ed. P. Lujala and S. A. Rustad. London: Earthscan.

Sisk, T. 2010. Sustaining peace: Renegotiating postwar settlements. In *Strengthening peace in post-civil war states: Transforming spoilers into stakeholders*, ed. M. Hoddie and C. A. Hartzell. Chicago: University of Chicago Press.

Spittaels, S., and F. Hilgert. 2009. Mapping conflict motives: Central African Republic. Fatal Transactions. International Peace Information Service. http://reliefweb.int/sites/

reliefweb.int/files/resources/3889CF0B221B33268525756300534ED9-Full_Report.pdf.
Stedman, S. J. 1997. Spoiler problems in peace processes. *International Security* 22 (2): 5–53.
Stewart, F. 2000. Crisis prevention: Tackling horizontal inequalities. *Oxford Development Studies* 28 (3): 245–262. http://economics.ouls.ox.ac.uk/14104/1/Frances_Stewart_Paper.pdf.
Sung, H. E. 2004. Democracy and political corruption: A cross-national comparison. *Crime, Law and Social Change* 41 (2): 179–193.
Taylor, M. B., and M. Davis. 2012. Taking the gun out of extraction: UN responses to the role of natural resources in conflicts. In *Governance, natural resources, and post-conflict peacebuilding*, ed. C. Bruch, C. Muffett, and S. S. Nichols. London: Earthscan.
UN (United Nations). 2011. *Civilian capacity in the aftermath of conflict: Independent report of the Senior Advisory Group*. A/65/747-S/2011/85. www.civcapreview.org/LinkClick.aspx?fileticket=K5tZZE99vzs%3d&tabid=3188&language=en-US.
UN DPKO (United Nations Department of Peacekeeping Operations). 2003. *Handbook on United Nations multidimensional peacekeeping operations*. www.peacekeepingbestpractices.unlb.org/Pbps/library/Handbook%20on%20UN%20PKOs.pdf.
UNEP (United Nations Environment Programme). 2009. *From conflict to peacebuilding: The role of natural resources and the environmet*. Nairobi.
UNGC and PRI (United Nations Global Compact and Principles for Responsible Investment). 2010. *Guidance on responsible business in conflict-affected and high-risk areas: A resource for companies and investors*. www.unglobalcompact.org/docs/issues_doc/Peace_and_Business/Guidance_RB.pdf.
UNSC (United Nations Security Council). 2003. Resolution 1509. S/RES/1509 (2003). September 19.
———. 2004. Resolution 1562. S/RES/1562 (2004). September 17.
———. 2008. Resolution 1856. S/RES/1856 (2008). December 22.
UNSG (United Nations Secretary-General). 2009. *Report of the Secretary-General on peacebuilding in the immediate aftermath of conflict*. A/63/881-S/2009/304. June 11. New York: United Nations.
———. 2010. *Report of the Secretary-General on peacebuilding in the immediate aftermath of conflict*. A/64/866-S/2010/386. July 16. New York: United Nations.
———. 2011. Letter dated 20 April 2011 from the chair of the Security Council Committee established pursuant to resolution 1572 (2004) concerning Côte d'Ivoire addressed to the president of the Security Council. S/2011/271. April 27. www.un.org/ga/search/view_doc.asp?symbol=S/2011/271.
USAID (U.S. Agency for International Development). 2006. Interviews of local USAID staff conducted by P. Le Billon in Kono District, Sierra Leone.
Vircoulon, T. 2009. Matières premières: Regulation internationale et états rentiers. *Etudes* 410:593–604.
———. 2011. Derrière le problème des minerais des conflits, la gouvernance du Congo. International Crisis Group. www.crisisgroup.org/en/regions/africa/central-africa/dr-congo/derriere-le-probleme-des-minerais-des-conflits.aspx.
Wallace, J., and K. Conca. 2012. Peace through sustainable forest management in Asia: The USAID Forest Conflict Initiative. In *High-value natural resources and post-conflict peacebuilding*, ed. P. Lujala and S. A. Rustad. London: Earthscan.

Waugh, J. D. 2010. *Assessment and recommendation for a national benefit sharing trust fund*. Monrovia, Liberia: Land Rights and Community Forestry Program, U.S. Agency for International Development.

———. 2011. *Implementing the national benefit sharing trust fund and social agreements: Issues and options for building capacity*. Monrovia, Liberia: Land Rights and Community Forestry Program, U.S. Agency for International Development.

Wennmann, A. 2010. Wealth sharing beyond 2011: Economic issues in Sudan's North-South peace process. Working Paper 1, Centre on Conflict, Development and Peacebuilding. Geneva: CCDP.

———. 2012. Sharing natural resource wealth during war-to-peace transitions. In *High-value natural resources and post-conflict peacebuilding*, ed. P. Lujala and S. A. Rustad. London: Earthscan.

Wiig, A., and I. Kolstad. 2012. Assigned corporate social responsibility in a rentier state: The case of Angola. In *High-value natural resources and post-conflict peacebuilding*, ed. P. Lujala and S. A. Rustad. London: Earthscan.

World Bank. 2008. *Democratic Republic of Congo: Growth with governance in the mining sector*. Report No. 43402-ZR. http://siteresources.worldbank.org/INTOGMC/Resources/336099-1156955107170/drcgrowthgovernanceenglish.pdf.

———. 2011. *World development report 2011*. Washington, D.C. http://wdr2011.worldbank.org/sites/default/files/pdfs/WDR2011_Full_Text.pdf.

Wright, C. 2012. The Kimberley Process Certification Scheme: A model negotiation? In *High-value natural resources and post-conflict peacebuilding*, ed. P. Lujala and S. A. Rustad. London: Earthscan.

APPENDIX 1
List of abbreviations

ABG: Autonomous Bougainville Government
AFRC: Armed Forces Revolutionary Council (Sierra Leone)
ANE: Bureau for Asia and the Near East (U.S. Agency for International Development)
ANEEJ: African Network for Environment and Economic Justice
APC: All People's Congress (Sierra Leone)
APOA: Affected Property Owners Association (Sierra Leone)
ARD: Associates in Rural Development
ASM: artisanal and small-scale mining
AWS: Agreement on Wealth Sharing (Sudan)
BCL: Bougainville Copper Limited
BP: British Petroleum
BRA: Bougainville Revolutionary Army
BRIC: Brazil, Russia, India, and China
CAO: Office of the Compliance Advisor/Ombudsman (International Finance Corporation)
CAR: Central African Republic
CDC: Chiefdom Development Committee (Sierra Leone)
CDF: Civilian Defense Force (Sierra Leone)
CFUG: community forest user group (Nepal)
CIRI: Cingranelli-Richards Human Rights Dataset
CNPC: China National Petroleum Corporation
CPA: comprehensive peace agreement
CPN(UML): Communist Party of Nepal (Unified Marxist-Leninist)
CSCW: Centre for the Study of Civil War (Peace Research Institute Oslo)
CSNPD: National Revival Committee for Peace and Democracy (Comité de Sursaut National pour la Paix et la Démocratie) (Chad)
CSR: corporate social responsibility
CTP: Conflict Timber Project (U.S. Agency for International Development)
DACDF: Diamond Area Community Development Fund (Sierra Leone)

DCHA: Bureau for Democracy, Conflict and Humanitarian Assistance (U.S. Agency for International Development)
DDR: disarmament, demobilization, and reintegration
DRC: Democratic Republic of the Congo
ECOMOG: Economic Community of West African States Cease-Fire Monitoring Group
EIA: environmental impact assessment
EITI: Extractive Industries Transparency Initiative
ELI: Environmental Law Institute
EP: Equator Principles
EPA: Environmental Protection Agency (Liberia)
EU: European Union
FAR: Federation, Action for the Republic (Fédération, Action pour la République) (Chad)
FARC: Revolutionary Armed Forces of Colombia (Fuerzas Armadas Revolucionarias de Colombia)
FARDC: Armed Forces of the Democratic Republic of the Congo (Forces Armées de la République Démocratique du Congo)
FARF: Armed Forces for a Federal Republic (Forces Armées pour la République Fédérale) (Chad)
FDA: Forestry Development Authority (Liberia)
FDLR: Democratic Forces for the Liberation of Rwanda (Forces Démocratiques de Libération du Rwanda)
FLEGT: Forest Law Enforcement, Governance and Trade (European Union)
FMC: forest management contract
FN: New Forces (Forces Nouvelles) (Côte d'Ivoire)
G8: Group of Eight
GAM: Free Aceh Movement (Gerakan Aceh Merdeka) (Indonesia)
GDP: gross domestic product
GEMAP: Governance and Economic Management Assistance Program (Liberia)
GLE: governor-led eradication (Afghanistan)
GOS: Government of Sudan
GOSS: Government of Southern Sudan
HIV/AIDS: human immunodeficiency virus/acquired immune deficiency syndrome
HLDSC: High Level Diamond Steering Committee (Sierra Leone)
HRIA: human rights impact assessment
ICG: International Crisis Group
ICJ: International Court of Justice
IDP: internally displaced person
IFC: International Finance Corporation
IFC-PS: International Finance Corporation's Performance Standards on Social and Environmental Sustainability
ILO: International Labour Organisation

INL: Bureau of International Narcotics and Law Enforcement Affairs (U.S. Department of State)
ISAF: International Security Assistance Force (Afghanistan)
iTSCi: International Tin Research Institute Tin Supply Chain Initiative
JEM: Justice and Equality Movement (Sudan)
KP: Kimberley Process
KPCS: Kimberley Process Certification Scheme
KRG: Kurdistan Regional Government (Iraq)
LEITI: Liberia Extractive Industries Transparency Initiative
LFI: Liberia Forest Initiative
LFP: Livelihoods and Forestry Program (Nepal)
LOGA: Law on the Governing of Aceh
MCAFC: Managing Conflict in Asian Forest Communities (U.S. Agency for International Development)
MCN: Ministry of Counter Narcotics (Afghanistan)
MDTF: multi-donor trust fund
MEND: Movement for the Emancipation of the Niger Delta (Nigeria)
MINUCI: United Nations Mission in Côte d'Ivoire (Mission des Nations Unies en Côte d' Ivoire)
MMR: Ministry of Mineral Resources (Sierra Leone)
MNDA: Ministry of Niger Delta Affairs (Nigeria)
MOI: Ministry of Interior (Afghanistan)
MONUA: United Nations Observer Mission in Angola (Mission d'Observation des Nations Unies à l'Angola)
MONUC: United Nations Organization Mission in the Democratic Republic of the Congo (Mission de l'Organisation des Nations Unies en République Démocratique du Congo)
MONUSCO: United Nations Organization Stabilization Mission in the Democratic Republic of the Congo (Mission de l'Organisation des Nations Unies pour la Stabilisation en République Démocratique du Congo)
MOSOP: Movement for the Survival of the Ogoni People (Nigeria)
MOU: memorandum of understanding
MPLA: People's Movement for the Liberation of Angola (Movimento Popular para a Libertação de Angola)
NAD: Nanggroe Aceh Darussalam (Indonesia)
NATO: North Atlantic Treaty Organization
NCDDR: National Committee for Disarmament, Demobilization and Reintegration (Sierra Leone)
NCP: National Congress Party (Sudan)
NDCS: National Drug Control Strategy (Afghanistan)
NDDC: Niger Delta Development Commission (Nigeria)
NDPVF: Niger Delta People's Volunteer Force (Nigeria)
NDRDMP: Niger Delta Regional Development Master Plan (Nigeria)
NFRL: National Forestry Reform Law (Liberia)

NGO: nongovernmental organization
NMJD: Network Movement for Justice and Development (Sierra Leone)
NPR: Nepalese rupee
NPRC: National Provisional Ruling Council (Sierra Leone)
NRF: natural resource fund
NRM: natural resource management
OECD: Organisation for Economic Co-operation and Development
OEF: Operation Enduring Freedom (Afghanistan)
OMPADEC: Oil Mineral Producing Areas Development Commission (Nigeria)
OPEC: Organization of the Petroleum Exporting Countries
OSD: Operational Support Division (Sierra Leone)
OTI: Office of Transition Initiatives (U.S. Agency for International Development)
PAC: Partnership Africa Canada
PDK: Party of Democratic Kampuchea (Cambodia)
PEP: Poppy Elimination Program (Afghanistan)
PNG: Papua New Guinea
PRI: Principles for Responsible Investment
PRIO: Peace Research Institute Oslo
PRML: Petroleum Revenue Management Law (Chad)
PRT: provincial reconstruction team
PSAC: Public Service Alliance of Canada
RAFT: Responsible Asia Forestry and Trade Program
RUF: Revolutionary United Front (Sierra Leone)
SFCG: Search for Common Ground
SGBV: sexual and gender-based violence
SGS: Société Générale de Surveillance
SLA: Sierra Leone Army
SLPP: Sierra Leone People's Party
SLST: Sierra Leone Selection Trust
SODEC: Society Development Centre (Nepal)
SPLM/A: Sudan People's Liberation Movement/Army
StAR: Stolen Asset Recovery Initiative
STAREC: Programme of Stabilization and Rebuilding of Former Conflict Zones (Programme de Stabilisation et de Reconstruction des Zones sortant des Conflicts Armes) (Democratic Republic of the Congo)
TAL: Law of the Administration for the State of Iraq for the Transitional Period
TCND: Technical Committee on the Niger Delta (Nigeria)
TFD: The Forests Dialogue
TNI: Indonesian National Armed Forces (Tentara Nasional Indonesia)
ToT: trainers of trainees
TRC: truth and reconciliation commission
TSC: timber sales contract

UCDP: Uppsala Conflict Data Program
UK: United Kingdom
UN: United Nations
UNAMA: United Nations Assistance Mission in Afghanistan
UNAMSIL: United Nations Assistance Mission in Sierra Leone
UNAVEM: United Nations Angola Verification Mission
UNCAC: United Nations Convention against Corruption
UNDP: United Nations Development Programme
UNICEF: United Nations Children's Fund
UNIOSIL: United Nations Integrated Office for Sierra Leone
UNIPSIL: United Nations Integrated Peacebuilding Office in Sierra Leone
UNITA: National Union for the Total Independence of Angola (União Nacional para a Independência Total de Angola)
UNMIL: United Nations Mission in Liberia
UNOCI: United Nations Operation in Côte d'Ivoire
UNODC: United Nations Office on Drugs and Crime
UNSC: United Nations Security Council
UNTAC: United Nations Transitional Authority in Cambodia
UNTAES: United Nations Transitional Administration in Eastern Slavonia, Baranja, and Western Sirmium (Croatia)
USAID: U.S. Agency for International Development
USFS: U.S. Forest Service
VDC: village development committee (Nepal)
VPA: Voluntary Partnership Agreement (Forest Law Enforcement, Governance and Trade initiative)
VPSHR or VPs: Voluntary Principles on Security and Human Rights
WDC: World Diamond Council

APPENDIX 2
Author biographies

Mishkat Al Moumin is the former minister of the environment for the interim Iraqi government. She is a well-known Iraqi lawyer and an assistant professor of human rights at the University of Baghdad School of Law. Because Iraq did not have a ministry of the environment before she took office, Al Moumin designed its entire structure. During her tenure as minister of the environment, she developed new environmental laws, led campaigns to assist Iraqi people who were living in environmentally dangerous areas, and initiated environmental awareness and remediation projects. Throughout these efforts, Al Moumin engaged community leaders and community-based nongovernmental organizations. Most notably, it was during Al Moumin's tenure that the ministry issued the first environmental status report in modern Iraqi history.

Stephanie L. Altman is an attorney advisor at the National Oceanic and Atmospheric Administration's Office of General Counsel for International Law. She formerly worked as a legal advisor to Liberia's minister of agriculture. Before assuming that post, she was a law fellow at the Environmental Law Institute, where she participated in the Liberia Forest Initiative, assisting with the development of Liberia's new wildlife conservation law and model forest management contract. Before beginning her career as an attorney, Altman spent four years working in West Africa—as a field team leader for the Overseas Processing Entity, assisting refugees seeking admission to the U.S. Refugee Resettlement Program, and as an agroforestry extension agent for the Peace Corps, in Senegal. Altman received her J.D. cum laude from Vermont Law School.

Michael D. Beevers is an assistant professor of environmental and international studies at Dickinson College. His research interests are in the domains of environmental policy and politics, development, international relations, globalization, peacebuilding, and African politics. He holds a Ph.D. in political science from the University of Maryland and an M.P.A. and M.S. from the University of Washington. Before joining the Dickinson faculty, Beevers was awarded a Harrison Fellowship from the University of Maryland and was a Jennings Randolph Peace Scholar at the United States Institute of Peace. He also served as a research associate at the Science, Technology and Environmental Policy Program of the Woodrow Wilson School, Princeton University, and as a consultant for the World Resources Institute and the Post-Conflict and Disaster Management Branch of the United Nations Environment Programme. Beevers was a Peace Corps volunteer in Niger and has worked in South Asia and West Africa on a range of development and environmental issues.

Volker Boege is a research fellow at the School of Political Science and International Studies, University of Queensland, where his work focuses on natural resources, environmental degradation, and violent conflict. He holds a Ph.D. in political science from the University of Hamburg. In the 1990s, Boege participated in the Environment and Conflict Project financed and coordinated by the Swiss Peace Foundation (Berne) and the ETH Zurich. From 2002 to 2005, he worked for the Bonn International Center for Conversion on issues related to water, conflict, and cooperation, with a focus on Southern Africa. Since 2006, he has served as the coordinator of ConCord UQ, the University of Queensland's consortium on community building and responsible resource development. Boege has done extensive research on violent conflicts and peacebuilding in the Pacific, including fieldwork in Papua New Guinea and Bougainville, and has published numerous books, articles, and papers on peace and conflict research.

Andrew Bone is director of International, Industry and Government Relations (International Relations) at De Beers, a director of the World Diamond Council and the Diamond Development Initiative, a board member of the Extractive Industries Transparency Initiative, and a visiting lecturer at the Westminster Business School. The mission of International Relations is to engage positively with key stakeholder groups and exchange views and experiences on issues of mutual interest and concern. International Relations develops and maintains relationships with governments; intergovernmental organizations (such as the United Nations); international organizations, including think tanks and academic institutions; industry groups; and international advocacy nongovernmental organizations. International Relations also deals with international policies, directives, and norms—such as the Kimberley Process and the Millennium Development Goals—that have an impact on De Beers Group.

Duncan Brack is a senior research fellow in the Energy, Environment and Development Programme at Chatham House (the Royal Institute of International Affairs), in London. His work focuses on international environmental regimes and institutions, the interaction between environmental regulation and international trade rules, and international environmental crime. Brack runs Chatham House's program to address illegal logging and the trade in illegally logged timber, which includes maintaining a web site; running twice-yearly update and consultation meetings; and carrying out research, mainly into mechanisms designed to exclude illegal products from consumer markets.

David M. Catarious Jr. is a Special Assistant at the U.S. Department of Energy. He was formerly an analyst and project director at CNA, a nonprofit think tank that provides analysis and solutions for national security leaders and public sector organizations. At CNA, he directed a group of analysts and retired military officers in an initiative that examined the role of the U.S. Department of Defense in achieving a more energy- and climate-secure future. Catarious coauthored (with Sherri Goodman, Ronald Filadelfo, Henry Gaffney, Sean Maybee, and Thomas Morehouse) a pivotal CNA report, "National Security and the Threat of Climate Change," and contributed a chapter to *Ideas for America's Future: Core Elements of a New National Security Strategy* (Center for Transatlantic Relations, 2008). Before joining CNA, Catarious worked on energy policy issues for Rep. Ed Markey, as a Congressional Science Fellow for the American Association for the Advancement of Science. He holds a doctorate in biomedical engineering from Duke University and degrees in mathematics from Virginia Tech. Catarious is also a principal and fellow at the Truman National Security Project.

Binod Chapagain has more than fifteen years of experience engaging in capacity building and addressing poverty and exclusion, women's rights, and people's rights to land and forest resources in South Asia. He was formerly a monitoring and communications advisor for the Livelihoods and Forestry Programme (LFP) in Nepal, where he was directly involved in strategy and operations. The LFP, which is funded by the United Kingdom Department for International Development, works directly with more than 4,500 community forest user groups (CFUGs), including those in areas that have been most affected by conflict. Chapagain has conducted research on the economic impact of CFUGs, the forest-poverty link, and the impact of nongovernmental organizations (NGOs) on the rural poor, among other topics. He has published manuals on NGO capacity building and participatory monitoring and evaluation, as well as a book titled *Healthier Civil Society*. Chapagain holds master's degrees in sociology and business administration and is a Ph.D. student at the Australian National University.

Paul Collier, CBE, is a professor of economics and director of the Centre for the Study of African Economies at the University of Oxford. From 1998 to 2003, he was the director of the Development Research Group of the World Bank. He is the author of three books: *The Bottom Billion: Why the Poorest Countries Are Failing and What Can Be Done about It* (Oxford University Press, 2007); *Wars, Guns and Votes: Democracy in Dangerous Places* (HarperCollins Publishers, 2009); and *The Plundered Planet: How to Reconcile Prosperity with Nature* (Allen Lane, 2010). His research covers the causes and consequences of civil war, the effects of aid, and the problems of democracy in low-income and naturalresource-rich societies.

Ken Conca is a professor of international relations at the School of International Service at American University, where he directs the Global Environmental Politics Program. His research and teaching focus on global environmental politics, environmental policy, water governance, social movements in world politics, and peace and conflict studies. He is the author or editor of seven books, including *The Crisis of Global Environmental Governance* (Routledge, 2008), *Governing Water* (MIT Press, 2006), and *Confronting Consumption* (MIT Press, 2002). Conca received the Chadwick Alger Prize, awarded by the International Studies Association (ISA), for the best book on international organization, and is a two-time recipient of the ISA's Harold and Margaret Sprout Award for the best book on international environmental affairs. Conca is an associate editor of *Global Environmental Politics* and a member of the Expert Advisory Group on Environment, Conflict and Peacebuilding of the United Nations Environment Programme.

Indra de Soysa is a professor of political science and the director of globalization research at the Norwegian University of Science and Technology and an associate scholar at the Centre for the Study of Civil War, Peace Research Institute Oslo. He has a Ph.D. from the University of Alabama. His primary research focuses on the economic, political, and social outcomes of globalization and the causes of political violence and civil war. He has a special interest in the governance of natural resources in support of development and peace. De Soysa has published a number of articles in leading journals and is on the editorial committees of the *Journal of Peace Research*, *International Studies Quarterly*, and the *American Journal of Political Science*.

Daniel M. Franks is a senior research fellow at the Centre for Social Responsibility in Mining, Sustainable Minerals Institute, University of Queensland. Since 1999, he has worked with government, industry, and community stakeholders to address the challenges that resource extraction poses to sustainable and equitable development. He has conducted research in Australia, Cambodia, Canada, and Latin America; one of his current research projects explores the links between extractive resources and mass atrocities. Franks has held senior positions in the Queensland government and has served as a consultant to the mining industry. He earned a B.S. (with honors) in earth sciences from the University of Queensland and a Ph.D. in resource politics and governance from Griffith University, for which he was awarded the Chancellor's Medal. He is an honorary research fellow at the Asia-Pacific Centre for the Responsibility to Protect.

John A. Gould is chair and associate professor of political science at Colorado College. He received his Ph.D. from Columbia University, an M.A.L.D. from Tufts University, and a B.A. from Williams College. Gould maintains a research program in the fields of comparative and international political economy, with a particular focus on the relationship between post-communist economic policies and political, domestic, and international institutions. His regional focus is on Central and Eastern Europe and the Balkans. He is the author of *The Politics of Privatization: Wealth and Power in Postcommunist Europe* (Lynne Rienner Publishers, 2011) and has written or coauthored articles that have appeared in *Comparative European Politics*, *Europe-Asia Studies*, *Business and Politics*, and the *Review of International Political Economy*. Gould has won a number of teaching awards, including the Ray O. Werner Award for Exemplary Teaching in the Liberal Arts, and the Lloyd E. Worner Teacher of the Year.

J. Andrew Grant is an assistant professor in the Department of Political Studies at Queen's University, Ontario. In 2009, he received an Early Researcher Award from the Ontario government to serve as principal investigator for a research project examining governance and competitiveness in mining. During the 2005–2006 academic year, he was a Social Sciences and Humanities Research Council of Canada postdoctoral fellow with the Center for International and Comparative Studies at Northwestern University. Grant is coeditor (with Fredrik Söderbaum) of *The New Regionalism in Africa* (Ashgate, 2003); editor of *Darfur: Reflections on the Crisis and the Responses* (Queen's Center for International Relations, 2009); and coeditor (with Timothy M. Shaw and Scarlett Cornelissen) of *The Research Companion to Regionalisms* (Ashgate, 2011). His recent publications focus on conflict diamonds and the Kimberley Process, regional security, transitional justice, post-conflict reconstruction, and governance issues relating to natural resource extraction. He has conducted field research in Botswana, Ghana, Namibia, Sierra Leone, and South Africa. Grant is also a senior fellow with the Queen's Centre for International Relations, a faculty associate with the Queen's Southern African Research Centre, a research fellow with the Centre for Foreign Policy Studies at Dalhousie University, and the chair of the International Political Science Association Research Committee #40 (New World Orders).

Karen Hayes is director of corporate engagement, Africa Region, for Pact, an international nongovernmental organization (NGO) based in Washington, D.C. Since 2000, she has worked for governments, NGOs, the United Nations, and bilateral and multilateral agencies, focusing on natural resource management (notably mining and governance) issues in Africa, including the Democratic Republic of the Congo (DRC), Ghana, Guinea, and Tanzania. Most of her work has centered on developing and implementing practical solutions to the challenges of the artisanal mining sector in the DRC. She is currently working on the ITRI Supply Chain Initiative, a mineral tagging and traceability scheme for staniferous metals in eastern DRC. Hayes has an M.B.A. from the Judge Institute, University of Cambridge.

Anke Hoeffler is a research officer at the Centre for the Study of African Economies and a research fellow at St. Antony's College, University of Oxford. Her research focuses on the macroeconomics of developing countries and the economics of conflict and political economy. She has published a range of articles on the causes of war, military expenditure, post-conflict economies, the effect of aid, and the problems of democracy in low-income and natural-resource-rich societies. She has a degree in economics from the University of Würzburg, Germany; an M.S. in economics from Birkbeck College, University of London; and a D.Phil. in economics from Oxford.

Kazumi Kawamoto is a Ph.D. candidate in the Human Security Program at the University of Tokyo Graduate School of Arts and Sciences, majoring in international relations. She holds an M.A. in human security studies and a B.A. in international relations from the University of Tokyo, and is currently pursuing a second master's degree at Columbia University's School of International and Public Affairs, where she is concentrating on international security policy. Kawamoto's research interests center on legitimacy building and peacebuilding in post-conflict countries, especially in sub-Saharan Africa, with a special focus on governance issues and the role of the United Nations and regional organizations. She worked for the Japanese Ministry of Foreign Affairs from 2008 to 2010 and has conducted fieldwork in Cambodia, Indonesia, Sierra Leone, and Togo.

Ivar Kolstad is a research director at the Chr. Michelsen Institute, in Bergen, Norway. He has conducted research on corruption, natural resources, business ethics, inequality, foreign direct investment, trade, aid, and public financial management. He has a Ph.D. in game theory from the Norwegian School of Economics and Business Administration.

Philippe Le Billon is an associate professor at the University of British Columbia (UBC), where he is affiliated with both the Department of Geography and the Liu Institute for Global Issues. Before joining UBC, he was a research associate with the Overseas Development Institute and the International Institute for Strategic Studies (IISS), in London. Le Billon's research interests focus on the links between environment, development, and security, with a focus on primary commodity sectors. He has published widely on the connections between natural resources and armed conflict, and is the author of *Fuelling War: Natural Resources and Armed Conflicts* (IISS/Routledge, 2005) and the editor of *The Geopolitics of Resource Wars* (Cass, 2005).

Päivi Lujala is an associate professor of geography at the Norwegian University of Science and Technology (NTNU) and a senior researcher at the Centre for the Study of Civil War at the Peace Research Institute Oslo. She holds a B.Sc. in geography from the University of Helsinki, an M.Sc. in economics from the Helsinki School of Economics, and a Ph.D. in economics from NTNU. Her research interests focus on the impact of natural resources on armed civil conflict. Lujala is the author of several articles that examine the role of diamonds, other gemstones, oil, gas, and drug cultivation in initiating, intensifying, and prolonging conflict.

Roy Maconachie, a human geographer by background, is a lecturer in international development at the University of Bath. Before joining the University of Bath, he held research positions at the University of Manchester and the Institute of Development Studies, University of Sussex. His research focuses on the political economy of natural resource management, with a specific interest in the socioeconomic dimensions of small-scale mining in West Africa. His recent work in Sierra Leone explores the increasing tension between artisanal mining and large-scale extraction, with a focus on how civil society groups are impacting the mining sector.

Annegret Mähler, a political scientist and research fellow at the German Institute of Global and Area Studies (GIGA), in Hamburg, is pursuing her Ph.D. at the GIGA Institute of Latin American Studies. Her current research is concentrated on the economic and political impact of natural resources, with a special focus on violent conflict. She is the author of two case studies, "Oil in Venezuela: Triggering Conflicts or Ensuring Stability? A Historical Comparative Analysis" (*Politics & Policy*, August 2011) and "Nigeria: A Prime Example of the Resource Curse? Revisiting the Oil-Violence Link in the Niger Delta" (GIGA Working Papers No. 120, January 2010), both of which were undertaken as part of a GIGA research project titled "Is Resource Wealth a Risk Factor? On the Importance of Contextual Conditions for the Connection between Natural Resources and Violence in Non-OECD States."

Harrison Mitchell, a researcher and analyst specializing in investigations of corruption, beneficiation, commodities, and minerals, is the codirector of Resource Consulting Services, a research and investigations consultancy. He previously worked for the *Financial Times* as a senior researcher and for Global Witness's conflict diamond campaign. Mitchell published groundbreaking investigations of militarized mining undertaken for the United Kingdom Department for International Development, the London School of Economics, and the *Financial Times*; has worked as a researcher and writer on several investigations into corruption and conflict in Central Asia and Africa; and has undertaken audits of China and Lebanon for the Kimberley Process Certification Scheme. Mitchell has worked in Africa, the Middle East, South America, and Asia. He is currently completing an M.Sc. in human rights at the London School of Economics.

Sandra S. Nichols is a senior attorney at the Environmental Law Institute, where her work focuses on the protection of water resources and biodiversity, climate adaptation, and improving environmental governance in the United States and internationally. She also works on capacity-building programs for public officials, judges, and citizens, and is an adjunct professor at Troy University, where she teaches environmental ethics, environmental law, and environmental economics. As a staff attorney with WildLaw, in Montgomery, Alabama, she represented citizens' groups on issues that included national forests, water, endangered species, pollution, resource extraction, environmental justice, and land use. Nichols served as an urban environmental management volunteer in the Peace Corps in Côte d'Ivoire. She holds a B.S. in earth and environmental science from Wesleyan University and a J.D. from the University of Virginia School of Law.

Adam Pain has combined theory and practice in the field of rural development. From 1976 to 1987, while a lecturer in natural resources at the School of Development Studies at the University of East Anglia, United Kingdom, he also worked in natural resource management in Africa and Asia. From 1987 to 1991, he led a SADDC (Southern Africa Development Coordination Conference) regional research program. From 1992 to 2000, he worked as principal advisor to the minister of agriculture in Bhutan, focusing on research and extension policy and natural resource management. In 2001, he rejoined the School of Development Studies as a senior research fellow. Since then, he has done extensive work in Afghanistan, on rural economy, and in Nepal and India, with research programs on natural resource management. Since January 2006, he has been a visiting professor in rural development at the Swedish University of Agricultural Sciences, Uppsala, which he combines with postgraduate teaching and support for a master's in rural development at a group of Vietnamese universities and continuing work on the opium economy and policy-making practices in Afghanistan. He is the coprincipal investigator of a research program on livelihood trajectories in Afghanistan funded by the Economic and Social Research Council.

Luke A. Patey is a research fellow at the Danish Institute for International Studies. His research focuses on the influence of oil on civil war, the peace process in Sudan, and the rise of national oil companies from China, India, and Malaysia. He coedited (with Daniel Large) *Sudan Looks East: China, India and the Politics of Asian Alternatives* (James Currey, 2011) and has written several articles on Sudan's oil sector: "Crude Days Ahead? Oil and the Resource Curse in Sudan" (*African Affairs*, 2010); "Against the Asian Tide: The Sudan Divestment Campaign" (*Journal of Modern African Studies*, 2009); and "State Rules: Oil Companies and Armed Conflict in Sudan" (*Third World Quarterly*, 2007).

Rachel Perks is a doctoral candidate at the School for Agriculture, Policy and Development at the University of Reading, United Kingdom. Her thesis will explore the role of small-scale mining in Zimbabwe. She graduated from Trinity College, University of Toronto, in 2000, with a B.A. (honors) in peace and conflict studies. From 2000 to 2010, she lived in Africa, primarily the Democratic Republic of the Congo (DRC), Kenya, and Sudan, where her work focused on peacebuilding and conflict resolution programming. Her most recent post was as the DRC country director for Pact, Inc., an international nongovernmental organization based in Washington, D.C.

Eddie Rich has nearly twenty years of experience in development. From 1996 to 1998, when BP was seeking a concession, he worked for the United Kingdom Department for International Development (DFID). When Publish What You Pay approached him, in 2001, he was heading up the DFID Corporate Social Responsibility team and was very interested in exploring the opportunity to be involved in a multi-stakeholder process for governance of the oil sector. Over the next few years, Rich was closely involved in DFID's role as the secretariat for the emerging Extractive Industries Transparency Initiative (EITI). Following four years in Kenya, Rich was appointed deputy head of the EITI International Secretariat, which was by then based in Oslo. At EITI, he has responsibility for Anglophone and Lusophone Africa and the Middle East.

Michael L. Ross is a professor of political science and director of the Center for Southeast Asian Studies at the University of California, Los Angeles. He previously taught at the University of Michigan and was a visiting scholar at the World Bank. He has served on advisory boards for the Revenue Watch Institute, the Bonn International Conversion Center, and the World Bank, and is a member of the Technical Group for the Natural Resource Charter. Ross has published widely on the political and economic problems of resource-rich countries, civil war, democratization, women's rights, and the politics of Southeast Asia. His article "Oil, Islam, and Women" received the 2009 Heinz Eulau Award from the American Political Science Association for the best article published in the *American Political Science Review*. His most recent book is *The Oil Curse: How Petroleum Wealth Shapes the Development of Nations* (Princeton University Press, 2012).

Alison Russell is an analyst at CNA, a nonprofit think tank that provides analysis and solutions for national security leaders and public sector organizations, where she specializes in Middle Eastern political-military affairs. She has conducted several assessments of the social, political, economic, and security environment in the Middle East. Among other topics, Russell's projects have focused on maritime security, global maritime strategies for partner capacity building, international support for global fleet stations, U.S. Navy–U.S. Coast Guard integration, military partnerships with nongovernmental organizations, and the future development of the Iraqi navy in the post-counterinsurgency environment. She holds an M.A. in international affairs from American University and a B.A. in political science and French literature from Boston College. Russell is currently a doctoral candidate at the Fletcher School of Law and Diplomacy, Tufts University.

Siri Aas Rustad is a researcher at the Peace Research Institute Oslo and a Ph.D. candidate at the Norwegian University of Science and Technology. Her main research interests are the role of natural resources in conflict and post-conflict situations, the ways in which different natural resource management mechanisms work in particular situations, and pitfalls to avoid in natural resource management. The role of oil in the Niger Delta, both as a contributor to the conflict and as an avenue for helping to resolve the conflict, through different distribution schemes, is a particular focus of her work. Rustad has published in *Political Geography* and *Conflict Management and Peace Science* and coedited (with Cyril Obi) *Oil and Insurgency in the Niger Delta: Managing the Complex Politics of Petro-Violence* (Zed Books, 2011).

Martin E. Sandbu is an editorial writer for the *Financial Times* and a senior fellow at the Zicklin Center for Business Ethics Research, the Wharton School. He received his B.A. in philosophy, politics, and economics from Oxford University and his Ph.D. in political economy and government from Harvard University. Sandbu writes for academic and nonacademic publications on topics in economic theory, economic policy, political economy, international development, and moral and political philosophy. He has held academic positions at Columbia University and the Wharton School.

Tina Sanio has a master's degree in social anthropology and a juridicum in international law from Ludwig-Maximilians-University, Munich, as well as a certificate as a peace and conflict facilitator from the Academy for Conflict Transformation of the Forum Civil Peace Service, Bonn. Sanio has research and field experience in Nepal, Thailand, and Mongolia, where her work focused on human rights and the management of conflict over natural resources. She is currently working in Germany as a conflict consultant, trainer, and author of training and facilitation guides for GIZ/InWEnt—Rural Development in Southeast Asia.

Jill Shankleman is director of J. Shankleman Limited, a business consulting firm she founded in 2000. She has worked as a consultant for oil and gas firms in Algeria, Angola, Bolivia, China, Indonesia, South Africa, the former Soviet Union, and elsewhere, helping the firms to assess the social impact of investment. Shankleman has published articles on oil companies in conflict areas and on the globalization of Chinese oil and mining companies. She was a senior fellow at the United States Institute of Peace (2003–2004) and a public policy scholar at the Woodrow Wilson International Center for Scholars (2009–2010).

Jennifer Wallace is a Ph.D. candidate in the Department of Government and Politics at the University of Maryland and an affiliate of the Harrison Program on the Future Global Agenda. Her research interests focus primarily on environmental linkages to conflict, with particular attention to natural resource management and environmental degradation. Wallace previously worked in Switzerland as a training course coordinator at the Geneva Centre for Security Policy, part of Switzerland's contribution to the Partnership for Peace, a program of bilateral cooperation between individual partner countries and the North Atlantic Treaty Organization. She holds a B.A. from Sarah Lawrence College, a Certificate of Advanced Studies in Environmental Diplomacy from the University of Geneva, and an M.A. in political science from the Graduate Institute of International and Development Studies in Geneva.

T. Negbalee Warner was the head of the secretariat of the Liberia Extractive Industries Transparency Initiative (LEITI) from October 2007 to January 2010; in that capacity, he helped develop and implement a comprehensive communications strategy for the LEITI. He is also credited with having been central to Liberia's having become EITI-compliant in record time, in October 2009. The EITI compliance process provided a unique opportunity to hear and respond to the disappointments, expectations, and fears of ordinary, poor, and vulnerable Liberians regarding the state of natural resource management in the country, and to demonstrate the critical link between natural resources, poverty, and conflict in Liberia. Warner is a lawyer by profession, and currently practices and teaches law in Liberia.

Achim Wennmann is a researcher at the Centre on Conflict, Development and Peacebuilding of the Graduate Institute of International and Development Studies,

Geneva, and executive coordinator of the Geneva Peacebuilding Platform. His research interests relate to the political economy of conflict and armed groups, state fragility, peacemaking, war-to-peace transitions, and the dynamics of armed conflict and violence. Wennmann is the author of *The Political Economy of Peacemaking* (Routledge, 2011) and coeditor (with Mats Berdal) of *Ending Wars, Consolidating Peace: Economic Perspectives* (International Institute for Strategic Studies and Routledge, 2010). Other publications related to natural resources include "Breaking the Conflict Trap? Addressing the Resource Curse in Peace Processes" (*Global Governance*, 2011); "Income Sharing from Natural Resources: Guidelines for Mediators" (*CCDP Issue Briefs*, 2010); "Economic Provisions in Peace Agreements and Sustainable Peacebuilding" (*Négociations*, 2009); and "The Political Economy of Conflict Financing: A Comprehensive Approach beyond Natural Resources" (*Global Governance*, 2007).

Arne Wiig, an economist with twenty years of experience in research, consulting, and policy analysis, is research director for the Poverty Reduction Group at the Chr. Michelsen Institute, in Bergen, Norway. Wiig's work focuses on international trade and foreign direct investment, poverty analysis, resource economics, and corporate social responsibility. His current research collaboration initiatives include projects on regional trade and poverty in the Southern African Development Community, and entrepreneurship and human capital. Wiig has undertaken long-term fieldwork in Angola, Bangladesh, Botswana, and Namibia, and has published extensively on policies for beating the resource curse, corporate social responsibility, barriers to exports of agricultural products, and the impact of trade preferences for least-developed countries.

Matthew S. Winters is an assistant professor in the Department of Political Science at the University of Illinois at Urbana-Champaign. His research focuses on foreign aid and development. Winters has published articles in *World Politics*, the *Annual Review of Political Science*, *International Studies Review*, and *Business and Politics*, and is currently working on a book about corruption in World Bank projects. Winters holds a Ph.D. from Columbia University, where he was a part of the Integrative Graduate Education and Research Traineeship Program in International Development and Globalization. Before joining the University of Illinois, he was a postdoctoral research fellow at the Niehaus Center for Globalization and Governance, Princeton University.

John Woods attended the College of Forestry at the University of Liberia, holds an undergraduate degree from the University of Kentucky at Lexington, and earned a master's degree in natural resource economics from the University of British Columbia, Vancouver. In 1972, he established the Concession Secretariat within the Ministry of Finance in Liberia, which provides technical research and advisory services to the government on the fiscal and legal obligations of concession and concessionlike arrangements for the extraction of natural resources. Woods became the managing director of Liberia's Forestry Development Authority in 1977, one year after it was founded. He also headed the Project Department of the Fund for Cooperation and Development of the Economic Community of West Africa States in Lomé, Togo. He coordinated the Liberia Forest Initiative in Liberia and retired as the managing director of the Forestry Development Authority in 2009.

Clive Wright is a British career diplomat who joined the Diplomatic Service in 1977, after serving in the Royal Marines. He has served in embassies around the world, including Austria, Libya, South Africa, Turkey, and the United States. Between overseas tours, Wright had several periods in the Foreign and Commonwealth Office in London. From February 2001 to December 2004, he was head of the United Kingdom (UK) delegation to the Kimberley Process Certification Scheme (KPCS) negotiation. During that period, he also established and ran the Government Diamond Office, the UK government's implementation arm for the KPCS. Since 2009, Wright has been in Ottawa, working closely with the Canadian government on foreign policy issues of mutual interest.

APPENDIX 3
Table of contents for *Post-conflict peacebuilding and natural resource management*

This book is one of a set of six edited books on post-conflict peacebuilding and natural resource management, all published by Earthscan. Following is the table of contents for the full set.

HIGH-VALUE NATURAL RESOURCES AND POST-CONFLICT PEACEBUILDING
Edited by Päivi Lujala and Siri Aas Rustad

Foreword
President Ellen Johnson Sirleaf

High-value natural resources: A blessing or curse for peace?
Päivi Lujala and Siri Aas Rustad

Part 1: Extraction and extractive industries

Introduction

Bankrupting peace spoilers: Can peacekeepers curtail belligerents' access to resource revenues?
Philippe Le Billon

Mitigating risks and realizing opportunities: Environmental and social standards for foreign direct investment in high-value natural resources
Jill Shankleman

Contract renegotiation and asset recovery in post-conflict settings
Philippe Le Billon

Reopening and developing mines in post-conflict settings: The challenge of company-community relations
Volker Boege and Daniel M. Franks

Diamonds in war, diamonds for peace: Diamond sector management and kimberlite mining in Sierra Leone
Kazumi Kawamoto

Assigned corporate social responsibility in a rentier state: The case of Angola
Arne Wiig and Ivar Kolstad

Part 2: Commodity and revenue tracking

Introduction

The Kimberley Process at ten: Reflections on a decade of efforts to end the trade in conflict diamonds
J. Andrew Grant

The Kimberley Process Certification Scheme: A model negotiation?
Clive Wright

The Kimberley Process Certification Scheme: The primary safeguard for the diamond industry
Andrew Bone

A more formal engagement: A constructive critique of certification as a means of preventing conflict and building peace
Harrison Mitchell

Addressing the roots of Liberia's conflict through the Extractive Industries Transparency Initiative
Eddie Rich and T. Negbalee Warner

Excluding illegal timber and improving forest governance: The European Union's Forest Law Enforcement, Governance and Trade initiative
Duncan Brack

Part 3: Revenue distribution

Introduction

Sharing natural resource wealth during war-to-peace transitions
Achim Wennmann

Horizontal inequality, decentralizing the distribution of natural resource revenues, and peace
Michael L. Ross, Päivi Lujala, and Siri Aas Rustad

The Diamond Area Community Development Fund: Micropolitics and community-led development in post-war Sierra Leone
Roy Maconachie

Direct distribution of natural resource revenues as a policy for peacebuilding
Martin E. Sandbu

Part 4: Allocation and institution building

Introduction

High-value natural resources, development, and conflict: Channels of causation
Paul Collier and Anke Hoeffler

Petroleum blues: The political economy of resources and conflict in Chad
John A. Gould and Matthew S. Winters

Leveraging high-value natural resources to restore the rule of law: The role of the Liberia Forest Initiative in Liberia's transition to stability
Stephanie L. Altman, Sandra S. Nichols, and John T. Woods

Forest resources and peacebuilding: Preliminary lessons from Liberia and Sierra Leone
Michael D. Beevers

An inescapable curse? Resource management, violent conflict, and peacebuilding in the Niger Delta
Annegret Mähler

The high cost of ambiguity: Conflict, violence, and the legal framework for managing oil in Iraq
Mishkat Al Moumin

The capitalist civil peace: Some theory and empirical evidence
Indra de Soysa

Part 5: Livelihoods

Introduction

Counternarcotics efforts and Afghan poppy farmers: Finding the right approach
David M. Catarious Jr. and Alison Russell

The Janus nature of opium poppy: A view from the field
Adam Pain

Peace through sustainable forest management in Asia: The USAID Forest Conflict Initiative
Jennifer Wallace and Ken Conca

Women in the artisanal and small-scale mining sector of the Democratic Republic of the Congo
Karen Hayes and Rachel Perks

Forest user groups and peacebuilding in Nepal
Tina Sanio and Binod Chapagain

Lurking beneath the surface: Oil, environmental degradation, and armed conflict in Sudan
Luke A. Patey

Part 6: Lessons learned

Building or spoiling peace? Lessons from the management of high-value natural resources
Siri Aas Rustad, Päivi Lujala, and Philippe Le Billon

LAND AND POST-CONFLICT PEACEBUILDING
Edited by Jon Unruh and Rhodri Williams

Foreword
Jeffrey Sachs

Land: A foundation for peacebuilding
Jon Unruh and Rhodri Williams

Part 1: Tools and techniques

Introduction

Land tenure and peace negotiations in Mindanao, Philippines
Yuri Oki

The Abyei territorial dispute between North and South Sudan: Why has its resolution proven difficult?
Salman M. A. Salman

Snow leopards and cadastres: Rare sightings in post-conflict Afghanistan
Douglas E. Batson

Community documentation of land tenure and its contribution to state-building in Afghanistan
J. D. Stanfield, Jennifer Brick Murtazashvili, M. Y. Safar, and Akram Salam

Title wave: Land tenure and peacebuilding in Aceh
Arthur Green

Beyond land redistribution: Lessons learned from El Salvador's unfulfilled agrarian revolution
Alexandre Corriveau-Bourque

Transboundary resource management strategies in the Pamir mountain region of Tajikistan
Ian D. Hannam

Part 2: Laws and policies

Introduction

Return of land in post-conflict Rwanda: International standards, improvisation, and the role of international humanitarian organizations
John W. Bruce

Angola: Land resources and conflict
Allan Cain

Refugees and legal reform in Iraq: The Iraqi Civil Code, international standards for the treatment of displaced persons, and the art of attainable solutions
Dan E. Stigall

Title through possession or position? Respect for housing, land, and property rights in Cambodia
Rhodri C. Williams

Land conflicts and land registration in Cambodia
Manami Sekiguchi and Naomi Hatsukano

Legal frameworks and land issues in Muslim Mindanao
Paula Defensor Knack

Post-conflict land tenure issues in Bosnia: Privatization and the politics of reintegrating the displaced
Rhodri C. Williams

Unexplored dimensions: Islamic land systems in Afghanistan, Indonesia, Iraq, and Somalia
Siraj Sait

Customary law and community-based natural resource management in post-conflict Timor-Leste
Naori Miyazawa

Part 3: Post-conflict return and dispute resolution

Introduction

Institutional aspects of resolving land disputes in post-conflict societies
Peter Van der Auweraert

646　High-value natural resources and post-conflict peacebuilding

The role of restitution in post-conflict situations
Barbara McCallin

Land issues in post-conflict return and recovery
Samir Elhawary and Sara Pantuliano

Rebuilding peace: Land and water management in the Kurdistan Region of northern Iraq
Nesreen Barwari

Part 4: Lessons learned

Lesson learned in land tenure and natural resource management in post-conflict societies
Jon Unruh and Rhodri C. Williams

WATER AND POST-CONFLICT PEACEBUILDING
Edited by Erika Weinthal, Jessica Troell, and Mikiyasu Nakayama

Foreword
Mikhail Gorbachev

Shoring up peace: Water and post-conflict peacebuilding
Jessica Troell and Erika Weinthal

Part 1: Basic services and human security

Introduction

The role of informal service providers in post-conflict reconstruction and state building
Jeremy Allouche

A tale of two cities: Restoring water services in Kabul and Monrovia
Jean-François Pinera and Robert Reed

Conflict and collaboration for water resources in Angola's post-war cities
Allan Cain and Martin Mulenga

Thirsty for peace: The water sector in South Sudan
Sam Huston

Community water management: Experiences from the Democratic Republic of the Congo, Afghanistan, and Liberia
Murray Burt and Bilha Keiru

Environmental management of the Iraqi marshlands in the post-conflict period
Chizuru Aoki, Sivapragasam Kugaprasatham, and Ali Al-Lami

Part 2: Livelihoods

Introduction

Lessons of water resource management from perspectives of irrigation water-use management and flood control: A case study of Japan after World War II
Mikiko Sugiura, Yuka Toguchi, and Mona Funiciello

Refugee rehabilitation and transboundary cooperation: India, Pakistan, and the Indus River system
Neda A. Zawahri

Despite the best intentions? The political ecology of water resource management in northern Afghanistan
Jennifer McCarthy and Daanish Mustafa

Water's role in security and stabilization in Helmand Province, Afghanistan
Laura Jean Palmer-Moloney

Part 3: Peace processes, cooperation, and confidence building

Introduction

The Jordan River Basin: A conflict like no other
Munther J. Haddadin

Transboundary cooperation in the Lower Jordan River Basin
Munqeth Mehyar, Nader Khateeb, Gidon Bromberg, and Elizabeth Ya'ari

The Sava River: Transitioning to peace in the former Yugoslavia
Amar Colakhodzic, Marija Filipovic, Jana Kovandzic, and Stephen Stec

Transnational cooperation over shared water resources in the South Caucasus—Reflections on USAID interventions
Marina Vardanyan and Richard Volk

Water security and scarcity: Potential destabilization in western Afghanistan and Iranian Sistan and Baluchestan due to transboundary water conflicts
Alex Dehgan, Laura Jean Palmer-Moloney, and Medhi Mirazee

Water resources in the Sudan north-south peace process and the ramifications of the secession of South Sudan
Salman M. A. Salman

Part 4: Legal frameworks

Introduction

Management of waters in post-Dayton Bosnia and Herzegovina: Policy, legal, and institutional aspects
Slavko Bogdanovic

648 High-value natural resources and post-conflict peacebuilding

The right to water and sanitation in post-conflict legal mechanisms: An emerging regime?
Mara Tignino

Part 5: Lessons learned

Harnessing water management for more effective peacebuilding: Lessons learned
Jessica Troell and Erika Weinthal

LIVELIHOODS, NATURAL RESOURCES, AND POST-CONFLICT PEACEBUILDING
Edited by Helen Young and Lisa Goldman

Foreword
Jan Egeland

Managing natural resources for livelihoods: Helping post-conflict communities survive and thrive
Helen Young and Lisa Goldman

Part 1: Natural resource conflicts, livelihoods, and peacebuilding approaches

Introduction

Social identity, natural resources, and peacebuilding
Arthur Green

Swords into ploughshares? Access to natural resources and securing agricultural livelihoods in rural Afghanistan
Alan Roe

Forest resources in Cambodia's transition to peace: Lessons for peacebuilding
Srey Chanthy and Jim Schweithelm

Post-tsunami Aceh: Successful peacemaking, uncertain peacebuilding
Michael Renner

Manufacturing peace in "no man's land": Livestock and access to resources in the Karimojong Cluster of Kenya and Uganda
Jeremy Lind

Resolving natural resource conflicts to help prevent war: A case from Afghanistan
Liz Alden Wily

Part 2: Innovative livelihoods approaches in post-conflict settings

Introduction

The opportunities and challenges of protected areas for post-conflict peacebuilding
Carol Westrik

A peace park in the Balkans: Cross-border cooperation and livelihood creation through coordinated environmental conservation
J. Todd Walters

Mountain gorilla ecotourism: Supporting macroeconomic growth and providing local livelihoods
Miko Watanabe, Annette Lanjouw, Eugène Rutagarama, and Doug Sharp

The interface between natural resources and disarmament, demobilization, and reintegration: Enhancing human security in post-conflict settings
Glaucia Boyer and Adrienne Stork

Demobilized combatants as park rangers: Post-conflict natural resource management in Gorongosa National Park
Matthew Pritchard

Utilizing alternative livelihood schemes to solve conflict problems in Sierra Leone's artisanal diamond mining industry
Andrew Keili and Bocar Thiam

Value chain development for biodiversity conservation and peacebuilding: BioTrade experiences from Asia and Latin America
Lorena Jaramillo Castro and Adrienne Stork

Part 3: The institutional and policy context

Introduction

Fisheries policies and the problem of instituting sustainable management: The case of occupied Japan
Harry N. Scheiber and Benjamin Jones

Developing capacity for natural resource management in Afghanistan: Process, challenges, and lessons learned by UNEP
Belinda Bowling and Asif Zaidi

Building resilience in rural livelihood systems as an investment in conflict prevention
Blake Ratner

Improving natural resource governance and building peace and stability in Mindanao, Philippines
Cynthia Brady, Oliver Agoncillo, Maria Zita Butardo-Toribio, Buenaventura Dolom, and Casimiro V. Olvida

Commerce in the chaos: Charcoal, bananas, fisheries, and conflict in Somalia
Christian Webersik and Alec Crawford

Part 4: Lessons learned

Managing natural resources for livelihoods in post-conflict societies: Lessons learned
Lisa Goldman and Helen Young

ASSESSING AND RESTORING NATURAL RESOURCES IN POST-CONFLICT PEACEBUILDING
Edited by David Jensen and Steve Lonergan

Foreword
Klaus Toepfer

Can peacebuilding succeed without environmental remediation and natural resource restoration?
David Jensen and Steve Lonergan

Part 1: Post-conflict environmental assessments

Introduction

Evaluating the impact of UNEP's post-conflict environmental assessments
David Jensen

Mitigating the environmental impacts of post-conflict assistance: Assessing USAID's approach
Charles Kelly

Environment and peacebuilding in war-torn societies: Lessons from the UN Environment Programme's experience with post-conflict assessment
Ken Conca and Jennifer Wallace

Environmental assessment as a tool for peacebuilding and development: Initial lessons from capacity building in Sierra Leone
Oli Brown, Morgan Hauptfleisch, Haddijatou Jallow, and Peter Tarr

Challenges and opportunities for mainstreaming environmental assessment tools in the post-conflict setting
George Bouma

Using economic evaluation to integrate natural resource management into Rwanda's post-conflict poverty reduction strategy paper
Louise Wrist Sorensen

Medical and environmental intelligence in peace operations and crisis management
Birgitta Liljedahl, Annica Waleij, Louise Simonsson, Christina Edlund, Björn Sandström, Claes Nyström, and Sture Sundström

Part 2: Planning for environmental risks

Introduction

Thinking back-end: Improving post-conflict analysis through consulting, adapting to change, and scenario building
Alexander Carius and Achim Maas

Evaluation in post-conflict natural resource assistance: Designing for accountability and real-world consequences
Suppiramaniam Nanthikesan and Juha I. Uitto

Peacebuilding and adaptation to climate change
Richard Matthew and Anne Hammill

Part 3: Identification and remediation of high-risk environmental threats

Introduction

Salting the Earth: Environmental health challenges in post-conflict reconstruction
Chad Briggs and Inka Weissbecker

Remediation of polluted sites in the Balkans, Iraq, and Sierra Leone
Muralee Thummarukudy, Oli Brown, and Hannah Moosa

The risks of depleted uranium contamination in post-conflict countries: Findings and lessons learned from UNEP field assessments
Mario Burger

Linking demining to post-conflict peacebuilding: A case study of Cambodia
Nao Shimoyachi-Yuzawa

Part 4: Restoration of natural resources and ecosystems

Introduction

Restoration of damaged land in societies recovering from conflict: The case of Lebanon
Aïda Tamer-Chammas

Ecological restoration and peacebuilding: The case of the Iraqi marshes
Steve Lonergan

Haiti: Lessons learned and way forward in natural resource management projects
Lucile Gingembre

Part 5: Infrastructure and reconstruction

Introduction

Addressing infrastructure needs in post-conflict reconstruction:
An introduction to alternative planning approaches
P. B. Anand

Natural resources, post-conflict reconstruction, and regional integration:
Lessons from the Marshall Plan and other regional reconstruction efforts
Carl Bruch, Ross Wolfarth, and Vladislav Michalcik

Making best use of domestic energy sources: The Priority Production System
for coal mining and steel production in post-World War II Japan
Mikiyasu Nakayama

Road infrastructure reconstruction as a peacebuilding priority in Afghanistan:
Negative implications for land rights
Jon Unruh and Mourad Shalaby

Part 6: Lessons learned

Natural resources and post-conflict restoration, remediation, and
reconstruction: Lessons and way forward
David Jensen and Steve Lonergan

GOVERNANCE, NATURAL RESOURCES, AND POST-CONFLICT PEACEBUILDING
Edited by Carl Bruch, Carroll Muffett, and Sandra S. Nichols

Natural resources and post-conflict governance: Building a sustainable peace
Carl Bruch, Carroll Muffett, and Sandra S. Nichols

Part 1: Frameworks for peace

Introduction

Reducing the risk of conflict recurrence: The relevance of natural resource
management
Christian Webersik and Marc Levy

Stepping stones to peace? Natural resource provisions in peace agreements
Simon J. A. Mason, Pilar Ramirez Gröbli, and Damiano A. Sguaitamatti

Considerations for determining when to include natural resources in peace agreements ending internal armed conflicts
Marcia A. Dawes

Peacebuilding through natural resource management: The UN Peacebuilding Commission's first five years
Matti Lehtonen

Preparing for peace: A case study of Darfur, Sudan
Margie Buchanan-Smith and Brendan Bromwich

Part 2: Peacekeepers, the military, and natural resources

Introduction

Environmental experiences and developments in United Nations peacekeeping operations
Sophie Ravier, Anne-Cécile Vialle, Russ Doran, and John Stokes

Crime, credibility, and effective peacekeeping: Lessons from the field
Annica Waleij

Environmental stewardship in peace operations: The role of the military
Annica Waleij, Timothy G. Bosetti, Russ Doran, and Birgitta Liljedahl

Taking the gun out of extraction: UN responses to the role of natural resources in conflicts
Mark B. Taylor and Mike Davis

Military-to-military cooperation on the environment and natural disasters: Engagement for peacebuilding
Geoffrey D. Dabelko and Will Rogers

Civil-military coordination and cooperation in peacebuilding and natural resource management: An enabling framework, challenges, and incremental progress
Melanne A. Civic

Part 3: Good governance

Introduction

Burma's cease-fire regime: Two decades of unaccountable natural resource exploitation
Kirk Talbott, Yuki Akimoto, and Katrina Cuskelly

Taming predatory elites in the Democratic Republic of the Congo: Regulation of property rights to adjust incentives and improve economic performance in the mining sector
Nicholas Garrett

Process and substance: Environmental law in post-conflict peacebuilding
Sandra S. Nichols and Mishkat Al Moumin

Post-conflict environmental governance: Lessons from Rwanda
Roy Brooke and Richard Matthew

Corruption and natural resources in post-conflict transition
Christine Cheng and Dominik Zaum

Stopping the plunder of natural resources to provide for a sustainable peace in Côte d'Ivoire
Michel Yoboue

Sartor resartus: Liberian concession reviews and the prospects for effective internationalized solutions
K. W. James Rochow

Social benefits in the Liberian forestry sector: An experiment in post-conflict institution building for resilience
John Waugh and James Murombedzi

Preventing violent conflict over natural resources: Lessons from an early action fund
Juan Dumas

Part 4: Local institutions and marginalized populations

Introduction

Legal pluralism in post-conflict environments: Problem or opportunity for natural resource management?
Ruth Meinzen-Dick and Rajendra Pradhan

The role of conservation in promoting sustainability and security in at-risk communities
Peter Zahler, David Wilkie, Michael Painter, and J. Carter Ingram

Integrating gender into post-conflict natural resource management
Njeri Karuru and Louise Yeung

Indigenous peoples, natural resources, and peacebuilding in Colombia
Juan Mayr Maldonado and Luisz Olmedo Martínez

Part 5: Transitional justice and accountability

Introduction

Building momentum and constituencies for peace: The role of natural resources in transitional justice and peacebuilding
Emily E. Harwell

Peace through justice: International tribunals and accountability for wartime environmental wrongs
Anne-Cecile Vialle, Carl Bruch, Reinhold Gallmetzer, and Akiva Fishman

Legal liability for environmental damage: The United Nations Compensation Commission and the 1990–1991 Gulf War
Cymie Payne

Reflections on the United Nations Compensation Commission experience
Lalanath de Silva

Part 6: Confidence building

Introduction

Environmental governance and peacebuilding in post-conflict Central America: Lessons from the Central American Commission for Environment and Development
Matthew Wilburn King, Marco Antonio González, Mauricio Castro-Salazar, and Carlos Manuel Rodriguez

Promoting transboundary environmental cooperation in Central Asia: The Environment and Security Initiative in Kazakhstan and Kyrgyzstan
Saba Nordström

The Perú and Ecuador peace park: One decade after the peace settlement
Yolanda Kakabadse, Jorge Caillaux, and Juan Dumas

Transboundary collaboration in the Greater Virunga Landscape: From gorilla conservation to conflict-sensitive transboundary landscape management
Johannes Refisch and Johann Jenson

Part 7: Integration of natural resources into other post-conflict priorities

Introduction

Consolidating peace through the "Aceh Green" strategy
Sadaf Lakhani

Natural resource management and post-conflict settings: Programmatic evolution in a humanitarian and development agency
Jim Jarvie

Mainstreaming natural resources into post-conflict humanitarian and development action
Judy Oglethorpe, Anita Van Breda, Leah Kintner, Shubash Lohani, and Owen Williams

Mitigating natural resource conflicts through development projects: Lessons from World Bank experience in Nigeria
Sandra Ruckstuhl

Natural resources and peacebuilding: What role for the private sector?
Diana Klein and Ulrike Joras

Part 8: Lessons learned

Fueling conflict or facilitating peace: Lessons in post-conflict governance and natural resource management
Sandra S. Nichols, Carroll Muffett, and Carl Bruch

Index

Abacha, Sani, 394n6
Abe, Ken-Ichi, 370
absolute poverty, 583n19
absorptive capacity, 309
Aceh
   distribution of revenues, 243–246,
      258, 573, 585, 586
   Law on Special Autonomy (NAD
      law), 242–244, 246, 595
   map, 241
   oil and gas, 241, 244, 301
   secessionist movement, 8, 234–235,
      241–243, 246, 258, 301, 307, 595
   tsunami of 2005, 242
Afghanistan, 38–39, 463–464
   agricultural redevelopment
      programs, 485, 486–487
   alternative livelihood programs,
      480–483, 485, 498
   Bonn Agreement, 470, 499
   China's copper concession, 601
   civil conflicts and wars, 468–471
   corruption, 479
   counternarcotics policies, 467–468,
      470–471, 475–487, 491–492,
      495n8
   CTP profile, 512, 513*t*
   farmer contexts, 471–475, 478–
      481, 484–487, 492–493, 574
   foreign aid, 499
   foreign direct investment, 58n17
   institutional capacity building,
      499–500, 599
   international opium sanctions, 26–27
   International Security Assistance
      Force (ISAF), 39
   map, 469, 493
   Ministry of Interior, 476, 479
   National Drug Control Strategy
      (NDCS), 475–476
   natural resources, 38n19, 571
   peace spoilers, 32*t*, 38–39
   poppy cultivation, 471*t*, 482*t*, 485,
      574
   Poppy Elimination Program (PEP),
      476, 482–483
   population demographics, 468
   state building, 499–500
   Taliban, 468–471, 472nn4–5,
      474n9, 479, 481–484
   UN expert panels, 576n8
   United Front/Northern Alliance,
      468, 479
   Uruzgan province, 481–484
   U.S. redevelopment policies, 486
   wheat production, 481
   See also opium
The Agenda for Change, 382
Ahmad, E., 256
aid effectiveness, 309
Alaska Permanent Fund, 224, 232,
   235n11, 275, 285–287
Algeria, 3–4, 8, 231
Alley, Patrick, 507
Alliance for the Renewal of the
   Congo. *See* Democratic
   Republic of the Congo: civil
   conflict
allocation of revenues, 293–295,
   315–317, 582–588, 613
   Chad, 322–334
   escrow accounts, 323n11
   Extractive Industries Transparency
      Initiative, 158, 201–208, 307, 584

Iraq, 413–414, 424–428
liberalized approaches, 367n1, 437–453
Liberia Forest Initiative, 348–349, 385
management overview, 611*t*, 612*t*
Nigeria, 396–397
patronage and rent seeking, 299–300, 313–314, 324–326
stabilization funds, 235–236, 276, 280, 309, 317, 584–585
transparency and accountability, 158, 201–208, 307, 583–584
winners-take-all distribution models, 316
win-win distribution models, 316–317
See also distribution of revenues
All People's Congress (APC). *See* Sierra Leone: civil war
alluvial diamonds, 597
alluvial mining, 11
al Qaeda, 39, 469–470, 474n9, 576
Altman, Stephanie L., 294
Americo-Liberians, 339–340, 374
Amnesty International, 162–163, 184
Angola, 70n4
  asset recovery, 82, 83
  assigned CSR projects, 147–153
  civil war, 148n4, 161–162, 168–170, 234, 302
  conflict diamonds, 161–163
  diamond revenues, 4, 31, 162, 171, 302
  diamond sanctions, 26–27, 163, 170, 227
  distribution of revenues, 586
  environmental law reforms, 65
  Kimberley Process, 170–173, 186, 580
  Lusaka Protocol, 174, 606
  map, 149, 161
  oil and gas industry, 151, 602
  oil and gas revenues, 3–4, 147

  patronage system, 602
  peace spoilers, 31–33, 606, 607
  resource curse, 147–148
  secessionist movements, 8n5, 253*t*
  UN expert panels, 576n8
Annan, Kofi, 192–193
Araf, Abed Alrahman, 422
Árbenz Guzmán, Jacobo, 103
armed civil conflict, 7–10
  abuses against civilians, 44
  definitions, 6n3, 513*t*
  economic freedom contexts, 443–448, 453–455
  financing, 10–11, 293
  global trends, 443
  grievance-based conflict, 8
  opportunistic objectives, 44
Armed Forces for a Federal Republic (FARF). *See* Chad: armed conflicts
arms sanctions, 28
artisanal and small-scale mining (ASM), 11, 14, 161, 529n1, 573–574
  Central African Republic, 574
  child labor, 535
  Democratic Republic of the Congo, 464, 529–542, 573–574, 591, 608
  diamonds, 167n13, 169, 171, 196, 199, 381, 588–589
  due diligence guidelines, 541n12, 581
  local economies, 465
  miner earnings, 540
  Pact program, 535–542
  public-private partnerships, 541
  Sierra Leone, 125, 166–167, 169, 172, 264
  women miners, 464, 529–542
Asari, Dokubu, 403n25
asset recovery, 22, 69–70, 80–83
  freezing of assets, 69, 80, 82
  tracking of assets, 80–81

assets (definition), 6
assigned-responsibility model, 23, 148–153
　Angola, 149–152
　incentives, 152–153
Australia, 298
autarkic systems, 439, 440–442
Autonomous Bougainville Government (ABG), 98
　See also Bougainville
Auty, Richard M., 299n1, 583n21
Azerbaijan
　Baku-Tbilisi-Ceyhan pipeline, 59, 62–64
　Extractive Industries Transparency Initiative, 584
　natural resource fund, 235n11
　oil production, 51n5
Azevedo, Mario Jaoquim, 320n7

Ba'ath Party of Iraq, 415–418, 422, 424
Banks, Glenn, 112
Bannon, Ian, 197
Basedau, Matthias, 395n8
al-Bashir, Omar, 328
basic services, 6
Beevers, Michael D., 294, 590
Belgium, 181
Bevan, David L., 287
Biafra, 8, 234, 253t, 301, 393–394
　See also Nigeria
biased commodity pricing, 74n10
bilateral development banks, 55, 56
Binningsbø, Helga Malmin, 7, 12
blood diamonds, 121, 126–131
　See also diamonds
Boege, Volker, 22, 99n23, 598
Bolivia, 251, 581
Bone, Andrew, 158
Bonn Agreement, 470
border monitoring, 28, 30
Botswana, 181, 186
Bougainville (Papua New Guinea), 8

Autonomous Bougainville Government (ABG), 98
　community relations, 98–102
　distribution of revenues, 585
　hybrid governance, 98
　map, 97
　Panguna gold and copper mine, 95, 99–100, 111–112, 113
　secessionist movement, 95–98
Brack, Duncan, 158
Brautigam, Deborah A., 303
Brazil, 161, 600
BRIC, 600
British legal system, 448n19, 449t, 455–456
Brosio, G., 256
Brown, Taylor, 271
Bryant, Gyude, 342n10
Bure, Benaiah Yongo, 239
Bureau of International Narcotics and Law Enforcement (INL), 478
Burma. See Myanmar
Burr, Millard, 320n7
Burton, John, 550
Burton, Matthew, 421
Bush, George W., 356, 486n17

cadastres, 574, 610t, 612t
Cambodia
　commodity sanctions, 26–27
　CTP profile, 512, 513t
　democratization, 593
　forest conflict management, 515
　forestry reforms, 522, 523
　gem mining, 33
　institutional capacity building, 599
　peace spoilers, 32t, 33
　timber wealth, 33, 302, 505
　UN peacekeeping mission, 28n6
Cameroon
　Chad-Cameroon pipeline, 59, 62–64, 314
　FLEGT initiative, 212, 214, 581
　wealth sharing, 587

Canada, 232, 286
capitalist free markets. *See* liberalized economies
capricious governance, 441n4
carbon capture, 360–361
Carter Center, 79
Castillo Armas, Carlos, 103
Catarious, David, Jr., 463–464, 574
Central African Republic
  artisanal mining, 574
  diamonds, 4, 574
  Extractive Industries Transparency Initiative, 584
  FLEGT initiative, 212, 581
  forest resources, 4, 212
  Kimberley Process, 580–581
  resource revenues, 4
  wealth sharing, 587
centralized distribution of revenues, 223, 233–234, 586
Centre for Humanitarian Dialogue, 242
Ceppi, Jean-Philippe, 161–162
Chad
  armed conflicts, 314, 318–322, 327–331
  Darfur conflict, 314, 327–328, 331–332
  distribution of revenues, 586
  foreign aid, 319, 320
  Future Generations Fund, 223, 330, 585, 594
  human rights abuses, 321
  institutional capacity building, 314–315, 322–324, 594–595
  map, 315, 319
  oil fields, 313, 318–321
  oil revenue management, 3–4, 293, 313–334
  patronage politics, 313–314, 324–334, 598
  Petroleum Revenue Management Law and *Collège,* 322–327, 329–333, 594–595
  stabilization funds, 317n5
  Sudanese-Darfur conflict, 314, 327–328, 331–332
Chad-Cameroon pipeline, 59, 62–64, 594–595
  cash compensation payments, 286
  construction, 325–326
  World Bank, 293, 321–324, 327, 328–334
chain-of-custody initiatives. *See* tracking schemes
Chapagain, Binod, 464–465, 574
child labor, 535
China
  extraction industries, 600–601
  forestry reforms, 522
China EXIM, 56–58
Cingranelli-Richards (CIRI) Human Rights Dataset, 448
civil conflict. *See* armed civil conflict
Civilian Capacity in the Aftermath of Conflict, 603–604
civil peace, 439–453
civil society, 91–92, 355–356, 359–360, 405, 603–604
Cleaver, Frances, 271
Clinton, Hillary, 276n3
coca, 11
Coleman, Paul D., 101
Colleta, Nat J., 104
Collier, Paul
  on conflict resources, 8, 148, 293
  on democratic systems, 594n36
  on development aid, 309
  on direct distribution, 287
  on economic liberalization, 452
  on income expectations, 253
  on the Kimberley Process, 197
  on oil and conflict, 9
  on sequencing of interventions, 609
  on viability of armed conflict, 440
Collins, Robert O., 320n7
Colombia, 4, 8, 43n31, 300
commercial banks, 55, 57*t*

commercial liberalism, 439
commodity chains. *See* tracking schemes
commodity sanctions. *See* sanctions
commodity tracking. *See* tracking schemes
community forest user groups (CFUGs), 464–465, 545–561, 574, 591
   conflict transformation process, 550–552, 557–561
   IDP reintegration, 552–556, 559
   leadership, 557–558
   membership, 546, 547, 557–558
   political affiliations, 558n27
   structure and organization, 546–548
community relations, 22–23, 87–114, 604–605, 613
   Bougainville, 98–102
   civil society organizations, 91–92, 603–604
   compensation for environmental damage, 111, 286, 588–589
   conflict relevance, 87–88
   conflict sensitivity, 87, 88n2
   context-based conflict analysis, 112, 471–475, 478–481, 484–487, 492–493, 574
   customary structures and institutions, 90–92, 94, 110, 552n15
   developing familiarity, 109, 112–113, 538
   distribution of revenues, 131–132, 139, 141, 224, 261–272
   free, prior, and informed consent (FPIC), 105n32, 106–107
   goals, 92–93
   Guatemala, 104–109
   human rights impact assessments (HRIA), 107–109
   hybrid institutions, 89–90, 109–110
   IFC-PS standards, 60, 106n36
   Liberia, 348, 356, 358, 376, 378–379, 382–383
   limitations, 93–95
   management overview, 612*t*
   official state institutions, 91
   Papua New Guinea, 98–102
   prioritizing reconciliation, 110–112
   public forums, 605
   Sierra Leone, 123, 131–141, 265–271, 597–598
   See also local resource economies
Conca, Ken, 464
concessions (definition), 230n5
   See also contract reappraisal and renegotiation
conflict episode, 12n16
conflict prevention, 88n2
conflict relevance, 87–88
conflict resources (definitions), 10n12, 26n2, 73n8
   See also high-value natural resources
conflict sensitivity, 87, 88n2
Conflict Timber Project (CTP), 503–504, 507–513
   action plan, 507–508
   analytic categories, 511
   case studies, 511–512, 513*t*
   conceptual framework, 509–512, 517
   country profiles, 512, 513*t*
   implementation, 508–509
   timber commodity chain, 509–511
   Type I conflicts, 509
   Type II conflicts, 509, 511n8
conflict transformation, 550–551, 557–561
Congolese army (FARDC). *See* Democratic Republic of the Congo
consumers, 44
context-based analysis, 15, 112, 596–598, 613

contract reappraisal and renegotiation, 22, 69–80, 83–84, 575, 577–579
   applications, 75–80
   corruption risks, 74
   Democratic Republic of the Congo, 76–80, 83–84, 577–579
   domestic options, 71–72
   liberalized conditions, 70
   Liberia, 75–76, 83, 344–345, 348–349, 351, 373, 385, 578–579
   long-term impacts, 71–72
   odious contracts, 22, 73n7, 575
   project delays, 74–75
   reappraisal teams, 74n12, 83–84
   timing, 72–73
   transitional authorities, 83, 592–593
coordination of interventions, 607–612
coping economies, 573n3
Corden, W. M., 303n9
Cornwall, Andrea, 271
Corporación Andina de Fomento (CAS), 55n15
corporate social responsibility (CSR), 23, 26, 600–601
   assigned-responsibility model, 23, 147–153
   community development programs, 568
   Global Compact, 26, 181, 605
   incentives, 152–153
   voluntary standards for resource extraction, 22, 49–65, 93, 601–603
corruption, 14, 207, 405, 479, 595–596
   direct distribution of revenues, 278
   peacekeeping operations, 42n28, 577
   UN Convention against Corruption (UNCAC), 82
   See also patronage systems

Côte d'Ivoire
   civil war, 26, 41, 175 580
   cocoa, 4, 41
   diamonds, 158, 175, 196, 580n16
   diamond sanctions, 26–27, 163, 197
   FLEGT initiative, 581
   Kimberley Process, 159n1, 175, 191n3, 197
   natural resource revenues, 4
   natural resources, 41
   peace spoilers, 32*t*, 41
   UN expert panels, 576n8
Croatia, 32*t*, 33–34
cross-cutting issues, 596–607
   context-based analysis, 15, 112, 596–598, 613
   external actors, 598–604
   multi-stakeholder initiatives, 604–605
   peace spoilers, 605–607
   public engagement, 604–605
Cullen, Michelle L., 104
currency exchange, 124n3
customary governance, 597
   informal power relationships, 598
   land rights, 53–54, 58, 597n42
   legal pluralism, 91, 100, 107
   structures and institutions, 90–92, 94, 110, 552n15

Darfur, 314, 327–328, 331–332, 564
De Beers, 189n1
   diamond smuggling, 124, 125n6, 159–160, 162
   Kimberley Process, 184, 189
debt forgiveness, 594n37
Déby, Idriss, 313–314, 320–322, 324–330, 585n24
Deeks, Ashley, 421
de Jong, Wil, 370
democracy/democratization, 448n19, 449*t*, 451–452, 592–593
Democratic Forces for the Liberation of Rwanda (FDLR), 34–36

Democratic Republic of the Congo, 8
  artisanal mining, 464, 529–542, 573–574, 591, 608
  asset recovery, 82
  child labor, 535
  civil conflicts, 234, 253t, 301, 530–531, 537–539
  commodity tracking initiatives, 581–582
  Congolese army, 34–35, 36n16
  contract renegotiations, 76–80, 83–84, 577–579
  CTP profile, 512, 513t
  diamonds, 158, 581
  disarmament, demobilization, and reintegration, 531
  FLEGT initiative, 212, 581
  foreign direct investment, 54
  gender-based violence, 530, 537–539
  HIV/AIDS, 535n7, 541
  illegal taxation, 36
  institutional capacity building, 599
  Interministerial Commission for the Revisitation of Mining Contracts, 79–80
  Kimberley Process, 34n12, 186, 196n4, 581
  Kingamhambo Musonoi Tailings project, 59n21
  Kinsevere Stage II mine, 54
  liberalized mining sector, 75
  map, 78, 530
  mineral resources, 158, 532–533, 581
  mineral revenues, 4, 36, 37, 308n16, 532
  Pact program, 535–539
  peace spoilers, 32t, 34–38, 42–43, 45, 576–577, 607
  political parties, 78–79
  Programme of Stabilization and Rebuilding of Former Conflict Zones (STAREC), 38
  regulation of mining, 529n1
  secessionist movement, 253t, 301
  security standards, 65
  sex trade, 534–535, 538
  Tenke Fungurume copper mine, 54, 59n21
  Transitional Parliament Commission, 77–79
  UN expert panels, 576n8
  UN Mission in the Democratic Republic of the Congo (MONUC), 32t, 34–38, 42–43, 45
  UN Organization Stabilization Mission in the DRC (UNOSM), 577
  UNSC sanctions, 227
  wealth-sharing, 587–588
  women artisanal miners, 530, 533–542
Democratic Republic of the Congo v. Uganda, 81
derivation principle, 232
de Soysa, Indra, 9, 295, 306, 591–592
Deutsche Investitions- und Entwicklungsgesellschaft mbH (DEG), 55n13
development. *See* economic contexts; institutional capacity building
development aid, 55, 56, 304, 309, 486, 599–601
  See also International Monetary Fund; U.S. Agency for International Development; World Bank
development banks, 55, 56
development prices, 75n13
Diamond Area Community Development Fund (DACDF), 131–132, 139, 141, 261–272, 587
  funding, 265
  transparency, 265, 266–267, 270
  use of funds, 265–266

diamonds, 3–4, 10, 11
  alluvial deposits, 597
  artisanal mining, 167n13, 169, 171, 196, 199, 381, 588–589
  certificate-of-origin system, 373
  as conflict resource, 161–163, 302
  Kimberley Process. *See* Kimberley Process Certification Scheme
  kimberlite mining, 122–124, 133, 137–141, 590n32
  quality measures, 171n17
  sanctions, 196n4
  secondary mining, 122
  smuggling, 126, 128, 158, 168, 169–170, 196
  See also Sierra Leone
Dietrich, Jean-Paul, 35
diffuse resources, 302
direct distribution of revenues, 223, 224, 232, 233t, 254n4, 275–288, 588
  advantages, 278–282
  applications, 285–288
  disadvantages, 285
  feasibility, 283
  implementation, 283–284
  means testing, 277
  poverty reduction programs, 287–288
  tax policies, 277, 279–280, 586
  variable approaches, 276–277
disarmament, demobilization, and reintegration programs (DDR), 28, 229, 531, 551n14, 559
distribution of revenues, 14, 223–227, 582–589, 613
  Aceh, 243–246, 258, 573, 585, 586
  Angola, 586
  Bougainville (Papua New Guinea), 585
  centralized approaches, 233–234, 252n2, 586
  Chad, 586
  community-led decision making, 131–132, 139, 141, 224, 261–272
  company-to-government transfers, 226, 229–232
  compensation programs, 286, 588–589
  corruption, 278
  decentralized approaches, 233–234, 251–258, 281, 586
  derivation principle, 232
  direct distribution. *See* direct distribution of revenues
  horizontal distribution, 223, 232, 233t
  horizontal inequality, 251–254
  impact on development, 234–236
  impact on peacemaking, 227–229
  Indonesia, 243–246, 254, 573, 586
  institution building. *See* institutional capacity building
  Iraq, 276n3, 294–295, 413–414, 424–428, 586, 587
  Kurdistan Regional Government (KRG), 586, 587
  Kuwait, 413n2
  management overview, 611t, 612t
  NGO roles, 232
  Niger, 251, 253, 255
  Nigeria, 279, 287–288, 294, 394–397, 400, 406, 583–584, 586, 588
  Norway, 235n11, 584
  oil and gas revenues, 52n8, 406n29, 588–589
  Papua New Guinea, 582
  remediation bonds, 589
  rent seeking, 226–227
  Sierra Leone, 224, 261–272, 589
  stabilization funds, 235–236, 276, 280, 584–585
  strategies, 245–246
  South Sudan, 236–241, 245–246, 255–256, 585, 588–589

Sudan, 236–241, 245–246, 251, 255–256, 587, 588–589
  vertical distribution, 223, 232, 233*t*
  wealth-sharing transfers, 226, 232–233, 254–257, 587–588
  See also allocation of revenues; political economies
Dodd-Frank Wall Street Reform and Consumer Protection Act of 2010, 308n16, 582, 593
Doe, Samuel, 340
donor conditionality, 599–600
Donovan, Deanna, 370, 506
dos Santos, José Eduardo, 82
Dutch disease, 235, 275n2, 303–305
  definitions, 235n12, 275n2, 323n12, 395n9
  detachment effect, 304
  diversification, 309
  Nigeria, 395n9
  saturation points, 304–305

Easterly, W., 309
East Timor. *See* Timor-Leste
Economic Community of West African States, 408
Economic Community of West African States Cease-Fire Monitoring Group (ECOMOG), 126n10, 128–130
economic contexts
  autarkic systems, 439, 440–442
  Dutch disease. *See* Dutch disease
  income expectations, 252–253
  institution building, 295
  internal conflict, 443–444
  liberalism, 438n2, 439
  liberalized markets, 70n2, 367n1, 437–453, 591–592
  local economies. *See* local resource economies
  National Resource Charter, 50n4, 74, 307
  peacemaking, 227–229

power-sharing agreements, 229
price shocks, 305
resource curse. *See* resource curse
revenue allocation. *See* allocation of revenues
revenue distribution. *See* distribution of revenues
stability, 6
stabilization funds. *See* stabilization funds
sustainable livelihoods, 385–386, 540, 545
wealth sharing. *See* wealth sharing
See also political economies
EIA. *See* environmental impact assessment
Eisenstein, Alisha, 132
Ekaette, Obong Ufot, 399
elections, 592–593
elite capture, 264n10
employment, 53–54
Ensign, John, 276n3
environmental degradation, 14, 60, 367–368, 372, 588–589
  compensation programs, 111, 286, 588–589
  local economic impact, 465
  Niger Delta, 394, 402–403, 588
  oil and gas extraction, 394, 402–403, 465, 563–568, 588–589
  remediation bonds, 589
  Sierra Leone, 589
  Sudan, 465, 563–568, 570, 588–589
Environmental Film Festival, 517
environmental impact assessment (EIA), 52–53, 60, 63, 602–603
Environmental Law Institute, 346–347
Equator Principles (EPs), 49–50, 56–59, 602
Erdimi, Timane, 329
Erdimi, Tom, 329
Esau, Bernhard, 176

escrow accounts, 323n11
ethnic fractionalization, 448n19, 454
European Coalition on Oil in Sudan, 568
European Union (EU)
  Forest Law Enforcement, Governance and Trade (FLEGT) initiative, 14, 157–158, 211–219, 351n26, 581, 584, 593, 599
  Kimberley Process, 183
excise taxes, 256, 258, 586
Executive Outcomes, 43n31, 578
expert panels, 576
export credit agencies, 55, 56–58
external partners, 598–604
extraction, 12–13, 21–23, 575–582
  asset recovery, 22, 69–70, 80–83
  assigned corporate social responsibility model, 23, 147–153
  commodity tracking systems. See tracking schemes
  community relations, 22–23, 60, 87–114, 123–124
  contract renegotiations, 22, 69–80, 83–84, 575
  environmental impact assessments, 52–53, 60–63, 602–603
  financing, 54–55
  international commercial interests, 600–601
  liberalization of extractive sectors, 70n2
  management overview, 610*t*
  peace spoilers, 21, 25–46
  postponement, 591
  resource rush, 575
  voluntary standards. See voluntary standards for resource extraction
extraction contracts, 230n5
  See also contract reappraisal and renegotiation
Extractive Industries Network, 536n8, 541n13, 602

Extractive Industries Review (EIR), 56, 106n35
Extractive Industries Transparency Initiative (EITI), 158, 201–208, 307, 584
  community relations, 605
  goals, 201
  impact, 206–208
  Liberia, 158, 202–208, 593–594
  Nigeria, 408
  oil and gas, 14, 50n3, 152
  rubber and forestry products, 202, 578
  Sierra Leone, 140–141
  validation methodology, 201

Fanthorpe, Richard, 126n7
FARC. See Colombia
FDA Reform Manual, 346–347
Fearon, James, 9, 305–306, 440
Federation, Action for the Republic (FAR). See Chad: armed conflicts
Federation of Community Forest User Groups of Nepal, 559
Fiji, 299–300
Financial Action Task Force, 82
Firestone, 41, 75, 578
Fisher, Ronald J., 550
fisheries, 11
FLEGT. See Forest Law Enforcement, Governance and Trade initiative
forced prostitution, 530
Forces Nouvelles (FN). See Côte d'Ivoire: civil war
foreign aid. See development aid
foreign direct investment, 21–22
  asset recovery, 22, 69–70, 80–83
  contract renegotiations, 69–80, 83–84
  governance, 51–54, 58–62, 74
  high risk/low returns cycle, 70–71
  peace spoilers, 21, 25–46
  project financing, 54–55

voluntary standards, 22, 49–65
See also international partners
Forest Conflict Initiative of USAID, 464, 503–527
  achievements and limitations, 524–526
  analytic categories, 511, 519–520, 526
  Conflict Timber Project (CTP), 503–504, 507–513
  country-level missions, 523–524
  governance characteristics, 520, 521
  Managing Conflict in Asian Forest Communities (MCAFC), 503, 504, 514–524
  map, 504
  military actors, 522–523
  private sector actors, 521–522
  target actors, 521–524, 526
  target countries, 504*f*, 512, 513*t*, 514
  timber commodity chain, 509–511, 518, 519, 525–526
  types of forest conflict, 509, 511n8, 518, 519, 525, 526
Forest Law Enforcement, Governance and Trade initiative (FLEGT), 14, 157–158, 211–219, 581, 584, 593, 599
  Cameroon, 212, 214, 581
  Central African Republic, 212, 581
  Côte d'Ivoire, 581
  Democratic Republic of the Congo, 212, 581
  Gabon, 581
  Ghana, 212, 215–216, 581
  goals and scope, 213–215
  government capacity building, 215–216
  impact, 218–219
  Indonesia, 581
  Liberia, 212–213, 216–218, 351n26, 581
  limitations, 214
  Republic of Congo, 212, 214, 215–216, 219, 581
  Sierra Leone, 581
  Vietnam, 212, 581
  voluntary partnership agreements (VPAs), 212
forest resources, 4, 10, 11, 14, 597
  Asia, 503, 504, 506, 514–524, 598n43
  Central African Republic, 4, 212
  community forest user groups (CFUGs), 464–465, 545–561, 574, 591
  comprehensive forest reforms, 368–369
  as conflict resources, 302, 370–372, 504–507, 515
  Extractive Industries Transparency Initiative, 202
  Forest Law Enforcement, Governance and Trade Initiative, 14, 211–219, 581
  institutional capacity building, 520, 521
  Liberia. *See* Liberia
  Liberia Forest Initiative reforms, 293–294, 337–362, 368–369, 375–379
  local economies, 464, 465, 503–527
  Responsible Asia Forestry and Trade program, 598n43
  Sierra Leone, 379, 505–506
  timber commodity chain, 509–511, 518, 519
Forestry Development Authority (FDA). *See* Liberia
Forest Stewardship Council, 214n5
formal trade, 199n7
Fowler, Robert, 27
fragile states, 87n1, 89–90, 109–110, 234
Franks, Daniel M., 22, 598

Fraser Institute, 444
free, prior, and informed consent (FPIC), 105n32, 106–107
Free Aceh Movement (GAM). *See* Aceh: secessionist movement
free markets. *See* liberalized economies
freezing of assets, 69, 80, 82
Fujimori, Alberto, 82
Fujita, Yayoi, 506

Gabon
  CTP profile, 512, 513*t*
  FLEGT initiative, 581
  wealth sharing, 587–588
Gai, Taban Deng, 567
Galtung, John, 550n12
Garrett, Nicholas, 198
Gelb, A., 299n1
gemstones, 4, 10, 11, 14
  See also diamonds
gender-based discrimination, 529, 534–535, 537
gender-based violence, 530, 531n3, 537–539, 541
gender mainstreaming, 540–541
Georgia, 59, 62–64
Ghana
  diamonds, 196n4
  Extractive Industries Transparency Initiative, 584
  FLEGT initiative, 212, 215–216, 581
Gini coefficient of income equality, 147n1
Global Compact. *See* UN Global Compact
Global North, 88n3
Global South, 88n3
Global Witness, 160
  on conflict diamonds, 162–163
  on conflict resources, 73n8, 302
  on conflict timber, 507

Kimberley Process, 172n18, 183, 184
  on LEITI, 206
  on Liberia, 40, 75, 377
  sanctions monitoring, 576
gold, 10–11, 174
  Afghanistan, 571
  Bougainville, 95, 99n26
  Colombia, 8
  Democratic Republic of the Congo, 42n28, 81, 532, 534–535
  Guatemala, 102–107, 603
  Indonesia, 253*t*
  Liberia, xiii, 202, 208, 340
  Niger, 4
  Papua New Guinea, 253*t*
  Sierra Leone, 264
Gonzalez-Acosta, Edward, 263n7
Goodin, R. E., 149–150
Gould, John A., 293
governance, 6
  foreign direct investment, 51–54, 58–62, 74
  institution building. *See* institutional capacity building
  low state capacity, 9, 306, 315–317
  personnel: soldiers, police, bureaucrats, 317
Grant, J. Andrew, 157
greed-based conflict, 279n8
grievance-based conflict, 8, 279n8
grievance thesis, 264
Grossman, Herschel, 299
Group of Eight (G-8), 211
Group of Seven (G-7), 82n25
Group of Twenty (G-20), 201n1
GTZ, 267, 398, 401
Guatemala, 102–109
  civil conflict, 103–104
  community relations, 104–109
  hybrid governance, 104–105
  map, 104
  Marlin gold and silver mine, 102–103, 112, 113

Guéhenno, Jean-Marie, 44n33
Guidolin, Massimo, 152
Guinea
   CTP profile, 512, 513t
   Kimberley Process, 191n3
   Liberian involvement, 341
Gunning, Jan Willem, 287

Habibie, Bacharuddin Jusuf, 242
Habré, Hissen, 319–320
Hayes, Karen, 464
health and safety standards, 60, 63
The Heart of the Matter (Partnership Africa Canada), 129
heroin, 467n1, 474n9
high risk ventures, 70n4
high-value natural resources, 3–15
   armed civil conflict. *See* armed civil conflict
   management. *See* resource management
   resource dependence. *See* resource curse
   revenue allocation. *See* allocation of revenues
   revenue distribution. *See* distribution of revenues
Hilson, Gavin, 196n4
HIV/AIDS, 535n7, 541
Hobbes, Thomas, 90
Hoeffler, Anke
   on conflict resources, 8, 148, 293
   on democratic systems, 594n36
   on economic liberalization, 452
   on income expectations, 253
   on oil and conflict, 9
   on viability of armed conflict, 440
Holbrooke, Richard, 498–499
Holmes, John, 539
horizontal inequality, 251–254
humanitarian assistance, 6
human rights
   free markets, 445, 448–452
   international standards, 105n32, 108
   Voluntary Principles (VPs), 60–62
human rights impact assessments (HRIA), 107–109
Human Rights Watch, 61n24, 162
Hume, David, 438n2
Humphreys, Macartan, 9, 306
Hussein, Saddam, 81–82, 415–418, 421, 424, 426
hybrid states, 89–90, 109–110

IFC. *See* International Finance Corporation
illegal taxation, 36
illiberal governance, 313n1, 316–317
immediate aftermath of conflict, 5, 609–612
income expectations, 252–253
income inequality, 286
income taxes, 230
independent country conflicts, 6n3
Index of Economic Freedom, 443–444
India, 512, 513t, 600
Indonesia
   CTP profile, 512, 513t
   distribution of revenues, 243–246, 254, 573, 586
   FLEGT initiative, 581
   forestry reforms, 212, 520, 522
   gas fields, 241
   Law on Special Autonomy (NAD law), 242–244, 246, 595
   secessionist movements, 8, 234–235, 241–243, 253t, 258, 301, 307
   See also Aceh; Timor-Leste
Industrial Bank Co. Ltd., 56
institutional capacity building, 14, 27–28, 306–309, 367, 589–596
   addressing corruption, 595–596
   Afghanistan, 499–500, 599
   allocation of revenues, 293–295, 315–317

Chad, 314–315, 322–324
diversification, 309
economic contexts, 295, 297–309
forest resource management, 520, 521
free market (liberalized) systems, 367n1, 437–453, 591–592
institutional reforms, 589–593
legal reforms, 593–595
Liberia, 342–357, 358–361, 375–379, 383–386
management overview, 611*t*
Nigeria, 397–408
post-conflict resource management, 11–12, 293–295, 313–334, 383–387
postponed extraction, 591
public-private partnerships, 541
resource cursed states, 441–442
scrutiny of revenues, 307–308
Sierra Leone, 381–386
Sudan, 238, 599
timing, 608–609
tracking schemes, 131–141, 215–216, 238, 308, 594
transitional authorities, 83, 592–593
transparency of revenues, 158, 201–208, 307, 583–584, 595–596
institutional consolidation, 316n3
Inter-American Development Bank, 55n13
internal conflict. *See* armed civil conflict
International Centre for Asset Recovery, 82
International Council on Mining and Metals, 584
International Court of Justice, 81
International Covenant on Civil and Political Rights, 108
International Covenant on Economic, Social and Cultural Rights, 108

International Crisis Group, 330
International Finance Corporation (IFC)
Performance Standards on Social and Environmental Sustainability, 49–50, 49n1, 55n13, 56–65, 602
resource management reform, 599
internationalized internal conflicts, 6n3
International Labour Organization standards, 63n29, 105n33
International Monetary Fund (IMF)
Santiago Principles, 585
structural adjustment programs, 444n10
international partners, 598–604
commercial interests, 600–601
donor countries, 599–601
extractive industries, 600–603
Liberia Forest Initiative (LFI), 342n11, 343, 355–356, 358, 598
Nigeria, 398
nongovernmental organizations, 603–604
See also foreign direct investment; U.S. Agency for International Development
International Security Assistance Force (ISAF), 39, 470, 477, 481–482, 486
See also Afghanistan
International Tin Research Institute, 582
Iran, 415–417
Iraq, 8
asset recovery, 81–82, 83
civil war, 418, 425
Coalition Provisional Authority, 418, 592
Constitution of 1970, 415–418
Constitution of 2005, 413, 418–424, 427–428, 432–435, 595

distribution of oil revenues, 276n3, 294–295, 413–414, 424–428, 586, 587
Gulf War of 1990–1991, 416–418, 426n18
Kirkuk Governorate, 425–426
Kurdistan Regional Government, 8, 414, 423–424
Law No. 97, 422
map, 415–417
oil and gas revenues, 4
oil field development, 414
Oil-for-Food Programme, 81–82, 418
oil management, 421–424, 427–428, 592, 595
population demographics, 414, 416, 424, 425
Transitional Administrative Law (TAL), 418–419
UN oil embargo, 26, 417
U.S. invasion, 43, 418
war with Iran, 415–416

Jackson, Paul, 267
Janjaweed militia, 328
Jarstad, Anna, 606–607
Johnson Sirleaf, Ellen
  climate change policies, 360–361
  forest sector reforms, 337, 347, 353–354, 357, 375, 578–579
  presidency, 75, 202, 206–207, 294, 342n10, 350n25
  See also Liberia
Joint Mission Analysis Cells, 42
joint ventures, 230, 231
Joubert, Jan, 134n31, 138
Justice and Equality Movement (JEM), 564

Kabbah, Ahmed Tejan, 122, 127–129, 131, 607
Kabila, Joseph, 36, 578–579, 591, 608
Kabui, Joseph, 98, 101

Kamara, Usman Boie, 168
Kant, Immanuel, 438n2
Kaplan, Robert, 379n33
Karzai, Ahmed Wali, 479
Karzai, Hamid, 476, 479, 486
  See also Afghanistan
Kazakhstan, 235n11
Keen, David, 380
Keleiboer, Marieke, 550
Kenya, 287
Khmer Rouge (PDK). *See* Cambodia
Kimberley Process Certification Scheme (KPCS), 14, 26, 50n3, 157–199, 371n8, 580–581, 599
  Angola, 170–173, 186
  conflict-related sanctions, 197
  Côte d'Ivoire, 159n1, 175, 191n3, 197
  creation, 130, 157, 163, 181–186
  Democratic Republic of the Congo, 34n12, 186, 196n4
  European Union, 183
  global reach, 158
  Guinea, 191n3
  impact, 186, 189–199
  inclusiveness goals, 173–175
  institutional capacity building, 165–166, 172, 308
  limitations, 195–199
  membership, 159n1, 163, 175, 190, 580n15
  monitoring and confiscation process, 164, 380n37
  multi-stakeholder governance, 159–160
  NGO participation, 160
  Russia, 43n30
  Sierra Leone, 121–122, 132–133, 139, 141, 167–168, 171–173, 261n3, 580
  South Africa, 181, 186
  structure and organization, 163–166, 172n20, 190–194
  suggested reforms, 192–194

suspensions for noncompliance, 165, 176, 185
transparency, 172n18, 197, 198*t*
United States, 181
Venezuela, 159n1, 165, 176, 191n3
See also diamonds
kimberlite mining, 122–124, 133, 137–141, 590n32
Kiribati, 235n11
Kirkuk Governorate (Iraq), 425–426
Knack, Stephen, 303
Koehler, Jan, 498
Koidu diamond riots, 133–139
Kolstad, Ivar, 23, 602
Kosovo, 599
Kouwenhoven, Guus van, 80n22
Kurdistan Regional Government (KRG), 8, 414n4
  distribution of revenues, 586, 587
  oil revenues, 414, 424–427
  Petroleum Act of the Kurdistan Region, 423–424
Kuwait
  distribution of revenues, 413n2
  General Resource Fund, 235n11, 584
  Gulf War of 1990–1991, 416–418, 426n18
  oil fields, 416
Kwamoto, Kazumi, 22–23
Kyrgyzstan, 584

labor conditions, 60, 63
Lacey Act, 215n6
La Ferrera, Eliana, 152
Laitin, David, 9, 306, 440
land rights, 60
  customary traditions, 53–54, 58
  IFC-PS standards, 60
  Liberia, 344n14, 349, 352–355, 374, 386
  Nepal, 549nn8–10, 557
  Sierra Leone, 380–381, 386

Laos
  CTP profile, 512, 513*t*
  forest resources, 506
  forestry reforms, 522
Lebanon, 185, 191n3
Le Billon, Philippe
  on Cambodia's timber, 505
  on contract renegotiation, 22
  on direct distribution of revenues, 278, 279
  on the Kimberley Process, 580
  on point and diffuse resources, 302
  on political geography of oil, 318, 327, 331–332
  on UN peacekeeping missions, 21, 391
Lederach, John Paul, 550
legal pluralism, 91, 100, 107
  See also customary governance
legal reforms, 593–595
  See also institutional capacity building
Levitt, Jeremy, 374
liberal democratic consolidation, 316n3
liberal governance, 313n1, 316
liberalism, 438n2, 439
liberalized economies, 70n2, 367n1, 437–453
  correlations with civil peace, 439–452
  correlations with civil war, 445–448
  correlations with human rights, 445, 448–452
  market-supporting institution building, 452–453, 591–592
  privatization, 442, 452–453
  self-interested activity, 438–439
  short-term destabilizing effects, 443
LiberFor, 350–351, 360
Liberia, 28, 337–362, 372–379
  Abuja II treaty, 130, 606

Index 673

agriculture, 372
allocation of revenues, 584
asset recovery, 80–81, 82, 83
civil service employees, 350n25
civil society, 355–356, 359–360
civil war, 126n10, 130n20, 131n21, 158, 174, 202, 212n3, 340–341, 373–375, 606
colonization and independence, 339–340
Community Rights Law, 361, 378–379
comprehensive peace agreement, 342, 606
conflict timber, 212, 340–341
contract renegotiations, 75–76, 83, 344–345, 348–349, 351, 373, 385, 578–579
corruption and patronage, 207, 374
County Social Development Fund, 588
CTP profile, 512, 513*t*
diamond smuggling, 126, 128, 130, 161, 340–341
FLEGT initiative, 212–213, 216–218, 351n26, 581
Forest Concession Review Committee (FCRC), 344–345
Forest Reform Monitoring Committee, 347, 375
Forestry Development Authority (FDA), 337, 340, 343–352, 355n30, 357–362, 376–379, 384–385, 589–590
forestry reforms. *See* Liberia Forest Initiative
gold, 340
Governance and Economic Management Assistance Program (GEMAP), 27–28, 349, 354, 376, 385, 590
Governance Reform Commission, 386n46

informal economies, 352–353
institutional capacity building, 337–338, 342–361
involvement in Guinea, 341
involvement in Sierra Leone, 126, 128, 130, 341, 379–380
iron mines, 340n6
Johnson Sirleaf presidency, 75, 202, 206–207, 294, 337, 342n10, 347, 353–354
land ownership system, 344n14, 349, 352–355, 374, 386
legal and regulatory framework, 346–350, 595
Liberia Extractive Industries Transparency Initiative (LEITI), 158, 202–208, 584, 593–594
map, 77, 203, 217, 338, 339, 368, 370
Mittal Steel, 75n15, 76*t*
National Forestry Reform Law (NFRL), 347–350, 354, 375–379, 384, 595
natural resources, 40–41
peacebuilding process, 370–379, 383–387
peace spoilers, 32*t*, 40–41, 356, 576, 606
Poverty Reduction Strategy, 357
Press Union of Liberia, 347, 348
rubber, 340, 578
three Cs focus, 375–377
timber concessions, 344–345, 348–349, 351, 373, 385, 578–579, 590
transitional government, 342, 349, 353–354
Truth and Reconciliation Commission (TRC), 81
UN arms embargo, 80n22, 341, 371n8
UN expert panels, 576n8
UN Human Development Index ranking, 372n11

UN Security Council timber
sanctions, 26, 216, 227, 341,
342, 347, 355, 371n8, 373–374,
375
wealth sharing, 588
Liberia Forest Initiative (LFI),
293–294, 337–362, 375–379,
589–590
assessment phase, 343–345
goals, 342–343, 353, 375–376
international partners, 342n11, 343,
355–356, 358, 598
lessons learned, 357–361
plan of action, 343
political context, 368–369
public participation, 348, 356, 358,
376, 378–379, 382–383
recommended reforms, 345–347
revenues, 385
training and implementation,
350–353, 377–378
U.S. financial support, 348–349,
356, 358–359
Liberia Media Centre, 347, 348
Libya, 3–4, 26–27
license agreements, 230–231
license fees, 230
local resource economies, 14,
463–465, 573–574, 613
community forest user groups
(CFUGs), 464–465, 545–561,
574, 591
conflict transformation, 550–552
environmental degradation, 465,
563–568
forest resources, 464, 503–527
management overview, 612*t*
mineral rights cadastres, 574
opium cultivation, 463–464,
467–487, 491–500
peace dividends, 566–567, 601
public engagement and multi-
stakeholder initiatives, 604–605
sanctions, 196n4

Sudan, 465
sustainable livelihoods, 385–386,
540, 545
taxation, 256, 586
women miners in the DRC,
529–542
See also community relations
Locke, John, 438n2
looting, 10–11, 440
Lujala, Päivi, 8, 9, 223, 224, 306,
585–586, 587
Luong, Pauline Jones, 442
Lutundula, Christophe, 77, 79, 578

Maconachie, Roy, 223–224
Mähler, Annegret, 294, 573
Malaquias, Assis, 170
Malaysia, 212, 581
al-Maliki, Nouri, 423, 426n18
Malloum, Félix, 319
management of high-value natural
resources. *See* resource
management
management of revenues. *See*
allocation of revenues;
distribution of revenues
Managing Conflict in Asian Forest
Communities (MCAFC), 503,
504, 514–524
analytic categories, 519–520
communications strategy, 515,
517
community stakeholder workshops,
515–516
conceptual framework, 517–520
holistic approach, 514n10
international forums, 515,
516–517
timber commodity chain, 518, 519
Type I conflicts, 518, 519
Type II conflicts, 518, 519
Manchester School, 438n2
Mandeville, Bernard, 438
Mansfield, David, 478

maps, 13
   Aceh, 241
   Afghanistan, 469, 493
   Angola, 149, 161
   Bougainville Island, 97
   Chad, 315, 319
   Democratic Republic of the Congo, 78, 530
   Forest Conflict Initiative of USAID, 504
   Guatemala, 104
   Iraq, 415–417
   Liberia, 77, 203, 217, 338, 339, 368, 370
   Nepal, 547
   Niger Delta, 393
   Nigeria, 392, 393
   Papua New Guinea, 96, 97
   Sierra Leone, 122, 123, 160, 263, 369, 370
   Southern Sudan, 237, 565
   Sudan, 237, 565
Martin, Adrian, 506
Massey, Simon, 330
May, Roy, 223
McMillan, John, 151
means testing, 277
Meekamui Movement. *See* Bougainville: secessionist movement
Mehlum, Halvor, 589
Mellor, John, 498
mercantilism, 439
Mexico, 287–288, 441
migration, 52n9, 53–54
Milton, John, 438n2
mineral rights cadastres, 574
mining
   community impacts, 93–94
   complaint and grievance mechanisms, 93n11
   post-conflict community relations, 87–114

   tributor-supporter systems of labor, 264n9
   See also artisanal and small-scale mining; mineral rights cadastres
MINUCI (UN Mission in Côte d'Ivoire), 32*t*, 41
mission creep, 29
Mitchell, Harrison, 158, 198, 580
Mitee, Ledum, 399
Mobutu Sese Seko, 532
Moene, Karl, 589
Moiwo, Daniel, 267
Momoh, Joseph Saidu, 125–126, 127
Mongolia, 584
Montesinos, Vladimiro, 82
Montesquieu, 438n2
MONUA (UN Observer Mission in Angola), 31–33
MONUC (UN Mission in the Democratic Republic of the Congo), 32*t*, 34–38, 42–43, 45, 577
Moore, M., 303n7
Morocco, 234
morphine, 467n1, 473n6, 491, 493n5
   See also opium
Mottu, E., 256
Al Moumin, Mishkat, 294
Mousseau, Demet Yalcin, 439–440
Mousseau, Michael, 439–440
Movement for Democracy and Justice in Chad. *See* Chad: armed conflicts
Movement for the Emancipation of the Niger Delta (MEND). *See* Nigeria: armed conflicts
Movement for the Liberation of the Congo. *See* Democratic Republic of the Congo: civil conflicts
Movement for the Survival of the Ogoni People (MOSOP). *See* Nigeria: armed conflicts

MPLA (Movimento Popular para a Libertação de Angola). *See* Angola: civil war
multidimensional peacekeeping missions, 576–577
multilateral development banks, 55
Multilateral Investment Guarantee Agency, 59
multi-stakeholder approaches
  multi-stakeholder initiatives, 604–605
  resource compacts, 26, 181, 399, 604–605
  tracking schemes, 159–160, 202, 205–206, 214–215, 227
Myanmar, 4, 253*t*, 512, 513*t*, 581

Namibia, 181
naming and shaming campaigns, 27
Nanggroe Aceh Darussalam. *See* Aceh
narcotics trafficking. *See* opium
Nasser, Mahmat Hassan, 330
National Advocacy Coalition on Extractives, 266–267
National Congress Party (NCP), 236, 563
National Patriotic Front of Liberia. *See* Liberia: civil war
National Revival Committee for Peace and Democracy (CSNPD). *See* Chad: armed conflicts
National Transitional Government of Liberia. *See* Liberia
NATO (North Atlantic Treaty Organization), 39, 470
Natural Resource Charter, 50n4, 74, 307, 584, 602n51
natural resource funds, 235–236, 276, 280, 309, 317, 584–585
natural resources (definitions), 6, 10
natural wealth accounts, 282
The Nature Conservancy, 522
Neary, J. P., 303n9

Nederlandse Financierings-Maatschappij Voor Ontwikkelings Landen (FMO), 55n13
neoliberal economic policies, 444
  See also liberalized economies
Nepal
  civil war, 548–550, 552
  community forest user groups (CFUGs), 545–548, 552–561, 574, 591
  comprehensive peace agreement (CPA), 552, 558n27
  conflict transformation process, 550–552, 557–558
  Constituent Assembly, 557
  CTP profile, 512, 513*t*
  Forest Act of 1961, 546, 549n10
  Forest Act of 1993, 558
  forest resource management, 465, 549n10
  forestry reforms, 523
  IDP reintegration, 552–556
  land ownership, 549nn8–10, 557
  Local Self-Governance Act of 1999, 558
  map, 547
  village development committees (VDCs), 547, 557n23
Network Movement for Justice and Development (NMJD), 167, 267, 268
Neumayer, Eric, 9, 306
new wars of the 1990s, 367–368
NGOs, 603–604
Nichols, Sandra S., 294
Niger
  distribution of revenues, 251, 253, 255
  Extractive Industries Transparency Initiative, 584
  uranium and gold revenues, 4
Niger Delta. *See* Nigeria

Niger Delta Development Commission (NDDC), 397–402, 405
Niger Delta People's Volunteer Force (NDPVF). *See* Nigeria: armed conflicts
Niger Delta Regional Development Master Plan (NDRDMP), 398–399, 401, 405, 406
Niger Delta Vigilante. *See* Nigeria: armed conflicts
Nigeria, 8–9
 amnesty program, 407
 armed conflicts, 391–396, 403–404, 406–408
 Biafran secessionist movement, 8, 234, 253t, 301, 393–394
 civil society, 405
 civil war, 393–394
 colonial era, 399
 corruption and patronage, 300, 405, 595–596
 distribution of revenues, 279, 287–288, 294, 394–397, 400, 406, 583–584, 586, 588
 Dutch disease, 395n9
 economic stagnation, 305
 environmental degradation, 394, 402–403, 588
 Extractive Industries Transparency Initiative, 408, 584
 institutional capacity building, 397–408, 595–596
 international partners, 398
 map, 392–393
 Ministry of Niger Delta Affairs (MNDA), 398–399, 401–402
 Niger Delta region, 391n2
 oil and gas industry, 3–4, 52, 393, 395–396, 583
 oil and gas revenues, 405–406
 population density, 405
 public participation, 404, 605
 resource management initiatives, 396–402
 socioeconomic indicators, 402
 sustainable employment plan, 407
 Technical Committee on the Niger Delta (TCND), 398–399, 401, 405, 406, 605
 weak central government, 52, 393–394, 396n11, 400, 407–408
Nilsson, Desiree, 606–607
nongovernmental organizations, 603–604
 See also civil society; names of specific organizations, e.g., Global Witness
nonrenewable resources, 10
Norland, Donald, 322
Northern Alliance. *See* Afghanistan: civil conflicts and wars
Norway
 Extractive Industries Transparency Initiative, 584
 primary commodity dependence, 298
 State Petroleum Fund, 235n11, 584

Obama, Barack, 486, 582
Obasanjo, Olusegun, 397n12, 398
obsolescing bargain theory, 330n22
Odingar, Noël Milarew, 319
odious contracts, 22, 73n7, 575
OECD Due Diligence Guidance, 581
Office of National Drug Control Policy, 478
Oglethorpe, Judy, 506
oil and gas, 9
 assigned-responsibility model, 148–153
 correlations with political repression, 449t, 451–452, 602–603
 distribution of revenues, 52n8, 406n29, 588–589
 environmental degradation, 394, 402–403, 465, 563–568, 588–589

Extractive Industries Transparency
  Initiative, 14, 50n3, 152,
  201–208, 408
Iraq, 4, 81–82, 276n3, 294–295,
  413–414, 418, 421–428, 586,
  587, 592, 595
  links with conflict, 301, 314–318,
    327, 331–332, 391–396,
    403–408
  local resource economies, 566–567
  local taxation, 256, 586
  Nigeria, 3–4, 52, 393, 395–396,
    405–406, 583
  as point resource, 318
  produced water, 564–566
  profit-sharing arrangements, 52n8
  sabotage, 403n24, 403n26
  security requirements, 60–62
  slant drilling, 416–417
  Southern Sudan, 237, 240, 563–
    564, 573
  Sudan, 3–4, 563–564
oil dependence, 298
Oil-for-Food Program, 81–82
Ojukwu, Odumegwu, 394n4
Olson, Mancur, 441
Mullah Omar, 469
Oomen, B., 552n15
Operation Enduring Freedom (OEF),
  469–471
opium, 4, 11, 38–39, 463–464,
  467–487, 597
  alternative livelihood programs,
    480–483, 485, 498
  conflict-related trade, 468–471,
    472nn4–5
  counternarcotics policies, 463,
    467–468, 470–471, 475–487,
    491–492, 495n8
  demand, 492
  economic dynamics, 496–498
  economic value, 467, 473–474,
    494–495

eradication programs, 479–480,
  484, 486n17, 493
farmer-based contexts, 471–475,
  478–481, 484–487, 492–493,
  574
as footloose crop, 495–496
international sanctions, 26–27,
  492n4
poppy cultivation, 471t, 472–473,
  482t, 485, 493, 494, 574
public information programs, 483
security/protection, 474–475,
  479–480
strategic management options,
  498–500, 574
uses, 467n1, 493n5
See also Afghanistan
Oppenheimer, Nicky, 189, 193
Organisation for Economic
  Co-operation and Development
  (OECD), 581
Organization of Petroleum Exporting
  Countries (OPEC), 416
overheated economies, 584n23
Overseas Private Investment
  Corporation (OPIC), 55n15
Oxfam, 184

Pact, 464
  artisanal mining community work,
    540–542
  Democratic Republic of the Congo,
    535–539
  gender-based violence prevention,
    537–538
  gender mainstreaming, 540–541
  literacy training, 536
  social and economic empowerment,
    536–537
  WORTH program, 536, 537
Pain, Adam, 464, 478, 574
Pakistan, 512, 513t
Papua New Guinea

Bougainville secessionist
movement, 8, 95–98, 234, 253*t*
community relations, 98–102
map, 96, 97
Panguna gold and copper mine, 95,
99–100, 111–112
revenue distribution conflicts, 582
paradox of plenty, 8, 583n21
See also resource curse
Paris, Roland, 367n1
Partnership Africa Canada (PAC),
129, 160
on conflict diamonds, 162–163
Kimberley Process, 172n18, 183,
184
Patey, Luke A., 465, 588–589
Patriotic Salvation Movement. *See*
Chad: armed conflicts
patronage systems
Chad, 313–314, 324–334, 598
definition, 3, 148n2, 263n7
Liberia, 374
patron-client relationships, 313n1
rent seeking, 9n8, 148n2, 226–227,
299–300, 437n1, 591n34
Sierra Leone, 263–264, 381
peacebuilding, 297, 613–614
actors, 5
conflict sensitivity, 88n2
definition, 26n3, 367
distribution of revenues. *See*
distribution of revenues
foreign direct investment. *See*
foreign direct investment
immediate aftermath stage, 5,
609–612
institution building. *See*
institutional capacity building
local economies. *See* local resource
economies
market promotion, 441, 450–453
natural resource management. *See*
resource management
objectives, 5–6, 367

peace consolidation, 5, 609–612
priorities, 372n9, 381–382,
385–387
secure communities, 531
sequencing of interventions,
608–612
sustainable livelihoods, 385–386,
540
voluntary standards for resource
extraction, 49–65
peace consolidation, 5, 609
peace dividends, 239–240, 278, 531,
566–567, 601
peacekeeping
combat operations, 42–43
corruption, 42n28, 577
definitions, 26n3
disarmament, demobilization, and
reintegration programs, 28, 229,
531, 551n14, 559
environmental impact, 40n26
gender-based violence, 531n3
human rights abuses, 577
Joint Mission Analysis Cells, 42
multidimensional peacekeeping
missions, 576–577, 599
peace spoilers. *See* peace spoilers
robust peacekeeping, 44
See also names of specific
peacekeeping missions, e.g.
UNTAC
peacemaking, 6
definitions, 26n3
economic contexts, 227–229
power-sharing agreements, 229
peace periods, 12n16
peace spoilers, 21, 25–46, 574,
605–607, 613
combat operations, 42–43, 44
commodity sanctions, 26–28
control of production sites, 29–30
demand-side enforcement, 30–31
economic and political concessions,
606–607

revenue sharing plans, 607
severing resource controls, 30
sovereignty considerations, 43
trade route control, 29–30
UN missions, 31–41, 575–577
Pegg, Scott, 600n47
People's Party for Reconstruction and Democracy (DRC). *See* Democratic Republic of the Congo
per capita income, 448n19, 449*t*, 453–454, 455
Performance Standards on Social and Environmental Sustainability, 602
Perks, Rachel, 464
permits, 230n5
Peru, 82
petroleum products. *See* oil and gas
Phanvilay, Khamla, 506
Philippines, 512, 513*t*, 515–516
point resources, 302, 318
political economies, 297–309
  institutional capacity building. *See* institutional capacity building
  of oil and conflict, 314–318, 327, 331–332, 448–452
  resource curse. *See* resource curse
  revenue allocation. *See* allocation of revenues
  revenue distribution. *See* distribution of revenues
political geography, 314, 318
political repression, 448–452
Political Risk Services, 589n30
Polity IV scale, 454
Polity Project measures of democracy, 148n3
pollution. *See* environmental degradation
poppy cultivation. *See* opium
population size, 448n19, 454
post-conflict period, 5, 11–12

institution building. *See* institutional capacity building
management of resources. *See* resource management
power sharing, 229
precocious marriage, 530
Press Union of Liberia, 347, 348
price shocks, 9, 305
primary commodities. *See* high-value natural resources
Principles for Responsible Investment (PRI), 605
Pritchett, Lant, 499
privatization, 442, 452–453
produced water, 564–566
production excise taxes, 256, 258, 586
production sharing, 230, 231
Programme for the Endorsement of Forest Certification, 214n5
property taxes, 586
prostitution, 530, 534–535, 538
public engagement, 604–605
  See also civil society
public-private partnerships, 541, 598n43
public relations. *See* community relations
Publish What You Pay campaign, 584n22

Qaddafi, Muammar, 286–287

Rally for Congolese Democracy, 78
Rally of Democratic Forces. *See* Chad: armed conflicts
ransom, 11
rape, 529, 530
reappraisal teams, 74n12
rebellion-specific capital, 441
redistribution of revenues. *See* distribution of revenues
regime types, 454
remediation bonds, 589
renewable resources, 10

Reno, William, 371n6, 373
rentier states, 227, 442, 499n20
rents (definition), 316n4
rent seeking
   allocation of revenues, 299–300
   definitions, 9n8, 148n2, 437n1, 591n34
   distribution of revenues, 226–227
   See also patronage systems
reparations
   asset recovery, 81–82
   environmental degradation, 111, 286, 588–589
republican liberalism, 439
Republic of Congo
   diamond smuggling, 165, 185
   FLEGT initiative, 212, 214, 215–216, 219, 581
resource appropriation, 43n31
resource capture, 8
resource compacts, 26, 181, 399, 604–605
resource curse, 8–9, 147–148, 280–281, 297, 583–584
   challenges to development, 299–309
   definitions, 65n31
   detached governments, 302, 304, 307
   development aid, 304, 309
   diversification, 309
   duration of conflict, 298–299
   Dutch disease, 235, 275–276, 303–305, 309, 323n12, 395n9
   institutional capacity, 306, 441–442
   patronage systems, 148n2
   political economies, 281–282
   price shocks, 305, 308–309
   rebellion financing, 301–302
   rent seeking, 148n2
   risk of conflict, 298, 304, 306, 307, 314–318
   saturation points, 304–305
   secessionist movements, 300–301, 307
resource dependence. *See* resource curse
resource management, 11–14, 293–295, 313–334, 571–614, 596–607, 613–614
   Chad, 293, 313–318
   context-based analysis, 572–573, 596–598
   coordination of interventions, 607–608
   enhancing institutions. *See* institutional capacity building
   external actors, 598–604
   extraction, 12–13, 21–23, 58–62, 106n36, 575–582
   local resource economies. *See* local resource economies
   multi-stakeholder initiatives, 604–605
   peacebuilding, 372, 375–379, 381–388
   peace spoilers, 605–607
   pre-conflict approaches, 597–598
   public engagement, 573, 604–605
   sequencing of interventions, 608–612
   UN mandate, 40
   See also names of specific resources, e.g. forest resources
resource rush, 575
resource sanctions. *See* sanctions
Responsible Asia Forestry and Trade program (RAFT), 522, 598n43
revenues, 3–4, 10–11, 14
   allocation. *See* allocation of revenues
   distribution. *See* distribution of revenues
   sharing. *See* wealth sharing
   tracking. *See* tracking schemes

Revolutionary Armed Forces of Columbia (FARC). *See* Colombia
Revolutionary United Front (Sierra Leone). *See* Sierra Leone: civil war
Reyna, Stephen, 327
Ribot, Jesse, 270
Ricardo, David, 438
Rich, Eddie, 158
Richards, Paul, 268
Robinson, J. A., 299n1
Rosales, Manuel, 286
Ross, Michael L., 223, 224, 305, 585–586, 587
royalty arrangements, 230, 231, 586
rubber, 202, 578
rule of law. *See* governance; institutional capacity building
Russell, Alison, 463–464, 574
Russia, 43n30, 584, 600
Rustad, Siri Aas, 6–7, 12, 223, 224, 507n3, 585–586, 587

Sachs, J., 299n1, 305, 309
Saideman, Stephen M., 439–440
Sala-i-Martin, X., 583n19
sanctions, 371n8, 575–577, 593
　arms sanctions, 28
　commodity sanctions, 25–28
　Kimberley Process, 197
　local impact, 196n4
　monitoring, 576
　monitoring mechanisms, 26–28, 31, 129–130, 163, 227, 599
　peace spoilers, 607
　secondary sanctions, 31
　See also names of specific countries, e.g. Liberia; UN Security Council
Sandbu, Martin E., 224, 278–279
Sanio, Tina, 464–465, 574
Sankoh, Foday, 126, 129, 130, 167, 299–300, 606–607
Santiago Principles, 585
São Tomé and Principe, 235
Saro-Wiwa, Ken, 394
saturation points, 304–305
Saudi Arabia, 584
Savimbi, Jonas, 169, 170
savings funds, 223, 330, 584, 585
Scotland, 300–301
Search for Common Ground (SFCG), 266
secessionist movements, 8, 300–301, 318
secondary diamond mining, 122
secondary sanctions, 31
security, 6
　diamondiferous regions, 271
　Voluntary Principles (VPs), 60–62
　voluntary standards, 53–54, 65
　wealth sharing, 229
September 11, 2001 attacks, 469–470
sequencing of interventions, 608–612
service agreements, 230, 231
Sese Seko, Mobutu, 82
sexual violence, 530, 531n3, 537–539, 541
shadow states, 371n6, 441, 492n1
Shankleman, Jill, 22
sharecropping, 497n13
sharing of revenues. *See* distribution of revenues; wealth sharing
sheltering of liabilities, 74n10
shifting cultivation system, 372n12, 381
Sierra Leone
　Addax Bioenergy project, 59n21
　The Agenda for Change, 382
　agriculture, 381
　artisanal mining, 125, 166–167, 169, 172, 264
　civil war, 8, 121, 126–131, 162, 166–167, 262–264, 271, 379–381
　commodity tracking systems, 607

conflict diamonds, 121, 126–131,
    161, 380
CTP profile, 512, 513*t*
Diamond Area Community
    Development Fund (DACDF),
    131–132, 139, 141, 261–272,
    587, 597–598
diamond industry management,
    121–122, 124–126, 131–141,
    167–168
diamond revenues, 3–4, 34, 121,
    124–131, 133, 168, 224,
    263–264, 381
distribution of revenues, 224,
    261–272, 589
economic freedom levels,
    446–447
environmental degradation, 589
extraction contracts, 578
Extractive Industries Transparency
    Initiative, 140–141
FLEGT initiative, 581
forest resources, 379, 505–506
Forestry Act, 382
forest sector reforms, 294, 369,
    381–383, 384, 590
institutional capacity building, 599,
    600
Kimberley Process, 121–122,
    132–133, 139, 141, 167–168,
    171–173, 186, 261n3, 580
kimberlite mining, 122, 133,
    137–141
Koidu diamond riots, 123–124,
    133–139
land ownership system, 380–381,
    386
land reforms, 386n46
Liberian involvement, 126, 128,
    130, 216, 341, 373, 379–380
Local Government Act, 262,
    270–271
Lomé Peace Agreement, 129, 130,
    167, 174, 606–607

map, 122, 123, 160, 263, 369
mining industry, 578
National Recovery Strategy, 264
patronage system, 263–264, 381
peacebuilding process, 379–387
peace spoilers, 32*t*, 34, 44n34,
    576–577, 594n38, 606–607
Poverty Reduction Strategy Paper,
    264
rent-seeking, 299–300
Revolutionary United Front (RUF),
    8, 26, 126, 131, 162, 264, 299,
    302, 379, 505, 606
secondary diamond mining, 122
traditional power relationships,
    267n12, 268–272
Truth and Reconciliation
    Commission, 263–264
UN diamond sanctions, 26–27,
    129–130, 227, 371n8, 373, 380,
    607
UN expert panels, 576n8
UN Human Development Index
    rank, 379n31
Wildlife Act, 382
Skaperdas, Stergios, 441
small-scale mining. *See* artisanal and
    small-scale mining
Smith, Adam, 438, 443n8
social fractionalization, 448n19,
    454
social impact assessment, 603
socialist legal system, 455–456
Somalia, 576n8
South Africa
    Angolan civil war, 169
    apartheid, 169n16
    Kimberley Process, 181, 186
    resource appropriation, 43n31
Southern Sudan
    Agreement on Wealth Sharing,
        237–241, 572–573
    Comprehensive Peace Agreement
        (CPA), 237, 240–241

distribution of revenues, 236–241,
  245–246, 255–256, 585,
  588–589
environmental degradation,
  563–568, 570, 588–589
environmental regulation, 567–568
institutional capacity building, 238
map, 237, 565
oil fields, 237, 240
oil revenues, 563–564, 573
secessionist movement, 8, 236, 563
Sudan People's Liberation
  Movement/Army (SPLM/A),
  236, 563
Soviet Union, 468
Sri Lanka, 515
stabilization funds, 235–236, 276, 280,
  309, 317, 584–585
state building. *See* institutional
  capacity building
state capacity, 315n2
  See also governance; institutional
  capacity building
State Oil Company of Azerbaijan
  (SOCAR), 51n5
stationary banditry, 441n4
Steinberg, David A., 439–440
Stevens, Siaka, 125, 262n4, 263, 268,
  381
Stolen Asset Recovery (StAR)
  Initiative, 82
Strasser, Valentine, 127
structural adjustment programs,
  444n10
Subramanian, A., 583n19
Sudan
  Agreement on Wealth Sharing,
    572–573
  civil wars, 8, 236, 253*t*, 328,
    563–564
  Comprehensive Peace Agreement
    (CPA), 237, 240–241, 563, 567
  Darfur conflict, 314, 327–328,
    331–332

distribution of revenues, 236–241,
  245–246, 251, 255–256, 587,
  588–589
environmental degradation, 465,
  563–568, 570, 588–589
environmental regulation, 567–568
institutional capacity building, 238,
  599
local economies, 465
map, 237, 565
National Congress Party (NCP),
  236, 563
natural resource fund, 235n11
oil and gas revenues, 3–4, 563–564
refugees, 329
secessionist movement, 8, 236
secession referendum of 2011,
  563–564
UN expert panels, 576n8
  See also Southern Sudan
Sudan People's Liberation Movement/
  Army. *See* Southern Sudan:
  secessionist movement
Suharto, President, 242
Sukarnoputri, Megawati, 242–243
survival economies, 573n3
sustainable development, 584
sustainable livelihoods, 385–386, 540,
  545

Taiwan, 184
Taliban, 468–471, 472nn4–5, 474n9,
  479, 481–484
  See also Afghanistan
Tanis, James, 101
tantalite, 37
tax policies, 586
  direct distributions of revenues,
    277, 279–280
  export taxes, 265
  illegal taxation, 36
  income taxes, 229
  production excise taxes, 256, 258,
    586

property taxes, 586
royalty arrangements, 230, 231, 586
tax base adjustments, 223, 232, 233
tax evasion, 73–74
tax holidays, 74
windfall profit taxes, 231
Taylor, Bob, 340
Taylor, Charles, 82
    involvement in Sierra Leone, 126, 128, 130, 216, 373, 379–380
    Liberian civil war, 340–341, 373–375
    presidency of Liberia, 128, 212n3
    See also Liberia
Temple, Paul, 132
terrorism
    money laundering, 131
    narcotics trafficking, 39
    U.S. war, 330
    See also al Qaeda
Tilly, Charles, 303n8
timber. See forest resources
Timor-Leste
    Extractive Industries Transparency Initiative, 584
    independence, 242
    natural resource fund, 235n11
    resource sector reforms, 27
    UN peacekeeping mission, 599
Tin Supply Chain Initiative (iTSCi), 582
Tocqueville, Alexis de, 439
Toe, Chris, 216
Tolbert, William R., 339–340
Tombalbaye, François, 318–319
Torvik, Ragnar, 299n1, 589
tracking schemes, 13–14, 157–158, 227, 525–526, 580–582
    applications, 166–173, 202–208
    asset recovery, 80–81
    Dodd-Frank Wall Street Reform and Consumer Protection Act, 308n16, 582, 593

    Extractive Industries Transparency Initiative, 158, 201–208, 307, 584
    Forest Law Enforcement, Governance and Trade initiative. See Forest Law Enforcement, Governance and Trade initiative (FLEGT)
    forestry resources, 509–511, 518, 519
    institutional capacity building, 131–141, 215–216, 238, 308, 593
    Kimberley Process. See Kimberley Process Certification Scheme
    management overview, 610t
    multi-stakeholder approaches, 159–160, 202, 205–206, 214–215, 227
    OECD Due Diligence Guidance for Responsible Supply Chains of Minerals, 581
    peace spoilers, 607
    Tin Supply Chain Initiative (iTSCi), 582
traditional governance. See customary governance
train-the-trainers programs, 482n13
transfer pricing, 74n10, 75
transitional authorities, 83, 592–593
transparency and accountability, 613
    Extractive Industries Transparency Initiative, 158, 201–208, 307, 584
    extractive projects, 601–602
    tributor-supporter systems of labor, 264n9

UCDP/PRIO Armed Conflict Dataset, 446
UK Department for International Development (UfID), 599
UNAMA (UN Assistance Mission in Afghanistan), 32t, 38–39

UNAMSIL (UN Assistance Mission in Sierra Leone), 129–131, 576–577
  diamond trading, 130n18
  peace spoilers, 32t, 34
UNAVEM (UN Angola Verification Missions), 31–33
UN Charter, 42–43
UN Convention against Corruption (UNCAC), 82
UN Declaration on the Rights of Indigenous Peoples, 105n32, 106–107
UN Development Programme (UNDP), 270, 437, 599
UN Disarmament, Demobilization, and Reintegration Resource Centre, 559
UN Environment Programme (UNEP), 391, 568, 599
UN Food and Agriculture Organization (UN FAO), 599
UN Global Compact, 26, 181, 605
UN Human Development Index
  Liberia, 202, 372n11
  Sierra Leone, 270, 379n31
UNIOSIL (UN Integrated Office for Sierra Leone), 131
UNIPIL (UN Integrated Peacebuilding Office in Sierra Leone), 131
UNITA *(União Nacional para a Independência Total de Angola). See* Angola
United Arab Emirates, 413n2, 584
United Front. *See* Afghanistan: civil conflicts and wars
United Front for Change. *See* Chad: armed conflicts
United Kingdom, 181
United Nations, 575–577, 613
  environmental protection mandate, 40
  peace spoilers initiatives, 26–28, 31–41
  resource management mandate, 40
  See also peacebuilding; peacekeeping; peacemaking; UN Security Council (UNSC)
United States
  Afghanistan counternarcotics efforts, 467–468, 470–471, 475–487, 491–492, 495n8
  Afghanistan war, 469–471
  Alaska's direct distribution program, 224, 232, 235n11, 275, 285–287
  Angolan civil war, 169
  counternarcotics policies, 475, 477–478
  Dodd-Frank Wall Street Reform and Consumer Protection Act, 308n16, 582, 593
  Iraq invasion and occupation, 43, 418
  Kimberley Process, 181
  Lacey Act, 215n6
  Liberian aid, 356, 358–359
  Operation Enduring Freedom/ Afghanistan war, 469–471, 475
  resource appropriation, 43
  USA PATRIOT Act, 302n6
  war on terror, 330, 469–471
Universal Declaration on Human Rights, 108
UNMIL (UN Mission in Liberia), 353, 576
  administration of natural resources, 342
  peace spoilers, 32t, 41–42, 342, 356
  See also Liberia
UNOCI (UN Operation in Côte d'Ivoire), 32t, 41
UN Office on Drugs and Crime (UNODC), 39, 82
UNOSM (UN Organization Stabilization Mission in the DRC), 577
UN Peacebuilding Commission, 613

UN Secretary-General, 4, 192, 604, 609n55, 613
UN Security Council, 225, 575–577
  arms embargoes, 341
  asset recovery, 69–70
  expert panels, 576
  freezing of assets, 69, 80, 82
  Iraq oil embargo, 417
  Liberian timber sanctions, 216, 341, 342, 347, 355, 371n8, 373–374, 375
  Oil-for-Food Programme, 418
  resolutions on women in peace processes, 531n3, 541
  revenue management authority, 28, 31, 45, 83
  sanction-monitoring mechanisms, 26–28, 31, 129–130, 163, 170, 227, 599
  sanction programs, 25–28, 31, 196n4, 371n8, 575–577
  Sierra Leone diamond sanctions, 26–27, 129–130, 227, 371n8, 373, 380
  See also peacekeeping
UNTAC (UN Transitional Authority in Cambodia), 32*t*, 33
UNTAES (UN Transitional Administration in Eastern Slavonia, Baranja, and Eastern Sirmium), 32*t*, 33–34
Upper Guinean Forest, 339, 377n22
Uppsala Conflict Data Program/Peace Research Institute Oslo, 6–7, 513*t*
U.S. Agency for International Development (USAID), 599
  Afghanistan counternarcotics programs, 477, 478, 481–484, 486
  Bureau for Asia and the Near East (ANE), 507
  Extractive Industries Network, 536n8, 541n13
  Forest Conflict Initiative, 464, 503–527
  functional bureaus, 507n4
  Liberia Forest Initiative, 348–349
  Office of Transition Initiatives (OTI), 507
  regional bureaus, 507n4
  Responsible Asia Forestry and Trade program, 598n43
U.S. Department of Defense, 478
U.S. dollars, 124
USA PATRIOT Act, 302n6

value chain approach, 492n2
Venezuela
  diamond smuggling, 165
  Kimberley Process, 159n1, 165, 176, 191n3
Verdier, T., 299n1
Vietnam
  CTP profile, 512, 513*t*
  FLEGT initiative, 212, 581
  forestry reforms, 522
village development committees (VDCs), 547
Voluntary Principles on Security and Human Rights (VPSHR), 49–50, 106n36, 602
  origins, 56–58
  requirements, 58, 60–62
voluntary standards for resource extraction, 22, 49–65, 93, 593, 601–603
  applications, 62–64, 351n26
  foreign direct investment, 49–56
  impact assessment guidelines, 64
  limitations, 65
  origins, 56–58
  requirements, 58–62, 106n36

Wallace, Jennifer, 464
war-booty futures, 302n5
war crimes, 81
Warner, A. M., 299n1, 305

Warner, T. Negbalee, 158
Warri South West, 394–395
wealth sharing, 225–227, 232–233, 254–257, 587–588
See also distribution of revenues
Weber, Max, 499n21
Weinstein, J., 44
Weinthal, Erika, 442
Wenar, Leif, 148–153
Wennmann, Achim, 223, 224
Wiig, Arne, 23, 602
Williams, Glyn, 268
windfall revenues, 231n7
winners-take-all distribution models, 316
Winters, Mathew S., 293
win-win distribution models, 316–317
Wolfensohn, James, 321, 325
Wolfowitz, Paul, 330
women
  artisanal mining, 464, 529–542
  child-care responsibilities, 535
  community forest groups, 547, 557–558
  gender-based discrimination, 529, 534–535, 537
  gender-based violence, 530, 531n3, 537–539
  gender mainstreaming, 540–541
  health and reproductive services, 541
  Pact program, 535–539
  sex trade, 534–535, 538
  UNSC Resolution 1325, 531n3, 541
  UNSC Resolution 1820, 531n3, 541
Woodrow Wilson International Center for Scholars, 517
Woods, John T., 294
Woolcock, Michael, 499
World Bank, 613
  on certification schemes, 197

Chad-Cameroon pipeline, 293, 313–314, 321–324, 327, 328–334, 594–595
  on economics of political violence, 227
  Extractive Industries Review, 56, 106n35
  on forest resource conflict, 518
  Independent Evaluation Group, 64
  liberalization of extractive sectors, 70n2, 75
  poverty line (definition), 583n19
  resource management reform, 599
  on Sierra Leone, 167, 381–382
  social and environmental impact policies, 56, 59
  stabilization funds, 317n5
  Stolen Asset Recovery (StAR) Initiative, 82
  structural adjustment programs, 444n10
  World Development Indicators, 454
World Diamond Council, 159–160, 165–166, 184, 190–191, 192
World Wildlife Fund, 516, 522
WORTH, 536, 537
Wright, Clive, 157

Yar'Adua, Umaru Musa, 398, 401
Ydígoras, Miguel, 104
Yemen, 4, 253t, 584
Yorongar, Ngarlejy, 322
Yusuf, Irwandi, 244

Zaghawa Justice and Equality Movement. See Sudan: civil wars
Zaïre. See Democratic Republic of the Congo
Zimbabwe, 158, 176, 186, 191n3
Zuercher, Christoph, 498